Courts

and

Country

To Linda Bertoldi and to our daughter
Amelia Bernice Bertoldi Bogart

Courts and Country

The Limits of Litigation and the Social and Political Life of Canada

W.A. Bogart

Toronto New York London
OXFORD UNIVERSITY PRESS
1994

Oxford University Press
70 Wynford Drive, Don Mills, Ontario M3C 1J9

Toronto Oxford New York
Delhi Bombay Calcutta Madras Karachi
Kuala Lumpur Singapore Hong Kong Tokyo
Nairobi Dar es Salaam Cape Town
Melbourne Auckland Madrid

and associated companies in
Berlin Ibadan

Oxford is a trade mark of Oxford University Press

Canadian Cataloguing in Publication Data

Bogart, W.A.
  Courts and country : the limits of litigation
and the social and political life of Canada

Includes bibliographical references and index.
ISBN 0-19-541035-1

1. Law — Canada. 2. Courts — Canada. I. Title

KE444.B64 1994   349.71   C93-095434-3
KF385.B64 1994

Extracts reprinted from *Continental Divide: The Values and Institutions of the United States and Canada*, Lipset, Seymour Martin (1990), by permission of the publisher, Routledge, New York.

Copyright © Oxford University Press 1994

Design: Heather Delfino

1 2 3 4 — 97 96 95 94

This book is printed on permanent (acid-free) paper ∞

Printed in Canada

Contents

Acknowledgements vii

Introduction ix

PART ONE: THE COUNTRY

Chapter One

'Preserving Its Identity
by Having Many Identities' 3

PART TWO: COURTS AND THEIR ROLE

Chapter Two

Litigation and the Question of Impact 37

Chapter Three

The Forms of Litigation 71

PART THREE: LITIGATION AND ITS CONTEXTS

Chapter Four

The Administrative State
and Judicial Review 107

Chapter Five

Women and the Courts:
'. . . how things must be, forever?' 134

Chapter Six

The Judges and Tort: Purpose and Limit 165

Chapter Seven

The Courts and Two Models
of the Criminal Law 190

Chapter Eight

Nation Building, Regionalism, and Federalism Litigation 223

Chapter Nine

The Charter: The Invigoration of Rights,
the Enfeebling of Democracy? 255

PART FOUR: CONCLUSIONS

Chapter Ten

The Courts and the Country 301

Index 324

Acknowledgements

A good many people helped this book along its way, though, of course, I alone am responsible for its shortcomings. I would like to begin by thanking sociologist — and neighbour — Bob Brym for introducing me to Oxford University Press, publisher Brian Henderson for his (critical) enthusiasm for the manuscript, and my editor Valerie Ahwee for her sharp pencil.

I would like to thank my research assistants: Laurie Letheren, Ian Laird, and Faeron Trehearne. In particular I am grateful to Meena Radhakrishnan who also contributed her strong editorial skills to an earlier draft of the book.

A number of people aided me greatly by reading or discussing parts of the book or by supporting grant applications: Annalise Acorn, Jeff Berryman, Susan Bertoldi, Donna Eansor, Brian Etherington, Scott Fairley, M.C. Havey, Patricia Hughes, Maureen Irish, Bert Kritzer, Diane Labrèche, Dick Moon, Mary Jane Mossman, Jacqueline Murray, Helena Orton, Erna Paris, Greg Richards, Peter Russell, Elisabeth Scarff, Bob Sharpe, John Sproat, Doug Stollery, Leigh West, and Neil Vidmar.

Four reviewers undertook the substantial task of reviewing the manuscript, pointing out areas for improvement. Sandra Burt and Kent Roach initially read a number of chapters and later became 'official' reviewers and were wonderfully critical and supportive throughout. There were also two (then) anonymous reviewers: Christopher Manfredi and Ted Schrecker.

The University of Windsor helped the initial stages of the enterprise by awarding me a research professorship for 1989. In addition, I received financial aid for research assistance from the Ontario Law Foundation, Block Grant to the Faculty of Law, University of Windsor.

Finally, I would like to thank my daughter Amelia Bernice Bertoldi Bogart, who, at five, is about the same age as this project, and to thank my wife — and editor — Linda Bertoldi who ever demonstrates that corporate law, love of literature, and fine Italian cooking make an exceedingly good combination.

Introduction

This is a book about the limitations of litigation in Canada. This may seem odd. Given the Charter of Rights and Freedoms, the growing coverage of the courts in the media, and the increasing influence of law, a book about the expansion of litigation and its growing significance might be more in order. In fact, I believe this book is about the growth of litigation and its increasing role — but it is also a reaction to that role, a plea to consider that the effects of courts should lead us to contemplate the limits of litigation and how as a society we might observe those boundaries.

This work derives from a simple proposition: law, whatever its origins, is fundamentally connected to the social and political life from which it arises and which, in turn, it seeks to influence. That obvious proposition is frequently thrust into the background or just plain ignored when we begin to speculate about the role of law — particularly a role for the law that comes to us from the judges in Canada. Many examples of such disassociation pervade this book. Conversely, its goal is to provide a discussion of the role of litigation firmly anchored in the social and political life of this country and to use the depiction of that social and political life to argue, quite specifically, for a limited (which is not to say unimportant) role for litigation.

Of course litigation before the courts is not in itself the issue. Litigation obviously performs an important function in resolving disputes that occur in society from breach of contract to suits for damages for defective goods to dissolving marriages and other kinds of domestic arrangements and, in the case of criminal law, dealing with questions of guilt. Nor, in principle, is there controversy in this context over resolution of disputes by tribunals created by the legislatures (the Ontario Municipal Board, the Canadian Radio-television and Telecommunications Commission, etc.) and subject to their control.

The litigation that is of concern involves complex and difficult social and political questions. Such issues are many and varied, but include abortion and other questions focused on the situation of women, the protection of minorities, issues concerning the environment, education, and the control of crime. Historically, these issues in the courts have arisen in two areas — constitutional litigation concerning the respective powers of the central and provincial governments (federalism litigation) and issues concerning the workings of the administrative state. More recently such issues are at the fore because of the Charter of Rights and Freedoms (and to some extent because of the Charter's predecessor, the Bill of Rights). The Charter equips courts to review all sorts of issues concerning the workings of government, including actually striking down legislation passed by the politicians. It is this converging of litigation and the role of the judiciary with the political process that is the focus of this book. Even more specifically, the book examines the capacity of litigation involving difficult political choices to improve the working of the legislatures and their bureaucracies or, in contrast, to weaken popular politics' capacity and willingness to deal with such difficult issues in our national life.

To use phrases like 'social and political' and 'national life' presupposes that one will offer such an account of this country. Yet from the beginning, we have been awash in uncertainty. Quite possibly our strongest bond has been our collective angst about who we are. We have engaged in what Barbara Frum called 'the dance of adjustment'[1] as we delayed, compromised, and connived. But the music for that dance is slowing and growing more faint with the dancers fatigued, awkward, and ill-tempered. The rubble of the Charlottetown Accord and the dreariness of an intense recession cast gloom over any attempts at national policy.

But perhaps it is at times of stress that there is the greatest need for accounts of what makes this country a country, in this case viewed through a particular lens: litigation. My response to our national troubles is to seek to enhance debate about a particular aspect of it: the role of the courts. Strong clashes — with wide participation — about the courts' function in Canada will not undermine that institution but rather treat it in a way similar to any of the institutions of government in this country. Indeed, whatever its other weaknesses, this book will totally fail if it does not persuade the reader that we need more rousing arguments about the role for judges in Canada so that we can consciously and with deliberation determine how this largely unexamined form of power ought to be exercised.

In Chapter One I hazard a description of the essential characteristics of our social and political life: variegated ideology, nationalism, government presence and lack of competition in the economy, deference to authority and hierarchy, regionalism, the English and the French. Not surprisingly, this is a complex and in some ways uncertain account subject to diverse interpretations. For example, it is argued that our lack of identity is a virtue for it is the basis upon which our aptitude for compromise and moderation (even now being sorely tested) rests. From this perspective, uncertainty and tentativeness can be seen to be a strength, not a weakness. Similarly, I emphasize the role of ideology in our political life and how we have allowed a number of organizing ideas to contend for influence in shaping our beliefs and, more importantly, our governmental policies. 'Ideology' is a word that may put off some readers. It has come to have a pejorative connotation with whiffs of extremism and rigidity. But understanding will suffer if readers are not open to a discussion of ideology defined simply (and much more calmly) 'as a doctrine or a set of ideas which claims to provide an adequate explanation of political arrangements'.[2] Chapter One seeks to demonstrate the rich politics that we have enjoyed by allowing a number of ideologies to compete in our national life. A discussion of ideology is vital because, as we shall see later in the book, a number of commentators from different perspectives point to liberalism as one ideology that is frequently buttressed by the values litigation most often fosters. This affiliation of courts and liberalism with its emphasis on individualism, the free market with its capacity to create wealth, and restraint of government can be a great strength in society, but it is also a critical reason for limiting the role of courts in Canada.

As I said, I realize that the depiction of Canada I offer is not without controversy, a point I discuss particularly at the beginning of Chapter One. Some of the greatest challenges to that portrait come from those who have been historically marginalized: women; gays and lesbians; visible, linguistic, and cultural minorities; Amerindians; and the disabled. Significantly, many from these groups are among those who also have the highest expectations concerning the capacity of litigation to effect a reordering of this society. Many of these voices contend that since the existing structures of power and (particularly the political process) have been indifferent at best and even hostile to the interests represented by these challenges, they ought to turn to litigation and harness principle and rationality to effect the recognition of rights that dulled legislatures and unresponsive bureaucracies have long denied them. Turning to judicially created rights as a method of restructuring society also has the potential to draw us closer to the United States, the society that has looked to the courts the most to resolve complex social and political issues, but with little success. At the same time, our relationship with that country has been one of the most elemental aspects of our identity.

Part Two deals with two topics that are an important bridge to the discussion of particular kinds of litigation and their connection to Canada in Part Three. The first of these topics (in Chapter Two) deals with the question of impact. If we are going to discuss what the role of litigation is and ought to be in the social and political life of the country, we surely require some understanding of how we ascertain its effects. Yet the focus of this chapter is to demonstrate that ascertaining the precise influence of litigation on important issues is very difficult. This is not because litigation is without influence but rather because very complex issues of causation come to the fore in such a discussion. The chapter sounds a very strong note of caution concerning claims for and about litigation and its capacity to respond to political issues, particularly in the name of reform. In this last regard, specific issue is taken with progressive forces in this country who have announced high hopes that courts will improve the lot of the disadvantaged.

The second topic in Part Two deals with the structure of the lawsuit itself (parties, costs, remedies, etc.) and how litigation is conducted. As such, Chapter Three may provide important background, particularly for readers unfamiliar with law. But there is a deeper purpose as well. The traditional structure of litigation mirrors liberal values of individualism, free choice, and limited government. Yet a number of challenges to the traditional model of litigation seek to allow for a broader range of values and to alter the very structure of litigation. Such challenges are discussed at some length in Chapter Three. Still, such an altered model of litigation is faced with an entirely different set of reservations, essentially, that it leads the judiciary to usurp functions that are better left to the legislatures and their agencies. These, too, are very real reservations about litigation. Nonetheless, Chapter Three argues that the solution does not lie in insisting upon the rigidities of the traditional model.

Having offered a portrait of the country in Part One and examined the question of the impact of litigation and fundamental ideas concerning its structure in Part Two, Part Three then looks at litigation itself. It does so by analysing six areas, each in a separate chapter: the administrative state, women, tort, criminal law, federalism, and the Charter of Rights and Freedoms. These six areas cover the essential terrain of litigation. The approach assesses how courts affect important social and political issues in contemporary Canadian society, but also examines such questions historically, beginning roughly with the turn of the twentieth century, while bearing in mind the difficulties of such assessments discussed in Part Two. These six chapters can be briefly summarized.

Chapter Four deals with the relationship between courts and the administrative state. The judiciary in the twentieth century impeded many progressive initiatives addressing broad social and economic questions, such as compensation for injury in the workplace, unionization, and human rights, with the result that legislatures replaced the courts in these areas with the administrative state and its mechanisms for decision making. Competition law furnishes a more ambivalent instance where courts' hesitation in enforcing such policy reflected a similar vacillation in politics.

Courts persist in exerting at least ideological influence through a review process (essentially fashioned by themselves) of the decisions of administrative tribunals and other entities. Such a process has the capacity to prune administrative programs, many addressing progressive initiatives, in the name of the highly contentious concept of 'jurisdiction'. This suggests that there is little basis for concluding that courts will fashion solutions that will displace traditional liberal values, particularly when powerful economic forces are involved.

Chapter Five addresses women's issues and their treatment by the judiciary. Before the Charter there was a clear pattern in the relationship between courts and legislatures: women were almost always defeated in cases brought before the courts, but there was reform of those same issues by politicians and their agencies. The coming of the Charter and the courts' (particularly the Supreme Court's) recognition of feminist analysis brings to the fore the paradox of victory. There is a contradiction arising from court successes that may actually impede more widespread and long-lasting reform. This paradox is discussed with regard to abortion and related questions. There have been a number of successful court cases that established women's legal right to an abortion, particularly the Supreme Court's decision to strike down the Criminal Code's prohibition of abortion except in certain circumstances. Yet these victories did nothing to address issues related to women's access to abortion. Meanwhile there is evidence, admittedly incomplete, that such access is, if anything, less available. Simultaneously, solutions to related issues critical in addressing women's disadvantage, such as maternity leave, pre- and postnatal care and day care, appear even further away.

Chapter Six examines tort litigation and analyses the courts' role in dealing with 'private' interests, which is in itself a problematic description. There are a number of areas of 'private' litigation that could be analysed: corporate, contracts, and trusts, but for several reasons, the most fruitful is torts. First, torts is the most wide-ranging of these areas; basically any action is tortious if the law regards it as wrong and orders some form of redress. Second, theoretical analysis is most highly developed in terms of torts, particularly the function of litigation generally and, more specifically, its limitations in Canadian society. Finally, there are reforms that remove important kinds of tort litigation — such as compensation for injuries from motor vehicle accidents and compensation for injuries sustained as a result of mishaps involving medical care — from the courts either entirely or in important aspects. Again, the reasons for such reforms and the reaction to them tell us much about Canadian society's expectations concerning courts.

Tort litigation strongly reflects liberal values of autonomy, self-regarding behaviour, and responsibility for injury caused to others that is engaged only when the fault of the person causing the injury has been established. Yet Canada has been quite willing to devise other ways of dealing with issues arising in tort litigation when there has been popular judgement that courts are not the best forum for dealing with such issues. This is not to say that debate about such questions is easy or free from ideological commitment. What does emerge is a view of litigation that acknowledges its usefulness while imposing limitations on its role. Such a perspective delivers important messages in terms of this book's larger themes about creating an important but contained role for courts regarding complex social and political issues.

Chapter Seven deals with the courts and their treatment of issues focused on the administration of criminal justice. There have been two models of criminal justice that have been very influential. The first — due process — reflects theories of the liberal state and thus emphasizes the rights of the accused as protection against abuse of official power. Thus this model underscores exclusionary rules of evidence, the right to counsel, the right to a speedy trial, and other procedural safeguards directed to shielding individuals from abuses by the state. In contrast, the second mode — crime control — has its foundations in reaction to individuals' unqualified claims and asserts that civil liberties are meaningful only in orderly societies. Thus this model emphasizes the suppression of criminal conduct. It does not ignore the treatment of individuals, but insists that order must be preserved before any of us can enjoy personal freedom. Until recently, the courts of Canada and the United States have each reflected the way the two nations have differed in their treatment of crime: the United States emphasizing due process with Canada underscoring crime control. Thus historically (and unlike in many other areas) the Canadian courts were reflecting dominant values in this society. But with the Charter of Rights and Freedoms, Canadian courts have moved significantly towards the due process model, providing the best example of the contention that the one change which is drawing the two societies together the most is the adoption in Canada of the Charter.[3] Such possibilities are illustrated by a discussion of the controversies surrounding Supreme Court cases on speedy trials and on the 'rape-shield' law, and by an analysis of the criminal rights 'revolution' in the United States.

Chapter Eight addresses federalism litigation and its relation to the tensions between the central and provincial governments. Examining the history of federalism reveals that it has been changed and influenced in many ways in which the courts have not been key or even marginal players: the discontinuance of the disallowance and reservation powers, constitutional amendment, the spending power, etc. Court judgements have mostly been bargaining chips employed in negotiations by the various interests. There is, therefore, a basis for arguing that courts have, at times, assisted in achieving the required alterations to federalism.

Yet federalism litigation appears to be on the rise. The danger is that such an expanded judicial role will be too easily used as a substitute for the necessary bargaining and negotiation if our federalism is to survive. Such pressure to turn to the courts may have been intensified because of the failure of constitutional rearrangement exemplified by the debacle of Meech Lake and the Charlottetown Accord.

Chapter Nine addresses the greatest potential for judicial power, the Charter of Rights and Freedoms. With the Charter the courts are able to say that *no* government may pass legislation (subject to the s. 33 override of the Charter, which permits legislatures to declare a statute to be valid, notwithstanding any arguments about the enactment violating certain other provisions of the Charter) or that no agency of government may engage in a particular form of questioned activity. The chapter examines two very different models of democracy. The first recognizes the power of the ballot, but one curbed by the judiciary, who will champion rationality and principle prevailing over insensitive legislatures, inflexible bureaucracies, and an ignorant populace. The second retains faith in popular politics and fears that an elitist, unaccountable, and unrepresentative judiciary will blunt democracy because of regressive decisions, progressive decisions that nevertheless sap legislative and administrative responses to complex problems, and greater barriers to the litigation process because of costs.

The chapter also examines the debate surrounding the judicial role under the Charter by first analysing the theoretical arguments for and against such power for courts. In conjunction with this general account, there is a specific examination of the putative benefits and pitfalls for the Aboriginals in invoking judicial power in their struggle for recognition in this society. Secondly, the chapter looks at existing evidence of the Charter's influence in its first decade. While the evidence is undefinitive, it indicates that the Charter is exerting a strong influence on this society, and that it is '"Americanizing" the practice of politics in Canada'.[4] In addition, studies of decisions in the area of criminal justice establish the point made in Chapter Seven that most of the Charter decisions in the Supreme Court are focused on such issues and that these judgements are moving us from the crime control model to the due process model. Further, one study reveals that of the few cases under the Charter that dealt with gender equality, the majority involved men attacking legislation or programs designed to alleviate disadvantages for women. Finally, the chapter examines a claim by one of the leading students of Canadian constitutionalism that the Charter has resulted in only a 'modest expansion'[5] of the judicialization of politics, suggesting that such a claim is not sustainable based on the accumulated evidence and its effects over the long haul.

Parts One, Two, and Three are a lengthy development of an attempt not to claim certainty about the impact of litigation but, rather, to engender scepticism concerning its consequences. At this stage let me attempt to sum up the introduction to those three parts even more succinctly.

Tracing the effects of litigation on society is very difficult. In twentieth century Canada, both court decisions and the very structure of litigation (parties, costs, remedies, etc.) have reflected a strong liberal orientation. Whether litigation has a positive effect on social change is far from clear. Indeed, litigation can deflect groups interested in reform from the legislative process where more ambitious and far-reaching change might be and, in important instances, has been realized. Such deflection may prompt politicians ultimately to do less rather than more in grappling with issues on reform agendas or with any critical social or political issue.

At the same time, there is strong evidence that Canadian courts are involving themselves in such questions. This is clearest because of the Charter and its expanded scope for the courts' role (especially their capacity to strike down legislation passed by all levels of government), but also because of federalism review and judicial review of administrative action. Such increasing 'judicialization' of issues has critics in many countries (including its homeland, the United States), but it may be particularly ill-suited to Canada. This nation's varied ideologies and tradition of moderation and compromise for effecting solutions could be strongly at odds with the claims of rights and the win-lose stance of litigation, particularly if liberalism continues to dominate the courtroom. Some of the most difficult questions arise not when progressive forces lose in the courts but when they win.

Part Four attempts to construct a role for litigation in Canada based on the discussion in the first three parts. Assuming an acceptance of limitations on that role, it suggests how boundaries might be drawn while examining the proper relation between the judiciary and other agencies of power in Canada. Those espousing the possibility for complementary roles for courts and political processes talk in terms of 'conversations' and 'dialogue', asserting that '[a] society that cannot imagine its disadvantaged going to court to achieve reform will have an impoverished sense of justice; one that relies on such Herculean efforts will have an illusory one'.[6] But this laudable goal to make judicialized rights and the common good not adversaries but partners in a 'dance of adjustment' is far easier to express in the abstract than to realize. Achieving such a balance is difficult because of the pressure to turn to litigation and because of the failing faith in the political process. The debris of the Meech Lake and Charlottetown accords and the dismal state of our national finances spread gloom about popular participation and its ability to enable us to reach common understanding and mutual ends. Yet the hope is that the defeat of Charlottetown will lead to consensus that constitutionalism is to be turned from. More broadly, there is hope that the discourse of rights is to have its limits so that solutions coming from popular politics will provide the best chance for our common life.

To that end I discuss a number of ways for bridging the gulf between law and politics. Regarding the Charter, I discuss s. 1 and its capacity to structure deference by the judiciary to solutions reached by the legislatures and s. 33 and the power it gives to parliaments to override curial pronouncements. More generally, I tackle the quandary of the judiciary being unrepresentative and unaccountable by discussing who gets appointed, including whether it is necessary for judges — at least members of the Supreme Court — to be lawyers, the process by which the judiciary are appointed, and the advantage of having limited terms to their appointments. Finally, I argue that programs to facilitate access to courts are necessary so that courts are not the preserve of the economically privileged. At the same time, there is a plea for a politics that will eliminate the barriers to those who have been long excluded, particularly women. Although they make up over half of the population, they are still severely underrepresented in legislatures.

Yet I conclude ambivalently. Will the Charter and the trail of litigation in other areas of the law enable us to realize the common good through political processes? Or are we headed to an atomistic consciousness and behaviour, each of us becoming increasingly isolated as official inaction increases?

I would like to dispel fears at the outset that the reader is in the grip of some romantic who is blinded to failings of the electoral process and politicians. (Conversely, we will see that a much-emphasized argument for courts, made by others, is that they will help reclaim democracy from the foibles of the legislature.) I think I am quite schooled in the myopia and plain wrong-headedness of elected officials. Nor do I cling to some fanciful notion that the exercise of governmental power is always about improvement. Too often tragic choices are involved, and whoever exercises power must answer the bleak question of which alternative will do the least harm. One indelible example of our government's failure is Canada's treatment of Jews who attempted to flee slaughter during the Second World War. As Abella and Troper documented in *None Is Too Many*,[7] our government's official indifference and, in many instances, overt hostility led to the deaths of thousands who might have been given sanctuary on our shores. While not unique, Canada's response may have been the worst.[8] Nor were our sins merely of neglect. We had deliberate choices to make. We made them with deliberation.

Yet for all democracy's tragedies, there are no true competitors by which to govern ourselves, so each generation must decide how its particular version will work while facing the limits of its politics. That judges may have an enhanced role during our time is a fair issue, but that democracy should come to hinge on courts is truly romance — perhaps dangerous romance.

NOTES

[1] S. Godfrey, 'Frum on Frum', *The Globe and Mail*, 1 February 1992, C1, quoting Frum describing us before we became locked in the constitutional embrace: 'My view of Canada was that you shift it around and make it work. I liked the non-explicit adjustments we were making — but now we're into a cold, crass, explicit trading of advantages. We've lost that dance of adjustment.'

[2] W. Christian and C. Campbell, *Political Parties and Ideologies in Canada* (2nd ed.) (Toronto: McGraw-Hill Ryerson, 1983).

[3] S.M. Lipset, *Continental Divide: The Values and Institutions of the United States and Canada* (Toronto: C.D. Howe Institute and Washington: National Planning Association, 1989): 225–6.

[4] F. Morton et al., *The Supreme Court's First One Hundred Charter of Rights Decisions: A Statistical Analysis* (Calgary: Research Unit For Socio-Legal Studies, University of Calgary, Research Study 6.1, n.d.): 2.

[5] P. Russell, 'Canadian Constraints on Judicialization from Without', Conference on 'The Judicialization of Politics' address to the Interim Meeting of the Interna-

tional Political Science Association Research Committee on Comparative Judicial Studies, University of Bologna, Forli, Italy, June 1992, 17–18, forthcoming in the International Political Science Review, 1993–4.

[6] K. Roach, 'Teaching Procedures: The Fiss/Weinrib Debate in Practice' (1991) 41 *University of Toronto Law Journal*, 247–86.

[7] I. Abella and H. Troper, *None Is Too Many — Canada and the Jews of Europe 1933 –1948* (Toronto: Lester & Orpen Dennys, 1982).

[8] Actually, Newfoundland's record was the worst of all Allied countries. See G. Bassler, 'Attempts to Settle Jewish Refugees in Newfoundland, 1934–1939', (1988) 5 *Simon Wiesenthal Center Annual*, 121–44.

PART ONE

The Country

CHAPTER ONE

'Preserving Its Identity by Having Many Identities'

INTRODUCTION

We live in a society in search of itself, one in which there has been a mixture of ideologies, tensions between the regions and central Canada, clashes between the two founding languages and cultures, and a long struggle for recognition by the First Peoples. Canada is a nation that has shown compassion for its less fortunate members, that has been committed to universal health care, but is also one that has tolerated concentration of wealth and lack of economic competition and that has had a liking for élitism and order tinged with authoritarianism. It is a society of insecurities and obsessiveness about questioning fundamentals that drives those who study it (let alone those who live in it) to distraction. It is a country whose citizens may have become profoundly distrustful of all popular politics.[1] Yet when the UN Development Program ranked 160 countries in terms of life span, literacy, educational and health-care systems, absence of discrimination and violent crime reported in 1991, Canada was second in the world; it was first in 1992, and second in 1993.[2]

Whatever the historic building blocks of this society, its fabric is being exposed to deep questioning. Foremost among these challenges is the sovereigntist movement in Quebec, a strong reaction to what is claimed to be inadequate recognition of the aspirations of the French language and culture within established accommodations. In addition, some of the concerted challenges are coming from those who have been excluded from the existing arrangements: women, visible and linguistic minorities, lesbians and gays, the disabled, and Aboriginals.[3] They are aware of such plaudits as the UN Development Program report, but they nevertheless focus upon the institutions of this society, which they view as unrepresentative and unaccommodating, denying them their share of power and unresponsive to their claims whether for accessible and high quality daycare, basic entitlements regardless of sexual orientation, or self-government, to give but a few examples. Whatever the merits of the structure of our society, historically it was exclusionary and élitist and there are demands that it be drastically altered. The Meech Lake and Charlottetown accords fell for a number of reasons, but prominent among them was a mistrust of official and unrepresentative élites, an unwillingness to leave them in charge of constitutional ordering.

It is no surprise then that many of those who have long felt denied basic participation in the fundamentals of representative politics might be tempted by courts and the discourse of judicially recognized rights to secure what they claim as basic entitlements, particularly with the coming of the Charter and its recognition of the courts' capacity to be arbiters of such claims. When the dishevelled state of our politics is surveyed and the newspapers continually refer to the 'rights revolution'[4] and the 'court party'[5] — interest groups said to be using lawsuits to promote their agendas — litigation appears to be a main channel for questioning the fundamental arrangements of this society, especially by those who have felt left out for so long.

This exclusion is nowhere better illustrated than with the plight of Amerindians.[6] The wrongful taking of lands, the Indian Act with its policy of assimilation through control and domination of Aboriginals' communal and individual lives, the residential schools dividing families and subjecting children to abuse, were only some elements of the bitter legacy of the 'White Man's Burden'.[7] The consequences have been appalling. To cite but one aspect, the suicide rate among Amerindians is six times that of the rest of Canada and for Aboriginals under twenty-five, it is the highest in the world.[8] Little wonder that almost anything — specifically courts — would appear to have a more promising response to this plight than the chaos and betrayal of politics and its administrative processes.

Yet much of this book is a plea against overreliance on litigation to achieve any kind of common understanding, perhaps particularly among those seeking reform. There are no doubt serious deficiencies in this country and its public institutions, but the hope for change cannot rest with courts, the least accountable and unrepresentative of all. This chapter, while providing an account of the main building blocks of Canada's identity, will describe how they have been related to the courts and how a major challenge to that identity is now coming from litigation, particularly the judicialization of rights under the Charter. Part Three will explore the terrain of litigation in detail.

Litigation's shift from having an important but not determinative role in our identity to occupying a central place in our construction and the consequences that could ensue can be vividly put by discussing the ideas of Charles Taylor.[9] Taylor, one of our philosophical giants, contrasts the rights model, which is now being asserted and which is linked closely with centralization, with the model of citizen participation (affiliated more with decentralization), which has historically reflected us to a greater degree.

The rights model's origin is in the United States, which has turned to courts and centralization as instruments of policy since at least the end of the Second World War. The courts, it is claimed, provide an alternative to the legislative process, so the more unwieldy popular politics becomes, the more individuals and groups will be tempted to have recourse to them. But in addition, '[T]he sense of the dignity of the free agent has been identified more with the bearer of rights than with the citizen participator.'[10]

In contrast, the participatory model reflects more who we were as a nation. A conspicuous element, therefore, was decentralization with its capacity to accommodate a lack of a unified vision in this country. While various political arrangements were negotiated by political élites who may have had a common understanding, no such common national formula was ever widely shared by Canadians so that we have been focused more on regional identities and loyalties: 'This close link between community and region has been most deep and enduring in the case of Quebec but has a strong lineage in the west and the maritimes as well.'[11]

It is not a question of the participatory model not respecting rights or granting means to enforce them. Rather, it is the case that rights recognition (especially through the courts) is not the fundamental element of citizen dignity, which instead 'is based on having a voice in deciding the common laws by which members live. . . . Special importance attaches to the fact that we as a whole, or community, decide about ourselves as a whole community.'[12] Instead, the rights model provides a ticket out of the community while simultaneously weakening its underpinnings: '[This] model goes very well with a more atomist consciousness . . . I cannot be too willing to trump the collective decision in the name of individual rights if I haven't already moved some distance from the community which makes these decisions. . . .'[13]

Of course, Taylor's account of the participatory model's virtues is flawed to the extent it does not face the fact squarely of how many have been excluded from full participation. The list of those who continue to be excluded — women, lesbians and gays, the First Peoples, the disabled, visible and linguistic minorities — is a long one. But we must not respond to the problems of the participatory model by abandoning it for the rights one, which over time may demonstrate greater weaknesses for facing the issues in our common life, including those questions about alleviating disadvantage.

To make that central argument, the book must do several things. This chapter will start by offering an account of this society and the building blocks that are now open to question. To do so, it looks at variegated ideology, nationalism and national identity, government presence in and lack of competition in the economy, deference to authority and hierarchy, regionalism, the English and the French. A story of a nation bearing questions in its heart.

VARIEGATED IDEOLOGY

The uncertainty enveloping the country began with the American Revolution. This country started as the leftover when Americans took to arms against Great Britain. The fragment that remained to become Canada was in some ways truly reactionary. The United States was said to be Whig, classically liberal with its attendant antistatism, populism, egalitarianism, voluntary religions, and veneration of individualism. Canada, outside of Quebec, was claimed (at least in part in reaction to what was occurring in the United States) to take its values from toryism with its statism, deference to authority, curbing of the individual, and hierarchical religions.[14]

Such contrasts may be put too starkly. Yet comparisons with the United States are an important clue to how Canada seeks its identity. This nation's uncertainty is bound together with the giant presence to the south. As Margaret Atwood has put it, 'If the national mental illness of the United States is megalomania, that of Canada is paranoid schizophrenia'[15] and Seymour Martin Lipset has observed, 'Much of what Canadian intellectuals, both scholars and creative artists, write about their own country is presented in a comparative context — that is, with reference to the nation to the south. They frequently seek to describe what Canada is about by stressing what it is not: the United States.'[16]

This attempt at identification by continually contrasting ourselves with Americans can go too far. After all, we share a common language (for the English-speaking majorities), a common legal tradition (again for the majority of jurisdictions), the largest undefended border in the world, issues concerning Aboriginal peoples, and large and ever-integrating economies. Indeed, significant differences, at least stemming from the inception of the two countries, have been doubted.[17]

Nevertheless, Horowitz, in contrast, found in Canada tory and ultimately socialist ideas allowing for differences in ideology that more closely resembled those of nations of Europe that have accommodated liberalism while retaining these other ideologies.[18] In this conception, the United States stands out with its overpowering liberalism, whereas Canada enjoys an ideological diversity and an affinity with western Europe[19]: 'Here Locke is not the one true god; he must tolerate lesser tory and socialist deities at his side.'[20] This basic assertion of variegated ideology as a vital element in the way we fashioned ourselves, making us more committed 'to collective provision'[21] when compared with the United States, has been echoed by many others. Such assertions are by no means beyond controversy,[22] but what may be critical is that while 'Canadian practice may be not as much better as many of us believe . . . the important point is that this is seen as a difference worth preserving'.[23]

Liberalism has been the dominant ideology of the West in the twentieth century. A stark reaction to the hierarchy and privilege that ruled before, liberalism places its faith in the individual and his or her promise. Government exists only because free and independent individuals contract for its existence. It provides the structure of order: repelling invaders, keeping the peace, providing means of resolving disputes through the courts, but it is to do little else, allowing the maximization of self-interest to rule the day. The market is the great sorter and distributor, rewarding the quick and the resourceful and eliminating the weak and indolent. These values enjoyed renewed vigour in the eighties in Thatcher's Britain,[24] Reagan-Bush's America,[25] and, as a paler variant, Mulroney's Canada[26] prompted by the Reform Party, among other forces.[27]

But liberalism, for all its pervasiveness and variants, did not stand alone. It co-existed with toryism and socialism. These ideologies, although antagonistic in their positions on the political spectrum, were aligned in their support (for different reasons) of collectivism. From the right came toryism — sometimes labelled 'red toryism' to highlight its support for communitarian values though extracting support for collectivism at a price. While it valued restraint of individual desire to further the public good, it did so in a framework that assumes a hierarchy in society and the sway of privilege for those at the top. In this it had a decided aversion to egalitarianism. Its linkage with the monarchy as the embodiment of the general welfare and the restraints on passionate majorities seems now only an artefact of a glory that is gone and never to be again.[28] Still its connection with communitarian values caused it to support government action from control of the economy to the erection of the welfare state.[29]

At first blush, socialism is the antithesis of toryism. It mocks such tory values as belief in the monarchy, the nation's connection with England, and hierarchy and élitism. Instead it emphasizes the betterment of ordinary people and the necessity for social and economic equality, at least at some minimum level. Yet both these ideologies turn their face against the pervasive claims of individualism as the race for happiness so cherished by liberalism. Indeed the presence of a vital collectivist tory strain in Canada left space in the Canadian political terrain for socialism to take root as a force that led to a vibrant political party, the NDP. It has formed the government in a number of provinces and territories in the early 1990s and has been a critical third party at the federal level,[30] though it is in tumult as it faces the clash between social democratic principles and huge government deficits.[31]

In Canada, however, the presence of and competition among several organizing ideas kept the nation moderate and centre-left. In comparing the two countries, Robertson Davies talked of Canada's 'deep affinity with

Scandinavia': 'It's hard for people in the [United] States to recognize this, but Canada is a socialist monarchy, like Sweden, Denmark and Norway. We have a leg in both camps, a limited welfare state and also a monarchy that causes a kind of clinging to the past.'[32]

However, one of the main themes we will explore is how dominant liberalism has been among the judiciary. We will see that veneration of individualism, including protecting economic and property rights, has often dominated the judges' decisions. This is not to contend that liberalism is to be shunned. Far from it. Individual responsibility, autonomy, choice, and respect for free markets capable of generating wealth are values that ought to be at the heart of society. This century is full of tragic examples to the contrary. But it is another matter to contend that such individualism should be the only value that is officially promoted. In many important ways a country's success will depend on supporting individualism, particularly around economic and property rights, in constructive tension with shared goals and ends. The judiciary's failure (until recently) to even contemplate such balancing is a deep and enduring criticism.

In contrast, it is the variegated ideology in Canada's political system that allowed this nation to make its way and hold in balance the many forces and strains present in this huge and complex country. There was rarely one ideological litmus test to be a Canadian.[33] Instead, it was ideological diversity, sometimes to a fault, that was depended upon to forge necessary solutions: 'Canada was in its origins and is still a country of rich ideological diversity . . . the explicit expression and acknowledgement of these differences gives our country a much greater chance to resolve the question of the kind of social life we wish to share as fellow citizens.'[34]

NATIONALISM AND NATIONAL IDENTITY

The uncertainties concerning our national identity have given rise to strong reactions. One set of views takes as a point of pride that 'Canada was from its depths experimental and conditional'.[35] This continuing search for who we are and for the best in this country is by and large the form of nationalism that has predominated. Its linchpin is not a push to organize the state along racial, linguistic boundaries but to enhance the particular characteristics of this state, to protect it from external influences, and to ensure independence of social, political, and economic policy, what Robert Stanfield has called 'simply a feeling for the nation'.[36]

Yet another reaction to our search for identity has been tinged by a hostility to the United States, or to put it starkly, 'Without at least a touch of anti-Americanism, Canada would have no reason to exist.'[37] Whatever economic impact free trade will have in the 1990s, it has, at least in the short run, brought a renewed awareness of the differences between Canadians and Americans and a commitment, at least by some, to preserve those differences, particularly with regard to our 'much more generous' welfare state.[38] The pact with Mexico may well evoke similar responses, though some argue that the policies of the Mulroney government, including free trade, have done irreparable damage to the cause of nationalism.[39]

Whatever the outcome, it is the case that throughout our history, our nationalism has been dominated by an attempt to imagine ourselves as something separate from the United States, a point already raised in the preceding section of this chapter.[40] This differentiation appears in many forms. One of the most interesting to contemplate is literature, where two themes related to a sense of difference from American society surface. The first is the vast unpopulated territory of Canada and coming to grips with it, particularly as a northern country.[41] The overwhelming brooding wilderness often claims central attention and takes on mystical proportions. Whether Frye's imposition of the natural world upon the Canadian psyche,[42] Atwood's theme of survival,[43] or Moss's exploration of isolation through what he calls the 'geophysical imagination',[44] we are left to ponder 'if any other national consciousness has had so large an amount of the unknown, the unrealized, the humanly indigestible, so built into it'.[45] Though perhaps out of fashion with those focused on the moment, such sentiments continue to appeal, especially for those who view their identity as connected to the past and to future generations: 'every year, whisking back and forth across Canada, the memories of the land return, restoring faith, inspiring hope, inducing humility, bringing perspective.'[46]

The second theme in Canadian literature in terms of national identity is the presence and treatment of women. Suggesting that our place beside the much more powerful United States can be compared with the traditional roles of men and women,[47] commentators have claimed that Canadian writers identify with women more than Americans, and that there are proportionately more female writers in Canada.[48] The metaphor of gender and Canadian-American relations has appeared repeatedly in the past: 'the sexual metaphor of national relationships [has] real importance in the Canadian imagination and in the Canadian self-conception. The metaphor reappears constantly. . . .'[49]

As feminism has increased in its efforts to empower women so too has Canadian literature undergone change in the presentation of the metaphor.[50] Canadian heroines are often strong characters and men are more gentle and reserved than in American fiction regardless of the gender of the author. In turn, women writers occupy more central positions in both English and French Canadian literature: 'Perhaps it is because female voices have a special resonance for the culture as a whole that, in Canada, women writers have assumed such an important role in defining a reality that is not uniquely feminine but, rather, profoundly Canadian.'[51]

Do the courts have a role in these elements of nationalism? Historically courts have attempted to nurture a connection between Canadian and

British law[52] and have been wary of American intrusion.[53] It is ironic then that the biggest threat to the Canadian identity in the future may come from judicial pronouncements. In his comparative work, *Continental Divide: The Values and Institutions of the United States and Canada*,[54] Lipset sifts through the similarities and dissimilarities of these two societies and sums up the differences between them — again not without controversy[55] — by entitling his last chapter 'Still Whig, Still Tory', referring to the United States as reflecting 'the influence of its classically liberal, Whig, individualistic, antistatist, populist, ideological origins' and to Canada as mirroring 'Tory-mercantilist, group-oriented, statist, deferential to authority' system.[56] When he considers the forces drawing the two societies together — Canada's assimilation to the ways of the United States — the one factor he considers the most influential is the Charter of Rights and Freedoms and the role of litigation and the judges in administering it:

> Perhaps the most important step that Canada has taken to Americanize itself — *far greater in its implication than the signing of the free trade treaty* — has been the incorporation into its constitution of a bill of rights, the Charter of Rights and Freedoms, placing the power of the state under judicial restraint . . . [T]he Charter makes Canada a more individualistic and litigious culture. . . . The greater institutional emphasis on individualism ultimately should be reflected in the country's values. By enacting the Charter, Canada has gone far toward joining the United States culturally. Whether it can continue to be 'a socialist monarchy', a deferential welfare state, will be its basic issue for the 21st century[57] [emphasis added].

Pursuing the significance of this view, particularly in light of observations that the legal élites in the two countries may be much more closely aligned than the populations generally,[58] will be one of the tasks of this book. Pressure on our courts to adopt American values and reasoning features prominently in debates about the Charter, particularly in issues of the administration of criminal law and women's issues. In addition, the Charter is the main vehicle for embracing a rights model of society, the model most closely associated with the United States. Judicially enforced rights carry many potential consequences, not the least of which is to mould the way we think of any society. Important differences between the United States as the home of judicial rights and any other country can be homogenized so that solutions to problems come from the particular right recognized and enforced by the courts, with the responses of American judges ever a background.

GOVERNMENT PRESENCE IN AND LACK OF COMPETITION IN THE ECONOMY

From the discussion of ideology and nationalism, we have seen that the government has played a strong role and continues to do so in the lives of Canadians. From the railways and nation-building programs of John A.

Macdonald,[59] to the Macdonald Commission,[60] government presence in the economy, regardless of party, has often been substantial. Indeed it has been argued that the willingness of Canadian élites to employ the state so broadly in economic issues was actually the source of tory ideology and not vice versa.[61] A related aspect was the fact that the Canadian economy has been so resource dependent. A land rich in resources is blessed with a source of wealth, but it is a type of wealth that individuals can do very little to alter,[62] which results in an almost antirisk-taking ethos compounded here by the massive amount of foreign ownership[63]: 'We are not an entrepreneurial country and never have been. . . . There is a feeling in the Canadian establishment that it is a little bit vulgar to go after things too hard.'[64]

Perhaps this lack of entrepreneurial spirit is best demonstrated by our attitude towards competition policy. While several incarnations of anticombines legislation have existed over the decades, they have been weak and sporadically enforced, and the few litigated cases have received a hostile reception in the courts. This slack presence of competitive enforcement, combined with the concentration of wealth,[65] brought warnings from Tom Keirans, vice-chairperson of McLeod, Young, Weir, that 'privatization' of Crown corporations must be done cautiously since if they are bought up by the few wealthiest interests, the consequence would be even greater concentration, making our economy even more of an oligopoly. In the same piece Keirans contended that there is 'no larger blot on the public policy record than our failure to come to terms with competition policy'.[66] A recent national study came to similar conclusions and also charged that among such problems of lack of competition is the high concentration of foreign-controlled firms that perform little research and development or sophisticated production in Canada.[67]

The courts' primary role concerning government presence in the economy and lack of competition has been to tolerate them. Most prominently, they have undercut whatever feeble attempts there have been to create and enforce a competition policy. Critics have continually charged the judges with defying legislators and regulators regarding enforcement of antitrust measures. Much of the criticism is accurate but may to a marked degree be beside the point. The courts may in fact have been reflecting the ethos that prevailed, at least until recently. This is one area, for better or worse, where they may have been reflective of the consensus, however wise it was. We shall also see that Parliament's reaction to the courts' record has been ambiguous.

DEFERENCE TO AUTHORITY AND HIERARCHY

There has always been a strong element of élitism and hierarchy in this country.[68] This attitude assumes that stratification in society is the inevitable result of some having greater endowments than others, and that far from being a bad thing, it is a good thing since it enables those who are best able to lead to do so.[69] Moreover, when aligned with a collectivist sense, it means that those who rule should do so for the public good and should exercise their power as if it were a trust. In exchange, there should be a strong deference to this authority.[70]

The unifying of the colonies in British North America was effected by Conservatives who were empire-oriented and who feared expansion by the United States and were apprehensive about the growth of influence within Canada of reform-minded 'pro-American' frontier settlers who favoured local autonomy. Likewise, giving Canada a strong central government that, in contrast to that of the United States, would be empowered to 'disallow' provincial laws was designed to resist the democratic threat from within or from across the border.

This attitude towards the need to preserve order and authority, to enhance respect for institutions can also be seen in the opening of the Canadian frontier, which was achieved with caution and care against the perceived American aggression. Accordingly, '[i]t was the established tradition of British North America that the power of civil authority should operate well in advance of the spread of settlement'.[71] As a result, the Northwest Mounted Police, centrally controlled, established themselves in the frontier settlements at the same time as the occupants. It is argued that an important effect of this was that Canada avoided, in large part, the bloody struggles with Amerindians that characterized the final advance of settlement in the United States.

These élitist and hierarchical values instilled in our society are said to have implications for civil liberties. It is contended that the élites' control, together with the diversity in this country, has led to a nation noted for its tolerance and respect for civil liberties. For example, it was argued that the unified and influential élites in this country chilled the development of a populism that produced the political intolerance associated with McCarthyism, Coughlinism, and the Ku Klux Klan in the United States. Yet it was also contended that this chilling of political intolerance resulted in less freedom: 'More careful examination of the American community in general, and perhaps of the academic community in particular, would probably reveal that, in spite of witch hunts in that country, the people of the United States enjoy in fact a much greater degree of freedom than do the people of Canada.'[72] In contrast, Kenneth McNaught argued that these same factors have resulted in Canada being the freer society where 'confidence in the social order minimizes resort to witch hunting. Genuinely conservative societies feel less need to require ideological conformity than do those [like the United States] in which the power of government is forever suspect.'[73]

Yet events such as the invocation by the Liberal government of the War Measures Act during the FLQ crisis in 1970 and the public support for it (when it appeared even then to be unjustified in light of the overwhelming majority in Quebec who disavowed violence[74]) indicates a country that is ready to allow everyone's basic freedoms to evaporate in the face of a tragic but otherwise controlled and controllable situation. And while the War Measures Act has been repealed, it is questionable whether the underlying attitudes have drastically altered. A poll in 1989 indicated that more Americans than Canadians (by 56 to 49 per cent) opposed the federal government's capacity to 'remove all civil rights' during 'times of crisis'. This difference increases when the comparison is confined to Americans and anglophone Canadians. Of French Canadians, 67 per cent were opposed, but such opposition shrank to 45 per cent among anglophones.[75]

What has been the courts' role in such issues? The themes of order and deference to authority have been largely reflected by the judiciary. An élite itself, the judiciary has been sympathetic to the goals of other Canadian ruling classes. This is reflected most clearly in its judgements on civil liberties and criminal law enforcement. With regard to the former, its record as protector of individual liberties has been excoriated by prominent authorities.[76] Respecting the latter, the due process model found in the United States has been less well recognized and instead judges have reflected a crime control model much more clearly emphasizing repression of criminal conduct so that law-abiding citizenry will be free and secure.[77] With the inception of the Charter, there has been a dramatic shift in the courts towards due process values. Such a change raises important questions regarding this society and, in particular, the future for the administration of criminal justice.

REGIONALISM

'Some countries have too much history but Canada has had too much geography.'[78] In a way, Mackenzie King said it all. Vast and sprawling with much of the land cold and forbidding for much of the year and settled by a ribbon of population stretched from coast to coast, this country's mass has had a great influence on what we have become. The gravitational pull has been to the centre. Ontario and Quebec may have had much that separates them, but they have been considered by the rest of Canada as the heartland, the core that regards itself as the focus of the nation and the rest of the country as the hinterland, which has to be cared for, coordinated, and dominated when necessary. Regionalism in Canada has defied a modern trend towards greater centralization.[79] Instead, change in this country has led to a more robust regionalism in Canada.[80] Indeed, it is generally agreed that this country is one of the most decentralized of industrialized nations, and that since the early 1960s, there has been a clear trend to such decentralization as measured by spending and tax shares.[81]

Though the various parts of Canada may be united in their resentment of central Canada, they have many differences among themselves in social, economic, and political arrangements — and, of course, geography. Indeed, the diversity among the various regions is an important factor in explaining the dominance of Quebec and Ontario. Despite the formidable barriers raised by two languages and two cultures, Quebec's and Ontario's economies and Montreal's and Toronto's anglo establishment were linked much more closely then any other segment of the country. To a large extent, such an arrangement continues today. The critical question for Canada's future, particularly in the wake of the constitutional tumult of the 1980s and early 1990s, is how to accommodate the needs of the various regions and how to change the perception that the federal government by and large equates the national interest with the interests of central Canada and still have a political and economic arrangement that results in one country.

Nowhere is this theme of diversity more patent than in the Atlantic provinces with substantial differences even within each of the four. For instance, the French and English of New Brunswick are located in different economic and geographic segments, and Cape Breton and the remainder of Nova Scotia have had to deal with deep and long-standing divisions.[82] Moreover, there are substantial economic variations among the four provinces. The image of the Atlantic provinces being poorer than the rest of Canada is borne out by statistics that show an average family income lower than that of the rest of the country. However, disaggregating that data for each of the Atlantic provinces shows that Prince Edward Island has fewer low-income families than the national average and Nova Scotia is at the national level. The depressed statistics are derived from Newfoundland and New Brunswick, which have significantly greater numbers of low-income families.[83]

Central Canada hogging the economy is a well-developed theme in the Atlantic region. The contention is that Atlantic Canada's poor economy is not a consequence of the region's lack of valuable natural resources nor of its geography.[84] In the nineteenth century, there were industries that prospered, but Confederation saw the exertion of control by central Canada and the Depression resulted in the collapse of industry and the important trades of forestry and fishing. Blame is attributed to the federal government for reflecting central Canada's business interests to disproportionately increase maritime freight rates.

With this economic fragility and diversity within the region, the notion of Quebec sovereignty is a disheartening threat. Quite apart from the philosophical antagonism that surely exists, the idea of Atlantic Canada being physically separated from the rest of the country is hard to imagine. Ontario, along with the western provinces and the territories, might be a more cohesive whole. But with Quebec gone, the Atlantic provinces would dangle precariously.[85]

The Yukon and Northwest Territories make up virtually 40 per cent of this country's land mass, but only 80,000 people live there.[86] A vast tract of land inhabited by so few who themselves are different in many ways creates a paradox that lies at the base of uncertainty about its future. History has viewed the North as large and barren, but beginning in the late 1950s through to the early 1970s with programs such as Diefenbaker's 'Roads to Resources', the North began to be seen as a source of assets that could be exploited for the entire country.

But into the 1970s there was a growing assertion that the North was not just a repository of resources but a home, however large and foreboding, to the Inuit, Amerindians, and whites. Such sentiment was documented and dramatized most notably by the Berger Inquiry into certain aspects of northern development. This assertion produced a 'no development' reaction, but in the 1980s, some need for — and benefit from — development has been acknowledged, and the focus has been on enterprises that minimize the effect on the way of life of those who have had a long-standing relationship with the North. Training, employment opportunities, and joint ventures contain the potential for First Peoples to enjoy the tangible benefits from the projects. Thus for First Peoples, the issues into the twenty-first century involve land claims and development that respects their needs. For whites, the object is for control of the territory of land and resources, culminating in its admission as a province.[87]

Though British Columbia is part of the 'West' in relation to the competition with and resentment of central Canada, historically it has been different from the three prairie provinces because it relies upon mining and lumbering rather than wheat farming as its base industry and its economy is tied to large corporations from central Canada and the United States. Recently it has been argued that BC differs in two fundamental ways: it is part of the Pacific Rim and beginning in the 1980s, there was an aggressive embrace of the 'new right' ideology.[88]

These two factors have been linked so that it has been argued that ideology has allowed the welfare system, public sector, and unions to be attacked in order to effect the substantial change necessary to accommodate global restructuring of industry so touted by the Pacific Rim environment. This can be seen as consistent with the traditional response of BC governments to external events and international capital and aided by an electorate that is polarized so intemperateness more easily takes hold.[89] The recent election of the NDP signals change yet again, particularly in turning from a right ideology. But what this will mean in terms of substance remains to be seen.

British Columbia is linked as part of the 'West', but the core of that sense of regionalism belongs to the three prairie provinces. A sense of alienation from the country itself has been a continuing presence in these three provinces, surging and waning just as the economy has gyrated in boom and bust. Financial stability and a secure share of political power are possible but are never securely grasped, and the course of life is determined elsewhere.[90]

The feeling of being marginalized was there from the beginning. The economic rule of the West by central Canada mirrored political rule. The governor of the prairie territory appointed by the Dominion was often decisive in his role until the coming of responsible government in 1897. Before the prairie provinces obtained control of natural resources in 1930, the Dominion's Department of the Interior shaped settlement and development. In 1905, Alberta and Saskatchewan became provinces, but their boundaries were designed by federal politicians and did not take into account the needs of the respective provinces. These provinces' first premiers were chosen by the Laurier government. And the federal government frequently used its powers of disallowance against legislation of the western provinces.[91]

Even during snatches of prosperity the West seethed at the centre's dominance and ignorance of their problems.[92] Reviewing the relationship between the two, Smiley suggested that, in fact, central Canada controlled the West through policies grounded in classic mercantilism: the hinterland has been confined to the production of staple products that are exported in a raw or semi-finished state; the hinterland has been required to buy the manufactured goods of the heartland; the hinterland's capital development has been controlled by institutions of the heartland; the hinterland's interests have been subordinated to the heartland in external economic relations; the hinterland and heartland have been connected by transportation operated for the benefit of the heartland; hinterland-heartland relations have been managed through large business aggregates shielded by the heartland from hinterland and foreign competition.[93] To the West, there was no more provocative example of such control than the ill-fated National Energy Program, a major source of contemporary alienation. Another reason for this disaffection (that had surfaced by the 1960s) was the ascendancy of the issue of language and culture in the heartland, with its incarnation, Pierre Elliott Trudeau. To the West, the contention that cultural duality was the linchpin of Canada was a claim that was irrelevant at best and (to many) destructive of the very Confederation it presumed to sustain.[94]

Nonetheless, talking about the West's reaction as 'alienation' may misdescribe an already complicated phenomenon. The revolts of the West have not exemplified the characteristics of political alienation: apathy towards the polity and the product of dispossessed and marginal groups. Instead it is a reaction that became widely shared during a period of increasing (if uncertain) prosperity and it is sustained by the upper echelons of the society. Moreover — as contrasted with Quebec — there are no serious separatist movements and indeed the clamour is not for withdrawal but for greater rights of participation in the Confederation. Meanwhile, the rise of the Reform Party[95] provides a political vehicle specifically for such interests and for assorted right-wing aspirations regarding bilingualism, multiculturalism, immigration, tax policy, and welfare.[96]

The rounds of constitutional reformulation in 1982 and Meech Lake did little to assist. On the whole, the premiers of the West were reactive in the negotiations leading to the Constitution Act of 1982, which was not a significant response to their concerns. Meech Lake reflected the concerns of Quebec, but aside from putting Senate reform on the agenda, it did little to respond to the hinterland's needs. While the Accord was initially endorsed enthusiastically by western provincial leaders, it was received with a chill by the people, and events in the Manitoba legislature played a significant part in its downfall.[97] A similar set of explanations could account for the rejection of the Charlottetown Accord in addition to the complexities surrounding recognition of Aboriginals' right to self-government.[98]

Regionalism is one area where the impact of the courts appears direct. The British North America Act provides for division of powers between the provinces and the federal government. But the division of powers, in many cases, overlap. Drawing the boundary lines — and shifting them — became the courts' task. And much of federalism litigation has been fuelled by themes discussed in this section: most prominently control of the economy by the federal government and chiefly in ways alleged to benefit central Canada.

The harder issue to tackle is the impact of this judicial role compared with other ways in which issues arising from regionalism have been manifested and responded to. Essentially, we will see that the courts have mostly acted to create bargaining chips that are then used by the respective parties in the continuing negotiations surrounding regionalism issues, though with various contentions, at different times, that either the provinces or the federal government were being preferred by the judges. Nevertheless, there is a basis for claiming that judges have had a positive role in the endless adjustments that our federalism demands. What can be a problem is the increasing velocity with which the judicial role is expanding, particularly when it is occurring alongside other forms of judicialization such as judicial review of administrative action and, most prominently, the Charter.

THE ENGLISH AND THE FRENCH

'. . . I found two nations warring in the bosom of a single state: I found a struggle not of principle, but of races. . . .'[99] — Lord Durham

'Canada and the French-Canadian question is really the Canadian question.'[100]

— Ramsay Cook

The Meech Lake Accord called Quebec the 'Distinct Society', but other phrases such as 'pas une province comme les autres', 'statut particulier', etc., reflect a social and political structure different from the rest of Canada. Quebec is both part of the central Canada that the rest of Canada envies and resents and is set apart from the rest of Canada because of its linguistic, political, and cultural heritage.

The matter is further complicated because 'English' Canada has for some time been increasingly heterogeneous in terms of its cultural and linguistic composition. Historically, especially in the West, many settlers' first language was not English. Instead, it was often a language of eastern Europe or elsewhere. In the last decades, there has been a large influx of immigration from Third World countries, particularly to the large urban areas.[101] It is no exaggeration to say that at least with regard to 'English' Canada, multiculturalism is a separate force in society; it has been the federal government's official policy for over two decades.[102] The pressure to accommodate multiculturalism is particularly strong around issues of race relations and there are claims to alter the institutions of power to allow for full participation by visible minorities.[103]

Quebec is a much more homogeneous society, at least in terms of the linguistic and cultural goals it officially promotes, especially in terms of first language, with Quebec the only province where the people are primarily French. In 1981, 82 per cent spoke French at home. The next closest province was New Brunswick, where only 31 per cent spoke French at home, while in Ontario the comparable figure was 4 per cent, and in all other provinces 3 per cent or less. Politically, Quebec's law has always been based on the Civil Code rather than the common law, and in the last decades the provincial government has had an important role in immigration and activities such as book publishing and film distribution.[104]

Preserving the French identity and yet co-existing with the English has been the dual but often contradictory mission since the conquest.[105] Indeed, it was a French-English duality in government that was the premise for Confederation negotiations. Many of the fathers of Confederation would have preferred a unitary government, but to the French Canadians, such an arrangement was unacceptable. As George Brown stated; 'We had either to take a Federal union or drop the negotiations.'[106]

The pact sealed, Quebec and the rest of Canada settled into a co-existence, the framework of which endured for almost 100 years until the beginning of the 1960s. This is not to say that there were no conflicts between the French and English. There was bitter strife concerning the treatment of French Catholic minorities outside Quebec and the orientation of Canada in external affairs in which the English overwhelmingly prevailed. These battles made Quebec a prominent defender of provincial rights, though in this period Ontario was the real leader of such assertions, probably because that province never had concerns in bolstering federal power against other provinces while Quebec did as it attempted to protect French Catholic minorities outside its borders, particularly as Manitoba flagrantly ignored the rights of that minority.[107]

Yet despite those issues of conflict, French-English relations were remarkably stable during this long period. Smiley pointed to a number of elements that were the foundation of this stability.[108] For example, there was the division of legislative powers. For its part, Ottawa used its powers, particularly up to the First World War, to develop the national economy, a matter in which there were no essential differences between the French and English. Conversely, the federal government did not involve itself in those matters within provincial jurisdiction that were considered critical to the French language and culture. In addition, there was institutional self-segregation. From the conquest there was developed and sustained in Quebec a culture in opposition to that dominating the rest of Canada: the French language, Catholic religion, authoritarianism, and the values of agrarian and rural life were set against the English language, Protestant religion, democracy, materialism, and commercial (and sub-sequent industrial) economy.[109]

Yet by the 1960s and Quebec's Quiet Revolution, the agreement was coming apart. The beginning of its undoing can be traced to many years earlier. The established institutions and their bases were ill-suited to a changing, industrializing North America and the Catholic Church as the focal point of culture was losing its grip. Similarly, reacting to a complex social order, the federal government respected federal-provincial boundaries of legislative activity less and less and entered into areas initially reserved for local governance. While not directed at Quebec, its impact was to erode the foundation upon which the francophone culture was built. By the 1960s, the government in Ottawa had invaded areas that were initially used by Quebec to foster the francophone culture. Predominantly because of its spending power, which was subject to little constitutional restraint, the federal government was directly involved in health, welfare, higher education, and vocational training. Conversely, Quebec governments came to see survival as dependent upon the province's control of its own economic development with an ensuing challenge to established federal powers. While other reasons could be discussed, what was evident was that as a result of the upheaval in Quebec during and after the Quiet Revolution, Canada now had two modernized linguistic communities.[110]

The furor surrounding three events in the late 1980s and the early 1990s would demonstrate that the francophones' aspirations to make Quebec their secure homeland remained intense regardless of whatever government was in office. The first concerned the Supreme Court of Canada's treatment of Bill 101. This bill had a number of provisions designed to make French the pre-eminent language in Quebec. In December 1988, the Supreme Court of Canada struck down the sections requiring French-only commercial signs as violating the Charter of Rights and Freedoms and Quebec's Human Rights Act. The Bourassa government responded with legislation that restricted outdoor signs to French but allowed other languages to accompany French within stores and used the notwithstanding clause to immunize the enactment from further judicial scrutiny.[111]

The second event that demonstrated the intensity of francophone feeling was the failure of the Meech Lake Accord. Whatever the achievements and failings of the 1982 Constitution, it was clear that it had not responded to francophones' demand that the government of Quebec be given the status and power to represent their aspirations. Quebec had refused to be a signatory to it, charging that last-minute negotiations among other parties had betrayed its interests.

The Accord responded to these aspirations, but even then in a limited way. Quebec was acknowledged to be a 'distinct society', but this was offset by a preceding clause involving a linguistic duality extending throughout Canada and was further qualified by a provision insisting that the federal government's 'powers, rights or privileges' could not be diminished. A provision existed for opting out with compensation from federal spending programs if it were established that the provincial substitute was compatible with 'national objectives' set by Ottawa. There was a provision allowing provinces to enter into agreements with the federal government concerning immigration, but this formalized what had been existing practice. There was some shift concerning the Senate and the Supreme Court with the provinces providing lists of those from whom the federal government would choose to make the appointments.

After initial indications that it would pass, agreement for the Accord in the provinces unravelled, most prominently in Manitoba and Newfoundland. Its failure sent waves through the country and the Mulroney government reeled for about a year in dislocation. In the summer of 1991, the country girded itself for yet another attempt, this time coordinated by Joe Clark, federal minister for constitutional affairs. Quebec was officially absent from these talks until the last stages, signalling that the status quo was untenable and that what Meech Lake offered might no longer be enough.[112]

As these events led to the Charlottetown Accord and its eventual fall, yet another force became a critical constitutional player, giving rise to the third factor concerning feelings of intensity around Quebec as the homeland for the French. Aboriginals had long pressed a number of issues from land claims and treaties to self-government to sovereignty, demands by no means limited to Quebec.[113] Yet in that province, Aboriginal assertions clashed with Quebec's own claims for autonomy from the rest of Canada. For example, there were critical questions concerning the fate of Amerindian land claims if Quebec should separate, since those claims were also tied to the First Peoples' relationship with the federal government.

In Quebec the immediate flashpoint during this period was the armed stand-off by Mohawk warriors over land claims in the summer of 1990 (the 'Oka crisis') and also the struggles of the Cree in the north to block Hydro-Quebec's Great Whale power project, which would flood thousands of acres of their land.[114] More positively, there was an acceleration of the process to deal with land claims, the review of the Indian Act by the Assembly of First Nations, and the appointment of a Royal Commission on Aboriginal Peoples. Furthermore, Amerindians became unstoppably involved in the 1992 round of constitutional negotiations, and self-government was eventually recognized in the document. Yet Charlottetown struggled to mesh the assertion of Aboriginal self-government with Quebec's claims for autonomy.[115]

But Charlottetown failed. Why? Explanations abound. It was insufficiently responsive to the needs of Quebec to have the constitutional means to protect itself as a distinct and minority society. It gave too much to Quebec and would have privileged it at the expense of the rest of Canada. It was unintelligible in terms of what changes would actually be effected. It was insufficiently attentive to the needs of women, particularly minority women (and especially Aboriginal women), possibly depriving them of the Charter's protection. It gave too much discretion to the courts on these and other issues, and so on. One thing is certain: issues surrounding Quebec — its claim to be a distinct society, its claim to be sovereign — will not disappear. The same can be said for Aboriginal issues, particularly the claim to recognition of the right of self-government, including its relationship to claims made by Quebec.

The courts have had an important role regarding Quebec's place in the country, particularly since the Second World War. One study we will examine indicates that the Supreme Court was often the federal institution most attuned until the 1980s to various strains of political thought in Quebec. The Charter of Rights and its interpretation by the Supreme Court regarding Quebec is an entirely different question. Claims that the Charter would unite Canada have foundered regarding that province; the contrary is the case.

The courts and Aboriginals is a different matter again. Unclear about self-government — perhaps unwilling to clarify lest concreteness dissolve tenuous agreement — the participants in the Charlottetown round seemed set upon giving the courts dominion over this abstract concept. We will discuss Amerindians and the courts directly in the chapter on the Charter, including the implications of what Charlottetown attempted and failed to do regarding their claim to self-government. Such a discussion will also be an occasion to observe radically different views of courts in this society: one that is optimistic about the transformative powers of the judges regarding Aboriginal issues; the other alienated by the hegemony of the dominant culture's courts, particularly regarding rights and the Charter.

CONCLUSION

'Our leadership groups — including artists, intellectuals and even journalists — must stop being so much part of the problem in refusing to face up to change. Whether it be economic nationalism, the nature of social programs, the state of Canada's democracy or the monarchy, the truth will win out.'[116] So goes an essay by the editor-in-chief of *The Globe and Mail*. Its burden was to alert us to how much about our national belief system and its related structures should be myth. The editor is not alone. He is joined by a chorus ready with the torch, convinced we must soon lay ourselves upon a pyre of fragmentation and disunity.[117] With the rejection of Meech Lake and then Charlottetown, the woeful death rattle may have begun. It is all so inevitable — undefended borders, increasingly integrated economies, common language and culture (Quebec will stay on its wilful own), with capitalism and liberalism the true order of the day — Canada merged with the United States, the true fulfilment of manifest destiny.

Is that the sticking point? Even many unreserved enthusiasts of free trade and pronounced sceptics of Meech Lake and the 1992 round and their attempts at rapprochement bridle at unity with the United States. One can debate the notion of 'variegated ideology', its existence and its effect. One can question the comparative significance of women writers and feminism in literature or the attitudinal differences between the peoples of the two countries. But the safety and cleanliness of streets, the continuous efforts to provide quality in public education, capital punishment as a reaction to crime, the level of violent crime, gun control, universal accessibility to sound medical care, the more elaborate social safety net, and the presence of Quebec as a home for the French language and culture tell a tale.

In 'Canadians Do It Better', *The Economist* compared Detroit and Toronto.[118] Characterizing the latter as 'virtually crime-free' and extolling its capacity to manage growth while constructing a positive urban environment on the idea that 'busy and lively streets are the best deterrent against crime',[119] the article says this of Detroit:

> Within a mile of the Renaissance Centre, Detroit's landmark skyscraper, stand hundreds of handsome redbrick houses. They are similar to the turn-of-the-century houses that fetch $400,000 plus in a gentrified downtown area of Toronto known as Cabbagetown.... Yet the Detroit houses are worthless. They have been abandoned by their owners. A few still house squatters: the poverty-stricken as well as drunks, whores, crack addicts. . . .[120]

To counter the comparison, it could be said that in terms of the complexities of cities, Toronto represents the best of Canada, Detroit the worst of the United States. This is arguable, including for many in the rest of Canada who are resentful of Toronto's claims. Nevertheless, a number of metropolitan centres in the United States have murder rates that have increased markedly faster than Detroit's.[121] The claim is that Canadian urban areas hug the pole of the spectrum occupied by Toronto with the reverse the case for American cities and Detroit.

Yet Canada may unravel. The problems of regionalism and Quebec are serious and pressing. The events leading to the failure of Meech Lake showed intolerance between the English and French at an all time high: 'Never in our post-war history has English-speaking Canada felt cooler to

Quebec as a partner in nationhood. And never in our post-war history have Quebec's political, intellectual and economic élites felt more common cause in testing the rest of Canada's desire for continued union.'[122] And in the end, who knows what the demise of Charlottetown demonstrated,[123] but surely there is potential in it for critically aggravating Quebec's relationship with the rest of the country.

But two points need to be borne in mind in this gloom. First, they call us the peaceable kingdom, but the way we govern ourselves is anything but. The promise of democracy does not rest on a tranquil base. Disagreements — sometimes the stormiest clashes — are necessary to bring out competing values so that the largest number of interests and needs can be taken into account.[124] The optimistic believe this is what is occurring, not only in terms of Quebec, but also regarding the claims of the excluded: women, lesbian and gays, visible minorities, the disabled, and Aboriginals. But even if Quebec cannot be accommodated within this country, there is still hope that Canada can be a model in demonstrating how divorce can be achieved and a new association established through peaceful means. Second, recent pronouncements about our impending doom[125] join a long chorus that we must end so that our integration with the United States can be fulfilled. From Goldwin Smith[126] to George Grant[127] to that magnate turned seer, Conrad Black,[128] our ending has been announced.[129]

But we continue hesitantly. And in this there is surely virtue, for it is not tentativeness that has immersed us in blood in this dangerous century. Rather, it is the terrorism of dictators, the rigidity of ideology and imperialism that have ignited war. Temperateness is not boring weakness but an essential bulwark in responding to problems that will always beset us. Yet so many contingencies abound that the course of this nation over the next decade could easily take several routes, some with sobering implications.

To conclude this attempt to portray us, I give the last word to one of our titans, capturing as it does both our aspirations and apprehensions. Northrop Frye said, shortly before his death, that 'Canada is the Switzerland of the twentieth century, surrounded by the great powers of the world and preserving its identity by having many identities.' Still, a statue emblematic of Canadian patriotism would depict 'someone holding his breath and crossing his fingers'.[130] The worry is that such tentative enduring may have come to the end of the road.

NOTES

[1]The Citizens' forum in 1990–1, as part of attempts at constitutional renewal, heard from over 400,000 Canadians regarding their views about Canada and its problems. It reported that the most common complaint of those participating was that they 'have lost faith in both the political process and political leadership': see 'Citizens' Forum on Canada's Future', *The Globe and Mail*, 2 July 1991, A9; see also J. Hall, 'We Liked Politicians Better in the Old Days, Gallup Says', *The*

Toronto Star, 3 August 1992, A1 and 'Only 9% Have Respect For Political Parties', *The Toronto Star*, 16 March 1992, A15.

[2] L. Schein, 'Canada Second Only to Japan in Survey of Best Places to Live', *The Globe and Mail*, 23 May 1991, A1; 'First Column', *The Globe and Mail*, 17 May 1993, A1; P. Lewis, 'The New UN Index Measures Wealth as Quality of Life', *The New York Times*, 23 May 1993, A6.

[3] The literature on these diverse voices questioning traditional arrangements is vast and by no means limited to this country. It also occupies many disciplines. A mere sampling would include: S. Burt, L. Code, L. Dorney (eds), *Changing Patterns — Women in Canada* (2nd ed.) (Toronto: McClelland & Stewart, forthcoming), A. Cairns, 'The Constitutional World We Have Lost', unpublished, a paper presented at the annual meeting of the Canadian Political Science Association, University of Prince Edward Island, June 1992 (political science); R. Brym with B. Fox, *From Culture to Power — The Sociology of English Canada* (Toronto: Oxford University Press, 1989), especially Chapter 5 'The Feminist Challenge: A Reconsideration of Social Inequality and Economic Development' (sociology); C. Gilligan, *In a Different Voice* (Cambridge: Harvard University Press, 1982) (psychology); O. Dickason, *Canada's First Nations: A History of Founding Peoples* (Toronto: McClelland & Stewart, 1992) (history); P. Williams, *The Alchemy of Race and Rights* (Cambridge: Harvard University Press, 1991) (law); L. Hutcheon, *The Canadian Postmodern* (Toronto: Oxford University Press, 1988), and R. Kroetsch, *The Lovely Treachery of Words* (Toronto: Oxford University Press, 1989) (literature).

[4] See, for example, S. Fine, 'The Rights Revolution — the Courts Lead the Charge', *The Globe and Mail*, a two-part series, 24 and 25 November 1992, A1.

[5] A. Strachan, 'The Hidden Opposition', *The Globe and Mail*, 11 January 1992, D3.

[6] See O. Dickason, *Canada's First Nations — A History of Founding Peoples From Earliest Times* (Toronto: McClelland & Stewart, 1992): 16, for a discussion of the problem of a general name for the New World peoples. 'Amerindian' is Dickason's (herself a Métis) preferred term because it avoids the ambiguities of 'Indian' and 'native' and is more specific than 'Aboriginal'. See also R. Wright, *Stolen Continents* (Toronto: Penguin, 1993): xi. I will use 'Amerindian', 'First Peoples', and 'Aboriginals' interchangeably.

[7] Dickason, ibid.

[8] Ibid., 418.

[9] C. Taylor, 'Alternative Futures — Legitimacy, Identity, and Alienation in Late Twentieth Century Canada' in A. Cairns and C. Williams (eds), *Constitutionalism, Citizenship and Society in Canada* (Toronto: University of Toronto Press, 1986): 183. See also C. Taylor, 'Can Canada Survive the Charter?' (1992) 30 *Alberta Law Review*, 427.

[10] Ibid., 209.

[11] Ibid.

[12] Ibid., 211.

[13] Ibid.

[14] S.M. Lipset, *Continental Divide: The Values and Institutions of the United States and Canada* (Toronto: C.D. Howe Institute and Washington: National Planning Association, 1989): 2.

[15] M. Atwood, *The Journals of Susanna Moodie: Poems* (Toronto: Oxford University Press, 1970): 62.

[16] *Supra*, note 14 at xiv–xv.

[17] For example, Louis Hartz, an American political scientist, argued some time ago that overseas European societies, including the United States and Canada, were settled by the middle class and so were 'fragment cultures' with neither the aristocracy nor the peasantry of Europe. Thus, he contended that an ideological left could not exist in these overseas societies because of a lack of a hereditary aristocracy to provide a true conservative or tory view as the counterweight, because there is no feudal tradition to ground an enduring sense of class identity, and because the foundation upon which an ideological left would be grounded had been institutionalized by the liberal and even radical founding premises of these new countries. Though Hartz duly noted the presence of toryism in Canada as a reaction to the American Revolution, he contended that the countries were far more united in their similarities and the true differentiation was as against the older European societies. See L. Hartz, *The Founding of New Societies* (New York: Harcourt, Brace and World, 1969): 34; Lipset, *supra*, note 14 at 9–10, contrasts his thesis with Hartz's. For further discussion of Hartz, see K.D. McRae, 'The Structure of Canadian History', an essay in ibid., 219–74. See also D.V. Bell, 'The Loyalist Tradition in Canada' (1970) 5 *Journal of Canadian Studies*, 22–3; and K.D. McRae, 'Louis Hartz' Concept of the Fragment Society and Its Application to Canada' (1978) 5 *Etudes Canadiennes*, 17–30.

[18] G. Horowitz, *Canadian Labour in Politics* (Toronto: University of Toronto Press, 1968): Chapter 1, 3.

[19] W. Christian and C. Campbell, *Political Parties and Ideologies in Canada* (2nd ed.) (Toronto: McGraw-Hill Ryerson Limited, 1983): 27–8.

[20] *Supra*, note 18 at 18.

[21] Taylor, 'Can Canada Survive the Charter?', *supra*, note 9 at 429.

[22] For example, R. Brym with B. Fox, *From Culture to Power — The Sociology of English Canada* (Toronto: Oxford University Press, 1989): 61–6. By contrast, see H. Forbes, 'Hartz — Horowitz at Twenty: Nationalism, Toryism and Socialism in Canada and the United States' (1987) 20 *Canadian Journal of Political Science*, 287, reviewing the substantial literature on these ideas, evaluating the criticisms, and basically agreeing with Horowitz's contentions when linked to Canadian nationalism.

[23] Taylor, 'Can Canada Survive the Charter?', *supra*, note 9 at 429.

[24] Editorial, 'A Season of British Discontent', *The Globe and Mail*, 27 February 1993, D6.

[25] K. Philips, *The Politics of Rich and Poor* (New York: Harper Perennial, 1991).

[26] A. Freeman, 'Major Economic Reform Mulroney Legacy', *The Globe and Mail*, 25 February 1993, A14.

[27] A party whose prospects heading into the 1990s may be mixed: K. Whyte, 'Nice Guys Finish Last' (July/August 1993) *Saturday Night*, 15.

[28] *Supra*, note 19 at 28:

These tory ideas have . . . contributed to the long-standing Canadian tendency to use the power of government to effect common goals or objects; and, moreover, to use it with equanimity and often with enthusiasm. This can be seen in a multitude of instances from the railway and canal building of the last century to the initiation of public enterprises such as the CBC, Air Canada, Ontario Hydro and Petro-Canada in more recent times.

[29] While there is controversy about this, the principle sources of toryism have been said to have derived from the Loyalists who fled the American Revolution, repulsed by their countrymen's embrace of liberalism, and from the massive wave of nineteenth-century British immigration. Others have pointed to the lawful taming of the Canadian West, contrasted to the lawless and violent American frontier, as well as to the Canadian adoption of British institutions such as the monarchy and the acceptance of the role of government in building the economy as other sources and reflections of toryism. Canadians' chilly attitude to egalitarianism and tolerance for stratification, élitism, and privilege have also been seen as a source: see Horowitz, *supra*, note 18 at 15–16.

[30] Ibid., 16, and *supra*, note 19 at 29: '[Toryism] helped to keep Canada open to imported socialist ideas because through collectivist toryism, socialism had a ready-made point of contact, or introduction, to Canadian society. It was not an exotic foreign growth; it "fitted" into the Canadian ideological structure.'

[31] G. York, 'Has the Left Sold Out?', *The Globe and Mail*, 17 July 1993, D1.

[32] J. Mitgang, 'Robertson Davies, A Novelist of the North', *New York Times*, 29 December 1988, 11.

[33] If anything, the fierce holding of a forceful, unrelenting set of ideas was considered un-Canadian. In *A Prayer for Owen Meany*, a main character, American-born, is living in Toronto and is taken to task for his vehemence: 'It's very Canadian to distrust strong opinions. . . . Your anger — that's not very Canadian either.' J. Irving, *A Prayer for Owen Meany* (New York: William Morrow, 1989): 203–4.

[34] *Supra*, note 19 at 3.

[35] W.L. Morton, *The Canadian Identity* (2nd ed.), (Toronto: University of Toronto Press, 1972): 131.

[36] Christian and Campbell, *supra*, note 19 at 194, quoting Robert Stanfield, Notes for 1978 Josiah Wood Lectures, 'Nationalism: A Canadian Dilemma', Mount Allison University, 7–8 February 1978, First Lecture, 3.

[37] B. Fraser, *The Search for Identity: Canada, 1945–67* (Garden City: Doubleday, 1967): 301. See also S.D. Clark in H.F. Angus (ed.), *Canada and Her Great Neighbor: Sociological Surveys of Opinions and Attitudes in Canada Concerning the United States* (Toronto: Ryerson Press: 1938): 243, 245.

[38] S. Schlefer, 'What Price Economic Growth?', *The Atlantic*, December 1992, 113, 115:

> The concerns of Canadian critics center on erosion of the welfare state, which is much more generous in Canada than in the United States. For example, in Canada both health care and Old Age Security are universal — eligibility for the latter, unlike the US Social Security, is based not on work history but on age alone. The differences between Canadian and US unemployment insurance are staggering. In 1988 seventy percent of unemployed Canadians received insurance covering 60 percent of their wages, while 32

percent of Americans received benefits covering 35 percent of their wages. In other words, nearly 70 percent in the United States got nothing. In both countries unions push for broad social programs (which reduce unemployed workers' incentive to break strikes), but Canadian unions represent 36 percent of employed workers (outside agriculture), while US unions represent 18 percent. The whole attitude toward unions is different. Canada Year Book 1992, a more colorful if less figure-packed counterpart to the Statistical Abstract of the United States, features in its chapter on employment a photo of a miners' strike and a chart on 'Unions With Largest Membership'.

[39] For a rousing journalistic account of this point, see L. Martin, *Pledge of Allegiance — The Americanization of Canada in the Mulroney Years* (Toronto: McClelland & Stewart, 1993). See also M. Barlow and B. Campbell, *Take Back the Nation* (Toronto: Key Porter Books, 1991) and M. Hurtig, *The Betrayal of Canada* (2nd ed.) (Toronto: Stoddart, 1992).

[40] Lipset, *supra*, note 14 at xiv: 'Much of what Canadian intellectuals, both scholars and creative artists, write about their own country is presented in a comparative context — that is, with reference to the nation to the south. They frequently seek to describe what Canada is about by stressing what it is not: the United States.'

[41] See also Morton, *supra*, note 35 at 88, and C. Bissell, 'The Place of Learning and the Arts in Canadian Life' in R. Preston (ed.), *Perspectives on Revolution and Evolution* (Durham: Duke University Press, 1979): 208, arguing that novels in Canada are more a part 'of European than American literature'.

[42] N. Frye, *The Bush Garden* (Toronto: Anansi, 1971).

[43] M. Atwood, *Survival* (Toronto: Anansi, 1972).

[44] J. Moss, *Patterns of Isolation* (Toronto: McClelland & Stewart, 1974): 109.

[45] *Supra*, note 42 at 220.

[46] J. Simpson, 'Where Every Prospect Pleases, and Government Seems Irrelevant', *The Globe and Mail*, 1 July 1992, A12, and W. Davis, 'In the Snow and Silence, Breaking Trail', *The Globe and Mail*, 28 December 1992, A15.

Robertson Davies, speaking directly about Canadian literature and the influence of the North upon it, characterized writing in this country as more closely connected with Scandinavian countries than with America:

> I like to think that Canada's greatest writers are Ibsen and Chekhov [he said, laughing]. When I go to Scandinavia and step off the plane, I ask myself if I've really left home. There is that very powerful sunlight and the wind-torn pine trees. The real Canadian is a Northerner. I'm a great believer in the influence of the climate and the land in plays and novels.

See Mitgang, *supra*, note 32.

[47] H. MacLennan, 'The Psychology of Canadian Nationalism' (1949) 27 *Foreign Affairs*, 414–15. This same point is sometimes put even more starkly. Consider this passage from a novel of the early 1980s and how the protagonist in a nineteenth century marriage describes her relationship:

> I feel I am acting out America's relationship to the Canadas. Martin is the imperial ogre while I play the role of the gentle mate who believes that if everyone is well-mannered, we can inhabit a peaceable kingdom. That is the national dream of the Canadas, isn't it? A civilized garden where lions lie

down with doves. I did not see the difference until I married Martin. We possess no fantasies of conquest and domination. Indeed, to be from the Canadas is to feel as women feel — cut off from the base of power.

See S. Swan, *The Biggest Modern Woman of the World* (Toronto: Lester and Orpen Dennys, 1983): 273–4.

[48] See Lipset, *supra*, note 14 at 63–4, 71–3, and, in particular, 242n.7 for further references.

[49] R. Brown, 'A Search for America: Some Canadian Literary Responses' (1980) 2 *Journal of American Culture*, 676.

[50] Ibid., 679: 'Feminine Canada has broken away from the traditional sex roles at a time when they were in actuality being abandoned, has ceased trying to play the "good wife" in a harmonious, supportive relationship with her dominant "husband" nation.'

[51] M.J. Green, 'Writing in a Mother Land' (Hanover: French Department, Dartmouth College, 1984).

[52] H.E. Read, 'The Judicial Process in Common Law Canada' (1959) 37 *Canadian Bar Review*, 265.

[53] J.M. MacIntyre, 'The Use of American Cases in Canadian Courts' (1964–6) 2 *University of British Columbia Law Review*, 478.

[54] *Supra*, note 14.

[55] For criticism of some of Lipset's earlier ideas about this country, see R. Brym with B. Fox, *supra*, note 22 at 24 *et seq*; specifically regarding *Continental Divide*, see D. Baer et al., 'The Values of Canadians and Americans: A Rejoinder' (1990) 69 *Social Forces*, 273, and see also 'The Values of Canadians and Americans: A Critical Analysis and Reassessment' (1990) 68 *Social Forces*, 693.

[56] Brym and Fox, ibid., 212.

[57] Lipset, *supra*, note 14 at 225–6 (emphasis added).

[58] M.A. Glendon, 'A Beau Mentir Qui Vient du Loin: The 1988 Canadian Abortion Decision in Comparative Perspective' (1989) 83 *North Western University Law Review*, 569, 589.

[59] P. Berton, *The National Dream: The Last Spike* (Toronto: McClelland & Stewart, 1974).

[60] *Royal Commission on the Economic Union and Development Prospects for Canada* (Ottawa: Ministry of Supply and Services, 1985), informally known as the Macdonald Report, named after its chair.

[61] R.T. Naylor, 'The Rise and Fall of the Third Commercial Empire of the St Lawrence' in G. Teeple (ed.), *Capitalism and the National Question in Canada* (Toronto: University of Toronto Press, 1972).

[62] R. Gwyn, *The 49th Paradox: Canada in North America, Past, Present and Future* (Toronto: McClelland & Stewart, 1985): 197:

> As is common among people who earn their living by selling resources, Canadians have never taken economics particularly seriously. After all, it was God and nature . . . who put the resources into the ground in the first place. Thereafter, the value of those resources is determined more by events elsewhere — wars, depressions, booms, bumper harvests, droughts, and floods — than by the ingenuity of those who happen to live on top of the resources.

Among Canadians, this tendency to economic passivity is heightened by the massive extent of foreign ownership and by the comprador character of so many Canadian businesses, as order-takers rather than as decision-makers.

[63]M. Hurtig, *The Betrayal of Canada* (2nd ed.) (Toronto: Stoddart, 1992), and G. Laxer, *Open for Business: The Roots of Foreign Ownership in Canada* (Don Mills: Oxford University Press, 1989).

[64]Lipset, *supra*, note 14 at 120–1, quoting Berton from a 1986 TV documentary, 'O Canada, Eh!'.

[65]On the concentration of wealth in Canada, see: *The Distribution of Wealth in Canada* (5th ed.) (Ottawa: Statistics Canada, 1977); C. McWatters, *The Changes Behind Canada's Income Distribution: Cause for Concern?* (Kingston: Industrial Relations Centre, Queen's University, 1989).

[66]*Supra*, note 62 at 221.

[67] G. Pitts, 'Porter Report Stokes Nationalistic Fires', *The Financial Post*, 9–11 November 1991, 1; G. Gherson, 'Porter Study Takes a Chilling Look at Our Competitive Failings', *Financial Times of Canada*, 28 October 1991, 7.

[68]S.M. Lipset, 'Revolution and Counter-Revolution — The United States and Canada' in T. Fond (ed.), *The Revolutionary Theme in Contemporary America* (Lexington: University of Kentucky Press, 1965): 38–44.

[69]Ibid., 20–4.

[70]S.D. Clark, *The Developing Canadian Community* (Toronto: University of Toronto Press, 1962): 192–8.

[71]E. McInnis, *The Unguarded Frontier* (Garden City: Doubleday Doran and Company, 1942): 307, and S.M. Lipset, *supra*, note 68 at 49–53.

[72]S.D. Clark, 'The Frontier and Democratic Theory' (1954) 48 *Transactions of the Royal Society of Canada*, 72. See also Morton, *The Canadian Identity*, *supra*, note 35 at 105–6.

[73]K. McNaught, 'Canada's European Ambience', a paper read at the annual meeting of the Italian Association for Canadian Studies, Sicily, May 1988, 6.

[74]K. McRoberts, *Quebec: Social Change and Political Crisis* (3rd ed.) (Toronto: McClelland & Stewart, 1988): 200–2.

[75]Lipset, *supra*, note 14 at 94 and at 110–12 describing various studies done in the 1980s:

. . . Americans were disposed significantly more than Canadians to voice a preference for liberty in contrast to the perceived danger to society of disruption. . . . Basically the study found that Canadians divided almost evenly in their willingness to take risks to maintain freedom of speech and assembly, while two-thirds of Americans would do so.

The national differences invert, however, when the questions posed deal with feelings about having deviants and extremists as neighbours, rather than with their possible impact on society . . . [Americans] were more likely (48 percent) than English Canadians (40 percent) or French Canadians (30 percent) to say that they were opposed to having 'people with a criminal record as neighbours'. Americans were also more disposed to find 'emotionally unstable people' offensive as neighbours (47 percent) than were Anglophones (33 percent) or Francophones (13 percent) . . .

It is difficult to interpret these results other than to infer that Canadians are more concerned than Americans with maintaining social order, even at the price of restricting the liberties of minorities, but are more lenient at the level of interpersonal behaviour.

[76] P. Weiler, *In the Last Resort — A Critical Study of the Supreme Court of Canada* (Toronto: Carswell/Methuen, 1974): Chapter 7, 'The Defender of Our Civil Liberties', and A. Borovoy, *When Freedoms Collide* (Toronto: Lester and Orpen Dennys Ltd, 1988): 208–13.

[77] J. Hagan and J. Leon, 'Philosophy and Sociology of Crime Control' in H. Johnson (ed.), *Social System and Legal Process* (San Francisco: Jossey-Bass, 1978). See also C. Griffiths, J. Fiklen, S. Verdon-Jones, *Criminal Justice in Canada* (Toronto: Butterworths, 1980); L. Tepperman, *Crime Control: The Urge Toward Authority* (Toronto: McGraw-Hill Ryerson, 1977); J. Hagan, 'Crime, Deviance, and Legal Order' in J. Curtis and L. Tepperman (eds), *Understanding Canadian Society* (Toronto: McGraw-Hill Ryerson, 1988): 426–7, 435–9; and J. Hagan, *The Disreputable Pleasures* (3rd ed.) (Toronto: McGraw-Hill Ryerson, 1991).

[78] W.L. MacKenzie King, House of Commons *Debates*, 18 June 1936, as quoted in *The Dictionary of Canadian Quotations and Phrases*, R.M. Hamilton and D. Shields (eds), (Toronto: McClelland & Stewart, 1979): 394.

[79] S. Beer, 'The Modernization of American Federalism' (1973) 3 *Publics: The Journal of Federalism*, 52.

[80] D.V. Smiley, 'Public Sector Politics, Modernization and Federalism: The Canadian and American Experience' (1984) 14 *Publics: The Journal of Federalism*, 59.

[81] R. Simeon, 'Some Questions of Governance in Contemporary Canada' (Kingston: School of Public Administration, Queen's University, 1987): 17. Lipset, *supra*, note 14, discussing this trend to decentralization and comparing it with a contrary movement in the United States, comments (194):

> The differences show up strikingly with respect to revenues. In the United States, federal authorities control most of the funds raised and spent by all the country's governments — federal, state, county, and municipal. In contrast, Canada has typically 'become the most decentralized federation in the western world. . . . Canada's provinces [and municipalities] have surpassed the Federal Government in total spending and tax revenues'. The ratio is the highest among the countries of the Organisation for Economic Co-operation and Development. As of 1985, the federal share of total Canadian tax revenue, *not* including social security funds, was 47.6 percent; the equivalent figure for the United States was 56.3 percent [emphasis in original; citations omitted].

[82] P. Boswell, 'The Atlantic Provinces' in M. Whittington and G. Williams (eds), *Canadian Politics in the 1990s* (Toronto: Nelson Canada, 1990): 119.

[83] Ibid., 123.

[84] Ibid., 125.

[85] D. Smiley, *Canada in Question: Federalism in the Eighties* (3rd ed.) (Toronto: McGraw-Hill Ryerson, 1980): 262.

[86] M. Whittington, 'Canada's North in the 1990s' in Whittington and Williams, *supra*, note 82 at 23.

[87] However these issues are resolved, it is clear that the North has become a focus

of attention for the rest of the country: '[T]he mainstream Canadian economic and political élites now see a need to develop the resources that for more than a century have been permitted to lie in "cold storage" undiscovered or at least unexploited. The North (and its people), traditionally ignored by southern politicians, has become economically significant to the rest of Canada.' Ibid., 35.

[88]M.P. Marchak, 'British Columbia: "New Right" Politics and a New Geography' in Whittington and Williams, *supra*, note 82 at 45. See also N. Ruff, 'Pacific Perspectives on the Canadian Confederation: British Columbia's Shadows and Symbols' in D. Brown (ed.), *Canada: The State of the Federation 1991* (Kingston: Institute of Intergovernmental Relations, 1991): 183.

[89]Ibid., 56.

[90] [T]he economic hopes of the region have always proved delusory. . . . It is not surprising therefore that for all the wealth of the region, there is a sense of underlying insecurity among Westerners. Boom in the past has always been followed by bust and the fear is that the cycle will be repeated. . . . As it was in the case of the economy, so it has been in the case of political power. . . . With population and finance centred elsewhere other things followed. The cultural institutions of the nation — the CBC, major arts, and theatre companies remained in the East. . . . [T]he populations of Ontario and Quebec, if they thought of the West at all, conjured up hazy visions of rural rustics or reactionary cowboys. The West, in short, was a hinterland in cultural, economic, and political terms.

D. Owram, 'Reluctant Hinterland' in L. Pratt and G. Stevenson (eds), *Western Separatism: The Myths, Realities and Dangers* (Edmonton: Hurtig Publishers Ltd, 1981), as reproduced in R. Blair and J. Mcleod (eds), *The Canadian Political Tradition—Basic Readings* (Toronto: Methuen Publishers, 1987): 106–7.

[91]*Supra*, note 85 at 264, 261–9.

[92]R. Gibbins, 'The Prairie Provinces' in Whittington and Williams, *supra*, note 82 at 60, observing at 62: '[T]he wheat economy bound the prairie provinces into a single economic unit within which individuals shared the same interests and faced the same problems; it supported a distinctive "regional way of life" that extended naturally to the political arena.'

[93]*Supra*, note 85 at 263; also see D. Smiley, *The Federal Condition* (Toronto: McGraw-Hill Ryerson, 1987): 158–62.

[94]*Supra*, note 85 at 263–4.

[95]M. Cernetig, 'Reform at the Crossroads', *The Globe and Mail*, 22 March 1993, A11.

[96]A. Stark, 'English-Canadian Opposition to Quebec Nationalism' in K. Weaver (ed.), *The Collapse of Canada?* (Washington: The Brookings Institute, 1992): 123, 141–50.

[97]*Supra*, note 92 at 70-4.

[98]Surveying these issues and attempts at resolution to give the West a full role in the life of the nation, Gibbins suggested two critical questions: first, which institutions of federalism could best be used to realize such a role and second, how can Canada both accommodate the needs of the West and those of Quebec? He put these dilemmas before the fall of Charlottetown, but its rejection only emphasizes these issues: 'Little prospect for their immediate resolution is apparent on the horizon as the prairie provinces enter the 1990s.' Ibid., 74.

[99] G. Craig (ed.), *Lord Durham's Report* (Toronto: McClelland & Stewart, 1963): 22–3.

[100] R. Cook, *Canada and the French-Canadian Question* (Toronto: Macmillan of Canada, 1966): 2.

[101] A. Malcolm, 'Beyond Plain Vanilla: Immigration Has Accentuated Canada's Diversity', *The New York Times*, 8 July 1990, E2.

[102] The debates such change can cause in the institutional arrangements of society are illustrated in C. Taylor, *Multiculturalism and 'The Politics of Recognition'* (Princeton: Princeton University Press, 1992) (commentary by A. Gutmann et al.); see also W. Kaplan (ed.), *Belonging — The Meaning and Future of Canadian Citizenship* (Montreal-Kingston: McGill-Queen's University Press, 1993), especially R. Fulford, 'A Post-Modern Dominion: The Changing Nature of Canadian Citizenship', 104.

[103] B. Etherington et al., *'Preserving Identity by Having Many Identities': A Report on Multiculturalism and Access to Justice* (Windsor: 1991) an unpublished report prepared for the Department of Justice, Canada; *Report of the Special Committee on Visible Minorities in Canadian Society: Equality Now!* (Ottawa: Supply and Services, 1984).

[104] It has also been innovative in regulation of labour relations by being the first government in North America to grant the right to strike in the public sector and the only government with an 'antiscab' labour law. Further, separateness can be seen in the substantial differences between the media in Quebec and the rest of Canada. For example, the network publicly owned (and dedicated to national unity) is divided between Radio Canada in Montreal and the CBC in Toronto: K. McRoberts, 'Quebec: Province, Nation, or Distinct Society?' in Whittington and Williams, *supra*, note 82 at 98, 98–9.

[105] Governed by the English, the people nevertheless preserved their language and culture by buttressing the role of the Catholic Church and the agrarian model in their lives. By the 1830s, Lord Durham's solution to the isolationist French was to have them disappear through assimilation and his vehicle for this was legislative union of the two Canadas. The Act of Union of 1841 provided for a single legislature with equal representation from the two Canadas. Such equality was intended to swallow the French, with the idea that the English of Upper Canada would join the minority of Lower Canada to frustrate the furtherance of the goals of the French majority of Lower Canada. But such a simple solution was not to succeed for the French were far more cohesive than the English. A series of devices developed — the double majority procedure, legislative groupings confined to English or French members, the official recognition of the two languages — that assisted the French in preserving the autonomy that had been established in Lower Canada and that led to the rejection of the assimilationist premises of the Durham Report. Smiley, *supra*, note 85 at 215–17, and Smiley, *The Federal Condition, supra*, note 93 at 126.

[106] *Parliamentary Debates on the Subject of the Confederation of the British North American Province, 1865* (Ottawa: King's Printer, 1951): 108.

[107] When Manitoba became a province in 1870, official language status for French and separate schools was guaranteed in the Manitoba Act. The Manitoba Legislature passed legislation contrary to these guarantees: see J. Staples, 'Consociationalism at the Provincial Level: The Erosion of Dualism in Manitoba, 1870–1890', in

K.D. McRae (ed.), *Consociational Democracy: Political Accommodation in Segmented Societies* (Toronto: McClelland & Stewart, 1974).

[108] *Supra*, note 85 at 219–21.

[109] Third, there was mediation 'at the summit'; that is, the most critical elements of the relationship were negotiated by an élite corps drawn from the two groups. Anglophone leaders had a Quebec lieutenant. In the Quebec Cabinet there was a member from the anglophone community who was given a powerful portfolio to respond to the business interests of the English.

The fourth element creating stability was the traditional French Canadian distrust of the state. French Canadians had democracy thrust upon them by the English conquest so they valued democracy not for itself but only to the extent it would assist in ethnic survival. The Church was jealous of its privileges and encouraged social and religious thought grounded upon authoritarianism and antistatism. Finally, there was the defence of historic, prescriptive rights. From the 1880s onward, such interests were often seen to be embodied in the terms of Confederation as a pact between anglophones and francophones. From this it followed that the terms could not be changed without the consent of both groups.

[110] Smiley, *supra*, note 85 at 222–5.

[111] In the background was a January 1989 survey demonstrating the deep cleavage concerning the government's action. Francophones (69 per cent) believed that the government had the right to restrict Quebec anglophones' freedom of expression in order to protect the French language, but 81 per cent of non-francophones disagreed: 'Language Law Poll Finds Most Opposed', *The Toronto Star*, 22 January 1989, A19.

[112] D. Brown, 'An Overview' in D. Brown (ed.), *Canada: The State of the Federation 1991* (Kingston: Institute of Intergovernmental Relations, 1991): 4.

[113] The earlier attempts to deal with the First Peoples' demands constitutionally are described in P. Russell, *Constitutional Odyssey — Can Canadians Be a Sovereign People?* (Toronto: University of Toronto, 1992): Chapter Nine.

[114] Regarding Aboriginal concerns in general, see D. Hawkes and M. Devine, 'Meech Lake and Elijah Harper: Native-State Relations in the 1990s' in F. Abele (ed.), *How Ottawa Spends, 1991–92: The Politics of Fragmentation* (Ottawa: Carleton University Press, 1991): 33–62. Regarding the Mohawk uprising, see R.M. Campbell and L.A. Pal, *The Real Worlds of Canadian Politics: Cases in Process and Policy* (2nd. ed.) (Peterborough: Broadview Press, 1991): 187–266.

[115] *Supra*, note 112 at 6–7.

[116] W. Thorsell, 'Let Us Compare Mythologies' (May 1990) *The Globe and Mail Report on Business Magazine*, 105, 111.

[117] For example, M. Valpy, 'Myths Central to Country's Nationhood', *The Globe and Mail*, 13 July 1990, A8. Also see D. Frum, 'Canada? Who'd Want It?', *Wall Street Journal*, 17 May 1990.

[118] *The Economist*, 19 May 1990, 17.

[119] Ibid., 18.

[120] Ibid., 17.

[121] M. Hinds, 'Number of Killings Soars in Big Cities Across US', *The New York Times*, 18 July 1990, A1. Comparing periods in 1989 and 1990, Detroit's murder

rate grew at 6 per cent whereas, to name only a few, New York's was 45 per cent, Boston's was 56 per cent, and Seattle's was 75 per cent.

[122] *Supra*, note 116 at 110.

[123] L. Gagnon, 'The Losers Were Not Punished, the Winners Didn't Gain a Thing', *The Globe and Mail*, 28 November 1992, D3.

[124] L. Nader, 'The ADR Explosion — The Implications of Rhetoric in Legal Reform' (1988) 8 *Windsor Yearbook of Access to Justice*, 269.

[125] J. Grimond, 'For Want of Glue — A Survey of Canada', *The Economist*, 29 June 1991, 14: '[A] club in which the dues (taxes) keep going up while the services (links to Britain, the railways, CBC and Air Canada) keep being cut: no wonder the members are tempted not to renew their subscriptions.'

[126] G. Smith, *Canada and the Canadian Question* (Toronto: University of Toronto Press, 1971).

[127] G. Grant, *Lament for a Nation: The Defeat of Canadian Nationalism in Canada* (Toronto: McClelland & Stewart, 1965).

[128] C. Black, 'Enough Is Enough', *Saturday Night* (September 1990), 12. Black, the 'proprietor', is countered by his editor, John Fraser, in the same issue. 'Our Own Meech Shoot-Out', 11, 12: 'The Canadian compromise has never been fixed, any more than the definition of a coherent nation state has to abide by rules formulated for countries that have not experienced what we have experienced. In any event, whatever our crowd of governing clowns comes up with, I'm not moving on — in spirit or body. As Al Purdy once said, "I have no other place to go."'

[129] This predicted disintegration of the country is aided and abetted by the popular media's — particularly television — glamorizing many aspects of things American: C. McInnes, 'Teens' Preference For Things American Found in Study', *The Globe and Mail*, 11 September 1992, A1.

[130] R. Fulford, 'Newsletter For a Man of Letters', *The Globe and Mail*, 14 June 1990, A18.

PART TWO

Courts and Their Role

CHAPTER TWO

Litigation and the Question of Impact

INTRODUCTION

Reaction to the consequences of litigation (and law for that matter) can be quite assertive. Whether in scholarly journals, television talk shows, or over the back fence, one continually hears remarks and declarations like: 'The judges and the Charter are changing how the country is governed'; '_____ (case) has been a great victory for _____ (group, interest)'; 'This cluster of cases indicates a marked shift from the crime control model to the due process model.' But how exactly do we know what effect any case or any group of cases have? How can we be sure that others besides those immediately involved in litigation comply with the ruling or even know about it? How do we determine that the change a case is supposed to effect actually occurs and what other effects — perhaps unpredicted — may occur as well? Beyond this lie significant and difficult questions concerning the kinds of decisions about social and political issues that should be made by judges, as opposed to other divisions of government, or whether they should be left to other forces like the market.

In this chapter we will examine many such questions relating to impact. We will see that though there are boisterous claims made for the advantages of litigation, particularly in terms of shaping the social and political structure, upon closer inspection, such claims are very hard to establish. This is not because courts do not have an impact but rather because their impact is hard to isolate and analyse separately from many other influential forces. Courts' decisions can also provoke political backlash.

But aside from any specific case or group of cases, litigation can send strong and complex messages about how to deal with social and political problems. It has always done that. More recently — mostly but not exclusively due to the Charter — claims for the courts' capacity to handle such questions and the desirability of their doing so have increased, often accompanied by the public's growing disenchantment with politicians and the legislative process. These assertions on behalf of courts are both promising and threatening. Promising because who can argue that government institutions do not need improvement? Who cannot understand the hope that our courts will become a positive influence on society? Threatening because although governments can improve, they can also become worse because of the consequences of litigation.

But this quandary about the problems of ascertaining the effects of litigation might be met by insisting that measuring the impact of any law, including statutes passed by the legislatures, has the same problems. This is an important point. Indeed, litigation suffers from many of the same uncertainties regarding measuring consequences as any other law or policy making. Such a basic observation, though, is quite in opposition to the claims made by unqualified supporters about the impact of litigation. Moreover, courts are the more problematic route for attending to complex social and political issues, particularly in the name of reform.

Litigation can force responses from stubborn governments or bureaucracies, which is one of its strengths, particularly on behalf of those who are otherwise excluded. Yet this also means that those who invoke legal action are not required to observe any agenda other than their own or to take into account any of the other pressing demands on the legislative timetable or constraints on the public purse. And, of course, a court's decision always involves the risk that it will be a negative one: those who turn to litigation may face rejection. Further, some of the greatest risks — particularly for those who seek reform — may result in victories. These wins, when disassociated from the political process, can produce a much greater level of backlash, including disagreement over the implementation of those court decisions, from other public institutions.

Finally, while it may be true that filing a lawsuit can require a response from those sued, the litigation process is not equally accessible. This is not to say that access to the political process or to administrative officials is completely evenhanded, but it is not as comparatively costly and complex as litigation. At the same time, the use of litigation by those seeking change — who can afford it — may divert scarce resources from popular processes that might achieve more long-lasting, widespread, and broadly acceptable compromises.

LAW, LAWYERS, AND LEGALIZATION: 'THE AUTHORITY OF THE TRAPEZE ARTIST'

The belief that law can be used to run society is widespread and most closely associated with instrumentalism. It asserts that law is an autonomous instrument that can be used to effect or curb various social, political, and economic consequences and, therefore, the law can be turned to for important explanations of such results. The core of instrumentalism is that 'legal rules do cause social phenomena because of what they prescribe, and that prescription in legal rules must therefore figure in the explanation of social phenomena'.[1] The manifestation of these beliefs is heard in virtually every debate about law: 'it simply does not occur to lawyers (or, for that matter, to most sociologists of law) to discuss legal rules without involving, implicitly or explicitly, their supposedly intended consequences.'[2]

A high watermark for this attitude came with public policy analysis of law, its foremost proponents being Lasswell and McDougal of Yale Law School.[3] A crude version of a cruder belief was that good public analysis would produce good law and good law would produce good societies with lawyers as the agents. Such a version has been characterized as:

> probably the most exaggerated conception ever imagined of the importance of lawyers. With arrogant assurance complemented by a lack of any empirical support, the authors proclaim that the lawyer 'is an important causal variable ... [who could] be acted upon to produce change' ... if only legal education were reoriented 'toward achieving the distinctive values and conditioning variables of a free society' ... their proposed changes would, they assert, 'increase the probability that the lawyers of the future will be more effective instruments for the achievement of the public good than they have been in the past' ... .[4]

We may be confident about one thing: law and lawyers are flourishing. In many ways the increase in the number of lawyers is a worldwide phenomenon in industrialized countries and even in some that are in the process of industrializing.[5] In England and Wales, the two branches of the profession (barristers and solicitors) increased about 147 per cent from the early 1960s to the mid-1980s.[6] In the United States during this same period, the number of lawyers increased by 129 per cent.[7] And Canada led the way with a 253 per cent increase in the legal profession during the same period.[8]

Not only are there more lawyers, but they are much more diverse in terms of age, education, and ethnic background, and now include more women.[9] In the early 1960s, women accounted for about 3 per cent of the profession in England, Canada, and the United States. In the late 1980s, women comprised about 15 per cent of lawyers in the United States and over 20 per cent in England and Canada, and almost half the number of law students were women.[10] The rapid influx of women into the profession leads to much speculation about possible changes based on gender.[11] Along with many more diverse lawyers, societies have come to depend more on law itself. In the United States, the portion of the national income and product derived from legal services almost doubled from the early 1960s to the mid-1980s. A larger portion of these increasing expenditures was spent by businesses as compared with individuals. No such comparable figures are available for Canada and the UK, but it has been suggested that the growth in the number and size of firms that focus on business is similar.[12]

With more lawyers and greater expenditures has come an exponential increase in the amount of law.[13] A sampling of growth spurts indicates how law has come to mediate a bewildering range of social, political, and economic quandaries. In 1955, the *Canada Gazette* (which contains notices about the federal government's laws and regulations) was a 3,120-page, four-volume consolidation; by 1978 it was a 14,420-page, eighteen-volume set.[14] In 1960, the annual output of the *Dominion Law Reports*, which publicizes judgements, was five volumes of 3,902 pages. By 1989, it was eleven volumes of 8,448 pages.[15] The number of law journals increased by 195 per cent from 1958 to 1980.[16] Moreover, such statistics from printed sources scarcely do justice in measuring the frantic level of activity. The use of new inventions is widespread in law: 'a rapid succession of new technologies — photo reproduction, computerisation, on-line data services, overnight delivery services, electronic mail and fax machines — have multiplied the amount of information that can be assembled and manipulated by legal actors and have greatly increased the velocity with which it circulates.'[17]

There is also an increase in the role of law. Marc Galanter, who examined 'law abounding'[18] in Canada, Great Britain, and the United States, observes that there has been an extension of judicial oversight and related legalization regarding whole areas of activity that were previously not regarded to be in need of legal structuring.[19] Examining three disparate areas — health care, employment, and sports — Galanter shows that, despite some important differences, there is a pattern of growth harnessing legal norms and institutions regarding various problems in diverse areas such as the environment or safety regulation.[20] For example, health care is provided in very different ways in the three countries, yet has undergone legalization in important aspects in each. Entitlement to treatment has undergone substantial regulation and users are increasingly turning to law as a recourse for alleged deficiencies.

But how confident can we be that promulgation of legal rules and methods for their enforcement will have the contemplated or indeed any impact? Those who have considered this question can be highly sceptical about the effects of law. Roger Cotterrell, in *The Sociology of Law: An Introduction*, observes that:

Undoubtedly it seems natural to many observers of legal processes to see law as counterposed to 'society' as a discrete mechanism acting upon social life. Current conception of legislation presupposes such a view. Yet it is vital to recognize the 'law . . . is only one component of a large set of policy instruments and usually cannot [be] . . . and is not used by itself.' Therefore, focusing of exclusive attention on law as a tool of direct social change is a case of tunnel vision which lacks the minimum perspective necessary for making sense from the observed phenomena.[21]

There are potentially a number of direct, indirect, and independent effects that can make it difficult to trace and isolate the impact of any law. This is even more so when the analysis of the law's consequences attempts to separate the effects of legal rules from those of the political decisions that created them.[22] Finally, there may be unintended effects that were unforeseen by those involved with the enactment of laws.

We can illustrate these complexities by thinking about a law against drunk driving. The efficacy of such a law is not dependent on how many individuals refrain from driving while intoxicated (primary direct effects) nor on the rate of its enforcement (secondary direct effects), but rather how this law affects the accident rate. This indirect effect (lowering accident rates) is of the most interest in gauging the law's impact. Yet because there can be so many indirect effects and corresponding causes, it is very difficult to ascertain whether the accident rate has decreased and, if so, whether the law against drunk driving was the cause.[23] The issue becomes even more complex if we attempt to ascertain the presence or absence and degree of political will that led to the passage of the law as contributing to achieving the desired goal, the lowering of accidents. Then, too, there may be shifts in attitudes towards the desirability of drinking moderately that may explain declining drunk-driving accident rates.[24] Finally, unintended consequences, such as a possible increase in pedestrian accidents involving intoxicated people who attempt to walk rather than drive, should also be considered when assessing the impact of a law against drunk driving.[25]

The point is that, in this world of ever-increasing legalization, it is easier to document the increase in law than to draw straightforward conclusions about its effects. Such complexities about the impact of law generally are an important backdrop to the discussion of the consequences of litigation. A comparison of the effects of all law, particularly litigation, would no doubt assist the discussion, but is beyond what is being attempted. What we can say with some assurance is that such a study would probably make statements about the impact of litigation even more complicated. But this, in any event, adds to caution concerning any analysis about such consequences — a central message struck here.

Nevertheless, law's powerful hold on the popular imagination is an important frame for examining litigation's role in our national life. That it can simultaneously tantalize and infuriate is part of law's grip, even as medicine is revered while doctors are seen as cold and aloof, even as science pronounces with certainty in the face of so many unanswerable questions: 'The law, too; shares what might be called the authority of the trapeze artist.'[26]

COURTS AND THEIR IMPACT

The Claims of Importance and Challenges to Those Claims

We have talked about the increase in law and lawyers over approximately the last two decades. Litigation also increased during this same period, though the pattern is not as clear. There has been an increase in the number of lawsuits. For example, in the United States, which is regarded by some as the leader in the use of litigation, total civil filings in the federal courts increased from 59,284 in 1960 to 273,670 in 1985.[27] In Canada, precise longitudinal data is not available, but substantial growth is indicated by the fact that the number of judges increased by 177 per cent from 834 to 2,315 between 1961 and 1986.[28]

But increasing numbers, whatever their extent, are only part of the claims about the influence of courts. More importantly, the contention is that their growing significance has a qualitative dimension — that judges, with their attentiveness to reasoned argument and dispassionate analysis, have a key role in sorting through the complexities that plague society. They will deliver solutions and the processes used to arrive at them can inspire the citizenry. While the legislatures may have many lawyers, it is not exclusively that profession's domain; in any event, politicians are animated not by legal 'values' but political considerations created through brokering, negotiation, compromise, and, more darkly, favouritism and connivance. Litigation and judgement, by contrast, are produced by lawyers in various roles. Judicial decisions are said to be determined through rationality, principle, and detachment. Such hallmarks are the sources of the courts' legitimacy and effectiveness, inspiring knowledge of and respect for them.

Nowhere are such claims made about litigation and its effects with more flourish than in constitutional law. Some American writers are unqualified in their extravagance. Consider, for example, Lawrence Tribe, who is the author of perhaps the leading treatise on American constitutional law:

> [T]he most basic ingredients of our day-to-day lives are sifted and measured out by the Supreme Court. When parents send their children to parochial schools, when men and women buy contraceptives, when workers organize a union, when friends share their intimate secrets in a telephone conversation without fear that others are listening, they enjoy rights and opportunities that would not exist if the Supreme Court had not secured them for us.
>
> ... [M]ore than half of all Americans — those who are women — now enjoy

the rights to 'equal protection of the laws' because a majority of the Burger Court has declared that government may not discriminate on the basis of gender . . .

In every aspect of our lives . . . not even the most passive, restrained, low-profile Supreme Court imaginable can any longer avoid playing a decisive role.

In fact even the term 'role' is misleading: it suggests that the Supreme Court is but one more actor on the legal and political stage — an actor who could, if the casting were just right, be reduced to a bit part. But . . . the Justices are not just so many actors on the stage. To them has fallen a large share of a far more basic function — that of playwright and director. It is the Justices who decide which roles will be played by whom; which decisions about hours and wages will be made by government regulators and which will be left to the play of private bargains; which things of value — housing, medical care, legal services, voting opportunities — will only be sold on private markets and which will be available to all as a matter of right; which decisions about birth and death will be made by lawmakers, which will be reserved to medical professionals, and which will be left to the men and women most intimately involved.[29]

Tribe is by no means alone in such hyperbole. He is joined by any number of others, including Owen Fiss, whose work we will examine later in the book. Fiss is perhaps the foremost proponent of using litigation to articulate and realize public values. The United States' genius for doing this is a matter to be countenanced:

To conceive of the civil lawsuit in public terms as America does might be unique. I am willing to assume that no other country . . . has a case like *Brown* v. *Board of Education* in which the judicial power is used to eradicate the caste structure. I am willing to assume that no other country conceives of law and case law in quite the way we do. But this should be a source of pride rather than shame. What is unique is not the problem, that we live short of our ideals, but that *we alone among the nations of the world seem willing to do something about* it [emphasis added].[30]

And while Canadians may not have quite reached the rhetorical flourishes that characterize Tribe and Fiss, there seems little doubt that some are determined to head in that direction. Shortly after the entrenchment of the Charter, one Canadian commentator felt sufficiently confident about the effects of litigation to characterize *Brown* v. *Board of Education* as 'such a moral supernova in civil liberties adjudication that it almost single-handedly justifies the exercise'.[31] John Whyte, a Canadian constitutional scholar, in the midst of decrying the notwithstanding clause in the Charter and its potential to override judicial policy making, asserted:

As a matter of principle we have adopted the notion that there are adjudicable public issues. Furthermore, we have come to terms with these issues being *ultimately* adjudicable — not subject to legislative review and revision. If Canada wants to say about human rights claims that not only are they adjudicable at the first stage of resolution, but they are adjudicable as a matter of ultimate resolution, this would be entirely consistent with our commitment to legalism in public ordering [emphasis in original].[32]

Yet as an antidote to such flourishes, evidence can be offered not only of the courts' lack of influence but of people's plain ignorance of their pronouncements. For example, despite Fiss's and Tribe's claims regarding the pervasiveness of the courts in the lives of citizens of the United States, studies indicate that people are only dimly familiar with judges' pronouncements. Studies in the 1960s and 1970s showed that less than half of the population could name a single decision or select three correct topics from a list of eight areas in terms of the court having rendered a judgement.[33] The public had an even lesser sense of lower court decisions.[34]

In a discrete area of Canadian law, a study by Robertson on informed consent has shown how even very intelligent and well-educated individuals can be totally unaware of a Supreme Court pronouncement that is directly relevant to their professional activities.[35] Robertson sought to study the effect of the decision in *Reibl* v. *Hughes*[36] on the practice of medicine. That case addressed the test to be applied in determining what information doctors are required to disclose to patients in order to comply with applicable standards of care and thus avoid liability to patients based on an allegation that the patient had not given informed consent to the treatment received. Particularly relevant was the importance of what was taken to be the Supreme Court's adoption of a 'reasonable patient' test; that is, that doctors should know or ought to know what their patients should be told in order for them to give informed consent to the proposed treatment.

Again, lawyers were quick to assert a great practical impact for the decision. The General Counsel to the Canadian Medical Protective Association contended that 'No legal event in the last fifty years has so disturbed the practice of medicine as did the decision of the Supreme Court of Canada in *Reibl* v. *Hughes*.'[37] Similarly the author of a leading book on torts, himself a judge, opined that 'The ultimate effect of [*Reibl* v. *Hughes*] should be medical practitioners who are even more sensitive, concerned and humane than they now are. Moreover, the doctor-patient relationship should be improved greatly by the better communication between doctors and their patients.'[38]

To test these claims, Robertson asked a series of questions about the case addressed to surgeons throughout Canada. His findings virtually contradict such pronouncements. Seventy per cent of the respondents were not even aware of the decision and those who were aware did not seem to appreciate its importance. Even a majority who knew of the decision expressed views inconsistent with it and there was no significant variation in answers from respondents who appreciated the importance of the decision and those who did not.[39] Robertson takes strong issue with sweeping contentions about litigation's capacity to effect change since the study:

> [P]rovides evidence, not only of medical practitioners being impervious to change by judicial decision, but more generally, of the impotence of law (and judicial decision in particular) as an instrument of social change. Even assuming that the medical profession were to become aware of the implications of *Reibl* v.

Hughes, to suggest that this would have any meaningful effect, such as doctors becoming 'more sensitive, concerned and humane' is to attribute to judicial decisions in general, and to *Reibl* v. *Hughes* in particular, a degree of influence which they probably do not possess.[40]

Robertson did a follow-up study of the decision ten years after the judgement.[41] He concluded that *Reibl* had had little significance on the severity and frequency of claims about malpractice. Further, it had little impact on developments in other areas of health law or jurisdictions outside Canada. Moreover its effect on medical practice is unclear. There is some evidence that doctors now spend more time discussing pertinent benefits and risks of treatment with their patients. But it is difficult to assess to what extent *Reibl* is the cause because there is evidence that the amount of information doctors give patients concerning proposed treatment has also increased in jurisdictions that have expressly declined to follow *Reibl*.

Robertson suggests that the real significance of this case is its 'symbolic importance'[42] in recognizing the substantial differential in knowledge and power that can exist between doctors and patients and in aligning itself with the patient's perspective.[43] However, if the decision has had little or no effect, what exactly does it mean to say that it has had a symbolic one? Is this just a tactful way of saying that it is irrelevant? Or maybe we ought to say the *Reibl* case is symbolic if we mean that those who are convinced of the power imbalance between physicians and patients and want to bring about change concluded that much was effected by the decision when in fact little had changed.

The claim here is not that courts will invariably be ineffectual in changing behaviour, including that of doctors. There are studies that demonstrate a complicated relationship between courts' decisions and behaviour based on those pronouncements.[44] Rather, the assertion is that any substantial effect (including the one that seems to arise from a judgement) is by no means certain. Moreover, when a court's pronouncement does little to change the situation, those seeking change may be misled into believing that they were successful when in fact their victory will not go beyond the courtroom door.

Litigation's ability to produce symbolic as opposed to actual change can be one of its most troubling illusions. This is an issue that surfaces in the discussion of women's issues, particularly abortion and related questions, and in the discussion of due process's dominance in the administration of criminal justice later in the book.

A Theory of 'Impact'?

We have already seen the difficulties with ascertaining the effect of law in general and litigation in particular. Why is it so difficult to develop a theory of impact and to ascertain its application? We ask this question to better understand how difficult it is to analyse the effect of courts' decisions and as a prelude to one particular theory of impact discussed at the conclusion of this part.

A frontal assault on a theory of impact was launched by Malcolm Feeley, a co-editor of *The Impact of Supreme Court Decisions*.[45] Feeley does not argue that the effect of court activity should not be assessed. He does, however, seriously question whether there is any developed theory about this institution and its consequences. The hallmarks of a developed theory are systematic explanations and predictions and Feeley argues that no idea about impact has ever acquired those critical characteristics.[46]

It will be useful first to try to define impact. Feeley compares it with the notions of aftermath and compliance.[47] Aftermath refers to direct and indirect consequences of a specified event. There is no requirement that the nature and scope of the relationship be indicated precisely, nor is there concerted effort to distinguish the 'significant' from the 'insignificant'. For instance, if a hurricane strikes, there will be many deaths, looting, lost birds' nests, etc. All of these are the 'aftermath' of the storm, but what is the relationship of the hurricane to those who died of heart attacks? How can one prove that the storm caused the looting? Aftermath is too open-ended and indiscriminate a concept.

In contrast, compliance is more precise: it inquires into why individuals knowingly obey or disobey specified rules. Compliance then is closely linked to attempts to formulate general theories of social control and social contract. But compliance examines the rule-recipient more closely than the rule-creator. This can actually detract attention from the courts. Furthermore, compliance might not adequately include side-effects that may be particularly important in studying courts. For instance, a reaction to judgements that do not easily fit within compliance would be, in the American context, legislative attempts to overturn a particular decision by either constitutional amendment, alteration of court personnel, or limitation of the Supreme Court's jurisdiction. Legislative (or executive) challenges to courts can exist quite apart from the extent to which decisions are otherwise complied with. So compliance may be too narrow a concept in these important ways.

Finally, 'impact' can be defined as 'all policy-related consequences of a decision', so it can refer not only to compliant behaviour but to other responses as well, such as attempts at legislative nullification. It also provides a guide to determine the scope and nature of relevant consequences. But because impact is encompassing, it is also imprecise. In fact almost all discussions of impact do not develop a full-blown theory but rather acknowledge and identify the inevitable imprecisions and attempt to determine their influence on any particular issue. Such efforts may raise more questions than they answer: 'courts can legislate morals [b]ut it is far from clear yet under what conditions, to what degree, and through which methods optimum attitudinal changes can be rendered.'[48] These difficulties are illustrated by Jesse Choper's attempt to assess litigation's impact, particularly regarding the United States Supreme Court and its protection of constitutional rights. Choper, a well-known American constitutional scholar, analysed what he regarded as five fundamental points.[49]

First, any kind of measurement is complicated, particularly because of its open-endedness. The greatest difficulty is the interrelatedness of all government actions, including judicial decisions, with public and private phenomena. Sometimes these ramifications cannot be identified and when they are, they sometimes cannot be quantified.[50] So when reforms come in the aftermath of courts' decisions, it cannot be confidently asserted that such changes would not have happened otherwise. Instead, the court's judgement may have simply reflected, anticipated, or at best reinforced the inevitable: 'Even the most careful study cannot establish whether alleged changes were not merely coincidentally but actually consequentially related.'[51] In some instances the invalidated laws could have been repealed by the political process without judicial intervention.[52] By contrast, the degree to which the symbolic effect of a judicial ruling or series of rulings can be a catalytic force for change in terms of equality, children's rights, or whatever, is generally not measurable.[53]

Handler made a related point in his evaluation of the success of public interest groups and their efforts at litigation. As part of that assessment, he focused on gauging the effects of law reform on social change. He asserted that it is generally very difficult to separate independent effects of legal changes, particularly regarding litigation, from results brought about by the interaction of such changes with broader elements such as the impact of timing, public opinion, and social and economic conditions. Conversely, such changes may result in largely symbolic victories, as mentioned earlier in the discussion of the Robertson study on informed consent.[54]

Further, litigation's indirect effects, particularly in conjunction with other activities, are very difficult to evaluate. Litigation from one vantage provides a measure in assessing wins and losses. Long-term impact, by contrast, may come from consultation and negotiation when they are employed by public interest groups, yet there is substantial difficulty in gauging such impact. For example, participation in these consultations and negotiations cannot be the criterion for establishing effectiveness since these may only be methods used to assuage social reform groups without creating any substantial change.[55] Or, to put the matter another way, social reform groups are not the only agents of influence. Major new government policies may come about through broad changes in public opinion as a result of dramatic events, vital leaders, or the media. Organizations may be able to aid change and make the case for it, but they cannot bring it about on their own.[56]

Choper's second point asserts that there is nothing that guarantees that the Court's decisions will be complied with. One variable is the effort required to enforce compliance. It is true that some decisions are comparatively self-enforcing. For instance, a person facing a prison sentence will have a clear incentive to assert the constitutionally recognized right to a lawyer, and trial judges will want such representation, otherwise the proceedings can be reversed on appeal. In contrast, other rights may be much more difficult to enforce if they require their own proceedings. For example, if a public school continues Bible-reading in defiance of the United States Supreme Court's prohibitions on school prayer, then stopping the practice will require litigation with the attendant costs.[57]

This point about compliance can be focused further by returning to the problem of measurement.[58] Since there is no clear unit of measurement, it is impossible to assess systematically the impact of decisions in terms of compliance. For instance, it could be asserted that the Supreme Court of the United States had greater impact with the reapportionment decision (*Baker* v. *Carr*[59]) because of quick and complete compliance than it had in school desegregation (*Brown* v. *Board of Education*[60]) because of the initial hesitancy with which lower courts approached desegregation.[61] Or should an opposite set of conclusions be drawn because the former judgement resulted in redrawing a few boundaries and replacing a few elected officials while the latter judgement, it is claimed, 'sparked' a social movement?

Third, even assuming compliance, the extent to which the Court's decisions are of any real benefit to those receiving the protection may vary considerably. On the one hand, if a court invalidates capital punishment, the effect on death-row prisoners would be very clear. On the other hand, mandated representation of indigents accused of crime does not guarantee the quality of the representation or, even if the defence is of acceptable standard, whether it will make any real difference to the verdict. This issue of actual benefit to those who are sought to be protected by the Court's order is illustrated by the *Miranda*[62] decision's aftermath, which held that the accused facing custodial interrogation must be told that they have a right to remain silent. Numerous studies can be cited establishing that after some initial resistance, police substantially complied with its requirements.[63] However, other studies also suggest that a substantial percentage of accused fail to understand the substance of the warnings.[64] The failure to understand in conjunction with pressure from the police, subtle and otherwise, leads many to waive these rights so that 'the data strongly suggest that giving the *Miranda* warnings has no significant impact on a suspect's decision to talk to police interrogators'.[65]

Fourth, even when there are benefits from the Court's rulings for some, Choper points out that it is usually at the expense of others' welfare, and that there is no agreed-on scale to weigh the costs and benefits to the competing interests as in, for example, the conflict over abortion and the interests of women who wish to end a pregnancy versus the interests of the foetus.[66]

Fifth, even if it is asserted that the United States Supreme Court's holdings have, on balance, effectively countered many constraints on personal liberty, account still has to be taken of the effects of the other decisions declining such action and how they may or may not have exacerbated the infringement of interests for which protection was sought. On the one hand, the Court's upholding of a political majority may prompt that majority to work its will more broadly. For example, within a year of *Ginsberg*,[67] in which the Court held that the states have broad regulatory power over the distribution of sexually related material to minors, at least twenty city councils across the country passed similar statutes. On the other hand, the possibility that the Court will nullify government regulation may result in officials' hesitation in passing controversial legislation on the grounds that it may be unconstitutional.[68]

Mindful of all these difficulties, Choper remains undeterred and soldiers on a 'best efforts' basis. He evinces a faith in litigation's properties despite the vagaries that he uncovers:

> [T]here appears to be no way to conduct a scientifically controlled inquiry to determine whether, all things considered, the state of freedom within the nation is 'better' than it would have been without the Justices' involvement.... But that all of the five sets of imponderables sketched above may be incapable of systematic resolution should not deter us from determining what is and can be known about some things.[69]

Yet in a very recent book, Gerald Rosenberg has specifically examined the effect of litigation on achieving social change and has arrived at very negative conclusions.[70] He examined several important areas in the United States where change has occurred or at least was expected to occur, including civil rights, women's rights (particularly abortion), the environment, reapportionment and electoral rights, and criminal law. His studies will be discussed in this book and his overall conclusions will be examined later in this chapter. Here we will discuss his understanding of causality and its bearing on two models of the judiciary he depicts, as well as the model of impact he constructs.

For Rosenberg, causality is best understood by discussing judicial and extrajudicial paths.[71] The judicial path emphasizes the direct outcome of court judgements and examines whether any change required by the courts was made. For instance, with regard to civil rights, if a United States Supreme Court decision ordering an end to possible segregation caused such a result, one ought to be able to observe lower courts requiring officials to comply, a community to respond accordingly, and, of course, segregation to actually disappear. With regard to abortion, if striking down the laws restricting or prohibiting abortion results in direct change, one should observe the disappearance of obstacles to abortion and the availability of such services where there is need.

The extrajudicial path makes claims about change other than those brought about by the courts. These other contentions suggest that judgements may lead to substantial change because they cause individuals to act or to examine and alter their views. In this way Supreme Court decisions may be powerful symbols for reform by transforming the intellectual climate. Judgements can bestow a salience on certain issues and place them on the political agenda. That effect is particularly valuable when other institutions wish to muffle these pleas. Manifestations of such impact might be seen in media coverage, public opinion data, and public responses that support change. For example, *Brown* v. *Board of Education* and *Roe* v. *Wade* are commonly said to have produced substantial extrajudicial impacts from focusing attention on civil rights and igniting that movement to convincing the American public of the acceptability of a woman's choice concerning abortion.

The second issue Rosenberg examines that is of immediate relevance is the nature of courts themselves in dealing with issues relevant to change. To do this he constructs and examines two very different models: the constrained and the dynamic. The constrained model in many ways has the finer historical pedigree since there is a tradition of scholarship that sees the judiciary as the 'least dangerous' branch of government, to quote Alexander Hamilton's famous phrase.[72] Because (to quote Hamilton again) they lack power of the 'sword or purse', their capacity to effect political and social change is limited. As a result, courts are able to do little besides indicate how actions have failed to comply with legislative or constitutional obligations. More specifically, the constrained model claims that those asking courts to effect substantial change will meet with real barriers. First, the limited nature of constitutional rights,[73] the constraints of legal culture, and the general caution of the judiciary will make it very difficult for proponents of change to persuade courts that the (often novel) rights they are claiming are required by either the Constitution or the language of a particular statute. Second, because of their deference to other government institutions and potential limitation by these institutions' actions, courts may be reluctant to move away from the mainstream of politics. Third, even if the first and second barriers are overcome, litigants still need to have judicial orders implemented. Because courts do not have tools of enforcement, their decisions can be stymied if there is strong opposition to them. In any event, the strong prescriptive claim for this model is that American society is left to govern itself without interference from nonelected officials.

In marked contrast is the dynamic court model espoused by those who have increasingly in the last decades turned to courts to effect change.[74] Initiated by prominent litigation brought by civil rights advocates and followed by suits on behalf of women's groups, environmental groups, and political reformers, American courts have been hailed as vital arenas for progress. In addition, such litigation victories have frequently been secured, it is said, in the face of paralysis in other governmental institutions, which are quiescent or even hostile to the issues in question. It is thus not a point of regret but rather of pride that America's version of democracy includes 'the world's most powerful court system, protecting minorities and defending liberty, in the face of opposition from the democratically elected branches'.[75]

A key claim on behalf of the dynamic court is that access and influence are not premised on political and economic leverage. Professional lobbying, with the persistence and compromise required for effective influence on bureaucracies or legislation, is not necessary for victory in litigation.[76] From this vantage, groups with few resources can harness litigation not only to achieve change directly but also to strengthen their presence with other branches of government, thus obtaining validity to assert their positions when they receive a response from courts. Independent and tenured (at least at the federal level) courts are able to offer a sanctuary 'from the pathologies of rigid bureaucracies, ossified institutions, and a reluctant citizenry'.[77]

Combining the constrained and dynamic models, Rosenberg concludes that theoretically, courts can be effective causes of significant change, but only under certain conditions. Briefly, these are that: (1) there is ample legal precedent for change; (2) there is support for change from substantial numbers in Congress and from the executive; and (3) there is either support from some citizens or at least minimal opposition from all citizens and (a) positive incentives are offered to induce compliance, or (b) costs are imposed to induce compliance, or (c) court decisions allow for market implementation, or (d) key administrators and officials are willing to act and see court orders as a tool for leveraging additional resources or for hiding behind.[78]

Careful reading of these circumstances posited by Rosenberg reveals an intricate set of conditions for effectiveness. Shortly, we will discuss his conclusions that these conditions are almost never met and, therefore, that the constrained model is a much more powerful view of courts. Whether his analysis is entirely accurate is not the point so much as the fact that his work injects a substantial degree of scepticism about litigation's power and efficacy in determining or shaping social and political forces.[79] What Rosenberg does contend is that litigation can have significant impact in deflecting the forces of change. This more specific question of the relationship between litigation and social progress is the subject of the next section.

Litigation and Social Change

Gauging the effects of litigation in achieving change is fundamental since frequently a society's betterment will be set off as the premium to be achieved against the loss to democracy that increased judicial power necessarily brings. To justify such dilution, at least among progressives, it is claimed that litigation and the acknowledgement of rights will effect reform, empowering the marginalized in ways that the political process and/

or an unresponsive majority has blocked. But how effective have the courts been in bringing about social change and what evidence exists to answer this question? The hope of realizing reform through the courts has been an abiding aspiration of many public interest groups in the United States, at least since the Second World War. The presence of public interest groups and their effect on the courts has in general been historically less marked in Canada. However, with the coming of the Charter of Rights and Freedoms, there are many claims about the importance of litigation and its capacity to achieve reform; so it is important not to lose sight of the experiences over the last decades of those groups in the United States who sought to use courts to achieve their goals.

In a 1978 study,[80] Handler looked at thirty-five case-studies in four principal areas of law-reform activity: (1) environmental litigation; (2) consumer issues and rights; (3) social welfare, including welfare reform, health and mental health; and (4) occupational health and safety issues. Each case-study was designed to illustrate a separate kind of social reform and legal activity. Handler's efforts to measure 'success' and his conclusions are directly pertinent to our discussion of impact. But he also shed light on our earlier question of why people turned to litigation for responses to these issues in the first place.

By the 1960s in the United States, one could talk about a public interest law movement. Typified by the work of Ralph Nader, it sought to make law an instrument of social change. Nader employed reports, publicity, and exposure to require enforcement of existing laws and to convince legislatures to pass other laws to protect the interests he represented. By the 1970s, there were public interest law firms known particularly for representing environmentalists and consumers, but they also represented such other groups as the physically and mentally disabled, minorities, children, juveniles, and women.

Though there were various tools, the focus of activities was on litigation. Handler encapsulates the history of the movement, with the lawsuit as its centre-piece from the 1950s to the end of the 1970s, the period of Handler's study. He documents how this came about by pointing to judicial activism that encouraged litigation. Further, the number of client groups that turned to the courts increased. Initially, the most conspicuous groups were blacks, but they were subsequently joined by other interest groups, including the poor, environmentalists, consumers, and women. Finally, these other developments stimulated the rise of lawyer organizations that, in turn, were interested in law reform through test-case litigation.[81]

A number of overarching reasons emerge in Handler's study concerning why so much time and energy was focused on litigation as a reforming strategy. Perhaps first and foremost is the enduring belief that courts and their procedures will help to rectify power imbalances on behalf of the disadvantaged:

It is because social-reform groups lack the power to seek their demands through the normal political processes or through direct action that they turn to the legal system for help. Courts have always been used by those who find the balance of political forces against them. The powerless seek to neutralize inequities in bargaining power or at least to extract some concessions from their opponents. The use of the courts often appears to be a less dangerous and less costly means than nonlegal struggles against formidable opponents.[82]

A second reason why these groups used the courts was for public relations value. A high-profile case gives the group a certain standing among the media and élites whether in law or society at large. A positive result in litigation repels any political attack since such a conclusion justifies the group's position. Handler puts the point sharply in terms of legitimacy: 'Law reformers and foundations feel the need for legitimation from courts. . . . [C]ases, particularly when they stop a bulldozer or unmask some outrageous practice, can be dramatic and newsworthy, and provide the legitimacy so necessary for support from élites.'[83]

Third, public interest lawyers on the whole seemed unsuited by preparation and temperament to lobbying activities. Lobbyists were older and more experienced than public interest lawyers, had long experience, patience, and the capacity to react to delay and frustration. Handler observes, 'Although the experience varied, many reported that behind-the-scenes negotiations, especially if carried out over a long period of time, were not satisfactory. The lawyers felt that they were less powerful in this role, and the lack of publicity was viewed as a detriment to their interests and the interests of their clients. They felt more comfortable in the litigation setting.'[84]

Fourth, Handler links the propensity of such lawyers to turn to litigation to their education. Legal education venerates appellate court judgements as the source of the law. Even highly critical perspectives of law still retain judicial decisions as their focus. Legislation and the day-to-day functioning of agencies and links with relevant political and social studies are subordinated: 'Law schools emphasize the appellate court decision, rather than the skills of the lobbyist and office negotiation. And the models for these social reformers are the great Supreme Court litigators of civil liberties cases.'[85]

From a different stance some of those seeking change argue for a role for litigation if for no other reason than the 'lack of alternatives' (again, a commentary on the democratic process) and because 'they can provide both ideological and institutional leverage that social movements cannot afford to ignore'.[86] The 'leverage' is frequently seen in terms of claiming rights. Such claims of entitlement will not easily be foregone by those who historically have not had them, particularly if matched with an aspiration that the very disadvantage can be used to transform the discourse: '"Rights" feels so new in the mouths of most black people. It is still so deliciously empowering to say. It is a sign for and a gift of selfhood. . . . The concept of rights, both positive and negative, is the marker of our citizenship, our participatoriness, our relation to others.'[87]

In this view courts become 'arenas of struggle'[88] with judicial decisions serving 'as mobilizing devices'.[89] In this conception, warnings about lawyers taking control away from individuals and groups with the problems are given an about-face. Instead, lawyers' detachment from the movements and issues they represent is an asset. For example, Scheingold portrays lawyers as 'cultural mediators' who transform problems of the disadvantaged into transcendent claims about 'universalized grievances': 'The language of the law enables lawyers to reform client problems in terms of the broad standards of American law and culture and, thus, to convey the plight of the have nots in terms that maximize the likelihood for a sympathetic response culturally as well as legally.'[90]

Yet even some of those who advocate rights in courts in order to achieve change admit its hazards. Chief among such dangers is that rights discourse will not be changed on behalf of progressive movements but will instead come to corral, divide, and deflate them. Thus, Scheingold's enthusiasm is sobered:

> The drawbacks of a politics of rights are ... extensive. [T]he mobilizing opportunities that are at the heart of a politics of rights are, when subject to careful scrutiny, suspect on two grounds. First, constitutional and legal symbols are not likely to be particularly useful for rallying those most in need. Second, with litigation at its core, mobilization tends to be divisive in so far as its principal long-term consequence is merely to broaden the pluralist political arena. The net effect is to pit have not segments of the society against one another in a zero sum struggle over scarce resources.[91]

This ability of rights litigation to buttress the most conservative values in the name of rights while enervating any capacity for change through democratic processes has been pursued by Mary Ann Glendon, a renowned student of comparative law.[92] We will deal in detail with her ideas in Chapter Five when discussing litigation and women's issues. What needs to be emphasized here is that both upholding and striking down legislation in the name of some progressive cause can, in the long run, curb what would have been more far-reaching restructuring in the legislatures:

> American experience suggests that the real danger represented by regular invalidation of legislation on constitutional grounds is not that elected representatives will rise up in anger against the courts. On the contrary, legislators are often relieved at being able to say their hands are tied by the courts, especially where controversial matters are concerned. One danger is, rather, that of atrophy in the democratic processes of bargaining, education, and persuasion that take place in and around legislatures. Another is that by too readily preventing compromise and blocking the normal political avenues for change, courts leave the disappointed majority with no legitimate political outlet.[93]

Asserting that the United States has been the country to most privilege notions of individual liberty in the Constitution while creating official indifference to many other issues,[94] Glendon sends this warning: '[T]he most important reason for being wary of current American models of judicial review and individual rights is that our "two hundred years of experience" is, to a great extent, a history in which accident, drift, and impotence in the face of seemingly insoluble problems of bigness, heterogeneity, and racial tension have played at least as much of a role as reason, deliberation, and choice.'[95]

Handler came to an even more sobering set of conclusions. Sifting through the evidence of the study discussed earlier in this section, he concludes that success for public interest groups was decidedly mixed. By turning to law and lawyers, public interest groups may lose control of the problem if only because the wrong set of tools — litigation and the courts — may be used instead of the devalued skills of lobbying and consultation.[96]

Lawyers often dominate with regard to tactics and the membership of interest groups is confounded by the law's mysterious language and procedures. As a result, there are dangers that the group's non-legal activity will falter and the membership itself will be sapped. The arguments may be soundly framed legally but at the same time may lose larger political and social appeal. And, of course, there is always the possibility of failure in the courts.[97]

Ultimately, Handler concludes that by turning to the law, these social reform groups have achieved only incremental change (if at all) since the legal system and the values it represents inevitably limit their claims. This is because in turning to litigation, progressive groups must inevitably take a role in the most established of institutions and their claims must be grounded in traditional American constitutional values. Such activity, therefore, is unlikely to disturb fundamental political and economic arrangements.[98]

Perhaps most cautionary is Rosenberg in his recent book, *The Hollow Hope*, referred to in the last section for its ideas on causality and models of judicial decision making. Rosenberg contends that a key element in understanding such ideas is ascertaining to what extent and under what conditions courts can produce political and social change rather than becoming absorbed by abstract arguments for and against the courts. As a result, he examined in detail several crucial areas in the United States where change was expected to occur. Rosenberg's conclusions are blunt: 'US courts can *almost never* be effective producers of significant social reform.'[99] Though major victories in the courts can be cited, Rosenberg concludes that almost invariably their long-range impact was minor, 'often more symbolic than real', so that there was 'only an illusion of change'. And while Rosenberg could find no evidence that court decisions mobilized supporters of significant social reform, he contends that there is evidence that litigation may actually galvanize opponents who are already very aware of the issues and related developments. Courts give rise to the 'fly-paper' phenomenon. Litigation is a 'lure' that entices groups and organizations to use it as they hope to provoke responses from bureaucracies, to counter the advantages of the better-endowed in the legislative processes, and to force recalcitrant majorities to desist from their unprincipled ways. Instead what occurs overwhelmingly is that these groups exhaust sparse resources that could have been better spent in the electoral, legislative, and administrative processes to make democracy live up to its ideals.[100]

Perhaps Rosenberg's conclusions may best be illustrated by discussing what could be the most controversial example he employs, the aftermath of *Brown* v. *Board of Education*. He contends that in the ten-year period after that decision (1954 to 1964), virtually nothing occurred to end segregation in public schools. For example, in 1964 only 1.2 per cent of black children in the South attended school with whites.[101] Instead, he argues that it was only after the enactment in 1964 of the Civil Rights Act that any real progress was made towards desegregation and that by 1971, 85.9 per cent of black children in the South were attending desegregated schools. Rosenberg asserts, therefore, that it was not the Supreme Court but Congress and the executive branch that effected desegregation.

Yet even if his account of what caused desegregation were to be accepted, an entirely different response to him would be to argue that it was the decision in *Brown* that propelled the awakening of civil rights. More specifically, the contention would be that *Brown* altered the way race relations were viewed so that legislation and government action to end discrimination followed: *Brown* may have not been the immediate cause, but it was the ultimate one. Yet Rosenberg also refutes this argument. His research on the structure of civil rights organizations and public opinion polls found no evidence that the judgement mobilized concern for civil rights or was influential in moulding opinion. To the contrary, he alleges that after the holding, the press did not devote more attention to civil rights issues, that organizations did not use *Brown* as a basis for fund-raising or membership recruitment, and that civil rights legislation of the 1950s and 1960s proceeded with few references to the decision.[102] What did occur was the galvanization of opposition, so that after *Brown* there was growth in the membership and activities of pro-segregation groups, such as the White Citizens Councils and the Ku Klux Klan.[103]

Still, if some have been at fault for making sweeping assertions about the efficacy of litigation, issue has been taken with Rosenberg for being too unqualified in the other direction. In reviewing *The Hollow Hope*, Sunstein points out that the principles of *Brown* may have been deeply internalized by blacks so as to profoundly alter their sense of entitlement.[104] He suggests that if in fact the decision was rarely mentioned in the press, this may have been because the Court's holding was so patently right that people did not think it was necessary to constantly refer to it. Further, Martin Luther King did refer to Supreme Court decisions and to the Constitution, and from this Sunstein suggests it is possible to conjecture that *Brown* must have been a nurturing (if unmentioned) moral influence.

Yet if Sunstein takes issue with Rosenberg for being too unqualified in his conclusions, he nevertheless recognizes the vigour of *The Hollow Hope* as a force in bringing up short those who simplistically draw conclusions about the impact of litigation: '[H]e has shown that there is room for much uncertainty about this matter [of consequences]. In any case, he has put into question the assumption of people who now believe . . . that litigation is an especially promising approach to social reform.'[105] For the moment, the last word on using courts to achieve progressive reform will be given to Rosenberg himself and his blunt warning: '[W]hile romance and even naïveté have their charms, they are not best exhibited in court rooms.'[106]

What, in sum, is being said in this part? The main contention is that gauging the impact of judicial activity on any specific issue is a much more problematic exercise then first meets the eye. I am not suggesting that all such attempts should be abandoned. At a number of places in the book I will discuss examples of very relevant and helpful studies or suggest why they ought to be done. I am emphasizing that sweeping generalizations about the effect of litigation upon particular questions ought to be viewed very sceptically. As the discussion of the works of Choper, Handler, Scheingold, Glendon, and Rosenberg illustrate, litigation used to further political reform can produce consequences that are particularly cloudy. What evidence there is, in some critical ways, points in an opposite direction: such court activity may actually deflect and corral these movements.

Litigation and Ideology: We of the 'Pragmatic and Empirical'

Some of the strongest reservations about courts have come from those willing to speak directly in ideological terms. From this perspective, courts are indeed capable of protecting rights, but that is precisely the problem because rights are almost always linked to a traditional liberal and individualistic sense of ordering. Thus, courts will excel at protecting property and economic entitlements and some political rights, but will, conversely, be indifferent or even hostile to assertions concerning group or community interests or non-traditional claims such as those made on behalf of women, minorities, the disabled, and the environment. In this section the influence of litigation is not gauged by focusing upon specific social and political issues but its relationship to ideology. The claim is that while the impact of litigation on particular issues may be difficult to assess (for reasons discussed in the preceding part), its relationship with political ideas and its influence in buttressing some while limiting others and the consequences of this activity are more easily analysed.

It is in the United States where the influence of litigation upon the ideological structure of the country and, conversely, those ideas upon the judiciary are most strongly felt. It is in that country where traditional liberalism most clearly structures the judicial enterprise. Almost from the beginning Americans accepted the notion of a judiciary capable of striking down legislation that conflicted with the Constitution as part of their embrace of 'a government of laws and not of men'.[107] Thus, that country quickly endorsed Alexander Hamilton's assertion that 'Constitutional limitation can be preserved in practice in no other way than through the medium of Courts of Justice, whose duty it must be to declare all acts contrary to the manifest tenor of the Constitution void.'[108]

But also from the beginning it was seen that a paradox existed because commitment to fundamental law conflicted with another bedrock principle: popular sovereignty so that 'democratic government under law' is a slogan that simultaneously pulls in different directions.[109] McCloskey has characterized the incompatibility and how Americans deal with it:

> Popular sovereignty suggests will; fundamental law suggests limit. The one idea conjures up the idea of an active, positive state; the other idea emphasizes the negative restrictive side of the political problem . . . [I]t seems unlikely that Americans in general ever achieved such synthesis and far more probably . . . that most of them retained the ideas side by side.[110]

This paradox has sometimes immersed the United States Supreme Court in controversy. It was said that the capacity of judicial rulings to generate heated debate was clear in the 1950s when the Court made decisions about desegregation, most conspicuously in *Brown* v. *Board of Education*. Such rulings led commentators to assert that the Court, if well-intentioned, was coming perilously close to overstepping its boundaries. Its place in the United States' governance was endangered 'when the judges seek the hottest political cauldrons of the moment and dive into the middle of them'.[111]

But instead of drawing back, the Court plunged forward and increased its activities during the 1960s. Consequently, it has been argued that its decisions over the past twenty-five years have had a more pronounced effect on American politics and society than those of any other period. Not only substantive law was altered but remedial law as well, so that the federal judiciary could directly supervise institutions such as federal prisons, schools, and hospitals to bring them into constitutional conformity.[112]

As such activity increased, so too did the warnings that the judicial role was being imperilled. For example, Justice Powell, writing in 1974, warned that '[w]ere we to utilize this power as indiscriminately as is now being urged, we may witness efforts by the representative branches drastically to curb its use'.[113] Justice Harlan asserted that 'The powers of the federal judiciary will be adequate for the great burdens placed upon them only if they are employed prudently.'[114] Finally, Felix Frankfurter, dissenting in the critical reapportionment case of the Warren Court, warned that '[T]he

Court's authority — possessed of neither the purse nor the sword — ultimately rests on sustained public confidence in its moral sanction. Such feeling must be nourished by the Court's complete detachment, in fact and in appearance, from political entanglements and by abstention from injecting itself into the clash of political forces in political settlements.'[115] This judicial chorus has always been joined by any number of scholars who issue grave warnings that the more the power of invalidation is exercised, the more imperilled it becomes. So Jesse Choper wrote, 'Since public antagonism, resistance and retribution appear to have a spill-over effect if one or another of the Court's rulings sparks a markedly hostile reaction, then the likelihood that subsequent judgements will be rejected is greatly increased.' He concluded that the Court 'in some principled fashion, must ration its power of invalidation'.[116]

These sentiments were buttressed by conventional political science that held there were any number of ways that the other branches of government could tame a too ambitious Court. Even before the Constitution was ratified, Alexander Hamilton set this tone when writing that the Court 'is beyond comparison the weakest of the three departments of power, it can never attack with success either of the other two, and . . . all possible care is requisite to enable it to defend itself against their attacks'.[117] A modern embodiment of this view goes as follows: 'Congress can increase the number of Justices, enlarge or restrict the Court's appellate jurisdiction, impeach and remove its members, or propose Constitutional amendments either to reverse specific decisions or drastically alter the judicial role in American government. . . . A President to whom the nation looks for leadership can throw the entire authority of his office against that of the Court, just as can a senator, congressman, or governor.'[118]

Yet in *The Limits of Judicial Power — The Supreme Court in American Politics*, William Lasser confronts the assertion about the Court's fragility and comes to quite the opposite conclusion:

> [D]espite all of the controversy and criticism of the past thirty years, the Court is as powerful and effective today as at any time in its history. Its unprecedented activism, far from endangering its place in American politics, seems to have given the Court even more power. Its critics have been unable to reverse outright even one of the Court's controversial decisions and the Court shows no signs of retreating from its activist approach to Constitutional decision making. The justices, having ignored all the advice proffered to the Court, have been rewarded instead of punished.[119]

He arrives at his conclusion by examining three periods of crisis prior to the Court's post-Second World War record: the events surrounding the *Dred Scott* case in which the Court rejected the claims of a runaway slave to his freedom; the Reconstruction cases in which the Court was deprived of its power to rule on the constitutionality of the Reconstruction acts; and the New Deal crisis, which became focused around the aborted Court-packing plan. Heated criticism of the Court and rejection of its views around these three controversies are often used as warnings to today's Court. But in reviewing these severe episodes of crisis, Lasser suggests that they were in many respects aberrant and did not, in any event, occur in isolation. Instead, they were part of a larger crisis for the country as a whole in which the Court as part of the controversy had many allies as well as enemies, so that in many ways it entered the more contemporary period from a position of strength that it drew upon and subsequently solidified.[120]

There may be several reasons why the Court's place in the United States is so strong, but a fundamental aspect is the broad consensus about its powers. The Court's critics in Congress have very rarely, if ever, used the powers they theoretically possess to curb the Court, such as the spending power, impeachment, or constitutional amendment. Nor has opinion ever coalesced effectively against the Court. When a crisis related to the Court's decisions has occurred with regard to race, for example, the decisions have either been supported by a majority or the issues have not created so great a concern as to lead to irresistible demand for reaction. Even on these infrequent occasions, when pressure for reaction developed — for example, regarding school busing in 1972 or the national security cases in the late 1950s — other issues quickly distracted public opinion. No court issue has ever dominated a modern presidential election. Congressional reaction to the Court's decisions, including those around school prayer, abortion, and busing, has been unorganized and sporadic. Attempts to alter the ideological structure of the Court have suddenly failed; the ill-fated Bork nomination for a seat on that Court only served to show the consensus around (or at least tolerance for) the Court's controversial decisions on equal protection, religion, and privacy.

At the heart of the acceptance of the Court and its substantial powers is fundamental agreement about the principles it invokes in its work: 'The removal of high policy to the realm of adjudication implies a prior recognition of the principles to be legally interpreted.'[121] Lasser cites Louis Hartz and his view that the linchpin of American governance was deep agreement that 'liberal' or 'Lockean' individualism should prevail.[122] As Hartz asserts, '[J]udicial review as it has worked in America would be inconceivable without the national acceptance of the Lockean creed, ultimately enshrined in the Constitution.'[123]

This question of ideology and its relationship to the judiciary and litigation has been addressed directly for England by J.A.G. Griffith in his *The Politics of the Judiciary*.[124] He analysed judicial activity in that country in five critical areas: industrial relations, civil liberties and personal freedoms, property rights and land-use planning, conspiracy law, and a comparison of the rights of trade union members against their union with the rights of students in disciplinary hearings. Griffith concluded that while judges are usually impartial, that is, not blinded by overt prejudice, they are not neutral to the extent of having no view of the 'public interest' in the cases they decide. To Griffith, the judges' overriding sense of the 'public interest' has three aspects: 'first, the interests of the state (including its moral welfare) and the preservation of law and order, broadly interpreted; secondly, the protection of property rights; and thirdly, the protection of certain political views normally associated with the Conservative Party'.[125] Even more bluntly, he asserted that 'their interpretation of what is in the public interest and therefore politically desirable is determined by the kind of people they are and the position they hold in our society. . . .'.[126]

Griffith accounted for these values by looking to the homogeneous backgrounds of the English judges and their membership in a small integrated élite.[127] Cotterrell, another English scholar, commenting on Griffith's work points to the force of legal ideology and doctrine and its emphasis on individualism:

> Much that Griffith describes as the political predilection of the judges can be interpreted as aspects of individualism which is deeply rooted in legal ideology and strongly supported by certain basic conditions and experiences of legal professional practice particularly in the Anglo-American context. Judges who have been appointed to the bench after long years of such practice are surely not unlikely to have their outlook powerfully shaped by the doctrine and ideology they ceaselessly analyze and faithfully serve in their judicial work.[128]

The heightened interest in litigation in Canada, augmented by the coming of the Charter, has produced a strong reaction among a group of leftish academics (some critical legal scholars, neo-Marxists, and feminists). They are scarcely content with the product of the Canadian political process, but even less so with the judicial role. There is very little that is equivocal about these writings and their conclusions. In these depictions, judges are at one in preserving established institutions and litigation is part of the ideological superstructure designed to enhance the status quo:

> [C]onstitutional litigation and adjudication are special social activities that do not cause or condition, but comprise and are constitutive of extant social conditions: '[it] is not so much that the court is the natural expression of popular justice, but rather that its historical function is to ensnare it, control it and to strangle it, by re-inscribing it within institutions which are typical of a state apparatus'. To participate in the litigation process as lawyer or litigant, however radical the claim or cause, is to sanction and reinforce existing social relations.[129]

This animosity takes several forms. The Charter is denounced for focusing upon 'rights' of individuals against government. Such a focus shields from scrutiny as 'private' social and economic relations (that are untouched by any form of governmental action and thus not subject to scrutiny under the Charter) that are as much or more responsible for any unjust and unequal conditions as any governmental action.[130] Furthermore, the claim that litigation protects minorities from insensitive majorities through principled decisions is viewed as a means of blunting representative institutions. In a clash between judges and democracy, the latter will lose: 'In allowing individuals to short circuit representative institution and groups, and to advance claims which "trump" more representative claims on the basis of consistency with abstract rights embedded in the status quo, [the Charter] is a perversion of democracy.'[131]

Such animosity towards the Charter does not stand alone but is coupled generally with a condemnation of the common law: both are charged with reflecting the same individualistic assumptions and hostility towards government. The record of legislatures is scarcely praised, dominated as they have been by entirely the wrong set of interests and political parties. Nevertheless, whatever progress has been achieved 'has come . . . through political action aimed at displacing the common law vision of unbridled individual autonomy with a countervision of collective responsibility'. The flaws of the Charter are 'predicated on the same hostility to legislative action, and the same reverence for individual autonomy, that animated the common law'.[132]

Such pronouncements may seem extreme, particularly in conjunction with what these critics might aspire to in terms of political change. Nevertheless, one should be careful not to reject the entire analysis on these grounds alone. There are portions of this critique of litigation and particularly of the Charter that can be part of apprehensions regarding overreliance upon litigation contouring our social and political life. Linked to such critiques, an overall assessment of litigation in this country was undertaken for the Royal Commission on the Economic Union and Development Prospects for Canada.[133] Guy Rocher examined such areas as labour relations, the environment, and federal and provincial intervention in the economy, and relied on the work of others for the commission in these areas that arrived at much the same conclusion. He drew a fundamental distinction between courts and legislatures with courts buttressing private property, capitalism, and individualism and with legislatures supplying at least some counter by recognizing collective interests and blunting the exercise of individual property rights: '[The] common law thus leans in favour of the pre-eminence of individual rights over public and community rights.'[134]

Connecting the work of judges with ideology in Canada is not just reserved for the left. Peter Russell, one of Canada's foremost political scientists and a student of the judiciary, reviewed the political role of the Supreme Court on its centenary in 1975. In the context of discussing the Court's troubled history with civil liberties (particularly its lack of enforcement of the Bill of Rights), he warned about entanglements with extravagant claims of individualism as a driving force for political and social construction even in the context of civil liberties. Pointing to some cases where courts had afforded protection, Russell explained that 'Our judges have been at their best in the field of civil liberties when, instead of being asked to theorise about such abstractions as "equality before the law" or "due process of law", they have been called upon to identify the rights implicit in the working of our basic institutions of government . . . .'.[135]

In blunting calls for an entrenched Charter and an enhanced role for courts in complex social and political questions, Russell turned not to the left but to the right, a direction in which others have looked as well.[136] The Burkean ideal of order, responsibility, and gradual change consistent with careful working out of community (including hierarchical) needs was (and should continue to be) our watchwords:

> [The approach] which is truest to our experience and most in keeping with our capabilities is that of Edmund Burke, not John Locke. Canadians — neither their judges, nor their politicians — are creatures of the Enlightenment. Their forte is not abstract, rationalist philosophising. The American Republic may be built on self-evident principles and universal rights, but Canadian political and legal thought is far more pragmatic and empirical.[137]

'Pragmatic and empirical': not very glamorous, scarcely a call to arms and, indeed, it is a description of the country with which Russell may no longer agree.[138] Yet it is evocative of more than a few of the political and social arrangements that, until recently, have guided Canada along its way. Pragmatic and empirical, while decidedly lacking glitter, is certainly consistent with the complex ideas and variegated ideology that we discussed in Chapter One. Still, they are scarcely consoling words for those who have felt left out and marginalized. Nor does 'pragmatic and empirical' fit well with the discourse of rights, the win-lose outcomes, and the call for clear-cut determinations that we may be embracing if we are indeed turning to litigation as a means of answering difficult social and political questions.

CONCLUSION

The message of this chapter is that simple and sweeping claims about the effects of litigation ought to be viewed sceptically. Such wariness is buttressed by studies like Robertson's, which demonstrated that a ruling by the Supreme Court of Canada on informed consent had little of the substantial consequences predicted for it. There is much to question regarding assertions that courts have been agencies of effective reform and of protection for the interests of minorities and the disadvantaged, as we saw in our discussion of the works of Choper, Handler, Glendon, Scheingold, and Rosenberg. That the evidence is, at best, unclear in this regard is particularly significant since solicitude for these interests is a cornerstone for validating judicial authority and, indeed, enhancing it.

The evidence that does exist mainly points the other way. With some exceptions, litigation in the name of reform has achieved little real change. What it frequently has done is act as a lure to deflect groups and their limited resources away from the political process where more deep and longlasting change might have been secured, though the fact that such resources were not spent on political activities also means that there can be no certainty about what would have happened outside the courts.

What litigation may do is send out ideological messages, not so much about any particular case or group of cases but to reinforce particular sets of values. Such messages are not in themselves bad; sets of beliefs about how a society is to be constructed are a part of that society. Yet in Canada a number of ideologies have played out in our national life. When litigation boosted liberalism, there were strong countervailing tendencies from the legislatures that built upon the resilient communitarian traditions bolstered by toryism with its emphasis on order and hierarchy and the restraint of individualism for the public good, as well as by social democracy with its insistence that individualism takes its meaning from concern for the general welfare.

In growing weary of our politics, such subtleties in our ideological make-up, even if still present, may seem beside the point as we cast about for new channels for our aspirations and our attentions are drawn to litigation. Such a shift may seem inevitable in order to exit the dreariness and connivance of legislatures and their bureaucracies, to come to a place of rationality and principle, to say nothing of decorum. Just let there be no illusions: either about the courts' considerable strengths or, then again, about their limits.

NOTES

[1] J. Griffiths, 'Is Law Important?' (1979) 54 *New York University Law Review*, 339.

[2] Ibid., 347.

[3] H.D. Lasswell and M.S. McDougal, 'Legal Education and Public Policy: Professional Training in the Public Interest' (1943) 52 *Yale Law Journal*, 203.

[4] *Supra*, note 1 at 372n.74.

[5] See R. Abel, 'Lawyers in the Civil Law World' in R. Abel and P.S. Lewis (eds), *Lawyers in Society: The Civil Law World* (Berkeley: University of California Press, 1988).

[6] M. Galanter, 'Law Abounding: Legalisation Around the North Atlantic' (1992) 55 *Modern Law Review*, 1, 4, citing R. Abel, *The Legal Profession in England and Wales* (Oxford: Basil Blackwell, 1988).

[7] B. Curran, 'Supplement to the Lawyer Statistical Report: The US Legal Profession in 1985' (1986) 20 *Law & Society Review*, 19–56.

[8] D. Stager and H. Arthurs, *Lawyers in Canada* (Toronto: University of Toronto Press, 1990): 149.

[9] Galanter, *supra*, note 6 at 4.

[10] Ibid., for Canada, *supra* note 8 at 149.

[11] For example, M.J. Mossman, '"Shoulder to Shoulder": Gender and Access to

Justice' (1990) 10 *The Windsor Yearbook of Access to Justice*, 351; and by J. Hagan et al., 'Cultural Capital, Gender, and the Structural Transformation of Legal Practice' (1991) 25 *Law and Society Review*, 355.

[12] Galanter, *supra*, note 6 at 5–6.

[13] Ibid., 6.

[14] Ibid., 6.

[15] Ibid., 7.

[16] Consultative Group on Research and Education in Law, *Law and Learning* (Ottawa: Social Sciences and Humanities Research Council of Canada, 1983): 82.

[17] Galanter, *supra*, note 6 at 7.

[18] Ibid.

[19] Ibid., 13.

[20] Ibid.

[21] R. Cotterrell, *The Sociology of Law: An Introduction* (London: Butterworths, 1984): 55, 70, and 72 for quote in text citing Y. Dror, 'Law as a Tool of Directed Social Change: A Framework for Policy-Making' (1970) 13 *American Behavioral Scientist*, 553, 554.

[22] *Supra*, note 1 at 357.

[23] Ibid., 352–3.

[24] M. Tolchin, 'Drinking Is Safer Than Ever, Since Sobriety Sank In', *The New York Times*, 17 January 1993, E3.

[25] Some of these issues and others are discussed in H. Ross, 'The Law and Drunk Driving' (1992) 26 *Law & Society Review*, 219.

[26] Galanter, *supra*, note 6 at 23.

[27] M. Galanter, 'The Life and Times of the Big Six; or, The Federal Courts Since the Good Old Days' (1988) *Wisconsin Law Review*, 921.

[28] Occupational Trends, 1961-86 (Ottawa: Statistics Canada, 1988): 2–29, as found in Galanter, *supra*, note 6 at 8.

[29] L. Tribe, *God Save This Honourable Court* (New York: Random House, 1985): xviii, 111, 139–40, quoted in A. Hutchinson, 'Charter Litigation and Social Change: Legal Battles and Social Wars', in R. Sharpe (ed.), *Charter Litigation* (Toronto: Butterworths, 1987): 358.

[30] O. Fiss, 'Against Settlement' (1984) 93 *Yale Law Journal*, 1073 at 1089.

[31] A. Gold, 'The Legal Rights Provisions — A New Vision or Déjà Vu' (1982) *Supreme Court Law Review* 4, 108, quoted in C. Manfredi, *Judicial Power and the Charter* (Toronto: McClelland & Stewart, 1993): 27.

[32] J. Whyte, 'On Not Standing for Not With Standing' (1990) 28 *Alberta Law Review*, 347, 351.

[33] W.F. Murphy and J. Tavenhaus, 'Public Opinion and the United States Supreme Court' (1968) 2 *Law & Society Review*, 357, and A. Sarat, 'Studying American Legal Culture: An Assessment of Survey Evidence' (1977) 11 *Law & Society Review*, 427, cited in A. Hutchinson, *supra*, note 29 at 364.

[34] R. Lehne and J. Reynolds, 'The Impact of Judicial Activism on Public Opinion' (1978) 22 *American Journal of Political Science*, 896, cited in A. Hutchinson, ibid., 364.

[35]G. Robertson, 'Informed Consent in Canada: An Empirical Study' (1984) 22 *Osgood Hall Law Journal*, 139. For a study demonstrating that professionals can play an important role in mediating knowledge of court's decisions and their clients' reaction to these judgements, and that this role can lead to a distorted understanding on the part of clients, see L. Edelman et al., 'Professional Construction of Law: The Inflated Threat of Wrongful Discharge' (1992) 26 *Law & Society Review*, 47.

[36][1980] 2 *Supreme Court Reports*, 880.

[37]*Canadian Medical Protective Association Annual Report* (1981): 39, cited in Robertson, *supra*, note 35 at 140.

[38]Linden J. in *White* v. *Turner* (1981) 120 *Dominion Law Reports* (3d) 269, 290 (Ont. SC) aff'd 14 May 1982 (unreported, OCA) cited in Robertson, ibid., 140.

[39]Robertson, *supra*, note 35 at 159–61.

[40]Ibid., 160–1.

[41]G. Robertson, 'Informed Consent Ten Years Later; The Impact of *Reibl* v. *Hughes*' (1991) 70 *Canadian Bar Review*, 423.

[42]Ibid., 439.

[43]Ibid., 440.

[44]For example, D. Givelber et al., 'Tarasoff, Myth and Reality: An Empirical Study of Private Law in Action' (1984) *Wisconsin Law Review*, 443, and yet compare J. Wiley, 'The Impact of Judicial Decisions on Professional Conduct: An Empirical Study' (1982) 55 *Southern California Law Review*, 345.

[45]T. Becker and M. Feeley (eds), *The Impact of Supreme Court Decisions* (New York: Oxford University Press, 1973).

[46]M. Feeley, 'Power, Impact and the Supreme Court', ibid., 227.

[47]Ibid., 211–13.

[48]C. Sheldon, *The American Judicial Process: Models and Approaches* (New York: Dodd, Mead & Co., 1974): 163.

[49]J. Choper, 'Consequences of Supreme Court Decisions Upholding Individual Constitutional Rights' (1984) 83 *Michigan Law Review*, 1.

[50]S. Wasby, 'The Impact of the United States Supreme Court' (Homewood: The Dorsey Press, 1970): 32, quoted in Choper, ibid., 7.

[51]S. Krislov, *The Supreme Court and Political Freedom* (New York: The Free Press, 1968).

[52]S. Scheingold, *The Politics of Rights* (New Haven and London: Yale University Press, 1974).

[53]*Supra*, note 49 at 8–9.

[54]This may be particularly true of regulatory reform that may provide 'tangible benefits to élites and symbolic benefits to mass publics, to quiet potential unrest, to deflect potential demands, and to blur the true allocation of rewards . . . [because] large, dispersed groups (the kind that press for reform) are not in a position to evaluate the situation and thus seize upon the symbolic reassurances that the situation is well in hand'. J. Handler, *Social Movements and the Legal System: A Theory of Law Reform and Social Change* (New York: Academic Press, 1978): 38.

[55]Ibid., 39.

[56]There can be real difficulty, if success does come, in concluding that public

interest organizations have caused it — 'Social-reform groups and law reformers are only one set of actors in the complex process of social change; their precise role is often impossible to ascertain with any degree of precision.' Ibid., 40.

[57] *Supra*, note 49 at 8.

[58] Becker, *supra*, note 45 at 221–2.

[59] *Baker* v. *Carr* (1962) 369 US 186.

[60] *Brown* v. *Board of Education* (1954) 347 US 483; (1955) 348 US 294.

[61] Sheldon, *supra*, note 48 at 143, quoting J. Peltason, *Fifty-Eight Lonely Men: Southern Federal Judges and School Desegregation* (New York: Harcourt, Brace and World, 1961): 93: '. . . six years of litigation produced negligible results'.

[62] (1966) 384 US 436.

[63] For example, N. Milner, *The Court and Local Law Enforcement* (Beverly Hills: Sage Publications, 1971): 229; Note, 'Interrogation in New Haven: The Impact of Miranda' (1967) 76 *Yale Law Journal*, 1519; G. Spohn, 'The Supreme Court's Post-Miranda Rulings' (1981) 3 *Law & Policy Quarterly*, 29.

[64] Note, 'A Postscript to the Miranda Project: Interrogation of Draft Protestors' (1967) 77 *Yale Law Journal*, 300.

[65] *Supra*, note 49 at 9n.27.

[66] Ibid., 10.

[67] *Ginsberg* v. *New York* (1968) 390 US 629.

[68] *Supra*, note 49 at 11.

[69] Ibid., 12.

[70] G. Rosenberg, *The Hollow Hope — Can Courts Bring About Social Change?* (Chicago: University of Chicago Press, 1991).

[71] Ibid., 7 *et seq*.

[72] Ibid., 3 *et seq*.

[73] Ibid., 21 *et seq*.

[74] Ibid., 2.

[75] Ibid.

[76] Ibid, 27.

[77] Ibid., 25.

[78] Ibid., 36.

[79] See the review of *The Hollow Hope*: C. Sunstein, 'How Independent Is the Court', *New York Review of Books*, 22 October 1992, 47.

[80] J. Handler, *Social Movements and the Legal System: A Theory of Law Reform and Social Change* (New York: Academic Press, 1978).

[81] Ibid., 2.

[82] Ibid., 22.

[83] Ibid., 31.

[84] Ibid., 30.

[85] Ibid., 31.

[86] S. Scheingold, 'Constitutional Rights and Social Change: Civil Rights in Perspective' in M. McCann and G. Houseman (eds), *Judging the Constitution — Critical Essays on Judicial Lawmaking* (Boston: Scott, Foresman/Little, Brown, 1989): 83.

[87] P. Williams, 'Alchemical Notes: Reconstructing Ideals from Deconstructed Rights' (1987) 22 *Harvard Civil Rights — Civil Liberties Law Review*, 401, 431.

[88] Scheingold, *supra*, note 86 at 76.

[89] Ibid., 80.

[90] Ibid., 83.

[91] Ibid.

[92] M.A. Glendon, 'A Beau Mentir Qui Vient De Loin: The 1988 Canadian Abortion Decision in Comparative Perspective' (1989) 83 *North Western University Law Review*, 569.

[93] Ibid., 588.

[94] Ibid., 589.

[95] Ibid.

[96] *Supra*, note 80 at 32.

[97] Ibid., 33.

[98] Ibid., 233.

[99] *Supra*, note 70 at 338.

[100] Ibid., 341.

[101] Ibid., 52.

[102] Ibid., 111, 118, 155.

[103] Ibid., 341.

[104] *Supra*, note 79 at 49.

[105] Ibid., 50. See also J. Simon, '"The Long Walk Home" to Politics' (1992) 26 *Law & Society Review*, 923; I. Holloway, Review (1992) 15 *Dalhousie Law Journal*, 664; and see the critical reviews of M. Feeley and M. McCann and Rosenberg's response in 'Review Section Symposium — The Supreme Court and Social Change' [1993] *Law & Social Inquiry*, 715.

[106] Ibid., 341.

[107] John Adams quoted by W. Lasser, *The Limits of Judicial Power — The Supreme Court in American Politics* (Chapel Hill and London: The University of North Carolina Press, 1988): 249.

[108] *Federalist* No. 78.

[109] A. Bickel, *Least Dangerous Branch: The Supreme Court at the Bar of Politics* (Indianapolis: Bobbs-Merrill, 1962): 27.

[110] R. McCloskey, *The American Supreme Court* (Chicago: University of Chicago Press, 1960): 12–13.

[111] Ibid., 229–31.

[112] Lasser, *supra*, note 107 at 2. The activity has been encapsulated as follows:

> The Court moved beyond school desegregation to school integration and busing; banned organized prayer in the public schools; virtually transformed the nation's criminal justice system by imposing strict procedural requirements on state and local law enforcement officials; redrew the national political map by requiring legislative apportionment on the one person, one vote standard; and struck down state laws prohibiting abortion, at least in the first two trimesters of a woman's pregnancy. Even this list, impressive as it is, abbreviates the historical

record; virtually every area of constitutional jurisprudence, from free speech to women's rights, to capital punishment, has been transformed.

[113] *United States* v. *Richardson*, 418 US 166 (1974) 192 (Powell, concurring).

[114] *Flast* v. *Cohen* (1968) 392 US 83, 131 (Harlan, dissenting).

[115] *Baker* v. *Carr* (1962) 369 US 186, 267 (Frankfurter, dissenting).

[116] J. Choper, *Judicial Review and the National Political Process: A Functional Reconsideration of the Role of the Supreme Court* (Chicago: University of Chicago Press, 1980): 156.

[117] *Federalist* No. 78.

[118] W.F. Murphy, *Congress and the Court* (Chicago: University of Chicago Press, 1962): 2–3.

[119] *Supra*, note 107 at 4.

[120] Ibid., 7.

[121] L. Hartz, *The Liberal Tradition in America: An Interpretation of American Political Thought Since the Revolution* (New York: Harcourt, Brace and Co., 1955): 9.

[122] *Supra*, note 107 at 250.

[123] *Supra*, note 121 at 9.

[124] J.A.G. Griffith, *The Politics of the Judiciary* (London: Fontana, 1981).

[125] Ibid., 217.

[126] Ibid., 230.

[127] Ibid., 241.

[128] Cotterrell, *supra*, note 21 at 249.

[129] A. Hutchinson, 'Charter Litigation and Social Change: Legal Battles and Social Wars' in R. Sharpe (ed.), *Charter Litigation* (Toronto: Butterworths, 1987): 357, 380, quoting M. Foucault in C. Gordon (ed.), *Power (Knowledge): Selected Interviews and Other Writings 1972–1977* (Brighton: Harvester Press, 1980): 1.

[130] J. Fudge, 'What Do We Mean By Law and Social Transformation?' (1990) 5 *Canadian Journal of Law and Society/Revue Canadienne droit et société*, 47, 60.

[131] M. Mandel, *The Charter of Rights and the Legalization of Politics in Canada* (Toronto: Wall & Thompson, 1989).

[132] A. Petter, 'Immaculate Deception: The Charter's Hidden Agenda' (1987) 45 *The Advocate*, 857, 858–9.

[133] G. Rocher, 'Canadian Law — a Sociological Perspective' in I. Bernier and A. Lajoie (eds), *Law, Society and the Economy*, vol. 46 (Toronto: University of Toronto, Royal Commission on the Economic Union and Development Prospects for Canada, 1986): 137.

[134] Ibid., 161–4.

[135] P. Russell, 'The Political Role of the Supreme Court of Canada in Its First Century' (1975) 53 *Canadian Bar Review*, 576, 592–3.

[136] R. Cheffins and P. Johnson, *The Revised Canadian Constitution — Politics as Law* (Toronto: McGraw-Hill Ryerson, 1986): 151. 'Canada has a much more distinctly European flavour than the United States. Its thinking owes much more to the great philosopher, Edmund Burke, than to another great English philosopher, John Locke. Locke emphasized the individual. Burke emphasized the community.'

[137] *Supra*, note 135 at 593.

[138] See P. Russell, *Constitutional Odyssey — Can Canadians Be a Sovereign People?* (Toronto: University of Toronto, 1992). Documenting the constitutional torment of the last decades and the shift that has taken place because of the Charter, he now writes (11): 'Canadians now are basically Lockean, not Burkean, in their constitutional aspirations.'

CHAPTER THREE

The Forms of Litigation

INTRODUCTION

In this chapter we discuss the structure of a civil lawsuit. (Criminal litigation, in both form and content, is driven in important ways by different considerations that will be examined in Chapter Seven.) Aside from giving useful context, particularly for those not familiar with the intricacies of law, we will see that the configuration of traditional civil litigation reflects some core ideas espoused in common-law decision making. Similarly, the challenges to the traditional structure of a lawsuit are propelled by a set of ideas that in turn are a basis for critiquing the values buttressed by the judges over time.

The core criticism of the traditional model is that it denies access while privileging a limited range of interests. In contrast, the essential reservations about the expanded model are that it leads the judiciary to usurp functions better left to the legislatures and their agencies. Either way we are left focused upon the limitations of litigation. A fair question is whether the choice of models must necessarily be so stark or whether there is a combination that may take account of the potential and limits.

In crafting the traditional model, the common law focused on the lawsuit as a mode of dispute resolution centred upon the individual determination of rights and remedies and emphasized protection of proprietary or economic entitlement. The traditional lawsuit was a claim on the part of a plaintiff and an assertion of a defence in reply heard by an aloof, passive judge (or jury) who would find relevant facts and apply the applicable rule. If the plaintiff prevailed, the remedy was simple and straightforward, usually a monetary payment or sometimes a directive to return something or do a clearly defined act. If the plaintiff lost, he was to slink away. In either case, the court's involvement was contained and minimal and the lawsuit was perceived as a self-contained, episodic event.[1]

The reasons for this structure are not mysterious. With important exceptions, Canadian courts have long been dominated in many areas by classic liberal ideology, emphasizing individual rights, autonomous and private ordering, and minimal state involvement. It is, therefore, not surprising that the structure designed to resolve disputes would reflect such values: 'the adversary system can be seen as reflecting the political and economic ideology of classic English liberalism. . . .'[2] The active parties, the passive judge, restrictive rules concerning standing and intervention, and a costs regime that rewarded victorious litigants by making losers pay costs helped to reinforce such claims.

But this model has been subject to searching criticism during the last two decades. Several organizing ideas have influenced the legislative process of this country. Individualism in Canada is highly prized, but it has been restrained by a resilient collectivism — on the right embodied in toryism and on the left in social democratic principles. The contention is that this variegated ideology, which has been prominent in formulating laws in the administrative and legislative processes, should also play a role in the judicial creation of the law. Those who wish to alter the model of litigation bridle at the suggestion that the traditional form created a neutral framework for resolving disputes. In challenging and pushing for an expanded model, they insist that the relative strength of parties be examined and, on this basis, claim that governments, large corporations, and sometimes unions have a much greater capacity to litigate. This is because they can absorb or pass on the costs of litigation so that the economic aspects are not a deterrence and, moreover, the propensity to litigate equips them with a sophistication that individuals' one-time experience cannot. In addition, critics of the conventional paradigm point to its emphasis on individual parties as ill-equipping it in assessing the full ramifications of decisions. Those favouring change want intervention expanded to allow all critical aspects of issues to be presented to the court, including by those not directly implicated by the immediate decisions, but who are concerned with the ramifications of the decision. Linked to this is a conviction that the court should be prepared to create a remedy that will respond to systemic and institutional harm. Such ambitions for litigation are often grouped together and referred to as the 'public' or expanded model.

These challenges to the traditional model, which seek to accomplish the changes just discussed, will occupy a large portion of this chapter. However, such challenges have also been a major reason for some turning away from the courts altogether. Such ideas were a powerful impetus in propelling the growth of tribunals' dispute resolution mechanisms as part of the growth of the administrative state. More recently, a push to use other means of decision making — alternative dispute resolution (ADR) — has arisen for many of the same reasons. Finally, we look at such attempts to alter the traditional structure of litigation itself in terms of the implications for the courts' larger role in society, returning to the question of whether we must choose between one model or the other.

CHALLENGES TO THE TRADITIONAL CONCEPT

The challenges to the traditional conception of a lawsuit that have gained momentum over the last two decades in Canada are reflections, in important ways, of the American faith in litigation's capacity to mediate important societal issues. Yet the success of these challenges in revamping litigation in this country is by no means certain. These challenges are united in questioning the highly individualistic premises of the traditional lawsuit, at least in terms of how it bars access to courts. An important focus of such challenge is upon the power of institutions in moulding social policy and how such power should be a proper and necessary subject of litigation and — critically, for the subject at hand — how that litigation is conducted.

Class Actions

The fundamental premise behind class actions is to permit aggregation of claims based on common issues so that they may be resolved at once. This aggregation has a number of objectives. It can save repetitive litigation when the claims are substantial and would have been brought in any event. It can allow claims to be brought that would otherwise not have had access because their individual monetary values would not justify the costs of litigation. Finally, and most controversially, class actions can perform an essentially deterrence function where, though the harm sustained by individual plaintiffs is so small as to make compensation incidental, the benefit to the defendant, wrongly obtained, is substantial so that the goal is more to prevent the wrongdoer from acquiring any ill-gotten gain than to compensate victims on an individual basis.[3] The assertion of rights based on mass harms, the representation of members of a class whose interests may vary, the assessment and distribution of monetary relief by new methods, the tailoring of other remedies (sometimes based on divergent viewpoints even within the class), and the procedural aspects of the class action, such as the motion for certification (a procedure early in the litigation in which a judge decides whether the litigation can be brought in this form), all mark it as a substantial break from the traditional approach to litigation.

Class actions were initially fashioned by the English chancery courts. During the eighteenth century they were allowed to develop, if unenthusiastically. However, by the early twentieth century the English courts, quickly followed by their Canadian counterparts, turned away from this form of collective action. They did so by erecting barriers that required the claims to be essentially identical in all respects rather than allowing class actions for common issues, as well as individualized proceedings, if necessary, for particular issues.[4]

This reaction by the courts was fuelled by the challenge of class actions to the traditional paradigm. But hidden behind this was the philosophical foundation of the common-law courts.[5] One such idea was formalism, the attitude that courts should relinquish their claim to creativity and adaptability and instead defer to precedents and the supremacy of Parliament by a literal interpretation and application of legislation.[6] This approach dictated that the meagre legislative guide in the codified rule concerning class actions represented the outer limit rather than a basic guide for further judicial embroidery.

A second and related factor was the social and political context in which claims to an expansive class action were made. By the early twentieth century, Anglo-Canadian courts were developing an antipathy towards group and collective interests that class actions, by definition, represented. In addition, the rise of leftist parties suggested that any movement towards social goals at odds with nineteenth-century laissez-faire individualism would be the work of legislatures with no need for aid from courts who viewed themselves as the preserve of a particular individualism that now seemed threatened. Thus actions by such groups as consumers, environmentalists, and civil rights activists — who often wanted to use class actions to fortify small or weak individualized claims — were unlikely to find favour with courts, which were developing biases against such interests and in favour of interests they considered more consistent with a nineteenth-century individualism.[7]

Beginning in the 1970s, the Canadian courts began to re-examine the strictures on class actions and to loosen their grip. They did this because the groups and associations — environmentalists, civil rights activists, and consumer representatives — had become much better organized and had achieved substantive rights, mostly through the legislatures, which they wanted the courts to enforce. In addition, there was the influence of the United States' Federal Rule 23 and the class actions brought under it, a trend that began in the mid-1960s. Whatever the reality, the perception that the Americans had fashioned a powerful device for judicial remedy of mass wrongs increased the movement for liberalization of class actions in Canada.[8]

In the late 1960s and 1970s, various provincial courts, including some appellate courts, hesitatingly loosened the strictures around class actions, for example, moving to reject the view that individualized claims for monetary relief would be a bar to class actions.[9] It was in the 1978 case of *Naken v. General Motors of Canada*[10] that the Ontario courts had to undertake their most extensive examination of class actions to that point. In that case, the plaintiff sued to represent purchasers of new models of cars manufactured or distributed by the defendant in 1971 and 1972. The plaintiff argued that the sale of the cars breached a collateral warranty of the defendant, resulting in each class member sustaining $1,000 in damages because of the reduced resale value of the cars.

Because the same damages were claimed for each individual, a separate stage for ascertaining damages was not necessary and thus the claim for damages presented no obstacle. However, the defendant argued that, as a matter of substantive law, each member of the class would have to rely on the warranty in order to recover any damages resulting from its breach. The Court accepted that each proceeding might be necessary, but was willing to allow the action to continue, subject to some modifications, even while urging that class actions be examined carefully by the Ontario Law Reform Commission (which was then studying the question) to ascertain whether comprehensive legislative reform was warranted. This willingness of some Canadian judges to at least begin an inquiry into the proper methods for courts to handle the widespread problems that are inevitable in the industrialized and regulated twentieth century all came to an abrupt halt when *Naken* reached the Supreme Court of Canada, which rejected the class proceedings.[11]

The Supreme's Court decision has been excoriated even at the technical (but nonetheless important) level of misstating the antecedent English and Canadian case-law.[12] However, most disturbing is the fact that the Court ignored lower courts' changing attitude towards class actions in the 1970s and 1980s and shrouded its own analysis in unrepentant formalism by focusing on the meagre text of the then existing rule of procedure governing class actions.[13] It is understandable that the text of the rule should determine the appropriateness of a class action, but the error is to decide that since various procedures are not explicitly addressed by the rule, these procedures must be strait-jacketed.[14] The Court said nothing about the fact that the rule was drafted over 100 years ago and that there is plenty of evidence to suggest that courts before and after did not regard it as an exhaustive code but simply a general statement concerning flexible and evolving procedures. The Court was completely unwilling to analyse why this litigation ought to be accommodated or why it should be shunned. Only once did Justice Estey, the author of the judgement, recognize the need for class actions and the consequences of not allowing the action to proceed, yet even then the Court claimed that these needs had to be answered by legislative rather than judical reform.[15]

As with so many other areas that we will see in this book, it was the legislative process that then became the hope. In 1978, before the Supreme Court decision in *Naken*, Quebec passed a comprehensive statute addressing class actions.[16] In 1982, the Ontario Law Reform Commission issued its *Report on Class Actions*, which dealt comprehensively with the existing problems, evaluated the case for reform, and proposed reform through a detailed draft act.[17] Praised for its comprehensiveness and insightful treatment,[18] but criticized for its alleged radicalism,[19] the report was the basis of legislation that was finally passed in 1993.[20]

The judiciary's hostility towards class actions centres on its form: 'the ad hoc collectivity that organizes its members for a specific purpose and limited time'.[21] The notion that judges should accept such activity and indeed adjudicate issues raised by a collectivity strikes directly at the image of the law and litigation that courts have created and reflected. This hostility has been taken up and developed by Glenn,[22] who believes that class actions must fail as a vehicle because collective litigation runs afoul of the essence of the judicial function in the adversarial system.[23] Glenn is concerned by the burdens he perceives class actions will impose. He points to low levels of filing of such suits,[24] and he maintains that in resolving issues for the class on the common questions, courts will somehow confer judgement on the class without taking account of class members' individual issues, which may be critical in deciding whether or not any particular member ought to recover.[25]

This celebration of litigation's classical paradigm can be responded to on several levels. First, the charge that class actions are unduly burdensome is very complex and Glenn makes it without due attention to the studies that have attempted to assess the relevant questions. Careful comparisons of class with non-class actions suggest that in some contexts and for some substantive areas of law, class actions may indeed be more burdensome.[26] However, other studies suggest that there is no significant difference in the amount of judicial time employed to hear class and non-class cases,[27] and that there is a basis for suggesting that any additional judicial time class actions may require is outweighed by their capacity to generate more substantial amounts of relief.[28] The point here is to emphasize that any view of class actions that fails to sift through the many relevant studies is open to serious question.

Second, the lower than expected level of filing under the Quebec legislation is a strange criticism since class actions initially had to fight allegations that they would flood the courts.[29] Class actions have also declined in the United States during this period, but several explanations have been offered that question the supposition that this form of litigation is unsuited to our court system. Prominent among these is the suggestion that class actions are often filed in response to some government litigation or investigation that unearths the cause of action and the evidence to establish it.[30] When such activity declines, so too can class actions.[31] A similar explanation could account for a lower rate of class actions in Quebec. There is no indication of the extent to which any of these class actions have had the benefit of prior government investigation or the extent to which original predictions concerning the volume of class actions contemplated were related to government investigation or litigation.

Third, when Glenn worries that courts fail to distinguish between individual questions and common questions, thus giving judgement to plaintiffs when they would not otherwise have succeeded, he does not point to cases either in Quebec or the United States in which this has actually occurred. Indeed, he has indicated a certain judicial hostility in the United States towards class actions for mass torts.[21] That courts should reject such claims as candidates for class actions is open to serious question,[33] but it hardly suggests that they are embracing the problem he fears.

Finally, his arguments that the essence of the judicial function demands rejection of class actions seem wrong-headed in two ways. First, research into what courts have historically done suggests that they have been much more intrusive and active than the paradigm he described. Such common matters as default judgements, long-arm provisions, prejudgement remedies, and levy and execution have all involved the courts persisting in forcing obstinate litigants to obey.[34] Again, common procedures in probate cases or bankruptcy and receivership matters show how courts can be involved in extensive, sometimes complex, and prolonged tasks that require their ongoing involvement and supervision.[35] Second, his description takes no account of the radical societal transformation in this century. The social structure has been transformed by the growth of aggregates of power, such as corporations, governments, and unions.[36] These aggregates and the consequences of their actions are the root of the need for change in decision-making forms. What will call the courts' legitimacy into question is an insistence upon immutable forms of dispute resolution that were shaped by social forces and needs of the past.

Yet these lawsuits also gives us an opportunity to examine the impact of litigation in a specific context. Again, as with litigation generally, class actions have been the subject of vaunted claims concerning their capacity to effect reform or wreak havoc on the affairs of those subject to them: '[M]ost unfortunate is the exaggerated rhetoric and imagery with which both proponents and opponents of class actions often have carried on their debate.'[37] However, a recent study of class actions in the United States demonstrates that such characterizations, at least in terms of class actions' capacity to effect reform, are badly inflated. Garth conducted an extensive study of successful and unsuccessful class actions brought in the federal court in a district of California over a six-year period that involved a wide range of claims.[38] By no means unsympathetic to the concerns of those who might bring class actions, he concluded that such litigation can have a positive effect upon plaintiffs by helping them mobilize regarding injustices that they may have suffered. Yet there was no basis for asserting class actions' ability to make major contributions to progressive reform: '[C]lass actions cannot measure up to any interpretation that loads them with political significance for their overall contribution to social change. . . . [W]e do not see . . . the mobilization of disadvantaged groups or the winning of momentous litigation that translates into social change.'[39]

So what role is left for class actions between the refutation of Glenn's indictment of them on the one hand and their severe limitations in achieving significant reform on the other? The answer draws upon a classic function of courts: dispute resolution. Resolving disputes is at the heart of what courts can and should do. A desirable role for class actions harkens back to that classic function. Do not look to them for regulatory or systemic reform — disappointment awaits. Instead, expect them to have the more modest but important role of giving access to claims about and resolving those disputes concerning mass harms in ways that are not possible without this procedural device. A limited role for litigation? Yes. One that is therefore likely to return us to legislatures and administrative agencies to argue about more far-reaching and long-lasting solutions? Yes. Messages consistent with the overarching plea of this book.

Standing

The central question asked by standing is whether a court will recognize someone's entitlement to sue so that the law, through a judicial decision, will protect a particular claim. Formulations of the standing dilemma have focused upon the kind of interest necessary for a plaintiff to be allowed to litigate. The traditional view was that an allegation of harm or injury, translated into some invasion of a particular economic or proprietary right or claim to individual liberty, formed the basis for the court conferring status. Without such a showing, plaintiffs were likely to be turned away.[40] In a world dedicated to providing a framework for individual ordering, to allowing individuals to assert specific claims of entitlement, this made sense. The problem with this depiction of a universe of autonomous organization is that it took no account of aggregates such as trade unions, corporations, and government, as well as their activities and impact; it refused to value claims that were not wrapped up in economic, pecuniary, or proprietary questions, but that often reflected concerns about the behaviour of these large entities.[41]

When aggregates act, their behaviour affects many individuals and groups. But the impact may not be felt in ways that are translatable into personal, specific, monetary claims of entitlement to which courts have been so naturally responsive. There may be, for example, concern about the legality of pollution, articulation, and execution of government policy or certain kinds of union activities, but simultaneously there may not be infringement that is likely to produce a plaintiff aggrieved in the traditional sense.

It was alien to a system focused upon the celebration of the individual to recognize expressions of shared values as the basis of entitlement to litigate. Thus, courts took refuge in shifting such claims to the public domain where the Attorney-General — a 'public' official — could be relied upon to protect these interests without further consideration of why interests that did not depend on property rights or claims of personal liberty should not be recognized.[42] But this shift to the Attorney-General added formalism to formalism. How could one person determine public rights? Why should a politician be expected to be the gatekeeper of litigation whose objects were frequently the government, its agencies, or other large entities, all of which could pressure someone who had to keep an eye on the political impact of any of his decisions?[43]

Indeed, the conventional reasons in support of restrictive rules largely miss the point. As indicated, casting the Attorney-General as the oracle for and guardian of the public interest is simply impossible.[44] So too is the suggestion that strict standing rules are necessary to avoid a flood of claims. There are a number of examples where standing rules have been liberalized by legislation and in no instance has there been a subsequent dangerous increase in litigation. The costs of litigation (quite apart from a plaintiff's obligation to pay costs if unsuccessful) and pervasive aversion to being involved in the legal system ensure that a dangerous level of claims is unlikely. The suggestion that restrictive rules are necessary to spare courts from trivial issues seems equally unsound. To accept this reason, we would have to assume that the issues brought before courts by all traditional interests are important or at least are always more important than those raised by non-economic claims. But if we consider judges determining who caused the breakup of a marriage (this is not to argue that dissolution of relationships is trivial, but only to suggest that finding of fault may be an unnecessary aspect) or making a once-and-for-all guesstimate of the damages caused by mayhem on the highway, we hesitate before agreeing that traditional interests always bring important issues to court and, conversely, that diffuse interests would always present insubstantial ones. It may be that some claims presented by other than traditional legal interests would be too abstract, but this has rarely been the reason why courts have declined to recognize new interests in the past. In any event, lack of concreteness and absence of traditional legal interest certainly do not go hand in glove. A regime that recognizes only traditional individual claims does not prevent insubstantial or abstract issues from being litigated.

Yet it is difficult to decide which interests not based on claims of property or personal liberty should be recognized. Once these claims are no longer the exclusive ordering principles, how can we determine what interests should be recognized? We need to distinguish sincere interests (but ones that are nevertheless too embryonic or idiosyncratic) from those that represent a common interest of sufficient importance to merit the law's protection. With all the hazards involved, we are dependent on judges for this enterprise. This is especially so when there is no relevant guide, but is also true when the legislature has spoken because much legislation says little if anything about what interests are to be protected by the particular enactment. Even quite elaborate legislative initiatives seem capable of giving no more than a sort of constrained discretion.[45]

Since 1975, the Supreme Court of Canada has examined the issue of standing five times and has on each occasion (except the last) relaxed the requirement that the ability to sue must be based on a traditional legal interest, i.e., a pecuniary, proprietary, or economic claim or one to personal liberty.[46] In doing so, the Court abandoned one of the central tenets of the classical adversarial system, venturing into terrain to an extent charted by possibly no other common-law court. The Court devised a vague requirement that the plaintiff must have a 'genuine interest', meaning that a traditional legal interest is no longer the boundary between those who are and those who are not entitled to litigate. On none of the five occasions did the Court really attempt to square its loosening of standing strictures with the traditional adversarial model.[47] It seemed convinced that the need to ensure some means to test the question at issue was reason enough to grant standing. Reason enough it may be, but what is significant is how the Court relinquished the classic paradigm in the context of standing (in a manner that might amaze many American observers as their courts largely adhere to a traditional vision of standing) while adhering to it in other contexts such as class actions.

What will be achieved by broadening standing to encompass a diverse range of interests? A vital result will be an acknowledgement by courts that their function is directed to ends more diverse than economic quests and personal liberty. Values such as good health, a safe environment, individuality, and position in social organization, may be tentative and abstract but they are values that can be realized and nurtured by courts. To broaden standing is to depart from a regime absorbed with the protection of individual proprietary, economic, and pecuniary values and to recognize other values, many of which may be more collective than individualistic, and more inspired by altruism than self-interest.[48]

Yet a danger in such broadening is to cast judges in the role of omnipotent overseers. This country has a rich ideological tradition, and altruism and collectivism have been values often nurtured by legislatures and their agencies. Broadened standing should not be part of extravagant claims for the judicial role. Yet whatever the limits and definition of that role ought to be, it cannot be realized by pretending that only certain aspirations should count, that only a particular view of societal organization ought to be embodied in determining how the judiciary discharges its function. For the courts to continue to adhere to the conventional strictures on standing would not inhibit any overreaching on their part, but it would confine the courts to dealing with a limited range and kind of interests that would not reflect the complexity of Canadian society. In this way the range of political ideologies discussed in Chapter One can come to be reflected in litigation: the communitarian and collectivist traditions fed by such disparate ideologies as toryism — with its emphasis on order and hierarchy but restrained individualism for the public good — and social democracy with its insistence that individualism and general welfare go hand in hand.

Intervention

Intervention focuses upon the ability of strangers (that is, non-parties) to participate in existing proceedings, at their request or upon the court's invitation. Intervention provides another useful perspective of competing tensions within litigation. The traditional concept of litigation was decidedly sceptical of allowing others aside from the immediate parties to become involved in litigation. Suits were a private matter 'owned' by the named parties to resolve their disputes. Any law and policy that was modified and created was seen as entirely incidental, and so the considerations and processes involved were regarded as even more so. At the other end is a more public concept of litigation that to some degree views all use of courts as a governmental matter that should take account of all reasonable interests. This is particularly so where new law or a novel or controversial application of existing law may be involved in a case. In such a situation control by the immediate parties is only one aspect of the model, albeit an important one. The traditional and public models will be explored in more detail and the utility and disadvantages of liberal intervention will be assessed.

The common-law courts were reluctant to allow broad intervention by non-parties because intervention conflicted with a major tenet of the traditional model of civil litigation — party control of proceedings and definition of issues. A related concern was that of fairness to the original parties, who might be subject to extra expense and delay if third parties were allowed to intervene. There were also ill-defined fears about the courts becoming a political forum or being flooded with applications for intervention in every imaginable case. Finally questions were raised about the courts' capacity to recognize and define non-traditional, diffuse interests, or to determine who best represented those interests.[49]

Conventionally, these apprehensions were responded to by requiring the applicant to demonstrate a 'direct interest' or 'very real interest' in the litigation; that is, where the applicant had a proprietary interest in the subject matter of the dispute, or where he or she could be legally affected by the outcome.[50] Even when the applicant had the requisite 'interest', intervention could still be denied on two other grounds: that the intervention would 'broaden the lis', that is, by introducing new issues or causes of action; or that the intervenor's interest was 'adequately represented' by one of the original parties to the proceedings.[51] The two caught most applications in a kind of conceptual crossfire. On the one hand, if they sought to address issues raised by the original parties, the court could take the view that their interests would be adequately represented by the parties, and therefore intervention was unnecessary. On the other hand, if the proposed intervenor attempted to raise concerns or issues other than those defined by the original parties, or even to offer alternative perspectives on the issues originally raised, intervention could be refused on the ground that the litigation was being broadened to the prejudice of the original parties.[52]

In the late 1960s and early 1970s when there was pressure for alterations in standing and class actions, there were also calls for liberalization of intervention. While many courts have continued to cling to the traditional model since then,[53] a group of cases arose in which courts have attempted to recognize the capacity of others besides the immediate parties to develop issues and implications of a case. Whether these courts consider the public interest aspect of litigation, or focus on the particular relevance of the would-be intervenor's role, or balance the value of intervenors' contributions against any need to control their participation so as not to unduly interfere with or burden the parties to the litigation, a core group of cases seem to accept a different idea of the purposes of litigation, at least when the law is clearly being developed.[54] Some courts have gone so far as to allow intervenors to carry the case forward when one of the original parties did not wish to proceed, in that instance with an appeal,[55] or to order notice to be given so that all interests reasonably connected to the issues raised would have an opportunity to be heard.[56] This openness to the participation of varied perspectives has recently been demonstrated by the Supreme Court. While in 1982 interventions were allowed in only one case, since 1987 many more groups participated in an increased number of cases a year.[57]

In endorsing such an approach to intervention, the Ontario Law Reform Commission links its role to more liberal standing, which it also supports. While it is clearly the case that issues of wide consequence can arise in the context of a purely private dispute involving traditional legal interests, litigation involving non-traditional legal interests, facilitated by broadened standing, can involve many diffuse interests. The greater the number of persons that may be affected by the outcome of a proceeding, the greater the likelihood that there will be many different, often contradictory or conflicting views of what constitutes the 'public interest', and of what principle or policy should govern the resolution of the issues raised by the litigation.[58] Intervention can promote better informed and more satisfactory decision making by ensuring that the court is fully armed with all relevant information and viewpoints from a spectrum of affected interests that will give the court a fuller appreciation of the consequences of the questions before it and an idea of the broader impact of the principles it is about to shape. It can also be an important means of facilitating access to justice for many citizens, particularly interest groups advancing non-traditional interests, who may be unable to initiate litigation due to the expense, or who wish to address a single issue arising in the context of more complex litigation. Finally, intervention, used in a flexible and creative manner, can promote efficiency and certainty in the administration of justice by preventing multiple proceedings and possibly inconsistent results.[59]

Remedies: Structural Injunctions and 'Reading In'

In traditional litigation, the remedy granted to a successful party is usually a monetary payment or sometimes a directive to return something or do a clearly defined act. But at the core of the public model is investigation of a policy and its ramifications. Redress may be sought for a named plaintiff, but the consequences of that lawsuit will be felt by many since it is the actions of a powerful entity — government, corporation, or sometimes trade unions — that are being scrutinized. When the plaintiff is successful, the question arises as to the form and content of the remedy: to what extent should a court supervise the behaviour of the defendant until the offending behaviour is eradicated? Though not confined exclusively to litigation about alleged Charter violations, such issues clearly arise in that context, particularly in light of s. 24's invitation to courts to grant a remedy that is 'appropriate and just' when responding to any particular Charter violation.

Experience in the United States claims that some kinds of constitutional infringement are not rectified by a once-and-for-all proclamation of the court. Such infringements are so pervasive and systemic that the court must supervise the remedial process over an extended period. In these 'structural' or 'complex' injunctions, 'orders in institutional litigation', or simply 'decrees', the focal point is not the individual or class of plaintiffs but, it is said, the unyielding institution or bureaucracy that must be reshaped and redirected towards constitutional conformity.[60]

Not every injunction issued for a constitutional violation in the United States requires the courts' extended involvement. Many such orders bear a family resemblance to those ordered in litigation adhering closely to the traditional model. Thus the court will often issue a preventative injunction forbidding parties from committing certain acts held to have infringed a constitutional right. Or more intrusive but still easily recognizable within established concepts is a reparative court order that requires the defendant to effect defined action to redress past wrongs or to discharge some obligation held to be owing. Such injunctions are often found in cases of discrimination where the harm of the past is sought to be eradicated.

The decree is said to be the remedial form marked off as new, defined by characteristics with no counterpart in the traditional model of litigation. Traced by some to origins in the American courts' reorganization of railroads and divestiture proceedings in antitrust cases in the earlier part of the century, its uniqueness lies in the courts' acknowledgement that they must become much more involved in supervising the offending entity in order to reshape it to conform with the Constitution. In doing so, courts are not led inexorably to any one set of solutions dictated by the infringement of anyone's rights but fashion a range of orders to redirect the entire course of the institution. This disassociation of right and remedy remains one of the most controversial aspects of the regime.[61]

The target of these orders is often some institution such as a prison, hospital, school system or other government bureaucracy, or even the legislature itself in the case of challenges to electoral boundaries, but the details of the relief ordered can vary enormously. In school cases where discrimination has been found, orders have involved redrawn district boundaries, magnet schools, remedial education, consolidation, busing, etc. The combination ordered by any particular court has not been dictated by the proven infringements but has resulted after the court considered the resources available, the operation of the school system, and the preferences of the parties. Similarly, a decree dealing with unconstitutional conditions in a prison or mental institution will be directed at a number of issues that are not necessarily related to a particular violation: staffing ratios, space availability, health, recreation, job training, sanitation, nutrition requirements, and so on. And as with school cases, critics of the decree have tried to contain or even eliminate them by insisting upon a return to tight and inexorable linking of right and remedy.[62]

Yet the differences between litigation that leads to a structural injunction and the traditional model must not be exaggerated. Defenders point to the fact that such orders are very rare and occur only after courts have attempted more gradualist solutions. Further, it has been asserted that traditional litigation may be much more intrusive than comparisons that put intrusiveness exclusively on the decree side of the ledger might suggest. Thus the proper comparison may be between courts that routinely order prejudgement attachment, enter default judgements, and attempt to locate hidden assets and courts that are more specific regarding their orders responding to constitutional non-compliance but only after trying a number of less active and less intrusive alternatives.[63] In addition, traditional litigation has engaged in much more complex supervisory tasks than the starkness of the contrasting paradigms has acknowledged. For example, bankruptcy and receivership provide many instances in which courts have stepped in to supervise assets of debtors, either in an attempt to put them back on a sound footing or to ensure their orderly liquidation and distribution. In such scenarios, courts have been caught up in many complex and difficult business transactions and decisions. While there have been varied criticisms about particular orders or decisions of courts in specific cases, there have been few serious challenges to the courts in engaging in such tasks.[64]

So far, however, Canadian courts have been tentative regarding structural injunctions. But their openness in doing so has been demonstrated by several members of the judiciary,[65] including former Chief Justice Dickson.[66] To this point the greatest potential for such orders appears to come from litigation regarding language rights.[67] The Supreme Court itself provides one such example.[68] In 1985, the Court invalidated Manitoba's English-only statutory law because it offended the constitutional requirement of bilingualism in that province, effectively striking down all English-only statutes enacted since the nineteenth century. However, to avoid what the

Court termed 'legal chaos',[69] it proceeded to deem that all legislation was temporarily valid in order to allow for a 'minimum'[70] period for the statutes to be translated and enacted in French and to 'uphold the rule of law'.[71] The Court 'as presently equipped'[72] was unable to determine the period during which it would be possible for the Manitoba legislature to comply with its constitutional duty. So, it required that the Attorney-General of Canada or of Manitoba request a special hearing within 120 days, at which time the Court would accept submissions from them and from intervenors concerning the logistics of bringing the legislation into constitutional conformity.[73] The Court subsequently issued a detailed order providing for a schedule for translating the law in stages until 1990 and providing for reapplication by any of them to ensure that the orders were carried out.[74]

Such structural injunctions raise important issues about the proper role of courts, questions that do not exist or that are submerged in the traditional model of litigation. Since this remedy is much more widely used in the United States than in this country, there has been considerable discussion of its merits in American legal literature. The first line of criticism looks at the success or failure of these orders. Basically, the argument is that courts ought to resolve bipolar disputes because that is what they do best and, conversely, when they attempt to reform institutions through decrees, there is a significant possibility of error in defining rights in this context and in bringing obstinate entities in line because they may become mired in the attempt.[75] Defenders respond by asserting that, although the complexity of structural litigation may increase the likelihood of error, a proper evaluation must also weigh the positive impact when it succeeds. Because of its breadth, a decree, if only partially successful, may be much more effective than a string of individual suits and may eliminate the need for them altogether.[76]

A second attack lies in the threat decrees pose to the power of the purse since structural relief, by its nature, is often more costly than any remedy that is granted on a one-on-one basis. Some courts refuse to order defendants in these cases to raise funds to comply, but others reject lack of money as excusing violations of constitutional standards and thus will force allocations of public money.[77] This attack is rebuffed by the fact that virtually every court order directly or indirectly affects allocation of private or public resources. While it is true that ordering busing or requiring fewer inmates in a cell may require more expenditures, so too will damage awards, sometimes on a scale more threatening than any decree.[78] Even when orders are made for non-monetary relief, they can cause substantial allocative shifts, as in the fashioning by Canadian courts of the doctrine of fairness and the extent to which it increased the range of circumstances requiring public officials to provide opportunities to reply to official action.[79]

A third line of criticism points to the public's lack of consent; while consent was historically given to courts to solve disputes between individual parties, the governed have never consented to institutional litigation.[80] The primary response has been to challenge the consent theory itself by questioning whether consent — which is clearly necessary for the legitimacy of a democratic government — is always vital for the legitimacy of particular parts. It has been argued that the courts' legitimacy depends not on implied or explicit consent of the people but rather on their competence: 'the special contribution they make to the quality of our social life'.[81] The people may approve or disapprove of what the courts do, but they can be permitted no more immediate control than that, otherwise the judiciary's independence in interpreting and carrying out the Constitution would be destroyed.

A fourth challenge focuses upon the necessity of according the individual an opportunity to participate in any decision that affects him or her directly. Structural litigation offends this basic premise, not because it denies representation but because it shifts the focus of that representation from individuals to groups and organizations, and because it requires a judge to engage in polycentric tasks — something that Fuller, the American legal scholar, said that courts could not do or, in any event, do well.[82] Fuller never offered a clear definition of polycentrism, but it seems to refer to a multifaceted issue — he used the image of a spider's web — so that any solution of one aspect must have ramifications for all others. Running any institution, such as a welfare agency, hospital, or school, could be seen in that sense as polycentric, since the task is not to focus upon any individual violations but to restore the entire entity to constitutional conformity.

These criticisms are responded to at several levels. While Fuller is regarded as correct in celebrating the connection between reason and adjudication, the relationship between adjudication and participation of the individual as an axiom is challenged. Taken to its full implications, polycentrism would include all adjudication that created rules of law — public norms — whether constitutional or otherwise. Most of the important rules of law — fellow-servant, doctrine of fairness, contributory negligence, hearsay rule and exceptions — have come from a polycentric process; that is, these doctrines have been formulated from an array of possible solutions. Finally, allowing the need for individual participation its widest scope would result in the triumph of form over substance.[83]

One is struck by an element arising on both sides of the argument despite the elaborateness and force of each. Scarcely any of the commentators refer to or call for evaluative and follow-up studies of courts' actual performances. Empirical studies, of course, cannot settle all normative debates, but they can often narrow the range of differences by unearthing and testing factual allegations embedded in opposing arguments. There are some evaluative studies of the decrees of United States courts,[84] but there have been reservations even about those studies. Gerald Rosenberg (whose book, *The Hollow Hope*, was discussed at length in the previous chapter) is critical of such investigations dealing with structural injunction and related topics: '[T]hey either focus on unrepresentative time periods, or on unimportant and noncontroversial cases, or they overstate their findings. In addition, many of the studies . . . are theoretical rather than empirical. They mistake what conceivably could happen with what actually has happened. Further, the empirical studies tend to examine only one case.'[85]

In the end, have prisons been brought into constitutional conformity? Has discrimination ended in schools subject to such orders and, when it has, at what costs? Has the blight of discrimination been eradicated at the price of quality of education? When decrees have been successful (having decided the measure of success), what has made them so? Is their success (or failure) noticeably different when compared with success or failure of courts' orders in traditional litigation? It could be that such careful and inclusive examination would reveal patterns, that effectiveness or its absence depend on a mix of factors not solely — or even principally — determined by the judge's personality and vision.

'Reading in' is an issue that is closely related to structural injunctions in terms of remedial complexity. A prominent basis for attacking legislation, usually under the equality provisions of s. 15 of the Charter, is that the statute excludes some groups from its provisions. In other words, those attacking the provision do so only because they have been left out of it: the discrimination occurs because they have been excluded from otherwise valid legislation. If a court agrees with such arguments, it must decide what remedy should be granted. Should it strike down the legislation because it has wrongly discriminated, or should it 'read into' the legislation the excluded group? The problem with striking down is that it has been called 'equality with a vengeance';[86] that is, no one benefits from the legislative program. By contrast, there are difficulties with 'reading in' because the courts are rewriting legislation, sometimes with substantial fiscal consequences, as this remedy expands the scope (and likely the cost) of the infirmed program. A recent decision in the Supreme Court, *Schachter*,[87] illustrates why the remedy of reading in needs to be available, but also how it can become part of the entanglement of courts and social policy, even when the courts understand the limits of their role.[88] Developments regarding gay and lesbian rights arising in part as a result of *Schachter* illustrate something different: attributing progress to courts when such change as has been achieved is the product of combined forces that may also be the best prospect for further change.

Shalom Schachter wanted to stay home after his child was born in 1985. At that time mothers (but not fathers) received fifteen weeks of maternity benefits under the Unemployment Insurance Act. In addition, another section allowed adoptive parents fifteen weeks that could be divided between the adoptive mother and father in any way they wanted. Schachter applied under that section, arguing that not allowing natural parents the same choice of dividing the benefits discriminated against them. Schachter won in the lower courts, but as the case was proceeding, Parliament amended the act so that adoptive and natural parents are entitled to the same benefit. However, the maximum period was reduced to ten weeks.

The Supreme Court heard the case, but was troubled by it since the federal government (presumably because of the amendments just described) simply admitted the constitutional violation and only wished to argue about the remedy. Nevertheless, the Court proceeded and concluded that in circumstances where a group has been wrongfully excluded, three options are available: ordering the extension of benefits, immediately striking down legislation and ending programs, or giving legislators time to bring laws into line. In acknowledging the power to extend programs, the Court emphasized that there should be caution in doing so. Courts should look at the legislation's intent (a difficult search) to ascertain whether the program would have been established with the excluded group in light of potential costs. Another important factor is determining whether the benefit is a constitutional right, thus favouring reading in, or simply a benefit extended by government for a particular social purpose.

The case illustrates the need for more expansive remedies to respond to structural and broad-based harms. The Court also demonstrated an awareness of its role in using such desirable remedies, yet was also wary of intruding into legislative decision making. However, the case itself also reflects the havoc litigation can play in terms of the larger context of social policy, in this case day care. In the end, this decision won benefits for fathers.

There are many forces at play and only time will show the effect of the *Schachter* decision on similar cases. Nevertheless, we can record three items of note all related to day care policy: (1) the *Schachter* case attacked the constitutionality of legislation; (2) an amendment of the legislation *reduced* the benefits to ten weeks, and (3) the Mulroney government announced in February 1992 (after the *Schachter* case was initiated but before the Supreme Court's decision) that it was abandoning a national day care policy. Cause and effect? Probably not in any simple and straightforward way. The basis for scepticism about where such litigation leads? Quite probably yes.

Shortly after the *Schachter* decision was announced, other events were set in motion. Lesbians and gays, similar to other disadvantaged groups, had been pressuring for some time to have their fundamental position recognized and to receive official protection from discrimination. The scourge of AIDS added tragic immediacy to gay men's struggle for the state's assistance. Using the *Schachter* decision's approval of 'reading in' in at least some circumstances and soon after that judgement was released, the Ontario Court of Appeal held that sexual orientation was to be read into the federal Canadian Human Rights Code as a prohibited ground of discrimination so that that legislation, otherwise silent on the matter, would now become a source of protection for lesbians and gays.[89] That decision was followed in quick succession by an administrative tribunal holding that the Ontario Human Rights Code, which contained protection for gays and lesbians, nevertheless offended the Charter to the extent that one of its sections defined marriage as applying only to male/female relationships (though the couple could be merely cohabiting without having gone through any kind of ceremony).[90] This decision was not about whether gays could 'marry' but whether, as in the actual facts of the case, partners of gays could claim legal benefits from being a 'spouse', such as pensions, health care, tax concessions, etc.[91] Soon thereafter in an unrelated case, the federal government settled a lawsuit over discrimination against a lesbian in the military by paying damages to the named plaintiff and by acknowledging that its policy against employing gays violated the Charter.[92]

Such holdings set off a flurry of news stories and political reactions. For example, they were a focus of a two-part front-page story in *The Globe and Mail* on 'The Rights Revolution — The Courts Lead the Charge', in which one law professor was quoted as saying, 'It seems to be something that courts have to lead us in' and another observed that gay and lesbian issues make politicians nervous so they say 'Let the courts do it. They bear the heat.' Meanwhile, then Justice Minister Kim Campbell first indicated she would do nothing,[93] but shortly thereafter introduced amendments to the federal Canadian Human Rights Code, which expressly protected sexual orientation, but also incorporated a definition of marriage that made clear that gays and lesbians could not be 'married'.[94] This action was greeted with derision on the part of the lesbian and gay community, who felt the legislation made them worse off: it protected sexual orientation, but that was coming about through the cases and, at the same time, it seemed to defy the administrative ruling that stipulated gays could not be excluded from benefits enjoyed by cohabiting straight couples.[95] About the same time, the Alberta Human Rights Commission announced that because of all the holdings recognizing gays' and lesbians' rights based on the Charter, it too would begin to protect gays even though the province's applicable human rights legislation did not cover sexual orientation.[96] This led Dianne Mirosh, minister for community development and the member of Cabinet responsible for the Commission, to blurt, 'it looks as though gays and lesbians are having more rights than anybody else'.[97] Such a comment resonated with a statement by Progressive Conservative back-bencher (and Family Caucus member) John Reimer, who opposed Campbell's legislation despite its limitations: 'Simply, homosexuality is changeable. The fact is indisputable.'[98]

Then in the *Mossop*[99] decision in early 1993, the Supreme Court put on the brakes by holding that as a matter of statutory interpretation — the effect of the Charter was not argued in this case — the existing Canadian Human Rights Code's provision prohibiting discrimination based on family status could not be extended to lesbians and gays. Immediately at issue was whether a gay man could claim time off to attend the funeral of his partner's father. The majority reasoned that since the existing code did not expressly prohibit discrimination based on sexual orientation, no such protection could be extended to cohabiting gays and lesbians within 'family status'. A vigorous dissent argued that the absence of any definition of family status in the code afforded an opportunity to extend some protection to lesbians and gays, and that the decision to do so was a matter for the Canadian Human Rights Commission and its tribunals, which ought to be respected by the courts.

Do these developments recognize the need for courts to protect minority rights and the desirability of equipping judges with the tools, such as reading in, to do so? Or is protecting minority rights more complicated than ceding responsibility to the judges so that they can bring about the 'rights revolution'?

There may be substantial shifts in judicial attitudes to lesbians and gays, at least as evidenced in the one judgement of the Ontario Court of Appeal reading sexual orientation into the Charter. But we should at the same time also note that this judgement contrasts with the courts' hostility towards gays, which lasted well into the late 1970s.[100] (The *Mossop* decision is taken by some to be evidence of that continuing pattern.) In addition, there are other points about this 'revolution' that have much less to do with the courts. First, when the Ontario Court of Appeal 'read in', it did so not in isolation or defiance of political action but rather against a background in which the majority of provinces and the Yukon already expressly protected sexual orientation in their human rights legislation — protection that was brought about through the political process.[101] Second, it is true that the protection was restricted to the extent that it came up against the definition of marriage (specifically 'spouse') in the codes. The process to rectify that has been started by an administrative hearing under the Ontario Code. Third, beginning in the late 1970s, public opinion polls have shown increasing public support for the protection of gays.[102]

The point is that the courts, to the extent that they are responding, are not acting alone or in defiance of stated majoritarian preferences but are joining a current of public opinion and legislative and administrative activity that is grappling[103] with the injustices against lesbians and gays. To say, as the law professor quoted earlier said, that the courts must lead us is not only inaccurate but helps to foster, no doubt unintentionally, the comments of the politicians also cited.[104] The law professor and the politicians become strange allies as they wave their banners about in the rhetorical winds of the Charter, all the while cloaking the possibility for acceptable compromise that would allow the majority of Canadians to demonstrate their capacity to protect minorities.

The situation may in fact be at a critical juncture. It is absolutely essential to avoid a divisive atmosphere: courts as protectors of an oppressed minority holding back the majority's instinct to crush; legislators standing up for majoritarian concerns and family values as yet another unruly interest group presses its selfish demands. Instead, those who are interested more in long-term solutions than high-mindedness need to promote and foster the underlying reality that there is no sharp divide between majoritarian and minority interests: gays wish simple dignity and legal entitlements for intimate relationships; the majority will tolerate such recognition (they need not approve) because to do so reflects simple fairness and justice, whose shelter we may all need to seek in our lives.

A compromise that allows for 'registered partnerships' for gays while reserving the term 'marriage' for heterosexuals, but with essentially the same legal entitlements for both (religious possibilities or prohibitions would remain untouched) would require a lot of good will all round.[105] Yet with many in the media focusing on anything that undermines politics and giving prominence to courts creating rights as the empowerments and boundaries of our lives, the fear is that those strange allies' accounts — the law professor's, those politicians' — will each come to be accurate: whatever gays' and lesbians' status is, it will hinge on judicial pronouncements, while the legislators and the people will abdicate responsibility, abandon tolerance, forsake compromise.

Costs

As an abstraction the traditional rules seem an adequate trade-off. If I win, I recover a significant portion of my costs. If I lose, I must pay such costs. Thus meritorious claims and defences are encouraged; unfounded ones are chilled. The difficulty is that this system of incentives and disincentives may discourage meritorious claims and defences as well because of the consequences of failure. The degree of such discouragement will largely depend on a party's ability to absorb or shift the costs. Thus those who can afford it are obviously better positioned to litigate; this is particularly so for governments or large corporations that can absorb such costs into a vast budget or, if need be, pass them on more directly to shareholders, consumers, or taxpayers.[106]

Such disincentives can be most pronounced in cases that clearly conform to the public model because the individual will have little or no economic incentive to launch such litigation even though important issues of policy or conduct are being raised. Class actions are a good example in which the monetary relief claimed could be substantial, but the damages sought by the individual plaintiffs may be small indeed compared with the total costs of litigation, and the risks in terms of having to pay the defendant's costs can be enormous.[107]

One suggestion for alleviating the problem is not to change the regime of costs but to have all those who could potentially directly benefit from the decision contribute to the litigation. But it is doubtful that this is a realistic means for underwriting the finances of litigation because of 'the free rider problem'; that is, when potential contributors can enjoy whatever benefits can be obtained by an action without payment and without incurring risk, they ordinarily will not donate funds voluntarily. It is true that the free rider argument does not recognize motivations for contributions other than economic self-interest. Some individuals, for example, may donate funds out of a certain ideological commitment or a sense of outrage against a defendant. Yet the problem of the 'free rider' remains, since idealism and altruism will not have the force of economic self-interest. Solicitation of contributions also involves transaction costs that may have to be absorbed personally by the individual who is requesting donations in case the funds collected are insufficient.

The difficulties of relying on private contributions may be exacerbated in the case of the plaintiff (usually an individual) who is engaging in 'one shot' litigation. Organizations that engage in fund-raising, such as the Consumers' Association of Canada or the Canadian Environmental Law Association, can distribute, rationalize, and thereby reduce the transaction costs of solicitation. For the individual litigant, such economies are unattainable. Another problem for the individual litigant, as distinct from the organizational litigant, is the necessity of collecting sufficient funds to cover both her costs and the potential liability of paying the other side's costs before the action is commenced or, at the very latest, prior to its conclusion. Otherwise, if the action is unsuccessful and she is ordered to pay the adversary's costs, the litigant will have to secure donations to indemnify her in respect of a losing action. Measured against the economic logic of the 'free rider' argument, contributions would be most unlikely in such circumstances.[108] Again philosophical questions are raised. Those who regard litigation primarily as a form of dispute resolution that reflects the values of autonomy and individualism will be content with a uniform set of costs rules in Canada, with losers paying the winners' costs. Those embracing a more ambitious role for litigation will be more open to altering the costs regime.

One model suggested is the American system of 'no costs' in which both sides are responsible for their own costs, win or lose. With contingency fees, the party (usually the plaintiff) pays her lawyer's fees only in the event of success, so that the lawyer is the bearer of risk in terms of the litigation. This combined with contingency fees (also of American origin) is seen to be more conducive to plaintiffs bringing forward claims. Indeed, it has been argued that these differences are key in understanding the more enhanced role that American courts have played in developing and enforcing law.[109] But there are problems here as well. First, such a regime only operates when the litigation can generate a sufficient monetary award to make the contingency fee attractive, so much 'public litigation' will be excluded. Further, the model is indiscriminate in the litigation it encourages and inevitably some unmeritorious litigation will go forward that would not otherwise.

Another basis of reform is through public underwriting of certain kinds of litigation.[110] This has long been the case with legal aid for the economically disadvantaged. A source of funds for some Charter litigation was the Court Challenges Program administered by the Canadian Council on Social Development. This program funded certain Charter challenges, primarily focusing on equality issues. Funding for most of these grounds was limited to federal policies or enactments. These constraints illustrate the disadvantages of such programs and there are other drawbacks, such as ceilings on funding and the possibility that such programs will be curtailed or even eliminated because of political factors.

A frontal assault on the traditional scheme of costs has been provided by the Ontario Law Reform Commission, to some extent drawing on American initiatives in this regard.[111] To facilitate access to courts and to raise important public issues against any kind of defendant (i.e., not just governmental), it recommends that winning plaintiffs be awarded costs, while losing plaintiffs are not liable for costs (except for misconduct in the litigation) when the following criteria are met: (1) the proceeding involves issues whose importance extends beyond the immediate interests of the parties; (2) the plaintiff has no personal, proprietary, or pecuniary interest in the outcome of the proceeding or, if he or she has such an interest, it clearly does not economically justify the proceeding; (3) the issues have not been determined previously by a court in a proceeding against the same defendant; (4) the defendant has a clearly superior capacity to bear the costs of the proceeding. While this recommendation may encourage some unmeritorious litigation, the criteria will assist in limiting such possibilities. Yet another frailty, from a different perspective, is this scheme of costs' reliance on the judiciary to interpret and implement it in light of the courts' commitment to the two-way (losers pay winners) costs regime and the underlying premises it reflects.

COURTS AND ALTERNATIVES FOR DISPUTE RESOLUTION

The limitations and high costs of traditional courtroom adjudication in providing effective and satisfactory justice has long stimulated proposals for change. The Alternative Dispute Resolution (ADR) movement seeks to divert conflict from courts and resolve them by less formal and costly methods. This movement builds on and tries to increase the use of alternatives such as mediation and arbitration. The movement started in the United States, originating from two camps that have conflicting goals. The first seeks to ease the pressure in the courts because, it is said, the culture is besieged by hyperlexis — excessive law, too many lawyers, and overburdened courts. The second camp is concerned that the poor and middle class need more appropriate remedies delivered by more accessible methods of dispute resolution.

Most discussion and debate surrounding ADR takes place in an atmosphere not well grounded in fact: there is no Canadian study that clearly establishes that civil courts are in fact overloaded. There are also no studies that demonstrate generally that the alternatives are faster and less expensive in resolving disputes than court proceedings or settlement, nor has it been shown that people are indeed more satisfied with alternatives. Further, most suits and potential suits in the court system are resolved not by trial but by negotiated settlement, often before formal proceedings have even begun. Thus any proper study would have to at least compare alternatives with litigated cases and those settled through negotiation and compromise.

ADR has made significant progress, accompanied by equal controversy, in resolution of domestic disputes. At a conceptual level, it is not difficult to understand why ADR was attractive. The court system is adversarial; it is meant to produce a winner and a loser if the parties do not otherwise negotiate a settlement. Because permission of the state is required in a divorce, a proceeding before a judge is always needed except in limited circumstances. But dissolution of such a relationship should not take place in a contested atmosphere. The mode of resolution should help cool antagonisms, not inflame them, particularly where children are involved because the parents will have to continue to relate to each other, at least for the sake of the offspring.

From this perspective, mediation is held out as a method for dissolving relationships that minimizes the financial and emotional costs of a divorce. Mediation is said to lessen conflict around the termination of the relationship because — in contrast to the adversarial system, which requires a trial or at least bargaining in a confrontational atmosphere — its goal is to arrive at a solution through active consensus. This process, which the parties control, is said to augment the stake the parties have in the agreement and ultimately to foster greater compliance with postdivorce arrangements. The mediation model is also said to reduce both the time required to secure a divorce and the financial cost to the parties. Lastly, it is claimed that mediation assists parents to focus on what is best for their children and to reduce animosity and challenges to the agreed-upon settlement; this model is praised as encouraging what is best for children in an otherwise unfortunate circumstance.[112]

Given this attractive depiction, mediation has grown substantially in the United States as an alternative in the adversarial system for dissolving domestic relationships. Though no level of government in Canada has passed legislation specifically directed towards regulating mediation, interest in it has certainly increased in the last several years. There are books that approach mediation from a number of perspectives, ranging from discussing its potential to providing a how-to manual. Some of these publications are written by those who practise the craft. Court-connected mediation programs are attracting greater attention and mediation studies are being conducted at several of these courts. Mediation organizations have been formed, including the national Family Mediation Canada. Family law legislation, including Ontario's Family Law Act, has begun to expressly recognize the practice of mediation.[113] The federal Divorce Act (1985) requires all practitioners to inform clients of the option to mediate before proceeding with a traditional divorce.[114]

But cautionary notes have been sounded. Part of the critique of mediation in domestic disputes comes from general criticism concerning ADR. Here the argument is that out-of-court settlements may harm the justice system by removing from judicial consideration cases crucial for the development of the parameters of the law. Some of these critics further allege that informal procedures actually increase state control over the individual rather than increase the individual's control over the dispute by expanding the range of issues and problems that become the business of a state apparatus.[115]

But scepticism about mediation in family issues also comes from many feminists. It is surprising because feminists have been highly critical of the adversarial system and courts in general. Some see it as male-dominated and reflective of traditional patriarchal values that celebrate tactics, winning, private control with minimum state involvement, etc. Yet these same critics have even stronger reservations about mediation and such scepticism sheds light on the value of courts, even if their value is realized all too imperfectly.[116] At the core is a concern that the mediation model may be unsuitable for traditional marriages. Ideally in mediation, there are equally situated parties, which may not be the case in many male-female relationships. The most glaring example is the use of mediation in wife abuse. Mediation is the mode of resolution in such cases in some states in the US.[117] But beyond wife abuse, a clear instance in which mediation is inappropriate, there is general concern that the inequality of bargaining power in traditional marriages will result in a process dominated by the husband and, therefore, in an agreement that reflects the husband's needs to the detriment of his wife's, all exacerbated by the absence of procedural safeguards in mediation.

There are further concerns about the impact of 'private ordering'. The fear is that removing domestic conflicts from a public forum will allow the power imbalances associated with traditional marriages to prosper. The same objections may very well be present in the judicial-adversarial process, but they are public and recorded and therefore open to scrutiny and challenge. Some feminists are particularly critical of mandatory mediation because it bars access to the court system until a mode is exhausted, which may be antagonistic to the resolution of a couple's problems. This imposition of mediation may be especially harmful to women who could have the most to lose from removal of formal legal protections. In the absence of sound empirical assessment, it is difficult to tell the extent to which these criticisms are justified.[118] This is not to denigrate the potential of ADR in domestic relations, nor to resist a search for ways to minimize any weaknesses. For example, Shaffer, although she is sceptical about mediation, suggests three ways to ameliorate it: it must be voluntary; the parties must have access to comprehensive legal advice; and legislatures should enact standards for mediation that secure a high level of competence.[119] Nevertheless, problems remain regarding the consequences of inequality for those involved in these processes.

This scepticism about ADR alerts us to the strength of courts in dispute resolution. There is no argument about the courts' actual and potential deficiencies, particularly concerning policy making. Yet these mistakes must not blind us to the fact that their activities are subject to public scrutiny. Moreover, the criticism is often directed towards our expectations that the courts will do justice and administer rights, regardless of any power imbalances between the parties. That courts fall short of this ideal does not negate it and their openness at least allows for searching criticism of their efforts.

All this is not to argue against alternatives. It is, however, to caution that we do not trade away the benefits of court litigation in searching for other ways to handle conflict. It may well be that our society may be more open to ADR because it has traditionally relied less on courts to develop policy and because it accepts the administrative state's alternative methods of resolving disputes.[120] If this is so, such openness should lead us to engage in discriminating experiments.

CONCLUSION

The traditional structure of litigation reflected traditional liberal values: individualism and autonomous ordering with minimal state involvement. Losers paying winners' costs without regard for their resources or lack thereof, the virtual exclusion of non-parties no matter how important the development of the law, the hostility to collective action, the tight linking of remedy to individual rights, and the confining of standing to those with pecuniary and proprietary entitlement all buttressed the concept of the lawsuit as a private matter about which the state, other than providing a decision maker, should maintain a position of official indifference. Such a structure has also led to experiments with ADR with largely inconclusive results thus far.

The challenges to the traditional model, which would nevertheless maintain issues in courts, reflect values that mirror the various ideologies in Canadian politics: a recognition that equality of access requires equality of resources; an acknowledgement of the legitimacy of communitarian values; and a concern for the workings and impact of large institutions as part of a revamped understanding of respect for the individual. At the heart of this challenge lies the contention that the process of litigation significantly affects its outcomes and determines how legal rules are shaped: the form of litigation reflects the substance of the law. Thus the state should not be officially indifferent about all these questions.

There is little doubt that the implication of reforming the traditional model is an increased role for the judge. Almost all the proposed modifications would add to the judiciary's obligations in the conduct of the litigation. This is not necessarily a bad thing and certainly the exercise of power in shaping proceedings would not be new — after all, excluding such issues and interests from the litigation was a form of power too. Yet it is critical not to confuse a need for judges to participate effectively in shaping laws with the boundaries of the judicial role in law making. It may be desirable, even necessary, for public interest groups and those they represent — environmentalists, women, the differently abled, Aboriginals, consumers, etc. — to engage in litigation to shape certain laws in ways that they believe would be conducive to their interests. It is quite another thing for them or, in a larger sense, Canadian society, to shift from politics to litigation so that courts are seen as the primary stage for dealing with complex social and economic issues.

This is the difficult distinction that must be maintained: altering litigation so that a diverse range of views can shape the law without displacing legislatures and administrative agencies as the primary means of government for achieving social and political ordering. By contrast, those who would return to traditional forms of litigation in order to corral the role of courts in democratic life will exclude diverse viewpoints from the courts. The traditional model of litigation, fastidiously observed, would still leave ample scope for an expansive judicial role of another kind because the financially well-endowed would have ample access to challenge legislative and bureaucratic acts that are not in their interests. Furthermore, such actors would rarely be impeded by restrictive standing rules since usually their motive in litigating is to protect financial or economic interests, the basis for granting standing in the traditional model. Such interests in court would advocate that the judges shape the process and substance of the law in ways that are favourable to them, a pressure enhanced by the absence of other voices shut out by the traditional model.

But suppose there was agreement that the paradigm of litigation should reflect, at some level, the 'public'-expanded elements discussed in this chapter. How, then, would we define and limit the judicial role? A short answer, often coming from progressives, is that litigation is 'only a tool'. Like many pithy responses, it carries with it an air of dispositiveness. Alas, such confidence of response dissipates upon any close examination. For if it is 'only a tool', it is an extraordinarily complex and unpredictable one with questionable effect. The vital issues around the judicial role and its boundaries cannot be responded to with such ease, especially when circumstances push both the courts and the public to expect so much more from litigation, as it becomes a habit of mind to expect so little from politics.

NOTES

[1] A. Chayes, 'The Role of the Judge in Public Law Litigation' (1976) 89 *Harvard Law Review*, 1281.
Part of this chapter appeared earlier in sections of W.A. Bogart, '"Appropriate and Just": Section 24 of the Canadian Charter of Rights and Freedoms and the Question of Judicial Legitimacy' (1986) 10 *Dalhousie Law Journal*, 81.

[2] N. Brooks, 'The Judge and the Adversary System' in A. Linden (ed.), *The Canadian Judiciary* (Toronto: Osgoode Hall Law School, 1976); R.J. Halfnight, 'Third Party Procedure: Some Problems of Purpose and Scope' in E. Gertner (ed.), *Studies in Civil Procedure* (Toronto: Butterworths, 1979): 87.

[3] Ontario Law Reform Commission, *Report on Class Actions*, 3 vols (Toronto: Ministry of the Attorney General, 1982) [hereinafter OLRC, *Class Actions*].

[4] *Markt & Co. Ltd* v. *Knight Steamship Co. Ltd* [1910] 2 *King's Bench* 1021 (CA) is the leading English case restricting class actions. It was largely followed by Canadian cases up to the 1970s. For the history of class actions, see J. Kazanjian, 'Class Actions in Canada' (1973) 11 *Osgoode Hall Law Journal*, 397; N.J. Williams, 'Consumer Class Actions in Canada — Some Proposals for Reform' (1975) 13 *Osgoode Hall Law Journal*, 1; OLRC *Class Actions* (vol. I, Chapter 2 and vol. II, Chapter 14).

[5] J. Bankier, 'Class Actions for Monetary Relief in Canada: Formalism or Function' (1984) 4 *Windsor Yearbook of Access to Justice*, 229, 245–8.

[6] P. Atiyah, *The Rise and Fall of Freedom of Contract* (Oxford: Clarendon Press, 1979): 660–1 quoted in Bankier, ibid., 234n.21.

[7] Atiyah, ibid., 665–6, quoted in Bankier, ibid., 247n.72.

[8] *Supra*, note 3, vol. I.

[9] For example, *Shaw* v. *Real Estate Board of Greater Vancouver* (1973) 36 *Dominion Law Reports* (3d) 250 (BCCA). The action was dismissed at trial (1974) 5 *Western Weekly Reports*, 193 (BCSC); *Chastain* v. *British Columbia Hydro & Power Authority* (1972) 32 *Dominion Law Reports* (3d) 443 (BCSC); *Farnham* v. *Fingold* (1973) 33 *Dominion Law Reports* (3d) 156 (Ont. CA). These and other cases are discussed in W.A. Bogart, 'Questioning Litigation's Role — Courts and Class Actions in Canada' (1986–7), 62 *Indiana Law Journal*, 665, 676–8.

[10] *Naken* v. *General Motors of Canada* (1978) 92 *Dominion Law Reports* (3d) 100 (Ont. CA).

[11] *Naken* v. *General Motors of Canada* (1983) 144 *Dominion Law Reports* (3d) 385 (SCC).

[12] See Bankier, *supra*, note 5; Bogart, *supra*, note 9; L. Fox, '*Naken* v. *General Motors of Canada*: Class Actions Deferred' (1984) 6 *Supreme Court Law Review*, 335; R. Prichard, 'Class Actions Reform: Some General Comments' (1984) 9 *Canadian Business Law Journal*, 309, 311 ('Naken is a bad decision in every sense of the word: bad as a matter of interpreting Rule 75; bad as a matter of understanding the case law of the past decade concerning class actions, bad as a matter of judicial craftsmanship; bad as a matter of being a further example of judicial formalism and conservatism; bad as a matter of an appreciation of the judicial role; and bad as a matter of public policy').

[13]*Supra*, note 11 at 408: 'The sole duty of the Court is to ascertain the proper interpretation by the application of the canons of construction to the words adopted by the maker of the rule and its application to these proceedings.'

[14]See Bogart, *supra*, note 9 at 680–1.

[15]*Supra*, note 11 at 408.

[16]Que. Stat. Ch. 8 (1978) now part of the Code of Civil Procedure. For an assessment of the experience under this legislative reform, see A. Prujiner (ed.), *Class Actions in Ontario and Quebec* (Montreal: Editions Wilson et Lafleur, 1992).

[17]*Supra*, note 3.

[18]B. DuVal, Review (1983) 3 *Windsor Yearbook of Access to Justice*, 411; T. Cromwell, 'An Examination of the Ontario Law Reform Commission Report on Class Actions' (1983) 15 *Ottawa Law Review*, 587. I worked for the commission on the Class Actions Report.

[19]W. Macdonald and J. Rowley, 'Ontario Class Action Reform: Business and Justice System Impacts — A Comment' (1984) 9 *Canadian Business Law Journal*, 351.

[20]Class Proceedings Act, SO 1992, c. 6; Law Society Amendment Act, SO 1992, c. 7 — an act to amend the Law Society Act to provide for funding to parties to class proceedings.

[21]W.A. Bogart, 'Naken, the Supreme Court and What Are Our Courts For' (1984) 9 *Canadian Business Law Journal*, 280, 308.

[22]P. Glenn, 'Class Actions in Ontario and Quebec' (1984) 62 *Canadian Bar Review*, 247; P. Glenn, 'Class Actions and the Theory of Tort and Delict' (1985) 35 *University of Toronto Law Journal*, 287; P. Glenn, 'The Dilemma of Class Action Reform' (1986) 6 *Oxford Journal of Legal Studies*, 262.

[23]Ideas that are in many ways parallel to those of Weinrib and his views of the limits of litigation, a discussion we will take up in Chapter Six.

[24]Glenn, 'Ontario and Quebec', *supra*, note 22 at 265–7.

[25]Ibid., 270–1.

[26]See B. DuVal, 'The Class Action as an Antitrust Enforcement Device: The Chicago Study Revisited' (1979) *American Bar Foundation*, 449, discussed in DuVal, *supra*, note 18 at 427n.35.

[27]See DuVal, *supra*, note 18 at 426, discussing S. Flanders, *The 1979 Federal District Court Time Study* (Federal Judicial Center, 1980).

[28]R. Bernstein, 'Judicial Economy and Class Actions' (1978) 7 *Journal of Legal Studies*, 349.

[29]*Supra*, note 3 (vol. I) at 169.

[30]See B. Garth, 'Studying Civil Litigation through the Class Action' (1987) 62 *Indiana Law Journal*, 497; B. Garth et al., 'The Institution of the Private Attorney General; Perspectives from an Empirical Study of Class Action Litigation' (1988) 61 *Southern California Law Review*, 353.

[31]Ibid., both references.

[32]Glenn, 'Tort and Delict', *supra*, note 22. But there is some evidence that this is changing: see M.K. Kane, 'Group Action in Civil Procedure: The United States

Experience' (*A Report for the XIII Congress of Comparative Law*, Montreal, 1990).

[33]G. Rosenberg, 'Class Actions for Mass Torts: Doing Individual Justice by Collective Means' (1987) 62 *Indiana Law Journal*, 561.

[34]T. Eisenberg and S.C. Yeazell, 'The Ordinary and the Extraordinary in Institutional Litigation' (1980) 93 *Harvard Law Review*, 465; W.A. Bogart, '"Appropriate and Just": Section 24 of the Canadian Charter of Rights and Freedoms and the Question of Judicial Legitimacy' (1986) 10 *Dalhousie Law Journal*, 81, 86.

[35]Eisenberg and Yeazell, ibid., 481.

[36]Ibid.

[37]*Supra*, note 3 (vol. I) at 102.

[38]B. Garth, 'Power and Legal Artifice: The Federal Class Action' (1992) 26 *Law & Society Review*, 237.

[39]Ibid., 238.

[40]For a description and analysis of standing in the Anglo-Canadian tradition, see such works as T. Cromwell, *Locus Standi — A Commentary on the Law of Standing in Canada* (Toronto: Carswell, 1986).

[41]*Supra*, note 1 at 1285.

[42]For studies of the Attorney-General and his historical role, see J. Edwards, *The Law Officers of the Crown* (London: Sweet and Maxwell, 1964) and *The Attorney General, Politics and the Public Interest* (London: Sweet and Maxwell, 1984).

[43]Ontario Law Reform Commission, *Report on the Law of Standing* (Toronto: Ministry of the Attorney General, 1989): Chapter 3 [hereinafter OLRC, *Report Standing*].

[44]Ibid; W.A. Bogart, 'Standing and the Charter: Rights and Identity' in R. Sharpe (ed.), *Charter Litigation* (Toronto: Butterworths, 1987): 1.

[45]*Supra*, note 43, Chapter 4 and Draft Act; Appendix I, especially s. 2.

[46]*Thorson v. Attorney-General of Canada* (1975) 1 *Supreme Court Reports*, 138; *Nova Scotia Board of Censors v. McNeil* (1976) 2 *Supreme Court Reports*, 265; *Minister of Justice of Canada v. Borowski* (1981) 2 *Supreme Court Reports*, 575; *Minister of Finance of Canada v. Finlay* (1986) 2 *Supreme Court Reports*, 607; *Canadian Council of Churches v. R* [1992] 1 *Supreme Court Reports*, 236. For comment including on *Canadian Council of Churches*, see S. Fairley, 'Is the Public Interest Falling From Standing' (1993) XI *The Philanthropist*, 28.

[47]W.A. Bogart, 'Understanding Standing, Chapter IV: *Minister of Finance of Canada v. Finlay*' (1988) 10 *Supreme Court Law Review*, 377, analysing the first four cases regarding the point made in the text.

[48]*Supra*, note 43 at 53, quoting P.P. Craig, *Administrative Law* (London: Sweet and Maxwell, 1983): 446; W.A. Bogart, 'The Lessons of Liberalized Standing?' (1989) 27 *Osgoode Hall Law Journal*, 195.

[49]*Supra*, note 43 at 113.

[50]*Supra*, note 43 at 115; P. Muldoon and D. Scriven, 'Intervention as Added Party: Rule 13 of the Ontario Rules of Civil Procedure' (1985) 6 *Advocates Quarterly*, 129, 140–1; citing *Re Ronark Developments and City of Hamilton* (1974) 4 *Ontario Reports* (2d) 195 (Div. Ct) aff'd on consent (1974) 5 *Ontario Reports* (2d) 136 (CA); *Re Orangeville Highlands Ltd and Township of Mono* (1974) 5 *Ontario Reports* (2d)

266 (Div. Ct); and *McDonald's Restaurants of Canada Ltd* v. *Corporation of the Borough of Etobicoke* (1977) 5 *Carswell's Practice Cases*, 55 (Ont. Div. Ct).

[51]For example, *Re Clark and the Attorney General of Canada* (1977) 17 *Ontario Reports* (2d) 593 (HC).

[52]J. Welch, 'No Room at the Top: Interest Group Intervenors and Charter Litigation in the Supreme Court of Canada' (1985) 43 *University of Toronto Faculty of Law Review*, 204, 211–12; K. Swan, 'Intervention and Amicus Curiae Status in Charter Litigation' in R.J. Sharpe (ed.), *Charter Litigation* (Toronto: Butterworths, 1987): 27, 29.

[53]Welch, ibid.

[54]For example, *Wotherspoon* v. *Canadian Pacific Ltd* (1982) 35 *Ontario Reports* (2d) 449 (CA) and see the discussion in OLRC, *Report Standing, supra*, note 43, 115–28.

[54]*Re Association of Parents for Fairness in Education, Grand Falls District 50 Branch and Société des Acadiens du Nouveau-Brunswick Inc.* (1984) 8 *Dominion Law Reports* (4th) 238 (CA).

[56]*Re Canadian Labour Congress and Bhindi* (1985) 17 *Dominion Law Reports* (4th) 193 (BCCA).

[57]S. Lavine, 'Advocating Values: Public Interest Intervention in *Charter* Litigation' (1992) 2 *National Journal of Constitutional Law*, 26, 53–4: 'Contrary to the pessimism and concern expressed by Welch, Swan and others, in the last 5 years the Supreme Court has shown itself to be extremely receptive to public interest intervenors . . . [with] a very low threshold for the granting of an intervenor application.' See also the remarks of the Supreme Court on the desirability of intervention compared to initiation of litigation by public interest groups in *Canadian Council of Churches, supra*, note 46.

[58]*Supra*, note 43 at 112–13.

[59]Welch, *supra*, note 52; Swan, *supra*, note 52; P. Bryden, 'Public Interest Intervention in the Courts' (1987) 66 *Canadian Bar Review*, 490.

[60]W.A. Bogart, '"Appropriate and Just": Section 24 of the Canadian Charter of Rights and Freedoms and the Question of Judicial Legitimacy' (1986) 10 *Dalhousie Law Journal*, 81; R. Sharpe, 'Injunctions and the Charter' (1984) 22 *Osgoode Hall Law Journal*, 473; B. Wildsmith, 'An American Enforcement Model of Civil Process in a Canadian Landscape' (1980–1) 6 *Dalhousie Law Journal*, 71.

[61]A. Chayes, 'The Supreme Court, 1981 Term-Forward: Public Law Litigation and the Burger Court' (1982) 96 *Harvard Law Review*, 4, 46: '[I]t [is] impossible to identify a unique remedial regime that follows ineluctably from and is measured by the determination of substantive liability. Control of remedial discretion is therefore an insistent problem. . . .'

[62]Bogart, *supra*, note 60 at 90–1.

[63]T. Eisenberg and S.C. Yeazell, 'The Ordinary and the Extraordinary in Institutional Litigation' (1980) 93 *Harvard Law Review*, 465.

[64] R. Sharpe, *Injunctions and Specific Performance* (Toronto: Canada Law Book, 1983): 23.

[65]J. Sopinka, 'Constitutional Remedies and Their Limitations' in J. Berryman (ed.), *Remedies — Issues and Perspectives* (Toronto: Carswell, 1991): 357; F. Kaufman, 'The Canadian Charter: A Time for Bold Spirits, Not Timorous Souls' (1986) 31 *McGill Law Journal*, 456, 464: 'The very wording of this section [s. 24 of the

Charter] — "such remedy as the Court considers appropriate and just" — is, of course, a call for judicial ingenuity or, if you will, an open door to activism. Indeed, some might say, and not without reason, that Parliament, in giving this power to the judges, virtually opened the door to the promulgation of laws by the judiciary.'

[66]B. Dickson, 'The Public Responsibilities of Lawyers' (1983) 13 *Manitoba Law Journal*, 175, 187.

[67]See N. Gillespie, 'Charter Remedies: The Structural Injunction' (1989–90) 11 *Advocates' Quarterly*, 190, discussing such cases as: *Société des Acadiens du Nouveau Brunswick Inc. v. Minority Language School Board No. 50* (1983) 48 *New Brunswick Reports* (2d) 361 *Queen's Bench* and (1983), 50 *New Brunswick Reports* (2d) 41 and (1983) 51 *New Brunswick Reports*, 219; *Marchand v. The Simcoe County Board of Education* (1986) 55 *Ontario Reports* (2d) 638 (HC) and (1987) 61 *Ontario Reports* (2d) 651 (HC); *Lavoie v. Nova Scotia* [1988] Nova Scotia Judgement No. 57 and [1988] Nova Scotia Judgement No. 102 and 312. See also S. Fine, 'Let Francophones Control Schooling, Manitoba Ordered' *The Globe and Mail*, 5 March 1993, A4.

[68]*Reference Re Language Rights under the Manitoba Act 1870* (1985) 19 *Dominion Law Reports* (4th) 1.

[69]Ibid., 29.

[70]Ibid., 37.

[71]Ibid., 21.

[72]Ibid., 37.

[73]Ibid.

[74]Order of Court, 30 October 1985.

[75]For example, D. Horowitz, *The Courts and Social Policy* (Washington: Brookings Institute, 1977), especially Chapter Two, 'Attributes of Adjudication'.

[76]For example, O. Fiss, 'The Supreme Court 1978 Term — Foreword: The Forms of Justice' (1979) 93 *Harvard Law Review*, 1.

[77] For example, G. Frug, 'The Judicial Power of the Purse' (1978) 126 *University of Pennsylvania Law Review*, 715 and P.J. Mishkin, 'Federal Courts as State Reformers' (1978) 35 *Washington & Lee Law Review*, 949.

[78]For example, *supra*, note 63 at 507.

[79]For example, *Re Nicholson and Haldimand — Norfolk Regional Board of Commissioners of Police* (1979) 88 *Dominion Law Reports* (3d) 671 (SCC) and Bogart, *supra*, note 60 at 96.

[80]Bogart, *supra*, note 60 at 96.

[81]*Supra*, note 76 at 38.

[82]L. Fuller, 'The Forms and Limits of Adjudication' (1978) 92 *Harvard Law Review*, 353.

[83]*Supra*, note 76 at 43–4.

[84]Bogart, *supra*, note 60 at 99–100.

[85]G. Rosenberg, *The Hollow Hope — Can Courts Bring About Social Change?* (Chicago: University of Chicago Press, 1991): 28–30.

[86]*The Queen v. Schachter* [1992] 2 *Supreme Court Reports*, 679, 702. The judgement

of Chief Justice Lamer citing factum of Women's Legal Education and Action Fund.

[87]Ibid. See J. Sallot, 'Judges Can Order State to Pay Social Benefit', *The Globe and Mail*, 10 July 1992, A3; Editorial, 'The Limits of Judicial Rule', *The Globe and Mail*, 10 July 1992, A12; J. Simpson, 'How the Courts Expand Rights and Whittle Away at Government', *The Globe and Mail*, 12 August 1992, A10.

[88]For three legal articles dealing with such issues, see N. Duclos and K. Roach, 'Constitutional Remedies as "Constitutional Hints": A Comment on R. v. *Schachter*' (1991) 36 *McGill Law Journal*, 1; A. Lajoie, 'De l'Interventionnisme judiciare comme apport à l'émergence des droits sociaux' (1991) 36 *McGill Law Journal*, 1338; C. Rogerson, 'The Judicial Search for Appropriate Remedies under the Charter: The Examples of Overbreadth and Vagueness' in R. Sharpe (ed.), *Charter Litigation* (Toronto: Butterworths, 1987).

[89]T. Claridge, 'Ontario Court Uses Power to '"Read in" Words Not in Law', *The Globe and Mail*, 8 August 1992, A1.

[90]The *Ontario Human Rights Code*, s. 9(1)(j) states that 'spouse' 'means the person to whom a person of the *opposite* sex is married or *with whom the person is living in a conjugal relationship outside marriage*' [emphasis added].

[91]S. Fine, 'Legal Triumphs Sure Signal for MPs', *The Globe and Mail*, 24 November 1992, A1; see also P. Edwards, 'Special Benefits Ruled a "Must" For Gay Couples', *The Toronto Star* 4 August 1993, A1.

[92]Ibid., A8.

[93]'Court Ruling Leads Ottawa to Drop Move on Gay Rights', *The Toronto Star*, 2 November 1992, A12.

[94]G. Fraser, 'Rights Protection Extended to Gays', *The Globe and Mail*, 10 December 1992, A8.

[9]G. Fraser, 'Bill Protects Gay and Lesbian Rights', *The Globe and Mail*, 11 December 1992, A4; H. Solomon, 'Campbell Accused of Compromising on Promise to Entrench Gay Rights', *Law Times*, 21–7 December 1992, 1.

[96]T. Arnold, 'Gays Favored over Others, Minister Says', *The Edmonton Journal*, 3 January 1993.

[97]Ibid.

[98]*Supra*, note 93.

[99]R. v. *Mossop*, unreported, 25 February 1993, SCC.

[100]See *Gay Alliance toward Equality* v. *Vancouver Sun* [1979] 2 *Supreme Court Reports*, 435.

[101]Canadian Human Rights Commission, *Annual Report*, June 1993.

[102]P. Girard, 'Sexual Orientation as a Human Rights Issue in Canada 1969–1985' (1986) 10 *Dalhousie Law Journal*, 278, 277–81 and D. Rayside, 'Gay Rights and Family Values: The Passage of Bill 7 in Ontario' (1988) 26 *Studies in Political Economy*, 109, 129–30.

[103]There have been recommendations at the federal level that sexual orientation should be protected from discrimination: *Report of the Parliamentary Committee on Equality Rights* (Ottawa: Queen's Printer, 1985): 29.

[104]See the stinging rebuttal to Ms Mirosh and to Premier Klein: *The Edmonton Journal*, editorial, 5 January 1993, A6.

[105] For example, in the United States some municipalities are moving to something like this solution: see J. Hicks, 'A Legal Threshold Is Crossed by Gay Couples in New York', *The New York Times*, 2 March 1993, A1.

[106] The literature on costs rules and their impact on litigation is vast: e.g., see Watson et al., *Civil Litigation — Cases and Materials* (Toronto: Emond-Montgomery, 1991): Chapter Four, 'The Economics of Litigation.'

[107] See discussion of the issues and proposed solution in OLRC, *Class Actions, supra*, note 3 at vol. III, 711–31. The Quebec Act establishes a fund to assist plaintiffs with the cost of litigation; 1982 Que. Stat. ch. 37, art. 23–5. The Ontario Act also establishes a fund and recipients will be shielded from paying costs to defendants. Bill 29, 'An Act to Amend the Law Society Act to Provide Funding to Parties to Class Proceedings,' Royal Assent, 25 June 1992. S. 3 of the Bill Amends s. 59 to establish a class proceedings fund.

[108] *Supra*, note 43 at 147 *et seq*.

[109] R. Prichard, 'A Systematic Approach to Comparative Law: The Effect of Cost, Fee and Financing Rules on the Development of the Substantive Law' (1988) 17 *Journal of Legal Studies*, 451.

[110] L. Fox, 'Costs in Public Interest Litigation' (1989) 10 *Advocates' Quarterly*, 385.

[111] *Supra*, note 43 at Chapter 6, 'Costs'.

[112] M. Shaffer, 'Divorce Mediation: A Feminist Perspective' (1988) 46 *University of Toronto Faculty of Law Review*, 162, 163.

[113] Ontario Family Law Act, RSO 1990, c. F. 3, see especially s. 3.

[114] Divorce Act 1985, RSC 1985, c. D-3.4.

[115] For example, O. Fiss, 'Against Settlement' (1984) 93 *Yale Law Review*, 1073; R. Abel, 'The Contradictions of Informal Justice' in R. Abel (ed.), *The Politics of Informal Justice*, 2 vols (New York: Academic Press, 1982).

[116] M. Bailey, 'Unpacking the "Rational Alternative": A Critical Review of Family Mediation Movement Claims' (1989) 8 *Canadian Journal of Family Law*, 61; N. Hilton, 'Mediating Wife Assault: Battered Women and the "New Family"' (1991) 9 *Canadian Journal of Family Law*, 29.

[117] L.G. Lerman, 'Mediation of Wife Abuse Cases: The Adverse Impact of Informal Dispute Resolution on Women' (1984) 7 *Harvard Women's Law Journal*, 57.

[118] C.J. Richardson, *Court-Based Divorce Mediation in Four Canadian Cities* (Ottawa: Supply and Services, Canada, 1988); *Report of the Attorney General's Advisory Committee on Mediation in Family Law* (Toronto: Ministry of the Attorney General, 1989).

[119] *Supra*, note 112 at 199–200.

[120] K. Roach, 'Teaching Procedures: The Fiss/Weinrib Debate in Practice' (1991) 41 *University of Toronto Law Journal*, 247, 250–3.

PART THREE

Litigation and Its Contexts

CHAPTER FOUR

The Administrative State and Judicial Review

INTRODUCTION

One of the most dramatic changes in the country in this century, paralleled by similar alterations in other Western nations, has been the growth of government. This increase has been accomplished largely by a shift of power from Parliament and the legislatures to the Cabinet, agencies, and bureaucracies. Growth of regulatory activity and governmental budgets underlie the pattern.[1] The Economic Council of Canada once established that Parliament had passed as many statutes addressing regulation of economic activity in a nine-year period as it had in the previous thirty years.[2] This growth has elicited many reactions often from those who experienced the benefits or drawbacks of any particular program. Two polarized views have emerged that are instructive in understanding the role courts have come to play in the administrative state.

The first view focuses on the possibilities for government to plan for and referee the most powerful forces in society, so that they can be used to achieve common purposes. From this perspective, government agencies are viewed mostly as benign influences that benefit ordinary people and their aspirations. This image reflects a segment of opinion that began in the nineteenth century and grew more widespread as a result of the Great Depression. That economic and social crisis led governments to become more active in redressing the severe problems caused, many contended, by the worst excesses of laissez-faire capitalism.[3]

The second view regards government as a marauder that feeds on its own sense of power, dampening entrepreneurial activity, corralling incentive, and harassing individual freedom, particularly in these days of huge budgets and deficits. Much of this depiction is propounded by those who equate freedom with economic liberty and the reliability of the market to distribute virtually all goods and services, to reward merit and hard work, and to castigate indolence and passivity. This view contends that not only is the economic élite hampered, but ordinary people are also entrapped by a faceless, unresponsive bureaucracy.[4]

Before pursuing these views further, it can at least be said that they both acknowledge the extent and complexity of government in virtually every facet of Canadian life. There are government agencies and commissions that perform a vast range of tasks and implement an array of policies. A study in the late 1970s that focused upon only permanent agencies (thus excluding specifically appointed commissions, public inquiries, etc.) reported that there were more than 640 agencies in Canada. A late 1970s survey of similar bodies in Ontario identified thirty-six regulatory bodies, forty-four licensing appeal tribunals, eight compensation boards, nineteen arbitral agencies, and ninety-five advisory boards.[5]

A recent work on administrative law has suggested a taxonomy of boards and commissions and offered reasons for their creation while warning against any simple generalizations.[6] Boards, the first group identified, relate to the administration of income support programs. These agencies exist because of the immense volume of decisions necessary to determine entitlements under the various programs. For example, the Ontario Workers' Compensation Board received 460,972 claims in 1979. There were 3,665 appeals of the board's decisions, of which 1,577 were disposed of by the highest level of appeal within the board's structure.[7]

The second group is comprised of commissions that regulate the economy or some related aspect, and can be divided into two subgroups: independent regulatory agencies and professional organizations. Examples of independent regulatory federal agencies are the Canadian Radio-television and Telecommunications Commission, the Canadian Transport Commission, the National Energy Board, and the National Farm Marketing Boards; provincial agencies include environmental assessment boards, public utilities boards, and other marketing boards. Examples of the second subgroup — professional organizations — are law societies (agencies that govern admission into and regulation of the practice of law), colleges of nurses and physicians, and societies of architects and teachers.[8]

The third group is composed of non-partisan specialists that deal with a diverse range of matters. Federal examples are the Immigration Appeal Board, the Tariff Board, and the Anti-Dumping Tribunal; provincial examples include liquor licensing boards, labour relations boards, and planning appeal boards. The rationale for the existence of such boards varies with the type of agency. For example, labour relations boards offer important points of departure from the judicial function. These boards resolve such issues as the certification of unions and determine whether there have been unfair labour practices or whether strikes or lockouts are sanctioned.

This chapter deals with the relationship between courts and the huge administrative state that has developed in Canada and may be summarized as follows. First, courts over the last century blocked many progressive attempts to deal with widely applicable issues such as compensation for injury in the workplace, unionization, and human rights, with the result that the administrative state frequently displaced courts in dealing with such issues. Competition law provides a more complex example where the courts' failure to enforce laws regarding economic competition echoed vacillation in the political process that continues today. Second, courts continue to exert at least ideological influence through a review process (that is mostly constructed by themselves) of administrative actors' decisions. Such a process has the capacity to prune administrative programs in the name of the highly contentious concept of 'jurisdiction'. Finally, the foregoing suggests little basis for concluding that courts are capable of or willing to intervene systematically and to devise effective solutions to social problems in the face of powerful economic forces.

THE ADMINISTRATIVE STATE: GOVERNING IDEAS AND NATION BUILDING

Given the level and degree of the administrative state's activities, it is no surprise that reactions have been strong and often polarized. So J.E. Hodgetts, one of the most respected students of public administration, once felt compelled to write that the 'shift from laissez-faire to collectivism has been accompanied by an unprecedented shift in the balance of real power, discretion and initiative — away from courts, legislatures and even cabinets to public servants. [The public fears] that their rights are being invaded even as they are ostensibly being served by [these] public employees.'[9] Yet government and its employment grew significantly, and such growth often led to complex and contradictory demands: 'the voices which complain about the overpowering anonymity, control, and impenetrability of bureaucracy are often the same as those demanding the regulations, the controls, and the productivity which are the daily concerns of bureaucracy.'[10]

And yet these alarms about the leviathan have to be balanced by views more supportive of or at least compatible with the first image of government agencies as planners and referees. This is evident when the work of Canadian students of government is compared with their American counterparts. Broadly speaking, the latter are sceptical of increasing administrative powers, an attitude consistent with the liberal philosophy of minimalism, which is the underpinning of the constitutionalism of that country. This is in marked contrast to Canadian scholarship, which, while focusing upon the extent and cause of the growth of government, is at least more tolerant and, at times, supportive of it. It is 'generally characterized by a much more sympathetic attitude towards governmental intrusions in society'.[11]

At one level, this is explained by the pragmatism for which Canadians are famed. There were jobs to do, institutions to build and if governments could accomplish the goals, so be it: 'No Delphic phrases and fundamental philosophies about government preoccupy our thoughts on the nature of governmental institutions.'[12] Yet at another level, one can harken back to the ideas of complex ideology that were explored in Chapter One. Such government intervention was consistent with tory and socialist notions of the legitimacy of restraining the individual and the use of government to achieve common ends. From this perspective, 'pragmatism' becomes a code word to disguise a much more complex set of ideas about how society ought to function than that depicted by the minimalist state of liberalism, particularly as manifested in the United States.

In addition, government has played a vital role in nation building in this country. For, as it has been remarked, 'the role of the state in the economic life of Canada is really the modern history of Canada'.[13] To make the country grow and coalesce, government had to exert a strong influence from the start. The contention is that because of the vastness of the subcontinent, the imperial sweep of settlement after 1867, and the speedy reaction to industrialization, government was encouraged or forced to act.[14] Other countries allowed the administrative state to develop to transform the role of government and act as a brake on the rapacious aspects of capitalism. This was also the case in Canada, but was combined with the need to make a nation.

In important ways the 'national policy' included all policies that had the purpose of transforming the territories of British North America into one political and economic unit. This national policy existed prior to Confederation, that union being regarded as its primary tool constitutionally.[15] Ideology was not seen as limiting the state in the achievement of this purpose: 'in a period where laissez faire policies were at their peak of respectability, the Canadian attitude to the question of public versus private enterprise was purely pragmatic. In the vital field of railway transportation there was not generally any clear view on the merits of public versus private action so long as the railways were actually built.'[16] A good example of the government's commitment to the instrumental character of its growing bureaucracy was the Department of the Interior.[17] Its mandate was to manage the West for the wave of immigrants and any export boom. For almost fifty years, this office furthered the hinterland development. Yet by the 1930s when its duty was accomplished, the Liberal government simply eliminated it.[18]

A further example of ideology not limiting the state is provided by Canadians' attitude (at least historically) towards government and economic regulation. This is an important element since the regulatory functions of government have been regarded since the Second World War as one of the prime sources of bureaucratic influence and growth. Yet much of the writing about regulatory activity comes from the United States, for American regulation performs a policing role to ensure that economic activity reflects competitive market conditions. From that viewpoint, the usefulness of regulation in the United States is measured by its efficiency.[19]

Not so for us. Regulation and its activity stemmed from what has been called the 'three p's': policing, promoting, and planning; much of this to build the nation.[20] Freight rates and air fares were set at least partly to foster national unity. Again, agricultural marketing boards were created in a deliberate attempt to transfer income from consumers to producers.[21] And in performing these functions Canadian agencies, unlike many of their American counterparts, were less 'independent' and much more controlled by executive action and decrees, partly reflecting the fact that they were meant to carry out these larger governmental policies: 'The instrumental and, indeed, beneficent role of bureaucracy as the core of modern government is a theme which is well developed in the literature of public policy and administration.'[22]

THE ROLE OF THE JUDICIARY IN THE ADMINISTRATIVE STATE

Introduction

But the 'beneficent role of bureaucracy' would not be the way many, including our courts, have characterized the regulatory state. In administrative issues our judges have mostly been the keepers of pure liberal ideology: the state assigned minimalist policing functions, and the market was the best distributor of goods and services. Whether it was in such matters as occupational health and safety, the development of human rights, or the advent of unions and collective bargaining, the courts' activities wove a pattern of indifference, even hostility towards state activities. With a few notable exceptions, judges have raised the sanctity of the common law, which brought market principles to bear on the resolution of such issues: that everyone should be free to contract and negotiate the terms on an individual basis, and that only establishing fault should determine the basis for compensation of injury. Yet, under the guise of principles that seemed to treat everyone equally, the health and safety of workers were ignored with abandon, poisons were dumped into the environment, and the most insidious acts of prejudice were taken as a hallmark of self-regarding behaviour.

Change to curb the most dire consequences of such rules came from the legislatures, but was resisted by the courts. This opposition had two clear consequences. First, it led to the removal of several important areas of law from the courts. Second, when the areas were taken from the courts and a new regime was established and carried out by an administrative board, the courts insisted on overseeing their activities through a process of judicial review, which provoked much controversy among legal commentators.[23]

The Establishment of Tribunals as Alternatives to Courts

While many instances exist (for example, regarding the environment[24] or in terms of public interest groups participating in the process itself[25]) three prominent illustrations spanning the better part of the twentieth century will be discussed regarding the courts' resistance to change aimed at altering the minimalist state. As a result of such resistance, the legislatures not only had to alter judge-made law but also took the task of implementing the new regime away from the courts. We will look at a fourth example — competition policy and law — which illustrates a more complex set of attitudes on the part of the courts and legislatures and a more ambiguous solution.

Workers' Compensation, Labour Relations, and Human Rights The first illustration of resistance by courts and intervention by the administrative state concerns compensation of workers who were injured as a result of industrial accident.[26] By the mid-nineteenth century, it was clear that only the most hardened could be indifferent to the toll industrialization had taken on human lives. Mishaps in the workplace injured and killed workers with alarming frequency, but the courts' response to this demonstrated a distressing rigidity. They insisted that fault must be established as a basis for recovery. In such a regime, individual workers fighting over a specific claim were almost always no match for employers, who were better organized and more financially able to resist. Courts placed workers at an even greater disadvantage with such holdings as that negligence of fellow workers would bar injured ones from recovering on the theory that they must have agreed to the joint enterprise that resulted in the damage.[27] This 'fellow servant' rule and other doctrines propounded by the courts were compatible with broader ideas about the role of the common law. Its purpose was to augment autonomy by creating spheres where individuals were free from state or any other interference. Accompanying such independence was a person's responsibility for his own fate. Such responsibility depended upon free will, with fault both a moral failing and a condition of liability.[28]

Studies done of court cases just before substantial change was effected by legislation suggest that despite impediments, those workers who turned to litigation may have been successful more often than the rules would suggest, but these few cases may illustrate how pathetic some work conditions actually were. These results conveyed a possibility for compensation while leaving untampered a severe regime weighted against the injured labourer:

Recovery by a few workers could satisfy the impulse of sympathy without challenging the settled doctrine and without making a shift in the balance of power between employers and labour or a threat to the established economic order. It may also be seen as giving the subtle control that can come from being merciful.[29]

After much debate, the legislatures in many industrialized countries, including Canada, established a regime to compensate workers injured on the job. The details varied markedly, but the schemes had two characteristics. First, recovery was to be based on 'no fault'; that is, the injured worker had to prove that she was injured as a result of an accident in the workplace, regardless of whose responsibility it was. Second, the regime of compensation was taken from the courts and handed to an administrative agency. Injuries were compensated by a system that provided for filing and adjudication of claims (where necessary) and for a system of appeals, all housed within an administrative structure established by the statutory regime.

A similar pattern developed with workers' rights to organize and bargain collectively, providing the second example of resistance by courts and intervention by the administrative state. During the nineteenth century, employees began to consolidate to demand some minimum benefits that came with the Industrial Revolution. Concerns for safety, exploitation of women and children, limits to hours worked, and the desire for increased wages all drove the union movement on. When it was not attacked by brute force, it was assaulted in the courts, where judges were mostly the allies of management. The cudgel was the concept of restraint of trade. Liberal values, at least in this context, espoused free markets where goods and services could flow unimpeded. Any clog was to be removed, hence any agreements or activities that restrained trade were to be suppressed. Courts used this concept to pummel any formal organizing by workers and attempts to bargain collectively.[30]

Again, it was for the legislatures to reformulate the structure between employees and management by recognizing the workers' rights to form unions and requiring employers to bargain with them collectively and, of course, freeing them from the threat of criminal conspiracy for asserting their own interests: 'the statutory freeing of unions from criminal responsibility for conspiracy or combination in restraint of trade is the cornerstone on which the trade movement rests. From it flows also collective bargaining and the later legislation dealing with labour relations.'[31]

Further, the implementation of such a regime was ultimately handed to administrative tribunals. A number of attempts to leave the issues with the courts foundered. Their focus on one-time disposition based on winners and losers, their adherence to a passive model where all aspects of an issue were to be brought and shaped by the parties, and their abiding hostility to the notion that workers should be able to bind together to improve their lot doomed the courts' role to failure. Ultimately, all legislatures in Canada ousted them from a direct role in collective bargaining issues.[32] Yet the courts did not ease silently away but reasserted themselves in another role, a matter discussed below.

The last example of resistance by courts and intervention by the administrative state comes from the law's treatment of discrimination. One of the most cherished ideals of justice is the law's equal treatment of everyone. But like so many ideals, it is utterly compelling as an abstraction and extraordinarily difficult as a reality. Does everyone have at least a basic claim to society's economic resources for minimum food, shelter, medical care, education, and access to the justice system? Does equality always mean equal treatment or is it sometimes necessary to treat individuals differently so as to achieve equal results?

Whatever equality should convey, it has come to mean at least a claim to treatment freed from discrimination based on religion, race, and sex. A man's chances for being hired for a job should be based on his competence as compared with that of other applicants. His ethnic background should be irrelevant. A black woman's desire to rent an apartment should depend on her ability to pay and her willingness to use the premises reasonably. The fact that she is a woman and black should be beside the point. Even this negative sense of equality can be problematic. Should it allow for affirmative action programs to rectify past injustices? Should a criminal record be taken into account when hiring or should it be regarded as irrelevant like religion, at least for some positions? Is it appropriate to allow certain institutions that overtly espouse a particular religion or set of beliefs to hire only those who adhere to those beliefs in order to foster the institution itself?

These issues illustrate the complexity of the concepts of equality and discrimination regardless of which government agency grapples with them. What is clear from the historical record is the courts' antagonism to even minimum notions of equality of freedom from discrimination. For decades the courts were given a number of opportunities to nurture or at least tolerate the concepts, but, with few exceptions, they were hostile and unyielding.[33]

The market was once again the frequent watchword. The free and uninterrupted flow of goods and services needed to be enhanced, while individual proprietors of those goods and services decided to contract with whomever they wished. If an owner refused to serve blacks, that was his right, subject to discipline by the market, because he would be deprived of that group's commerce. That a group as weak and diffuse as blacks in this country at that time could actually discipline bigotry through market forces was a fantasy that escaped the courts' notice.

This fidelity to freedom of contract was not subtle in any way. In one of the most notorious cases in Quebec before the Second World War, a black was refused service by a tavern owner. In upholding his right to do so, the Supreme Court of Canada made these comments:

> [T]he general principle of the law of Quebec was that of complete freedom of commerce.... Any merchant is free to deal as he may choose with any individual member of the public. It is not a question of motives or reasons for deciding to deal or not to deal; he is free to do either. The only restriction to this general principle would be the existence of a specific law, or, in the carrying out of the principle, the adoption of a rule contrary to good morals or public order ... [and it cannot] be argued that the rule adopted by the respondent in the conduct of its establishment was contrary to good morals or public order.[34]

Over time, there were a number of cases dealing with similar issues that venerated contract and dishonoured human dignity.[35]

A similar atmosphere surrounded the 'Persons' case, which raised the question of whether women could be appointed to the Senate as 'qualified persons', a case we will return to in the next chapter.[36] In denying the entitlement to women, the Supreme Court of Canada engaged in tortuous reasoning based on the historical intent when the provision was created in 1867.[37] That is how things would have stood had an English appellate court, the Judicial Committee of the Privy Council (at that time Canada's highest court of appeal), not disagreed, ruling that women were qualified.[38] This case is but one example of how the courts treated women, a topic that will receive full treatment in Chapter Five.

To be sure, the legislatures perpetuated their own discriminatory horrors.[39] But again, challenges to these wrongs, particularly against the Chinese, were continually rebuffed by the courts.[40] Often the legislation restricted the rights of the Chinese to gain a livelihood or employ certain people, particularly 'white women'. On these occasions freedom of contract was subordinated to the higher cause of 'morals' and 'bodily health'. This is typical judicial reaction:

> It would require some evidence of it to convince me that the right and opportunity to employ white women is, in any business sense, a necessary condition for the effective carrying on by Orientals of restaurants and laundries and like establishments. . . . Neither is there any ground for supposing that this legislation is designed to deprive Orientals of the opportunity to gain a livelihood.[41]

Hesitantly and piece by piece, the legislatures eradicated discrimination after the Second World War. Though fragmentary and incomplete, the idea behind the statutes was basic: equal treatment for all individuals without regard to particular characteristics that are irrelevant to the decision being made.[42] It is well to remember that the process is still unfolding and is almost always controversial. In Ontario, it has only been a few years since gay men and women have received at least some of the law's protection,[43] and in a few jurisdictions in Canada, it is still denied to them altogether.

Yet the process continues and these issues have been removed from the courts' jurisdiction. Human rights commissions have been established to implement the legislation, fight discrimination with education, conciliation and, if necessary, through adjudication that brands particular actions as wrong and awards compensation to victims when the allegations are proven. Reviewing the courts' performance and legislative reaction, a leading text on discrimination concludes, '[I]t is no wonder, then, that the legislatures, with no aid from the judiciary, had to move into the field and start to enact anti-discrimination legislation, the administration and application of which have largely been taken out of the courts.'[44]

The examples drawn from these three areas are merely illustrative of a pattern: initially, the courts' propounding of rules that mostly honoured strict liberal notions of individual responsibility, autonomy, and freedom centred on economic entitlement; then a reaction by legislatures that adopted a more communitarian perspective, inquired into the actual results, and recognized other values (such as need for compensation, legitimacy of collective action, and claims to equal treatment), frequently combined with the creation of an administrative body. Finally, the removal of these issues, in large part, from the courts, at least in terms of initial decision-making and the creation of some administrative agency to decide such questions. Other contemporary examples include pay equity,[45] redress for environmental harm,[46] and compensation for injuries from motor vehicle accidents.[47] Issues concerning the last example will be taken up in Chapter Six regarding tort litigation.

This is not to say that the legislative response has been flawless. Workers' compensation boards, grappling with rising costs, have come to be seen as unresponsive to very serious issues that affect health in the workplace, such as occupational disease,[48] though most standard claims are handled promptly and to the satisfaction of the injured.[49] Human rights tribunals are criticized for being slow and backlogged. Indeed, such problems have grown to crisis proportions in Ontario and have been the subject of a very critical report.[50] There are many examples of discrepancy between the high ideals espoused by these tribunals and related initiatives and the underlying reality.[51] For example, despite strict laws prohibiting discrimination against the disabled, Canada's record for employing people with disabilities appears to be among the worst.[52]

Yet in terms of responding with solutions other than those centred on economic individualism when it comes to issues that affect ordinary men and women, there has been a consistent division in this century between the courts and the legislatures and their agencies. Reviewing the historical record on this question, Arthurs has flatly asserted, 'the courts utterly failed to deal with the most significant legal repercussions of the Industrial Revolution in the nineteenth century and with the revolution of rising expectations in the twentieth.'[53] In suggesting that judges by and large should not deal with human rights cases, a former justice of the Ontario courts has observed recently that:

> Judges as a group have been traditionally drawn from social classes unsympathetic to social change. This has been perceived as clouding their judgement by inclining them to decide against the change the legislation seeks to achieve. Judges have been perceived as unsympathetic to the problems of the 'common-man'.[54]

Courts, Tribunals, and the 'Virtues of Competition' In Chapter One's discussion of the essential structure of Canada, we reviewed how the government's role in the economy and tolerance for large entities and concentration of wealth has long been a prominent aspect of the nation. It was by no means suggested that this was an unqualified good; this deference to economic concentration has important implications for such diverse questions as productivity and distribution of wealth.

The courts' tepid attitude towards competition has been obvious from nineteenth century common law to judgements rendered under contemporary legislation. But such judicial hostility to legislative intervention is more complex than the courts' attitude to the administrative state just discussed: in the context at hand, it can be strongly argued that courts were reflecting societal opinion as much as they were defying it. This is because of this country's deep ambiguity towards competition and any law used to enforce it. At the end of the 1970s W.T. Stanbury, one of the most prominent students of competition law, summarized our attitudes: 'There does not exist in Canada any fundamental belief in the virtues of competition as the method of allocating scarce resources and of diffusing economic and political power.'[55] Amplifying on this succinct summary, he suggested that the structured and authoritarian Canadian society assumed a high level of influence for business interests. In addition, there was the government's large-scale intervention in the nation's economic life. These and other factors combined to produce a state of affairs that ensure the dominance of producers' interests over consumer' interests; that is, high tariffs, high concentration, inefficient production, and extensive foreign ownership.[56]

Inevitably, Canada is compared with the United States. While there is sound scholarship urging that the two countries' differences on these issues not be exaggerated,[57] in fact disparities between American and Canadian society and their respective courts regarding such policies are frequent and pointed,[58] though there might be general agreement that a statement characterizing the Sherman Act (a main US antitrust statute) as 'one of the great foundations of American civilization'[59] sets a standard few countries, including our neighbour, would care to meet.

In all of this, it is clear that our courts have done little to advance competition law and policy. While liberalism and its relationship to the judges is complex (in ways we have discussed in a number of places already) the posture of the Canadian courts seemed a dilution of the liberalism they had often otherwise fostered in the sense that market forces and freedom of trade were slighted in favour of protectionism and individual freedom of contract, thus creating cartels and other anticompetition devices. Whether interpreting their own common-law rules,[60] or limiting the federal power to enforce criminal sanctions as a matter of constitutionalism,[61] or blunting provisions addressing conspiracies to restrict competition,[62] our judges almost always rendered decisions that deflected politicians' attempts to create vigorous policies. For example, here is an illustrative summary of the post-Second World War era:

> In the late 1950s, Canadian anti-combines officials began to question some significant mergers. In the early 1960s, however, the courts dismissed two merger prosecutions in terms which indicated that the existing legislation was unenforceable. When the merger and monopoly provisions were considered by the Supreme Court in the 1970s, they were again very narrowly interpreted. Further, after World War II, while Canadian courts generally interpreted the prohibition of anti-competitive agreements broadly, two decisions by the Supreme Court also cast doubts on the efficacy of this provision.[63]

Meanwhile, around the same time, the situation in the United States with its receptive courts was a marked contrast. Attacks on mergers and large corporations, the judiciary's enthusiasm for antitrust, and the heavy use of the private action all served to effectively distinguish American antitrust activity from its Canadian counterpart.[64]

The point is not simply to provide yet another example of courts blocking policy development through their common-law rules and subsequently defying legislative intervention. The story is more complex in this context because, quite apart from the courts, as a society we harbour a substantial ambivalence to these policies that has wound its way through our history. Examples abound, but consider just two. In discussing the 1930s, Cheffins observes:

> The unambitious nature of Canada's anti-combines policy can be attributed largely to the attitude of government. Neither the Liberals, who were in power until 1930, nor the Conservatives, who formed the government between 1930 to 1935, were enthusiastic about the legislation. Peter Heenan, who was the Minister responsible for the Combines Investigation Act between 1926 and 1930, said in 1933: '. . . the Combines Investigation Act is probably one of the most unpopular acts on the statute books and one of the most unpopular to administer. I can say that from experience'.[65]

Writing in the 1980s during a period of reform that would be ultimately successful, but that at the time had as yet undetermined results, and while giving judges the primary role of eviscerating policy to that point, Monahan suggested that commentators of a wide range of political views believed that competition policy was essentially bankrupt. Such lack of purpose was regarded as the result of political reticence to strong and sustained opposition to reform from the business community. The entire process was "'a national joke . . . a saga of delays and procrastination'".[66]

When reform that started in the 1970s was actually implemented, the design of the dispute resolution mechanism was significant. Neither fish nor fowl, it was a hybrid. While the body is called the Competition Tribunal and may have a maximum of eight other members, it may have up to four members of the Federal Court, Trial Division.[67] One of these judges must be the chair of the tribunal, and every panel in particular cases must also be chaired by one of the judges. Further, questions of law must be determined only by judicial members of the tribunal. So while the body carries a name that indicates it is part of the administrative process and has lay members, its decisions will be very heavily influenced by judges, especially since there is a right of appeal (not unique) to the Federal Court of Appeal.

There are many difficult questions surrounding competition policy. For example, influential opinion argues that in countries with smaller economies (like Canada) concentration is not necessarily a bad thing in terms of competing on global terms. However, it is essential that these economies be exposed to world competition, so governments should put their energies and resources into free trade and its consequences.[68] To express opinions on such issues would be beyond even the ambitious scope of this book. The essential point here is that courts undoubtedly had a role in restricting competition law, but to look only to the courts' record without linking it to the larger context and the roles of other actors would be distorting cause and effect. Whatever the consequences, the present Competition Tribunal affirms policy-makers' continuing ambivalence. Its design turns from the courts towards the administrative process. Its membership and rules lead back to the judiciary. Parliament continues to want it both ways — maybe several ways. Politicians frequently bemoan the ill-directed judges. When this occurs, look out for crocodile tears.

Judicial Review of Administrative Action The clash between the judiciary and the administrative state — illustrated by our discussion of workers' compensation, labour relations, and human rights — developed on another front. Even before the advent of industrialization and capitalism, the courts had claimed the right to review the workings of government, though actual review was unsystematic.[69] The growth of government was accompanied by the courts' increasing propensity to intervene and set aside orders made illegally.

But how was illegality to be determined? The courts vowed that this review was focused not on the correctness of the ultimate decision but on whether the decision-maker was empowered by the authorizing legislation to make the decision and the procedures the decision-maker was required to use. But even if this was the ambit of review, deciding what legislation empowered and what procedures could be used left plenty of scope for review. It was easy to see how a view that suggested the courts should not have such power of scrutiny would arise. Such an opinion was grounded in the belief that each administrative actor was as well situated or even better situated because of expertise to determine how his decisions ought to be made. Any review or appeal should come from that structure. The courts should keep out, as history indicates this was not a task for them, either as initial decision-makers or as reviewers of administrative actors' decisions, unless there was some appeal made to them that was authorized by statute.

Those who subscribed to this view were outraged that legislatures often inserted in relevant statutes sections declaring that the tribunal's decision was final and not to be reviewed in any way, specifically by a court. Yet these admonitions — known as 'privative clauses'[70] — were frequently defied by courts. To do this, they declared that all administrative tribunals had limited jurisdiction assigned to them by the legislatures. Therefore, whenever the tribunal made decisions that exceeded the limits of the jurisdiction assigned to them, they stepped outside the ambit of protection afforded by these clauses and the courts as protectors of the rule of law could — and indeed were obliged — to step in and corral them.

As logic, this manoeuvre was fine; as policy, it was highly dubious. It was true that administrative tribunals were assigned limited functions. Labour relation boards were to deal with issues arising between properly certified unions and management but were not to set milk production quotas. But the flaw was that issues submitted to the court as jurisdictional ones were far less clear than that. They almost always dealt with questions critical to the task the administrative actor was performing. The courts were frequently ignorant and even hostile to the thrust of the underlying legislative policy. When they brought to the interpretive exercise notions about the rule of law that idealized courts and the common law as its embodiment,[71] there were bound to be clashes.

Perhaps at this point an example would be helpful. Any number could be provided, but let us take a classic one from the wranglings between courts and human rights tribunals, since we have already looked at the courts' response to issues of discrimination in the previous section. In 1968 McKay, a black, phoned about renting an apartment in the home of Bell. When he arrived to look at it, Bell informed him that the flat was rented. McKay, who was suspicious of the circumstances, had an acquaintance of his phone Bell soon after and she was told it was still available. Faced with this revelation, McKay went to the Ontario Human Rights Commission and filed a complaint. Bell explained that he lied because he did not rent to young men who could be students, and lying was a means to avoid argument and confrontation. However, at the board of inquiry — the hearing to adjudicate whether a discriminatory act had taken place — Bell raised a more formidable point that, if accepted, would prevent the board from proceeding at all.

Preventing discrimination has been given a high value in our society through the statutory prohibitions against it, but compromises have been made. Rightly or wrongly — at the time of this case — the legislation only prohibited discrimination in rental accommodation for 'self-contained dwelling units'. The idea behind the qualification was that the physical set-up is likely to engender even more hostility between bigot and victim if the bigot is forced to accept the victim into what is basically her own home.

However, the matter for debate was what qualified as a 'self-contained dwelling unit' since this term was not defined in the code. Bell went to court to have the judges stop the board of inquiry on the grounds that the flat was not a self-contained dwelling unit and, therefore, the board had no 'jurisdiction' to decide whether acts of discrimination had occurred. Despite dissents, Bell won in the Supreme Court of Canada, the majority characterizing the issue as a 'perfectly simple, short and neat question of law'.[72]

What irks defenders of administrative tribunals is the attitude typified by this quote. In fact the issue is complex and heavily dependent on a sense of the entire antidiscrimination structure and where and how to draw boundary lines in terms of, on the one hand, resisting discrimination and, on the other, realizing that insistence on enforcing the Human Rights Code will result in even more rancour. Such a decision should not be reached in the abstract, but only after carefully examining the facts in the particular case and relating them to appropriate circumstances where boundary lines have had to be drawn to enforce human rights legislation and mindful of the fact that premises such as the one in the *Bell* case are likely to be rented by individuals most in need of protection from discrimination.

Instead the Court based the meaning it attributed to 'self-contained dwelling unit' on a mechanical and selective application of the previous formulation of the legislation. Initially the code forbade discrimination in 'any apartment in any building that contains more than six self-contained dwelling units'. An amendment in 1965 included buildings with more than three such units. Finally, in 1967 the legislation was altered again to prevent discrimination because of race to 'any self-contained dwelling unit'.[73] Responding to these evolving formulations, the Court asserted that: '[T]he premises leased by the appellant, located in his upstairs floors, may well be "dwelling units" but they were not "self-contained" dwelling units.'[74]

It is small wonder then, with the *Bell* case as an example, that courts' review of administrative action has been characterized as subjective, inconsistent, hostile to the purpose of the agency and the legislation being scrutinized, and just plain muddled. Adams, a leading author in labour law (and himself now a judge) explains that since substantive rules of law applicable to judicial control of administrative action are so general in nature, they may actually invite intervention based on 'subjective judicial opinion'. Statutes like those dealing with labour relations issues were enacted to reflect particular economic and social policy, but any number of judges' personal views may be quite contradictory and lead to any number of conflicting decisions.[75]

The terrain is even more complex because some judges have recognized how ill-equipped courts can be in deciding such jurisdictional questions. While antecedents existed,[76] the most recent architect of such an attitude has been former Chief Justice Dickson. In a famous decision dealing with the power of a labour relations tribunal to bar the substitution of management for employees during a strike — the CUPE case — Chief Justice Dickson was clear that judges should hesitate to second-guess such administrative actors without a showing of clear and unmistakable error demonstrating that 'the Board's interpretation [was] so patently unreasonable that its construction cannot be rationally supported by the relevant legislation and demands intervention by the court.'[77] This attitude reflects a tolerance for other forms of decision making and the working out of other policies.[78] If nurtured, it prevents the courts from projecting their own image onto tribunals, while still retaining their overseeing function for administrative law.[79]

Yet the cases in the Supreme Court of Canada that insist upon the supremacy of courts have been reinvigorated and may again dominate.[80] Mixed together with cases professing deference,[81] these are driven by antagonism towards the administrative state and its ends. The eye of the storm is interpreting ambiguous legislative provisions that address the scope of the tribunals' power: if courts with this view disagree with a board reading, then they take it as their duty to overturn the administrative actors' judgement. Some of the most difficult cases are those where the Court has found jurisdictional error over the scope of boards' remedial powers — the area where the need for flexibility may be the greatest as the various interests are kept in balance in the context of specific issues.[82]

Such intervention is accompanied by high-handedness. In these cases the courts have again demonstrated the arrogance that has earned such contempt.[83] This has led commentators such as Etherington to contend that, at least in the labour context, judges were only deferential when such restraint accorded with 'their own basic values and strongly held ideological preferences'.[84] They did, in fact, intervene (even during the brief period of deference) to 'protect deeply held traditional liberal values concerning property and management rights, freedom of contract, and the right to trade. . . .'[85] He reaches a similar set of conclusions after a detailed survey of labour relations cases under the Charter.[86]

From the perspective of this interventionist stance, legislatures and their administrative agencies are viewed as threats to the law spurred on by a popular will, contemptuous of the purity in the law that judges have created and must defend.[87] As Justice Beetz contended in a notorious case decided in 1984, 'The power of review of the courts of law has [an] historic basis . . . and . . . relates to . . . the supremacy . . . of the law of which the courts are the guardians.'[88] Meanwhile, those in the Court who still believe in deference to tribunals, have become quite vocal in dissent concerning the dilution and intervention that has reasserted itself:

> . . . [T]here has been a tendency in the post-CUPE era to return to a less stringent test for judicial review than the one established in CUPE. This backsliding has been largely predicated upon a rather Dicean view of rule of law and the role that courts should play in the administration of government. That approach to curial review in the administrative context is, in my opinion, no longer appropriate given the sophisticated role that administrative tribunals play in the modern Canadian state. I think we need to return to CUPE and the spirit which CUPE embodies.[89]

The Supreme Court's latest retreat from deference has been with regard to human rights. In fairness, it should be said that throughout the 1980s, on several occasions the Supreme Court approved a number of tribunals' ground-breaking initiatives under various human rights codes,[90] including issues dealing with discrimination based on pregnancy, treating sexual harassment as a form of discrimination, and affirmative action as a remedy for systemic discrimination. It also rebuffed an attempt to sue directly in courts for discrimination on the grounds that such action would weaken the comprehensive enforcement provisions in human rights codes.[91] But such initiatives may have been significantly chilled by the Court's recent decision in *Mossop*.[92] The immediate issue was the Court's spurning of attempts to protect cohabiting gays and lesbians through a liberal interpretation of 'family status'.[93] However, the majority also made it clear that it would generally not defer to human rights agencies concerning the interpretation of human rights codes — particularly in the absence of a privative clause — since boards of inquiry (the decision-makers for individual disputes) have 'no particular expertise'. Such a position was taken in spite of the courts' history of stifling initiatives to protect human rights in this country.

The landscape is even more complex. In addition, whatever should be the appropriate point for courts overturning administrative actors' decisions about the proper scope of their statutory regime, courts have also sought to fulfil a second function with their review.[94] In this second role, they recognize the importance of reviewing an administrative decision to ensure that one who has been affected by a decision has been accorded minimal procedural decencies. At first glance, this too may seem intrusive since the courts' power to intervene is so embracing. Still, most of the criticism of courts' interference with tribunals, much of it justified, has been directed towards their mangling of the agencies' substantive programs by second-guessing how their legislative mandate is to be carried out.

Critics have been much less bothered by the courts' role in assuring that decisions accord with appropriate procedural safeguards — free of bad faith and bias, and giving those who are affected adequate opportunities to participate in the process. That these two processes — supervising the scope of administrative agencies' power and scrutinizing the procedures used to arrive at their decisions — can be very different is obvious if one realizes that former Chief Justice Dickson, the primary architect of deference to boards working out their regulatory scheme, was also one of the judges who favoured the most intervention to ensure that individuals affected by administrative actors' decisions have an adequate opportunity to present their arguments and evidence.[95]

Deference to an agency's decisions in determining its mandate will alleviate problems of courts crippling tribunals' substantive programs. On the other hand, respect for persons — not just in terms of economic rights but in all aspects of individual integrity — should inform any kind of decision made by anyone empowered to decide. Even the staunchest defenders of administrative law are willing to admit that agencies' records at times have not been good in this regard.[96] While indicating their willingness to intervene on this basis, the courts have simultaneously indicated that they will not use a fixed and immutable standard for evaluating the decencies of the procedures used unless required to do so by some statutory directive.[97] The person affected must be given an adequate opportunity to participate and be treated fairly, but what is adequate and fair will vary from the most perfunctory right of oral reply to written submissions to a more formal hearing.

CONCLUSION

What does the description add up to? What has been the impact of courts on the administrative process? These questions have a particular bite in this context because, in the legal literature at least, debates about the proper role of courts as umpire of the administrative process have been considerable. Does this mean that courts have indeed had a pivotal role — whatever that may be — or have lawyers again fooled themselves into thinking that something central to their world is crucial to everyone else's?

Two consequences can be asserted with some confidence. First, with their continuous insistence on enforcing common-law rules antithetical to the social and political problems of society, courts acted, at some level, as a catalyst for change. Their indifference at best and hostility at worst to questions surrounding workers' rights to organize, human rights, environmental and consumer issues, to name but a few, was something that the legislature could react against and use as justification to create and expand the administrative state.

This is not to suggest that there was a direct cause-and-effect relationship between courts' obstinacy and the establishment of, for example, labour relations boards. Clearly many social, political, and economic forces interacted leading to sufficient acceptance of workers' collective bargaining and to the state's recognition of that right. But the courts' resistance was at least one such factor and there was a connection between their inflexibility and the legislatures' determination to replace them with tribunals to administer the scheme they propounded.

The second consequence is that in reviewing administrative decisions, judges have played an intensely ideological role in continuously articulating values at odds with those of the administrative state. Whether by resorting to high-flown concepts like the rule of law or by insisting that they are only interpreting the regulatory statute and setting aside incorrect interpretations (amounting to jurisdictional error so as to blunt the protection of privative clauses), with some notable exceptions, courts have acted as a brake on the administrative state as they tend towards liberal, individualistic values that centre on property entitlements and away from the communitarian values that the administrative state, on the whole, tends to advance.

Regardless of one's larger views of the matter, it is possible to agree that the courts have a role in assuring that appropriate procedures have been followed in making a decision. Such review, if it is sensitive to the many ways in which decisions can be made given the ends sought to be achieved, protects a sense of individuality and integrity not conditional on proprietary claims and guards against caprice, values that any civilized regime would want to nurture. Beyond this, however, one's view of court activity is likely to be heavily influenced by which pole, described in the introduction, one heads towards. If one sees government as the planner and referee of the powerful forces in society, harnessing them (at least in part) to achieve beneficial common ends, then the courts are looked upon as an embargo — at least at an ideological level — to attaining those goals. On the other hand, if one sees government as a powerful marauder that continually dampens entrepreneurial activity, corrals incentive, and harasses individual freedom, one is likely to applaud judges and urge them on.

One aspect that does emerge vividly is the courts' self-created and energized role in all of this. They have fashioned their role as overseer of administrative activity, not only without instructions from the legislature, but — in the case of privative clauses — in open defiance of statutory instruction. Whether creation of this role and ousting of privative clauses is good or bad may be debatable. What is manifest is the active entrepreneurial role of the courts in this context.

Still, is there more that can be said regarding the impact that judicial review of administrative action has actually had? One can certainly point to instances where the Supreme Court's action has been regarded as so inappropriate that the legislature passed enactments to overrule the particular decision. This occurred, for example, as a result of the *Bell* case discussed earlier — no mean feat, considering the difficulty of any issue getting on to the order paper.[98] Yet such reaction is quite exceptional. On the whole the administrative state continues with more regulatory schemes propounded and debated and with concerns about how to make its agents responsive and accountable. Meanwhile, the literature on the administrative state reflecting the debates and concerns has, aside from legal scholars, little to say about the utility or obstructiveness of judicial review.[99]

Nevertheless, the consequences of surveying courts' activities in the administrative state in the last century lead one to conclude that we should not rely on courts to devise solutions to social and political issues that shape our society. By the same token, the history of competition law and policy warns us that courts sometimes reflect us as much as they defy us and solutions will be elusive as long as political will vacillates. Nevertheless, courts' indifference and hostility would seem to make them ill-equipped in dealing with broader issues, particularly those that curb the excesses of powerful economic forces.

This is why liberal visionaries such as Beatty[100] seem to be on shaky ground when extolling the virtues of the Charter and its ability to enhance workers' rights, especially in relation to meaningful participation in economic and social decision making. After a selective summary of courts' activities regarding worker interests over the last century, Beatty asserts that there is 'some basis' to be sanguine, that under the Charter, the judiciary would be sensitive to workers' issues. On the basis of this modest claim based on wobbly foundations, he feels confident in giving the courts an ambitious agenda for the betterment of ordinary people. Some aspects of these goals are lofty; however, the means to attain them are highly doubtful.

Yet there is nothing inherent and predetermined about courts and what they can and cannot do. And a changed and progressive judiciary has become the new hope of many interest groups the seek reform in this country. We will see much more of this when we discuss the Charter of Rights and Freedoms and its impact, as well as the strengths and foibles of placing hope for a progressive democracy in the hands of the judiciary. The main point is that while it is good to be optimistic, one needs to remember history as well, particularly if the judicialization of issues is growing as a result of increased judicial review of administrative action. Such judicialization may not in itself be critical, but it becomes significant when linked with judges' potential under the Charter and a reinvigorated federalism review. In the end, the potential is sobering.

NOTES

[1]V. Seymour Wilson and O.P. Dwivedi, 'Introduction' in O.P. Dwivedi (ed.), *The Administrative State in Canada — Essays in Honour of J.E. Hodgetts* (Toronto: University of Toronto Press, 1982): 3: 'The steady growth of government, both at

the federal and provincial levels, has been one of the most distinctive and important developments in Canadian history during the twentieth century.'

[2] *Responsible Regulation* (Ottawa, 1979): 16.

[3] *Supra*, note 1 at 6:

Whether one dubbed the phenomenon the administrative state, the welfare state, or the positive state, the implications were clearly the same: namely, the instrumental nature of the state's institutions as rationally conceived means to the realization of expressly announced group goals. Its structures are understood as tools deliberately established for the efficient and effective realization of these group purposes.

[4] Ibid., 6–7.

[5] B. Bresner and T. Leigh-Bell with R.S. Prichard, M. Trebilock, and L. Waverman, 'Ontario's Agencies, Boards, Commissions, Advisory Bodies and Other Public Institutions: An Inventory', in *Government Regulation* (Toronto: Ontario Economic Council, 1978): 207–75.

[6] J. Evans et al., *Administrative Law Cases, Text and Materials* (3rd ed.) (Toronto: Emond-Montgomery, 1989): 5–7. The discussion in the text concerning the taxonomy of agencies depends heavily on this work.

[7] Ibid. The Ontario Workers' Compensation Act and Board has been restructured since, but the figures are indicative.

[8] Ibid.

[9] J.E. Hodgetts, 'Challenge and Response: A Retrospective View of the Public Service of Canada' (1964) VII *Canadian Public Administration*, 421.

[10] *Supra*, note 1 at 10–11.

[11] Ibid., 4.

[12] Ibid.

[13] A. Brady, 'The State and Economic Life' in G.W. Brown (ed.), *Canada* (Berkeley: University of California Press, 1950): 353.

[14] Ibid.

[15] V. Fowke, 'The National Policy — Old and New' (1952) 18 *Canadian Journal of Economics and Political Science*, 271–86.

[16] W.A. MacKintosh, 'Canadian Economic Policy: Scope and Principles' (1950) 16 *Canadian Journal of Economics and Political Science*, 317.

[17] *Supra*, note 1 at 8–9.

[18] H.G. Aitken, 'Defensive Expansionism: The State and Economic Growth in Canada' in H.G. Aitken (ed.), *The State and Economic Growth* (New York: Social Science Research Council, 1959): 79–114.

[19] *Supra*, note 1 at 9.

[20] R. Schultz, 'Comments for Panel Discussion on Regulation' (1979) 4 *Canadian Public Policy*, 486–90.

[21] G.B. Reschenthaler, 'Direct Regulation in Canada: Some Policies and Problems' in W.T. Stanbury (ed.), *Studies on Regulation in Canada* (Montreal: Institute for Research on Public Policy, 1978): 37–112.

[22] *Supra*, note 1 at 10.

[23] Similar themes and their influence in Great Britain are discussed by J. Griffith in

The Politics of the Judiciary (London: Fontana, 1978), discussed in Chapter Three.

[24]P. Emond, 'Environmental Law and Policy: A Retrospective Examination of the Canadian Experience' in *Consumer Protection, Environmental Law and Corporate Power*, vol. 50 of the research studies prepared for the Royal Commission on the Economic Union and Development Prospects for Canada (Toronto: University of Toronto Press, 1986), but see also J. Nedelsky, 'Judicial Conservatism in an Age of Innovation: Comparative Perspectives in Canadian Nuisance Law 1880–1930', in D. Flaherty (ed.), *Essays in the History of Canadian Law* (Toronto: The Osgoode Society, 1983): 281, arguing that, regarding the law of nuisance, the conservatism of the Canadian judiciary may have led them to resist the defences of industry during at least one phase of this country's development.

[25]M. Valiante and W.A. Bogart, 'Helping "Concerned Volunteers Working Out of Their Kitchens": Funding Citizen Participation in Administrative Decision-Making' (1993) *Osgoode Hall Law Journal* (forthcoming) and S. McWilliams, 'The Costs of Intervenor Funding and Their Control: The Experience of the Ontario Energy Board', 11 *Windsor Yearbook of Access to Justice*, 217–49, detailing development of intervenor funding for participation in the administrative process, its rejection by the courts and a legislative response for the administrative process in the Ontario Intervenor Funding Project Act; and W.A. Bogart and M. Valiante, *Access and Impact: An Evaluation of the Intervenor Funding Project Act, 1988*, a report to the Ontario Ministries of the Attorney General, Energy, and Environment, 1992.

[26]R.C.B. Risk, '"This Nuisance of Litigation": The Origins of Workers' Compensation in Ontario' in D. Flaherty (ed.), *Essays in the History of Canadian Law* (Toronto: The Osgoode Society, 1983): 418.

[27]See *Priestly v. Fowler* (1837), 150 ER 1030 (UK) 3 *Meeson & Welsby's Exchequer Reports* (150–3ER): 1836–47. *Farwell v. Boston and Worcester Railroad Corporation* (1842) 45 Mass. (4 Met.) 49.

[28]*Supra*, note 26 at 421.

[29]Ibid., 448. See also E. Tucker, *Administering Danger in the Workplace — The Law and Politics of Occupational Health and Safety Regulation in Ontario 1850–1914* (Toronto: University of Toronto Press, 1990) and in particular Chapter 8, 'Courting Risk: The Establishment of Market Regulation'. While Tucker concludes that the legislative response particularly in implementation was itself flawed, it was a clear improvement over how the judges had treated the issues (211): '[T]he judges chose to preserve the purity of the legal framework of market regulation by rejecting workers' legal arguments and by silencing the jury when it showed it was unwilling to cooperate with them in this project.'

[30]G. Adams, *Canadian Labour Law — A Comprehensive Text* (Toronto: Canada Law Book, 1985), Chapter 1, 'Historical Introduction'.

[31]A. Crysler, *Labour Relations and Precedents in Canada* (Toronto: Carswell, 1949): 10.

[32]*Supra*, note 30.

[33]Perhaps the most prominent was the trial level decision in *Re Drummond Wren* [1945] *Ontario Reports*, 778, in which the court held that a covenant not to resell land to 'Jews, or to persons of objectionable nationality' was invalid as contrary to public policy after reviewing several international proclamations. This decision was

overshadowed by *Noble and Wolf* v. *Alley* [1951] *Supreme Court Reports*, 64, where a similar covenant was upheld by the Ontario trial court and Court of Appeal and was finally held invalid by the Supreme Court of Canada, but only on the technical grounds of uncertainty and that it could not run with the land. A leading text on discrimination observes that 'It is possible to argue that the Supreme Court decision achieved the same result as [Drummond Wren]. However, one certainly could not look to the decision for any inspiration in attempting to achieve an egalitarian society.' W. Tarnopolsky, *Discrimination and the Law* (Toronto: DeBoo, 1985): 26 (revised by William Pentney).

[34]*Christie* v. *York Corporation* [1940] *Supreme Court Reports*, 139, 142, 144.

[35]*Loew's Theatres* v. *Reynolds* (1921) 30 *Quebec King's Bench*, 459; *Franklin* v. *Evans* (1924) 55 *Ontario Law Reports*, 349; *Rogers* v. *Clarence Hotel Co.* [1940] 3 *Dominion Law Reports*, 583 (BCCA); *King* v. *Borclay and Borclay's Motel* (1961) 35 *Western Weekly Reports* (NS) 240. A much earlier case in 1899 *Johnson* v. *Sparrow et al.* (1899) 15 *Quebec Supreme Court*, 104, aff'd (1899) 8 *Quebec Queen's Bench*, 379 illustrates the road not taken.

[36]See Chapter Five.

[37]*Re Meaning of Word 'Persons' in Section 24 of the BNA Act* (the *Edwards* case) [1928] *Supreme Court Reports*, 276.

[38]*Edwards* v. *Attorney-General for Canada* [1930] *Appeal Cases*, 124.

[39]Tarnopolsky, *supra*, note 33 at 1–4 to 1–5: '[T]here were federal laws restricting immigration from Asian countries and withholding the Franchise from Asiatics, as well as from the native peoples until after World War II. Similarly, there were provincial laws denying the franchise to Asiatics, imposing head taxes, restricting and segregating land ownership, restricting employment and business opportunities, and even going so far as making it an offence for white women to be employed by them' [citations omitted].

[40]Ibid., 1–7 to 1–21 discussing applicable cases.

[41]*Quong-Wing* v. *The King* (1914) 49 *Supreme Court Reports*, 440, 465.

[42]Detailed in Tarnopolsky, *supra*, note 33, Chapter II, 'The Rise and Spread of Anti-Discrimination Legislation'.

[43]Ontario Human Rights Code, RSO 1990 c. H. 19, s. 1, 2(1), 3, 5(1), 6.

[44]Tarnopolsky, *supra*, note 33 at I–26.

[45]*Employment Standards Act*, RSO 1990, c. E. 14, s. 32; M. Freudenheim, 'Ontario Law Matches Women's Wages to Men's', *New York Times*, 2 July 1989, A1. P.C. McDermott, 'Pay Equity in Ontario: A Critical Legal Analysis' (1989) 28 *Osgoode Hall Law Journal*, 381–407.

[46]In Canada see Emond, *supra*, note 24. See also 'Dam Exemption Illegal, MPs Say' *The Globe and Mail*, 24 May 1993, B1 (detailing the disagreement of a Senate-Commons Committee with the Federal Court of Appeal's decision upholding the Cabinet's exemption of a project from environmental assessment) and J. Simpson, 'A Fixed Link Is No Match for the Muscle-Flexing of the Courts', *The Globe and Mail*, 31 March 1993, A18.

For a discussion of the courts' complex role in protecting the environment in the United States, see G. Rosenberg, *The Hollow Hope — Can Courts Bring About Social Change?* (Chicago: University of Chicago Press, 1991): 269–92, discussed at length in Chapter Two. Rosenberg concludes that, while in specific situations some progress was made in the courts, 'environmental litigation, as a strategy for producing a clean and healthy environment, achieved precious few victories' (p. 292). See also K. Schneider, 'Thwarted Environmentalists find US Courts Are Citadels No More,' *The New York Times,* 23 March 1993, A1.

[47] For example, *Insurance Act,* RSO 1990, c. I. 8, s. 266, 268; *Motor Vehicle Accident Claims Act,* RSO 1990, c. M. 41.

[48] For example, P.S. Barth, 'Workers' Compensation and Asbestos in Ontario' (1982) a study for the Royal Commission on Matters of Health and Safety Arising from the Use of Asbestos in Ontario and L. West, 'Compensating Occupational Cancer in Michigan and Ontario: A Comparative Perspective' (1988) 3 *Journal of Law and Social Policy,* 138.

[49] W.A. Bogart and N. Vidmar, 'Problems and Experience with the Ontario Civil Justice System: An Empirical Assessment' in A. Hutchinson (ed.), *Access to Civil Justice* (Toronto: Carswell, 1990): 1.

[50] See *Achieving Equality: A Report on Human Rights Reform* (Toronto: Ministry of Citizenship, 1992), M. Cornish, task force chair; see also L. Hurst, 'Rosemary's Baby', *The Toronto Star,* 7 August 1993, B1 (discussing the problems of the Ontario Commission facing the new chief commissioner, Rosemary Brown).

[51] For example, S. Fine, 'Equity Law's First Report Card', *The Globe and Mail,* 30 December 1992, A1, and R. Platiel, 'Racial Harassment Ruling Denounced', *The Globe and Mail,* 19 January 1993, A6.

[52] V. Galt, 'Disabled Strive to Crack Job Market', *The Globe and Mail,* 18 January 1993, A1.

[53] H. Arthurs, 'Jonah and the Whale: The Appearance, Disappearance, and Reappearance of Administrative Law' (1980) 30 *University of Toronto Law Journal,* 225. Arthurs has developed this theme in more detail in a book, *'Without the Law': Administrative Justice and Legal Pluralism in Nineteenth-Century England* (Toronto: University of Toronto Press, 1985).

[54] *Supra,* note 50 at 94, quoting the Honourable R. Reid and a paper he prepared for the task force.

[55] W. Stanbury, *Business Interests and the Reform of Canadian Competition Policy, 1971–75* (Toronto: Carswell/Methuen, 1977): 45.

[56] Ibid.

[57] B. Cheffins, 'The Development of Competition Policy, 1890–1940: A Re-Evaluation of a Canadian and American Tradition' (1989) 27 *Osgoode Hall Law Journal,* 449.

[58] *Supra,* note 55 at 45; B. Dunlop et al., *Canadian Competition Policy: A Legal and Economic Analysis* (Toronto: Canada Law Book, 1987), 58 *et seq., Report of the Royal Commission on the Economic Union and Development Prospects For Canada,* Vol. II (Ottawa: Ministry of Supply and Services Canada, 1985): 170–1.

[59] Cheffins, *supra,* note 57, quoting W. Letwin, *Law and Economic Policy in America: The Evolution of the American Antitrust Act* (New York: Random House, 1965): 3.

[60] Dunlop et al., *supra,* note 58 at 280–1.

[61] *Supra,* note 57 at 487–8 citing *Transport Oil Ltd* v. *Imperial Oil Ltd* [1935] 2 *Dominion Law Reports,* 500 (Ont. CA) and *Direct Lumber Co.* v. *Western Plywood*

[1962] *Supreme Court Reports*, 646. See now *General Motors of Canada Ltd* v. *City National Leasing* (1989) 93 *National Reporter*, 326 (SCC).

[62] Royal Commission, *supra*, note 58 at 172.

[63] *Supra*, note 57 at 486–7.

[64] Ibid., 486.

[65] Ibid., 470. Describing the period up to 1940, he points the blame away from courts and towards the political process (479–80):

> The problem instead was the ambivalent or unsympathetic attitude of Parliament and Cabinet. For example, some legislation, such as that passed in 1919 and 1935, aimed as much at reducing as promoting competition. Further, the deferent tone used by King and others defending anti-combines legislation indicated that the business community had little to fear. The 1889 and 1910 legislation was also left on the books for significant periods of time when the legislation was clearly not being utilized. Finally, the machinery set up to administer anti-combines legislation was so poorly funded and understaffed that it was impossible to carry out any form of rigorous enforcement.

[66] P. Monahan, 'The Supreme Court and the Economy' in I. Bernier and A. Lajoie (eds), *The Supreme Court of Canada as an Instrument of Political Change* (Toronto: University of Toronto, 1986): 109.

[67] *Competition Tribunal Act*, SC (1986) c. 26, Part I, ss. 1–17, discussed in B. Dunlop et al., *supra*, note 58 at 284–5.

[68] Royal Commission, *supra*, note 58 at 220; Dunlop et al., *supra*, note 58 at 59–60.

[69] J.M. Evans, *DeSmith's Judicial Review of Administrative Action* (4th ed.) (London: Stevens and Sons Ltd, 1980): 108–10.

[70] A typical privative clause is found in the Ontario Labour Relations Act RSO 1980, c. 228, s. 108: 'No decision, order, direction, declaration or ruling of the Board shall be questioned or reviewed in any court, and no order shall be made or process entered, or proceedings taken in any court, whether by way of injunction, declaratory judgement, certiorari, mandamus, prohibition, quo warranto, or otherwise to question review, prohibit or restrain the Board or any of its proceedings.'

[71] The famous proponent of this view was the nineteenth-century English constitutional scholar, A.V. Dicey: see *The Law of the Constitution* (London: Macmillan, 1885). For Dicey's influence on administrative law and judicial review of administrative action, see H. Arthurs, 'Rethinking Administrative Law: A Slightly Dicey Business' (1979) 17 *Osgoode Hall Law Journal*, 1.

[72] *Bell* v. *Ontario Human Rights Commission* [1971] *Supreme Court Reports*, 756.

[73] Taken from P. Weiler *In the Last Resort — A Critical Study of the Supreme Court of Canada* (Toronto: Carswell/Methuen, 1974): 140.

[74] *Supra*, note 72 at 767–8.

[75] *Supra*, note 30 at 156.

[76] For example, see the dissent of Justice Rand in *Toronto Newspaper Guild* v. *Globe Printing Co.* [1953] 3 *Dominion Law Reports*, 561 (SCC).

[77] *CUPE Local 963* v. *NB Liquor Corp.* (1979) 26 *National Reporter*, 341 (SCC). The CUPE decision was rendered in the context of labour relations. It has spilled over into other areas, e.g., *Re Shulman and the College of Physicians and Surgeons of*

132   Part Three: Litigation and Its Contexts

Ontario (1980) 111 *Dominion Law Reports* (3d) 689 (Ont. HC Div. Ct) (medical professional tribunal) and *Re Evans and Workers' Compensation Board* (1982) 138 *Dominion Law Reports* (3d) 346 (BCCA) (workers' compensation board).

[78] It may also have had a hand in the Supreme Court's tolerance of tribunals that decide Charter issues in some instances, see: *Cuddy Chicks Ltd v. Ontario (Ontario Labour Relations Board)* (1991) 81 *Dominion Law Reports* (4th) 121 (SCC); *Tétrault-Gadoury v. Canada (Employment and Immigration Commission)* (1991) 81 *Dominion Law Reports* (4th) 358 (SCC); *Douglas College v. Douglas/Kwantlen Faculty Association* [1990] 3 *Supreme Court Reports*, 570.

[79] G. Gall, 'Judicial Review of Labour Tribunals: A Functional Approach' in *Proceedings of the Administrative Law Conference* (Vancouver: UBC Faculty of Law, 1979): 305; D. Mullan, 'Developments in Administrative Law: The 1978–79 Term' (1980) 1 *Supreme Court Law Review*, 20–32.

[80] A notorious case is the *Syndicat des employés de production du Québec et al., l'Acadie and* CLRB, [1984] 2 *Supreme Court Reports*, 412 (SCC) (sometimes known as the CBC case) and see also, for example, *Lester (ww) (1978) Ltd et al. v. United Association of Journeymen and Apprentices of Plumbing and Pipefitting Industry, Local 740* [1990] 3 *Supreme Court Reports*, 644.

[81] See, e.g., *Blanchard v. Control Data Canada Ltd* (1984) 14 *Dominion Law Reports* (4th) 289 (SCC) decided on the same day as the *l'Acadie* case, with neither referring to the other.

[82] See P. Cavalluzzo, 'The Rise and Fall of Judicial Deference' in N. Finkelstein and B.M. Rogers (eds), *Recent Developments in Administrative Law* (Toronto: Carswell, 1987): 213, 225.

[83] For provocative descriptions of the courts' intervention, see H. Glasbeek and M. Mandel, 'The Legislation of Politics in Advanced Capitalism: The Canadian Charter of Rights and Freedoms' (1984) 2 *Socialist Studies: A Canadian Annual*, 84; A. Hutchinson, 'The Rise and Ruse of Administrative Scholarship' (1985) 48 *Modern Law Review*, 293; T. Ison, 'The Sovereignty of the Judiciary' (1985) 10 *Adelaide Law Review*, 1.

[84] B. Etherington, 'Arbitration, Labour Boards and the Courts in the 1980s: Romance Meets Realism' (1989) 68 *Canadian Bar Review*, 405, 408.

[85] Ibid., 409.

[86] B. Etherington, 'An Assessment of Judicial Review of Our Labour Laws under the Charter: Of Realists, Romantics and Pragmatists' (1993) 24 *Ottawa Law Review* (forthcoming).

[87] Ibid., discussing other recent instances of intervention, particularly in the context of labour relations.

[88] *Supra*, note 80 at 444, and see also *Crevier v. Attorney-General of Quebec* [1981] 2 *Supreme Court Reports*, 220, holding that judicial review of administrative action is constitutionally required at least in relation to the provinces.

[89] See dissent by Justice Wilson in *Lester, supra*, note 80 at 650, 651.

[90] See the discussion and analysis of such cases in C. Manfredi, *Judicial Power and the Charter* (Toronto: McClelland & Stewart, 1993): 132–7; B. Etherington, 'Central Alberta Dairy Pool: The Supreme Court of Canada's Latest Word on the Duty to Accommodate' (1992) 1 *Canadian Labour Law Journal*, 311.

[91] *Bhadauria* v. *Seneca College* (1981) 37 *National Reporter*, 455 (SCC).

[92] *R* v. *Mossop*, unreported, 25 February 1993, SCC.

[93] See the discussion in Chapter Three.

[94] This supervision under the rubric of 'fairness' first received the sanction of the Supreme Court of Canada in *Nicholson* v. *Haldimand-Norfolk Regional Board of Commissioners of Police* (1979) 88 *Dominion Law Reports* (3d) 671 (SCC).

[95] See, for example, *Kane* v. *The Board of Governors of the University of British Columbia* [1980] 1 *Supreme Court Reports*, 1105; *Martineau* v. *Matsqui Institution Disciplinary Board* [1980] 1 *Supreme Court Reports*, 602; *Homex Realty & Development Co. Ltd* v. *Village of Wyoming* [1980] 2 *Supreme Court Reports*, 1011.

[96] Ison, *supra*, note 83 at 29–30.

[97] *International Woodworkers of America Local 2–69* v. *Consolidated Bathurst Packaging Ltd* [1990] 1 *Supreme Court Review*, 282. But see also *Québec (Commission des Affaires Sociales)* v. *Tremblay* (1992) 136 *National Reporter*, 5. At least in Ontario, it is the legislature that has imposed formal trial-type hearings on the administrative process: see *Statutory Powers Procedure Act*, RSO 1980, c. 484.

[98] *Supra*, note 73 at 142.

[99] For example, in the Wilson and Dwivedi book, *supra*, note 1, none of the essays deal with any aspect of judicial review, though they certainly do discuss limits to and accountability of administrative actors. Similarly, an essay dealing in a broad, general way with the directions of this form of government has only the scantiest reference to any aspect of the judicial role: see R. Schultz, 'Regulatory Agencies' in M. Whittington and G. Williams (eds), *Canadian Politics in the 1990s* (3rd ed.) (Toronto: Nelson, 1990). See also *University of Toronto Law Journal*, vol. 40 (1990) *Special Issue on Administrative Law*, where very few of the papers, mostly written by lawyers, focus on the judicial role in the administrative state.

[100] D. Beatty, *Putting the Charter to Work* (Kingston: McGill-Queen's, 1987): 40, and see the book's footnotes 30 and 31 on 197 and footnote 1 on 198.

CHAPTER FIVE

Women and the Courts: '... how things must be, forever?'

INTRODUCTION

Of all the areas of law and policy, those that have undergone the greatest transformation in the last twenty years have been the ones pertaining to women. The women's movement and feminism encompass many ideas and currents, some quite disparate. However, in the last decades, there has been a tremendous questioning of women's role in society. Issues regarding work, reproductive technology (such as birth control and abortion), violence towards women, the intersection of gender, race, and socio-economic status, and the structure of the family itself (within traditional marriage and otherwise) have all been intensely scrutinized and, to some extent, altered. In terms of both courts and legislatures, there has been substantial activity in law that has paralleled changes in society.

Of course, there is nothing unique to Canada when it comes to significant changes in the relations between the sexes. Such changes may not be universal, and they have been different in various countries, but they certainly have been prominent around the globe.[1] The purpose here, however, will be to concentrate on how such issues have been played out in Canadian society and to examine the courts' role in this phenomenon. But as elsewhere, when we focus on the court's role we do so on a comparative basis. A comparison of the courts' role and that of the legislatures is particularly appropriate because their interaction has been frequent and direct and, at least before the Charter, reveals a very distinct pattern in dealing with issues. Women virtually always lost in the courts, but received some form of redress from the legislatures and their agencies. The advent of the Charter and the success of some feminist issues, particularly in the Supreme Court, brings forth a paradox — the dangers of victory. This possible contradiction is evident in the abortion dilemma and related issues. A number of court cases have established a right to abortion. Most prominent in this regard was the Supreme Court's nullification of the Criminal Code's prohibition of abortion, except under specific conditions. However, such victories did nothing to ensure women's access to safe abortions and, in fact, there is some evidence suggesting that it is now more difficult to obtain an abortion. Meanwhile, related issues critical to addressing women's disadvantage, such as maternity leave, pre- and postnatal care and day care, remain unaddressed and possibilities for establishing public-sponsored programs seem even more remote.

The 'women's movement' and 'feminism' are terms that are used in many senses with some women disassociating themselves from any connection with these labels, while an increasing number of men consider themselves feminists and part of the women's movement. In this context I regard the two terms as embracing a wide range of ideas that are not always harmonious, but that have a common purpose — to advocate change because some laws treat women unequally or unjustly because of their gender.

What message am I conveying in this chapter on women and the courts? Am I signalling that federalism, criminal justice, torts, etc., are somehow men's issues? I hope not. In fact, feminist perspectives do appear elsewhere, but I believe these issues should be treated in a separate chapter because litigation on behalf of women as a disadvantaged group may be the most fully developed. In addition, the judges' response to such questions sheds significant light on how our courts have functioned historically and how they are grappling with a movement whose ideas are challenging the premises of our social and political life. Yet while there have been successes on a number of fronts, fundamental transformation on behalf of all women lies in the future. It will be a happy day when notions of equality between men and women are so well understood, agreed upon, and implemented that a chapter such as this can be viewed as a curiosity. That day is not yet.

LOSS IN THE COURTS, REDRESS IN THE LEGISLATURE

With works like Backhouse's *Petticoats and Prejudice*,[2] we have begun to benefit from fundamental historical research on women and the law in Canada. What we know of litigation concerned with women's issues suggests clearly that courts were consistent in their refusal to alter the law in response to claims of injustice based on sex. Reviewing these decisions up to the earliest Charter cases, Beverley Baines demonstrated how judges rendered decisions that failed to take account of the changing patterns in women's lives and how '[g]ender bias . . . explains why Canadian courts have rendered [such] decisions. . . .'[3]

What is also striking is that in virtually all instances, these decisions were countered by legislatures. In observing this fact, no simple statement about cause and effect is implied, particularly in light of the discussion concerning the impact of litigation in Chapter Two. Besides reaction to court judgements, other factors, such as lobbying, law reform reports, the growth of women's groups, and general shifts in public opinion, led to these legislative responses, and even then not in a straightforward manner. Furthermore, the responses were often imperfect and obtained only after lengthy battles. Still, whatever redress was achieved for the injustices of gender inequality was gained almost always through elected officials and not the courts. We can demonstrate this by discussing several groups of cases, roughly in chronological order.

The earliest group of five cases, all decided by 1930, involved the concept of 'persons' and its application to women. The fact that women needed to argue that they were embraced within the legal concept of persons indicates how fundamental the challenges were. Three of the cases involved women who were suing to be admitted as lawyers in New Brunswick, Quebec, and British Columbia.[4] These suits were not radical, even for their time. Several provisions had been made in the nineteenth century to admit women as lawyers in the United States. Clara Brett Martin, the first woman in the British Empire to be admitted to the practice of law, had already secured her position in Ontario, after a fight with the Law Society, by convincing the Ontario legislature to pass enactments admitting women.[5]

Yet in all three instances, the women lost in the courts. Though acknowledging that the word 'persons' was sufficiently broad to encompass both sexes, the judges refused to open the doors for women for reasons embodied by the Chief Justice of New Brunswick: 'I have no sympathy with the opinion that women should in all branches of life come in competition with men. Better let them attend to their own legitimate business.'[6] In all three instances, relief for women was gained by response from the legislatures, though not until 1941 in the case of Quebec.[7]

The fourth case dealt with the conviction of a prostitute, Lizzie Cyr, for vagrancy.[8] It had two interesting issues. The first was an argument that the woman police magistrate who presided over the prosecution of Cyr was incompetent because of her gender. In one of the few decisions favourable to women, this argument was rejected, possibly because to have accepted it would have meant a direct challenge to the elected officials who appointed her. The second issue involved an argument that only men could be convicted of vagrancy because the provision making it a crime used only masculine pronouns. This was rejected because the court referred to general provision for interpretation, stipulating that words of the masculine gender were to include women. This is a sensible (if sexist) approach to the economy of words. Revealingly, this same straightforward approach was completely rejected by the courts when hearing women's applications to enter the legal profession.

It was also rejected by the Supreme Court of Canada in the famous 'Persons' case, which addressed whether women were competent to be appointed to the Senate. Lest we are tempted by illusions concerning the yearning for justice by elected officials, it is well to remember that the case would never have been brought if the government had not raised the issue of women's competence. It did so at a time when women were eligible to sit in all legislatures except New Brunswick and Ontario, and when there were already at least two female Cabinet ministers appointed.[9] Nevertheless, the Supreme Court was unqualified in its rejection of women's competence based upon tortuous reasoning regarding the historical intent at the time the provision was drafted in 1867.[10] That is how things would have stood had not an English appellate court, the Judicial Committee of the Privy Council (at that time Canada's highest court of appeal), disagreed, ruling that women were qualified.[11]

The second group of cases concerning property and support issues on dissolution of a domestic relationship were decided mostly between the mid-1960s and early 1980s, but, in one important respect, continued into the 1990s. The economic consequences of marriage and its breakup have always been one of the most pressing issues for women. In a traditional marriage, the wife often stayed at home and therefore was economically dependent upon the husband. The husband's superiority often translated into denial of property rights to the wife, both during marriage and at its termination since the common-law rules did not confer any property rights and only very limited rights to support arising from the marriage itself.[12]

By the late 1960s a marriage was starting to be viewed as an economic partnership, so that the way legal title had been arranged by either of the spouses (usually the husband in the traditional arrangements) should not, in and of itself, determine the interests of the other spouse. This issue became galvanized in *Murdoch* v. *Murdoch*.[13] Mrs Murdoch was an Alberta farm wife. In 1968, upon the breakdown of her marriage, accompanied by some violence to her, she claimed an entitlement to a share in the family ranch (which was registered in her husband's name), based on her contribution to it. When the case finally reached the Supreme Court, her claim was denied despite the vigorous dissent of future Chief Justice Laskin. Many were amazed that although Mrs Murdoch's work included 'haying, raking, swathing, mowing, driving trucks and tractors and teams, quietening horses, taking cattle back and forth to the reserve, dehorning, vaccinating, branding' and actually running the farm for five months during some years, this labour amounted to the work of 'any ranch wife' and it would not 'give any farm or ranch wife a claim in partnership'. In the end,

Murdoch was granted a lump sum maintenance payment, but this implied there was no recognition of her role in the economic unit, the household. To many, the message of the judges' law was as clear as it was disturbing. Women could be entitled to support during marriage and to maintenance after breakup in exchange for domestic duties and sexual availability on an exclusive basis for the duration of the marriage. But without other bases for claims to property, women's role in marriage was not a foundation for acquiring such a claim.[14]

Murdoch v. Murdoch became a symbol to women for the need to change family property.[15] The lobbying and educating led to legislative action that was much broader than a favourable ruling in Murdoch would have been, thus demonstrating how a loss in the courts was a catalyst for broader and long-lasting legislative change. In 1978, Manitoba was the first[16] province to approve legislation that recognized that women's domestic activities in traditional marriages made it possible for wage-earners (husbands) to earn money and acquire property.[17] The Ontario Family Law Reform Act (1978) stated that 'child care, household management and financial provision' were 'the joint responsibility of the spouses'.[18] Further, it described marriage as entailing a 'joint contribution, whether financial or otherwise, by the spouses . . . entitling each spouse to an equal division of the family assets'.[19] But the disagreement between legislatures and courts concerning financial arrangements on the dissolution of marriage continued. The Ontario legislation, s. 8, provided that a court, upon the breakdown of a relationship, could award an interest in property (other than family assets) owned by the other spouse in circumstances where there had been a contribution of work, money, or money's worth by the non-titled spouse to that property's acquisition or maintenance.

In 1978, the Leatherdales separated after nineteen years of marriage; for about half of the marriage, Mrs Leatherdale did not work outside the home, but for approximately nine years she worked in a bank, using her bank earnings for family purposes. Upon separation, the couple agreed on the division of family assets, particularly the matrimonial home. But there was an issue over two non-family assets: shares in Bell Canada valued at about $39,500 and a registered retirement savings plan of $10,000, both registered in the husband's name.

When the case arrived at the Supreme Court of Canada in 1982, the majority took the position that Mrs Leatherdale's work outside the home (during her years as an employee of the bank) constituted 'work, money or money's worth' in the words of the section.[20] But the Court was adamant that her years of work in the home, either when she was employed at the bank or when she was not, did not qualify her for s. 8 since Mrs Leatherdale's contribution was recognized and accounted for by the presumption that family assets would be divided equally. It therefore awarded her $10,000 based on her 'contribution' during the time of the marriage that she was working outside the home.

This case demonstrated the real weaknesses of the Ontario Family Law Reform Act: first, it created a difficult distinction between family and non-family assets, and second, judicial discretion to order sharing of such non-family assets led to uncertainty. The distinction between assets was artificial because it failed to take into account the fact that most husbands and wives worked jointly towards the acquisition of property throughout marriage and that women often had no independent money with which to purchase property in their own name. The reaction to *Leatherdale* set off another flurry about the courts' inadequacies concerning domestic issues, leading to 1986 legislation that declared that business assets accumulated by spouses during marriage were to be joint property,[21] a direct legislative response to the judgement.

This disagreement between courts and legislatures continued in terms of spousal support. Until the late 1960s, spousal claims for financial support after separation were based on relatively clear views of the nature of the marriage and the role of women based on a regime created by the judges. In general, an 'innocent' wife (only the wife) was entitled to support. But if a woman was guilty (especially of adultery), she was not entitled to support, even though the husband may have also contributed to the breakup of the family. Generally, the courts applied a 'one-third rule' (in terms of the husband's income) to determine the basis upon which a faultless wife was to be maintained. The connection between a husband's responsibility to support his wife and exclusive sexual access was clear.

However, by the late 1960s society had changed sufficiently so that the direct connection between exclusive sexual services and support was broken down. Treating men and women equally without considering the impact of marriage and child-rearing upon women's ability to be financially secure led to enactments that severed the direct connection between exclusive sexual services and support. Yet this also allowed claims by husbands, throwing determination in specific cases back to the courts by a grant of broad discretion. For example, the 1968 Divorce Act stipulated that 'a court *may*, if it thinks it *fit and just to do so*, having regard to the conduct of the parties and the condition, means and *other circumstances* of each of them' (emphasis added) order spousal support.[22]

Such open texture of the legislation certainly ousted the rigidity (indeed, oppressiveness) of the former regime but its cost was to turn the award of support into a guessing game. One of the great difficulties was articulating a basis for support after marriage. Was support primarily an aid to child care or was it meant to allow for a continued standard of living enjoyed in the marriage, or was it based on a view that each spouse should be responsible for himself or herself and support should only be for a transitional period to enable them to become self-supporting? It is this last basis for support (or non-support) that courts increasingly adopted, to the detriment of women in traditional marriages.

The 1985 Divorce Act indicates that spousal orders should be made based on evaluating four factors so as to:[23] (a) recognize any economic advantages or disadvantages to the spouses arising from the marriage or its breakdown; (b) apportion between the spouses any financial consequences from child care beyond that provided for in a child support order; (c) relieve any economic hardship of the spouses arising from the breakdown of the marriage; and (d) in so far as practicable, promote the economic self-sufficiency of each spouse within a reasonable period of time.

However, there was strong consensus among practitioners and academics that the courts were emphasizing the fourth factor.[24] Though this factor, on the face of it, is neutral and applies to both men and women, there are still many traditional arrangements and in most instances, the economic disadvantages of marriage fall disproportionately on women. Studies show that 64 per cent of all reasons women give for employment interruption (which reduce their earnings) are directly related to marriage (16 per cent); pregnancy or child care (42 per cent); or relocation because of the husband's employment (6 per cent). In contrast, men interrupt their employment for such reasons less than 1 per cent of the time. Further, the opportunity cost (for example, missed possibilities for promotion and accumulation of seniority) of assuming the primary responsibility for the home and children can reduce lifetime earnings by up to twice the loss arising from the actual time out of the labour force.[25]

To the extent that courts overrated dependent spouses' (wives') ability to get back to work, a lot of women, particularly when children were involved, were being economically devastated by the dissolution of a marriage.[26] This was more the case when there were children because what Canadian data there is confirms the conclusion of international studies that child support orders are generally inadequate and bear no discernible relationship to the actual costs of raising children. Child support awards rarely cover even half of the direct costs of supporting children — such as housing, food, clothing, and day care — while the substantial indirect costs in terms of the custodial parent's time, energy, and detrimental impact on her career are not compensated at all.[27] Overarching concerns of a similar nature, not discussed here, have arisen concerning custody issues.[28] It was said, '[W]e need to have a public debate and reach a consensus on a legislative level as to a new policy dealing with the family, rather than allowing it to be created indirectly.'[29]

Finally, in late 1992 in *Moge* v. *Moge*,[30] the Supreme Court directed that the factor of economic self-sufficiency was not to dominate but that courts should take all four factors set out in the 1985 Divorce Act in reaching their decisions. In particular, the Court recognized that emphasizing economic self-sufficiency without examining the underlying reality of marriage and the burdens it can impose on women would only aggravate the feminization of poverty.

While the decision in this case is to be applauded in terms of its willingness to grapple with the burdens upon women that can result from marriage, the press's portrayal of the Court's centrality in bringing about change should not escape notice. Newspapers reporting the decision carried headlines such as 'Women Suffer Most in Many Divorces, Supreme Court Says . . .'[31] and 'Making the Law Make Sense'.[32] Even a fairly careful reader of some of these stories could get the impression that the judges were mainly responsible for establishing these more progressive principles. In fact, of course, the Supreme Court was correcting seven years (1985–92) of court decisions that had regressively interpreted the 1985 statute. Moreover, those cases were consistent with how courts had responded to related issues in the past, despite the legislatures and law reform agencies' movement in a progressive direction.[33] From this vantage point, the Supreme Court was finally recognizing and, yes, facilitating a longstanding trend of majoritarian choice acknowledging, despite judicial decisions, the changing role of women and how marriage can still put them at a disadvantage.[34]

The third group of cases, those decided under the Bill of Rights, reflect a general pattern. Overwhelmingly, the judiciary was unwilling to use that document to challenge the legislators. From one perspective, it can at least be said that the judiciary was consistent, since virtually all challenges, including a few brought by men disputing legislation aimed at benefiting women, were spurned. Yet two points should be made. First, judges professed deference to legislative judgement in cases concerning Bill of Rights issues. Yet they were non-deferential in other areas, for example, in relation to human rights and labour relations issues, where the courts pruned legislation that did not comport with individualistic values. That the context of the litigation might be different does not alter the fact of judicial willingness to supplant elected officials' decisions and their agencies despite their profession of deference concerning the Bill of Rights. Second, the cases under the Bill of Rights largely involved those who most need a careful assessment of their position, particularly in terms of power imbalance: women, Aboriginals, and those accused in the justice system. So judicial uniformity fell upon those least able to shoulder it. In reviewing the Bill of Rights cases involving women's issues, specifically sexual equality, Beverley Baines observes:

> [T]he judiciary denied every claim in which women relied on the guarantee of sex equality in the Canadian Bill of Rights. Although there were at least five lower court decisions that were favourable to women, every one of these cases was reversed — either on appeal or in a later case on the same issue — by a higher court. Thus, from the perspective of women, the judiciary effectively emptied the guarantee of sex equality in the Canadian Bill of Rights of any meaning.[35]

The first set of issues were those around the rights and status of Amerindian women. The court decisions against change fitted the mould, but also revealed a deep divide among native women themselves. The court cases circled around clause 12(1)(b) of the Indian Act, which gave Indian status to wives and children of Aboriginal men,[36] but denied it to Amerindian women who marry non-status men. The children of such unions were also classified as non-status. The Royal Commission on the Status of Women had criticized this as 'a special kind of discrimination'[37] and Aboriginal women began to organize against it. Often the rationale was directed towards white justice and away from Aboriginal men; that is, it was contended that sexist elements of the Indian Act came from white legislators who were attempting to assimilate the First Peoples.[38] Eventually the legislation was attacked directly in court using the Bill of Rights. In 1973, the Supreme Court of Canada confirmed that Jeannette Corbiere Lavell had forfeited her status by marrying a white man.[39] The same result occurred for Yvonne Bedard, who tried to return to the Six Nations Reserve after a failed marriage to a non-Indian.[40] The Court held that First Peoples women were entitled only to 'equality in administration and enforcement of the law'. The Bill of Rights did not forbid 'inequality within a group or class by itself, by reason of sex'.[41] While the Court's decision was harsh, we need to realize the complexities of these issues. Amerindian women were far from united in their opposition to such sections of the Indian Act, let alone attacking them directly in court. Women such as Kahn-Tineta Horn focused on the need for her race to increase and opposed not only interracial marriage but also birth control and abortion. It was she who urged Indian groups to appeal the Federal Court of Appeal decision in *Lavell* to the Supreme Court.

With the Supreme Court unresponsive to change, the process turned, as it often has for women's issues, to education, lobbying, and the legislative process and eventually to international organizations. The most prominent example in all this activity was Sandra Lovelace. Initially she camped out on the reserve with her small son. She then joined a three-month occupation of the band office by Indian women who were trying to draw attention to hardships faced by non-status Amerindian women. She finally took her case to the United Nation Human Rights Committee. Despite the publicity and public pressure mounted by a Native Women's Walk to Ottawa in July 1979, the Canadian government was unresponsive. In 1981, the UN committee found the Canadian government in breach of the International Covenant on Civil and Political Rights.[42] As a reply, the government granted the power to individual Indian bands to request that subsection 12(1)(b) not apply to them. However, by 1984, only ninety-five of the 577 Indian bands in Canada had made such a request.[43] Finally, the clause was repealed in 1985. Meanwhile, the underlying social and political problems of Amerindian women and their people largely continued.

Some of the best documented of cases involving women's issues and the political consequences challenge the discriminatory effects of unemployment insurance on pregnant women. By the 1970s, maternity leave was granted for most working women under provincial legislation passed in the 1960s and 1970s. These acts allowed pregnant employees to leave and then resume their jobs without loss of position or seniority. Wages were replaced, in part, under the federal program of unemployment insurance unless, of course, more ample provisions in specific jobs were available (usually through bargaining by unions). Such legislation stipulated a longer qualifying period than was required for unemployment on other grounds, seemingly assuming that otherwise pregnant women might seek employment just to get support.[44]

Stella Bliss was unemployed in 1976 after having been fired. At that point she had worked long enough to be eligible for normal benefits. However, she did not apply for them because she was pregnant and did not intend to seek work until after the baby was born. She then attempted to find work, was unsuccessful, and then applied for benefits and was refused. The grounds were that because she was pregnant when she became jobless, the only unemployment benefits she was entitled to were maternity benefits, but she was not eligible for them because she had not worked long enough. Claiming discrimination, she and her supporters engaged in a legal battle leading to the Supreme Court of Canada.[45] It held that there was no discrimination because Bliss was denied benefits, not because she was a woman, but because she was pregnant. This situation was not the making of any law but of nature, which enabled only women to become pregnant.[46]

This result and its justification, which were savaged by legal commentators,[47] galvanized broader protests. Bliss became a national symbol for the women's movement and, to a lesser extent, the trade union movement. Her case had originated in British Columbia and the Vancouver Status of Women described the Supreme Court's decision as a 'kick in the stomach' for all working women.[48] Many were aghast at a decision that they perceived as highly unfair.[49] Women and workers' supporters mobilized to respond to the decision and its implications. Such action produced legislative reaction in the 1980s. For example, in 1983, the Unemployment Insurance Act was amended so that it was not necessary to be in the workplace longer for maternity than for other unemployment benefits,[50] and the Canadian Human Rights Act was altered so that discrimination because of pregnancy was no longer allowed.[51] In 1986, Ontario made similar amendments to its Human Rights Code.[52] Furthermore, the *Bliss* case became a vital impetus for women pushing for a strongly worded equality section (s. 15) and a section specifically guaranteeing the rights and freedoms equally to men and women (s. 28) in the Charter.

In testimony before the Special Joint Committee on the Constitution, Lynn McDonald, then president of the National Action Committee on the Status of Women, directly referred to the case in order to urge a clearly articulated equality clause: 'In view of the Stella Bliss case especially, it is clear that more specific directions need to be given to the courts for the interpretation of equality.'[53] She maintained that the decision demonstrated how 'unacceptable women in the labour force are if they are pregnant or if they have very young children'.[54]

When the 'notwithstanding' clause was added to allow federal and provincial governments to exempt legislation from certain Charter provisions, including the equality section, many feminists across the country cited such cases as *Bliss* and *Lavell* to re-establish the 'unconditional' status of sexual equality. Through persistence and organized support, s. 28, which guarantees that Charter rights were to be enjoyed equally by both men and women, was added and the Charter became a focal point for women's issues.[55]

WINNING ONLY TO LOSE AGAIN?

Victories and Limits

In discussing the impact of judicial decisions, particularly *Bliss*, Pal and Morton suggest that the courts' policy-making function is limited in the sense that it is not final. A Supreme Court decision will favour one side or the other, but the ultimate resolution of the issues depends on the determination, organization, resources, and wit of the combatants.[56] They extend this point to the effect of the Charter suggesting that '[it] will doubtless encourage more judicial activism but it would be a mistake to assume that such activism will in itself create a regime of judicial supremacy over the legislature or executive. Court decisions will continue to be only one tributary in the broader stream of policy making.'[57]

Women's issues have had a critical role in court judgements since the inception of the Charter. One issue, abortion, takes up the tributary stream image and illustrates the dangers of overreliance on the judiciary's power, even when it acts progressively. Excessive reliance on the judiciary and overdrawn expectations of litigation may cause the stream to course in unexpected ways or may even reduce it to a trickle so that difficult problems are not tackled to achieve more effective and lasting results.

Since the inception of the Charter, there has been a perceptible turn, at least in the Supreme Court of Canada, regarding women's issues. Though not all of them were decided under the Charter, the cases reveal a newfound sensitivity to the problems faced by women, at least those arguing for acceptance of a changed role. This alteration upon the part of the Court extends to a willingness to examine some feminist claims on terms urged by them, including a focus upon the power imbalances between men and women in this society.

In 1989 the Supreme Court of Canada effectively repudiated *Bliss*. In *Brooks v. Canada Safeway*,[58] pregnant women had been denied benefits under an insurance plan because the terms specifically stated that benefits would not be payable to pregnant women during the period around the birth. The case arose in Manitoba and at that time there was no specific prohibition regarding discrimination based on pregnancy.[59] Because of the precedence of *Bliss*, the plaintiffs lost at every level until they arrived at the Supreme Court of Canada. In a stunning, unanimous decision, they were victorious, *Bliss* was repudiated and then Chief Justice Dickson, speaking for the court, embraced a vision of protection from discrimination that would require women be treated differently than men precisely because of women's difference:[60] '[I]t is unfair to impose all of the costs of pregnancy upon one half of the population. It is difficult to conceive that distinction or discrimination based upon pregnancy could ever be regarded as other than discrimination based upon sex, or that restrictive statutory conditions applicable only to pregnant women did not discriminate against them as women.'

This attitude was carried into the *Janzen*[61] case in 1989, where the Court was vigorous in its condemnation of sexual harassment and accepted a wider definition of what constitutes such objectionable activity.[62] The perpetrator need not victimize all women (or men) on the job, nor is it limited to situations where there are 'threats of adverse job consequences should the employee refuse to comply with the demands'.[63] Instead 'sexual harassment in the workplace may be broadly defined as unwelcome conduct of a sexual nature that detrimentally affects the work environment or leads to adverse job-related consequences for the victims of the harassment.'[64] Men can be subjected as well, but because of power imbalance, women are more vulnerable: 'women may be at greater risk . . . because they tend to occupy low status jobs in the employment hierarchy'.[65]

Though a number of other cases could be discussed,[66] *Lavallee*[67] further illustrates the adoption of a perspective that is sympathetic to the context of women's lives, in this instance concerning abuse. The Criminal Code had long accepted self-defence based on a reasonable apprehension of death or grievous bodily harm and a reasonable belief that it was necessary to avoid such dangers by using force.[68] However, in addition, the courts themselves had long interpreted these provisions to require that the danger had to be imminent as a precondition of reasonableness.[69] The requirement of imminence effectively precluded defences by women who through repeated battery and abuse came to believe that they would be killed if they did not disable their abuser first when his back was turned or when he was sleeping, etc. In recognizing that such retaliation could be self-defence, the Supreme Court reinterpreted case-law recognizing that 'imminence' had developed 'from the male model of a bar-room brawl between strangers of relatively equal size and ability'[70] so that 'reasonableness is not to be viewed, as it has been historically, solely from the male perspective'.[71]

Yet despite these victories and the Supreme Court's changed attitudes, there are substantial reservations. There have also been significant defeats in that Court, particularly the striking down of the 'rape-shield' provisions of the Criminal Code.[72] Because this case runs up against 'due process' concerns being developed by the courts in criminal law under the Charter, we will deal with it in detail in Chapter Seven. Even when there were victories, many of these cases (such as those dealing with pregnancy as a form of discrimination, with sexual harassment, or with support on the dissolution of a relationship) ratified changes begun in the legislatures that the courts had initially opposed. *Lavallee* removed a barrier to the creation of defences for abused women, but it was a barrier that had been placed there by the courts themselves. Finally, as we shall see in the chapter on the Charter when we discuss the matter in detail, systematic study of equality cases in all levels of courts on behalf of women reveals dismal results. A 1989 study demonstrated that of 600 court cases under the equality provision of the Charter, only forty-four (or 7 per cent) involved sexual equality.[73] Even more disturbing was the fact that of those cases, only seven were initiated by or on behalf of women, while the other thirty-seven sought to advance the interests of men, mostly by attacking legislation or government programs designed to alleviate disadvantage suffered by women.

The Abortion Dilemma and 'All the Pageantry of Institutions'

Nowhere are the benefits and pitfalls of court rulings (particularly favourable court rulings) for those seeking reform better illustrated than in the context of the abortion debate, a highly charged issue over which there is much conflict based on religious, political, and social ideals.

Termination of pregnancy, at least before quickening (the perceptible movement of the foetus at about the sixteenth week), was historically legal and, indeed, had not even been regarded as a moral dilemma.[74] During the nineteenth century, it was gradually condemned, in part because those of British origin feared the rise of other races, referring to abortion as 'race suicide',[75] and in part because of doctors' insistence that birthing and birth control practices be brought under their authority.[76] By 1892, sanctions against abortion and all methods of birth control had been included in the Criminal Code.[77]

This legislation was a cap on discussion since few at that point supported birth control, let alone abortion. But with the Depression, various groups composed of society women, some clergy, and business men endorsed birth control as a solution to economic problems, an acceptable rationale as opposed to a woman's right to control her own body.[78] Pressure continued, brought about in part by some unsuccessful prosecutions regarding birth control[79] and in part by the appalling statistics concerning illegal abortions,[80] until in 1969 the selling and advertising of contraceptives were legalized. At the same time, doctors could perform abortions if they were done in hospital and sanctioned by a committee of physicians who concluded that it would be in the interest of preserving the life or health of the woman.[81]

But even as the grounds were liberalized, the battle lines were being drawn. By 1971, the first of repeated demonstrations was held by antiabortion groups who called for an end to all abortions. Most of this activity focused on an important figure and symbol on the other side: Henry Morgentaler. Morgentaler, a concentration camp survivor who defined himself as a humanist, told the Commons Health and Welfare Committee in 1967 that abortion should be allowed freely to women through the end of the first trimester of pregnancy. After the passage of the 1969 amendments, he continued to perform abortions in defiance of the law, announcing that he was carrying on legitimate acts of civil disobedience. Although he was repeatedly arrested and brought to trial, three Quebec juries and one in Ontario refused to find him guilty.[82] In these processes, the abortion law was attacked under the Bill of Rights. Declining to invalidate the law, in 1975 the Supreme Court said, 'The values we must accept for the purposes of this appeal are those expressed by Parliament which hold the view that the desire of a woman to be relieved of the pregnancy is not, of itself, justification for performing an abortion'.[83]

Meanwhile antiabortion groups with broader antifeminist agendas were mobilizing. By 1984, REAL (Real, Equal, Active, for Life) women became highly visible. It denounced such groups as the National Action Committee on the Status of Women as representing only radical feminists. Instead it claimed that its opposition to abortion, the equality clauses of the Charter of Rights, no-fault divorce, legislation on equal pay for work of equal value, publicly funded child care, affirmative action in employment, and legal protection of the rights of homosexuals more accurately reflected the interests of women.[84]

Though feminists and antifeminists now had a range of issues over which they were opposed, the abiding one was abortion. With the inception of the Charter and its invigorated role for the courts, feminists began to hope that the 1969 law could be struck down on the basis that the law restricted the rights of women who might elect to terminate a pregnancy. In fact, the legislation was ruled invalid with the Supreme Court's decision in *R. v. Morgentaler* in 1988.[85]

Focusing on s. 7's right to 'life, liberty and security of the person and the right not to be deprived thereof except in accordance with principles of fundamental justice', the Court centred its analysis on the administrative unevenness in requiring abortion committees. Their unavailability in some areas of the country could lead to dangerous delay or outright denial of access to safe abortions. Except for Justice Wilson, who seemed to suggest that any restriction on abortion (at least in the early part of the pregnancy) would violate a woman's Charter right, the Court emphasized that constraints could be placed on abortion, but the one under attack did not survive constitutional scrutiny.

This nullification was greeted with cheers. At last the Supreme Court had rendered a decision on behalf of women who sought change from the dominance under which they had been held. Further, after the legislation was struck down, attempts to protect the foetus through a recognition of a constitutional entitlement to life were rebuffed by the Supreme Court as an abstract issue in the absence of any legislation;[86] so too was a father's attempt to restrain a woman from having an abortion.[87]

Yet this prominent victory can alert us to the dangers of having judges decide such sensitive issues. Such warning comes eloquently from the work of Mary Ann Glendon. Glendon has studied abortion law in many Western countries and concludes that the judicialization of the issue in the United States has made it much more difficult to achieve an acceptable solution, particularly compared with the countries of Europe.[88] The decision of the United States Supreme Court in *Roe* v. *Wade*[89] liberated women from the threat of oppressive legislation relating to abortion. It did not hold that there could never be restrictions, particularly regarding the point in the pregnancy when an abortion could be performed. Yet in a society that is so dedicated to minimalist government and rights and freedoms, the implication is that any attempt to regulate the manner and timing of abortion is taken to be an invasion of women's liberty. At the same time, there is a strong view that the state has no obligation to provide safe and accessible abortion; to curb the growth of private abortion clinics whose interest is profit; to provide counselling, prenatal education and nutrition, and child care.

Glendon's point is that abortion should be addressed by providing safe and accessible procedures, at least in the earlier part of the pregnancy, but also by concern for the circumstances surrounding pregnancy. Such concern could lead to state support for women and families, so that the need for abortion is minimized and adequate child care is available. She suggests that some countries of continental Europe, where pregnancy and abortion have been addressed primarily through the legislative process, have attempted to respond to such concerns: 'Continental legislatures typically have tried to maintain the value of protecting developing human life, while showing compassion for women who find themselves in extremely difficult circumstances, all the while striving to help avoid tragic choices.'[90] In particular, she cites the example of Sweden, where in 1973 abortion reform was part of enactments that also addressed sex education and birth control. As she indicates, it is difficult to demonstrate causation, but it is the case that by the mid-1980s Sweden could claim that its rates of teenage births and abortions were significantly reduced; that country's teenage pregnancy rates are almost three times lower than that of the United States.

In examining the decision nullifying Canada's abortion laws, Glendon was struck by the fact that, despite members of the Court's disclaimers, the judgement mirrored the style and discourse of American courts in the abortion decisions. This was particularly the case for Justice Wilson, who assumes that the 'liberty' of s. 7 should be comprehended as individual liberty inspired by John Stuart Mill. She proceeds to criticize other judges for taking a narrow, deferential, procedural approach when what is required is deep analysis of 'liberty'. But as Glendon observes, 'Like the majority judges in *Roe*, Justice Wilson did not see any similar compulsion to explore the implications of the right to "life" in section 7.'[91]

We should be careful not to infer from Mary Ann Glendon's work that outside the United States and Canada, abortion issues have been placidly resolved. Indeed, she has been criticized as painting an excessively conciliatory portrait of some of the countries of western Europe and for espousing lofty but vague conclusions.[92] Yet her work pushes us to confront the danger that in judicializing abortion, the opportunity to compromise, to emphasize rights and responsibilities, may be lost. Such litigation can represent the triumph of individualism and liberalism over the values of restraint, compassion, and fairness promoted by other organizing ideas like socialism and toryism. Indeed, the abortion debate and how it proceeds may tell us a great deal about the impact of litigation, particularly under the Charter, on such issues as the interactive processes between legislatures and courts and the waxing and waning of the various ideologies that have vied for influence in our national life.

In her observation of the experience in the United States (but with refreshing curiosity and tentativeness) Glendon sends us this warning: 'Canada . . . with its traditional concern for social welfare, neighbourliness, and future generations, may be legally and politically closer in important respects to the Continent than to the United States.'[93] She goes on to discuss what occurs when courts begin to exert such power — even unwillingly — in these sensitive areas. There may be a sapping of the legislative will as politicians use the role of the courts to be much more cautious or to take no action at all,[94] despite the fact that Canadian studies suggest that single issues, specifically abortion, do not have marked influence on voting patterns.[95] The worry is that unqualified victory in courts unaccompanied by any political resolution may lead to backlash, fragmentation, and a withdrawal of the legislative and administrative processes from not only abortion but related issues as well. The absence of any law on abortion, in one sense, completely frees choice, but it can also signal an official indifference that can spread to connected areas where active state involvement is needed if the burdens on women are ever to be successfully addressed. The rise of the Family Caucus and its opposition to any program or groups that challenge 'family values' — a term that could have many meanings — in the federal Conservative Party was not 'caused' by *Morgentaler*. Yet that decision may have promoted that organization and steeled it against any parliamentary initiatives aimed at alleviating women's inequality.

In his book, *The Hollow Hope*, Rosenberg analyses the impact that *Roe* v. *Wade* actually had in the United States. He concludes that most litigation on behalf of progressive issues in recent decades has had little positive and at times decidedly negative impact. His account of litigation concerning the issues around abortion and women's rights in general is no less dismal. Whatever progress has been made on behalf of women has occurred because of the momentum of social and economic forces that predate the bulk of such litigation: 'Court decisions joined a current of social change and a tide of history; they did not create it.'[96] In addition, what the court decisions did was take the momentum from political action and lobbying as proponents of change mistook the symbolism of these judgements for real reform.[97]

Regarding *Roe* v. *Wade*, fantastic claims about its effect were made by those who lauded it ('No victory for women's rights since enactment of the 19th Amendment has been greater than the one achieved Monday in the Supreme Court')[98] and those who abhorred it ('[*Roe* v. *Wade*] may stand as the most radical decision ever issued by the Supreme Court').[99] More specifically, proponents placed great faith in such litigation to mobilize ('litigation, because it attracts television, newspaper, and magazine attention, is critical in raising the consciousness of the American public').[100]

In sifting through court decisions, legislation proposed and enacted, press coverage, polls, and academic writing, Rosenberg concludes that such effects were far more problematic. He demonstrates that the percentages of abortions did not rise after the decision but were consistent with a trend that had already developed.[101] What did continue was a very serious problem of access.[102] It was so serious that one study concluded in 1986, some thirteen years after Roe, that most hospitals had never performed abortions or 'as recently as 1985, only 17 per cent of public and 23 per cent of private, non-Catholic, short-term, general hospitals performed any abortions. . . . Even among hospitals with the capability to perform abortions, only 35 per cent performed any in 1985.'[103] Meanwhile, there is evidence that medicine, particularly obstetrics and gynaecology, is increasingly *less* interested in such procedures: 'A 1985 survey of all such residency programs found that 38 per cent of them offer *no* training at all, a nearly fourfold increase since 1976. Approximately one-half of the programs make training available as an option, while only 23 per cent include it routinely . . . [T]he percentages that provide training for second trimester abortions are even smaller.'[104] And even these statistics may not adequately represent the extent to which such programs have withdrawn that training.[105]

Any increase of access, where it has occurred, can be attributed in large part to a discomforting source in this context: the market. During 1973–6, immediately after *Roe*, abortions in hospitals rose only 8 per cent, while those performed in clinics and physicians' offices increased 113 per cent.[106] By 1985, 87 per cent of all abortions were performed in non-hospital settings. Dollars and cents loomed large in all of this: 'At least some clinics were formed solely as money-making ventures.'[107] One legal activist observed, '[s]ome doctors are going to see a very substantial amount of money to be made on this'.[108] Another claimed, 'the people that are necessary to effect the decision are doctors, most of whom are not opposed, probably don't give a damn, and in fact have a whole lot to gain . . . because of the amount of money they can make'.[109]

Also in the aftermath of *Roe* was the galvanization of an antiabortion movement with its marching, lobbying, protesting, and harnessing of the legislative process (such as the Hyde amendment reducing abortions paid for by the federal government with whatever effect). More recently, such forces have turned to picketing and harassment, and even to illegal activities such as blocking clinic doors, vandalism, death threats, bombing of clinics,[110] and even murder.[111] In addition, they have turned back to courts, where the gutting or even overturning of *Roe* v. *Wade* looms as a possibility. During the same period, pro-choice forces succumbed to their own pronouncements about the impact of victories in the courts. A National Abortion Rights Action League (NARAL) activist observed; 'Everyone assumed that when the Supreme Court made its decision in 1973 that we'd got what we wanted and the battle was over. The movement afterwards lost steam.'[112] Failing to attend to the complex and difficult business of knitting these issues into the national life, the pro-choice forces found themselves in a questionable position. A former director of NARAL suggested that 'had we made more gains through the legislative and referendum processes and taken a little longer at it, the public would have moved with us'.[113] Whether the pro-choice movement can remobilize to turn back the momentum against it, including that in the courts, remains to be seen, though some hopeful signs appeared in the early days of the Clinton administration, including the nomination of a Supreme Court Justice, Ruth Bader Ginsberg, who seems much more sensitive to the intricate relationship of courts and the political process.[114] Nevertheless, related issues around prenatal care, counselling, day care, and pay equity are receiving very little attention.

In this country there has been insufficient study of the aftermath of *Morgentaler* and related decisions,[115] which is not to say that there has not been a considerable amount written about it. Nevertheless, there is evidence that suggests these judgements have directly resulted in backlash (particularly directed at access), an erosion of the ability to compromise, and a splintering of issues that need to be connected so that the barriers to women can be dismantled.

In 1989, the federal government attempted to recriminalize abortion. Bill C-43 would have made abortion an indictable offence punishable with a maximum of two years unless it was performed by a medical practitioner who was of the opinion 'that if the abortion were not induced, the health or life of the female person would be likely to be threatened'. The bill has been characterized as saying that 'abortion was wrong in principle, but available in practice. It still treated abortion as a crime, but created a broader and more efficient exemption procedure than the old abortion law.'[116] It may have been compromise to the extent that almost all legislation is, but it was a bad one if only because it left so much up to individual practitioners who would have no public statement to guide them as to when and when not to perform the procedure. There was a 'free vote' in the House of Commons and the bill narrowly passed, but it was defeated in the Senate (a tie vote), at least in part by a strange alliance between pro-life and pro-choice forces voting against it, though for very different reasons. That unrepresentative body having spoken, the government announced that it would not make further attempts. Then Minister of Justice Kim Campbell, in explaining the government's decision, made a questionable claim: 'The democratic process has functioned.' Earlier in the same interview, she made a statement with an even more disturbing linkage to the concerns we have been discussing: 'I think you'll find action by the provinces . . . that will generate . . . litigation. We will have to wait for . . . the Supreme Court . . . to provide the kind of *national certainty that people want*' [emphasis added].[117]

All federal law dismantled, there are no longer shackles upon women regarding abortion, at least at that level of government. Removal of laws criminalizing abortion responds to the first problem of legal barriers to obtaining an abortion. The other concern is access to abortions in a supportive environment. Having no law at all certainly removes restrictions to performing the procedure, but, paradoxically, may at the same time signal a lack of concern regarding when and how abortions are performed, if at all. This indifference may spill over to related issues where positive action on the part of government and public funds are required for sex education, family planning, research into better birth control, pre- and postnatal care, and day care.

While it is true that there was restricted access before *Morgentaler*, it is clear that these problems continue with even more complexities. In Prince Edward Island, access has been non-existent[118] and will apparently stay that way according to the new premier, Catherine Callbeck.[119] In Alberta, restrictions were increased using the province's constitutional control over health care services, so that abortions could be performed only in hospitals after a second opinion and with the government paying only a modest fee.[120] In Saskatchewan, there have been repeated attempts to drop the procedure altogether from Medicare and otherwise reduce access.[121] From the Northwest Territories have emerged horrifying accounts of women being subjected to the procedure without anaesthetics in racist and misogynistic circumstances.[122] In British Columbia, members have resigned from hospital boards rather than follow the government's directive to provide abortion services.[123]

In Newfoundland[124] and Ontario, abortions in clinics are now paid for and the number of such procedures in the latter province have increased substantially.[125] There is also litigation to force such payments in Manitoba[126] and to permit clinics in Nova Scotia.[127] However, the clinics in

Ontario are in Toronto, leaving serious questions about access to abortion in that province;[128] only about half of the obstetricians/gynaecologists and less than 1 per cent of family physicians perform the procedure.[129] The clinics have been the subject of harassment, court actions to obtain injunctions to eliminate picketing, and finally a bombing in May 1992.[130] A hopeful sign has been the Ontario health minister who, reacting to a governmental task force, has promised to take action to improve access.[131]

At the same time, the federal government has done nothing to encourage steps to clear for use the abortifacient, RU 486 (which would move termination a long way to being a private matter) despite pressure from doctors, Ontario's health minister, and others. The experience of women in France, Sweden, and Britain suggests that RU 486 eliminates pregnancies in the initial weeks and reduces physical trauma. Yet the French manufacturer of the drug refuses to submit it for approval, claiming it fears backlash from antiabortion groups.[132]

Meanwhile, related issues have been ignored or have splintered. The Royal Commission on Reproductive Technology is in shambles, the members having taken to using litigation on each other.[133] Charges of unrepresentativeness and insensitivity swirl around the Canadian Panel on Violence, despite the fact that it is headed by a woman who has dedicated herself to such issues and although the panel includes members of visible minorities and Aboriginal communities. The National Action Committee on the Status of Women leads the charge.[134] Child care, a critical vehicle for equality for women, barely wobbles on[135] as the federal government abandoned its commitment to a national day care policy in 1992[136] while *Maclean's*, in 1993, pronounced such a policy 'dead'.[137]

There is litigation awaiting hearing by the Supreme Court of Canada that attacks the Income Tax Act's restrictions on child-care allowance.[138] Significantly, if successful, the removal of limits to deductibility of child-care expenses would only apply to those who are independently employed and, of course, many in that position would be men. The challenge is being brought by a woman lawyer, a profession that has many independently employed partners in law firms who could claim such benefits.[139] The case is pending, but, win or lose, there are significant reservations about this strategy voiced even by those who are willing to recognize a role for litigation and rights. Such litigation has implications for the privatization of child care and 'It has divided the child care lobby, and indeed, significantly demobilized a powerful section of that lobby — upper income, self-employed professional parents — who stand to benefit from that business expense deduction.'[140] At about the same time, a main political result of the *Schachter* decision (discussed in Chapter Three) has been to include natural fathers in the unemployment insurance benefits after the baby is born, but at the price of having those benefits reduced from fifteen to ten weeks.

Yet these issues around reproduction and child care surge forward so that, however resolved, their significance is now indelible. Perhaps surprisingly, I will give the last words to a federal Cabinet minister. I frequently disagreed with the government of which Barbara McDougall was a member. I am not certain that I entirely agree with her here. Nonetheless, her 'pageantry of institutions' speech on the abortion Bill C-43 demonstrates that political debate is yet capable of great conviction and eloquence:

> This miscarriage of an unborn child is a natural abortion. It is the body saying 'no'. Why, if the woman is a whole being, cannot her mind, her intellect, her spirit make that same decision? . . . And make no mistake, women make the right choice, a far better choice than you or I or all the pageantry of institutions that have been invented . . . from the beginning of time.[141]

CONCLUSIONS

Until the Charter, there was a clear pattern of misunderstanding, even hostility, in the courts regarding women's concerns. Advancement, such as it was, came from the legislatures and administrative agencies and institutions, which even today are unrepresentative of women in terms of numbers. Since the Charter, there have been some significant victories, at least in the Supreme Court. Yet when women's interests are making a breakthrough in an institution that was unresponsive for so long, voices arise saying, 'This may not be such a good idea after all?' Can these reservations be just another deflection of feminism, parading as support? Suspicions may increase when other warnings about overreliance on litigation come from those whose sympathy for feminism is far from clear.[142]

Nor is it true that those most concerned about alleviating disadvantages of women have all seized on the courts as the solution. There are success stories in the last decade where courts have had a small role or none at all. One such example is legislation and administrative programs dealing with pay equity that alleviate inequality of remuneration between men and women through the concept of equal pay for work of equal value. Ontario's program, which began in the mid-1980s and was North America's most ambitious,[143] was largely brought about through lobbying and educational efforts that were by no means easy.[144] An account of LEAF, the organization so instrumental in much of the litigation on behalf of women, depicts many attempts to connect its efforts with those of diverse community groups that work for women in other ways.[145] Mary Eberts, one of the foremost litigators on behalf of women, freely discusses the limits of litigation[146] and has herself been a leader in the policy-making process for such issues as midwifery and pornography.

Yet the claims for litigation continue. Two examples of newspaper stories dealing directly with the issues can illustrate. In the first entitled 'Political Cowardice Blamed for More Active Role of Courts',[147] Peter Burns, the former dean of the University of British Columbia law school, and Justice Michel Proulx of the Quebec Court of Appeal appeared at a conference and discussed the *Lavallee* case, involving recognition that an abused woman might not necessarily have to show imminent danger to establish a defence. Both praised the decision, but neither indicated that the 'imminence' requirement was imposed by the courts in the first place. Instead, Justice Proulx is reported as saying that there would be no way a male-dominated Parliament would pass a law recognizing such a defence. This is quite possibly not true, but is beside the point, given that the courts had imposed the obstacle to the defence in the first place. So as not to be outdone, Burns is then reported as making remarks, not confined to *Lavallee*, about how politicians are afraid to address tough legal questions: 'It is the role of Parliament to act and it has abrogated its responsibilities so the court has filled the vacuum.'

The second newspaper article concerns the aftermath of the *Butler* decision in 1992, which upheld a federal antipornography law. The decision was hailed as a breakthrough. Catharine MacKinnon, the prominent American feminist who helped write an intervenor's brief in support of the law, declared in a front-page story in the *New York Times*: 'This makes Canada the first place in the world that says what is obscene is what harms women not what offends our values.'[148] But this cheering may be misplaced. The relationship between pornography and harm is deeply controversial, perhaps particularly among those seeking to improve the lot of women.[149] Another feminist perspective challenges such cause and effect and urges that 'equality and freedom of expression are not separable: they are two sides of the same coin. . . . Equal pay for work of equal value is no more or less important than the right of women to explore the range and depth of human experience.'[150]

The point here is not to determine the correct side in the debate but rather to suggest the dangers of constitutionalizing it and housing it in the domain of judges at a time when it is stormily unfolding in public opinion, including among feminists themselves. Meanwhile, a year after *Butler*, there was little evidence of any crack-down on degrading pornography, though there were accusations from the gay and lesbian community that police were using *Butler* as an excuse to seize and prosecute their erotica.[151] In any event, what the Court's ratification of the statute did involve was a long, hard court battle that drained and deflected the reserves of the groups that supported the legislation and prevented them from dealing with other issues.[152]

Meanwhile, in terms of both stories, one thinks of Glendon's expressive image: 'Court majorities with an expansive view of the judicial role, and their academic admirers, propelled each other, like railway men on a handcar, along the line that led to the land of rights.'[153] True, there have been imaginative attempts, including some by feminists, to transform rights discourse.[154] Nonetheless, Glendon's stark rendering needs to be before us:

'[I]n its simple American form, the language of rights is the language of no compromise. The winner takes all and the loser has to get out of town. The conversation is over.'[155] In fact, the observations of Sandra Burt raise serious questions about who is winning. Surveying changing feminist perceptions of justice in English Canada, Burt comes to this sober conclusion: 'The earlier focus by women's groups on lobbying for legislative changes has been diluted by a litigation strategy which has been disappointing. This disappointment is reflected in the observation of a women's group activist who works with victims of violence. "I can't tell yet. I think it's better now. But I don't personally know of one woman whose life has been changed [by the Charter]. It's not real to me yet".'[156]

It is sadly true that democracy is only what people make of it. There have been brilliant successes and dismal failures, sometimes simultaneously. It is not surprising, then, that those who make exaggerated claims for litigation and those who excoriate it both do so in the name of bettering democracy. Others are left to grapple with the territory between the two extremes where courts at one glance seem so much the hope to stir recalcitrant bureaucracies, jittery legislators and a dulled citizenry and then, at another, appear destined to separate questions from those who will have to live with the answers erecting fences of rights hammered together by the discourse of lawyers and judges. For litigation to be part of exposing the foibles of democracy is desirable, even necessary. But for the business of courts to replace democracy or even be perceived as a substitute is to enter dangerous terrain. Such a view is not based on a romantic depiction of our other agencies of government but quite the opposite: democracy must be constantly told to do its duty, for it is a sad truth that it will often shirk it if allowed.

Yet I have explored the problems of 'victories' in litigation in the context of feminism because of its strength. One cannot traverse the land of the law without being struck by how women's voices have been influential in law and politics during the last two decades. Though sniped at and blunted, though at times itself deeply divided by race, class, culture, and other fractures, feminism cascades forth: unstoppable, brimmed with promise.

> *Was a man who smiled in this way daring you not to believe, not to acknowledge, not to agree, that this was how things must be, forever?*
>
> — Alice Munro, *Friend of My Youth*[157]

NOTES

[1]D. Anderson, *The Unfinished Revolution: The Status of Women in Twelve Countries* (Toronto: Doubleday, 1991).

²C. Backhouse, *Petticoats and Prejudice — Women and Law in Nineteenth Century Canada* (Toronto: The Osgoode Society, 1991).

³B. Baines, 'Women and the Law' in S. Burt, L. Code, and L. Dorney, *Changing Patterns — Women in Canada* (2nd ed.) (Toronto: McClelland & Stewart Inc., 1993): 243 at 245.

⁴See *In Re Mabel P. French* (1905) 37 *New Brunswick Reports*, 359; *In Re Mabel Penery French* (1912) 17 *British Columbia Reports*, 1; *Dame Langstaff* v. *The Bar of Quebec* (1915) 47 *Cour Supérieure*, 131, (affirmed [1915]), 25 *Cour du Banc du Sov.* 2, 11.

⁵C. Backhouse, '"To Open the Way for Others of My Sex": Clara Brett Martin's Career as Canada's First Woman Lawyer' (1985) 1 *Canadian Journal of Women and the Law*, 37.

⁶In *Re Mabel P. French, supra*, note 4 at 361–2.

⁷Baines, *supra*, note 3 at 249–50.

⁸*Rex* v. *Cyr (Alias Waters)* (1917) 2 *Western Weekly Reports*, 1185 aff'd 3 *Western Weekly Reports*, 849.

⁹Baines, *supra*, note 3 at 254.

¹⁰*Reference re Meaning of the Word 'Persons' in Section 24 of the British North America Act, 1867* [1928] *Supreme Court Reports*, 276.

¹¹*Henrietta Muir Edwards et al.* v. *Attorney-General for Canada* (1929), (1930) *Appeals Court*, 124 (PC).

¹²This pattern of economic dependency had its antecedence in the nineteenth century. The economic power imbalance between husbands and wives contributed significantly to the continued suppression of women and women's rights in such matters as physical autonomy throughout marriage, access to divorce, and serious barriers to custody of children in the event of marriage breakdown. For an excellent socio-legal account of the role of women in nineteenth-century Canada, see Backhouse, *supra*, note 2.

¹³*Murdoch* v. *Murdoch* [1975] 1 *Supreme Court Reports*, 423.

¹⁴A. Prentice et al., *Canadian Women — A History* (Toronto: Harcourt Brace Jovanovich, 1988): 398–9.

¹⁵See M.J. Mossman, '"Running Hard to Stand Still": A Feminist Perspective on the Family Law Reform Process — Property and Support Entitlements on Marriage Breakdown' (unpublished, Osgoode Hall Law School, York University, May 1989): 27:

> Most commentators recognized that the problem faced by Mrs Murdoch now required legislative action. An editorial in the *Toronto Star* in 1973, for example, suggested that the decision was both 'a warning to women and a cue to legislators'; citing the recommendation of the Royal Commission on the Status of Women that the law should recognize 'the concept of equal partnership in marriage', the editorial suggested that reform was needed to prevent other 'Irene Murdochs [from being] left out in the cold with less than $60 a week to show for a quarter-century of labour'. This sentiment was echoed in other media comments and in letters to the editors, the *Globe and Mail*, for example, suggesting that $200 per month was 'not much for a lifetime of work'. An editorial

in *Chatelaine* magazine in January 1974 suggested that the Murdoch decision was a chilling warning: 'The Supreme Court protects males but not females' [citations omitted].

[16] First, that is, after *Murdoch*. Quebec had reformed its family law provision of the Civil Code beginning in the late 1960s; see e.g., SQ 1969, c. 77, SQ 1977, c. 72; SQ 1980, c. 39.

[17] Marital Property Act, SM 1978, c. 24 (M-45).

[18] Family Law Reform Act, RSO 1980, c. 152, s. 4(5).

[19] Ibid., s. 4(5).

[20] [1982] 2 *Supreme Court Reports*, 743.

[21] The *Family Law Act*, SO 1986, c. 4 provided for a strict equalization formula to divide assets at the time of marriage breakdown, thus removing judicial discretion for the most part. As well, it eliminated the distinction between family and non-family assets in keeping with the act's policy to ensure that both spouses shared equally in any economic gain during the marriage.

[22] Divorce Act, 1968, SC 1970, c. D-8, s. 11(1).

[23] Divorce Act, 1985, SC 1986, c. 3, s. 15(7).

[24] And see the trio of Supreme Court of Canada cases that emphasize this factor in the context of alteration of separation agreements: *Caron* v. *Caron* [1987] 1 *Supreme Court Reports*, 892; *Pelech* v. *Pelech* [1987] 1 *Supreme Court Reports*, 801; *Richardson* v. *Richardson* [1987] 1 *Supreme Court Reports*, 857.

[25] C. Schmitz, 'Courts' Emphasis on "Self-Sufficiency" for Divorce Act Support Awards Causing Hardships for Ex-Spouses, Kids?' *The Lawyers Weekly* 9, no. 16, 1 September 1989, 16.

[26] Ibid., 16.

[27] Ibid.

[28] S. Boyd, 'Child Custody Law and the Invisibility of Women's Work' (1989) 96 *Queen's Quarterly*, 831 at 852:

> Only through struggles for social and legal change in these other areas that affect parenting can we create conditions which give incentives to men as well as women to engage in parenting. Until we have achieved a more genuine form of 'equality' within families and within the social and economic structures shaping the decisions that individuals make concerning their families, putting a norm which assumes 'equality' of parenting in our family law is a mistake.

[29] *Supra*, note 25 at 17.

[30] *Moge* v. *Moge* (1992), unreported, 17 December 1992.

[31] S. Fine, 'Women Suffer Most in Many Divorces, Supreme Court Says', *The Globe and Mail*, 18 December 1992, A9. See also J. Middlemiss, 'Self-Sufficiency No Longer Key, Court Says', *Law Times*, 4–10 January 1993, 1.

[32] S. Fine, 'Making the Law Make Sense', *The Globe and Mail*, 10 April 1993, A1.

[33] See, for example, Law Reform Commission, *Maintenance on Divorce*, Working Paper No. 12 (1975).

[34] See also A. Mitchell, 'Common Law Spouse Wins Equal Share', *The Globe and Mail*, 26 March 1993, A3, discussing *Peter* v. *Beblow*, 25 March 1993, awarding a share of the assets to a woman in a common-law relationship.

[35]Baines, *supra*, note 3 at 259.

[36]Indian Act, RSC 1970, c. 1–6 s. 12(1)(b).

[37]*Report of the Royal Commission on the Status of Women* (Ottawa: Information Canada, 1970): 237–8; 'The Mohawk Women of Caughnawaga, '"The Least Members of Our Society"' (1980) *Canadian Women's Studies/Les cahiers de la femme* II, no. 2, 64.

[38]*Supra*, note 14 at 397. The social and political circumstances around status issues and the continuing state of turmoil is analysed at length in S. Weaver, 'First Nations Women and Government Policy, 1970–92: Discrimination and Conflict' in Burt et al., *supra*, note 3.

[39]*Attorney-General of Canada* v. *Lavell; Isaac* v. *Bedard* (1973), [1974] *Supreme Court Reports*, 1349.

[40]*Lavell* and *Bedard* were heard together (1973), [1974] *Supreme Court Reports*, 1349.

[41]*Lavell* 1350, *Bedard* 1372–3.

[42]*Supra*, note 14 at 398, and E. Hutcheson, M. Eberts, B. Symes, *Women and Legal Action: Precedents, Resources, and Strategies for the Future* (Ottawa: Canadian Advisory Council on the Status of Women, 1984): 17–18; C. Lachapelle, 'Beyond Barriers: Native Women and the Women's Movement' in M. Fitzgerald, C. Guberman, Margie Wolfe (eds), *Still Ain't Satisfied: Canadian Feminism Today* (Toronto: The Women's Press, 1982): 257–64.

[43]*Supra*, note 14 at 398.

[44]Ibid., 380–1.

[45]*Bliss* v. *Attorney-General of Canada* (1978), [1979] 1 *Supreme Court Reports*, 183.

[46]*Supra*, note 14 at 422–3.

[47]For example, D. Réaume, 'Women and the Law: Equality Claims Before Courts and Tribunals' (1979) 5 *Queen's Law Journal*, 3; J. MacPherson, 'Sex Discrimination in Canada: Taking Stock at the Start of a New Decade' (1980) 1 *Canadian Human Rights Reporter*, c. 7; M. Gold, 'Equality Before the Law in the Supreme Court of Canada: A Case Study' (1980) 18 *Osgoode Hall Law Journal*, 336.

[48]'Cabinet to Re-examine UIC Maternity Benefits', *The Globe and Mail*, 1 November 1978, 14.

[49]L. Pal and F.L. Morton, '*Bliss* v. *Attorney General of Canada*: From Legal Defeat to Political Victory' (1986) 24 *Osgoode Hall Law Journal*, 141 at 143. This article is an excellent analysis of the ramifications of the *Bliss* case.

[50]Unemployment Insurance Act, as am. SC 1980–81–82–83, c. 97 [s. 4].

[51]Canadian Human Rights Act, SC 1985, c. H-6 [s. 3(2)].

[52]Ontario Human Rights Code, RSO 1980, Ch. 340 [s. 4(6)].

[53]Canada, Special Joint Committee of the Senate of the House of Commons on the Constitution of Canada, *Minutes of Proceedings and Evidence*, vol. 9 at 59 (20 November 1980).

[54]Ibid., 64.

[55]C. Hosek, 'Women and the Constitutional Process' in K. Banting and R. Simeon (eds), *And No One Cheered — Federalism, Democracy and the Constitution Act* (Toronto: Carswell/Methuen, 1983): 280; *supra*, note 49 at 156.

[56]*Supra*, note 49 at 159–60.

[57]Ibid., 160.

[58]*Brooks* v. *Canada Safeway Ltd* [1989] 1 *Supreme Court Reports*, 1219.

[59]See Human Rights Code, SM 1987–8, c. 45; s. 9(2)(f) of the new code prohibits discrimination on the basis of 'sex, including pregnancy, the possibility of pregnancy, or circumstances relating to pregnancy'.

[60]*Supra*, note 58 at 1243.

[61]*Janzen* v. *Platy Enterprises* [1989] 1 *Supreme Court Reports*, 1252.

[62]See also the decision of the Manitoba Court of Appeal: (1986) 38 *Manitoba Reports* (2d) 20.

[63]*Supra*, note 61 at 1282.

[64]Ibid., 1284.

[65]Ibid., 1285.

[66]For example, see: *R.* v. *Butler* [1992] 2 *Western Weekly Reports*, 577 (SCC); *Norberg* v. *Wynrib* [1992] 4 *Western Weekly Reports*, 577 (SCC); *Mary Sullivan and Gloria J. Lemay* v. *R.* [1991] 1 *Supreme Court Reports*, 489; *M (K)* v. *M (H)* (1992) 96 *Dominion Law Reports* (4th) 289.

[67] *Lavallee* v. *R.* [1990] 4 *Western Weekly Reports*, 1, 55 *Canadian Criminal Cases* (3d) 97.

[68]See *Canadian Criminal Code*, RSC 1990, c. C-46, s. 34(2).

[69]For example, *R.* v. *Baxter* (1976) 27 *Canadian Criminal Cases* (2d) 96; *R.* v. *Whynot* (1984) 37 *Criminal Reports* (3d) 198.

[70]Justice McLachlin discussing the case in a more general treatment of the burdens of the criminal law may impose on women: B. McLachlin, 'Crime and Women — Feminine Equality and the Criminal Law' (1991) 1 *University of British Columbia Law Review*, 16.

[71]Ibid., 17.

[72]*R.* v. *Seaboyer* (1991) 2 *Supreme Court Reports*, 577.

[73]G. Brodsky and S. Day, 'Canadian Charter Equality Rights for Women: One Step Forward or Two Steps Back?' (Ottawa: Canadian Advisory Council on the Status of Women, 1989).

[74]*Supra*, note 14 at 165.

[75]Ibid.

[76]C. Backhouse, 'Involuntary Motherhood: Abortion, Birth Control, and the Law in Nineteenth Century Canada' (1983) 3 *The Windsor Yearbook of Access to Justice*, 61, and W. Mitchinson, 'The Medical Treatment of Women' in Burt et al., *supra*, note 3 at 391, 407–8.

[77]Ibid., 252.

[78]Mitchinson, *supra*, note 76 at 406.

[79]Ibid., 252, describing the prosecution of Dorothea Palmer.

[80]'Between 1954 and 1965 there were 226 therapeutic abortions performed in Canadian hospitals, and an estimated additional 50,000 to 100,000 illegal abortions. In British Columbia, abortion related deaths accounted for one in every five maternal deaths occurring between 1946 and 1968': *supra*, note 14 at 323.

[81]Canadian Criminal Code 1968, RSC 1970, c. C-34, s. 251.

[82] *Supra*, note 14 at 365.
[83] *Morgentaler v. The Queen* [1976] 1 *Supreme Court Reports*, 616, 671.
[84] *Supra*, note 14 at 365–6.
[85] *R. v. Morgentaler* [1988] 1 *Supreme Court Reports*, 30.
[86] *Borowski v. Attorney-General of Canada* (1989) 57 *Dominion Law Reports* (4th) 231.
[87] *Tremblay v. Daigle*, [1989] 2 *Supreme Court Reports*, 530.
[88] M.A. Glendon, 'A Beau Mentir Qui Vient Du Loin: The 1988 Canadian Abortion Decision in Comparative Perspective' (1989) 83 *Northwestern University Law Review*, 569.
[89] *Roe v. Wade* 410 US 113, 93 S. Ct 705 (1973).
[90] *Supra*, note 88 at 583–4.
[91] Ibid., 580.
[92] See, for example, L.P. Francis, 'Virtue and the American Family' (1988) 102 *Harvard Law Review*, 469; H. Ietswaart, 'Incomplete Stories' (1989) 69 *Boston University Law Review*, 257; M. Fineman, 'Contexts and Comparisons' (1988) 55 *The University of Chicago Law Review*, 1431; J. Cohen, 'Comparison-Shopping in the Marketplace of Rights' (1989) 98 *Yale Law Journal*, 1235.
[93] *Supra*, note 88 at 590–1.
[94] Ibid., 588:

> American experience suggests that the real danger represented by regular invalidation of legislation on constitutional grounds is not that elected representatives will rise up in anger against the courts. On the contrary, legislators are often relieved at being able to say their hands are tied by the courts, especially where controversial matters are concerned. One danger is, rather, that of atrophy in the democratic processes of bargaining, education, and persuasion that take place in and around legislatures. Another is that by too readily preventing compromise and blocking the normal political avenues for change, courts leave the disappointed majority with no legitimate political outlet. The West European experience has been instructive on this matter. There, leaving abortion primarily to legislative regulation has not put an end to controversy. Public debate about abortion in Europe is vigorous and often heated. But it is not marked by the degree of bitterness, desperation and outrage that occasionally erupts into violence in the United States.

[95] B. Kay et al., 'The Impact of Single-Issue Interest Groups on the Canadian Electorate: The Case of Abortion in 1988', a paper prepared for presentation at the 1989 Annual Meeting of the Canadian Political Science Association, Laval University, Quebec City, 3 June 1989 (on file).
[96] G. Rosenberg, *The Hollow Hope — Can Courts Bring About Social Change?* (Chicago: University of Chicago Press, 1991): 265.
[97] But see N. Devins, 'Judicial Matters' (1992) 80 *California Law Review*, 1027. This lengthy review of *The Hollow Hope* is generally critical of the book. It takes issue with Rosenberg's account of the abortion controversy arguing, for example, that subsequent decisions such as *Webster v. Reproductive Health Services* 492 US 490 (1989), while appearing to help pro-life forces by undermining *Roe*, actually set off a pro-choice reaction among legislators: 'That . . . transformation of the status quo involves not just judicial action but also market conditions, elected government,

and interest groups, is beyond dispute. The judiciary, however, is certainly a partner in this dynamic process' (p. 1065).

[98] *Supra*, note 96 at 173 for the quotes cited.

[99] Ibid., 173 for the quotes cited.

[100] Ibid., 236.

[101] Ibid., 178–9.

[102] See also L.A. Schreiber, 'What Kind of Abortions Do We Want?' *The New York Times Book Review*, 17 January 1993, 13, citing statistics showing that 83 per cent of the counties in the United States have no known abortion provider.

[103] *Supra*, note 96 at 190.

[104] Ibid., 194.

[105] See editorial 'The Unfinished Abortion Battle', *The New York Times*, 12 May 1993, A10: 'Over the last 20 years many residency programs in obstetrics and gynecology have made abortion training an elective, or stopped offering it at all. Today only 13 per cent require training in first-trimester abortions, and only 7 per cent require second trimester training. (Nearly 25 per cent required both in 1985.)'

[106] *Supra*, note 96 at 196.

[107] Ibid., 198.

[108] Ibid.

[109] Ibid.

[110] Ibid., 187.

[111] E. Goodman, 'Abortion War: From Mayhem to Murder', *The Detroit News*, 16 March 1993, 15A.

[112] *Supra*, note 96 at 339.

[113] Ibid., 340.

[114] E. Schmitt, 'Clinton Orders Reversal of Abortion Restrictions Left by Reagan and Bush', *The New York Times*, 23 January 1993, 1; D. Margolick, 'Judge Ginsburg's Life a Trial by Adversity', *The New York Times*, 25 June 1993, A1; N. Lewis, 'Judge Ginsburg's Opinions: At the Center, Yet Hard to Label', *The New York Times*, 27 June 1993, A1; N. Lewis, 'Ginsburg Deflects Pressure to Talk on Death Penalty', *The New York Times*, 23 July 1993, A1.

[115] Though an important initial contribution is J. Brodie, S. Gavigan, J. Jenson, *The Politics of Abortion* (Toronto: Oxford University Press, 1992); see also F.L. Morton, *Morgentaler v. Borowski: Abortion, the Charter, and the Courts* (Toronto: McClelland & Stewart, 1992); C. Manfredi, *Judicial Power and the Charter* (Toronto: McClelland & Stewart, 1993): 114–19.

[116] R. Knopff and F. Morton, *Charter Politics* (Toronto: Nelson Canada, 1992): 289.

[117] G. York, 'Senators Kill Abortion Bill with Tied Vote', *The Globe and Mail*, 1 February 1991, A1.

[118] A. Picard, 'One Year After Abortion Law Struck Down, Little Has Changed', *The Globe and Mail*, 28 January 1989, A13.

[119] K. Cox, 'Callbeck on Track to Being 1st Woman Elected as Premier', *The Globe and Mail*, 25 January 1993, A4.

[120] I. Urquhart, 'Federalism, Ideology, and Charter Review: Alberta's Response to

Morgentaler' (1989) 4 *Canadian Journal of Law & Society*, 157.

[121]Knopff and Morton, *supra*, note 116 at 31, describes one such attempt in the 1980s before the Morgentaler decision; see also A. Mitchell, 'Abortion Foe's Hope for Victory in Saskatchewan', *The Globe and Mail*, 6 May 1992, A1.

[122]M. Cernetig, 'NWT Orders Abortion Inquiry' *The Globe and Mail*, 2 April 1992, Al.

[123]D. Wilson, 'Hospital Ends Abortion Ban After Board Members Quit', *The Globe and Mail*, 2 April 1992, A8.

[124]See 'Newfoundland Changes Policy on Abortions', *The Globe and Mail*, 18 November 1992, A8.

[125]A. Mitchell, 'Clinic Abortions Soar, Figures Show', *The Globe and Mail*, 13 March 1992, A7.

[126]D. Roberts, 'Manitoba Must Pay for Clinic Abortions', *The Globe and Mail*, 3 March 1993, A6.

[127]D. Vienneau, 'Morgentaler Begins "Final" Battle over Abortion', *The Toronto Star*, 4 February 1993, A1.

[128]A. Mitchell 'Abortion Rate Reaches New High', *The Globe and Mail*, 3 June 1993, A6.

[129]R. Mackie, 'Lankin Promises to Make It Easier to Obtain Abortion', *The Globe and Mail*, 19 December 1992, A6.

[130]See 'Archbishop Condemns (Morgentaler) Clinic Bombing' *The Globe and Mail*, 29 June 1992, A9; 'Ontario to Rebuild Abortion Clinic: Arson Cited in Bombing', *The Globe and Mail*, 20 May 1992, A1.

[131]*Supra*, note 129; R. Mickleburgh, 'Ontario Seeks Court Order', *The Globe and Mail*, 20 April 1993, A5.

[132]'The Abortion Pill: A Question of Choice', editorial, *The Globe and Mail*, 9 October 1992, A28.

[133]See L. Hurst, 'Should This Inquiry Be Decommissioned?' *The Globe and Mail*, 5 December 1991, A20; L. Hurst, 'Battle Royal: Is Royal Commission on Reproductive Technology Self-Destructing?' *The Toronto Star*, 1 December 1991, B1, B7; H. Branswell, 'Renegade Royal Commission Members Expect to Be Fired Monday', *Montreal Gazette*, 14 December 1991, A9.

[134]J. Simpson, 'Shrug Off the Mosquito Bites and Get On With the Good Work', *The Globe and Mail*, 20 August 1992, A20; J. Rebick, 'Panel Refused to Deal With NAC's Concerns', *The Globe and Mail*, 26 August 1992, A13.

[135]S. Pigg, 'Day Care in Metro Nearing Collapse', *The Sunday Star*, 27 January 1991, Al.

[136]G. York, 'Government Scraps Day Care Commitment', *The Globe and Mail*, 27 February 1992, A1.

[137]N. Wood, 'Who Cares? — Why "National Day Care" Is Dead — Parents Seek Their Own Solution', *Maclean's*, 31 May 1993, 34.

[138]For a thoughtful article arguing that such deductions should be allowed, see D. Eamsor and C. Wydrzynski, '"Troubled Waters": Deductibility of Business Expenses under the Income Tax Act, Child-Care Expenses and *Symes*' (1993) *Canadian Journal of Family Law* (forthcoming).

[139]The case *Symes* v. MNR is pending in the Supreme Court as of writing. See E.

Newman 'Fair Tax Treatment for Child Care Takes Centre Stage in Canada', *Canadian Lawyer*, April 1993, 12.

[140]B. Cossman, 'Dancing in the Dark: A Review of Gwen Brodsky and Sheilagh Day's *Canadian Charter Equality Rights for Women: One Step Forward or Two Steps Back?*' (1990) 10 *Windsor Yearbook of Access to Justice*, 223 at 235.

[141]Quoted in J. Brodie et al., *supra*, note 115 at 76.

[142]*Supra*, note 116.

[143]M. Freudenheim, 'Ontario Law Matches Women's Wages to Men's, *New York Times*, 21 July 1989, A1; P.C. McDermott, 'Pay Equity in Ontario: A Critical Legal Analysis' (1989) 28 *Osgoode Hall Law Journal*, 381–407.

[144]I. Scott, 'Reforming the System: Consultation and Collaboration' (1990) 24 *Law Society of Upper Canada Gazette*, 42.

[145]S. Razack, *Canadian Feminism and the Law — The Women's Legal Education and Action Fund and the Pursuit of Equality* (Toronto: Second Story Press, 1991): 56–8, 131–2.

[146]M. Eberts, 'The Uses of Litigation under the Canadian Charter of Rights and Freedoms as a Strategy for Achieving Change' in N. Nevitte and H. Kornnerg (eds), *Minorities and the Canadian State* (Oakville: Mosaic Press, 1985); J. Kassel, 'Courts Not Only Solution to Fighting Inequality', *Law-Times*, 2–8 March 1992, 2.

[147]D. Vienneau, 'Political Cowardice Blamed for More Active Role of Courts', *The Toronto Star*, 11 July 1991, A12.

[148]T. Lewin, 'Canada Court Says Pornography Harms Women and Can Be Barred', *New York Times*, 28 February 1992, A1.

[149]W. Kaminer, 'Feminists Against the First Amendment', *The Atlantic Monthly*, November 1992, 111.

[150]C. Ruby, 'Law and Society', *The Globe and Mail*, 1 December 1992, A24, quoting Thelma McCormick, director of the Centre for Feminist Research at York University.

[151]S. Fine, 'Confusion about the Meaning of Porn', *The Globe and Mail*, 26 March 1993, A13.

[152]S. Noonan, 'Harm Revisited: *R. v. Butler*' (1992) 4 *Constitutional Forum*, 12, 16: '[I]n spite of juridic pronouncement sympathetic to the victimization of women and children, how much has actually been accomplished?'

[153]M.A. Glendon, *Rights Talk: The Impoverishment of Political Discourse* (New York: The Free Press, 1991): 7.

[154]For discussion of some important attempts; see J. Brodie et al., *supra*, note 115 at 117 *et seq*.

[155]*Supra*, note 153 at 9.

[156]S. Burt, 'What's Fair? Changing Feminist Perceptions of Justice in English Canada' (1993), forthcoming, *Windsor Yearbook of Access to Justice*, quoting L. Lakeman, Canadian Association of Sexual Assault Centres, interview September 1991.

[157]A. Munro, *Friend of My Youth* (New York: A Borzoi Book, Alfred A. Knopf, Inc., 1990): 86.

CHAPTER SIX

The Judges and Tort: Purpose and Limit

INTRODUCTION: THE REALM OF 'PRIVATE' LAW

In this chapter we look at litigation and 'private' interests, specifically through the eyes of tort law. There are two elements to this exercise that need to be examined at the outset: what do we mean by 'private' law and why are we focusing on 'torts'?

There have literally been volumes written on the public/private distinction in law and whether such a separation is tenable. Part of the difficulty is that the terms mean different things to different people in various contexts. Sometimes 'private' is used in a way similar to its popular meaning to suggest that the law should respect certain behaviour and moral choices as beyond its reach, for example, varied forms of sexual activity between consenting adults or the right of parents to choose when and under what circumstances to have children and to make decisions about how they should be raised and educated. However, at other times, 'private/public' means removing some areas from the law's scrutiny when instead it is critical that the state assert an interest, for example, in domestic situations where abuse of spouses or children is taking place.

When 'private' is applied to litigation, it often describes lawsuits involving non-governmental actors. It has long been asserted that when governmental actors are not present in the lawsuit, the legal issues are qualitatively different and courts must be particularly cautious not to trample on the rights of individuals because 'private' rights are being worked out in a neutral forum provided by the state. This linking of 'private' and a neutral forum echoes the traditional model of litigation we discussed in Chapter Three.

A decidedly liberal cast surrounds all of this: the talk of individuals and their rights, the suspicion of governmental actors, the insistence that individuals take responsibility for their actions. The reaction to these tenets has been equally predictable: an assertion that all law is the product of state action, that 'private' interests (particularly large corporations) can assert powerful influences on society and that every time a judge rules, she is engaging in a value-laden and 'public' task since the force of the state will be put behind the victor's judgement.

This chapter will refer to 'private' litigation, but only to denote a shorthand description of lawsuits that primarily involve disputes between individuals and non-governmental entities. Even this limited use will sometimes be inaccurate since we will see that many of the doctrines generated in private litigation have implications for governments and their agencies when they engage in certain activities. In any event, there is nothing 'private' about the law that is created since all rights and responsibilities do flow from the state through the judges' pronouncements.

There are a number of areas of private litigation that could be analysed: corporate, contracts, trusts. But, for several reasons, the most fruitful area is that of torts. First, torts is the most wide-ranging area. Fundamentally, any action is tortious if the law regards it as wrong and will order some form of redress. Second, theoretical and analytical writing is most highly developed in this area of law. In particular, Ernest Weinrib's ideas and reactions to them are highly pertinent to issues about the function of litigation generally in Canadian society and, more specifically, its limitations. Finally, there are impulses to reform that would remove some important tortious activities from the courts either entirely or in vital aspects. Again, the reasons for such reforms and the reaction to them tell us much about expectations concerning courts and their function in Canadian society.

These expectations are by no means disconnected from discussions concerning courts in other countries, particularly England and the United States. Here, Canada is considerably closer to the former rather than the latter. Focusing on those two countries and the role of tort law litigation, Atiyah asserts flatly, 'Nobody in England would regard tort law as playing more than a very peripheral role in the life of the society. . . .'[1] In stark contrast is his summary of the reach of tort in America: 'because so many areas of public life and activity are controlled by the courts in America (as opposed to being regulated by the legislature or the government, as they are in England), tort law is a more central part of the means of social control in America. Together with the free market, tort law thus plays in America very much the role set for it by liberal theorists who wish to minimize the collective role of the state and the legislatures.'[2]

Whether tort litigation (or other areas of 'private' law) has had anywhere near the effect claimed for it, even in the United States,[3] has been seriously doubted.[4] Such doubts lead back to many of the issues about impact raised in Chapter Two where we saw that the gap between the claimed and actual consequences of litigation can be substantial. What lawsuits may do is deflect attention away from other solutions to problems that might come from other divisions of government. Such channelling may, indeed, be the overarching consequence of tort litigation in the United States. In contrast, as indicated by Atiyah, the role of torts is much more closely circumscribed, and regarded as such, in Canada. This is not to say that discussions of the courts' role in Canada are easy or do not have a highly relevant ideological overlay. What does emerge, though, is a perspective about litigation that suggests a utility that is nevertheless limited. Such attitudes deliver important messages in terms of this book's larger themes concerning an important but bounded role for judges in determining complex social and political issues.

THE FUNCTIONS OF TORT LAW

Of all the rules created by judges, those involving torts may be the most pliant. This is because they are defined with a very broad range: 'a tort is a civil wrong, other than a breach of contract, which the law will redress by an award of damages.'[5] Or, to put it bluntly, a tort is what a judge characterizes as a wrong for which she will order some form of redress.[6]

Such a description is hardly crisp and orderly, but conveys the potential of tort law to put its stamp upon virtually any human interaction if someone involved believes she has been harmed. Consider the sense of its scope:

> The driver of every automobile on our highways, the pilot of every airplane in the sky, and the captain of every ship plying our waters must abide by the standards of tort law. The producers, distributors, and repairers of every product, from bread to computers, must conform to tort law's counsel of caution. No profession is beyond its reach: a doctor cannot raise a scalpel, a lawyer cannot advise a client, nor can an architect design a building without being subject to potential tort liability. In the same way, teachers, government officials, police, and even jailers may be required to pay damages if someone is hurt as a result of their conduct. Those who engage in sports, such as golfers, hockey-players, and snowmobilers, may end up as parties to a tort action. The territory of tort law encompasses losses resulting from fires, floods, explosion, electricity, gas, and many other catastrophes that may occur in this increasingly complex world. A person who punches another person in the nose may have to answer for it in a tort case as well as in the criminal courts. A person who says nasty things about another may be sued for defamation.[7]

As the great regulator of human conduct — at least in the eyes of the judges — torts provide an excellent opportunity to study how the judiciary believes society ought to be run in terms of bearing of loss and shifting of risk.[8]

Tort's most obvious goal is compensation of the victim for the injuries sustained because of a wrongdoer's activities. One of the critical issues that has arisen is the range of victims to be recompensed. This is because redress has focused on wrongdoing for a long time: only the injured who establish fault or negligence on the part of the perpetrator are successful; the rest are not compensated, no matter how sympathetic their plight. This limiting of recovery to some version of fault was clearly meant to reflect the individual's freedom of activity in the liberal state, to be curtailed only for a compelling reason. So Holmes in a classic version of such sentiment asserted, 'A loss must lie where it falls . . . [the state's] cumbrous and expensive machinery ought not to be set in motion unless some clear benefit is to be derived from disturbing the status quo. State interference is an evil, where it cannot be shown to be a good.'[9]

Such sentiments were complementary to the needs of capitalism's entrepreneurial activity. However, their harshness and the suffering that resulted caused a reaction. Through devices such as *res ipsa loquitur* ('the thing speaks for itself' — a provision to partially shift the onus of proof onto defendants) and negligence per se, the net of compensation was enlarged and a direct reaction to Holmes developed asserting that 'worthwhile "social gain" *is* achieved by shifting losses from innocent victims'.[10] The main fulcrum for this shift was the notion of loss distribution, which asserts that the consequences of accidents are no longer transferred from individual to individual but are shifted to those who are responsible for most such mishaps — industrial enterprises and other insured activities — with the loss ultimately spread to the larger community.[11]

A criticism of this shift to loss distribution is that, though it is well intended, it is a poor substitute for a proper scheme of social welfare benefits. What in fact has evolved in Canada is a three-level system of compensation. At the base are social welfare schemes that provide hospital and medical care and some income replacement for injury or illness. At the second level are several schemes that provide fuller compensation on a no-fault basis for special groups in society, such as workers, or victims of crime and, in some jurisdictions, auto accidents. At the third level is tort litigation, which provides the fullest compensation for those who are willing to sue and who can establish that their injury is the fault of the person they seek to hold responsible. What the right mix of these three levels may be is an important question. We will return to specific debates about these questions later in the chapter.

The second purpose of torts — deterrence — is said to act in two ways. First, someone who is ordered to pay damages for loss caused by her substandard conduct will try to avoid a recurrence. Second, a tort judgement stands as a warning to others. A judgement sends the message that tort, like crime, does not pay. Indeed, civil actions for tortious conduct can follow on the heels of criminal prosecution for the same act or be used in substitution where, for whatever reason, the criminal process is not proceeded with. Yet it is not clear to what extent deterrence is actually realized through tort law. The empirical evidence available is indeterminate and some tort scholars have alleged that the admonitory function is a myth[12] or at least that its possibility is 'of a low order'.[13] Realizing such a function is difficult for at least four reasons.[14]

First, some are simply unwilling to conform with the articulated standards. Second, some may be willing to conform, but simply are not able to. Third, the public, even those directly implicated by a certain rule, may be totally ignorant of it. This was clearly illustrated by the Robertson study on the standard of care for doctors regarding informed consent discussed in Chapter Two. Finally, the widespread availability of insurance has removed the sting (and the threat) of judgement. In the motor vehicle area, it has been argued there is little if any deterrent effect because of almost universal coverage. It may be the case that insurance companies may be interested in reducing accidents to reduce their pay-outs and they may attempt to effect deterrence through premium adjustment. However, it is also unclear to what extent the public actually understands the relationship between claims on an insurance policy and premium adjustment.[15]

Another device insurance companies can employ is to cancel insurance. But an American study disclosed that only 2 per cent interviewed thought their policy could be cancelled after an accident, which tends to suggest that 'an unperceived penalty cannot deter future deviant conduct'.[16] Deterrence, insurance, and their relationship will be returned to again when we discuss the debate over 'no-fault' and auto accidents later in this chapter.

Related to the function of deterrence is tort's third goal: education. Tort law is held to be a reinforcer of values by publicly marking wrongdoers and vindicating those they have injured. It is true that non-compliance with the standards of torts is not so egregious as arson, robbery, rape, or murder. But all these acts are both crimes and torts and both branches of the law operate to publicly denounce the acts. Of course, it is also the case that since moral values infiltrate the law so slowly, torts may continue to reflect precepts that no longer command obedience in the larger society or at least have been drastically modified.[17] Tort law can also be an outlet for vengeance and, indeed, it is said this was one of the primary reasons for creating torts: 'It is better to pursue a wrongdoer with a writ than a rifle.'[18] Linden also asserts that tort litigation can counter feelings of alienation in our large and complex societies. Such litigation can provide an opportunity, for those who can avail themselves of it, to regain some measure of control over their lives. In this light, the complex and arcane aspects of such lawsuits are seen as potential strengths: 'More and more of us, suffering from "future shock", are searching for bridges with the past, points of stability, to comfort us as the world races by. The traditions of litigation may supply some medicine for this ailment.'[19]

Finally, market deterrence differs from the deterrence discussed above as it functions indirectly. The central idea is that the cost of accidents should be borne fully by the activities that cause them. Again, there are other ways of reducing accidents, for example, through criminally backed prohibition of very dangerous activities and administrative regulation of activities that have a dangerous element. The idea is that market deterrence should function as a supplement to other means when the activity is one society wishes to continue with less stringent control. Moreover, it clearly reinforces a respect for free choice in a free market and, therefore, has a strong ideological component. So long as the prices of the various commodities reflect the full cost of providing them, consumers should choose because they are the ones to decide what is best for themselves.[20]

It is said that market deterrence operates in two ways to reduce the cost of accidents. First, financial incentives are created for people who are involved in dangerous activities to switch to safer ones. This is because if those involved in a hazardous undertaking have to pay for its full cost, some may transfer to a safer and cheaper activity. Second, this deterrence urges individuals to alter the *way* in which activities are conducted rather than the *type* of activities. Bearing the full cost will encourage individuals to eliminate aspects of the activity that are the cause of the injuries.

There are two shortcomings of market deterrence that question its efficacy. First, there is little empirical evidence to show that it actually operates or, if it does, the situations in which it works best and worst. Its success will turn at least in part upon the fluctuating demand for the product or activity. In addition, its impact will depend on the amount of the price made up by accident costs. If the proportion of accident costs in comparison with labour and material is very small, deterrence will not have much impact. Conversely, such deterrence would likely have more consequence if *all* costs of *all* accidents — whether premised on fault or otherwise — were reflected in the price of the enterprise.

Second, market deterrence discriminates against the poor. To some extent, this is a truism since any aspect of market functioning necessarily must discriminate against those less well endowed. Nevertheless, the consequence of market deterrence is to consciously allow the financially superior to embrace activities not available to the economically disadvantaged. In this sense market deterrence 'works like a regressive tax'.[21] It is one thing to acknowledge the market as an economic regulator. It is quite another to embrace all its consequences as a theory of justice.

WEINRIB AND CORRECTIVE JUSTICE

Whatever rationale one looks towards, notions of individualism and individual responsibility loom large. The fault system may be flawed because of cost, delay, difficulty of administration, and its denial to many who are injured. Yet the fact that it is a philosophical beacon in terms of individualism and notions of responsibility causes many to venerate its moral firmness in this age of 'adjustments', 'relativism', and assorted postmodern prescriptions: 'The philosophy of the age of reason, not determinism, still permeates tort law. The fundamental goal is individual restraint and respect for one's fellow creatures, something which is required more than ever in mass urban societies.'[22]

None have saluted this as high ground more than Ernest Weinrib. In a series of articles published in Canada, the United States, and England that span almost two decades, he has focused his ideas about how tort law ought to reflect notions of individual responsibility, particularly embodied in the concept of corrective justice. His writing is important to us in a number of ways. First, in Weinrib's prolific output, there is not only a theory of torts but also one of the few developed conceptions of litigation. We will see that it is not comprehensive and that is one of its obvious shortcomings. Nevertheless, it is a challenging attempt to explore the terrain. Second, in insisting upon a limited role for courts centred around individualistic values, Weinrib is not driven by hostility towards the welfare state and its underlying values. Indeed he is one legal scholar who has some insight into the diverse ideologies that construct our governance. Third, in supporting individualistic values as the heart and soul of litigation on the one hand, and as a firm supporter of progressive values in the legislature on the other, he launches a strong retort to those who focus on courts as a source, perhaps the primary resource, for enlightened governance. This latter position reaches its high-water mark with American adherents and Weinrib's exchange with one of its foremost proponents is illuminating in terms of the two very different perspectives. Finally, Canadian scholars' reaction to Weinrib's ideas pushes us further in a theory of torts, but also towards an understanding of litigation and our society.

Drawing on Aristotle's theory of corrective justice and Kant's concept of right, Weinrib has constructed a theory of tort law centred upon the defendant's action and the plaintiff's suffering as a result. The intimate relationship between the two gives torts a special morality.[23] This special relationship is an end in itself and renders irrelevant other justifications for tort — deterrence, compensation, and wealth maximization.

From this core arise five critical aspects.[24] First, tort law is not to concern itself with an ordering of an aggregate of transactions. As a consequence, loss-spreading through insurance cannot be the basis for liability since that distribution of losses functions across a set of potential transactions instead of within a single transaction. Second, treating each transaction as a unit suggests internal integration of all elements: if there is an integral relationship of doing and suffering regarding the harm, then the involved parties cannot be considered independently of each other. It follows that deterrence does not have a role because deterrence contemplates a focus on the doer regardless of the absence of any specific victim. Even compensation has no necessary role because it focuses on the victim. For compensation to be a rationale, there would be no basis for insisting on causation by the defendant or on making the wrongdoer pay. Third, the parties need to be equal. Thus, an objective standard of negligence must be applied so that the doer's personal qualities are irrelevant to the relationship. The fourth point follows from the third — that it is not open to tort law to award the victim compensation and in turn allow the wrongdoer to continue the activity on that basis. The defendant's duty to the plaintiff embraces the obligation to refrain from the harmful enterprise. Fifth, since tort litigation is limited to the defendant's doing and the plaintiff's suffering of the same harm, it is not for a court to engraft some independent policy that is judged to promote the general welfare: 'tort law is not public law in disguise.'[25]

It is important to emphasize that Weinrib is explicit in his support of the social welfare net woven in Canada. He points to the relative elaborateness of such schemes in Canada compared with the United States to explain a greater fidelity to his model in the former and great pressures to develop more expansive basis for compensation in the latter:

> [T]he callous and niggardly response of the world's richest democracy to the tragedies of sickness and disability means that often the injured person must seek compensation in tort or not at all. The courts are then tempted to produce what the political process has withheld, and tort law becomes an instrument of policy for achieving such goals as loss spreading, resource allocation, and the redistribution of wealth from the deeper pocket.[26]

He looks to the ideological diversity of Canada, a theme coursing through this book, to explain developments that run largely in a contrary direction than those in the United States:

> [T]he survival of a more pristine conception of private law in Canada was perhaps facilitated by the sustained liberal and even social democratic influence on the political process and by a conservative tradition that encouraged the realization of the common good through state action. When the pressures of change can thus be channelled through public law, there is perhaps less need for courts to trench on and tamper with the domain of private right.[27]

Having paid tribute to the social justice of welfare schemes, Weinrib rests content with a model of tort law that exists for doer and sufferer whatever the implications in the real world of loss and prevention of loss. Others may focus on such ends as deterrence or compensation as goals for torts and debate the extent to which such ends are realized. But for Weinrib, such discussion is essentially beside the point because it is far too goal-oriented: 'a symptom of our estrangement from the internal mode of justification represented by corrective justice. . . .'. Instead, the focus for a theory of corrective justice for torts must be a 'normative immanence' because it is 'the justificatory structure that renders tort law intelligible from within'.[28]

Weinrib does not have a great deal to say about the structure of litigation and its ability to either impede or facilitate access for those not financially endowed or, indeed, the relationship of issues concerning access to the 'immanence' of tort law. Nevertheless, corrective justice can rationalize the traditional bipolar structure of a lawsuit better than many other legal theories.[29] Since the only parties to the lawsuit are the plaintiff and the defendant, the only correct choice for a judge is to focus upon the wrong one has caused to the other (the 'doing', the 'suffering') without regard to broader policy aspects. So this tight and limited structure is a signal to eschew distributive implications that speak only to one party but implicate many who cannot be heard in that litigation. We saw a roughly parallel set of ideas when we discussed Glenn's opposition to class actions in Chapter Three.

This coincidence between corrective justice and the traditional structure of litigation has led Owen Fiss, an exemplar of the potential of litigation to cure society's — at least American society's[30] — ills to excoriate Weinrib's depiction of the lawsuit.[31] We looked at Fiss's ideas earlier in Chapter Two in connection with claims about the power of litigation to structure society and in Chapter Three regarding his boosting of a more public model of litigation. From this stance, he might not only agree with Atiyah's assertion but salute it: 'It is . . . no exaggeration to see American tort law as the major means for setting norms and standards for social and economic behaviour.'[32] Fiss believes adjudication has to respond to modern political and social failings and in doing so refocus from singular acts of wrong involving individuals to scrutinizing acts of institutions with their capacity for mass wrongs. For him, the paradigmatic action is a lawsuit on behalf of some group or other collective interests leading to a 'structural' remedy empowering the court to bring a recalcitrant institution — school, hospital, prison — to heel so that its fidelity to the Constitution or other public values is assured theoretically and practically.[33]

With this view of the litigation terrain, Weinrib's ideas are to be dismissed. Generally eschewing, in his eyes, the Canadian approach to law and litigation ('more oriented towards automobile accidents than the pursuit of equality')[34] none make a better target than Weinrib and his 'academic concoction':[35]

> [A]ny court system held to [the corrective model] would become an empty and trivial institution. The 'inner intelligibility' that Weinrib's model of corrective justice promises might be of great attraction to the scholastics and others drawn to formal systems, but of no interest to anyone else, especially to those seeking justice . . . [I]t would leave unfulfilled the deepest social aspirations of the law — to use reason to confront those who possess state power and to show them how that power might be used, and indeed must be used, to build a world that is worthy of the ideals we hold in common.[36]

In responding directly to this attack, Weinrib alleges that Fiss's realm of public values rests on little more than his say-so and can claim no transcendent legitimacy:

> The fundamental deficiency of Fiss's jurisprudence is that it moves too facilely to law from an inadequate conception of public value. Fiss's premise, often repeated, is that the function of adjudication is to give meaning to public values. Nowhere, however, does he satisfactorily explicate the 'publicness' of values. . . .
> . . . Fiss also believes that law has an inherent worth and dignity. Where does this inherent worth come from? It cannot derive from the public value of societies like Iran or Nazi Germany, because those particular values have, *ex hypothesi*, no worth or dignity. Neither can the law's inherent worth have some other source, if it did, the law's character would not be determined by the society's public values.[37]

Riveted by the gap between these two models of litigation, Roach has stepped in and, with admirable Canadian moderation, has called for 'synthesis'.[38] He reassures by asserting that 'there seems to be little immediate danger of falling in the trap set by the public law model of devaluing or ignoring alternatives to litigation'.[39] But then he cautions not to put too much faith in 'expansive strategies'[40] for legislatures and their agents. To do otherwise 'risks disenfranchising those who cannot get past legislative and administrative gatekeepers, while a traditional approach to adjudication only aggravates their powerlessness by depriving them of a credible threat of judicial intervention'.[41] He concludes, 'A society that cannot imagine its disadvantaged going to court to achieve reform will have an impoverished sense of justice; one that relies on such Herculean efforts will have an illusory one.'[42] This is an inspiring statement of balance — in the abstract. How to achieve it, in fact, is an entirely different matter and a central dilemma posed by this book.

From a different stance, it is a telling criticism of Weinrib's theory that, though he is supportive of other schemes to effect instrumental goals such as compensation and deterrence so long as they are propounded by legislatures, he gives virtually no clue when such arrangements should be struck and how, if at all, they should be connected to his model of litigation. For example, we can only guess what Weinrib would say about the schemes for 'no-fault' coverage of automobile accidents and the proposals for the elaborate interwoven framework between the administrative scheme and court adjudication for redress of damages caused by health care discussed later in this chapter. Moreover, in elaborating his model, Weinrib illustrates it with references to tort and to a lesser extent property and contract issues.[43] What, if anything, does he have to say about federalism, Charter, and administrative law issues where notions of fault and individual responsibility often fit awkwardly, if at all? Further, his model seems starkly ahistorical. One would have thought claims about discrimination were classic candidates for the doer, for the sufferer. Yet tort claims of discrimination, as we saw in Chapter Four, were systematically spurned by the courts. The legislatures were forced to act not to create a distributive scheme lying outside Weinrib's model but to fashion a scheme to expose the doer and to vindicate the sufferer of one and the same wrong, the goal that lies at the heart of his prescription.

Further, Weinrib has been taken to task for the divergence between the 'immanence' of his model and actual injuries and suffering and the way they are caused.[44] Alleging that Weinrib asserts the inner coherence of his model rather than ever demonstrating it, Hutchinson reminds us that the very implications of corrective justice are a matter of debate[45] with others suggesting it should lead to principles of strict liability,[46] and still others using corrective justice as a basis to shift to no fault.[47] Hutchinson alleges that, in consequence, Weinrib's theory fails to take account of the complex and mass-produced world out of which many tortious injuries now arise and which are so often perpetuated by powerful corporations, impersonal entities that cannot be equated with 'Kantian moral persons', 'noumenal selves', and 'freely purposive beings'. Meanwhile, to be indifferent to the capacity of these large corporations to either create risk or to avoid it is to callously ignore the real people who actually bear the injuries caused by these entities.[48] In such circumstances, doing and suffering are not 'unique and dichotomous' but 'probabilistic and continuous'. In the world of Agent Orange, Bhopal, DES, Chernobyl, the Dalkon Shield, and Three Mile Island, the interrelationship of many factors prevents confident attribution regarding any particular causes for any particular injuries: 'The attribution of responsibility is simply a conclusion based on a rebuttable hypothesis of probabilistic generality.'[49]

Such a powerful and persistent attempt to bound tort litigation and, incidentally, strongly buttress the traditional bipolar construction of a lawsuit was destined to draw strong reactions. While admiring his powers in describing and defending his ideas, few seem ready to enlist in Weinrib's cause. Yet his insistence on a core and limited value to litigation — as seen through tort laws — is yet another attempt to limit litigation, an enterprise we see throughout this book. Here the claim is that its legitimacy rests in devoting it to very circumscribed ends.

LINDEN AND TORT AS AN OMBUDSMAN

Faced with complex goals that are sometimes unattained and sometimes conflicting, Linden, a leading author on tort law, has struck out on an entirely different tack, one that does not answer Weinrib directly and, indeed, is some distance from his model. Linden proposes moving torts from the means through which individuals obtain redress by being awarded damages for wrongdoing to a tool to react to abuse of power, whether arising from common law or under statute, or whether perpetuated by governmental, corporate, or union actors. Tort law would become an ombudsman; administrative schemes would be largely to effect compensation. Whether the power abused is political, economic, or intellectual, torts would be there perhaps as 'the only recourse available to an aggrieved person, other than a protest march or an act of violence'.[50]

Linden sees torts playing this role in any number of areas. Through torts citizens will be able to prod government regulatory agencies to fulfil their mandate. It will serve as a weapon of change for products liability leading to a form of consumer democracy: 'a tool of immense potential in the movement for a more humane society'.[51] So, too, will the environment receive additional protection from this tool. And the professions will by no means be immune from such scrutiny: 'a healthy and vibrant profession must constantly justify its stewardship.'[52]

For Linden, there are three advantages to tort's roles as ombudsman. First, the judiciary's independence insulates it from pressures to stifle protest that are at work in the many areas where relevant issues will arise. Second, individual citizens are empowered to engage the supervisory machinery: both the defendant and the court itself must react to the filing of a suit. Third, litigation and its focus on specific issues reduce larger concerns to the concrete questions in contrast to anxieties about vague concerns like world competition, loss of jobs, professional autonomy, and technological expertise. Most lawsuits attract little attention other than from those involved, but when an action causes publicity, it may be the most threatening aspect of the litigation: 'damage awards and fines are relatively easy to forecast, whereas the result of bad publicity is impossible to prophesy.'[53]

Nevertheless, Linden recognizes institutional limitations on this role. First, the substantive law may not yield a decision consistent with the ombudsman model. The role of precedent and Canadian judicial conservatism and the values underlying it may constrain such an undertaking for torts: 'present negligence law may dictate a dismissal of a defective product claim, nuisance law may be unavailable against certain polluters, and an erroneous police arrest may be held to have been reasonable in the circumstances.'[54] Having said that, Linden adds a point about the capacity of a regressive decision having a more catalytic effect and leading to far more wide-reaching legislative change than one consistent with more progressive values. This is a phenomenon we saw loom large in Chapter Five in the discussion of women's issues, particularly before the Charter:

> Paradoxically, a harsh decision in a well-publicized tort case may stimulate legislative reform, whereas a decision that corresponds with our sense of justice may lull us into a false sense of security. Progressive scholars who assert that negligence liability has become strict because of *res ipsa loquitur* and other such devices may be impeding rather than accelerating the movement towards tougher controls on government and business. Legislators may think all is well, when it is not. A plaintiff who loses a tort case after a trial in the glare of the media

may be more help to future victims than one who wins. A judge who says no may do more good than one who says yes.[55]

Second, the expenses of the litigation process can constitute a serious limitation, one that we discussed in Chapter Three. The costs of one's own lawyer, the threat of paying the other side's costs in the event the case is lost, the expenses of investigating the claim and hiring experts can all be disincentives:[56] '[L]awsuits which test the frontiers of tort law are difficult to finance. Only the rare case, the rare litigant and the rare lawyer become involved in such litigation.'

Still, Linden remains optimistic and insistent. He recommends a number of devices to shore up this ombudsman model, for example, creating a rule of strict liability in products cases, allowing contingent fees where they do not exist to offset the risk of the plaintiff's lawyer's fees, limiting the number of tort trials, permitting wide intervention so that the implication of the litigation could be fully articulated, and improving the amount and quality of media coverage. He ends on a high note, concluding that 'tort law as an ombudsman and as a weapon of social reform may turn out to be its most promising function in the decades ahead. It may well become its primary raison d'être in the future.'[57]

TURNING FROM TORT?

Introduction

The administrative state in Canada fulfils many functions, a matter discussed earlier in Chapter Four. One of the more important ones is as a direct alternative to tort litigation. We saw in Chapter Four that for several reasons, such as inefficiencies in delivering compensation and judicial hostility in the recognition of new entitlements, administrative schemes were developed as alternatives to tort law in areas such as human rights-discrimination, collective organizing and bargaining, compensation for victims of crime, and workplace injuries — though, as we saw in that chapter, these schemes can themselves be flawed. For example, there are very serious problems that now surround administrative agencies enforcing human rights. In addition to such schemes, variants of which exist in many developed countries, there are social welfare nets — health care, unemployment insurance, welfare benefits, old age pensions — that are available to help fulfil basic needs, including those arising from personal injury.

The existence of such regimes as alternative models, on the one hand, and the deficiencies of tort litigation, on the other, have been the source of a movement, by no means confined to Canada, to scrap torts or at least greatly curtail its scope, particularly in the case of personal injury.[58] The allegation is that many personal injuries go uncompensated and that even when victims do receive compensation, they face enormous delays, costs, and psychological traumas that defeat any ambition to construct efficient and humane models for redress. Similarly, it is contended that the deterrence element of tort law has not been demonstrated to curb undesirable activities. Such proponents, therefore, would effect compensation through some form of administrative no-fault scheme or the social insurance system or both. The deterrence function would also be achieved by some element of an administrative scheme or, in more serious instances, through the criminal law.

While proponents of this position argue in a number of ways, depending on the context, three basic components can be distilled: horizontal equity, community responsibility, and different instruments for different objectives.[59] The first, horizontal equity, is a requirement that those whose needs are equivalent ought to receive equivalent benefits. From this perspective, torts is criticized for creating a regime where victims of accidents are favoured: those injured by others may be fully compensated, but those damaged in some other way receive nothing from that regime even though their needs could be equal to those compensated through the torts system. Likewise, workers' compensation schemes and existing no-fault administrative regimes, are criticized as preferring injured workers since they usually receive more comprehensive benefits than those sustaining similar or sometimes even the same damage off the job. Such criticisms ground an argument that financial need arising from illness ought to be treated much the same as those resulting from accidents. Once this train of argument is initiated, it is said the other causes of need like unemployment, retirement, congenital disabilities, or dissolution of domestic relationships ought to be treated alike.

The second component, community responsibility, asserts that responding to life's hazards should be viewed primarily as a collective rather than individual responsibility. This view of redress has two main elements. First, since society as a whole is the beneficiary of economic activities, it should bear the cost of unavoidable hazards of random incidents. Second, a collective response based on horizontal equity (the first component) would result in a publicly administered scheme with the related subordination of private insurance.

The third component, different instruments for different objectives, asserts that since one policy instrument cannot achieve many goals that are not always harmonious, different tools should be used to achieve different goals: criminal and regulatory instruments for deterrence; compensation schemes for redress to victims. Torts would deal with areas outside of personal injury, such as defamation.

What surfaces from these three arguments is faith that a more humane world lies outside the torts system and that that world should embrace collective responsibility rather than the atomistic notions that are the bedrock of tort. Again we return to an earlier theme. The world of the courts is one of traditional liberal values; a sense of individualism driven by economic entitlement. Its justice is a limited one and harsh for those who do not comply with its demands for initiative, persistence, and proof of wrongdoing without regard to the power and resources of those involved. The alternatives are about societal goals and responsibility where some limited refuge based on need, regardless of responsibility, is provided as some response to the hazards of the industrialized corporate state. It is too stark to describe it as social democrats against liberals, but there is no mistaking the parallel in sentiment and argumentation. We can examine these arguments against litigation and the resulting complexities by looking at compensation for auto accidents and health care, two areas of ongoing debate.

Automobile Accidents and
No-Fault Schemes of Compensation

It has been an article of faith among many progressives in Canada, especially social democrats, that redress for the mayhem on the highways should be taken from the courts' inhumane and unpredictable tort system and dealt with on a no-fault basis.[60] In *Quebec: Social Change and Political Crisis*, Kenneth McRoberts discusses how the Parti Québécois initially was decidedly social democratic in orientation and cites its introduction of a public regime of no-fault compensation for personal injury arising from auto accidents as one of the most important aspects of this program.[61] A scheme in Ontario for wide-ranging no-fault benefits, despite the fact that several government-sponsored studies recommended against such broad change, has intensified the national debate that has been played out in several provinces about which model and which components will provide the greatest justice and what justice means in this context.[62] Certainly criticism of the tort system's failure to compensate fairly and to deter effectively are reflected in debates about compensation for auto accidents. Tort's inability to deliver compensation to all who are injured because fault will not always be established, the mandatory once-and-for-all assessment of damages before a claim can be settled, and the amount of insurance dollars eaten up by the administrative and legal costs are among the frailties of the tort regime pointed to by its critics.

Any number of these critics of no-fault are driven by self-interest. Prominent among them are lawyers for whom disputes arising from auto accidents provide a steady stream of clientele. They are quick to point out that the savings imputed to no-fault schemes regarding legal and administrative expenses have been seriously disputed.[63] Such critics insist that proof of fact should be synonymous with individual responsibility, so that its abandonment would be one more sign that society and law are deserting a responsible social order.[64] But there have been thoughtful critiques of no-fault regimes that do not take issue with their goals so much as question their means. Trebilcock shares 'the vision of [the tort system's] critics that superior alternatives can be conceived', but suggests that many of the thorny issues around the fault system surface in the design of a no-fault regime, so that fault and no-fault may be 'a fundamentally misleading dichotomy'.[65]

Generally, Trebilcock believes that each of the three components of the critique of the tort system fail to take account of important aspects that any system must countenance.[66] First, horizontal equity does not in any way take account of the various trade-offs in terms of risks and incentives arising out of different types of accidents. Failure to have proper regard for such risks, incentives, and trade-offs could actually lead to fewer classes of those injured obtaining lower benefits at elevated costs compared to a social insurance scheme that took into account appropriate conduct variables, for example, victims' ability to adopt different strategies for coping in the wake of mishaps. Second, adoption of a community model of responsibility for accidents defies the reality that hazards are frequently influenced by individual conduct. If this is so, appropriately focused pricing and benefit structures along with some role for torts will have a significant influence. In other words, the community model asserts that individual behaviour is not influenced by economic incentives but neither evidence nor theory supports this contention. Third, a too-ready acceptance of the notion that separate policy objectives must be effected by separate instruments can ignore the reality that how instruments for compensation are designed can significantly affect the extent to which deterrence of the behaviour that is causing mishaps is actually achieved.

Applying these ideas to point out the complexities of compensation and deterrence, Trebilcock then comments upon a number of such schemes. Again, there are difficulties around impact with regard to automobile accidents. The empirical evidence respecting such schemes in the United States, Australia, and New Zealand is mixed. However, studies of the Quebec[67] regime, which is entirely no-fault, clearly have some troubling implications, particularly in Gaudry's assessment.[68] In Quebec all court actions for compensation for bodily injury from automobile accidents are banned. In exchange, an agency of the provincial government provides earnings-related benefits at a high level, though there is a maximum. The regime is funded by flat-rate levies.[69] Using multivariate analysis, Gaudry concluded that bodily injuries grew by 26.3 per cent a year and fatalities by 6.8 per cent after the initiation of the scheme. It may be the case that the increase in bodily injuries can reflect a reporting bias, but this would not be the case with fatalities. Gaudry suggests that the increase in both these rates is at least partly due to compulsory insurance requirements that cause previously uninsured motorists to drive less carefully and partly to flat premiums that significantly decrease insurance for high-risk drivers, permitting them to drive with attendant consequences whereas the previous differential rates would have discouraged them from driving.

In discussing the implications of these studies, Trebilcock urges that policy-makers take conduct variables into account in the pricing of coverage in order to reach the highest possible levels of traffic safety. While other policy instruments such as criminal and regulatory sanctions may also be used to encourage safety, it is the case, as with workplace accidents, that the evidence on the efficacy of these alternative safety measures is at best unclear and in many cases disappointing. As a result, Trebilcock concludes that well-defined and implemented risk-rating policies have an important role under a scheme of compensation.[70]

The point here is not to reach a conclusion about any of these studies or about the most desirable attributes of a compensation scheme for traffic accidents. Rather, our purpose is to draw attention to the debate concerning the role of litigation regarding compensation for personal injuries generally and the complex and yet unbounded nature of that discussion; it is one that the courts, to their credit, have mostly avoided.[71] Such free-flowing discussion of the respective roles of the courts and administrative schemes is an important element in assuring that they both serve society to the greatest extent possible. Danger comes when we begin to think of courts not as an important vehicle for addressing policy but as the ultimate arbiter for dealing with society's problems.

Compensation in Health Care

During the 1980s there was steady media coverage of health care that suggested a crisis. Particularly in the United States, there have been fears that malpractice suits have driven up the cost of insurance so that many insurers are denying coverage and a number of doctors are withdrawing from practice because of the threat of malpractice claims. Proferred reforms have included limiting the amount of damages recoverable, shortening the periods within which suits may be brought, resolving such disputes outside the courts by some alternative mechanisms, and establishing no-fault social insurance schemes like the debated model we have just discussed in the context of auto accidents. Meanwhile, Americans focus larger issues around a national plan of health care. Again, Trebilcock is insightful. He and others examined medical malpractice issues in England, the United States, and Canada and caution against seizing upon 'tort reform' as *the* solution: 'The three countries . . . have experienced similar growth in malpractice litigation during the 1970s and 80s. The parallelism suggests that this growth must arise less from isolated doctrinal changes in one country than from changes in medical malpractice and social mores, which occur roughly simultaneously in western countries.'[72]

A lesser version of these apprehensions has stalked medical-legal circles in Canada and resulted in *Liability and Compensation in Health Care: A Report to the Conference of Deputy Ministers of Health of the Federal/Provincial/ Territorial Review on Liability and Compensation Issues in Health Care.*[73] The report is a product of a national interdisciplinary advisory committee and wide consultation, and is supported by background papers by medical-legal academics. It is illuminating for the contextual approach it takes to the issues by examining what systemic devices are available to avoid health care hazards and for exemplifying this country's divided loyalties to tort litigation and what it represents, as well as the potential and pitfalls for social insurance schemes.

The report made seven principal findings upon which to base its recommendations.[74] First, there has been a major increase in claims against health-care providers in Canada between 1971–88. This growth rate has been comparable to the experience in the United Kingdom and United States during the same time (though the absolute levels of litigation are lower here) and the rate of increase in claims against physicians in this country has been higher than that for most other professionals. Second, the cost of insurance for health-care institutions and physicians in Canada in the 1980s grew faster than the underlying growth in claims. Third, these increases in claims were not due to any major change in legal doctrine. Fourth, the current liability and compensation system is very expensive, with insurance costs exceeding $200 million annually. Fifth, at present only a small number of injured patients annually receive any compensation from the liability and compensation system and this number represents only a modest per cent of those who suffer negligent injury. Sixth, in the absence of change, there will be an increase over time in the claims against health-care providers since at present there are no barriers to such growth and there are many injuries caused by negligence that are not now compensated. Seven, on balance, the possibility of litigation against health-care providers for negligence improves the quality of that care and decreases the frequency of avoidable health-care damages.

The findings led to three major sets of recommendations.[75] First, malpractice litigation should be kept because of its deterrent element. In addition, certain incidental recommendations were made to improve this form of litigation, including reforms covering calculation and payment of damages, reduction of frivolous actions, and faster and cheaper disposition of such suits. Second, since many injuries in health care occur systemically, changes need to be made at the institutional as well as individual level. Thus, initiatives with risk management, peer review and quality assurance are urged. Third, in order to compensate those injured by health-care services — a social justice concern — the report recommends developing a no-fault compensation scheme for persons suffering significant avoidable health-care injuries, but only as an *alternative* to a negligence action through a process of election by the injured person that would allow that person to choose either no-fault compensation or a tort action, but not both.

Defending himself against anticipated charges of failure to observe horizontal equity, Prichard, the chair of the advisory committee that wrote the report, reminds us of the benefits of taking identifiable forms of injury and responding with gradual progress. Such a strategy can have flaws, but he urges that it is a better one than the paralysis that may beset us if we insist on simultaneous progress in all respects for all forms of mishap. He believes that in a quarter of a century we will have moved towards a universal scheme of compensation — not in one leap — but in a series of important adjustments. He offers his recommendations regarding health-care injuries as one such step.[76]

Prichard may be right about incrementalism. After all, it is an abiding theme of this book that we have made a virtue of tentativeness. Moreover, his attempt to both deter and prevent medical injuries and to compensate its victims is to be praised. Yet the 'election' for fault or no-fault is problematic.

By Prichard's own estimates, no more than 10 per cent of those who suffer negligent injury from health-care providers are ever compensated — and this in a society where their only choice is to invoke the tort regime.[77] Faced with an election between a no-fault administrative system and a lawsuit, even if some greater compensation were potentially available, how many of those injured would ever elect litigation, particularly when it is remembered that under Prichard's regime if the suit is lost, then the individual cannot in any way avail herself of the no-fault benefits? Meanwhile, the mere possibility of lawsuits based on tort will allow health-care professionals and institutions to argue that the claims channelled through the no-fault regime indeed arise from a no-fault incident (otherwise they would be in court). So there may be a perverse effect here: a smokescreen for sloppy work and preventable harms when the overarching goal is to develop systems, routines, and sensitivities that will have precisely the opposite impact. Better to turn to a comprehensive and carefully structured regime of no-fault that takes into account critiques, like those discussed earlier, of rating experience, as well as of pricing and benefit levels. That would be incrementalism more consistent with Prichard's twenty-five year sightings.

CONCLUSIONS

When we think back to the introduction of this chapter and how tort litigation is viewed by some as a 'private' matter, many may be astonished. It is appropriate to say that it is 'private' only to the extent that the parties are often non-governmental. However, to suggest that such litigation is only about resolving disputes without significant implications for law and social structure is dismally wide of the mark.

An analysis of tort litigation quickly reveals how it reflects basic debates about societal structure and its values and, in turn, is meant to buttress a certain set of values with watchwords like autonomy, responsibility, redress, and deterrence. And it is no coincidence that one's larger view of politics may heavily influence perspectives on this kind of litigation.

The left, always suspicious of claims about individualism, focuses upon the frailties of tort — amassing evidence and arguments, demonstrating how it fails to compensate and deter. This leads, as it frequently does, to proposals for governmental intervention to abolish the structure and replace it with a publicly financed regime in which individual fault and responsibility is irrelevant. Yet there are a number of positions in between making the tort-fault and administrative no-fault models ends on a continuum. These positions cannot be said to be uniquely Canadian, but that their adherents are among the most influential scholars in the making of public policy is certainly consistent with larger views of the political process and litigation in this country.

Weinrib's critics are surely right when they see conservative potential in his 'immanence' model, but that is only part of the story. From another perspective, his depiction unshackles the administrative state and bids it to do the tasks that tort does inadequately, restricting tort to what it does well. We may not embrace his ideas, but we should not fail to notice that they are about division of labour in which the regulatory state and social insurance schemes are clearly legitimated. From a different perspective, Linden clearly contemplates a role for the administrative state, but he urges us to contemplate a *residual* role for tort in scrutinizing the exercise of power. Trebilcock and Prichard embrace the goals of social justice, particularly covering compensation, but urge us to contemplate that we do not necessarily free ourselves of complex issues around compensation and related questions by wholly abandoning the tort system and entirely embracing an administrative system that is completely indifferent to notions of individual performance and individual compensatory needs.

The evidence of how users of these systems regard them is unclear: one reason is that their opinions are rarely sought and their use or non-use of these systems rarely studied — which is surely ironic when there is so much talk about social justice. However, in a recent study done in Ontario, the data suggest that individuals' satisfaction with how a problem is resolved and the extent to which alleged harm is compensated may be far more influenced by the nature of the problem itself rather than how it would be ultimately resolved either in court or by an administrative regime.[78]

Respondents were asked if they or anyone in their household had experienced a significant problem related to the civil justice system and if they had, what they did about it.[79] Those claiming compensation for automobile accidents (the study was done at a time when such claims could have been resolved by court litigation) claimed at the highest levels, received compensation at the highest levels and expressed the highest levels of satisfaction, which were measured by such indicators as the length of time taken to resolve the matter and the cost of lawyers' fees. Very similar results surfaced for injuries sustained at work, damages that would be resolved formally through a no-fault workers' compensation scheme. This suggests that at least from the consumer's perspective, either model is capable of performing well, depending on the type of problem. By contrast, those who perceived they were victims of discrimination were highly dissatisfied with both the result and the process. Similar data were reported with regard to problems with professionals (including but not limited to health-care professionals). Again, each of these two problems represents a different model: discrimination (administrative but with a fault component); professionals (court/tort or perhaps breach of contract). Yet in both cases, high levels of dissatisfaction were reported.[80] This study and related ones[81] suggest that those willing to contemplate a middle ground in dealing with civil justice problems (i.e., a mixed use of courts and administrative schemes) need to examine with great care the nature of the kind of problem for which they are designing a scheme. The respective merits and frailties of torts and administrative schemes may have quite different effects, especially upon consumers, depending upon the different types of civil justice problems.

A number of strands keep surfacing in this chapter: the tension between the individual and community; the role of courts, and the role of administrative schemes. The left is most leery about tort litigation, but, significantly, reservations about courts in this area are by no means limited to that end of the spectrum. Though there may be substantial differences expressed in how change will be achieved, there is substantial consensus that achieving any generalized reform in redress for personal loss will be outside the courts. Affiliated with such consensus, Weinrib seeks to confine and focus the role of litigation, not expand it.

As a result, a claim (like Atiyah's characterization of the United States' version) that tort law is the 'major means for setting norms and standards for social and economic behaviour' would be grossly overdrawn. Conversely, the balance struck in Canada (and other countries) is possible because of government willingness and capacity to devise schemes that achieve the purposes of tort litigation better than the litigation itself. Such lawsuits can have an important role. But when goals can be better achieved by using other methods, very little is lost by shrinking the scope of lawsuits. Such attitudes in general are an important part of creating an effective but not overdrawn role for courts in Canadian society.

NOTES

[1] P.S. Atiyah, 'Tort Law and the Alternatives: Some Anglo-American Comparisons', *Duke Law Journal*, 1002, 1044; and see P.S. Atiyah and R.S. Summers, *Form and Substance in Anglo-American Law* (Oxford: Clarendon Press, 1987).

[2] Atiyah, ibid., 1044. He continues, 'Or at least it would do so, if it were not for the paradoxical fact that so much modern American tort law has fallen under the

control of a sort of proplaintiff party which seems to see its function as performing the redistributive exercises performed by legislatures in other democratic systems. That is why American tort law is in crisis; but that is another story.'

[3]R. Epstein, 'The Social Consequences of Common Law Rules' (1982) 95 *Harvard Law Review*, 1717.

[4]D. Dewees and M. Trebilcock, 'The Efficacy of the Tort System and its Alternatives: A Review of Empirical Evidence' (1992) 30 *Osgoode Hall Law Journal*, 57.

[5]J. Fleming, *The Law of Torts* (6th ed.) (Sydney: Law Book, 1983): 1.

[6]A. Linden, *Canadian Tort Law* (4th ed.) (Toronto: Butterworths, 1988): 2.

[7]Ibid., 1.

[8]Ibid., 3–20. Linden is a leading author on tort law. The analysis in the text of the purposes of tort law draws heavily on his work.

[9]O. Holmes, *The Common Law* (Boston: Little, Brown, 1881): 96.

[10]M.A. Franklin, 'Replacing the Negligence Lottery: Compensation and Selective Reimbursement' (1967) 53 *Virginia Law Review*, 774, 782 [emphasis in original].

[11]G. Priest, 'The Invention of Enterprise Liability: A Critical History of the Intellectual Foundations of Modern Tort Law' (1985) 14 *Journal of Legal Studies*, 461 and other sources cited by Linden, *supra*, note 6n.12.

[12]For example, T. Ison, *The Forensic Lottery* (London: Staples Press, 1967).

[13]C. Morris, 'Negligence in Tort Law — With Emphasis on Automobile Accidents and Unsound Products' (1967) 53 *Virginia Law Review*, 899, and C.J. Bruce, 'The Deterrent Effects of Automobile Insurance and Tort Law: A Survey of the Empirical Literature' (1984) 6 *Law & Policy*, 67.

[14]*Supra*, note 6 at 6–7.

[15]R. Bombaugh, 'The Department of Transportation's Auto Insurance Study and Auto Accident Compensation Reform' (1971) 71 *Columbia Law Review*, 207 at 233.

[16]Ibid.

[17]*Supra*, note 6 at 12.

[18]Ibid., 15.

[19]Ibid., 16.

[20]Ibid., 17–18.

[21]Morris, *supra*, note 13 at 903.

[22]*Supra*, note 6 at 13.

[23]For example, Weinrib's works: 'A Step Forward in Factual Causation' (1975) 38 *Modern Law Review*, 518; 'The Case for a Duty to Rescue' (1980–1) 90 *Yale Law Journal*, 247; 'The Intelligibility of the Rule of Law' in A. Hutchinson and P. Monahan (eds), *The Rule of Law: Ideal or Ideology* (Toronto: Carswell, 1987): 59; 'Toward a Moral Theory of Negligence Law' in *Law and Philosophy: An International Journal for Jurisprudence and Legal Philosophy*, vol. 2 (Dordrecht, Holland: D. Reidel Publishing Company, 1983); 'The Insurance Justification and Private Law' (1985) 14 *Journal of Legal Studies*, 681; 'Enduring Passion' (1985) 94 *Yale Law Journal*, 1825; 'Law as a Kantian Idea of Reason' (1987) 87 *Columbia Law Review*, 472; 'Causation and Wrongdoing' (1987) 63 *Chicago-Kent Law Review*, 407; 'Legal Formalism' (1988) 97 *Yale Law Journal*, 949; 'The Special Morality of Tort Law' (1989) 34 *McGill Law Journal*, 403.

[24] Ibid., 'Special Morality', 408–10.
[25] Ibid., 410.
[26] E. Weinrib, 'Liability Law beyond Justice', *New York Times*, 16 May 1986.
[27] Weinrib, 'The Insurance Justification and Private Law', *supra*, note 23 at 685.
[28] Weinrib, 'The Special Morality of Tort Law', *supra*, note 23 at 413.
[29] K. Roach, 'Teaching Procedures: The Fiss/Weinrib Debate in Practice' (1991) 41 *University of Toronto Law Journal*, 1, 8.
[30] This is the same Fiss cited in Chapter Two. It will be useful to reproduce again the quote from 'Against Settlement', (1984) 93 *Yale Law Journal*, 1073, since it so perfectly reflects his confidence in the superiority of American adjudication (1089):

> To conceive of the civil lawsuit in public terms as America does might be unique. I am willing to assume that no other country . . . has a case like *Brown* v. *Board of Education* in which the judicial power is used to eradicate the caste structure. I am willing to assume that no other country conceives of law and uses law in quite the way we do. But this should be a source of pride rather than shame. What is unique is not the problem, that we live short of our ideals, but that we *alone among the nations of the world* seem willing to do something about it [emphasis added].

[31] O. Fiss, 'Coda' (1988) 38 *University of Toronto Law Journal*, 229.
[32] Atiyah, 'Tort Law', *supra*, note 1 at 1018.
[33] *Supra*, note 29 at 1.
[34] Fiss, *supra*, note 31 at 231. Fiss met Ian Scott, then attorney general of Ontario and, impressed, went so far as to describe him as 'a Robert Kennedy of the North'. Alas, Scott's views of litigation failed, too, to measure up: 'His understanding of adjudication also seemed uniquely unsuited for the kind of constitutional litigation that was the principal subject of his concern and that will soon dominate the Canadian dockets.'
[35] Ibid.
[36] Ibid., 243–4.
[37] E. Weinrib, 'Adjudication and Public Values: Fiss's Critique of Corrective Justice' (1989) 39 *University of Toronto Law Journal*, 1, 4, 16.
[38] *Supra*, note 29 at 32.
[39] Ibid., 33.
[40] Ibid.
[41] Ibid., 33–4.
[42] Ibid., 39.
[43] See E. Weinrib, 'Legal Formalism: On the Immanent Rationality of Law' (1988) 97 *Yale Law Journal*, 949.
[44] A. Hutchinson, 'The Importance of Not Being Ernest' (1989) 34 *McGill Law Journal*, 233.
[45] Ibid., 251.
[46] R. Epstein, 'A Theory of Strict Liability' (1985) 2 *Journal of Legal Studies*, 681.
[47] J.B. Murphy and J.L. Coleman, *The Philosophy of Law: An Introduction to Jurisprudence* (Totowa: Rowman and Allenheld, 1984).
[48] *Supra*, note 44 at 257.

[49]Ibid., 259.

[50]*Supra*, note 6 at 27. A particularly negative reaction to this model is found in G. Fridman, *Introduction to the Law of Torts* (Toronto: Butterworths, 1978) who retorts that it is a 'monstrous idea' to allow tort law to behave as a 'legitimized busybody' or as a 'new-fangled inquisitor' to act as a method of keeping officials from 'straying away from the path of valid righteous conduct'. See also J. Henderson, 'Expanding the Negligence Concept: Retreat from the Rule of Law' (1976) 51 *Indiana Law Journal*, 467.

[51]*Supra*, note 6 at 23.

[52]Ibid.

[53]Ibid., 25.

[54]Ibid.

[55]Ibid., 25–6.

[56]Ibid., 26.

[57]Ibid., 27.

[58]An incomplete list includes: T. Ison, *The Forensic Lottery* (London: Staples Press, 1967); R. Keeton and J. O'Connell, *Basic Protection for the Traffic Victim* (Boston: Little Brown, 1965): Chapter 2; A. Calabresi, *The Costs of Accidents* (New Haven: Yale University Press, 1970); S. Sugarman, 'Doing Away With Tort Law' (1985) 73 *California Law Review*, 555; H. Glasbeek and R. Hasson, 'Fault — The Great Hoax' in L. Klar (ed.), *Studies in Canadian Tort Law* (Toronto: Butterworths, 1977); D. Harris et al., *Compensation and Support for Illness and Injury* (Oxford: Clarendon Press, 1984); Ontario Law Reform Commission, *Report on Motor Vehicle Accident Compensation* (Toronto: Ministry of the Attorney General, 1973).

[59]See M. Trebilcock, 'Incentive Issues in the Design of "No-Fault" Compensation Systems' (1989) 39 *University of Toronto Law Journal*, 19, 20–5.

[60]See, generally, C. Osborne, *Report of Inquiry Into Motor Vehicle Compensation in Ontario* (Toronto: Ministry of Attorney General, 1988).

[61]K. McRoberts, *Quebec: Social Change and Political Crisis* (3rd ed.) (Toronto: McClelland & Stewart, 1988): 267–8.

[62]C. Brown and J. Menezes, *Insurance Law in Canada: A Treatise on the Principles of Indemnity Insurance as Applied in Common Law Provinces in Canada* (Scarborough: Thomson Professional Publishing, 1991): see introduction.

[63]For the criticism and response to it, see Osborne, *supra*, note 60 at 506 *et seq.*

[64]B. Wright, 'The Future of Personal Injury Compensation' (1987) 18 *Revue Générale du Droit*, 23.

[65]*Supra*, note 59 at 54, and see generally Dewees and Trebilcock, *supra*, note 4.

[66]Ibid., 53–4.

[67]Ibid., 29–30.

[68]M. Gaudry, 'The Effects on Road Safety of the Compulsory Insurance, Flat Premium Rating and No-Fault Features of the 1978 Quebec Automobile Act' appendix to *Report of the Inquiry into Motor Vehicle Accident Compensation in Ontario* (Osborne Report) (Ontario: Queen's Printer, 1988), and R. Devlin, 'Liability Versus No-Fault Automobile Insurance Regimes: An Analysis of Quebec's Experience', a paper presented at the Canadian Economics Association Meeting, Windsor, Ontario, 3 June 1988.

[69] *Supra*, note 59 at 29.

[70] Ibid., 33. These ideas are developed more fully in M. Friedland, M. Trebilcock, K. Roach, *Regulating Traffic Safety* (Toronto: University of Toronto Press, 1990).

[71] *Reference re Workers Compensation Act, 1983* (1989) 56 *Dominion Law Reports* (4th), 765.

[72] D. Dewees, M. Trebilcock, P. Coyte, 'The Medical Malpractice Crisis: A Comparative Empirical Perspective' (1991) 54 *Law and Contemporary Problems*, 217, 250.

[73] R. Prichard, *Liability and Compensation in Health Care: A Report to the Conference of Deputy Ministers of Health of the Federal/Provincial/Territorial Review on Liability and Compensation Issues in Health Care* (Toronto: University of Toronto Press, 1990) KF/3825.3/L53 1990.

[74] Ibid., 3–5 and see Executive Summary.

[75] Ibid., 5–7 and see Executive Summary.

[76] Ibid., 7.

[77] Ibid., 5.

[78] W.A. Bogart and N. Vidmar, 'Problems and Experience with the Ontario Civil Justice System' in A. Hutchinson (ed.), *Access to Civil Justice* (Toronto: Carswell, 1990): 1.

[79] The survey was done by random digit dialling of 3,000 Ontario households: see ibid, 4–6.

[80] Ibid., 24–9.

[81] For example, H. Kritzer, W.A. Bogart, N. Vidmar, 'Context, Context, Context: A Cross-Problem, Cross-Cultural Comparison of Compensation Seeking Behaviour', a paper presented at the Law and Society Conference, Amsterdam, June 1991.

CHAPTER SEVEN

The Courts and Two Models of Criminal Law

INTRODUCTION

Why we criminalize and why we punish are questions that every society has to answer. For most, the core of the response begins by recognizing the public nature of criminal law.[1] From this perspective, a crime is not so much a wrong against the person harmed but a transgression against the community in violating its peace and sense of order. So the enforcement of criminal law is not left exclusively or even primarily to the victim but depends on the entire society, particularly those representing the state — the police or prosecuting authorities. Yet one still asks what wrongs will be criminal and subject to this public reaction. After all, there are many wrongs inflicted such as breaches of contract or trust that may cause much loss, at least in a monetary sense, but they are not crimes. There are a number of explanations for where the line is drawn, but none of them is wholly satisfactory, including structural ones that claim that '[t]he *real politik* of all law, not just criminal law, is that law is not a *social* instrument (in the sense of representing 'fundamental *social* values'), but a *state* instrument defining, upholding and enforcing a limited range of interests, interests which . . . represent the needs of the power elite.'[2]

A variation on the question of which acts should be criminalized is the debate about the appropriate relationship between criminal law and morality. In many instances there is no divergence: murder, rape, theft are morally reprehensible and cause objective harm. But there are other acts about which there can be vigorous disagreement as to whether they ought to be criminalized since the harm (if any) that they do is debatable and since their moral offensiveness is doubtful. Among such acts are gambling, consumption of erotica, abortion, and consensual sex. One view supports the criminalization of such acts if any of them are generally condemned by the public. But the other view argues that moral reprehensibility by the majority or otherwise is irrelevant, and unless acts are socially detrimental, they should not be criminalized.[3] The latter position has led to the decriminalization of many acts that were formerly sanctioned: homosexuality, prostitution *per se*, and attempted suicide. Abortion has been removed from the scope of criminal law, but only after great controversy, as discussed in Chapter Five. By contrast, decriminalization of such 'private' practices as euthanasia, incest, and possession of drugs are resisted for different reasons and by different segments of the populace, either on grounds of moral reprehensibility, social detriment, or both.[4]

But beyond a general description of criminal systems, can we say something about the Canadian criminal system, particularly the judge's role and its relation to our structure, our aspirations as a society? The answer to this question once again centres upon a comparison between ourselves and our American neighbour. Crime — particularly violent crime and responses to it — provides substantial points of comparison. Until recently, the two countries's courts and their societies' treatment of crime differed more or less in the same way: the United States emphasized due process, while Canada emphasized crime control. Thus historically (and unlike in many other areas), the Canadian courts were reflecting dominant values in this society. But the Charter has changed the role of Canadian courts quite significantly regarding criminal justice, perhaps providing the best example of Lipset's observation discussed in Chapter One that Canada's adoption of the Charter is drawing the two societies closer.[5]

The dangers of such a convergence can be summarized as follows. In the abstract, there is much to be said for a heightened sensitivity to the rights of the accused in the due process model, particularly when set against actual instances of harshness imposed by our courts in the past with their strict fidelity to the crime control model. Nevertheless, the crime control model in the hands of the courts is the more deferential: it places the responsibility for difficult decisions regarding criminal justice and its relation to other policies squarely with Parliament and its law enforcement officials. The hazards of undue reliance on courts and the due process model are that we substitute solicitude for the accused and convicted for the necessary care and attention to society's underlying attitudes and structures so that crime itself, particularly violent crime, can be suppressed to the greatest possible extent. Historically, we have been very successful suppressing violent crime compared with the United States. Analytically, all those concerns about due process, on the one hand, and prevention of crime, on the other, should be kept separate and accommodated. But underestimation of due process's capacity and its emphasis by courts to transform, channel, and control other interests can yield debilitating consequences for the administration of criminal justice and for related issues. Such possibilities are examined by analysing the questions surrounding Supreme Court of Canada cases on speedy trials and on the rape-shield law and by discussing the criminal rights 'revolution' in the United States.

No one is arguing that our criminal justice system is the model: problems of unfairness, including racism, are being documented with depressing regularity while disrespect for those charged with enforcing the law and maintaining order grows.[6] Yet given the route the courts are taking, the critical question is are they likely to do some good in addressing these problems, or will their activity deflect us from facing such problems head-on and forging workable solutions that suppress violent crime by responding to its causes?

DISREPUTABLE PLEASURES, DUE PROCESS, AND CRIME CONTROL

Important differences between the two countries are reflected, at least in part, in differing attitudes towards law itself, perhaps particularly criminal law: 'Efforts to distinguish Canada and the United States almost invariably point to the greater respect for law and those who uphold it north of the border.'[7] This difference is perhaps the most prevalent characteristic cited in comparisons of the two countries. The vitality of the distinction has been reiterated many times by writers and historians to illustrate the varying organizing principles of the two societies. As Atwood noted, 'Canada must be the only country in the world where a policeman [the Mountie] is used as a national symbol.'[8]

It is contended that such differences were there from the beginning stemming from successful, violent revolt in the one and affirmation of monarchical, gradual evolution to self-government in the other. As the countries expanded, the West in the United States refused to be centrally controlled and was instead populist-dominated — guns rather than the law often responded to disputes. But in Canada expansion was centrally controlled[9] and 'Alexander MacKenzie . . . founded the . . . North West Mounted Police for the specific purpose of ensuring a non-American type of development in the prairie west.'[10] Yet clearly there were important exceptions to this depiction of orderly development and change, as the Riel rebellion and the Winnipeg General Strike tragically illustrate.[11]

Still, the relative influence of and respect for law is apparent in comparing the order of mining camps during the gold rushes of the nineteenth century in California and British Columbia and in Alaska and the Klondike. Whereas those in what is now the United States were undisciplined and violent, those in what is now Canada were subject to the 'Queen's peace' and differed greatly from their American counterparts in terms of vigilantes or other forms of lawlessness.[12] And while both nations can be indicted for their subjugation of Amerindians, there is evidence that those in Canada were subject to less violence and that our justice system offered some avenue for redress for the First Peoples.[13]

This is not to suggest that the pervasiveness of law and deference to it in Canada has always been an unqualified good. The legality of and tolerance for the Canadian government in imposing a form of military control during the 1970 Quebec crisis has been strongly argued to show how respect for authorities can lead to authoritarianism.[14] That such attitudes are deeply ingrained is demonstrated by a 1989 *Maclean's*-Decima poll that found that, while 56 per cent of Americans opposed giving the national government the power to 'remove all civil liberties' during a national emergency, only 49 per cent of Canadians were opposed.[15] Such differences are even greater if the responses between Anglophone and French Canadians are subdivided, since two-thirds of the latter but only 43 per cent of the former supported suspension of civil liberties in such circumstances. A similar theme has been struck by A. Westin (a passage, incidentally, that also demonstrates a darker side to the Mounties):

> [I]n Canada there have been some incidents which, had they happened in the United States, would probably have led to great *causes célèbres*. Most Canadians seem to have accepted Royal Canadian Mounted Police break-ins without warrants between 1970 and 1978, and also the RCMP's secret access to income tax information, and to personal health information from the Ontario Health Insurance Plan. . . . [T]hese did not shock and outrage most Canadians.[16]

This concern with order, even if it trenches upon liberties, particularly those of minorities, is further reflected in survey evidence. In a 1987 study, four questions were used to measure concern for liberty in contrast to interest in an orderly society. The survey found that Americans are significantly more disposed than Canadians to voice a preference for liberty over risks of a disrupted society. More concretely, the study found that while only 50 per cent of Canadians are so minded, fully two-thirds of Americans are willing to take risks to maintain freedom of speech and assembly.[17] Yet in another study, Canadians were consistently more tolerant of deviant behaviour. In this regard, Americans were more likely than Canadians to oppose having 'people with a criminal record' or 'emotionally unstable people' or political 'extremists' as neighbours.[18] Reviewing these and other studies on Canadians' racial tolerance, Lipset concluded that while Canadians are more concerned than Americans with maintaining social order, even when this means restricting liberties, they are more tolerant of interpersonal behaviour that somehow deviates from the norm.[19]

There is evidence that such consistent attitudinal differences about law, particularly criminals and certain structural aspects such as race and poverty, do lead to concrete dissimilarities. The clearest indicator is the striking difference between the two with respect to rates for major crimes.

Canadians are far less likely to commit violent offences like murder, robbery, and rape. In 1985, Canada with 35 million people had 651 murders (2.2 per 100,000), while the United States with 234 million had 18,976 (8.3 per 100,000).[20] While there is evidence that crime is increasing in both countries,[21] there is also evidence to suggest that the disparity in rates of violent crime between the two countries is actually growing.[22] Similarly, the United States has greater evidence of political violence.[23]

Accompanying this safer, less violent culture in Canada is not an attitude of understanding towards those who transgress the law but one of tough-mindedness. Whether in support for police, attitudes to imposing stiff punishments, support for gun control, or willingness to suppress objectionable practices (such as smoking in public places), Canadians almost always significantly differ from Americans in their level of support.[24] One possible exception to this is Quebec residents who in some studies seem less willing than both Canadians and Americans to use stiffer punishments to reduce crime.[25]

What has been the courts' role in the criminal system in Canada? Again, the most insightful observation about their role in these areas comes from a comparison of Canada and the United States. At the most general level, Rocher suggests: 'Throughout the history of the United States, common law and the courts have been perceived and used as a check on the power of the State. "American jurisprudence reflects a concern for limiting a governmental coercion over individuals." In Canada, the courts have been much more closely identified with the State, and perceived as the arm of the State.'[26] This may be overstating the difference when one thinks, for example, of the courts' ideological opposition to the progressive programs of the administrative state as documented in Chapter Four. Yet the point of contrast seems accurate in terms of criminal law.

These differences have been put most forcefully and carefully by the sociologist J. Hagan in a number of places, most importantly in *The Disreputable Pleasures*.[27] Hagan begins with the insights of Packer, who suggested that responses to violation of the law fit within two basic models: due process and crime control.[28] The greatest difference between these two models arises regarding the rights they accord those facing the criminal law.[29] Due process, rooted in the Enlightenment, emphasizes the assertion of Locke and others that law could be employed in defending 'natural' and 'inalienable rights'. It follows that the model focuses upon exclusionary rules of evidence, the right to counsel, and other procedural safeguards deemed helpful in shielding the accused from unwarranted criminal sanctions. The plainest embodiment of this attitude is the notion that risk of error should be heavily on the side of allowing the guilty to go free rather than risking the possibility of convicting the innocent.

By contrast, crime control is buttressed philosophically from conservative reaction to Enlightenment thought. As such, the argument of Burke and others that civil liberties are meaningful only in orderly societies looms large. So this model underscores the necessity of suppressing criminal conduct since it asserts that order must be ensured before individuals can be assured personal freedom. It follows that this conception is not as ready to presume innocence of the accused. Some mistreatment may be tolerated when, on the whole, social order is preserved.

Both Canada and the United States lean much more towards the due process model, but there are critical differences within the two countries. Hagan quotes this Russell passage (which appears in a number of places in this book) to emphasize our connection with Burke as compared with the Americans' connection with Locke: '[the] approach which is truest to our experience and most in keeping with our capabilities is that of Edmund Burke, not John Locke. Canadians — neither their judges, nor their politicians —are creatures of the Enlightenment.'[30] The consequences that flow from the differences between the two models will occupy much of the rest of the chapter. One question that will be tackled is whether the differences drawn by Hagan are fading at least regarding the courts and their invoking of the Charter regarding criminal issues.

For the moment we can focus on some of Hagan's critical conclusions regarding the effects of such differences. Aside from the substantial dissimilarities concerning rates for violent crime and political unrest documented earlier, the United States spends more per capita on its police, substantially more on its courts and institutions of correction to produce 'a legal order that combines high levels of crime with a profuse and coercive police response'.[31] In contrast:

> ... Canada has been able to limit its resource commitment to crime control by reemphasizing its ideological commitment to the Burkean ideal of social order first and individual rights second. Thus, in Canada, the police role has become pre-eminently symbolic, a reminder that social order ideologically precedes individual liberties. . . . Whether the focus is restricted access to probation, discretionary right to counsel, the admissibility of illegally obtained evidence, or a range of other issues, Canadians have demonstrated a considerable willingness to accept laws that give social order precedence over individual rights.[32]

There is surely one more aspect of these differences to be pondered. Canada (along with almost all other countries of similar heritage) has forsaken capital punishment for some time while it has rapidly accelerated in the United States during the last decade. Texas leads the way (not all states have capital punishment), executing nine people from January to August 1992 and fifty-one individuals in that previous decade.[33] Meanwhile, serious debate — even litigation — has loomed over what may be the ultimate obscenity: whether execution ought to be televised.[34] A question is posed in leaving this point. Why is it that the country that is most solicitous about notions of due process for the accused is the same nation that exacts this ultimate penalty with such ferocious enthusiasm and in such determined isolation?

THE COURTS AND CRIME HISTORICALLY

Hagan is right in emphasizing that both Canada and the United States tend towards the due process model with its concern for protecting individuals from unwarranted conviction. However, he is also right in suggesting that, historically at least, Canadian judges were much more likely to embrace elements of the crime control model even when the consequences for the accused were harsh.[35] Moreover, existing evidence suggests that those judgements more or less reflected the views of the Canadian public. Many such instances could be cited, but four of the more notorious from the Supreme Court involving the defence of intoxication, the defence of duress, the felony murder rule, and, most prominently, the exclusion of illegally obtained evidence are particularly illustrative.

Again, it is important to emphasize that there were incidences where, in the clash between crime control and concern about its harshness towards an accused, the individual sometimes won. For example in *R. v. Beaver*,[36] the Supreme Court recognized the requirement of *mens rea* (criminal intent) even though the applicable statute appeared to make any possession of heroin without a licence an offence. The accused maintained that he thought the heroin was powdered milk and the Court agreed that however implausible, the defence should be considered by a jury. While the Court's reasons are not developed, it has been suggested it reached its decision because it was obviously repelled by the notion that Parliament meant to impose a sentence of at least six months even if it could be demonstrated that the individual, however mistakenly, truly believed he was handling powdered milk.[37] Such an exception noted, it is interesting that in that case there was a vigorous dissent that clearly subscribed to the efficacy of the crime control model, even in the face of the possibility of such untoward consequences:

> ... Parliament [intended] to deal adequately with the methods, which are used ... to defeat the purposes of the Act, ingenious as they may be. That enforcement of the provisions of the Act may, in exceptional cases, lead to some injustice, is not an impossibility. But, to forestall this result as to such possible cases, there are remedies under the law, such as a stay of proceedings by the Attorney General or a free pardon under the royal prerogative.[38]

Moreover, the Court subsequently confirmed in a later case that *mens rea* would not necessarily need to be established if the offence could be characterized as not criminal 'in the true sense' but rather one of a 'wide category of offenses created by statutes enacted for the regulation of individual conduct in the interests of health, convenience, safety and general welfare of the public'.[39]

The Court's treatment of drunkenness as a defence also indicated its tendency to prefer order over arguments about the accused's capacity to intend to commit a crime. The code historically was completely silent about the validity of the excuse of drunkenness. Our courts, led by the Supreme Court, created an implausible distinction between general and specific intent, which has been tortuously applied — most prominently in cases involving indecent assault and rape. Nevertheless, the thrust of these cases was to make drunkenness a very difficult defence to substantiate.[40]

Possibly one of the clearest instances of the Court's fidelity to the notion that once a guilty act is established, the circumstances allowing a defence to be raised should be tightly circumscribed is starkly illustrated in its treatment of duress as a reason for committing an act that would be otherwise criminal. While the Criminal Code provision required 'threats of immediate death or grievous bodily harm', the code also allowed the courts to recognize and create defences.[41] Yet despite this capacity, the courts continually interpreted the duress provision in the most limited way. For example, in one case a prisoner was threatened with death if he did not participate in the smashing of furniture and plumbing in his cell during a prison upheaval.[42] The threat was made by another prisoner who at the moment was in a separate cell. He could not immediately carry out the threat, but there was evidence to suggest that there were reprisals in similar circumstances in the same prison and the guards could not really prevent it.

Despite this, the Supreme Court held that because the threat could not be carried out at the moment it was made, the defence of duress did not apply. This is not to suggest that caution should not be exercised in extending the defence of duress; for example, it is possible for a story to be concocted by two offenders so that one may go free.[43] However, it does illustrate a pattern: whenever our courts, particularly the Supreme Court, were faced with a decision about the limits of a justifiable defence or the need to buttress the enforcement of the law, the latter almost always won.

This attitude is again illustrated in the application of what was referred to as the felony murder rule.[44] This rule expressed a basic idea: if a person committed an offence such as robbery and caused death in the course of it, then he was to be found guilty of murder. The rationale, of course, was to suppress the violence in conjunction with any other wrongdoing. However, our courts took this rule and by invoking provisions that made anyone who aids and abets an offence guilty of that offence, extended the felony murder rule to anyone else involved in the crime.[45] Such decisions were strongly criticized[46] and indeed the rule has been abrogated by the Supreme Court by invoking its powers under the Charter.[47] But the underlying rationale of the earlier decisions was quite consistent with the law enforcement model: if the primary actor is to be found guilty of murder, in order to properly reflect society's abhorrence of this act, an accomplice for any purpose should be treated in exactly the same way. For those who insist upon remembering the victims of violence first and foremost, the rule may yet hold appeal: its harshness was precisely the point.

But perhaps it is with the admission of illegally obtained evidence that the courts demonstrated that they were most aligned with the law enforcement model and most at variance (at that time) with the United States courts and their due process concerns. While courts in various countries have consistently held that for confessions to be admissible, they must be voluntary, there is considerable divergence in terms of what is to be done with other evidence secured because of involuntary confessions and the processes employed to obtain such evidence.[48] In the United States, such evidence was pretty uniformly excluded under the doctrine of the 'fruit of the poisoned tree',[49] but Canadian courts, and particularly the Supreme Court, insisted there was no discretion to exclude no matter how outrageous the means used to obtain it.

In *Wray*,[50] the accused was held for hours and given a lie-detector test while the individual administering the test finally got the accused to divulge where the weapon in question was hidden by alternatively offering inducements and raising threats. Meanwhile, a lawyer engaged by the accused's family was prevented from seeing him. When the case arrived at the Supreme Court, it came out resoundingly against any discretion to exclude otherwise probative evidence:

> This type of evidence has been admissible for almost 200 years. There is no judicial discretion permitting the exclusion of relevant evidence, on the ground of unfairness to the accused.... Judicial discretion in this field is a concept which involves great uncertainty of application. The task of a judge in the conduct of a trial is to apply the law and to admit all the evidence that is logically probative unless it is ruled out by some exclusionary rule. If this course is followed, an accused person has had a fair trial. The exclusionary rule applied in this case is one that should not be accepted.[51]

Of course, there are strong arguments about the integrity of the justice system on both sides of this issue. This is so because it is patently objectionable that someone should be convicted on the basis of evidence that was obtained through coerced means. Equally, however, it is wrong that someone who committed the crime should go free simply because of law enforcement officers' wrongful conduct. Clearly the answer to this dilemma that came from our courts was to guard against the second objection.

But we should focus more on this specific issue because it clearly illustrates a major theme in this chapter and indeed in this book: the effect of ideology upon judicial decision making and vice versa. Moreover, this controversy led directly to a section in the Charter that deals with exclusion of tainted evidence — s. 24(2) — that has been the subject of a debate and systematic study that will occupy our attention in the next section.

We can begin by observing the extent to which the debate about the exclusionary rule is a microcosm of our variegated ideology discussed at some length in Chapter One. It has been suggested that 'Canada, because of its "tory touch" and non-revolutionary origins, provides less fertile ground for an exclusionary rule than the United States with its traditional distrust of authority'.[52] More bluntly, it has been asserted by an American observer that *Wray* reflects 'a total commitment to the guilt determining function of a criminal trial. This approach is characteristic of a criminal justice system that emphasizes order and crime control'[53] and a related case, *Hogan*,[54] exemplifies our absence 'of awareness of individual rights'.[55] In contrast, it has been contended that 'Canada's finest non-liberals have never denied our liberal core, and respect for human autonomy, through adequately enforced constitutional prohibitions against arbitrary searches, seizures, detentions and imprisonments, and denial of counsel, is well within our ideological capacity. Discontent with the conviction of people such as Hogan, was crucial in gaining support for the entrenchment of s. 24 and legal rights.'[56]

A brief summary of the events after *Wray* and leading up to the Charter strongly reflects these two positions. Generally reform agencies urged some capacity for courts to exclude wrongfully obtained evidence, but provided only ill-defined guidance to performing such a task. The federal Law Reform Commission in its proposed Evidence Code[57] and the McDonald Commission in its report on surveillance practices[58] both made essentially the same recommendations.[59] The core was that courts should decide to exclude evidence by having regard to 'the extent to which human dignity and social values were breached in obtaining the evidence' and 'whether any harm to an accused or others was inflicted wilfully or not'[60] and whether such evidence 'would tend to bring the administration of justice into disrepute'.[61] They instructed courts to consider all relevant circumstances such as 'the seriousness of the case, the importance of the evidence, the existence of urgency to prevent the destruction of evidence, and the deliberation or degree of inexcusable ignorance demonstrated by the police'.[62] In contrast, the Federal-Provincial Task Force on the Rules of Evidence[63] flatly rejected such authority because it believed exclusion of such evidence was the greater injustice. Further, it believed that the criteria were 'ineffective to achieve uniformity of result [and] invariably incomplete, conflicting and subjective'.[64]

Nevertheless, once the cause of the Charter had gathered momentum, the rigidity of the Supreme Court, particularly in *Wray* and *Hogan*, in failing to contemplate virtually any circumstances where evidence should be excluded no matter how egregious the behaviour of the authorities, was used to propel the case forward for some entrenched exclusionary power. Despite dire warnings of police and Crown attorneys,[65] civil libertarian arguments prevailed as reform proposals were carefully distinguished from the American rule, which was seen to be inflexible from the other direction. The *Canadian Charter of Rights and Freedoms: A Guide for Canadians* reassuringly opined: 'This power to exclude evidence is limited and circumstances will permit the courts to preserve public expectations for the integrity of the judicial process.'[66] After a number of versions were debated, including ones that would have actually tended to reaffirm existing law,[67] s. 24(2) was accepted and provided that if 'a court concludes that evidence was obtained in a manner that infringed or denied any rights or freedoms guaranteed by this Charter, the evidence shall be excluded if it is established that, having regard to all the circumstances, the admission of it in the proceedings would bring the administration of justice into disrepute'.

THE COURTS AND CRIME — AND THE CHARTER

The Due Process Trajectory

Quite possibly the area where the Charter has made the greatest difference is in the administration of criminal justice. The greatest number of decisions, at least at the Supreme Court, has been in that area and in a qualitative sense, criminal law has experienced the greatest alteration because of these judgements. A study surveying the Supreme Court's first 100 decisions under the Charter (up to 1989) and assessing criminal justice decisions concluded, 'The Court has used the Charter to develop a new constitutional code of conduct for Canadian police officers in dealing with suspects and accused persons. In the process, it has pushed the Canadian criminal process away from the "crime control" toward the "due process" side of the ledger.'[68] How and why the shift in models is occurring and the implications for the influence of courts on public opinion are the issues that will occupy this subsection. The second subsection will examine two recent cases where the triumph of due process has subsumed other pervasive concerns with the danger that vindication of due process will be mistaken for a solution rather than an aspect of the problem. The last subsection is a comparative examination of the consequences of the 'criminal rights revolution' in the United States.

There is no question that the text of the Charter itself gives a strong indication that vigilance about the rights of accused persons was to be part of the fundamental law of the land with the 'legal rights' (as opposed to 'political' rights such as free speech, freedom of religion, equality, etc.) set out in ss. 7–14 at the core of this watchfulness.[69] S. 7 is the most encompassing provision declaring that '[e]veryone has the right to life, liberty and security of the person and the right not to be deprived thereof except in accordance with the principles of fundamental justice'. The remaining sections are more specific relating to investigative methods, and the conduct of trials and punishment upon conviction. Unreasonable searches and seizures (s. 8) and arbitrary detentions (s. 9) in the investigation of crime are prohibited. A person must be informed of the reasons for arrest or detention and of the right to retain and instruct counsel without delay (s. 10). At the trial, an accused has a number of rights. The right to have evidence excluded if other Charter provisions are infringed and the administration of justice will be brought into disrepute (s. 24[2]) has already been discussed. Other rights include a trial within a reasonable time; not to be compelled as a witness at the trial; the presumption of innocence until proven guilty according to law in a fair and public hearing by an independent and impartial tribunal; a jury trial if he or she faces five years' imprisonment or more; assistance by an interpreter; upon conviction or acquittal, not to be tried for the same offence again; and, upon conviction, not to be subjected to cruel or unusual punishment (ss. 11–14).

Moreover, earlier drafts leave little doubt that the evolution was towards a due process model. For example, in the 1980 draft, the Charter would have provided protection against searches and seizures, detentions, denial of bail only when they were not carried out 'on grounds, and in accordance with procedures established by law'.[70] In contrast in the 1981 incarnation, these provisions were altered so that even if authorized by law, a search and seizure is impermissible if 'unreasonable',[71] a detention cannot be arbitrary,[72] and reasonable bail cannot be denied 'without just cause'.[73] The 1981 version asserted that a person charged with an offence should not be compelled to be a witness in proceedings against him in respect to that offence,[74] that an accused must be informed of his or her right to counsel,[75] and that he or she has a right to a jury trial if the maximum punishment is five years or more.[76] None of these rights appeared in the 1980 version. As seen earlier, previous versions of the Charter actually tried to forestall any development of an exclusionary rule,[77] and it was only in the 1981 draft that the present s. 24(2) surfaced.

Yet those fully committed to a due process model have expressed dissatisfaction that the text of the Charter does not go far enough in its vigilance concerning the accused.[78] After a detailed comparison concerning the rights of the accused under the Canadian and United States constitutions, an American observer concluded that Canada still fell short of the mark regarding its solicitude for those charged: 'in areas where the danger of government abuse is great, the constitution provides few protections'.[79] Still, regardless of their stance on how the rights of accused should be formed, almost anyone would be struck by the quantity and breadth of decisions to date that have used the Charter. An initial study of the first year and a half after the enactment of the Charter found that the number of reported criminal cases on the Charter increased ten times compared with the same period after the enactment of the Canadian Bill of Rights in 1960,[80] though in that regard, it must be remembered that the latter only applied to the federal sphere. That said, a 1987 study of reported Charter cases between 1982 and 1985 established that 90 per cent of the Charter arguments presented to courts were based on legal rights (that is, those rights in ss. 7–14 described earlier).[81] Similarly, in a study of 800 Ontario Charter cases, it was found that 85 per cent raised legal rights provisions.[82] Finally, in terms of sheer numbers the aforementioned study of the first 100 cases decided by the Supreme Court under the Charter demonstrated that seventy-four of them involved legal rights.[83] The influence of criminal justice issues is highlighted even more if the interrelationship between these issues and other rights is considered. For instance, the legislative disenfranchising of inmates as interfering with democratic rights, various Criminal Code sections forbidding communication for the purpose of prostitution, and the wilful promotion of hate propaganda on the grounds of infringing freedom of expression have been challenged. The equality right provisions have been raised by young offenders and others alleging that they do not receive legal protection or benefit from the criminal law.[84]

Yet this potential for far-reaching activity by the courts has received less scrutiny than many other issues. The authors of the study of the first 100 Supreme Court cases make this point and go on to speculate at possible turn of events:

> Ironically, while this policy area represents the Court's most extensive *de facto* efforts at law reform, it has thus far escaped public notice. American experience shows that this type of judicial policy making can become an issue of partisan political conflict. Beginning with Richard Nixon's 1968 presidential campaign, the Republican Party has criticized liberal judges for being 'soft on criminals' and successfully exploited the 'law and order' issue, particularly as it relates to the appointment of federal judges. It will be of both theoretical and practical interest to see if a Canadian political party will try to make a political issue out of the Supreme Court's Charter inspired reform of the criminal law process.[85]

There have been a number of views about what the Charter and the courts will do to the administration of criminal justice. The first, appearing especially in early accounts, was 'the story of progressive continuity', suggesting 'an optimistic picture of the functioning of the Canadian criminal process with the Charter offering moderate improvements'.[86] These accounts extolled the Charter as 'an important yet incremental stage in legal development'.[87] Adherents of such a position underscored the fact that rights pertinent to criminal investigations were built by and large on existing legal doctrines relating to the admissibility of statements and arrest and search and seizure. Bail and habeas corpus to protect individual liberty were constitutionalized, but were rooted in familiar concepts. A similar characterization was made of the institution of the jury and the traditional burden of proof on the prosecutor. Further, the provision for exclusion of evidence was more akin to Commonwealth jurisdictions than to the United States with its emphasis on automatic ouster for any violation of constitutional rights.

The second account focuses on 'political conflict and change'.[88] It centres on the alterations in the various drafts of the Charter (discussed earlier) and the shift towards firmer protection for the individual despite the consequences for investigation and enforcement: 'The broader guarantees transferred power from elected representatives, prosecutors and police to judges, defence counsel and the accused. With this transfer, the conflict between due process and crime control values in the political arena became visible in the judicial process.'[89]

The third account is 'a much darker vision stressing the continued repressions of both the perpetrators and victims of crime'.[90] Here the inequality of access to the justice of the Charter is underscored. This depiction points to the fact that some of the biggest wins in civil libertarians' view have, in fact, been those on behalf of large corporations that seek to avoid government regulation.[91] Meanwhile, '[t]he legalization of criminal justice politics can take penal and social reform proposals off the agenda of politicians happy to avoid them, or engender a politics which is reactive to a symbolic discourse revolving around the new procedural rights' and 'the Charter's civil libertarian restraints on crime control are liable to have a disproportionate effect on women, minorities and the poor who are often victimized by crime'.[92]

Writing in 1991, Roach gave one assessment of activity under the Charter to that point. While allowing that judicial review of pretrial conduct may not be a full description of the day-to-day activities of law enforcement authorities, he did venture a synopsis of the extent to which due process values have been accepted by courts and concluded that the crime control model was still with us, at least regarding certain important elements:

> ... Canada has embraced some aspects of the due process model while eschewing many others. The right to counsel has become the preeminent legal right which is rigorously enforced by the exclusionary sanction. Interrogation law has developed along lines remarkably similar to the American *Miranda* doctrine with its emphasis on prophylactic standards against unfair self-incrimination. Rights against entrapment or unreasonably delayed trials have been protected by sacrificing convictions through stays of proceedings and the Supreme Court has expressed its preference for the prior judicial authorization of searches.
>
> On the other hand, Canadian courts have adhered to the traditional crime control model in their unwillingness to exclude relevant and reliable real evidence of crimes and in their sensitivity to the practical constraints placed on the police in the investigation of crime over a broad range of subjects such as searches incident to arrest and the authorization of electronic surveillance. The continued prevalence of guilty pleas and enthusiasm for the use of the criminal sanction suggest that, despite the addition of new elements of due process, the empirical reality of the criminal process still largely conforms to the crime control model.[93]

Yet in comparing the legal rights under the Charter and the Bill of Rights and how they have been interpreted by the Canadian and American Supreme Courts, others have come to stronger conclusions regarding the due process trajectory. A 1990 study examined Supreme Court of Canada cases in criminal law until February 1989.[94] This was before some other spectacular decisions on behalf of the accused.[95] The authors studied the cases up to February 1989 and their use of American precedent and the effect the Canadian cases had regarding protection of those charged. Their basic conclusion was that reference to American precedent (although increasing in Charter cases) was erratic, and that while an impression might be conveyed that our Court was a pale imitation of the American Supreme Court in terms of the due process model, the reality was frequently quite different. Such difference could not be attributed exclusively to recent, more conservative tendencies in the American Court:

> [O]nce the general value and relevance of United States law has been recognized, however cautiously, it ought not to be resorted to in a random fashion. The current selective, almost eccentric, use of precedent tends to create the misleading impression that the Court is either rejecting American law that is too liberal or, at the very least, is doing no more for the accused than the Americans do. In fact, in many cases, where United States law is cited peripherally or not at all, the Court is doing more. . . .
>
> . . . [I]n cases invoking issues such as the use of an accused's prior testimony, the seizure of blood samples, the right to counsel at line-ups and traffic stops, and even the substantive definitions of offenses and defences, . . . the Supreme Court of Canada now protects the interests of the accused more vigorously than its American counterpart. Moreover, this contrast seems due as much to the wording of the *Charter* and the philosophy and approach of the Supreme Court of Canada as to the conservative trend that many commentators believe has been operative in the United States Supreme Court recently.[96]

The authors were at pains to indicate that it is not on every issue that our Court has been more solicitous.[97] For example, it has flatly rejected American authority prohibiting random spot checks[98] and went on to hold that such stops were reasonable limits on the Charter's s. 9 right not to be arbitrarily detained.[99] However, the Court's treatment of involuntary blood samples is much more indicative of the point the authors make. In *R v. Dyment*[100] and a related case,[101] reference to American case-law was absent. There a physician had held a container under the accused's free-flowing wound and thereby obtained a sample for medical purposes. The police had not requested a sample, but in the course of investigation, the doctor handed it over. The Crown contended that such action was not a seizure, but, in any event, was not unreasonable. The Court excluded the evidence, holding that patients have a reasonable expectation that blood will be used for diagnostic purposes and not given to strangers for non-medical reasons. The police had 'seized' the sample within s. 8 of the Charter, there was no compelling reason to do so, and the evidence could not be admitted without bringing the administration of justice into disrepute contrary to s. 24(2).

In contrast, in the leading American decision not discussed in *Dyment*, such arguments were rejected. In *Schmerber* v. *California*,[102] several constitutional arguments were rejected, including one involving the Fourth Amendment's prohibition against search and seizure. This case involved a blood sample taken by a physician at the request of the police after the defendant had objected on the advice of counsel. The Court declared, 'The extraction of blood samples for tests is a highly effective means of determining the degree to which a person is under the influence of alcohol'[103] and in a subsequent case reinforced its view that blood tests 'do not constitute an unduly extensive imposition on an individual's personal privacy and bodily integrity'.[104] Yet in stark contrast, the Supreme Court of Canada insisted in *Dyment* that seizing the vial of blood 'infringed upon all the spheres of privacy . . . spatial, personal and informational'.[105]

After surveying these cases and the 'eccentric' use of American precedent and the due process findings by our Supreme Court, the authors concluded:

> [T]here is a tendency in the Court to cite United States law when it helps or, at least, does not stand in the way of a result it wishes to reach, but not otherwise. Certainly, that is what has been done, thus far, in a number of cases involving traffic stops, line-ups, breath and blood samples, and the case of the accused's prior testimony. . . . The Court's somewhat selective approach to the United States jurisprudence is matched by its relatively consistent commitment to liberal values.[106]

In a follow-up study published in 1992, the authors found that the Court was 'less inclined than in the past to imply that American law is more solicitous to the accused than Canadian law',[107] but reinforced their conclusions that the Court 'has jumped into rights review "head first", and has ended up protecting the interests of accused persons at least as much as, and often more than, the Rhenquist, Burger and, what is more surprising, the Warren Court'.[108]

Do we have any sense of the impact this shift has had on the public? Since the Charter is not yet fifteen years old, it may appear to have had little effect on the underlying criminal justice system as analysed by John Hagan and discussed earlier. Yet there is some specific evidence of disjunction between judges and the general public regarding the impact of the Charter, though the effects of this difference are unclear. The issues revolve around the admission or exclusion of illegally obtained evidence under s. 24(2) of the Charter, an issue discussed in a number of places in this chapter.

The courts have been 'clear and unequivocal'[109] that in deciding to exclude or admit tainted evidence, the standards to be applied are not the personal values of the judge but those of the ordinary reasonable Canadian:[110] 'The concept of disrepute necessarily involves some element of community views, and the determination of disrepute thus requires the judge to refer to what he conceives to be the views of the community at large.' Despite this, the Supreme Court has rejected empirical evidence of public opinion regarding what brings the administration of justice into disrepute because of fears of unreliability[111] and the costs involved. In addition, there are two other related reasons that seem to fly in the face of determining disrepute by community standards. The first is that the public's views might not be reasonable seemingly because they do not have a sufficient appreciation concerning the protection of the accused,[112] and the second is that the Charter 'is designed to protect the accused from the majority, so the enforcement of the Charter must not be left to that majority'.[113]

This is a circle leading back to judicial say-so. Disrepute is not to turn on the judges' personal opinion but rather on community standards. Yet possibly urgent evidence of those standards is not ever to be admissible and in any event the majority cannot be relied upon, so the judges need to make such determinations. Apart from being an ill-disguised imposition of what appear to be judges' highly personal views, this view carries with it a very impoverished notion of Canadian citizens' sense of justice. Further, it begs the question at issue: the majority's resiling at seeing a guilty person go free because of some violation may in fact be a greater disservice to the cause of justice than admitting the tainted evidence. What this circumlocution may offer is some indication of how the embrace of the due process model is insulating the judges from Canadian public opinion.

We can begin by noting that evidence exists to suggest that there is a high degree of consistency between judicial behaviour and public opinion in another area of the criminal justice system: sentencing. There is widespread belief that people are consistently harsher in their belief of what constitutes a just sentence compared with judges' opinions.[114] And if one looks only to opinion evidence about whether the public believe sentencing policy should be harsh, this is borne out: for example, 1987 data indicate that almost 80 per cent believe that sentences ought to be stiffer.[115] However, Roberts and Doob have shown that much of the public's attitude arises because of misinformation they receive about the criminal justice system in terms of sentencing practices, statutory maxima, criminal recidivism rates, parole release rates, and crime rates.[116] When more sophisticated survey questions are asked, results indicate greater leniency and more flexibility regarding the purposes of sentencing. Further, recent data that compares the public's views about using imprisonment with actual incarceration also contradicts the assertion of a popular wish for greater punitiveness. If the public's views were followed, there would actually be fewer, not more, convicted who would be incarcerated.[117] The authors conclude that reform initiatives directed to using incarceration more sparingly should not be constrained because of fears of reactionary public opinion:[118] 'Systematic research using a representative sample of Canadians demonstrates that the public favour the use of incarceration to no greater degree than the courts currently impose. . . . In fact, members of the public would probably support the use of greater restraint concerning this sanction.' The point here is that in an important area of criminal law, there appears to be consistency between the judges and the general public once the latter are apprised of the critical facts.

In contrast, a study concerning the admission of illegal evidence has demonstrated that there is disagreement between the judges and the general public with the latter more likely to exclude evidence.[119] In the larger context being discussed, there is the question of whether this difference should be taken as demonstrating the public's insensitivity to the rights of the accused or as a reasonable reaction to be set against the undue enthusiasm with which the courts have embraced the due process model. The study conducted in 1987 revealed some very interesting general findings. In an initial set of questions, 75.7 per cent had heard of the Charter and 77.7 per cent responded affirmatively to a question of whether the Charter is a good thing.[120] However, a very interesting set of responses was elicited depending on how a question about the Charter's effect on the way the justice system works was posed. Even if respondents were simply asked the question, only 56.1 per cent said it would have a positive effect, but when the questioner explicitly indicated it was possible to answer 'not sure', those answering 'positive' fell to 32.3 per cent while 52.3 per cent answered 'not sure'. Indeed, if one takes account of those who have not heard of the Charter (23.6 per cent), then those who know about the Charter and think it is a good thing represent only 58.8 per cent of the total population.[121]

The study found that the public seemed to utilize the same criteria as rationally as judges to make decisions to exclude or admit illegally obtained evidence.[122] However, the public was less likely to exclude evidence notably in cases where the accused had been drinking and driving and cases that involved violations of the right to counsel. Further, those who oppose the exclusion of evidence are more strongly committed to their view that excluding evidence brings the administration of justice into disrepute than are those who favour exclusion.[123] The authors of this study rightly point out that there should be no leaping to the conclusion that '[a]ny significant gap between judicial and public opinion will undermine public respect for the legal system, and the system will be thrown into a crisis of legitimacy'.[124] Nevertheless, '[w]hat does seem relatively clear is that a significant gap between public and judicial opinion might throw into question the adequacy of the stated rationale as a justification for the rule.'[125]

Two Examples

To illustrate the dangers of the due process trajectory, a discussion of two specific examples may be helpful. In both cases the 'rights' of the accused were recognized. For our purposes, those cases are not so important in terms of whether they are correctly decided (though there are strong reservations about the second) but rather the effect that judicial decisions have on the underlying issues. While it is possible the litigation could actually stimulate response to the larger questions from which it has sprung, the danger is that judicial activity will instead deflect attention away from such issues.[126]

The first is *Askov*[127] holding that a twenty-three month delay between committal and trial violated s. 11(b) of the Charter, which requires the accused 'to be tried within a reasonable time'. Evidence established that the judicial district of Peel, the location of *Askov*, was the slowest in Canada and substantially slower than the worst jurisdiction in the United States,[128] and that the delay in *Askov* was very bad even by Peel's deleterious standards. In holding that s. 11(b) was violated, the Court characterized the case as 'one of the worst from the point of view of delay in the worst district not only in Canada, but so far as the studies indicate, anywhere north of the Rio Grande'.[129]

The holding itself may be entirely defensible as an example of equipping courts to deal with clear cases of delay that have indeed prejudiced the ability of an accused to mount a defence. However, instead of responding to the specific circumstances alone, the Court went on to propound what was taken to be a standard: a period of delay in a range of some six to eight months between committal and trial might be deemed to be the outside limit of what is reasonable.[130] In fairness, elements of the judgement could have been interpreted as allowing flexibility in application. Instead, it became a lightning-rod for the polarization of due process versus crime control. Though possibly the worst jurisdiction in terms of delay, Ontario nevertheless stayed, dismissed, or withdrew some 43,000 charges in the wake of the Supreme Court ruling.[131]

This obvious impact was greeted with horror. That reaction displayed little curiosity about the underlying problems that lead to delay and what ought to be an appropriate balance in this context, but instead mostly seized law and order as the appropriate cudgel.[132] The Attorney-General called for the Supreme Court to review its decision.[133] Judges took to making comments on the bench ('the staying of so many charges . . . has eroded the public's confidence in the administration of justice')[134] and off it (Askov is 'a public relations disaster for the bench').[135]

In speeches and interviews, senior judges decided to weigh in with victims' 'rights' as the order of the day. Describing the system as having a 'black eye', the Chief Justice of the General Division of the Ontario Court of Justice then wondered: 'If you have your house broken into, and you see the guy walk out of a court with a smirk on his face, what do you think about the justice system?'[136] Putting aside qualms about the presumption of innocence, the Chief Justice of Canada opined, '[A] great many guilty people are roaming the streets for months and months and years and years. That is unacceptable.'[137] His solution to all of this was to set up a task force to study delay, its causes, and appropriate solutions (isn't this what legislatures are to do?) while denying the reasons for doing so had any connection with *Askov*.[138] Responding to this announcement, the chief of police in Ottawa (chair of the Law Amendments Committee of the Canadian Association of Chiefs of Police) warned, '[S]omething has to be done because the country is not in good shape with regard to increasing violence and serious crime. There are many people out on the street who are laughing at the justice system.'[139] Justice Cory, who authored *Askov*, publicly expressed his 'shock' at the ruling's impact.[140] This itself set off a furor over the propriety of the judiciary attempting to give 'off-the-bench reinterpretation of what [they] really meant'.[141]

Finally, in just seventeen months after *Askov*, the Supreme Court was able to hear, decide, and issue reasons in another case making time constraint requirements much more flexible.[142] But, of course, this flexibility itself will give rise to many issues in terms of how and when it can be successfully invoked. Refreshingly, the majority this time acknowledged the limits of its capacity: 'Embarking as we did on uncharted waters it is not surprising that the course we steered has required, and may require in the future, some alteration in its direction to accord with experience.'[143]

The fallout from *Askov* should not warn us off concerns for due process. The Charter obviously addresses this value and our history shows that we need continual reminding about its place in the administration of criminal justice. The warning from *Askov* and its aftermath is the danger of how overlitigation of due process concerns can mesmerize our attention to the neglect of the overall consequences for the administration of justice and society at large.

A vital underlying controversy here is a long-standing one over court administration and budgeting: 'Traditionally, the judiciary asserts that insufficient funding of the justice system is the cause [of delay] and the executive responds that inefficient practices and structures in the existing system are the cause . . . [while] it must be recognized that both sides have vested interests and they are not impartial in this debate.'[144] The real concern here is that litigation over delay will not promote workable solutions but will instead become yet another stage for ventilating tensions. It is true that '[r]eal leadership from the executive and the judiciary is required to achieve agreement on this difficult structural issue'.[145] The apprehension is that litigation — unsystematic, unrepresentative, and individually driven — will aggravate these tensions and obscure such structural problems: 'Until greater harmony is achieved, "speedy trials" will be used as a weapon in this institutional battle. This was never the purpose of "speedy trials" and they will suffer from being pressed into service as swords striking blows for ever larger court budgets.'[146] The effect may be that overarching questions around court administration, budgeting, and control, which are complex, sensitive, and linked to other policy and fiscal issues, will be harnessed to the due process trajectory with such litigation not answering these pressing questions but instead taking them further away from political and administrative resolution.

The second example involves the famous rape-shield law and its striking down by the Supreme Court in September 1991 in a case called *Seaboyer*.[147] The infirmities of the judgement have been fully analysed by others. Suffice it to say that, even confining this case to an analysis of 'rights',

Seaboyer was not just about the 'rights' of the accused to a fair trial under s. 7; it was about a clash between that right and 'rights' of equality for women under s. 15 and women's rights under the same s. 7 'to security of the person', points that were forcefully made in a stinging dissent.

The difficult question of how these 'rights' should be recognized in the context of criminal proceedings involving sexual attacks upon women was answered by the legislature over a number of years. It had done so with incremental deliberation,[148] propelled in large part by the careful documentation concerning the lack of redress for victims[149] in the face of the judiciary's persistence in acting upon sexual myths regarding those complaints that did get to trial.[150] The section that was struck down (which in fact did permit evidence of the complainant's sexual activities in limited specified circumstances) was the product of such deliberate change.[151] Nor could such enactments be said to be oblivious to minority interests for, while in some sense accused are a minority in sexual complaints, the clear minority are those victimized women who summon the strength to seek justice. Yet these modifications were set aside by the same body that has continuously reflected and reinforced myths about women's sexuality, even to the extent of gutting previous and more modest legislative attempts to protect women complainants in such criminal processes.

The Supreme Court's decision was greeted by a wave of reactions on both sides: as a rebuff to women in the justice system that would cause fewer assaults to be reported[152] and as a vindication of due process and a halt to feminist tamperings with the law.[153] Those defending the judgement pointed out that while the Supreme Court struck down the legislation, it provided strict guidelines for the admission of evidence of the complainant's sexual history.[154] Critics saw such guidelines as judicial intrusion. The Court may have agreed that sexual stereotypes concerning women are discredited. However, the effect of the judgement was to hand back to trial judges, who are notorious for acting on such myths, a discretion to admit evidence linked to these stereotypes.[155] Then Justice Minister Kim Campbell vowed to reintroduce legislation. Such legislation was reintroduced, involved broad consultation and heated debate among various interests, but progress was deliberate and it passed in June 1992.[156]

One might say at this point that the response to *Seaboyer* confronts one of the basic apprehensions expressed throughout this book: as issues become judicialized, democratic processes will become enervated. Doesn't the fact that the legislature reacted so quickly in taking account of the court's judgement and responding to it provide evidence to the contrary? It is fair to underscore this and to note further that women were involved in the processes in a way that was unthinkable even a decade ago: on the Supreme Court a woman wrote the majority opinion, a woman wrote the dissent, a woman minister of justice led the legislative response, and a diversity of women were actively involved throughout as counsel for various positions and involved in the legislative process.

Yet those sympathetic to women's position can be apprehensive. Let's recast the bidding. In the absence of Charter review, the rape-shield provisions would not have been attacked. This is not to sweep aside due process concerns. As indicated earlier, these legislative provisions were the result of incremental change in which such concerns were well represented and in the wake of more modest alterations that were rebuffed by the judiciary. But before Charter litigation, such legislative alterations were seen to be what they were: one small step in responding to systemic and pervasive inequality of women. They were part of a larger debate about 'how best to promote women's sexual autonomy under social relations which result in women's sexual subordination'.[157]

However, the successful attack on the rape-shield provisions has torn the legislation from this larger context and turned into a dangerous attack on constitutional principles. Yes, there has been a legislative response, but it is depicted as a substantial and dubious concession in the face of established and recognized constitutional ordering.[158] So what started out as a small step is now seen as an enormous concession. The aura of due process, a 'right' now capable of strong popular currency and one that has a legitimate core value may have converted and controlled women's outrage in a way that no political process ever could.

Lessons from a 'Failed Revolution'

We have referred to Rosenberg's *The Hollow Hope*[159] in a number of places. The book examines the effect of litigation on issues involving social change in the United States, especially over the last three decades. For reasons discussed earlier in Chapter Two, Rosenberg concludes generally that such lawsuits have had little or no positive impact and there have been other significant costs. As part of this inquiry, Rosenberg looked at court action to reform the criminal law. Specifically, he examined four areas concerning defendants: (1) protection against illegal search and seizure, (2) the right to remain silent and to be represented, (3) the rights of juvenile defendants, (4) and reform on behalf of prisoners. Since all of those topics have already or could become part of the Canadian judicial inventory, his analysis of the effects of court involvement is instructive.

After sifting through myriad court decisions and studies concerning their effect and acknowledging that 'the argument is more suggestive than definitive',[160] Rosenberg concluded that while the lawsuits were frequently successful in terms of having such 'rights' recognized by the United States Supreme Court,[161] very little about the administration of criminal justice changed for the better. For example, regarding protection from illegal search and seizure, 'a long list of studies ... conclude that the exclusionary rule has not deterred illegal searches and seizures to any significant extent'.[162] There are a number of reasons for this, but one important one is that the rules propounded by the courts were dependent upon the police for their efficacy. Such rules were seen as hampering law enforcement and treated as such: 'for the exclusionary rule to be routinely effective, either police officers must internalize the rule or the command structure must institute incentives for compliance or penalties for noncompliance. Studies suggest that neither has happened to any great extent, nor is likely to soon.'[163] There has been little impact in terms of the need to be informed of the right to remain silent. This is not because the police do not give the warning but rather that it is given in a tone and manner so as to convey 'a routine, meaningless legalism'.[164] Combined with a general lack of understanding and the need to make decisions under extreme pressure, this leads 'many, if not most suspects . . . [to] frequently make statements to the police even against the advice of their attorneys'.[165]

Those involved in prison reform proclaimed that the 'collective result of this litigation has been nothing less than the achievement of a legal revolution within a decade'.[166] This was true in the sense of courts becoming implicated in the running of prisons: by 1986, forty-five states had at least one such facility in litigation, while in thirty-seven states correctional administration prisons were actually operating under federal court orders.[167] Some are optimistic about where such judicial activity will lead.[168] Nevertheless, Rosenberg and others[169] insist that 'problems still abound'.[170] Such difficulties include serious overcrowding and rampant prison violence: 'despite . . . close scrutiny and mandated reforms, many prisons are less safe than they were in the pre-reform days'.[171] A particularly difficult element in achieving change is that its effectiveness depends on prison administrators.[172] Since prisons must be strictly regulated, it is comparatively easily to resist implementation of court orders for ostensibly legitimate reasons and by the same token, it is much more difficult for those who seek reform to monitor such implementation: 'when California corrections administrators were asked, in a survey if they could "comply with court orders through changes which meet the letter of the court order, but not its spirit, and thereby frustrate the intent of the court," a whopping 87 per cent said yes. As one administrator put it in a follow-up interview, "we can usually get around anything".'[173]

Of particular interest for our discussion is the response of those who have invoked court strategies in the face of such mixed results. A typical rejoinder is that there is no choice because it is all that is left: 'litigation is the clumsiest, most frustrating, costliest way of doing anything, but it's the only game in town because of the default of the other branches of government'.[174] But, in fact, Rosenberg maintains that there is scant evidence demonstrating that reformers have sought change on a concerted basis other than from courts. Such lack of actual impact has led some court reformers to embrace the emblematic potential of law: 'the symbolic effects of criminal procedure guarantees are important; they underscore our societal commitment to restraint in an area in which emotions easily run uncontrolled'.[175] But as Rosenberg responds; 'Reliance on courts will not bring much change. The political challenge must be faced directly.'[176] Otherwise symbols are indeed the result, while those relying on litigation 'may be misled (or content?) to celebrate the illusion of change'.[177] Rosenberg starkly concludes his study of litigation focused on criminal rights: '[t]he revolution failed'.[178]

CONCLUSION:
GLIMPSING THE 'GOLDEN CUPOLA'?

Any effective yet humane system of criminal justice must hold in tension the competing values of crime control and due process, but the balance can be struck in different ways in different societies. The effect of such balance on the society is (again harkening back to Chapter Two) a difficult question to answer in terms of cause and effect. Yet one may fairly ask if it is more than coincidence that the United States, the home of due process and litigation to effect reform of the criminal system, is one of the most crime-ridden societies in the world. Canada, by contrast, has historically accorded more influence to crime control in its justice system and has consistently experienced much less violent crime. Meanwhile, as documented earlier in this chapter, the United States has also spent more per capita on its police, courts, and institutions of correction and resorts to capital punishment with grisly frequency.

The danger of judicializing the models of criminal law is not so much that due process will, in itself, be given undue prominence by the judiciary. Judges are part and parcel of the administration of criminal justice and our history and awe of authority suggest that more heightened awareness of assuring that the accused receives fair treatment is not wrong-headed. The danger is that in harnessing due process to the 'rights' discourse, that value will be given a momentum in courts that blunts other concerns, such as protecting women from violence, fiscal responsibility for the administration of criminal justice, and punishing the guilty, even if relevant evidence is somehow tainted.

Further, there is a real fear that due process as the focus of reform will in fact change very little about the criminal justice system, but will nevertheless deflect attention away from underlying issues in terms of the causes of crime and the consequences for Canadian society. Outside the courts' praise for due process, even if matched at times with cries for law and order, could muffle concerns that are closely linked to achieving both an effective and fair justice system and low rates of crime. Sadly, such concerns are too well known: poverty, gender inequality, treatment of minorities and Aboriginals, and police forces that are not fully diverse and accountable but that are at the same time not supported.[179] The fear is that this harsh but evocative description of the American criminal justice system will come to accurately describe ours: 'the constitutional revolution in criminal procedure has amounted to little more than an ornament, or golden cupola, built upon the roof of a structure found rotting and infested, assuring the gentle folk who only pass by without entering that all is well inside'.[180]

NOTES

[1] Much of the section depends on the introduction to two Canadian treatises on criminal law. D. Stuart, *Canadian Criminal Law — A Treatise* (2nd ed.) (Toronto: Carswell Co. Ltd, 1987), and A. Mewett and M. Manning, *Criminal Law* (2nd ed.) (Toronto: Butterworths, 1985).

[2] R. Penner, 'Review of *Our Criminal Law* and *Limits of Criminal Law*' (1978) 20 *Canadian Journal of Criminology and Corrections*, 343, 345.

[3] Mewett and Manning, *supra*, note 1 at 12.

[4] Stuart, *supra*, note 1 at 51–2.

[5] S.M. Lipset, *Continental Divide: The Values and Institutions of the United States and Canada* (Toronto: C.D. Howe Institute, 1989): 225.

[6] See, for example, Manitoba, Public Inquiry into the Administration of Justice and Aboriginal People, *Report of the Aboriginal Justice Inquiry of Manitoba*, vols 1 and 2 (Winnipeg: Queen's Printer, 1991).

[7] *Supra*, note 5 at 90.

[8] Ibid., 90.

[9] Ibid., 91.

[10] K. McNaught, *The Pelican History of Canada* (Harmondsworth: Penguin Books, 1982): 146.

[11] Though see K. McNaught, 'Political Trials and the Canadian Political Tradition' in M. Friedland, *Courts and Trials: A Multidisciplinary Approach* (Toronto: University of Toronto, 1975), which argues that, with important exceptions — Riel, for instance — repressive reaction to insurrection would be followed by a retreat from such harshness (143): '[Canada was] a society which felt secure enough in its basic attitudes toward legitimacy to act quickly when these attitudes were challenged while showing extreme leniency once the threat appeared to have passed.'

[12] *Supra*, note 5 at 92.

[13] Ibid., 91, and O. Dickason, *Canada's First Nations: A History of Founding Peoples from Earliest Times* (Toronto: McClelland & Stewart, 1992): Chapter 19.

[14] A. Borovoy, *When Freedoms Collide* (Toronto: Lester & Orpen Dennys, 1988): 1–9.

[15] *Supra*, note 5 at 94.

[16] A. Westin, 'The United States Bill of Rights and the Canadian Charter: A Socio-Political Analysis' in W. Mckescher (ed.), *The US Bill of Rights and the Canadian Charter of Rights and Freedoms* (Toronto: Ontario Economic Council, 1983): 41.

[17] P. Sniderman et al., 'Liberty, Authority and Community: Civil Liberties and the Canadian Political Culture' (Centre of Criminology, University of Toronto and

Survey Research Centre, University of California, Berkeley, 1988): figures 9A–9D.

[18] *Supra*, note 5 at 111–12 discussing CARA — Gallup studies of the early 1980s.

[19] Ibid., 112.

[20] J. Hagan, 'Comparing Crime and Criminalization in Canada and the USA' (1989) 14 *Canadian Journal of Sociology*, 361, 365.

[21] Ibid., 367.

[22] Ibid. These conclusions have been challenged by R. Lenton, 'Homicide in Canada and the USA: A Critique of the Hagan Thesis' (1989) 14 *Canadian Journal of Sociology*, 163 and responded to by Hagan, ibid.

[23] C. Taylor and D. Jodice, *World Handbook of Political and Social Indicators* (3rd ed., vol. 2) (New Haven: Yale University Press, 1983): 19–25, 33–6, 47–51.

[24] *Supra*, note 5 at 97–100, citing a number of studies.

[25] D. Baer et al., 'Canadian and American Values; Reassessing the Differences' in J. Curtis and L. Tepperman (eds), *Images of Canada: The Sociological Tradition* (Scarborough: Prentice Hall, Canada, 1989).

[26] G. Rocher, 'Comments on Seymour Martin Lipset's "Canada and the United States: The Cultural Dimension"' (Montreal: Faculty of Law, University of Quebec at Montreal, 1988): 4, 7, 8–9.

[27] J. Hagan, *The Disreputable Pleasures* (3rd ed.) (Toronto: McGraw-Hill Ryerson; 1991).

[28] H. Packer, 'Two Models of the Criminal Process' (1964) 113 *University of Pennsylvania Law Review*, 1.

[29] *Supra*, note 27 at 225, and J. Hagan, 'Crime, Deviance and Legal Order' in J. Curtis and L. Tepperman (eds), *Understanding Canadian Society* (Toronto: McGraw-Hill Ryerson, 1988): 425, 426–7.

[30] P. Russell, 'The Political Role of the Supreme Court of Canada in Its First Century' (1975) 53 *Canadian Bar Review*, 577, 593.

[31] *Supra*, note 27 at 226.

[32] Ibid., 226–7.

[33] 'Texas Inmate Executed for Slaying in $8 Burglary', *The New York Times*, 12 August 1992, A12.

[34] The litigation was filed in California in the Federal Court. Prominent columnists, such as George Will and Anthony Lewis, treated the issues very seriously, accepting that there really is a set of advantages and disadvantages to such horror: see, e.g., L. Goodman, 'Executions on Television: Defining the Issues', *The New York Times*, 30 May 1991, B6.

[35] See also R. Ericson and P. Baranek, *The Ordering of Justice: A Study of Accused Persons as Dependents in the Criminal Process* (Toronto: University of Toronto Press, 1982).

[36] [1957] *Supreme Court Reports*, 531; 26 *Criminal Reports*, 193; 118 *Canadian Criminal Cases*, 129.

[37] P. Weiler, *In the Last Resort — A Critical Study of the Supreme Court of Canada* (Toronto: Carswell-Methuen, 1974): 92–5.

[38] *R. v. Beaver*, *supra*, note 36 at 554 (SCR) and elsewhere 547, 554:

> The plain and apparent object of the Act is to prevent, by a rigid control of the

possession of drugs, the danger to public health, and to guard against the social evils which an uncontrolled traffic in drugs is bound to generate. . . .

The enforcement sections of the Act manifest the exceptional vigilance and firmness which Parliament thought of the essence to forestall the unlawful traffic in narcotic drugs and cope effectively with the unusual difficulties standing in the way of the realization of the object of the statute.

[39] R. v. *Pierce Fisheries Ltd* [1971] 5 *Supreme Court Reports*, 13–14.

[40] See *R. v. George* [1960] *Supreme Court Reports*, 871 and Weiler, *supra*, note 37 at 104–8.

[41] *Supra*, note 37 at 109–10.

[42] R. v. *Carker* [1967] *Supreme Court Reports*, 114.

[43] *Supra*, note 37 at 111.

[44] Formerly s. 202 then s. 213 of the Criminal Code.

[45] R. v. *Trinneer* [1970] *Supreme Court Reports*, 638.

[46] *Supra*, note 37 at 112–15, and J. Willis, 'Case and Comment' (1951) 29 *Canadian Bar Review*, 784.

[47] See *R. v. Vaillancourt* [1987] 2 *Supreme Court Reports*, 636, and *R. v. Logan* [1990] 2 *Supreme Court Reports*, 731. For a discussion of the difficulties surrounding the Supreme Court's decisions in these cases, see R. Cairns Way, 'The Charter, The Supreme Court and the Invisible Politics of Fault' (1993) 12 *Windsor Yearbook of Access to Justice* (forthcoming).

[48] See K. Roach, 'Constitutionalizing Disrepute: Exclusion of Evidence After Therens' (1986) 4412 *University of Toronto Faculty of Law Review*, 209, 215–16.

[49] The doctrine of the 'fruit of the poison tree' was first enunciated in *Silverthorne Lumber Co. v. United States* (1939) 308 US 338: see K. Pye, 'The Rights of Persons Accused of Crime under the Canadian Constitution: A Comparative Perspective' (1982) 45 *Law and Contemporary Problems*, 221, 245n.150.

[50] [1971] *Supreme Court Reports*, 272.

[51] Ibid., 299–300 (Judson, J.).

[52] *Supra*, note 48 at 220. Roach articulates but does not agree with this view.

[53] L. Katz, 'Reflections on Search and Seizure and Illegally Seized Evidence in Canada and the United States' (1980) 3 *Canada-US Law Journal*, 103 at 124.

[54] (1975) 48 *Dominion Law Review* (3d) 427 (SCC) (breathalyser results obtained in violation of dependant's right to assistance of counsel were admitted).

[55] *Supra*, note 53 at 138.

[56] *Supra*, note 48 at 220.

[57] Law Reform Commission of Canada, *Report on Evidence* (Ottawa: Law Reform Commission, 1975).

[58] Commission of Inquiry Concerning Certain Activities of the Royal Canadian Mounted Police, *Freedom and Security under the Law: Second Report* (Ottawa: Commission of Inquiry, 1981).

[59] See also the *Report of the Canadian Committee on Corrections* (Ottawa: Information Canada, 1969): 70–5 (the Ouimet Commission) and the Ontario Law Reform Commission, *Report on the Law of Evidence* (Toronto: Ministry of the Attorney-General, 1976): 57–94.

[60]Law Reform Commission of Canada, *Report On Evidence* (Ottawa: Law Reform Commission, 1975): s. 15.

[61]*Supra*, note 58, and ibid.

[62]*Supra*, note 48 at 216.

[63]Federal-Provincial Task Force on the Rules of Evidence, *Report of the Federal-Provincial Task Force on Uniform Rules of Evidence* (Toronto: Carswell, 1982).

[64]Ibid., 231–2.

[65]R. McLeod, 'The Pitfalls in Americanizing the Canadian Criminal Law', *The Globe and Mail*, 11 March 1981, 7, and J. Ackroyd of the Association of Chiefs of Police, Special Joint Committee on the Constitution, Minutes of Proceedings and Evidence, *Minutes of Proceedings*, Issue 14 at 19.

[66](1982), as quoted in Roach, 'Constitutionalizing Disrepute', *supra*, note 48 at 218n.35.

[67]Roach, *supra*, note 48 at 218–21, discusses the various versions.

[68]F.L. Morton et al., 'The Supreme Court's First One Hundred Charter of Rights Decisions: A Statistical Analysis' (1992) 30 *Osgoode Hall Law Journal*, 1 at 22.

[69]This summary is taken from K. Roach, 'The Charter and the Criminal Process' in J. Gladstone, R. Ericson, C. Shearing (eds), *Criminology: A Reader's Guide* (Toronto: Centre of Criminology, University of Toronto, 1991): 197–8.

[70]Government of Canada, *The Canadian Constitution: Proposed Resolution 1980* ss. 8, 9, 11(d) [hereinafter the 1980 Proposals].

[71]*Canadian Charter of Rights and Freedoms*, Part I of the *Constitution Act, 1982*, being Schedule B of the *Canada Act 1982* (UK) 1982, c. 11, s. 8 [hereinafter The Charter].

[72]The Charter, s. 9.

[73]The Charter, s. 11(e).

[74]The Charter, s. 11(c).

[75]The Charter, s. 10(b).

[76]The Charter, s. 11(f).

[77]1980 Proposals, *supra*, note 70 at s. 26.

[78]K. Pye, *supra*, note 49.

[79]Ibid., 246.

[80]M. Friedland, 'Criminal Justice and the Charter' in *A Century of Criminal Justice* (Toronto: Carswell, 1984): 205–31.

[81]F.L. Morton and M.S. Withey, 'Charting the Charter, 1982–5: A Statistical Analysis' [1987] 4 *Canadian Human Rights Yearbook*, 65–90.

[82]P. Monahan, *Politics and the Constitution: The Charter, Federalism and the Supreme Court of Canada* (Toronto: Carswell, 1987), 37.

[83]*Supra*, note 68 at 21.

[84]*Supra*, note 48 at 198 for discussion and citations.

[85]*Supra*, note 68 at 22.

[86]*Supra*, note 48 at 200.

[87]Ibid., citing M. Friedland, 'Criminal Justice and the Charter' in M. Friedland, *A Century of Criminal Justice* (Toronto: Carswell, 1984), and R. Salhany, *The Origins*

of Rights (Toronto: Carswell, 1986).

[88] Ibid., 201.

[89] Ibid.

[90] Ibid., 201–2.

[91] Ibid., citing N. Boyd et al., 'Case Law and Drug Convictions: Testing the Rhetoric of Equality Rights' (1987) 29 *Criminal Law Quarterly*, 487; R. Ericson, *The Constitution of Legal Inequality* (Ottawa: Carleton University Information Services, 1983); P. Marshall, 'Sexual Assault, the Charter and Sentencing Reform' (1988) 63 *Criminal Reports* (3d) 216.

[92] Roach, *supra*, note 48 at 202, citing D. Kairys (ed.), *The Politics of Law: A Progressive Critique* (New York: Pantheon Books, 1982); M. Mandel, *The Charter of Rights and the Legalization of Politics in Canada* (Toronto: Wall & Thompson, 1989).

[93] Ibid., 203 (citations omitted).

[94] R. Harvie and H. Foster, 'Ties That Bind? The Supreme Court of Canada, American Jurisprudence, and the Revision of Canadian Criminal Law under the Charter' (1990) 28 *Osgoode Hall Law Journal*, 729.

[95] For example, *R. v. Lavallee* [1990] 4 *Western Weekly Reports*, 31 (SCC); *R. v. Askov* [1990] 2 *Supreme Court Reports*, 1199; *R. v. Seaboyer* [1991] 2 *Supreme Court Reports*, 517.

[96] Harvie and Foster, *supra*, note 94 at 734–5 and 782. See also C. Manfredi, 'The Use of United States Decisions by the Supreme Court of Canada under the Charter of Rights and Freedoms' (1990) 23 *Canadian Journal of Political Science*, 499.

[97] Harvie and Foster, ibid., 776–8.

[98] *Delaware v. Prouse* (1979) 440 US 648.

[99] *Hufsky v. R.* [1988] 1 *Supreme Court Reports*, 621.

[100] *R. v. Dyment* [1988] 45 *Canadian Criminal Cases*, (3d) 244 (SCC).

[101] *R. v. Pohoretsky* [1987] 1 *Supreme Court Reports*, 945.

[102] *Schmerber v. California* (1966) 384 US 757.

[103] Ibid., 771.

[104] *Winston v. Lee* (1984) 470 US 753 at 762.

[105] *Supra*, note 100 at 261.

[106] *Supra*, note 94 at 778–9.

[107] R. Harvie and H. Foster, 'Different Drummers, Different Drums: The Supreme Court of Canada, American Jurisprudence and the Continuing Revisions of Criminal Law under the Charter' (1992) 24 *Ottawa Law Review*, 39, 110.

[108] Ibid., 109.

[109] A. Bryant et al., 'Public Attitudes toward the Exclusion of Evidence: Section 24(2) of the Canadian Charter of Rights and Freedoms' (1990) 69 *Canadian Bar Review*, 1, 8; D. Gibson, 'Determining Disrepute: Opinion Polls and the Canadian Charter of Rights and Freedoms' (1983) 61 *Canadian Bar Review*, 377.

[110] *R. v. Collins* [1987] 1 *Supreme Court Reports*, 265 at 281–2.

[111] *R. v. Therens* [1985] 1 *Supreme Court Reports*, 613.

[112] *Supra*, note 110 at 281–2: 'Members of the public generally become conscious

of the importance of protecting the rights and freedoms of accused only when they are in some way brought closer to the system either personally or through the experience of friends or family.'

[113] Ibid.

[114] Including some academics: see, e.g., E. Fattah, 'Making the Punishment fit the Crime: The Case of Imprisonment' (1982) 24 *Canadian Journal of Criminology*, 1.

[115] J. Roberts and A. Doob, 'Sentencing and Public Opinion: Taking False Shadows for True Substances' (1989) 27 *Osgoode Hall Law Journal*, 491, citing Canadian Gallup Poll Limited, '78% Polled Say Courts Too Easy on Criminals', *The [Ottawa] Citizen*, 14 January 1987, 4.

[116] Ibid., 514–15 summarizing findings.

[117] Ibid., 514.

[118] Ibid., 515.

[119] Bryant et al., *supra*, note 109.

[120] Ibid., 14–15.

[121] Ibid.

[122] Ibid., 43.

[123] Ibid.

[124] Ibid.

[125] Ibid., 45.

[126] For a similar analysis focusing upon the Supreme Court's constitutionalizing fault in the context of criminal law, see Cairns Way, *supra*, note 47.

[127] *R. v. Askov*, [1990] 2 *Supreme Court Reports*, 1199.

[128] Ibid., 1239.

[129] Ibid.

[130] Ibid., 1240; R. Knopff and F. Morton, *Charter Politics* (Toronto: Nelson, 1992): 218.

[131] D. Downey, 'Courts Catching Up on Backlog of Cases Created by Askov Decision', *The Globe and Mail*, 11 July 1991, A10; D. Brillinger, 'Ont. CA Puts Brakes on 'Draconian' Result of SCC Askov Ruling', *Lawyers Weekly*, 14 June 1991, 1.

[132] Knopff and Morton, *supra*, note 130 at 220–1; P. Mathias, 'Supreme Court Lacks "Common Sense"', *Financial Post*, 1 September 1991, 9.

[133] Canadian Press, 'Hampton Calls for Review of Ruling in Askov Case', *The Globe and Mail*, 17 July 1991, A5.

[134] *R. v. Bennett* (1991) 3 *Ontario Reports* (3d) 193 (CA) at 196.

[135] 'Askov Case Created "Public Relations Disaster" for Judges', *The Lawyers Weekly*, 6 September 1991, 1, quoting BC Supreme Court Justice Stuart M. Leggatt.

[136] 'Judges May Have Misinterpreted *Askov*, Ont. Chief Justice Suggests', *The Lawyers Weekly*, 14 December 1990, 14.

[137] J. Middlemiss, 'Public Has Lost Confidence in the Courts: Chief Justice', *Law Times*, 26 August–1 September 1991, 1.

[138] Ibid., S. Bindman, 'Lamer Announces "Urgent" Study into "Unacceptable" Court Delays', *The Lawyers Weekly*, 6 September 1991, 7.

[139]Bindman, ibid.

[140]Editorial, 'Justice Cory Learns Lesson', *Law Times*, 22–8 July 1991, 6.

[141]Canadian Press, 'Hampton Calls for Review of Ruling in Askov Case', *The Globe and Mail*, 17 July 1991, A5.

[142]*R. v. Morin* [1992] 1 *Supreme Court Reports*, 771; *R. v. Sharma* [1992] 1 *Supreme Court Reports*, 814.

[143]Ibid., 784.

[144]M. Code, *A Comparative Study of the Impact of Constitutional Instruments on the American and Canadian Criminal Justice Systems: Procedure Governing Constitutional Hearings and Trial Within a Reasonable Time* (LL. M. thesis, University of Toronto, 1991): 264.

[145]Ibid., 268.

[146]Ibid., 267.

[147]*R. v. Seaboyer* [1991] 2 *Supreme Court Reports*, 517.

[148]Attempts to protect complainants were first enacted in 1976: see s. 142 of the Criminal Code enacted by the Criminal Law Amendment Act 1975, SC 1974–75–76, c. 93, s. 8.

[149]For example, L. Clarke and D. Lewis, *Rape: The Price of Coercive Sexuality* (Toronto: Women's Press, 1977).

[150]*R. v. Forsythe* [1980] 2 *Supreme Court Reports*, 268; *R. v. Kenkin* [1983] 1 *Supreme Court Reports*, 388. See C. Boyle, 'Section 142 of the Criminal Code: A Trojan Horse?' (1981) 23 *Criminal Law Quarterly*, 253, and E. Sheehy, 'Feminist Argumentation Before the Supreme Court of Canada in *R. v. Seaboyer, R. v. Gayne*: "The Sound of One Hand Clapping"' (1991) 18 *Melbourne University Law Review*, 450 at 452.

[151]S. 276 was struck down; another related one, s. 277, was upheld: see *The Criminal Law Amendment Act*, SC 1980–81–82, c. 125, 2.246.6, renumbered as s. 276, RSC 1985, Vol. 1, c. 19.

[152]S. Scott, 'Without Rape Shield Law, What Protection?' *Montreal Gazette*, 21 September 1991, B4; J. Baxter, 'Women Stage Rally Against Ending of Rape Shield Law', 29 August 1991, *The Vancouver Sun*, B3; P. Kulig, 'SCC Rape Shield Ruling Means Tough Times Ahead in Prosecuting Sex Assaults Says Crown Attorney', *Law Times* 23–9 September 1991, 10.

[153]L. Still, 'Critics of Judgment Jumping the Gun', *The Vancouver Sun*, 29 August 1991, B3; D. Paciocco, 'In Some Cases, Evidence of Prior Sexual Conduct Can Be Crucial', *The Toronto Star*, 8 October 1991, A17; D. Paciocco, 'The Charter and the Rape Shield Provisions of the Criminal Code: More About Relevance and the Constitutional Exemptions Doctrine' (1989) 21 *Ottawa Law Review*, 119 at 130.

[154]P. Kulig, *supra*, note 152.

[155]A. Acorn, '*R. v. Seaboyer*: Pornographic Imagination and the Springs of Relevance' (1991) 3 *Constitutional Forum*, 25.

[156]J. Sallot, 'Political Battle Looms over Sex Assault Bill', *The Globe and Mail*, 13 December 1991, A6; S. Fine, 'Sexual Assault Bill Wins Approval', *The Globe and Mail*, 16 June 1992, A12.

[157] J. Fudge, 'What Do We Mean by Law and Social Transformation' (1990) 5 *Canadian Journal of Law and Society/Revue canadienne de droit et société* 47 at 59.

[158] D. Stuart, 'Sexual Assault: Substantive Issues Before and After Bill C-49' (1993) 35 *Criminal Law Quarterly*, 241.

[159] G. Rosenberg, *The Hollow Hope — Can Courts Bring About Social Change?* (Chicago: University of Chicago Press, 1991).

[160] Ibid., 304.

[161] For example, *Mapp* v. *Ohio* 367 US 643 (1961) (search and seizure); *Gideon* v. *Wainright*, 429 US 335 (1963), *Miranda* v. *Arizona* 384 US 436 (1966) (rights of criminal defendants); *In Re Gault* 387 US 1 (1967) (rights of juvenile defendants).

[162] *Supra*, note 159 at 318.

[163] Ibid., 321.

[164] Ibid., 327.

[165] Ibid., 326, quoting H. Pollack, 'Comments' in 'Symposium: The Future of Criminal Justice under the Constitution', 25 *Crime Law Bulletin*, 3 (January/February 1989) at 26–7.

[166] Ibid., 306, quoting L. Orland, *Prisons: Houses of Darkness* (New York: The Free Press, 1975): 11.

[167] Ibid., 306, quoting J. Brakel, 'Prison Reform Litigation: Has the Revolution Gone Too Far?' (1986) 70 *Judicature*, 5.

[168] See M. Feeley and E. Rubin, 'Prison Litigation and Bureaucratic Development', [1992] *Law and Social Inquiry*, 125 (reviewing S. Martin and S. Ekland-Olson, *Texas Prisons: The Walls Come Tumbling Down*; B. Crouch and J. Marquart, *An Appeal to Justice: Litigated Reform of Texas Prisons*; J. DiIulio Jr, *Governing Prisons: A Comparative Study of Correctional Management*; L. Yackle, *Reform and Regret: The Story of Federal Judicial Involvement in the Alabama Prison System*) (145). 'the lasting impact of the prisoners' rights movement will be stronger, better organized, and more efficient institutions'.

[169] In the context of reform schools, but speaking more generally of such litigation, see J. Miller, *Last One Over the Wall — The Massachusetts Experiment in Closing Reform Schools* (Columbus: Ohio State University, 1991): 'Looking at the results [of lawsuits], one wonders whether the effort was worth it. Court decisions have no doubt moderated harsh prison conditions and softened some of the grosser brutalities [but they have] served to reinforce reliance on the failed institutional model as our primary correctional response to crime.' Quoted in D. Anderson, 'Let His Children GO', *New York Times Book Review*, 26 January 1992, 19.

[170] *Supra*, note 159 at 307. See also S. Rhodes, 'Prison Reform and Prison Life: Four Books on the Process of Court-Ordered Change' (1992) 26 *Law & Society Review*, 189 (reviewing Crouch and Marquart, *An Appeal to Justice*; Useem and Kimball, *State of Siege*; Wood (ed.), *Remedial Law*; Yackle, *Reform & Regret*). Rhodes is more optimistic (211):'[E]xisting information suggests that since the 1970's judicial intervention has made prison conditions significantly more humane than they would otherwise have been.' Nevertheless, she goes on to describe many problems and uncertainties, for example, (213): 'Tight budgets highlight the inadequacies . . . in the courts' capacity to make effective social policy. Further, courts' ability to secure implementation of orders that lack the backing of other

policy makers is very limited. When implementation fails and prison litigation becomes deadlocked . . . the legitimacy of the correctional administration is damaged.'

[171] *Supra*, note 159, 307, quoting Brakel (1986) at 6.

[172] There has been little study of the impact of any litigation on behalf of prison reform in Canada. In *Prisoners of Isolation* (Toronto: University of Toronto Press, 1983), M. Jackson discusses the effects of a Bill of Rights case, *McCann* v. *The Queen* (1976) 29 *Canadian Criminal Cases* (2d) 337 (Fed. TD) concerning solitary confinement. Though the plaintiff won, Jackson concludes the conditions were not reformed (181-2): '[b]ehind the thin veneer of physical changes, solitary confinement in maximum security was still characterized by virtually the same inhumanity and gratuitous cruelty that had existed before the trial'. Cited in K. Roach *Constitutional Remedies in Canada* (Toronto: Canada Law Book, 1994): Chapter 9 (forthcoming).

[173] Rosenberg, *supra*, note 159 at 310, quoting Project, 'Judicial Intervention in Corrections: The Californian Experience—An Empirical Study' (1973) 20 *UCLA Law Review*, 452 at 530–1.

[174] Ibid., 313, quoting W.B. Turner. Discussion in Colloquium, 'The Prison Overcrowding Crisis' (1984) 12 *New York University Law Review Law and Social Change*, 347.

[175] Ibid., 340, quoting Schulhofer, 'Reconsidering *Miranda*' (1987) 54 *University of Chicago Law Review*, 435 at 460.

[176] Ibid., 313.

[177] Ibid., 340.

[178] Ibid., 335.

[179] See, for example, Nova Scotia, Royal Commission on the Donald Marshall, Jr Prosecution, *Findings and Recommendations*, vol. 1, *Consultative Conference on Discrimination against Natives and Blacks in the Criminal Justice System and the Role of the Attorney General*, vol. 7 (Halifax: The Royal Commission, 1989).

[180] Rosenberg, *supra*, note 159 at 340, quoting M. Tigar, 'Forward — Waiver of Constitutional Rights: Disquiet in the Citadel' (1970) 84 *Harvard Law Review*, 1 at 7.

CHAPTER EIGHT

Nation Building, Regionalism, and Federalism Litigation

INTRODUCTION

It has been said, 'Probably no other Canadian political subject has been more controversial and more written about than the various aspects of federalism.'[1] As we saw in Chapter One, two themes have loomed large in these discussions. The first concerns primarily economic issues and to what extent they would be controlled by the federal or regional governments. A perennial subtext here was that federal superiority was not used for the good of the country as a whole but instead served the interests of the financial heartland — Quebec and Ontario — with the rest of Canada as its hinterland. This view was represented by the other provinces, most prominently the four Western provinces, led by Albera. The second subtext was about linguistic and cultural issues and from this perspective, the country was divided between Quebec as the homeland for the French language and culture and the rest of the country. Although Quebec is part of central Canada, the rest of Canada at times has set it apart because of its linguistic, political, and cultural heritage.

So from the beginning the country was in tension because of two competing ideas: regionalism and nation building. Their shared purpose was to construct an independent country, but the means to do that were widely divergent. The regionalists sought to recognize the existing diversity and to use it to form points of focus in a vast country with a dispersed population. These differences would allow the regions to build on their strengths that, taken together, would be forged into a vital Canada. On the other hand, the nation builders saw the provinces as a repository for *only* local interests. The prospect for a united and strong Canada lay with a robust national government, so regionalism was a force to be checked.

The claims around regionalism and nation building have often been garbed in the highest (yet competing) political values, even if this meant selective use of the evidence. From its great proponents like John A. Macdonald[2] down to F.R. Scott,[3] nation building has attempted to associate itself with the overarching public good evidenced in effective and equitable social and economic regulation and the enhancement of civil liberties: '[P]rovincial autonomy [means] national inactivity . . . the more we have of the one, the more we have of the other.'[4] In contrast, regionalists have chronically sought to associate themselves with claims about furthering democracy itself.[5] This is because small units will be able to better reflect the needs of the people living within them and their particular views about what constitutes sound economic and social policy rather than leaving such needs to the vagaries and dilution of the larger unit: 'an increase in the number of governmental units increases the probability that any person living in any jurisdiction will be a member of a majority able to secure for him or herself the quantity and quality of public policies that he or she (and others of his or her group) prefer.'[6]

This tension between the federal government and its claims to act for the national interest and the regions and their contentions that they reflect particular, more democratic concerns is housed in litigation regarding federal-provincial powers under the Constitution, with most of the information we have coming from studies focused upon the Supreme Court of Canada. At the same time, we will see that any number of devices have been used, sometimes cooperatively, sometimes competitively, to shift power between the provinces and the federal government in which the courts have had little or no role: the discontinuance of the disallowance and reservation powers, constitutional amendment, and the spending power. The role that the courts have played can be summed up by referring to three periods, roughly in chronological order. The first (before 1950) focuses upon the decisions of the Judicial Committee of the Privy Council (an English body, at that time Canada's final court of appeal) and their substantial decentralizing effect as a variety of powers claimed by the provinces were recognized. The second extends roughly from 1950 into the 1970s when the courts had relatively little influence because of prevailing norms concerning cooperative federalism. Such ideas stipulated that disagreements between Ottawa and the provinces ought to be resolved through negotiation and not in the courts.

The third period begins in the 1970s (but takes into account the relatively few cases from 1950) and extends to the present, a period in which there has been an appreciable rise in federalism litigation. The impact of the decisions is less clear. There is a charge of bias alleging that the courts preferred Ottawa, for which there is some but not definitive evidence. There are also grounds for asserting that the Supreme Court was the federal institution most sympathetic to Quebec's aspirations, at least until the latter part of the period. In general, the decisions were used as bargaining counters in the continuing adjustments between the levels of government — which were no longer as cooperative as they once were — but the precise effect of any of these decisions has been too little studied to assert any more confident conclusions.

As we enter the 1990s, the danger is not that there will be such litigation or even more of it but that it will be too easily viewed as a substitute for the necessary process of bargaining and negotiation that must lie at the heart of the federal-provincial pact if we are to survive. Attempts to renew federalism through constitutional overhaul have foundered as the debris of Meech Lake and Charlottetown attest. In the aftermath, the temptation is that we will too easily depend on the courts to sort through the tensions of the federal-provincial pact if a sense of drift begins to dominate our national life.

THE PURPOSES OF A FEDERAL SYSTEM OF GOVERNMENT AND THE ROLE OF JUDICIAL REVIEW

All federal systems of government reflect the idea that a country has taken hold, but the various blocs will not surrender what they believe to be their autonomy. Political, economic, social, and cultural requirements are simply too great. A country is formed, but the power to govern is divided between the central and regional governments in ways judged best to serve their respective interests. With the realization of a federation, the underlying tensions that resulted in it (rather than a unitary government) may remain. As we have seen, this was manifestly the case for Canada. Thus the impulse is to find an arbiter who will police the boundaries of power between the two levels of government. It is not surprising, therefore, that judicial review has sometimes been seen (at least by legal scholars) to hold a central role in Canadian federalism despite the fact that there is no mandate in the British North America Act to courts to perform this task. Instead, the bedrock for the role was the widely shared belief that there could not be boundaries to division of power without a means of enforcing those boundaries.[7]

However, there is nothing necessary or inevitable about courts arbitrating disputes between levels of government in a federal system. A point of comparison here is the United States where federalism lawsuits have languished for several decades, though Bill of Rights litigation proceeds apace. The meagre activity has been summarized by Hogg:

> In the last forty-nine years, the [Supreme] Court has rendered only two decisions in which a Congressional statute has been struck down (or limited in its application) on federal grounds, and one of those decisions has just been

overruled. The occasional state statute has been struck down on the ground that it unduly burdened interstate commerce, or on the ground that it was inconsistent with, and 'preempted' by a federal law. But that is about all.[8]

He concludes: '[J]udicial review on federal grounds has almost disappeared. . . . Very few American constitutional cases arise out of the federal distribution of powers.'[9]

There are two sets of reasons for this phenomenon.[10] The first is the courts' restraint with their strict rules of ripeness, mootness, and standing, particularly the state's inability to challenge a federal statute and the court's refusal to give advisory opinions. The second involves the national institutions' capacity to reflect state interests in legislation. The Senate, composed of two representatives from each state regardless of size, was designed to reflect these interests. The House of Representatives can also reflect local concerns because, with lack of party discipline, representatives from both parties can combine to assert the needs of a state, sometimes even to the extent of bloc voting.[11] Such reasons have led to the assertion that 'the constitutional issue of whether federal action is beyond the authority of the central government and thus violates "states' rights" should be treated as nonjusticiable, final resolution being relegated to the political branches— i.e., Congress and the President'.[12]

Even where there is conflict between levels of government, courts need not necessarily be the line-drawer. Arrangements can be structured so that one level of government has the final say over the other's legislation. This was precisely the route taken by Canada initially by giving the federal government the power to disallow provincial legislation within one year of passage.[13] It was this vehicle, not curial review, that was seen as the means to referee between the levels of government when the Confederation bargain was struck.[14] The use of the disallowance power declined and its employment is virtually unthinkable today. However, during the debates surrounding the establishment of the Supreme Court, not effected until 1875, strong reservations were expressed that the Court should pass on the constitutionality of federal legislation, especially when the disallowance power existed.[15] Proponents of such a position voiced objections against curial power that echo down the decades: the convention of ministerial responsibility would be undermined; it unwisely mixed law and politics — nullifying laws on federalism grounds was essentially a political exercise; and, a related argument, the provinces would have less protection of their claims in judicial review because any exercise of disallowance would have to be defended publicly in the Commons and the Senate, which were designed to reflect regional interests, whereas court opinions would face no such scrutiny.[16]

But the courts did come to have a role based on different ideas that centred on two disparate models.[17] The first model, which was mostly associated with the initial decades of the country, saw judges as oracles passively interpreting statutes and their compatibility with the division of powers so as to conform with the intention of those who had struck the bargain. Using a 'plain meaning' rule, judges were to be the agents of an objective process resulting in a neutral disposition of the particular issues that were raised. Courts were not an active branch of government that shifted power between the central government and that of the regions but were passive agents corralling legislatures' impetuous tendencies to exceed defined bounds.

The second model, which arose between the two world wars, asserted that judges actively engage in the interpretive process and that results should be influenced by values that judges brought to the exercise. This malleability in results was seen to be desirable in light of two other contentions: social and political change made the original pact outdated in terms of the respective roles of provincial and federal governments and, despite this, it was very difficult to formally rearrange the bargain, to amend the Constitution. Issues (such as the taxing of natural gas) had come to the fore requiring legislative action not initially contemplated. Values that were previously uncrystallized or even non-existent became recognized (for example, universal and equal access to medical services). The basic understandings of the pact had modified, yet the ability to change the constitutional order through amendment (while possible) was difficult because of the complexity of the process and the difficulty in reaching consensus about the precise nature of the alteration.

So courts over time came to alter the pact not directly but through a series of decisions that responded to the unforeseen issues that were then litigated because of their questionable fit within the original constitutional arrangement. Beginning about the 1930s, the broad sweep of legal constitutional scholars argued that this second model more accurately reflected the judicial enterprise. Writers described the shifts engendered by the courts and prescribed how the courts should redistribute legislative power based on the question of which level of government was better able to deal with the matter.[18]

Yet the recognition of the need for courts to respond to political and social change by shifting the institutional arrangements of federalism also led to some of the most trenchant criticism. Courts were seen as modifying arrangements inappropriate to the extraneous forces at work. They came to be perceived as the wild card of federalism equipped to reform it in light of changed conditions but exercising their power in an aloof and detached manner that exacerbated conditions. This was particularly seen to be the case in the age of cooperative federalism. After the Second World War until the 1970s, great store was placed in the notion of the two levels of government's 'interests' about which, of course, there could be conflict. But the prevailing view was that any disharmony should be worked out through mutual accommodation and negotiation.

In this atmosphere conventional wisdom held that there would be a turning away from the courts. By definition, court decisions imposed results antithetical to those achieved through negotiation and compromise by the implicated governments.[19] Even private actors, particularly business interests, seemed to accept the wisdom of not using the courts. In 1958, it was said that the Supreme Court was being removed from 'its post as supervisor of the federal balance in Canada . . . by forces outside itself'.[20] By 1970, Donald Smiley appeared to echo widely held views when he suggested that the curial role in federalism issues was in eclipse: 'Judicial review results in a delineation of federal and provincial powers where the perceived needs of the federal system are for a more effective articulation of these powers. In general, the prospects are remote that the courts will reassume a major role as keepers of the federal balance.'[21]

However, by the 1980s it was clear that this received wisdom was seriously mistaken. On the part of the provinces there were the two factors that are at the crux of Canadian federalism. The first was the coming of a strong sentiment for greater autonomy on the part of Quebec nationalists. Such demands ranged from a revamping of Quebec's powers under the existing constitutional arrangement to complete independence from Canada. The second was the regionalism of the rest of Canada other than the heartland of Ontario and Quebec. These demands were more economic and were largely concerned with revamping federalism to allow the provinces representing these interests to have a direct role in the institutions of federal government, such as the Senate and the Supreme Court. These two streams, in many ways themselves conflicting, were captured by the *Report of the Task Force on Canadian Unity*: '[T]he heart of the present crisis is to be discovered in the intersecting conflicts created by two kinds of cleavages in Canadian society and by the political agencies which express and mediate them. The first and most pressing cleavage is that old Canadian division between "the French" and "the English". . . . The second cleavage is that which divides the various regions of Canada and their population from one another.'[22]

Largely as a result of the resiliency of these two strains in challenging federal power, in the early 1980s the Liberal government began to respond unilaterally in dealing with areas that had clearly become the domain of negotiated federal-provincial arrangement. This reaction took place on a number of important fronts: fiscal arrangements, energy policy, and, most significantly, the Constitution. Ottawa would now leap over the clamouring provincial leaders and speak to and for all of the people as the one hope of unity.[23] Countering that reaction, the provinces often moved the disputes into the judicial arena. Thus the curial role regarding federalism was invigorated anew. The developments just described and the resurgence of the courts led to this observation in 1987:

> All of the indicators which suggested that judicial review was declining in importance have now dramatically reversed themselves . . . [The federal actions and provinces' attempted blocking in the courts] thrust the Supreme Court centre stage in crucial federal-provincial conflicts. . . .
>
> Nor did private interests appear reluctant about invoking federalism argu-

ments in order to avoid state regulation.... Finally, the courts themselves appear to be assuming an increasingly activist stand, more willing to invoke federalism norms to limit state activity.[24]

THE DEMARCATION OF POWERS

The federal government is given the upper hand in the text of the British North America Act. That government is accorded powers sufficient to restrict the independence of the provincial governments, even in areas assigned to them. As already noted, the federal government is empowered to disallow any statute enacted by a provincial legislature. Further, the lieutenant-governor of each province (a federal appointee) is able, as instructed by the central government, to reserve provincial bills for consideration by the Governor-in-Council. In addition, the lieutenant-governors may decline to assent to bills from provincial legislatures, further corralling provincial power. Moreover, Parliament is granted powers in at least two areas that could directly compromise regional autonomy. One is the declaratory power in paragraph 92(10)(c) of the British North America Act, which allows the federal legislature to declare works to be 'for the general advantage of Canada'. The other is s. 93 permitting remedial acts by the central government should Roman Catholics or Protestants be compromised in their rights of religious education.

Yet how these powers exist in the text and how they have been utilized is sufficiently divergent to allow for the characterization some time ago that 'the Canadian Constitution is quasi-federal in law, it is predominantly federal in practice'.[25] S. 93 has never been used. Paragraph 92(10)(c) has played a role in taking such enterprises as wharves, harbours, telephone companies, grain elevators, and railways into the federal sphere, but has not been a favoured instrument since the 1960s. The power of lieutenant-governors to reserve bills was used seventy times. However, the central government ceased to use it in the 1940s. When it was employed by Saskatchewan's lieutenant-governor in 1961, it was soundly condemned by then Prime Minister Diefenbaker. The power of disallowance was exercised with some frequency against 112 statutes of the legislatures. But, significantly, the federal government has not exercised such power since 1942.[26]

In fact, the battleground for federal-provincial legislative powers has become the various sections of the Constitution Act (1867) that create the boundaries. The courts have been the arbiter of where to draw lines. Several sections of the Constitution Act (1867) deal with division of powers: for example, 92A, 93, 94, 94A, 95, 96, 101, 109, 117, and 132.[27] Disputes over those sections have been important. For example, s. 96 empowers the federal government to appoint superior court judges and has been used, because of interpretations by the courts, as a brake upon the provinces, particularly regarding the creation of administrative tribunals. Nevertheless, ss. 91 and 92 are the key sections with respect to the division of legislative powers. An initial glance might argue for division based on an assignment of economic authority to Parliament and cultural and local matters to the legislatures. Yet closer scrutiny indicates that the central and regional governments were to each have power to control the economy, no matter how fractious the result. Both are allowed to tax directly with provincial authority supplemented by amendment (s. 92 in 1982), bestowing on the provinces the capacity to resort to indirect taxes with respect to certain types of non-renewable resources if they are part of interprovincial trade. And there is a fair measure of power that is explicitly concurrent. As mentioned, this occurs with direct taxation, but also with regard to old-age provisions and supplementary benefits (s. 94A) and agriculture and immigration (s. 95).

The main section for invocation of federal power has been its capacity to legislate 'for the Peace, Order and Good Government of Canada, in relation to all matters not coming within the Classes of Subjects by this Act assigned exclusively to the Legislatures of the Provinces'. It has been employed to justify acts responding to emergencies and residual matters not expressed in the other heads. Two other powers frequently invoked to buttress impugned Parliamentary legislation are 91(2), the regulation of trade and commerce, and 91(27), the criminal law and procedure jurisdiction.[28]

The provinces have relied mostly on two provisions. The first has been subsection 92(16): 'Generally all matters of a merely local or private nature in the province' argued to be a modified residual power to them. The second and most important provision has been subsection 92(13) 'Property and Civil Rights in the Province'. This assignment has been a potent weapon for provincial authority, since between them the concepts of property and civil rights touch almost all interests recognized by the law. So enactments of Parliament grounded in peace, order and good government, the criminal law, or trade and commerce could usually be viewed from another perspective as dealing with property or civil rights, or both, and therefore invading the provincial sphere.[29]

COURTS AS LINE-DRAWERS

How have the courts invoked their power to police federal-provincial legislative boundaries? Is any pattern discernible in terms of the court favouring central or regional interests and, if so, for what reason?

To begin, let us look at the decisions themselves in terms of ideas or theories concerning judicial review in federalism. Fundamentally, two such perspectives have emerged. The first suggests that, quite apart from their impact, the decisions and the reasons offered for them are incoherent and contradictory. This was the view of Weiler almost twenty years ago in his study of the Supreme Court. For example, taking a series of cases that were rendered within years of each other and that dealt with regulation of production and marketing of poultry products, he demonstrated how at odds they were with no theoretical structure animating the Court's decisions.[30]

About a decade later, Monahan made similar assertions.[31] He began with the premise that there must be an overarching theory that can guide judges in interpreting text, particularly the Constitution, which structures fundamental relations. Essentially agreeing with Weiler, he asserted that the precedents in federalism are so open to interpretation and inconsistency that they cannot be dispositive. The courts stumble because federalism by its nature cannot provide requisite theory. This is so since Canada is based on contentious views of the proper ordering of federalism that have developed over time. As such, judges are not able to draw upon arguments based on principle to resolve federalism cases. Rather such judging is largely 'a matter of a priori belief rather than rational argument'.[32]

In sharp contrast is the view most recently represented by Swinton in her 1990 study of the courts and federalism.[33] She acknowledges that judging requires 'value-laden determinations . . . because federalism itself is something of an indeterminate concept, for there is no perfect, uncontroversial division of responsibility between the nation and the regions'.[34] Elsewhere, she acknowledges that in this area the Supreme Court 'has a great deal of discretion'[35] and that its use of a 'formalist style' could lend support to claims of 'arbitrariness and confusion'.[36] Yet Swinton insists there is a critical distinction. Contending that the politics of interpretation should not be 'personal or partisan politics',[37] she argues that there are measures that discipline the judicial exercise to keep it from being 'arbitrary and totally subjective'.[38] The courts are validated 'by concerns for principle, respect for the constitutional text and for certainty, and yet also driven by visions of the "good" federal structure for this country at the time of the decision'.[39]

Whatever one may think about the first view (as illustrated by Monahan and Weiler) and its wholesale questioning of the legitimacy of the judicial role, one wants to respond to the very stark distinction Swinton attempts to maintain between 'political' decisions and judicial ones. In fact, such boundaries are not nearly so clear. We might all agree that arbitrariness and subjectivity are not desirable attributes in decision making and that concerns for values and principles and for previous decisions of those grappling with similar issues are to be valued. The difficulty comes in always imputing the former attributes to politicians and the latter attributes to judges. Swinton herself admits that judgements can bear the imprint of the former[40] while the political process can just as likely be the product of the latter. The processes by which 'politics' arrive at decisions are indeed complicated, but by no means exclude resort to 'ethical principles, political philosophy, economic theories, scientific findings, etc'.[41] In other words; 'We should not succumb to the dangerous delusion that the only decision-making process in which reason and justice can be had is the judicial arena. For such a delusion threatens to gravely overload the judicial process and ignore its limitations.'[42]

Concerning the courts themselves, three patterns can be detected. First, up to 1950, the series of decisions by Canada's ultimate appeal court, the Judicial Committee of the Privy Council in England, can be seen as a strong impulse to strengthen the hand of regional interests. The consequence of the Privy Council's decisions from the late 1800s to the mid-1940s was a judicial recognition that, despite the overarching powers the Constitution gave to the central government, the country was to be a federation. The driving force behind this was a widely shared realization that the powerful centralized nation was an unreality in view of the cultural, geographical, and economic disparities throughout Canada.[43]

This reformulation can be traced to one case, *Citizens Insurance Company of Canada* v. *Parsons*,[44] and its invigorating 'property and civil rights in the Province' interpretation of subsection 92(13). In that case an insurance company attempted to argue an Ontario statute was invalid because it invaded the federal trade and commerce power. Upholding the Ontario Act, the Privy Council interpreted expansively 'property and civil rights' to protect the provinces' capacity to legislate over contract and related matters. Conversely, the trade and commerce power was reduced to issues about interprovincial and international trade.[45]

While it was not the case that the Judicial Committee uniformly preferred the provinces, the decisions both in number and vigour were heavily weighted in their favour. *The Liquidators of the Maritime Bank of Canada* v. *The Receiver General of New Brunswick*[46] did much to transform the lieutenant-governor from a federal officer into a representative of the Crown. Similarly, *Hodge* v. *The Queen*[47] held provincial legislatures to be supreme within their legislative sphere of competence, which meant that if a court decided that a legislature was within the designated powers, its enactment would be valid. These two cases' significance lay in their emphasis that Canada was to be a federation and the provinces were to be on an equal footing with Parliament.

But it was the invigorated property and civil rights' power, referred to earlier, that turned back much of federal aggressiveness. The Privy Council used it to prune the general reserve of federal power: 'peace, order and good government'. Legislation buttressed by 'peace, order and good government' dealing with contracts or contractual relationships fell because it was seen to invade property and civil rights: contracts of employment including labour relations and labour welfare legislation, contracts of insurance, and commercial contracts that dealt with local trade.[48]

These decisions of the Privy Council occurred over many years and against a background of substantial change in a young and evolving nation. There can be disagreement about the precise nature of the influence of these decisions as they interacted with other cultural, political, and economic elements. Yet the thrust of the decisions appears unmistakable:

'[E]veryone agrees that the overall impact of the Judicial Committee's decisions was decentralizing — and significantly decentralizing at that.'[49]

The second pattern of cases is from 1950 into the 1970s. This was the age of cooperative federalism, where there was a relatively prevailing consensus that courts should not be used to resolve these tensions. One of the mainstays of such a mood was the idea that governments should carefully assess the impact of any initiative on the workings of any other government. Reflecting prevailing sentiment in 1965, Premier Lesage observed that 'a government may not do exactly as it pleases simply because it has legal authority in a given field'. Instead, even when its jurisdiction was clear, 'it must see that its actions are compatible with those of the other legislative authorities, and do not infringe on their rights and privileges'.[50] Such waning of the courts' influence led to the quip, 'The lawyers are moving out and the economists are moving in.'[51] By the 1970s, 'executive federalism'[52] with its participation by highest level bureaucrats and government leaders themselves was the order of the day. The significance here is the existence of conditions, widely agreed upon and external to the courts, which led to a significantly diminished role for the judges and to a prevailing norm that differences between governments were to be worked out through negotiation and accommodation.

The third pattern concerns a few cases from 1950, but begins in the 1970s. Regarding these cases, there is a contention that there was a marked shift in favour of centralization. As a matter of bare statistics, there is validity to the allegation: at least until recently, a much higher proportion of provincial statutes compared with federal enactments were held unconstitutional by the Supreme Court.[53] Moreover, those leading the charge also focus upon the breadth of the holdings. Lysyk voiced concern on a number of fronts.[54] He pointed to the Supreme Court's decision to strike down legislation regarding natural resources.[55] Further, he pointed to assaults on control of agriculture, decisions that shrink the economic sphere of provincial authority.[56] Similarly, he viewed decisions in the area of communications as bolstering the federal sweep,[57] as did the decision in the *Anti-Inflation Reference*[58] where he believed the courts too easily acquiesced to Parliament's contention about circumstances allowing it to enact sweeping powers regulating the national economy in an emergency.

One response to Lysyk was to point to the nature of federalism, and not judicial bias, as an explanation.[59] The provincial legislative bodies could be viewed as innovative 'social laboratories' with a leaning to more creative schemes. However, because the provinces are geographically limited, they are more vulnerable to challenge on the basis of extraterritorial impact. Related to this was the contention that technological developments made the courts more sympathetic to federal regulations than to provincial control. Seemingly an aspect of this 'nature of federalism' point is the contention that a proper understanding of the underlying values of the Court's judgements reveals it, in fact, to be dedicated to protecting regionalism.

Because 'regionalism continues to be a major force in politics, the Court has a responsibility to protect the autonomy of both national and regional communities'.[60]

An intermediate position, in terms of the allegation of bias, distinguished between economic and other issues.[61] That stance pointed to the fact that during the same period, the Court restricted the Federal Court of Canada's jurisdiction, thus preserving the established judicial structure whereby courts in the provinces have had most power. Further, the *Reference re Upper House*[62] and *Reference re Amendment of the Constitution of Canada*[63] could be seen as inhibiting unilateral moves by the federal government to amend the Constitution. But in decisions that affected economic control where the trade and commerce power was used to curtail provincial powers in marketing, taxation, and other terms of regulation, Lysyk's criticisms were judged sound.

Looking at Supreme Court decisions up to 1985, Monahan made a number of observations. First, federalism litigation was on the rise. There were almost as many federalism cases in the five years ending in 1985 as in the decade between 1970 and 1980. Whereas federalism issues appeared in only one of every thirty cases in the 1960s, by the early 1980s the Court was determining one out of every nine opinions on federalism grounds.[64] In addition, the Court was more likely to rule enactments as unconstitutional on federalism grounds than in any period during the past twenty years. Finally, he pointed to the alteration in success rates between challenges to provincial legislation and federal enactments with a substantial change in holdings that struck down federal enactments. In the period from 1950–70, the Court looked upon the laws of Ottawa as almost immune. Yet in the 1980s, there was a discernible move to have federalism challenges directed at both federal and provincial enactments and with almost equal success.[65]

Peter Russell agreed that recent decisions indicated a more balanced approach in terms of the likelihood of either provincial or federal enactments being struck down. Moreover, he too emphasized the about-face and increase of the entire court system's activity in refereeing federalism issues and the importance of the questions entertained, leading him to question whether 'the judiciary of any other federation is more active than Canada's in umpiring the federal system'.[66] He emphasized that curial influence is not only quantitative but qualitative as well so that '[o]ne victory in a big case on a major point of constitutional interpretation may be worth many losses in relatively minor cases'.[67]

Reviewing the series of cases in the major areas — peace, order and good government, trade and commerce, taxation, criminal justice, constitutional power with respect to the judiciary, culture, and, most dramatically, constitutional amendment — and assessing their effect, he concluded that the courts had struck an 'uncanny balance'. Why? No deep philosophical or theoretical view emerges from the myriad of cases. So mindful of the issues around exclusivity of the federal power to appoint senior judges, Russell proposes the 'cunning of institutional history':

> How often we have observed in other contexts — especially the sports arena — the pressure on umpires or referees to 'even things up'. Justices of Canada's Supreme Court must feel some of that pressure. After all, they are human too! They are umpiring a contest which the main protagonists — federal and provincial politicians — take very seriously. As umpires they know they have a credibility problem because one side, the federal government, appoints them and constitutionally controls their institution. It may, indeed, turn out that, if the Constitution is ever amended so that this federal control over appointments is modified and the Court becomes a creature of the Constitution, the Court will be under less pressure to retain its credibility.[68]

OUSTING THE COURTS?

In his 1974 book, *In the Last Resort*, a study of the Supreme Court of Canada and the reasoning behind judgements in several areas, Paul Weiler advocated minimizing the occasions when courts would be permitted to review legislation for infringement of the zones established by division of powers.[69] In light of judges' expanded domain under the Charter, such advocacy appears almost fanciful. Yet, it is worthwhile exploring Weiler's basis for that position and countervailing views because the exchange says much about what leading academics think courts should be about concerning federalism or other issues. It is also another illustration of how limiting the judicial role or even eliminating it in certain contexts has loomed as a continuous issue in Canadian discussions of law and policy.

The basis for Weiler's position was that the primary beneficiaries of judicial review in cases involving division of powers seemed to be business interests. Their assault on legislation was not fuelled by respect for conceptions of federalism but was to free themselves of any regulation to which they were antagonistic. So these interests were content to oscillate between provincial and federal heads of power, depending on which permitted attack on disfavoured legislation. Since the goal of federalism was to allocate governing power and not to enable groups to withstand regulation by government, he advocated that individuals be required to obtain the consent of the Attorney-General before being permitted to bring constitutional challenge based on division of powers except for questions of paramountcy (as between conflicting legislative enactments). In the main, governments were to be left to work out allocation of power from time to time based on ongoing negotiation. His arguments were part of his more general questioning of the capabilities of Canadian judges to deal with complex and broad issues. He contended that 'a federal system is precisely the kind of relationship for which an external umpire may not be necessary and in which the better technique for managing conflict is continual negotiation and political compromise'.[70] He argued that the Supreme Court is an institutionally inadequate forum for resolving the complex political, economic, and social dimensions inherent in federalism controversies.[71]

Not surprisingly, this view has been questioned from a number of angles. First, Weiler's concession that paramountcy challenges should be allowed when legislation of the two levels of government conflict was seen as leading back to all of the complexities he sought to avoid with his proposal. The myriad forms and types of legislation about a whole range of interlocking subjects from both levels of government would provide many occasions for paramountcy challenges.[72]

Second, it has been contended that the compromise at the heart of Weiler's proposal is not always possible, and that courts, whatever their limitations, have been and will be drawn into resolution of these issues. Conflict over resources, the control of their development and production, and the taxation of their revenues was but one example of an area where negotiated settlement was likely to prove difficult.[73]

Third, a number of commentators defend review by the courts as the best of the difficult and problematic alternatives, including Weiler's. There was the worry that 'the danger of this proposal is that it might have minority, regional and cultural interests, and civil liberties, insufficiently protected from the acts of powerful majorities'.[74] Further, there was[75] (and is[76]) the belief that an appropriate division of power within a federal structure should reflect both pluralism, that is, diversity within society, and a sense of unity within the country. To achieve this, it is necessary to confer a meaningful level of 'identity and particularity' to provincial and federal categories of powers: 'This assumes sophisticated and socially sensitive interpretation of the power-conferring words and phrases by impartial courts, especially the Supreme Court of Canada.'[77] Such a position was bolstered by the contention that indiscriminate infringement by one government of another's zone of powers threatened democratic process since accountability to the electorate was blurred and debate and argument inhibited.[78]

Fourth, it was argued that the fact that powerful private interests have historically shaped ss. 91 and 92 litigation should not defeat judicial review in that area but lead to providing means by which other interests can pursue this process. This position advocated allowing individuals and groups to litigate through liberal standing and intervention rules and assisting individuals and groups with the cost of such litigation.[79] Finally, Weiler's position was sought to be avoided by a kind of end-run argument. This contention urged that there were other ways for government to accomplish goals frustrated by impugning legislation. On that basis, judges should continue to have their say as part of an ongoing process of adjusting federalism.[80]

All these positions in their own way rest upon consequentialist arguments. Judicial review on federalism grounds has a certain impact and, depending on whether the impact is favoured (and which one is focused on), the process is characterized as mostly good or bad unless one is confident the results can be overcome, in which case an attitude of indifference may prevail. What is remarkable (but consistent with a central theme of this book) is that after over 100 years of experience, there is by no means universal agreement that there even ought to be a role for the judiciary, let alone what it is or should be. For example, in her very recent study, Swinton, a promoter of the courts in this context (as we have seen), feels compelled to engage the legitimacy argument for a full chapter and then returns to it several times in her book as she presents her defence of federalism review.

THE IMPACT OF JUDICIAL REVIEW FOR FEDERALISM QUESTIONS

Introduction

We should begin our discussion of the impact of judicial review for federalism questions by isolating areas of shifts of power between provinces and the federal government where the courts have had little or nothing to say. Because it is easy to isolate such areas, their significance may be overlooked as simply obvious. Yet the breadth of these areas and (in some instances) the fact that they were created by political consensus that has held through many governments and through many difficult situations indicates that significant shifts of power between the federal and provincial levels of government have been accomplished without involving the courts as main players.

To begin, we need to recall that the disallowance and reservation powers give the federal government a trump card in terms of any conflict between regional aspirations and notions of federalism prevailing in the central government. Historically, these powers were invoked with some frequency to give the central government the lead hand in contests. Equally significant is the fact that these powers have fallen into disuse basically since the 1940s. This is an enormous shift in power that the federal government has relinquished without any role for the courts. To say that it is a fantastic proposition for any federal government to invoke such powers may be correct, but that is to demonstrate how deeply ingrained is the belief that no matter how federal-provincial issues are to be managed, disallowance and reservation are not among the available tools. A similar set of comments could be made concerning the federal capacity to declare specific works and undertakings to be within its sphere.[81]

Concerning a different aspect, there are large areas of power accorded to both levels of government that are essentially untouchable by the courts. The taxing power is unqualified at the federal level. It is true that at the provincial level, taxes must be direct. But even here any number of ways have been found to get around court decisions that strike down provincial legislation. For example, when the Supreme Court struck down Saskatchewan's production tax on the gas and oil industry,[82] it was greeted with shrieks about interference.[83] In fact, that government soon imposed an income tax that allowed Saskatchewan to maintain the expected revenue.[84] Further, one of the best ways to redistribute income is through adjustments in taxes and transfer payments. Thus, so far as those measures are concerned, issues involving redistribution of wealth — an issue of sharp controversy in any democracy — and the federal and provincial governments' respective roles in this area have been largely untouched by the courts, allegations by respected commentators notwithstanding.[85]

In addition, redistribution of power has been achieved through constitutional amendment. Subsection 91(2A) addressing unemployment insurance was added to the federal jurisdiction in 1940. S. 94(A) gives concurrent jurisdiction to both Parliament and the legislatures regarding old-age pensions and supplementary benefits, but, in case of conflict, provincial legislation is to prevail. Finally, s. 92(A) increased provincial legislative jurisdiction regarding non-renewable natural resources. The provinces are allowed to employ indirect taxes regarding non-renewable natural resources, and they also have some power regarding the interprovincial export of non-renewable natural resources in the absence of federal enactment.[86] Of course, both the Meech Lake and Charlottetown accords contained ambitious attempts to address various dissatisfactions with federalism. The failure of one close on the heels of the other and, in particular, the emotions that the referendum accompanying Charlottetown generated, suggest that constitutional amendment is not a device that is likely to be turned to soon.

Finally, one of the most important ways power has been shifted to the federal government after the Second World War is through that government's spending, particularly in conditional grants. Yet this power has received virtually no judicial scrutiny and recent attempts to engage the courts' attention were rebuffed. A recent study of this phenomenon documented the growth of conditional transfers as an instrument of federal government policy over the past forty years.[87] Ottawa has initiated over 100 shared-cost programs, most of them of a continuing nature. In 1945 such conditional transfers to the provinces from the federal government cost $46 million, which was then less than 1 per cent of federal budgetary expenditures. In sharp contrast, by 1975 these transfers reached $6.7 billion (they declined in the 1980s). This was almost 20 per cent of federal expenditures: '[B]y expanding its revenue base and by channelling new revenues into shared-cost programs and direct grants, Ottawa has been able to circumvent limitations on its legislative jurisdiction and to have a major influence on public policy falling within the sphere of provincial legislative responsibility'[88] with virtually no means of accountability.

Such exercise of power by Ottawa without formal control has led critics to call for comprehensive alteration: first, the constitutional prohibition of conditional transfers with the 'tax room' required at the present to fund such transfers should be handed over to the government with legislative jurisdiction; second, both levels of government should agree to joint initiatives to end other conditional grants, loans, and tax expenditures that promote policies outside legislative authority; third, the federal government's commitment to regional equalization of the revenues should be made explicit in the Constitution; and finally, procedures regarding constitutional amendment should be made more flexible.[89] In light of the failure of Meech Lake and Charlottetown, this final suggestion is not likely to materialize soon.

Whether such formal controls are necessary or desirable is a debate that is noted but not entered into for our purposes. From a different perspective, the spending power is argued to be part of the equalization and sharing strategy that has been a particular characteristic of our federalism as opposed to others, especially that of the United States. To the extent that these developments in Canada have occurred largely through consultation and negotiation (though often without widespread popular participation), such arguments can be seen as a strength and not as a weakness.[90] The point is that whatever controls may be placed on the spending power, they are unlikely to be effected through the courts who have essentially rebuffed any invitations to become involved.[91]

This discussion of disallowance and reservation, the taxing power, constitutional amendment, and the spending power demonstrates the several vital elements of federalism that essentially lay beyond curial scrutiny. Instead, the courts' involvement has centred around 'command and control' legislation; that is, direct regulation by the state. Most cases dealing with federalism issues since 1949 that have impugned legislation have done so regarding that kind of enactment. Regardless of one's opinion of the appropriate role for judicial review of federalism issues, it is the case that the courts will never be able to proffer their views on many of the dimensions of this important aspect of our national life. On the other hand, excessive reliance on the courts to referee areas where they are involved may deflect energy and resources away from other means of handling the complex and sensitive issues concerning federalism.

For the moment, let us turn to impact. What effect have the courts had in refereeing 'command and control' laws?

Assessing the Impact

Monahan suggests the idea of 'bargaining chips'.[92] He draws upon the insights of Coase, who contended that in the absence of transaction costs, parties will bargain to the efficient result, regardless of the rule of liability announced by a court.[93] This proposition was insightful because it suggested that a court's determination of liability would not necessarily dictate the allocation of resources for those implicated by such determination. Taking this contention into the realm of federalism cases, Monahan argues that judicial pronouncements have often been far from determinative because the various levels of government factor in the result in a case or series of cases as part of a process of ongoing negotiation.

He cites several examples to illustrate his point, one of which centres on *R. v. Dominion Stores Ltd*[94] and *Labatt Breweries of Canada Ltd v. Attorney-General of Canada*.[95] In the first case, the Supreme Court decided that a scheme prescribing grade names and standards associated with those names could not be applied to those trading intraprovincially. In the second case, the Court struck down s. 6 of the Food and Drugs Act, ruling that s. 6 was a prohibited effort to regulate local trade. These decisions were widely criticized by commentators who contended that the cases assaulted national product standards and would lead to increased consumer ignorance and market confusion.

But in fact a decade later, there appeared to have been little impact on the way in which goods were packaged and sold in Canada or on public policy-makers' agenda. This inactivity is explained by the history of constitutional litigation that dealt with the regulation of farm products. Federal-provincial attempts to regulate the marketing of farm products date back to the mid-1930s. The Privy Council decided that the provinces were to regulate intraprovincial trade in natural products, while Parliament would regulate interprovincial and international trade. But the two levels of government struck a bargain: the relevant standards would be created through federal-provincial agreement with each province implementing the agreement for products traded locally and the federal government enacting legislation covering interprovincial and international trade. The scheme was in place for years and essentially continued after the *Dominion Stores* case. All that was successfully attacked was a part of the federal legislation that created a voluntary system of grade names and standards for products traded locally. All the decision did was require that the source of the product be known before laying a charge so that the appropriate legislation — federal or provincial — can be utilized.

However, as Monahan acknowledges, such iterative processes are not possible regarding all issues. He suggests that it is easiest to obtain agreement on issues that can be framed as 'technical' and focused on a specific and limited subject matter. These issues can be dealt with by officials adhering to a set of professional norms. Moreover, governments will be seen as sharing common interests and, therefore, explicit trade-offs or concessions from each side will not be required. Yet issues framed in explicitly regional or national terms require the involvement of the highest political levels of government with negotiations conducted under the glare of the media. Moreover, any bargain struck will be scrutinized publicly in terms of concessions made. This is not to say that agreements are impossible, but they are likely to be more difficult. Monahan suggests that the struggles over energy rents in the 1970–80s illustrate such highly charged issues. Finally, by his own admission, his 'bargaining chip' point so intricately made raises only the *possibility* that the Court's decisions will be circumvented. Moreover, when they are, it is only after the regulatory or negotiating process has taken account of the decisions, thus deflecting or even distorting the flow the process would have otherwise taken. Isolating and gauging that deflection or distortion may be essential in determining the effect of the judgements.[96]

A more encompassing account of federalism cases is suggested by Tremblay.[97] Surveying the federalism cases, particularly those since 1949, he concludes that the Supreme Court has erected a structure for federalism compatible with Canadian society by demonstrating continuity in the basic conception of the Canadian form of government, maintaining an equilibrium between federal and provincial powers, and trying to promote federal-provincial cooperation.

About the first point — demonstrating continuity in the basic Canadian form of government — Tremblay is unconvincing since it is an assertion about the very point at issue: what is and ought to be the Court's role. Statements such as 'if the Court has been more generous toward the federal power, it was not because of a changed perception of the internal workings of federalism, but rather because of its conception of what Canadian sovereignty requires at the international level'[98] and '[i]n fact, the Supreme Court has contributed in a variety of ways to reinforcing the principle of federalism in Canada insofar as this principle implies that certain rules of the game apply to the two levels of government'[99] simply put debatable points in vague terms.

The second and third points are more persuasive. The second concerns the maintenance of equilibrium between federal and provincial powers. Tremblay maintains that the Supreme Court has succeeded since 1945 in maintaining a balance of legislative powers comparable to those that existed previously. He does contend that there has been a bias in favour of federal power. Nevertheless, the decisions demonstrate a subtle blend of the dynamics of exclusiveness with that of overlapping powers between the two levels of government so that the Court maintains a regime that is both federal and flexible, one with a capacity to be moulded to new circumstances. He argues that the decisions reveal that 'the political actors . . . must establish a workable marriage between federal and provincial measures, because the judiciary will intervene only in cases of extreme conflict'.[100]

This point about the maintenance of equilibrium becomes more forceful when combined with the third point Tremblay makes — the Supreme Court has attempted to foster federal-provincial cooperation through its decisions. He argues that the Supreme Court has been an effective umpire that always pushes towards federal-provincial cooperation. A high point was the reference regarding the patriation of the constitution: the Supreme Court's justification for considering the existence of constitutional convention was its desire to influence a political settlement.

Tremblay does not accept the argument that federal-provincial collaboration would be encouraged if legal disputes dealing with the distribution of powers were eliminated or restricted. Rather, he contends that constitutional jurisprudence is itself a political resource that gives governments occasions for negotiation. In this view, cooperative federalism is more likely to develop when the respective powers have been clarified. Even if the Supreme Court divides the weapons in a relatively equitable way, such a balance will not be evident in each particular case. As a result, governments cannot abandon their call for judicial control, which in fact is often a prerequisite for intergovernmental cooperation. This explains why lost causes are pursued in order to establish a basis for negotiation. In these circumstances, a choice cannot be made between political and judicial solutions for the disputes between the two levels of government because they are interdependent in the context of a process where the dynamics of conflict appear normal and inherent.

Russell reaches similar conclusions as he begins with the proposition that such litigation will rarely be dispositive of any question but rather will be one of many sources that influence the ongoing development of an issue. Thus, there should be no expectation that the courts will tilt the balance decisively in any direction: 'Instead the practical impact of decisions should be studied in terms of how they combine with the other resources of federal and provincial politicians within a particular political or policy context.'[101]

Beginning from this perspective, Russell goes on to isolate two kinds of policy effects. First, when a law is found unconstitutional, the same policy objective may nevertheless be achieved through a law drafted to circumvent the constraint articulated in the case. For example, Saskatchewan recouped revenue with an oil well income tax when other forms of taxes were ruled unconstitutional in the *Canadian Industrial Gas and Oil Ltd* (CIGOL) case.[102] But such circumvention can be imperfect and the cost high. For instance, Privy Council decisions required federal anticombines law to be criminal. As discussed in Chapter Four, competition law in this country has not been successful partly because of the awkwardness of enforcement through the heavy-handedness of criminal sanctions.

A second kind of effect occurs when the decisions are used as bargaining counters: 'constitutional power should be viewed as a political resource just as popularity or a good international economic climate are resources for democratic politicians'.[103] It is the outcome of the case rather than anything the courts say in their reasons that is primarily the source of the bargaining chip. Yet there are a few instances where the Court seems quite direct in its attempt to create a framework for negotiation. The most conspicuous instance of this was the Patriation Reference,[104] preceding the constitutional reordering of 1982, where both sides were given something. The federal government was held to have the right to proceed unilaterally with its constitutional package, but at the same time the Court held that such unilateralism would violate a convention of the Canadian Constitution. Such a holding directed both sides back to the table with the result that all of the provinces, save Quebec, adhered to the package after the federal government made a number of concessions.[105]

An example of a straightforward bargaining chip also surfaced in this context. CIGOL,[106] in according the federal government exclusive power to impose indirect taxes on non-renewable natural resources regardless of their destination, had a substantial impact on how the central government could conduct its energy policies. But Trudeau offered to share that power by amending the Constitution in exchange for the NDP's support of the constitutional package. Yet a related case, *Central Canada Potash*,[107] while affirming the federal government's exclusive control over foreign trade, did not constitute a bargaining chip, at least not a useable one, since the central government viewed such power as so vital as to be inalienable.

Sometimes a court decision may not be directly 'tradeable', but instead creates a general resource that strengthens one side's hand. For instance, while the *Anti-Inflation*[108] case did not support as expansive a definition of peace, order, and good government as Ottawa would have liked, it did indicate that the federal government had effectively unlimited power to respond to an emergency and that courts would not second-guess that government's assessment of emergency conditions. Such a wide berth likely buttressed Ottawa in its quarrel with Alberta when the federal government rumbled about Alberta severely diminishing the supply of oil for the rest of Canada.

It is not always the case that the losing side can derive no value from a decision. This may be particularly so when there is a struggle for constitutional change. Thus we have Lévesque's pointed assault on the Supreme Court for its decision on the *Quebec Veto*[109] case as the 'end of all illusions' as a lightning-rod for that province's argument that the Supreme Court could not be relied upon as even an imperfect source of provincial aspirations. Also illustrative are provincial losses in s. 96 cases. These losses have been used by the provinces to ground an argument, as yet unsuccessful, that there is insufficient flexibility in the constitutional arrangement regarding their role in the administrative state, specifically their capacity to create administrative tribunals with sufficient adjudicatory powers.

In assessing overall judicial decisions on federalism questions in the last decades, Russell speaks in terms of an 'uncanny balance'.[110] Yet he believes that in conjunction with other factors, Ottawa has been more adroit in employing them at least in the context of constitutional ordering: '[D]espite a reasonable balance in terms of doctrine, as well as quantitatively, Supreme Court decisions on the division of powers have been more useful to federal than to provincial politicians in the struggle over constitutional change. This perhaps has had more to do with the skill and coherence of federal players in the constitutional game than with the inherent value of the resources the Supreme Court has given them.'[111]

While the images of 'bargaining chips', political resources, 'uncanny balance', and their underlying explanations are insightful in coming to grips with the consequences of federalism decisions, much remains unanswered. In particular, such analysis offers little advice to courts or the rest of us about the appropriate balance between litigation and negotiation-consultation to work out the recurring problems of federalism. Litigation may at times be an escape hatch for building pressures around federal-provincial relations and may at times offer a signal about where the balance should lie in a certain instance. Still, at what point does the balance shift so that litigation becomes a deflection, its availability turning our attention and energies away from the long and tiring processes of negotiation and accommodation, which have also been critical aspects of the pact? At what point does litigation impede rather than spur and energize those other processes?

The Special Case of Quebec

As we discussed in Chapter One, there is no issue more enduring than the relationship between Quebec and the rest of the country. From before the establishment of the nation to the present, this issue of how two cultures and two languages can coexist has always been prominent. It is a fascinating paradox that a question that threatens the very survival of Canada is at the same time one of the most prominent elements of its identity. Quebec and its continuance within Canada brings the nation to a precipice while simultaneously the relationship adds richness and wealth to the sense of ourselves.

This tension between Quebec and the other provinces and between Quebec and the federal government is repeated in federalism litigation. In a 1986 study for the Macdonald Commission, Lajoie, Malazzi, and Gamache examined the political ideas in Quebec and their relation to Canadian constitutional law from the end of the Second World War to 1985.[112] This is the period when the seeds of the Quiet Revolution were sown, sprang up, and have not yet been fully reaped. Their study is divided into three periods (not to be confused with the three we discussed earlier). In each of these three periods, constitutional and political thought in Quebec, whether dominant or in opposition, is examined from the perspectives of the distribution of powers, civil liberties, and institutions. The first, 1945–60, was a period of unilateral federalism with a strong centralist conception. The second, 1960–75, were the years of cooperative federalism that, though not embracing true decentralization, provided for devices such as opting out with compensation, which gave Quebec in particular more range. This was also the period of the Quiet Revolution in Quebec and the rise of movements to achieve economic, cultural, and, in varying degrees, political autonomy. The final period, 1975–85, was marked in 1982 by the patriation of the Constitution and the ushering in of the Charter, a preeminent federal goal accompanied by an even more aggressive version of the spending power. This was countered by provincial demands centred on the distribution of powers. For Quebec the focus was on immigration and social security.

The tone of the study is of a Quebec — province, society, nation — unheard by the rest of Canada in terms of its aspirations to build a secure homeland for francophones. Very little of any of the political thought in Quebec during the entire period was taken account of by the rest of Canada in institutions or federal-provincial relations. A limited exception (but one that stands out in contrast and confounds widely held expectations) are the decisions of the Supreme Court. Conventional wisdom might suggest that the relationship between changes in Canadian constitutional law and political thought in Quebec would be more readily detectable in legislative amendments and practice than in the decisions of the Supreme Court, but, in fact, the result was the opposite: '[T]he little ground gained by either dominant or opposition political thought in Quebec over the last 40 years has been won in the courts, not within the real forum of politics, where the Constitution is at a standstill.'[113]

In the first period (1945–60) the opposition to Duplessis found expression in the cases on civil liberties. During this time the Supreme Court of Canada handed down seven cases dealing with civil liberties, six of which originated in Quebec. These cases were a direct result of Duplessis's actions to repress any civil, political, or union liberties that challenged his vision of Quebec as 'conservative, oriented toward survival rather than toward progress, and [that] failed to distinguish between the interests of the Church and those of the nation'.[114]

As the authors note, such attitudes were supported, at least passively, by a dismayingly large section of the population. The opposition was left to be formed largely of progressives and unionists and by the circle surrounding *Cité Libre*, one of whom was Pierre Trudeau. These ideas were reflected, at the least in result, by the Supreme Court in these six cases based on distribution of powers arguments and with reference to the doctrine of implied rights in the preamble of the Constitution Act (1867) and the parliamentary form of government adopted in Canada.

These decisions are explained to some extent because this was an era of pronounced centralist tendencies by the Supreme Court. Though on this point it is important to note that other than the cases just discussed, Quebec had almost no role in litigation dealing with distribution of powers: of thirty-three decisions addressing such issues, only two concerned disputes in which the cause of action arose in Quebec.[115] The study explains these results by focusing on the prevailing political thought during that period. Duplessis and to some extent the Church maintained a strong distrust of government. Duplessis's animating view was that there should be no state intervention in the economy. Exceptions occurred to block any interference with capital, particularly union activity. Because Quebec was so inactive in passing legislation, there of course was little federalism litigation with its source in that province.[116]

Regarding the second period (1960–75), the authors conclude that there was a positive relationship between the Supreme Court's decisions for cases from Quebec and the growth of the neo-nationalist ideology until 1976 when proponents of sovereignty came to power. This positive relationship in judicial response stands in contrast to the negative relationship between the moderate dominant ideology — to say nothing of radical variants — and the results of constitutional practice in this era manifested in conferences, agreements, and programs.

The results are impressive in sheer numbers, particularly compared with other provinces. Depending on how the cases are counted, Quebec won between two-thirds and three-quarters of the cases, while other provinces were successful in only slightly more than one-third. Qualitatively the relationship between political thinking and results was even more apparent. The reasons for judgement do not establish this, but the results clearly reflect the neo-nationalist position as if to buttress it against the sovereignty/*indépendantiste* movement gathering momentum. After discussing the cases, Lajoie and her co-authors conclude:

> [T]he Court was responding to the aspirations expressed in the then dominant current political thought in Quebec, whose main demand was for a more decentralized form of federalism. But there is more to it. These decisions related to two areas of law included in the minimum constitutional demands of all the successive currents of thought that held sway in Quebec during this period, including the positions taken by the Bourassa government....
>
> However, the ideas that were undoubtedly best received were those of the Johnson government. All these decisions support its constitutional demands not only with respect to labour relations and communications and of course agriculture (*Re Farm Products Marketing Act*), but more particularly with respect to the doctrine of national dimensions, which was rejected in the *Anti-Inflation* decision.... By rejecting the doctrine of national dimensions, it made the two-nation concept of Canada, a pivotal point of Johnson's demands, a legal possibility.
>
> We can thus conclude that overall the dominant constitutional proposals of the Johnson government were relatively well received by the Supreme Court, and no doubt had some influence on the development of the law.[117]

In the third period (1975–85) the Supreme Court decisions in Quebec cases were not supportive of sovereignty. While many of the cases from Quebec during this period involved criminal powers, an area consistently decided in favour of Ottawa, it is also the case that qualitatively the cases affirming the federal government's power to unilaterally amend the Constitution, particularly the *Quebec Veto* case, dealt a massive blow to the position espoused by dominant political thought:

> [A]lthough the centralist tendency of the court after World War II had been tempered somewhat, the Court had never actually veered from that course.

Now, however, there seems to have been a reversal, at least in the numbers of decisions that favoured the provinces. Not only were a majority of decisions in favour of the provinces, but, with the exceptions of criminal law, the environment and the 'meta-power' to amend the constitutional rules themselves, the majority was of significant proportions. In fact, if decisions involving criminal law, which were overwhelmingly favourable to the federal government, had not accounted for more than half of all cases heard, the total proportion of cases representing gains for the provinces would appear far higher.[118]

As for civil rights and liberties, the Court recognized language rights as individual rights and not collective ones following cases in the second period. This was a vindication of the liberal opposition and a rejection of sovereignty position as espoused by the Parti Québécois.[119] The Supreme Court's decision in the *Signs* case in 1988[120] with regard to French-only signs is a further demonstration of the points made by the authors.

The Lajoie study also has implication for the bias charge made so prominently by Lysyk and others concerning the Supreme Court favouring federal institutions. On first impression, Lajoie's study undermines Lysyk's charges because it demonstrates a core of decisions that secure provincial interests (albeit represented by Quebec and its special cultural and linguistic claims) at least during the second period of the study (1960–75), one that was an important focus for Lysyk's and others' analysis.

However, at this juncture we need to recall that there are and have always been two challenges to the forces of federalism. The first concerns primarily economic issues and to what extent they would be controlled by the federal and regional governments. The four western provinces, particularly Alberta, were the leaders on this issue. The second challenge was about linguistic and cultural issues that divide Quebec as a homeland from the rest of the country. These concerns made Quebec simultaneously part of central Canada resented by the rest of Canada and set apart from the rest of the country linguistically and culturally.

If one reviews the Quebec cases from this period on the theory that the issues they raised focused upon linguistic and cultural questions more or less identified with Quebec rather than the other form of regionalism, Lysyk's charge is greatly strengthened at least during the 1960–75 period regarding the 'Western' form of regionalism. Of course it is possible to argue that there can be a coincidence of interests between Quebec and other provinces regarding some of these cases, and to that extent these cases should not be removed from the entire group of decisions examined in relation to the bias charge. But this more finely tuned exercise has not been done. Until it is completed, full analysis about the allegations of bias remains in limbo.

In addition, the systematic studies of the effect of all Supreme Court of Canada cases end around 1985 (most were related in some way to the Macdonald Commission),[121] so cases in the most recent years are missing. Nevertheless, recent cases suggest that the Supreme Court is buttressing a more vigorous use of federal powers for the 'general regulation of trade'[122] concerning 'matters of a national importance'[123] and immunizing federal powers from any impact by otherwise valid provincial legislation.[124]

CONCLUSION

It is an understatement to say that in this country we are confronted by many contradictions concerning federalism. The claims to power on behalf of the provinces are themselves often in conflict: Quebec and culture, the West and economic matters. The federal government voluntarily ceased using the disallowance power, but greatly expanded its influence through the spending power and conditional grants. Yet since the early 1960s, there has been a clear trend towards such decentralization as measured by spending and tax shares.[125]

Most will agree with Swinton who, despite writing a book that touches the question at many points, begins with the caution that '[a] systematic and complete evaluation of the political importance of the Supreme Court to Canadian federalism would be a book in itself, requiring a series of case studies on public policy and the role of the Court in various policy areas'.[126] What we do know is that while courts have had an impact on federalism, they have by no means had the final word. Whatever effect they have had has been encased in a number of tools and institutional arrangements that can render their influence provisional on any number of aspects of federalism. Their role was incidental in many aspects from about 1950 to 1970 because of prevailing norms.

Yet the politics of federalism, that great migraine of Canada, have only increased accompanied by a renewed turning to the courts.[127] This may be one instance where those great clashes so essential for a vigorous democracy come too frequently and from too many angles. Here Monahan's insight about federalism providing no theory because there is so little consensus about it cuts both ways in terms of the courts. From one perspective, as we have seen, it questions their legitimacy, revealing that there are no neutral principles they can draw upon. From another, it explains why courts are so controversial in this area. However they are made, their decisions are a reflection of the profound cleavages and disagreements about region and nation that simultaneously attract and repel. To attribute responsibility for those deep and enduring tensions, we should not look to the courts. We must look to ourselves.

Nevertheless, what we also must not do is confuse a role for litigation in federalism issues with the necessary process of bargaining and negotiation that lies at the heart of the federal-provincial pact. The burden of opinion may be against arguments denying litigation a role at all, but these arguments are surely a part of that scepticism about litigation we have seen throughout the book. Litigation has the capacity to provide another forum for arguments and reasons to be aired about the distribution of powers, as well as the ability to channel disagreement away from overheated political and bureaucratic processes. But in the end, elected officials must be responsible for holding together diverse provincial and federal interests since only they can engage in the tiring and tiresome process of adjustments. The United States is the leader in channelling critical issues into litigation and throughout the book, we examine many ways in which this statement is true. Yet it is significant that American courts have virtually absented themselves from federalism issues. In contrast, we have Russell's question (quoted earlier) of whether 'the judiciary of any other federation is more active than Canada's in umpiring the federal system'.[128]

The greatest hazard of federalism litigation is allowing it an excessive scope if only by default. The failure of the Meech Lake and Charlottetown accords and their futile attempts to rearrange the pact adds substantial pressure to turn to the courts. Politics could not deliver a new deal so perhaps these conflicts should be removed from these fatigued processes and turned over to one that at least provides an answer, where principle governs the disposition of conflict, even if we acknowledge that those principles contain many uncertainties and contradictions.[129]

This danger is heightened when growth of such lawsuits is combined with judicial review of administrative action (discussed in Chapter Four) and Charter litigation, discussed in the next chapter. All three strands are directed against governmental action and all three have the capacity to sweep complex social and economic issues into court while reinforcing the widespread sense that our politics cannot be relied on to deliver the compromises and settlements that are, in any event, now viewed as exclusionary and otherwise flawed.

NOTES

[1] R.I. Cheffins and P.A. Johnson, *The Revised Canadian Constitution: Politics as Law* (Toronto: McGraw-Hill Ryerson, 1986): 119.

[2] D. Creighton, *John A. Macdonald*, 2 vols (Toronto: Macmillan, 1965): 369: 'The British North American Provinces could avoid the mistakes of their (U.S.) neighbours if only they could agree upon forming a strong federal union. . . . If we can only attain that object — a vigorous general government — we shall not be New Brunswickers, nor Nova Scotians, nor Canadians, but British North Americans, under the sway of the British Sovereign.' Macdonald is quoted from the *Toronto Globe*, 21 September 1864, in a speech made at a dinner in honour of the colonial conference delegate's visit to Halifax.

[3] F.R. Scott, *Essays on the Constitution: Aspects of Canadian Law and Politics* (Toronto: University of Toronto Press, 1977).

[4] B. Laskin, 'Reflections on the Canadian Constitution After the First Century' (1967) 45 *Canadian Bar Review*, 395, 401.

[5] A. Petter, 'Federalism and the Myth of the Federal Spending Power' (1989) 68 *Canadian Bar Review*, 448, 464.

[6]A. Breton and A. Scott, *The Design of Federations* (Montreal: Institute for Research on Public Policy, 1980): 15.

[7]See, for instance, the work of W. Lederman, e.g., *Continuing Constitutional Dilemmas* (Toronto: Butterworths, 1981).

[8]P.W. Hogg, 'Judicial Review on Federal Grounds: Canada Compared to the United States' in G.A. Beaudoin, (ed.), *The Supreme Court of Canada: Proceedings of the October 1985 Conference* (Cowansville: Editions Yvon Blais, 1986): 25–6.

[9]Ibid.

[10]Ibid., 28–30.

[11]J. Choper, *Judicial Review and the National Political Process* (Chicago: University of Chicago Press, 1980): 179; 'national legislators generally choose to act and vote in conformity with their perceived regional interests, even when these are in conflict with the dictates of political party allegiance'.

[12]Ibid., 175.

[13]Constitution Act, 1867 (UK) 30 and 31 Vict., c. 3, ss. 56, 90.

[14]R. Vipond, 'Alternative Pasts: Legal Liberalism and the Demise of the Disallowance Power' (1990) 39 *University of New Brunswick Law Journal*, 126.

[15]J. Smith, 'The Origins of Judicial Review in Canada' (1983) 16 *Canadian Journal of Political Science*, 115.

[16]Ibid., 125–9 citing the views of Senator Haythorne: Canada, *Senate Debates*, 6 April 1875, 716–17.

[17]P. Weiler, *In the Last Resort — A Critical Study of the Supreme Court of Canada* (Toronto: Carswell/Methuen, 1974): 166–7.

[18]Ibid., 167–79.

[19]P. Monahan, *Politics and the Constitution: The Charter, Federalism and the Supreme Court of Canada* (Toronto: Carswell/Methuen, 1987): 149–51.

[20]J.A. Corry, 'Constitutional Trends and Federalism' in A.R.M. Lower et al., *Evolving Canadian Federalism* (Durham: Duke University Press, 1958): 92, 117–18.

[21]*Supra*, note 19 at 150.

[22]Task Force on Canadian Unity, *A Future Together* (Hull: Supply and Services Canada, 1979): 21.

[23]*Supra*, note 19 at 148.

[24]Ibid., 150. See also K. Swinton, *The Supreme Court and Canadian Federalism: The Laskin-Dickson Years* (Toronto: Carswell, 1990). Writing in 1990 and indicating that the numbers may have fallen off somewhat for part of the 1980s, during some period of less bitter conflict, she nonetheless indicates the comparative growth of federalism review (8): '[T]he Supreme Court became embroiled in many of the disputes between federal and provincial governments — and at a rate never before experienced in Canadian history. Between 1970 and 1989, the Court decided 158 cases raising distribution of power issues (although several did not ultimately turn on the constitutional issue).'

[25]K.C. Wheare, *Federal Government* (4th ed.) (London: Oxford University Press, 1964): 20.

[26]Cheffins and Johnson, *supra*, note 1 at 119–20; *supra*, note 14.

[27]Cheffins and Johnson, ibid., 121.

[28] Ibid., 124.

[29] Ibid., 124–5.

[30] Weiler, *supra*, note 17 at 156–64, discusses and compares *Carnation Co. v. Quebec Agricultural Marketing Board* [1968] *Supreme Court Reports*, 238 and *Attorney-General for Manitoba. v. Manitoba Egg & Poultry Association* [1971] *Supreme Court Reports*, 689.

[31] P. Monahan, 'At Doctrine's Twilight: The Structure of Canadian Federalism' (1984) 34 *University of Toronto Law Journal*, 47.

[32] Ibid., 87.

[33] K. Swinton, *The Supreme Court and Canadian Federalism: The Laskin-Dickson Years* (Toronto: Carswell, 1990).

[34] Ibid., 199–200.

[35] Ibid., 34.

[36] Ibid., 88: '[W]hile judges may feel that a formalist style gives an aura of neutrality, in fact, the appearance is often the contrary; when precedents are manipulated or revived after long periods of disuse to "justify" what seems to be a new departure in the law, the Court is seen not only to make policy decisions, but to do so in an arbitrary and unreasonable manner. . . . Those trying to deduce the Court's real reasons for decision and to predict the outcome of future cases can only speculate on the values influencing the judges.'

[37] Ibid., 200 citing, R. Dworkin, 'Law as Interpretation' (1982) 60 *Texas Law Review*, 527.

[38] Ibid., 200.

[39] Ibid.

[40] Ibid., 88, 198n.12, and 200n.17.

[41] P. Russell, 'The Politics of Law' (1991) 11 *Windsor Yearbook of Access to Justice*, 127, 131.

[42] Ibid.

[43] A. Cairns, 'The Judicial Committee and Its Critics' (1971) 3 *Canadian Journal of Political Science*, 301, and in response, see F. Vaughan, 'Critics of the Judicial Committee of the Privy Council: The New Orthodoxy and an Alternative Explanation' (1986) 19 *Canadian Journal of Political Science*, 495.

[44] (1882) 7 *Appeal Cases* 96 (PC).

[45] *Supra*, note 1 at 125–6.

[46] [1892] *Appeal Cases*, 437 (PC).

[47] (1883) 9 *Appeal Cases* 117 (PC).

[48] *Supra*, note 1 at 125–7.

[49] P. Russell, 'The Supreme Court and Federal Provincial Relations: The Political Use of Legal Resources' (1985) 11 *Canadian Public Policy*, 161, 162.

[50] J. Lesage, 'Opening Statement' (Federal-Provincial Conference, July 1965), quoted in D.V. Smiley, *Constitutional Adaptation and Canadian Federalism Since 1945* (Ottawa: Information Canada, 1970): 83.

[51] Quoted in R. Knopff and F. Morton, *Charter Politics* (Toronto: Nelson, 1992): 64, and see other quotes to the same effect and sources at 408n.5.

52 A term used by D. Smiley, *Canada in Question: Federalism in the Eighties* (3rd ed.) (Toronto: McGraw-Hill Ryerson, 1980). D. Smiley, *The Federal Condition in Canada* (Toronto: McGraw-Hill Ryerson, 1987): 83–99.

53 P. Hogg, 'Is the Supreme Court of Canada Biased in Constitutional Cases?' (1979) 57 *Canadian Bar Review*, 721, 727–9.

54 K. Lysyk, 'Reshaping Canadian Federalism' in *William Kurelek Memorial Lectures* (Toronto: Ukrainian Professional & Business Club of Toronto, 1979).

55 *Canadian Industrial Gas and Oil Ltd* v. *Government of Saskatchewan* [1978] 2 *Supreme Court Reports*, 545; *Central Canada Potash Company Ltd* v. *Government of Saskatchewan* [1979] 1 *Supreme Court Reports*, 42.

56 *Burns Foods Ltd* v. *Attorney General for Manitoba* [1975] 1 *Supreme Court Reports*, 494, and *Attorney General for Manitoba* v. *Manitoba Egg and Poultry Association* [1971] *Supreme Court Reports*, 689.

57 *Supra*, note 54 at 18.

58 Ibid., 21, *Reference re Anti-Inflation Act* [1976] 2 *Supreme Court Reports*, 273.

59 *Supra*, note 53.

60 *Supra*, note 33 at 55.

61 *Supra*, note 1 at 53–5.

62 [1980] 1 *Supreme Court Reports*, 54.

63 [1981] 1 *Supreme Court Reports*, 753.

64 *Supra*, note 19 at 150–2.

65 Ibid., 151–2.

66 *Supra*, note 49 at 162.

67 Ibid., 163.

68 Ibid., 164.

69 *Supra*, note 17 at 180–1, and see also Monahan, *supra*, note 31 at 96; and S. Blake, '*Minister of Justice* v. *Borowski*: The Inapplicability of the Standing Rules in Constitutional Litigation' (1982) 28 *McGill Law Journal*, 126, 137.

70 *Supra*, note 17 at 175.

71 P. Weiler, 'Of Judges and Scholars: Reflections in a Centennial Year' (1975) 53 *Canadian Bar Review*, 563, and P. Weiler, 'The Supreme Court and the Law of Canadian Federalism' (1973) 23 *University of Toronto Law Journal*, 307.

72 W. Lederman, 'Unity and Diversity in Canadian Federation: Ideals and Methods of Moderation' (1975) 53 *Canadian Bar Review*, 597, 618.

73 B. Strayer, *The Canadian Constitution and the Courts — The Function and Scope of Judicial Review* (2nd ed.) (Toronto: Butterworths, 1983): 297–8.

74 P. Hogg, Constitutional Law of Canada (2nd ed.) (Toronto: Carswell, 1985): 100.

75 *Supra*, note 72 at 619.

76 *Supra*, note 33.

77 Ibid., and see J. Whyte [Book Review] (1975) 82 *Queen's Quarterly*, 121.

78 P.E. Trudeau, 'Federal Grants to Universities' in *Federalism and the French Canadians* (Toronto: Macmillan, 1968): 79.

79 D. Mullan, 'Standing After McNeil' (1976) 8 *Ottawa Law Review*, 32, 48–9.

80 *Supra*, note 19 at 143.

81 *Supra*, note 1 at 119–21.

82 *Canadian Industrial Gas and Oil* v. *Government of Saskatchewan* [1978] 2 *Supreme Court Reports*, 545.

83 For example, the charge that the Supreme Court was 'not in the mainstream of the political process': 'Reform of the Supreme Court of Canada', British Columbia; Constitutional Proposals (Paper No. 4, October 1978): 8.

84 *Supra*, note 19 at 235–6, 241.

85 Ibid., 239–41.

86 *Supra*, note 1 at 127.

87 A. Petter, 'Federalism and the Myth of the Federal Spending Power' (1989) 68 *Canadian Bar Review*, 448, 453.

88 Ibid.

89 Ibid., 475–7.

90 P. Hogg, *Constitutional Law of Canada* (3rd ed.) (Toronto: Carswell, 1992): chapters 6 and 7.

91 See, for example, the recent cases of *Brown* v. YMHA *Jewish Community Centre of Winnipeg Inc.* [1989] 4 *Western Weekly Reports*, 673 (SCC) and *Re Canada Assistance Plan* [1991] 1 *Supreme Court Reports*, 525.

92 *Supra*, note 19 at 225–8.

93 R. Coase, 'The Problem of Social Cost' (1960) 3 *Journal of Law & Economics*, 1.

94 [1980] 1 *Supreme Court Reports*, 844.

95 [1980] 1 *Supreme Court Reports*, 594.

96 *Supra*, note 31.

97 G. Tremblay, 'The Supreme Court of Canada: final Arbiter of Political Disputes' in I. Bernier and A. Lajoie, *The Supreme Court of Canada as an Instrument of Political Change* (Toronto: University of Toronto Press, 1986).

98 Ibid., 182.

99 Ibid., 183.

100 Ibid., 194.

101 *Supra*, note 49 at 168. The following text relies very heavily on this article.

102 *Supra*, note 55.

103 *Supra*, note 49 at 165.

104 [1981] 1 *Supreme Court Reports*, 753.

105 *Supra*, note 19 at 199–203.

106 *Supra*, note 55.

107 Ibid.

108 *Supra*, note 58.

109 [1982] 2 *Supreme Court Reports*, 793.

110 *Supra*, note 49 at 162.

111 Ibid., 168.

112 A. Lajoie, P. Mulazzi, M. Gamache, 'Political Ideas in Quebec and the Evolution of Canadian Constitutional Law, 1945 to 1985' in I. Bernier and A. Lajoie,

(eds), *The Supreme Court of Canada as an Instrument of Political Change* (Toronto: University of Toronto Press, 1986).

[113] Ibid., 75–6.

[114] Ibid., 21.

[115] Ibid., 8.

[116] Ibid., 13–14.

[117] Ibid., 37–8.

[118] Ibid., 60.

[119] Ibid., 65.

[120] *Ford* v. *Quebec* [1988] 2 *Supreme Court Reports*, 712.

[121] *Royal Commission on the Economic Union and Development Prospects of Canada* (Hull: Minister of Supply and Services, 1985).

[122] See s. 91(2) and *General Motors of Canada Ltd* v. *City National Leasing* [1989] 1 *Supreme Court Reports*, 641.

[123] As part of the 'peace, order and good government' powers of the federal government: *R.* v. *Crown Zellerback Canada Ltd* [1988] 1 *Supreme Court Reports*, 401.

[124] See *Commission de la Santé et Securité du Travail* v. *Bell Canada* [1988] 1 *Supreme Court Reports*, 749 (also known as Bell 1988); *Commission de Transport de la Communauté Urbaine de Quebec* v. *Canada (National Battlefields Commission)* [1990] 2 *Supreme Court Reports*, 838; *Bank of Montreal* v. *Hall* [1990] 1 *Supreme Court Reports*, 121, but see OPSEU v. Attorney-General of Ontario [1987] 2 *Supreme Court Reports*, 2.

[125] S.M. Lipset, *Continental Divide: The Values and Institutions of the United States and Canada* (Toronto: C.D. Howe Institute and Washington: National Planning Association, 1989): 193–4.

[126] *Supra*, note 33 at 7.

[127] J. Whyte, 'On Not Standing for Notwithstanding' (1990), 28 *Alberta Law Review*, 347, 354: 'Our experience under federalism has clearly shown us that politics lives (that political initiatives are vital and that political mobilization makes an important contribution to the well-being of society) even when courts have the authority to protect constitutional values.'

[128] *Supra*, note 49 at 162.

[129] P. Meekison, 'Canada's Quest for Constitutional Perfection' (1993) 4 *Constitutional Studies*, 55, 56, 58.

CHAPTER NINE

The Charter:
The Invigoration of Rights,
the Enfeebling
of Democracy?

INTRODUCTION:
'THE COURTS WHICH GOVERN THEIR LIVES'

Currently in Canada we do have judges who regularly accept public speaking engagements. I believe this practice ought to be encouraged as it provides an excellent forum for the public to learn more about their judges, and the courts which govern their lives. As custodians of the Charter of Rights, judges are now performing a supreme public service.

— John Sopinka[1]

This is an extract from a speech given by Justice Sopinka soon after he was appointed to the Supreme Court. There were several interesting things about the address, including, of course, the valuable suggestion that judges should meet more frequently with the public, but I was struck by this paragraph and a number of its phrases: 'the courts which govern their lives', 'custodians of the Charter of Rights', 'supreme public service'.

Is it already the case, scarcely more than a decade after the Charter's advent, that a judge can claim to 'govern' the Canadian people? Can the courts describe themselves as 'custodians' of the Charter and not lay themselves open to accusations of overreaching in the face of s. 33 (and the last word it assigns to the legislatures) and, indeed, the role of the legislature and its agents in scrutinizing enactments and policies even before implementation? Or are we already regarding any number of actions by legislatures as intrusions into the curial sanctuary? How do we test the claim of 'supreme public service' in terms of ordinary Canadians in their everyday lives as others attempt to provide them with health care, educate their children, keep their streets and parks safe and clean, strive to establish safe and equitable work, all under the aegis of divisions of governments other than the courts?

In bluntest terms, two very different models of democracy are at stake. The first recognizes the power of the ballot that is curbed by independent and tenured judges who ensure that rationality and principle are never ejected by impetuous legislatures, rigid bureaucracies, and a dulled citizenry. In this model, courts will shelter the disadvantaged, who will harness that rationality and principle. The second model places its confidence in those who can claim the power of the ballot. Realistic about democracy's foibles, it is even more reserved about using judicial intervention to solve them. In this model, judges' independence and tenure make them unaccountable, élitist, and, at present in any event, unrepresentative. The apprehension is that far from invigorating democracy, judicial review will sap it with regressive decisions, progressive decisions that nonetheless blunt popular responses to societal problems, and barriers to access because of the costs of litigation. In this second model, those who seek social reform may have the most to lose in the courts.

In this chapter, we come to the eye of the storm: Where is the point of balance between the judges and our other agencies of government? How much judicial power is too much? We have seen this issue emerge repeatedly throughout the book. It could scarcely be otherwise in a study of litigation's effects upon social and political structure. Whether regarding federalism issues or torts, we found ourselves asking questions about the judiciary's influence in structuring an area of law and its relationship with society. But the Charter is quantitatively and qualitatively different: quantitatively because (especially in the Supreme Court) these kinds of issues are rapidly dominating, and qualitatively because the Charter gives the judiciary a special power. In the litigation discussed so far, parliamentary sovereignty dominated. Yes, the Supreme Court could tell Mrs Murdoch (see the discussion in Chapter Five) that despite her efforts and contribution, the law required that the registered owner (Mr Murdoch) had no duty to share that ownership. But the legislatures could and did intervene to say explicitly that the law required such contributions to be taken into account on an equitable basis. When the courts dealt with federalism issues, they had the capacity to strike down legislation, but only in a limited sense. There they were playing umpire: deciding whether the appropriate level of government had passed the legislation in question. That the legislation could be passed by one of the levels of government was not challengeable (leaving aside the Bill of Rights scrutiny of federal legislation in the 1960s and 1970s).

But this is precisely what can happen with the Charter (a constitutionally entrenched document), which is not subject to legislative repeal. The

Charter empowers the courts to say that *no* government may pass legislation (subject to the s. 33 override) or no agency of government may engage in a particular form of questioned activity. It is this power that is most controversial and that gives rise to the claims of supremacy. As we will see, giving an élite and unaccountable body such power is controversial in many societies, including the United States, which is really its homeland. Yet there are elements of the debate that are peculiar to Canada and play off many of the essential attributes of this country. Since various issues in many areas can take on a Charter dimension, it is difficult to confine the discussion to one chapter. We have seen Charter issues play a prominent role in the chapters on the structure of litigation, women, and the criminal law. Aspects of those discussions will be returned to in this chapter, but our focus here is on the strengths and foibles of an entrenched document subject to judicial interpretation, the evidence concerning the Charter's influence during the first decade, and analyses of its long-term impact.

This chapter could be subtitled 'Speculation' because making hard pronouncements about the differences an entrenched rights document will make, particularly over the long haul, is obviously impossible. But such uncertainty is at least as much a basis for scepticism as it is for Olympian pronouncements about the benefits of judges in our lives. Judging the impact of litigation upon any society is to enter the realm of cause and effect, a tricky issue if ever there was one, perhaps particularly in terms of social and political ordering. In this sense, we return to many of the issues concerning the impact of litigation that were discussed in Chapter Two. But if cause and effect are difficult to measure, there are complexities on both sides of the debate. Scepticism in the face of such uncertainty is no less reasonable than assured declarations that Canada has been on the road to betterment since 1982.

Meanwhile, the Canadian public is continually bombarded with claims about the importance of the Charter and, indeed, of all litigation in their lives. Within legal circles, it is self-evident that we are 'litigating the values of a nation'[2] and that 'as the Charter evolves so evolves Canada'.[3] But spectacular claims appear in the general media as well, documenting a 'rights revolution' in which the 'courts lead the charge'.[4] 'Top Court Becomes Supreme Player', a front-page story in a national newspaper, included a large photo of the present Chief Justice and quoted him as saying that the introduction of the Charter has been nothing less than 'a revolution on the scale of the introduction of the metric system, the great medical discoveries of Louis Pasteur, and the invention of penicillin and the laser'.[5] It will be noted that no upheaval of less benign consequences made the Chief Justice's list. His comments may, however, reflect the potential danger of the Charter and its trail of litigation: complex and problematic consequences ignored with high-mindedness and illusions the order of the day.

Here we will examine debates surrounding the judicial role under the Charter by first examining the document itself and looking at the range of decided cases to form an impression of its effect upon Canadian society. We then look at the theoretical arguments for and against the exercise of such judicial power under an entrenched document. In conjunction with this general account, there is a specific analysis of the potential benefits and pitfalls of litigation, particularly invoking the Charter, regarding one of the most critical issues facing Canadian society: the Amerindians' struggle for recognition. We then examine the existing evidence regarding the Charter's influence during the first decade. The evidence is not definitive for such a short period, but does suggest that in at least some critical ways, the Charter is exerting a strong influence on our society that belies any confident assurance of progressive results. Finally, we discuss a claim by one of the leading scholars of Canadian constitutionalism that the Charter has resulted in only a 'modest expansion' of the judicialization of politics and respond that such a claim is not sustainable based on the accumulated evidence and the effect of the Charter over the long haul, while freely' acknowledging that assessing the impact of this litigation is complex and dependent upon many factors.

THE CHARTER AND THE RANGE OF DECIDED CASES

Before further addressing the central question of what the Charter's impact might and ought to be, a brief description of the document itself and a survey of some decided cases to date and their possible consequences may prove helpful. Aside from providing useful background for those not immersed in constitutional issues, there is a fundamental point in such an overarching discussion: distinguishing between the Charter and the judges' pronouncements. Such a distinction is critical because it is one thing to agree or disagree about whether we ought to have a basic document enshrining fundamental principles about how we govern ourselves. It is quite another, however, to accept that a small group of unelected, unrepresentative lawyers and judges interpret these principles and the meaning that is to be attributed to them.

The Charter itself has sufficiently diverse and undefined elements to accommodate any number of views and values in specific circumstances. It is entirely conceivable that this statement of rights and freedoms could be used to stimulate and frame debate about Canadian society, including government and government institutions, but not limited to that source of power. Yet we face the prospect that curial pronouncement will be taken as the meaning, that litigation, lawyers, and judges will become the focus for fundamental debates about basic values so that wider and more popular discussion is inhibited rather than encouraged, and that attention is riveted upon court decisions rather than on the effects and implications of such judgements.

There are clearly a number of provisions that indicate that the freedoms recognized in the Charter are centred on liberal notions. Inclusion of such rights as freedom of expression in s. 2; the right to life, liberty, and security of the person in s. 7; legal rights in ss. 8 to 14; and the equal protection and legal benefit provisions in s. 15, as well as the reference to the rule of law in the preamble and the restriction of the Charter to governmental action in s. 32 all mark it as such a document. Yet the text also reflects other values. There is nothing in s. 15 to prevent equality of results being taken into account. Moreover, there are provisions in ss. 6(4) and 15(2) for affirmative action programs that cannot be gainsaid by the rights in those sections. Further, the guarantee of minority language rights in s. 23; the provision for Aboriginal rights in ss. 25 and 35; the dictate in s. 27 to interpret the Charter in a manner consistent with multiculturalism; the guarantee of s. 28 that the Charter applies 'equally to male and female persons', 'notwithstanding anything in this Charter'; and the absence of property rights all point to a view of the Charter as something beyond the land of liberalism conceived and expressed, for example, in the American Bill of Rights. Finally, whatever claims to individual freedoms there are in the Charter, s. 1 instructs that they are to be measured against 'reasonable limits prescribed by law as can be demonstrably justified in a free and democratic society' and s. 33 equips legislatures to override judicial decisions with which they disagree regarding many of the sections of the Charter.

In *Charter Politics*,[6] in a section entitled 'Public Policy Impact', Knopff and Morton discuss several Charter cases that give an idea of the range of issues that have been decided and their possible consequences. This mere sampling illustrates two important points. First, to equate judicial activism (that is, nullification of legislation or governmental action) with progressivism is a gross oversimplification. If the statute or official action serves a critical societal interest, judicial activism can just as easily be regressive. We have already seen this point illustrated in our discussion of the rape-shield decision and its aftermath. Second, even when judicial activism appears progressive in protecting interests that the legislatures have ignored, the overall consequences of the decision may give rise to substantial problems and may also create problems in related issues. We have encountered this point in our discussion of the range of remedies in Chapter Three (the *Schachter* decision and developments surrounding recognition of gay rights), abortion and related questions in Chapter Five, and the controversy around 'speedy trials' in Chapter Seven.

In 1985, in *Singh*,[7] the Supreme Court struck down a law dealing with the process for determining refugee status because the law did not provide for an adequate oral hearing and such provisions could not be justified under s. 1. Despite the burden that these cases imposed because of their high volume, the Court dismissed arguments addressing 'utilitarian considerations' and 'administrative convenience'.[8] This despite the fact that the process for determining such status had been lauded by the United Nations as a worthy model for other Commonwealth and European nations, many of which had no provision at all for appeals concerning refugee determination.[9] Initially, the government reacted by hiring more personnel to conduct oral hearings, but the decision had in fact affected 13,000 other refugee claimants and 7,000 unexecuted deportation orders. The government then declared a general 'amnesty' and introduced Bill C-55, a new process that provided a hearing before a two-member tribunal, either of whom could pass the claimant on to a full hearing before two other officials. By November 1989, the program had fallen nine months behind schedule and the estimated cost of $100 million had virtually doubled.[10]

The 1990 report of the Auditor-General includes a review of the results of the legislative response to the holding in *Singh*.[11] The review stated that refugee claims within Canada increased from 8,500 in 1985 to 35,000 in 1988, producing a backlog of 85,000 unprocessed claims by the end of 1988. According to the review, the procedures did not provide a 'means of dealing effectively and conclusively with claims that had no merit'. It found that the average direct cost of each such claim using these procedures was $2,600 or a total cost of $83 million for just 1989–90. Yet there was no demonstration that these procedures produced greater accuracy in determining refugee status.

Another area for which the Charter has had implications is Sunday closing. Initially, the Supreme Court ruled in *Big M Drug Mart*[12] (overruling a Bill of Rights precedent) that the federal Lord's Day Act violated the Charter's freedom of religion provision. Then in *Edwards Books*[13] two years later, the Court validated an Ontario Sunday-closing statute that had the explicitly secular goal of a common rest day with the majority holding that, although the law's effect was to interfere with the freedom of religion of some people, it was justified within the 'reasonable limit' constraint of s. 1. Nevertheless, reacting to political pressure, the Ontario government repealed the Sunday-closing provisions and substituted a local option for municipalities, more or less the same solution as the one chosen in Alberta. This, in fact, ultimately leads to wide-open Sunday shopping because once one municipality permits it, a domino effect is created, particularly in heavily urbanized areas. This appears to be what is happening in Ontario as the present government rolls towards a wide-open policy.[14]

Still another critical area where judicial rulings under the Charter have had a significant impact is the electoral system itself in terms of election campaigns and constituency boundaries. In *National Citizens' Coalition*,[15] a conservative public interest group successfully challenged provisions of the Canada Elections Act, which placed strict limitations on independent political action committees' expenditures on the grounds of violation of the Charter's freedom of expression provision. The government never replaced the legislation. Knopff and Morton contend that when the 1988 election became focused on free trade, pro-free trade groups were then able to spend freely to help reverse anti-free trade sentiment: 'Thus a 1984 Court of Queen's Bench interpretation of the Charter right to freedom of expression may have determined the fate of the 1988 free trade agreement, one of the most important decisions ever made by Canadians.'[16]

Regarding constituency boundaries, the Charter's 'right to vote' in s. 3 has triggered a spate of cases challenging the configuration of electoral boundaries. In 1989, the British Columbia Supreme Court struck down the province's system of electoral districting, interpreting s. 3 as guaranteeing a 'meaningful' right to vote that did not require 'one person, one vote' but did require that the population of an electoral district could not vary by more than 25 per cent from the provincial average.[17] Cases followed in Alberta, Saskatchewan, and the Northwest Territories. In 1991, Saskatchewan's provisions were struck down by that province's Court of Appeal, even though they complied with the 25 per cent rule approved in British Columbia. The Supreme Court of Canada overruled this decision, but articulated as the standard a right to 'fair and effective representation',[18] one that Knopff and Morton contend is 'certain to encourage further litigation'.[19]

Finally, there are examples of the courts using the Charter to rule on issues of health care policy. In 1985, British Columbia tried to remedy the undersupply of doctors in rural areas and an oversupply in the urban lower mainland by invoking a policy denying new doctors a billing number unless they practised in designated rural areas for a certain number of years. A group of doctors successfully challenged the new policy as a violation of their s. 7 rights,[20] though in fairness, given the present indications from the Supreme Court, similar challenges might no longer be successful.[21]

PERSPECTIVES ON LITIGATION

We could tear up the goddam country by this action but we're going to do it anyway.[22]

— Pierre Trudeau on the constitutional reformulation, 1982

The Charter and the Rise of the Legitimacy Debate

In many ways, the Charter will forever be a divide in terms of our focusing on the potential and limits of litigation. This is not to say that there were no debates about the work of Canadian courts before the Charter's inception. Still, since the Charter and its expansion of judicial power, there has been a considerable amount of work on the implications of litigation that extend even to the judiciary's legitimacy under the Charter.

In fact, there are several strands to these often heated and complex debates. While many of those positions are intricate and merit separate treatment and analysis, this section will try to capture and reflect the range of views. We will see that those who are doubtful about or even flatly opposed to Charter litigation draw upon a scepticism that is also diverse and embraces a range of political leanings. Nevertheless, such scepticism did not arise full-blown with the advent of the Charter. Rather, it builds upon the long-standing and deep questioning about the boundaries of litigation. In contrast, those who are advocates for the Charter and the judges do not deny history so much as call for a new order: a constitutionally entrenched document in the hands of judges who now understand their role.

The next two subsections will discuss the case for and against the Charter mapping those terrains at an essentially theoretical level. In a subsequent section, we will look at the available evidence of the Charter's impact. In particular, we will examine the conclusion of one of the most authoritative commentators that 'judicialization of politics' has experienced only a 'modest expansion' because of the Charter.

Before discussing these strands, it is important to respond to the assertion that since Americans have long had discussions about the limits of the judicial role, a legitimacy debate is just part and parcel of any entrenched rights document. Yet there may be a sharp difference: our debate questions the judicial role itself, whereas the American discussion is essentially about the mapping of that territory and its borders. This is not to suggest that there are no similarities in the debate, but there is an essential element to Americans' view of their Bill of Rights and judges as its agents that we may be missing. Unlike Canadians, Americans have long accepted liberal individualism as the guiding ideology in their governance, a matter we pursued at some length in Chapter Two in our discussion of the impact of litigation. Such a set of beliefs not only complements an entrenched bill of rights, it may be a necessary precondition for its acceptance: '[J]udicial review as it has worked in America would be inconceivable without the national acceptance of the Lockeian creed, ultimately enshrined in the constitution. . . . The removal of high policy to the realm of adjudication implies a prior recognition of the principles to be legally interpreted.'[23] It may be too stark but nevertheless instructive to suggest that fundamental agreement about ideology ensures fundamental agreement about the judicial role, but in its absence, the legitimacy debate is assured a long and vigorous existence. If indeed we are the possessors of a complex ideological framework, as suggested in Chapter One, do we lack the bedrock upon which a full-blown judicial enterprise must rest?

The Case For the Charter

A fundamental argument favouring an entrenched bill of rights is that such a document allows individuals, particularly those with minority interests, to seek vindication in an open, public, and responsive process as opposed to legislators who may be unresponsive and, in any event, are more attentive to majority concerns:

> Charter litigation provides a means for allowing individuals to insist that issues concerning fundamental rights and freedoms be considered in an open and public forum. Legislative and executive bodies can ignore a citizen complaint, and other priorities often mean that legitimate claims go without redress even though it would be provided if the complaint could attract the necessary attention. The judiciary does not have the option of refusing a claim on the ground that other matters are more pressing.[24]

Coupled with this argument is a claim that the coming of the Charter signals the full maturity of the Canadian legal system. This development, the end goal of which is an entrenched Charter, explains the Canadian courts' spotty record with the Bill of Rights:

> Canadian constitutional law has often been of intellectual interest and economic importance but, with notable exceptions, it has not attracted much attention outside law schools and a rather narrow segment of the legal profession. The Charter of Rights and Freedoms already has broken this pattern, and it is no longer surprising when a constitutional case becomes a featured news story attracting national attention. . . . [T]he Canadian Bill of Rights provided experience that was a necessary intermediate step in the change from a legal system steeped in the tradition of parliamentary supremacy to one incorporating entrenched constitutional rights.[25]

Yet another justification for the Charter is its ability to unite Canadians. Before its entrenchment, the structure of Canadian society was significantly influenced by executive federalism, that élite form of accommodation dominated by a very small, unrepresentative handful of white males. Indeed, this tradition of structuring by a small group of men from the two dominant cultures was part of the pacts of 1982 and Meech Lake and was largely responsible for a momentous negative reaction, which, in the case of Meech Lake, was a large part of its undoing.

In contrast, the Charter has recognized 'other' identities who can simultaneously gain strength and weaken the disjunctive tendencies of regionalism through their coalescence. No longer will the female Nova Scotian and the female British Columbian speak to each other through the tensions of regionalism; rather, they will be united by their gender. And if in this unification 'rights' of gays are set against the 'rights' of visible minorities, and the 'rights' of the differently abled are set against the 'rights' of Amerindians, and so on, this is only evidence that the new societal and constitutional discourse is taking hold:

> Federalism . . . speaks only to the territorial dimensions of our existence — our membership in Canadian, provincial and territorial communities, while the Charter addresses us as individuals and members of groups who are indifferent and sometimes hostile to federalism's categories. Federalism . . . 'lacks the

conceptual resources to respond to the claims of individuals and groups for justice and freedom'. That is why a Bill of Rights is so important in a federal state. Through it, individuals and groups are given recognition in a federal system, and their interests are placed on the same footing as those of other constitutional actors.... The chaos and babble of discordant voices to which this opening up seems to lead in the short run is in reality the early stage of a process of honest self-discovery on which we have embarked.[26]

Other more cautious bases for accepting the Charter stipulate certain conditions for its implementation. One condition rests on it being construed only to protect democracy's functioning and not to review substantive decisions made by elected officials.[27] Fundamental to this view is the assertion that the Charter does not oblige a court 'to test the substantive outcomes of the political process against some theory of the right or the good but, instead, its focus is to assure the integrity of politics by buttressing the opportunities for public debate and collective deliberation'.[28]

This mirrors an American theory of judicial review. Its adherents on both sides of the border cite two principal advantages to this conception of a Bill of Rights.[29] First, it provides a context for interpreting particular guarantees: free speech, for instance, ought to be viewed not as constitutive of personal autonomy (a substantive value) but as a vehicle of democratic government (a process value). Second, it claims to establish the legitimacy of judicial review because, with this theory, judges need not take positions on substantive issues. Courts should focus on the fairness of the process by which legislative bodies and their agents make decisions, but not the wisdom, justice, or rightness of the outcomes. Related to this second point, at least one proponent of this view sees it as a way of preserving our tory and social democrat traditions from judicial dilution.[30] But this strand, like its southern relation, has been criticized most prominently on the basis that the very text of the Charter (and the Bill of Rights) seems to speak to substantive entitlements.[31] Nor has the Supreme Court appeared very interested in self-limiting on the basis of this procedural-substantive distinction.[32]

Another condition to the acceptance and therefore justification of judicial review under the Charter is the existence and use of s. 33, which allows judicial decisions under most of the provisions of the Charter to be overridden by the competent legislative body. Indeed, the existence of s. 33 along with the fact that the Charter was adopted 'in full knowledge that the application of the Charter by non-elected, non-accountable judges would nullify the acts of elected legislative bodies and accountable officials, and would occasionally do so in unpredictable ways' prompts a leading commentator to suggest that the legitimacy of judicial review 'is a much less serious problem in Canada than it is in the United States'.[33] However, other commentators believe that s. 33 does not submerge the legitimacy question so much as provide a point of demarcation between the roles of legislatures and courts. The override clause should not be seen as repellant to a rights-protecting document that involves an election between rights entrenchment and the supremacy of legislatures.[34] Instead, s. 33, interacting with s. 1's containment of rights based on the justification of free and democratic societies, should be seen as creating an entrenchment of 'dialogue' between courts and legislatures: '[O]ur constitution is a seamless web, made up of constitutional text, convention and judicial pronouncement. The override can be understood as intensifying and strengthening its patterns of respect for democracy, difference and individual dignity.'[35]

An even stronger version of this focus upon s. 33 would use it to resist what is seen as the greatest danger of the Charter: 'not that it may result in decisions that run counter to the will of the majority, but that it may foster a political process in which ordinary citizens leave questions of justice to lawyers and judges and thereby withdraw from the central activity of human politics'.[36] In this conception, the legislative override in s. 33 is essential to maintain balance in the valuing of important social and political issues between popular and legal actors, yet is accompanied by anxiety about whether 'we have the intelligence and courage to use it'.[37]

But it is the most unqualified enthusiasts of the Charter who provide extreme statements about its purposes and effect. Dubbed 'Charterphiles',[38] they '[a]t an abstract level . . . believe that the Charter enshrines Canada's most important political truths and principles and therefore ought to be interpreted in the most generous manner'.[39] Indeed, at least initially, they were little prepared to countenance issues of legitimacy.[40] Stern warnings are delivered from this group about any tendency on the part of the courts to deviate from a strong interventionist stance to promote progressive — but frequently liberal — values so that there is '*only one* approach to constitutional review that [is] consistent with the "inner logic" of the Charter, and . . . this, and *only this*, vision [is] constitutionally correct'.[41] Indeed, in some quarters, such values are now hailed as triumphant: '[liberalism] has been our unexplained, unexplored, and unjustified political philosophy. . . Canada's intellectual origins are undoubtedly Whiggish. . .'.[42]

There is talk of the rational ('conversations of justification'),[43] of the uplifting ('moments of possibility'),[44] of symbolism ('perception has a substantive potential value independent of the truth of its contents'),[45] and of that perennial for progressives, 'consciousness raising': '[A] charter that promises not only freedom and justice for all but also equality provides a forum in which consciousness can be raised. Lawyers can aim to raise consciousness and provoke participation by focusing public attention on the ways in which society fails to live up to its formally enacted promise.'[46] It follows that s. 33, 'an alien feature in any Charter',[47] is anathema and must go. It is an affront to courts as guardians of these fundamental precepts. All issues of justice housed in the Charter should receive responses 'ultimately adjudicable'.[48]

Along the way, there is faith in rights extended to having them vie with the power of the ballot: 'Democracy relies on a full slate of rights which can be claimed by citizens, and an effective allocation of resources to groups who can benefit from rights. The process of claiming rights is as fundamental to democratic institutions as is the act of voting.'[49] Indeed, if there is a problem with rights, it is not that we are relying too much on them but rather that there are too few available for judicial enforcement: 'Our current set of rights is simply an incomplete set of rights. By omitting all of the social and economic rights that were contained in the Universal Declaration and the International Covenant on Economic, Social and Cultural Rights, our Charter denies rights to those who most need them.'[50]

The Case Against the Charter

In contrast, those who are opposed or at least indifferent to the Charter point out that the Charter and its accompanying judicial role did not come about because of the documentation of widespread abuse, nor did it arise from popular outcry.[51] It was born as a device to shore up the centralizing tendencies that Pierre Trudeau believed were vital to enhance Quebec's stake in the nation and to check the forces of separatism led by his rival, René Lévesque.[52] It rode piggyback on a widespread desire to claim the Constitution from England and deal with other issues between the federal government and the provinces. Its other terms and conditions were seen as negotiable in order to make a deal. Trudeau declared that there must be a strong federal government and that language rights had to be enshrined, but the rest was up for grabs.[53] The 'notwithstanding' clause, viewed by some as a critical counterbalance to the judiciary, was a last-minute concession to some of the hesitating provinces.[54] Conjecturing from these events, a depiction of the Charter as an indispensable document of governance with the judges as its inevitable guardians is preposterous.

Those who are opposed are hardly conspiratorial since many of them can agree about little else except their antagonism towards the document. The politics of many of them are left. For some of those so inclined, the vehemence against the judges arises because their role subverts any possibility of true democracy, which 'means the greatest possible engagement by people in the greatest possible range of communal tasks and public action'.[55] In this conception, the Charter is a 'reflection of the inherent contradiction of liberal ideology. . . .'[56] Such advocates have been criticized as being short on what would occur with this bursting forth of true democracy.[57] They unquestionably contribute to the vigour of the debate with their stark and trenchant criticism, but it is probably safe to suggest that calls by some for 'street theatre'[58] is as likely to simply puzzle as it is to attract adherents.

Yet those of more moderate or even right leanings have joined this loose consortium.[59] These sceptics — whatever their political bent — are among the most articulate and energetic academics,[60] but do not confine themselves to scholarly output. Several are or have been senior advisers to government, many have excellent contacts with the media, and a number are actively involved with a broad range of interest groups. Indeed, some prominent journalists affiliate themselves with this scepticism.[61]

There is something else that we should note. There is a rapidly growing movement for interdisciplinary studies in law. Boosters of this school are by no means universally sceptical of the courts' role, though their ranks contain many who are. This kind of scholarly work invites placing courts in a historical, economic, and social context. While it does not inevitably follow, most of this work results in highlighting the courts' political role. Their claim to moral and philosophical guardianship is duly noted, but the order of the day is to study the wax and wane of their influence on the structure of the country.

Further, there are many interest groups (such as those who want a stronger central government, environmentalists, and feminists) whose support for the courts may be highly conditional upon the fulfilment of their expectations. Should these be disappointed, the support may well abate. Indeed, both excoriating the role and taking the benefits of judgements conducive to particular ends may be housed together. Consider what Alan Borovoy, a leading civil libertarian, has to say in this regard. In a chapter in his book, *When Freedoms Collide*, he regrets the fact that courts, with their record on civil liberties, were ever given the role under the Charter:

> [T]he generalities of the Charter give the courts an abundance of power without the requisite guidelines. As a practical matter, of course, civil libertarians should press for the best Charter judgements they can get. But they should recognize that the Charter is no substitute for specific legislation addressed to specific problems. And they should also be grateful for whatever potential there is in the 'notwithstanding' clause to rescue the sovereignty of the people from possible usurpations by the judiciary.[62]

What is the basis for this leeriness, which ranges from scepticism to unbridled antagonism? Though presented in different forms, the arguments can be summarized in three points. The first concerns substantive outcomes and claims that the elected members of government and their agencies have been the more effective vehicle for improving the lives of most Canadians in many circumstances. The second relates to process and asserts that the best chance for a vigorous, responsive, and respected democracy comes from elected representatives. The third is about the costs of access to the courts which privilege the powerful and organized and thus allow them disproportionate use of judicial review, either to dismantle legislation and programs or to shield themselves from attack by government or other groups. These three points are comparative. This is not to deny that courts have sometimes acted in admirable ways[63] or that there have been some progressive — even visionary — judges: on the Supreme Court alone names such as Rand, Laskin, Dickson, and Wilson easily come to mind. Nor is it to claim that legislatures and their agents have always reached just outcomes by adequate processes. What is contended is that relatively, the chance for greatest justice will come from legislatures.

We have seen all three points surface in previous chapters. For example, the first contention regarding regressive decisions appeared prominently in Chapter Four on the administrative state, in Chapter Five concerning women's issues, and in Chapter Six on tort law and its harshness in limiting compensation. We saw echoes of the second argument about the effect on democracy in Chapter Five on women's issues, in Chapter Seven on the administration of criminal justice, and in Chapter Eight in the discussion of federalism. The third, focusing on problems of access, has long been an issue, a point demonstrated in Chapter Three's discussion of the structure of litigation. Nevertheless, the three arguments become most focused on Charter issues because the courts are now equipped with the power to directly nullify acts of elected officials. Such a shift of power raises the stakes significantly in terms of how our democracy will be shaped.

The first argument claims that assistance of the disadvantaged and the poor, as well as ordinary citizens, has more often happened because of legislative action.[64] Whether in health, occupational safety, workers' rights, housing, peace and order in the streets, or other aspects of life, the advancement has come because of the popular support of political will. In this view, government, while open to searing criticisms about waste and inefficiency, has also been the agent of civilizing and progressive change. It has mediated between those who wish *laissez-faire* and the enrichment of the few (regardless of the consequences) and those who insist upon a basic claim to entitlement for all. Conversely, this argument contends that the historical record reveals that courts, rather than achieving conditions to nurture and protect ordinary people in their everyday lives, have instead been uncaring or actively hostile. The explanation for this lies in an embrace of liberal ideology and an active suspicion of the political process as intrusion upon the purity of the judge-made common law that did not develop to meet these ends. State regulation and programs, designed to be responsive to the concerns of such people, have often been cut back under the guise of interpretation of statutes when in reality it was to allow the ideas of the judiciary to hold sway.

It is significant that boosters of the Charter and the judicial role rarely look to the history of courts to buttress their arguments. In his work urging judges to be the agents of progress for the rights of labour, Beatty advances what may be some insightful ideas about the conditions of working men and women in this country. But when he argues that judges should and will be a vital force for implementing these propositions, the record upon which he bases this claim is revealing in its caution and qualifications:

As with the law the courts contributed to the pre-industrial codes, some members of the judiciary were at least sensitive, even in the heyday of laissez-faire liberalism, to the most basic physiological needs workers pursue through their work.... [T]hey offer some basis to be optimistic that, in our time as well, courts can contribute legal rulings to our labour code which will be equally sensitive to the most important purposes each of us has in our work.[65]

In contrast, it is history that prompts many sceptics to be wary of judges and to prefer the hazards of the legislative processes to handle the complex social and economic problems of Canadian society. In discussing the intrusiveness of the courts in reviewing administrative action, Arthurs observed: '[T]o the extent that contemporary claims for judicial pre-eminence are based upon the perceived superior performance of the courts, it is necessary to remind ourselves, by an examination of the historical evidence, that the courts utterly failed to deal with most significant legal repercussions of the Industrial Revolution in the nineteenth century and with the revolutions of rising expectations in the twentieth.'[66] And even commentators, much more accepting of the judicial role in review of administrative action, point out the judicial indifference and awkwardness in responding to the complexities of twentieth-century society.[67]

What of civil liberties, as traditionally conceived, and the protection of minorities? There were a few valiant attempts by some judges in the implied Bill of Rights cases.[68] But we know all too well the list of cases under the actual Bill of Rights, which displayed the Supreme Court's lack of enthusiasm[69] even though it initially manifested some promise of vigour. Again, Alan Borovoy is instructive:

> Historically at least, Canadian judges have shown something less than enthusiasm for the principles of civil liberties. Since 1960 there has been a statutory Bill of Rights operating at least at the federal level. The language of the bill could have sustained some far-reaching protections for human rights and civil liberties. Regrettably, that same language could also support a more feeble construction. With few exceptions the senior Canadian courts chose the latter approach.[70]

So any initial flourishes under the Charter, admirable though they might be — former Chief Justice Brian Dickson's warning that the Charter must not be a club against the disadvantaged[71] — have to be put in the balance against that record.

The second argument urges that for democracy not to be sapped but invigorated, basic decisions affecting the people must be made by elected representatives. This point does not suggest that such a process has not led to mistakes, sometimes horrible ones, such as our failure to save as many Jews as we could have in the Second World War.[72] The tragedies that beset our Amerindians is surely another. Nor does it suggest that there are not major impediments to popular participation.[73] What it argues is that concerted efforts should be exerted to eliminate them and that we should not rely upon a small unelected corps. Unlike the first argument, the concern here is not so much that judges will impose their views on a democratic majority. Rather, the worry is that critical, social, and political questions will be translated into legal issues that will be left to judges and lawyers instead of the citizenry working out acceptable and supportable solutions.[74]

In this view, even a cycle of progressive and enlightened decisions entails costs, although the results may be desirable. There may be benefits, but they come from a small group of judges and lawyers who are bound together by a limited set of ideas and attitudes and who impose conclusions rather than persuade and build consensus among the electorate. The danger is that the basis for having citizens make their own decisions and face future issues will be eroded, and that the resentment felt by having solutions handed down will make future progress even more difficult and may even contribute to regressive backlash.

This process argument is sometimes put in terms so strong as to rob it of some persuasiveness. Adherents are heard to caption it by asserting that 'the people should be allowed to go to hell in a hand basket', 'the people and their representatives must prevail even when wrong'. Others would not put it in such absolute terms but base it on the particularities of the Canadian political culture. Each country must decide where the risk of error should lie. The argument then becomes specific to the country and asserts that because Canada has been a country of moderate politics and social construction, risk should lie with the people. This is a point underscored by the discussion in Chapter One and the words of Horowitz quoted there echo strongly: 'Here Locke is not the one true god; he must tolerate lesser tory and socialist deities at his side.'[75] The claim here is that this competition of ideas along with other factors has kept the nation moderate and centre left. It is not a perfect formula for anyone, but a mix with the potential for greater popular accountability but also for hostility to an enhanced role for a legal élite, no matter how well intended.

The third point focuses upon the costs of any court response. The contention is that whatever meaning is possible in interpreting the Charter, it will inevitably come to be slanted towards the rich and the organized. Obviously, access to the political and bureaucratic processes is imperfect, but it is not as expensive and complicated and is available without necessarily being mediated through the language of the law, a discourse largely available only to lawyers.[76] A number of isolated figures for the costs of litigation illustrates how expensive it can be[77] and the problems this engenders has been recognized by some judges.[78] The successful argument by Southam Newspapers that a search of its offices by anticombine officials should be struck down took over two and a half years and cost about $200,000. The unsuccessful suit by Operation Dismantle to have cruise missile testing declared unconstitutional cost about $50,000, despite the fact that its lawyers charged reduced fees and the action was determined at a preliminary stage.[79]

Though there are some programs to help the less powerful and the less organized to engage in Charter litigation, they are limited in application and amount,[80] and the most prominent one, the Court Challenges Program, was eliminated in February 1992. The ending of the Court Challenges Program is not so much a second thought about the potential of litigation. Rather, such termination sends a signal to the disadvantaged that lack of access is not a deficiency of court processes but only an unfortunate side effect for some implicated interests that is, in any event, those interests' problem. It can also be a backlash against disadvantaged groups that use the courts, regardless of whether they succeed or fail.[81] Such reaction is by no means an unforeseeable consequence, particularly regarding litigation in the name of reform.

We can further illustrate the benefits and pitfalls around Charter litigation by focusing on one of the most critical issues now facing us: Amerindians and their relationship to the rest of Canada. One can scarcely argue that historically politics and governments have done well by the First Peoples. The critical question is will litigation move us to constructive resolution or will it deflect us further?

The Difference: Aboriginals — Whose Law? Whose Culture?

All the Indian women in the world is playin' hockey now! World Hockey League, they call themselves. Aboriginal Women's WHL. My wife, Veronique St Pierre, she just got the news. Eegeeweetamagoot fax machine. . . .

Tomson Highway,
Dry Lips Oughta Move to Kapuskasing[82]

Their tale of hopelessness and squalor lies across our conscience. In a country with one of the highest standards of living in the world and proclaimed for its tolerance, the plight of Aboriginals is a searing exception. Yet Amerindians are no longer complacent. As with any movement for change, the law becomes a flashpoint, simultaneously reflecting inequities as well as possibilities for change. Land claims, international law, the criminal justice system and constitutional reform are prominent areas where the law and, for our purposes, the law of the judges have been closely examined. Such pressure for and expectation of change provides an excellent opportunity to examine how the ideas about the Charter and, generally, ideas about the effect of litigation are reflected in issues that make insistent claims upon our attention. Some of the sharply conflicting ideas about Charter litigation, discussed in the previous subsections, are thrown into relief by the oppressive circumstances that beset Aboriginals.

There is no serious challenge to the tale of misery. Death for Aboriginals comes mostly because of poisoning, accidents, and violence with an incidence for these three times that of Canadians as a whole. It is small wonder that there is such discrepancy in life expectancy: males, 72; native males, 60–2; females, 79; native females, 63–9. Aboriginals in federal prisons doubled between 1977 and 1987; while they are only about 3 per cent of the population, they constitute 10 per cent of inmates in federal prisons. A 1985 study by the Department of Indian and Northern Affairs revealed that 38 per cent of reserve housing did not have running water, indoor toilets, and/or a bath or shower and 47 per cent failed to comply with basic standards of physical conditions. The official unemployment level has been two and a half times the overall rate. In 1981, 36 per cent of the Canadian population had some form of postsecondary education with only 19 per cent of Amerindians achieving this level, and a decade later there is no indication that relative conditions have altered significantly.[83]

Behind these bare statistics lie tales of degradation that are scarcely describable. The media now confronts us with a continual documentation of broken communities and broken lives. Aboriginals have been relocated to accommodate mining, logging, hydroelectric dams, and for any number of other reasons, including the administrative convenience of the Department of Indian Affairs. Merely one example of this destruction through dislocation is provided by the fate of the Osnaburgh band of Ojibwa. In 1959, a small plot of land in northwestern Ontario was chosen for this band by the department because the highway made it easier to provide services. It was also the case that the nearest lake was too shallow and swampy to support the traditional fishing, housing was substandard, and the water undrinkable: 'Thirty years after the relocation, the Ojibwas were suffering a 97 per cent unemployment rate, and 80 per cent had serious alcohol problems. Children as young as 10 were drinking liquor and sniffing gasoline.'[84]

Yet documenting the suffering and the wrongs is one thing and redressing the tragedies is another. Substantial differences emerge in how to address this misery, particularly concerning the role of the judges. In fairness, thoughtful commentators, regardless of their views of litigation, at least make some attempt to place law in a larger context and acknowledge that undue emphasis on litigation may actually frustrate change by obscuring the circumstances that trap Amerindians in such fundamental inequality. There are, therefore, calls for reforms to specific institutional arrangements such as fiscal policy, education policy, health care, child welfare, policing, criminal justice, resource management, and economic development and changes in political responsibilities towards the First Peoples and the dominant culture's perception of responsibility.[85] Nevertheless, these more encompassing prescriptions are generally short on how this integration of law and such channels of reform could take place. For most, the emphasis sooner or later is on the judges' role.

This literature has a number of contributors who are undoubtedly well-intentioned and make genuine attempts to be sensitive, but who nevertheless create substantial pressure to assimilate the claims of the First Peoples. The difficulties are seen as redressable through more engaged and rigorous analysis, which will guide us in our use of litigation, particularly under the Charter, and obviate angst about cultural hegemony, even while acknowledging that anxiety.[86] Once better tests are formulated, particularly to balance individual and collective aspirations and to define Aboriginal claims more precisely, the First Peoples can shelter in the warm embrace of human rights dispensed by the judiciary. One such proponent asserts:

> [The Charter] is an interpretive prism, and the refraction which it provides will protect the rights and freedoms of the aboriginal peoples of Canada.[87]
> ... The key challenge that remains is to translate the theoretical generalities presented here into arguments in concrete cases, for it is only by this process that ... the Constitution Act, 1982 can serve to enhance the rights of the aboriginal peoples of Canada.[88]

Such attitudes have evoked strong responses charging that 'better' arguments and tests can actually disguise fundamental differences between Aboriginals and the dominant society. 'Solutions' from those outside the culture can actually add to the subjugation; human rights 'progress' that assimilates Amerindians' issues to those in the rest of society may itself be a form of oppression. One such reaction comes from Patricia Monture, legal academic and Aboriginal, when re-evaluating her experiences at a conference where these issues were treated with detached and clinical analysis:

> I do not have any control over the pain and brutality of living the life of a dispossessed person. I cannot control when that pain is going to enter my life. I had gone away for this conference quite settled with having to deal with racism, pure and simple. But, I was not ready to have my pain appropriated. I am pretty possessive about my pain. It is my pain. I worked hard for it. Some days it is all I have. Some days it is the only thing I can feel. Do not try to take that away from me too. That was what was happening to me in that discussion. My pain was being taken away from me and put on the table and poked and prodded with these sticks, these hypotheticals. 'Let's see what happened next.' I felt very very much under a microscope, even if it was not my own personal experience that was being examined.[89]

The extraordinary complexities of responding to the plight of the Amerindians without doing further harm can be illustrated by looking at the work of Patrick Macklem and Mary Ellen Turpel. Both are eloquent young legal academics. Macklem is a white male, and Turpel is a woman of Aboriginal origins. Macklem represents faith in post-Charter litigation and its capacity to respond to almost any problem. Turpel is the voice of scepticism about how oppression can parade as enlightenment.

Macklem's work begins with a fine documentation of the Aboriginals' insurgency against the squalor of their lives. He then analyses at length a number of areas of law, all with judicial amplification — Aboriginal title, treaty rights and interpretation, distribution of legislative authority over First Peoples, the Aboriginal section (s. 35[6]) of the Constitution — demonstrating clearly how First Peoples' aspirations for greater control over their lives has been and is being systematically denied: '[T]he law governing native people in Canada is resistant to claims to self-government because of the unquestioned adherence to basic categories of the Anglo-Canadian legal imagination effected by the denial and acceptance of native difference. The result is a set of principles which work to establish and maintain a hierarchical relationship between native peoples and the Canadian state.'[90] At this point, he invokes the ethereal to suggest that the law, particularly litigation, can be turned upon itself to redress the very problems it has created or at least ratified ('moments of transformative possibility').[91] There are two essential building blocks to all of this. First is his citing of the insights of 'post-realist scholarship' that the law is 'a set of practices that constitutes economic, social and political relations among individuals and groups in society which is itself open to transformation'.[92] Second, he asserts that the First Peoples have an abiding confidence in the Supreme Court: 'an institution which native people trust'.[93] He then goes on in some detail to show that in each of the categories discussed earlier, there are ways to reshape the existing law, which is mostly made and remade by the judges:

> ... [T]he common law of aboriginal title contains the seeds of a doctrinal approach to the nature and scope of native proprietary interests in ancestral and reserve lands which respects the fact of original occupation. The law governing the distribution of authority contains an interpretive approach with respect to the applicability of provincial laws of general application that could be extended to all forms of state regulation so as to carve out a sphere of activity immune from legislative intervention in which forms of native self-government could take root and flourish. Treaty jurisprudence ought to be refashioned so as to reconceptualize the purpose of treaties to be the protection of particular forms of self-government, and the broad and purposive method of interpretation currently accepted by the judiciary ought to be redirected so as to conform to such a purpose. Constitutional jurisprudence ought to deepen the requirement that native people be consulted in the formation of laws that affect their individual and collective identities so that native consultation and consent become preconditions of the constitutionality of laws that regulate native forms of life.[94]

Such invocation of the courts to not only change but be transformed into our standard-bearers is a regular characteristic of post-Charter scholarship. So too is the absence of an inquiry into a central question: if Aboriginal claims (as well as those of women, visible minorities, lesbians and gays, etc.) were systematically thwarted in courts before the Charter, should we not consider that the Charter with its enhanced powers for the judges will exacerbate their plight? To talk in terms of the judges' law as 'a powerful source of potential social transformation'[95] is to assume that which is highly questionable. To flatly assert that the Supreme Court is 'an institution which native people trust' is to deny evidence to the contrary. Consider just one reaction, that of an elder of the Teslin Tlingit band of the Yukon: 'The [C]harter puts the rights of the individual ahead of the group ... [i]n our culture, the rights of the group must come ahead of the individual.'[96] Even if there are progressive decisions from the courts — and there is some evidence of this[97] — do we not have to be fundamentally concerned that they would not 'transform' but rather convert and corral what little is left of a culture that is so very different from the dominant one, including substantial diversity within itself?

In contrast to Macklem, a deeply sceptical reaction comes from Mary Ellen Turpel.[98] One of the greatest sources of this wariness is the rights paradigm, particularly as manifested in the Charter. She begins by reminding us that good intentions are not enough, that it is possible to be killed by kindness: 'assistance aimed at human rights progress may actually be part of the oppression Aboriginal peoples experience'.[99] But in turn the very paradigm of rights through the adjudicative model is called into question. The courts as agents for this model animated by concerns for proprietary entitlement are argued to be alien to the Amerindians:

> A traditional concern with respect to the conceptual and institutional framework for judging rights claims is the elitist and culturally-specific (European) character of the court. This concern involves both the issue of the cultural difference which arises because such a formalized adversarial and impersonal institution is unknown amongst Aboriginal peoples, and the political problem of cultural hegemony raised by the fact that the representatives of the dominant (settler) communities write and 'interpret' the law for all Canadians, and do so within a conceptual framework of rights derived from the theory of a natural right to private property.[100]

As Turpel asserts, such a world view is antithetical to Aboriginals. She explains that Amerindians structure their societies around the Four Directions: trust, kindness, sharing and strength, responsibilities that each person owes to others in terms of social life. In such a context, it is difficult to even talk in terms of 'rights' since there is no ownership of private property and no exclusionary spheres of social life.[101] She ends on a depressed note, starkly different from Macklem:

> It is difficult for me to see any potential for sensitivity to the cultural differences of Aboriginal peoples in the constitutional rights paradigm.... I find it impossible to be reconstructive or instrumental in my analysis.... The rights paradigm and interpretive context of Canadian constitutional law is so unreceptive to cultural differences that, as a result, it is oppressively hegemonic in its perception of its own cultural authority.[102]

A drift to the judicialization of rights to deal with fundamental problems that beset us was vividly illustrated by the ill-fated Charlottetown Accord and how it would have treated Aboriginal issues by dealing in the courts at a fundamental level. The First Peoples pushed very hard in that round for recognition of the 'inherent right of self-government'. As part of a many-faceted deal, such a right — undefined and only briefly described — was incorporated.[103] All the while we heard much about empowerment and autonomy and control. These are noble, essential aspirations for people who have been so marginalized and ill-treated. But at the same time we heard little about illiteracy, life expectancy, infant mortality rates, substance abuse, and the other blights that plague Aboriginals. The hope was that self-government would untap and harness the wills and abilities of the people themselves to expel these demons.[104] The fear — largely unspoken — was that self-government would be a black hole that endlessly absorbs fractious debates about forms and procedures — perhaps mostly among the people themselves — while the list of woes would advance, conscribing ever more victims for its miserable cause.

At critical points courts would have been plunged into this. The agreement stipulated that there would be a five-year period during which the respective parties were to negotiate over the meaning and implementation of self-government.[105] In addition, there appeared to be some contemplation that a specialized tribunal would make some of these decisions. What is clear is that after five years, courts would have been called upon to make a myriad of judgements at a fundamental and structural level concerning Aboriginal governments 'as one of three orders',[106] to which the Charter applied,[107] even while there were charges (some made through lawsuits) from some Amerindian women that their Charter entitlements were not sufficiently protected.[108] With virtually no guidance, the judges would have made decisions about 'languages, cultures, economics, identities, institutions and traditions'[109] and, subject to any framework to be found in a subsequently negotiated accord, about 'federal and provincial governments . . . providing . . . Aboriginal peoples with fiscal or other resources, such as land, to assist those governments to govern their own affairs. . . .'.[110]

Such wrenching decisions with unforeseen long-term consequences would have been handed over to courts with their lack of accountability and lack of involvement in the ongoing negotiation and compromise that would have been absolutely essential if this arrangement was to work. It was a startling example of a phenomenon we have examined at several places in the book. In the face of increased judicial power, politicians may recede and allow courts to grapple with issues regardless of the courts' capacity, no matter how untoward the consequences.

Yet the Charlottetown Accord failed. It was rejected for many possible reasons, some of which have had little to do with the arrangements for self-government. Nevertheless, there is substantial evidence that the Amerindians themselves were divided along several lines, including gender and, in the end, a substantial proportion did not support the Accord.[111] One thing is certain: the rejection of the Accord was accompanied by deep dissatisfaction with popular politics. In the wake of such a mess, it would hardly be surprising if people turn increasingly to the courts, if only by default. In all of this, blaming the courts is beside the point. The critical question is whether we will have the patience and fortitude to see that judicialization of rights is no substitute for the rehabilitation of politics.

Such politics could confront the plight of our Aboriginals on a variety of fronts, including experiments with self-government that would be bold in concept and careful in execution.[112]

AN EARLY ACCOUNTING

Up to this point, we have focused primarily at a theoretical level on the reasons for and against the Charter, on the judges' role, and on the possible consequences for Canadian society. Though the Charter is just more than a decade old, what evidence exists relevant to these diverse positions? How do we weigh and assess such evidence in light of the many caveats about the impact of litigation discussed in Chapter Two?

This section will tackle these questions in two ways. First, by summarizing and analysing the empirical studies regarding the kinds and numbers of decisions that have been made. Such studies are of limited use in assessing the qualitative effect of court decisions. One high-profile case with a broad and encompassing holding can reverberate much more strongly and in more complicated ways than a dozen lesser known, more straightforward ones. Yet such studies are helpful in giving a sense of the overall terrain. Second, we will examine in detail and take issue with a qualitative assessment by one of the Constitution's most prominent scholars that the judges' role has seen only (and will not likely exceed) a 'modest expansion' under the Charter.

Studies Concerning the Impact of the Charter

Attitudinally we seem, on the surface, to be in fine shape concerning the Charter. Russell reports results from a study he and others did concerning what people thought of its presence and the judicial role.[113] A substantial number of Canadians think the Charter 'is a good thing for Canada', but most seem to possess scant knowledge of what the Charter does. Further, it is interesting to compare citizens and politicians in terms of who should have the final say when a law is found to be unconstitutional because it invades the Charter. Whereas over 60 per cent of people favoured the courts, over 60 per cent of politicians favoured the legislature. Russell goes on to suggest that 'the public regard the Courts as being ideologically neutral'. But he concludes, 'This level of support for judicial review may very well change if the courts — especially the Supreme Court's — interpretation of the Charter becomes associated in the public mind with unpopular policy positions.'[114]

He may be right on this last point. Still, it may not be even clear what the level of support for the Charter is among the people. In this regard, we should revisit a 1987 study discussed in Chapter Seven (on criminal law) concerning the admission of illegal evidence.[115] Of those interviewed, 75.7 per cent had heard of the Charter and 77.7 per cent indicated that the

Charter is a good thing. Yet if those individuals who had not heard of the Charter (23.6 per cent) are taken into account, then those who both knew about the Charter and thought it was a good thing represent only 58.8 per cent of the total population. Further, significant differences emerged, depending on how a question about the effect of the Charter on the way the system of justice works was posed. Even if respondents were simply asked that question, only 56.1 per cent said it would have a positive effect, but when it was possible to answer 'not sure', those indicating 'positive' fell to 32.3 per cent, while 52.3 per cent answered 'not sure'.

What of the actual decisions and their impact? Early empirical studies of reported cases suggest that the courts' initial forays were more modest and the charges of rule by judges were exaggerated.[116] One study attempted to measure the impact of Charter litigation since 1982 on the federal and provincial levels of government; that is, on the balance regarding their respective law-making capacities. It found that most such litigation had not involved legislative-judicial confrontations over statutes. In excess of two-thirds of all reported Charter cases have challenged the conduct of government officials (primarily the police). When litigation has directly challenged legislation, there was only a 28 per cent success rate compared with claims against executive-administrative functions (33 per cent). The centralizing impact of the Charter — one of the reasons for subscribing to it — was mixed since a greater number of federal statutes, as opposed to provincial statutes, had been struck down, but the success ratio was higher against provincial statutes (30 per cent compared to 23 per cent).[117]

However, a sharper picture emerges when one focuses upon the Supreme Court of Canada and courts of appeal (federal and provincial) decisions in which a statute has been ruled invalid in whole or in part. The study done by F.L. Morton and others[118] of cases up to and including 1988 concluded that the impact of the Charter on statute nullification is not (as some have contended) abating but rather increasing. The number of statutes struck down, in whole or in part, increased every year except 1986. 1988, the year of *Morgentaler* and *Ford* (Quebec public signs), among others, set a new record high of twenty-four, which was almost double the previous high set in 1987.

The authors go on to observe that different provisions of the Charter have affected the two levels of government dissimilarly. Legal rights have been the basis for 73 per cent of the successful Charter challenges to federal statutes, but only 34 per cent of the winning challenges to provincial enactments. Conversely, claims based on the Charter non-legal rights reveal a much higher percentage of successful challenges to provincial statutes (66 per cent) than to federal statutes (27 per cent). The impact of the mobility rights and minority language education rights sections have been exclusively on provincial law making.

Secondly, provincial statutes that have been struck down have been largely substantive in content (58 per cent), while only 19 per cent of federal statutes abrogated have been substantive. Thus the federal government has been mostly curtailed in the procedure and methods it has taken concerning statutes, but the provinces' policy-making functions have actually been limited more.

Further, provincial statutes struck down are of a much more recent 'vintage' than their federal counterparts. Of the latter, 66 per cent were enacted before 1970. In comparison, 84 per cent of the nullified provincial statutes have been enacted since 1970. The mean date of enactment for the nullified federal statutes is 1952 (but 1970 for provincial statutes). In the more recently enacted cases, the 'antidemocratic' character of judicial review is more pronounced, since the statutes involved represent the policy changes of contemporary governments and the political majorities that elected them. The authors cite the two decisions striking down parts of Quebec's Bill 101, dealing with the primacy of the French language, as illustrating the tension.

In a 1990 study, Morton and others reported their findings of the first 100 Charter of Rights decisions in the Supreme Court.[119] In many ways, this study simply buttresses the points already made. They found that the Charter constitutes one-quarter of the Court's annual workload, supplanting federalism as the primary source of the Court's constitutional business. Moreover, in three important aspects — composition of docket, nullification of statutes and success rate — there is no longer any significant difference between our Supreme Court and the United States' under the Bill of Rights. They conclude, 'This institutional parallel was unthinkable prior to the Charter'[120] and support 'Lipset's recent hypothesis that the Charter is "Americanizing" the practice of politics in Canada'.[121] This drawing together of the two court systems is the point made in the discussion of Lipset's work in Chapter One. Further, after a short initial period of consensus, there has been increasing division within the Court about proper Charter interpretation. At one extreme is the former Justice Wilson, who supported the Charter litigant in 53 per cent of the cases, followed by Lamer and Estey (retired) both at 47 per cent. The other extreme was represented by L'Heureux-Dubé at 15 per cent and the former Justice McIntyre at 23 per cent.[122]

A further glimpse of the effect of Charter decisions is gleaned by studies focusing on particular areas. The one area in which the Charter has had the most direct impact is the administration of criminal justice. In Chapter Seven on criminal law, we discussed these studies and their relevance to the courts moving from the law enforcement to the due process model of administration of criminal justice. Indicative are the results of the 1990 study by Morton and others. Seventy-four of these decisions involved legal rights (that is, those rights in ss. 7–14 predominantly focused on criminal issues). Morton and his colleagues assert: 'The Court has used the Charter to develop a new constitutional code of conduct for Canadian police officers in dealing with suspects and accused persons, and in the process has pushed the Canadian criminal process away from the "crime control" toward the "due process" side of the ledger.'[123]

In another area (related to women's concerns), a 1989 study examined the apprehensions raised in Chapter Five on women and the courts. The study by Brodsky and Day[124] documented the dismal record on behalf of women in terms of equality rights litigation. While continuing to maintain the belief that courts will rectify disadvantage, the report established that this had not yet happened. Three years of constitutional equality litigation (1985–8) produced 591 decisions.[125] Only forty-four were concerned with sex discrimination and challenges made by or on behalf of women were in only nine of these. The other thirty-five were made by or on behalf of men.[126] Men's success rate was somewhat lower, but because there were more than three times the challenges, the number of successes were more than double those of women.[127] 'Many of the men's challenges [were] to legislated protections and benefits such as rape law reforms and unemployment insurance pregnancy benefits, which women [had] fought for in the political arena. To defend their few hard-won gains against men's equality challenges, and to establish a voice for women in the courts, women [were] forced to seek the courts' leave to participate in equality litigation as intervenors,'[128] all the while consuming the limited resources they had.

The study recorded that the overwhelming proportion of cases under s. 15 were not about systemic inequality but about 'drunk driving, marketing boards, the regulation of airline landing fees, and the manufacture of pop cans. . . . The principal players are corporations, persons charged with criminal offences, government departments and Attorneys General.'[129] Of course this is not to say that those charged with drunk driving, manufacturing pop cans and men as a group should not be permitted to make arguments in their interests. But the evidence that s. 15 could be an arsenal for the disadvantaged, particularly women, was just not there. Instead, women (at least those who believe these protections are worth having) were on the defensive.

This study was done before the Supreme Court's decision in *Andrews*[130] and the authors hasten to point out that the concept of equality formulated in *Andrews*, emphasizing analysis focused on possible disadvantage, may alleviate the situation.[131] But they observed that no matter how attractive parts of *Andrews* are (and assuming they come to dominate), many problems of its applicability remain, doubtless giving rise to rounds of court jockeying regarding equality, its meaning, and implementation.[132]

The 'Modest Expansion' of Judicialization of Politics under the Charter

Another way of taking stock of the Charter's first decade is to pay careful heed to respected scholars' assessments of the process and to respond to them. In this vein, one of the most valuable estimations comes from Peter Russell.[133] Russell is internationally renowned for a lifetime of work on

Canadian constitutional issues and his work has been quoted and cited many times already in this book. His assessment of the Charter in the first decade in many ways could calm apprehensions about excessive use of litigation and influence of courts in our social and political life, but careful scrutiny of the basis for his judgement shows that, in fact, there remains much to be concerned about over the long haul.

Russell's conclusion is that 'judicialization of politics from without is not likely to exceed its modest expansion under the Charter of Rights'.[134] The primary basis for his assertion is that '[n]one of the key economic and social policy interests of governments — monetary and fiscal policy, international trade, resource development, social welfare, education, labour relations, environmental protection — have been significantly encroached upon by judicial enforcement of the Charter'.[135] In his opinion, '[t]he limitations on the Charter's policy impact stem both from the Charter itself and its interpretation by the judiciary'.[136]

Regarding the Charter itself, he points to three reasons why its impact has been blunted. First, 'the absence of property rights reduces the Charter's impact, especially its due process of law guarantees, on social, economic and environmental regulation'.[137] Second, '[o]f more fundamental importance is the fact that the Charter applies only to governments and legislatures. Charter rights and Charter freedoms can be claimed only against actions of governments or legislatures.'[138] Third, (and closely related to the second reason), 'the main barrier to full enjoyment or exercise of some rights, particularly equality rights, is not government action but government inaction in responding to problems emanating from the private sector and the very structure of society'.[139]

Russell refers to the 'Supreme Court's moderate performance'[140] and speculates that it 'has probably kept the Court in line with the mainstream of political opinion in the country'.[141] To demonstrate that 'the Supreme Court's jurisprudence has significantly restricted the scope of the Charter's impact and thus the ambit of judicialization',[142] he points to the following. First, a narrowing of 'the realm of state action to which the Charter applies by removing from that realm judicial decisions applying common law . . . in actions involving private parties'.[143] Then he contrasts a denial by the Court of the right to strike and other collective bargaining rights as included within the Charter's guarantee in s. 2(d) of 'freedom of association', a rebuff to organized labour[144] with a statement by then Chief Justice Dickson that 'the courts must be cautious to ensure that it does not become an instrument of better situated individuals to roll back legislation which has as its object the improvement of the condition of less advantaged persons'[145] and the former Chief Justice's view that the right to 'liberty' in s. 7 is not to be used to protect corporate commercial rights.[146]

Further, he points to the reduction of the potentially broad scope of s. 15, the equality provision, 'to laws which harm or prejudice groups covered by or analogous to the section's enumerated categories'.[147] This has immunized most areas of business regulation from judicial review. However, with the possibility of invoking s. 1, other equality issues have been left to legislative judgement, for example, the dismissal of a challenge by university professors to policies requiring mandatory retirement at age 65.[148] Next, he acknowledges the liberality of due process rights in the criminal area, but he insists (while recognizing the intrusiveness and confusion engendered by the Court's rulings on speedy trials discussed in Chapter Seven)[149] that the Court has not pushed its activism so far as to blunt broadly supported law enforcement programs, for example, its upholding of the gun control provisions of the Criminal Code[150] and random roadside tests aimed at apprehending drunk drivers.[151] Finally, he claims that '[m]ost of the members of the country's highest Court are conscious of the political reasons for exercising this constraint',[152] and quotes Chief Justice Lamer from a newspaper interview on the first decade of the Charter: 'I think now [governments] realize we haven't gone berserk with the Charter and we aren't striking down laws right and left. They know how far we'll go and how far we're not going to go because we've said so. . . .'[153]

Russell then examines cases dealing with 'moral issues' 'on which there are sharply opposed political interest groups and no strong or clear public consensus'.[154] The decisions dealing with abortion (discussed in Chapter Five)[155] and the 'rape-shield' sections of the Criminal Code that exclude evidence of a complainant's sexual conduct (discussed in Chapter Seven)[156] are examples of such issues where the Court struck down such legislation. Cases dealing with antihate propaganda,[157] restrictions on Sunday shopping,[158] prostitution,[159] and pornography[160] are examples where s. 1 was invoked and the legislation was upheld. He concludes that '[j]udicialization in these cases is best analyzed not as transferring decision-making authority from one branch of government to another but as judicial processing of social controversy'.[161]

Finally, he insists that there is no 'legitimacy crisis' regarding the judicial role: 'it is elected politicians . . . who are experiencing a legitimacy crisis. The *Citizens' Forum* which in 1990–91 heard from over 400,000 Canadians on their concerns about the country reported that the most common concern of forum participants was that they "have lost faith in both the political process and political leadership".'[162] Yet that said, he points to the reluctance to involve the judiciary in the then pending Charlottetown Accord regarding free trade within Canada and a Social Charter as continuing evidence of restraint on their role. Regarding the Social Charter, he refers to some on the left who insisted that the courts should enforce entitlements to comprehensive health care, quality education, reasonable standard of living, etc.,[163] but 'it is most doubtful that a majority of Canadians, left, right or centre, could come to believe in such judicial fairy tales'.[164]

In a sense, Russell's reassurances are part of the central message of the book that litigation and judicial decisions should never be a substitute for popular and accountable politics. His warnings against 'judicial fairy tales' and his claims that groups for social reform have not abandoned politics 'while some of their lawyer-members flail about in the courts'[165] may be harsh but are nevertheless equally consistent with concerns expressed in many ways throughout this work. The difficulty, therefore, is not with the message of his paper but the confidence with which he portrays the politics of the judiciary both after a decade and over the long haul. Three strong caveats about his descriptions and predictions can be expressed: first, some consequences that he acknowledges in the paper itself that seriously undermine his claim of a circumscribed role; second, his selection of pertinent material and analysis of it concerning the Charter and judicial interpretation; and third, the critical point concerning the Charter and judicialization and their effect on governments' willingness (as opposed to their capacity) to act.

Regarding some consequences that he does acknowledge, this is best illustrated by his discussion of s. 33 and the 'notwithstanding clause', which in his own estimation is 'almost unusable' and which 'tells us much about how constitutionalizing rights can affect the nature of politics'[166] — a critical point that those who fear the Charter wish to make. He goes on to describe how one of Quebec's uses of the override occurred when the Supreme Court struck down a section of Bill 101 requiring French-only signs[167] and the Bourassa government invoked the override to restore French-only commercial signs outdoors. All this took place during the time of ratification of Meech Lake: 'But so great was English Canada's furor over Quebec's use of the override . . . that from this point on "there was virtually no chance that the Meech Lake Accord would be ratified". . . . A constitutional bill of rights designed to unify the country may turn out to be the final instrument of the country's break-up.'[168] This is a dramatic statement and surely one at odds with a conclusion that asserts that there has only been a 'modest expansion' of the judicialization of politics under the Charter when the effects and consequences of such judicialization are taken into account.

The force of the judiciary under the Charter comes not only from what they do but how their decisions are put in the balance against other creators of public policy, particularly the legislatures and especially in terms of complex policy formulation. If, by Russell's admission, we have in less than fifteen years arrived at a point where judges' views are seen as uncontradictable, we are surely witnessing a substantial shift in power or, as Knopff and Morton express it, '[t]o the extent that judicial pronouncements are seen as the very embodiment of the constitution, rather than as debatable interpretations of it, the use of section 33 will be seen as illegitimate'.[169]

While insightful in many ways, his selection of pertinent material and analysis of it concerning the Charter and judicial interpretation of it suffer from sins of omission. Central to his ultimate claim is another, that '[n]one of the key economic and social policy interests of governments — monetary and fiscal policy, international trade, resource development, social welfare, education, labour relations, environmental protection — have been significantly encroached upon by judicial enforcement of the Charter'. First, it has been less than fifteen years and some of these interests — education[170] and labour relations[171] — have been the subject of much judicial activity, although it may be debatable the extent to which they have been 'encroached upon' as yet. Second, he may be right in some areas, but only depending on how he is using the term. Regarding 'monetary and fiscal policy', there are many cases that have placed substantial burdens on the public purse. Again he provides two such examples in his discussion of *Singh*[172] and *Askov*.[173] (*Singh* was discussed earlier in this chapter; *Askov* was discussed at length in Chapter Seven.) Further, he makes no mention of the *Schachter*[174] case and its implications for the breadth of remedies, especially in terms of financial burden (*Schachter* was discussed in Chapter Three). Third, he is surely wrong when he puts 'social welfare' on the list since most of the cases he discusses, whether striking down legislation or not, have some ramifications for that area almost however defined: conditions of work, abortion, pornography, language rights, etc. Moreover, there are many cases with implications for social welfare that he does not even refer to. Just two examples (discussed earlier in the chapter) that directly affect the democratic process are the cases involving election spending and those concerning constituency boundaries[175] where substantial encroachments took place.

Regarding the Charter itself, he highlights the fact that there is no protection of property right, thus reducing 'its due process of law guarantees, on social, economic and environmental regulation'.[176] What he does not say is that there is a concerted effort to have property enshrined, though admittedly not successful so far. In addition, s. 7, our 'due process' provision, has been interpreted by the Supreme Court to give it very wide scope. The Court has refused to confine the guarantees in s. 7 of 'life, liberty and security of the person' (all undefined) and the right not to be deprived of them except in accordance with 'fundamental justice' to procedural review. Instead, the Court has held[177] the section also has a 'substantive' component despite that fact that there was compelling evidence that the drafters expressly chose the wording to avoid 'substantive due process'. Historically in the United States, 'substantive due process' was at least as much a basis as the inclusion of 'property' for the courts' interference with a wide range of regulation,[178] though admittedly it is not clear, given the various messages from our Supreme Court, about how s. 7 ought to be interpreted and where its recognition of a substantive component will lead.[179]

When Russell discusses actual cases, he does so in a 'balanced' way. Whatever else it does, the inventory surely demonstrates the enormous range of issues with which the judiciary has become involved in less than fifteen years. In any event, one may question how he comes to that sense of balance. For example, in his discussion of equality and s. 15, nowhere does he discuss the Brodsky and Day study,[180] which demonstrates how that section, far from being an arsenal for the disadvantaged, has actually been used to attack programs meant to assist them. Nor does he discuss the ending of the Court Challenges Program and the implications that termination has for disadvantaged groups regarding access to the courts.

Finally, he leaves largely unexamined one of the central apprehensions of this book: the more judicialization there is, the less the democratic processes are inclined to grapple with difficult and sensitive issues to work out compromises that have been the hallmark of Canada. From that perspective, his indication that the Charter has essentially been confined to the public sector is a further indication that the focus of such litigation will be in corralling government while deflecting attention away from other sources of power, the exercise of which can have as much or more consequences than the public sector. Related to this apprehension concerning the sapping of the legislative process is his pointing to the fact that regarding the Social Charter and free trade within Canada, the judges had not been given a role (in any event a direct role) in the resolution of disputes related to these two aspects. Some critics might point out that in the case of the Social Charter, there was a grave risk of devaluation, not because the courts were not to enforce it, but because the politicians ducked the opportunity to construct a more representative, accountable, and sympathetic mechanism. Moreover Russell fails to confront the possibility, discussed earlier, that the courts would have become involved in working out one of the main and most contentious elements of the failed constitutional package: the inherent right to self-government for the Aboriginals with the implications for the judicial role. Of course Charlottetown failed, but its terms and conditions showed the degree to which the judicialization of rights was turned to resolve fundamental social and political issues.

At one point, Russell does seem to acknowledge this central concern about the weakening of politics by litigation: 'Although the Charter has not judicialized Canadian politics in the sense of bringing about a major transfer of policy-making power to the courts, it could have a long-term impact on policy by shaping how Canadians think about political values' if 'its concern about restricting government activities [came] to be identified in the public mind with social progress'.[181] Of course it is true that in one sense, judges do not prevent legislatures from acting. But, as explored a number of places in this book, the fear is that judicialization of politics will enervate the other parts of government as the lure of litigation parades before us. Kim Campbell (then minister of justice) echoed this concern:

> We must never lose sight of the central importance of the political process. Nor must we forget that it is legislatures — not courts — which are in the best position to assess competing demands and to conduct the necessary balancing of interests. . . .
>
> In this regard, I have begun to note a very disquieting trend among legislators

to leave difficult decisions to the courts. There is a great temptation to avoid dealing with contentious issues by saying, 'Let's wait until the courts force us to act'. This is a defeatist attitude and nothing less than an abdication of Parliament's role as the primary agent of social change in Canada.[182]

To demonstrate a developing sense of self-restraint on the part of the Supreme Court, Russell quotes Chief Justice Lamer's remarks that governments 'know how far we'll go and how far we're not going to go because we've said so. . . .' What he omitted was another set of remarks (quoted earlier in this chapter) from the same interview that the Charter 'has been nothing less than a revolution on the scale of the introduction of the metric system, the great medical discoveries of Louis Pasteur, and the invention of penicillin and the laser'.[183] The fact that these two statements could be given in the same interview is testimony that calming assurances and extravagant claims can exist simultaneously as we wander about in the land of the Charter.

Finally, suppose Russell's characterization of the court's role as one of 'modest expansion' is taken to be correct. Would we not then be left with a further question: Why do we have the Charter? Whatever else divides them, supporters and detractors of the judicial role agree in their supposition that the Charter does and will make a difference. They are, of course, deeply at odds in terms of what that difference will or should be.

If the courts' role is indeed 'modest', why have we gone to the expense and turmoil of enshrining this document and giving such a task to the courts? It is no answer to say that there are individual disputes that need resolution. Of course that is unarguable. And for such resolution, we may need courts, but that does not answer the question of why we need courts *and* the Charter. If the further response is, well, we do not just want resolution, we want justice then do we not thereby ascribe to courts and the Charter an essential, normative function? That function makes the judges' role deeply controversial for all the reasons we have discussed in this chapter and elsewhere in the book and defies characterization of that role as 'modest'. If, on the other hand, widespread agreement evolves that the courts' role is 'modest' should not democracy consider saving itself time, trouble, and expense and dispense not necessarily with the Charter but the judges' involvement with it?

CONCLUSION: THE CHARTER AS AN EXPERIMENT

None of us can confidently assert how the Charter will turn out: what issues will be presented to the courts, what judges will be appointed and how the various legislatures will react by using s. 33 or other powers. We especially do not know how the Canadian people will respond to this enhanced role of judges, whether they will accept it as part of their government, see it as enriching the political process, or turn from it. Given the resilience of the contending views concerning the Charter and the absence of experience, we need to recognize it for what it most surely is — an experiment. It is an ambitious and hazardous one with a scope too broad for some of us to have countenanced, but, at the same time, one that is underway.

In calling it an experiment, I make no particular claim for or against it. After all, democracy itself is an experiment, one in which a people learn to govern themselves, all too often by painful trial and error. Canada has long been willing (out of necessity if nothing else) to experiment with its government, whether in building the nation, sharing power among the various provinces, or deciding the basis for foreign investment.

Consider Quebec. About thirty years ago it was a regressive society dominated by the Catholic clergy and a petty tyrant who could declare, 'There is no great difficulty in governing Quebec. All one must do is to keep the Jesuits and Dominicans fighting.'[184] Through a combination of a people determined to claim a place in twentieth-century society and a series of governments of different stripes (though they had a shared purpose), the French majority has been able to assert itself. Except for a few tragic instances, this incredible transformation has been achieved peacefully. Whether this push towards self-determination can be contained within the borders of Canada as we know it remains to be seen despite or perhaps because of recent feverish and failed attempts to redo the constitutional order. Yet it will be solved, however it is solved, by Canadians adhering to the tradition of flexibility and risk taking and not by giving themselves over to a set of imposed solutions.[185]

As with all experiments, there is hope that the judicial role under the Charter will succeed, but there must be a realistic expectation of failure. Now there may be scoffs at the notion of an important aspect of government 'failing'. An enterprise may be flawed, may be controversial, but surely once it is started, it will be carried along by the rambunctious current of Canadian society. But perhaps not, for there is a riveting example of such breakdown. It is the Senate.

For a long time the Senate has been a deep embarrassment to almost everyone. It is seen as a meandering and expensive behemoth — mostly inert, stumbling on the rare occasion it takes any real action. Only a failure of political will has kept it in all its docility these many years. But when the Senate was created, hopes were high, at least in terms of the rhetoric surrounding it.[186] It was to be independent, its members appointed, and was to be a reactive body restraining the unruly democracy of the House of Commons, representing regional interests and defending rights. But over time very little of this occurred. Indeed, on the occasions when the Senate has roused itself and even made sound suggestions, calls have increased for radical reform of a body seen to be undemocratic and unaccountable.[187] It has been reduced to a pitiful state, new appointments greeted with sneers and guffaws: 'The Canadian Senate is a frustrating puzzle. . . . Its outstanding characteristic is not what it does, for that is not impressive, but that it has survived.'[188] It has come to a point where its continuation depends on the inability to concur on the details of change, agreement about the need for drastic modification having long since been established on a depressingly long record.[189]

I seek to draw no close parallel. I only say that Canadian politics has a number of ways of dealing with forces judged to be alien to it. One is simply to turn from an institution once it is realized that the fit is not there. This may be the real danger for the courts and the Charter. Of course, people cannot be prevented from invoking it and of course courts will pronounce upon it. But how much the electorate will embrace all this and how much it will come to see it as an obstacle to democratic governing is the question. Judicial review cannot be held accountable for the sense of drift in our national life, but its existence may well exacerbate it. Maybe the real danger is that in the meantime our politics will become so debilitated that we are left with little but that sense of drift as a characterization of our social and political policies.

In the same address quoted at the beginning of this chapter, Justice Sopinka described his distaste for the appointment process used for federal judges in the United States and clearly the appropriateness of such procedures in this country is a matter to ponder. But he cited in particular the protracted hearings around Robert Bork, who was ultimately rejected. Some thought this an odd example to fasten upon for, at this distance, if ever there was an instance of the utility of the confirmation hearings, those around the radical Bork would seem to be such. In any event, he warned that such procedures should not come to Canada, otherwise, as he curtly stated, much legal talent might say, 'Who needs it?'[190]

A good question. Yet, as this chapter has tried to explore, there may be a very different set of reasons why those of premium ability begin to find the bench not the cap it once was. Regrettably, not a few lawyers — to say nothing of the public — may come to say, 'Who indeed?'

NOTES

[1]'Limited Value in Confirmation Ritual', *Financial Post*, 15 August 1989, 14.

Parts of this chapter first appeared in W.A. Bogart '"And the Courts Which Govern Their Lives": The Judges and Legitimacy' in J. Berryman (ed.), *Remedies — Issues and Perspectives* (Toronto: Carswell, 1991): 49 and W.A. Bogart, 'Ambiguity' in Prujiner et Roy (eds), *Les Recours Collectifs en Ontario et au Québec* (Montréal: Wilson & Lafleur Ltée, 1992).

[2]See J.M. Weiler and R.M. Elliot (eds), *Litigating the Values of a Nation: The Canadian Charter of Rights and Freedoms* (Toronto: Carswell, 1986).

[3]Brochure advertising *Conference on the Tenth Anniversary of the Charter*, 14–15 April 1992, sponsored by the Canadian Bar Association and the Federal Department of Justice.

[4]S. Fine, 'The Rights Revolution — The Courts Lead the Charge', *The Globe and Mail*, a two-part series, 24 and 25 November 1992, A1, A8.

[5]J. Sallot, 'Top Court Becomes Supreme Player', *The Globe and Mail*, 6 April 1992, A1; 'How the Charter Changes Justice' (J. Sallot's interview with Chief Justice Lamer), *The Globe and Mail*, 17 April 1992, A11.

[6]R. Knopff and F.L. Morton, *Charter Politics* (Toronto: Nelson, 1992).

[7]*Singh et al. v. Minister of Employment and Immigration* [1985] 1 *Supreme Court Reports*, 177.

[8]Ibid., 220.

[9]Ibid., 218.

[10]M. Mandel, *The Charter of Rights and the Legalization of Politics in Canada* (Toronto: Wall and Thompson, 1989): 175; *supra*, note 6 at 24.

[11]Canada, Office of the Auditor-General, *Report of the Auditor-General of Canada: Fiscal Year Ended 31 March 1990* (Ottawa: Supply and Services Canada, 1990): 343, 351, as cited and discussed in C. Manfredi, *Judicial Power and the Charter* (Toronto: McClelland & Stewart, 1993): 166.

[12]*R. v. Big M Drug Mart* [1985] 1 *Supreme Court Reports*, 295.

[13]*R. v. Edwards Books and Art Ltd* [1986] 2 *Supreme Court Reports*, 713.

[14]*Supra*, note 6 at 24–5.

[15]*National Citizens' Coalition Inc. and Brown v. Canada (Attorney-General)* (1984) 5 *Western Weekly Reports*, 436.

[16]*Supra*, note 6 at 25.

[17]*Dixon v. Attorney-General for British Columbia* (1989) 59 *Dominion Law Reports* (4th) 247.

[18]*Reference re Provincial Electoral Boundaries* [1991] 5 *Western Weekly Reports*, 1 (SCC) at 3. See also G. Rosenberg, *The Hollow Hope — Can Courts Bring About Social Change?* (Chicago: University of Chicago Press, 1991): 269 *et seq.*, discussing the meagre impact reapportionment has had on political reform.

[19]*Supra*, note 6 at 26. For a more optimistic account of what is happening in these cases in terms of protecting constitutional values and yet taking account of our political culture, see K. Roach, 'Chartering the Electoral Map into the Future' in J. Courtney (ed.), *Drawing Boundaries — Legislatures, Courts, and Electoral Values* (Saskatoon: Fifth House Publishing, 1992): 200.

[20]*Wilson v. Medical Services Commission of British Columbia* (1988) 30 *British Columbia Law Reports* (2d) 1.

[21]See the authorities cited, *infra*, note 179.

[22]Quoted in S. Clarkson and C. McCall, *Trudeau and Our Times: The Magnificent Obsession*, vol. 1 (Toronto: McClelland & Stewart, 1990): 291.

[23]W. Lasser, *The Limits of Judicial Power — The Supreme Court in American Politics* (Chapel Hill: University of North Carolina Press, 1988): 250, quoting L. Hartz, *The Liberal Tradition in America: An Interpretation of American Political Thought Since the Revolution* (New York: Harcourt Brace, 1955): 9.

[24]W. Black, 'The Charter of Rights and Freedoms — Introduction' in J. Magnet, *Constitutional Law of Canada* (3d ed.) (Toronto: Carswell, 1987): 1.

[25]Ibid.

[26] A. Cairns, 'Constitutional Minoritarianism in Canada' in R. Watts and D. Brown (eds), *Canada: The State of the Federation 1990* (Kingston: Institute of Intergovernmental Relations, Queen's University, 1990): 71, 90, quoting S. LaSelva, 'Does the Canadian Charter of Rights and Freedoms Rest on a Mistake?' (1988) 8 *Windsor Yearbook of Access to Justice*, 223.

[27] H. Fairley, 'Enforcing the Charter: Some Thoughts on an Appropriate and Just Standard for Judicial Review' (1982) 4 *Supreme Court Law Review*, 217; P. Monahan, 'Judicial Review and Democracy: A Theory of Judicial Review' (1987) 21 *University of British Columbia Law Review*, 87.

[28] Monahan, ibid., 89.

[29] P. Hogg, 'The Charter of Rights and American Theories of Interpretation' (1987) 250 *Osgoode Hall Law Journal*, 87 at 105.

[30] P. Monahan, *Politics and the Constitution: The Charter, Federalism and the Supreme Court of Canada* (Agincourt: Carswell, 1987): Chapter 5.3 'The Canadian Tory Touch'.

[31] *Supra*, note 29 at 104–11.

[32] *Re BC Motor Vehicle Act (1985)* [1985] 2 *Supreme Court Reports*, 486.

[33] *Supra*, note 29 at 88.

[34] L. Eisenstat Weinrib, 'Learning to Live With the Override' (1990) 35 *McGill Law Journal*, 541.

[35] Ibid., 571.

[36] P. Russell, 'The Politics of Law' (1991) 11 *Windsor Yearbook of Access to Justice*, 127 at 133.

[37] Ibid., see also P. Russell and P. Weiler, 'Don't Scrap Override Clause — It's a Very Canadian Solution', *The Toronto Star*, 4 June 1989, B3.

[38] F. Morton et al., 'The Supreme Court's First One Hundred Charter of Rights Decisions: A Statistical Analysis' (1992) 30 *Osgoode Hall Law Journal*, 1 at 14.

[39] Ibid.

[40] D. Beatty, *Putting the Charter to Work: Designing a Constitutional Labour Code* (Kingston: McGill-Queen's University Press, 1987): x: 'I [will not] attempt to respond to those who question the legitimacy of the entire enterprise. I have started from the premise that our Charter of Rights and judicial review are accepted constitutional facts.'

[41] D. Beatty, *Talking Heads and the Supremes: The Canadian Production of Constitutional Review* (Toronto: Carswell, 1990): vi, and D. Beatty and S. Kennett, 'Striking Back: Fighting Words, Social Protest and Political Participation in Free and Democratic Societies' (1988) 67 *Canadian Bar Review*, 573.

[42] J. Whyte, 'The Future of Canada's Constitutional Reform Process' in D. Smith et al., (eds), *After Meech Lake — Lessons for the Future* (Saskatoon: Fifth House, 1991): 242.

[43] *Supra*, note 41 at vii.

[44] P. Macklem, 'First Nations Self-Government and the Borders of the Canadian Legal Imagination' (1991) 36 *McGill Law Journal*, 382 at 393.

[45] P. Zylberberg, 'The Problem of Majoritarianism in Constitutional Law: A Symbolic Perspective' (1992) 37 *McGill Law Journal*, 27, 79.

[46]D. Dyzenhaus, 'The New Positivists' (1989) 39 *University of Toronto Law Journal*, 361 at 378.

[47]D. Coyne, 'Commentary', in Smith et al., *supra*, note 42 at 140.

[48]J. Whyte, 'On Not Standing for Notwithstanding' (1990) 28 *Alberta Law Review*, 347 at 351.

[49]B. Porter, 'Claiming and Enforcing Social and Economic Rights', Conference on Social and Economic Rights, Toronto, December 1991, 4.

[50]Ibid., 4.

[51]For example, Hogg asserted in 1977 (shortly before the entrenchment process began): '[i]t is a fact . . . that in Canada — as in the United Kingdom, Australia and New Zealand — civil liberties are better respected than in most other countries'. P. Hogg *Constitutional Law of Canada* (Toronto: Carswell, 1977): 418.

[52]R. Romanow, J. Whyte, A. Leeson, *Canada Notwithstanding: The Making of the Constitution 1976–1982* (Toronto: Carswell/Methuen, 1984): Introduction, xv, quoting Trudeau's 'The Enemy Within' speech, House of Commons Debates, 32nd Parliament, 1st Session, 1:32–56 (15 April 1980).

[53]House of Commons Debates, 32nd Parliament, 1st Session, 21 May 1980, 2: 1264.

[54]Romanow et al., *supra*, note 52 at 188 *et seq.*, describing the hammering out of the details as 'a classic example of raw bargaining' (211).

[55]A. Hutchinson and P. Monahan, 'Democracy and the Rule of Law' in A. Hutchinson and P. Monahan (eds), *The Rule of Law: Ideal or Ideology* (Toronto: Carswell, 1987): 119.

[56]A. Hutchinson and A. Petter, 'Private Rights/Public Wrongs: The Liberal Lie of the Charter' (1988) 38 *University of Toronto Law Journal*, 278, 283.

[57]D. Galloway, 'No Guru, No Method . . .' (1988) 8 *Windsor Yearbook of Access to Justice*, 304.

[58]A. Hutchinson and P. Monahan, 'Law, Politics, and the Critical Legal Scholars: The Unfolding Drama of American Legal Thought' (1984) 36:1 *Stanford Law Review*, 199, 243: 'The ultimate goal must be to promote "street theatre", the spontaneous involvement of people in everyday situations.'

[59]For example, Knopff and Morton, *supra*, note 6.

[60]A mere sampling of the work that ranges from scepticism (for different reasons and about different aspects) to unqualified hostility:

K. Banting and R. Simeon (eds), *And No One Cheered: Federalism, Democracy and the Constitution Act* (Toronto: Methuen, 1983).

J. Bakan, 'Constitutional Interpretation and Social Change: You Can't Always Get What You Want (Nor What You Need)' (1991), 70 *Canadian Bar Review*, 307.

A. Borovoy, *When Freedoms Collide: The Case for Our Civil Liberties* (Toronto: Lester & Orpen Dennys, 1988).

R. Cheffins and P. Johnson, *The Revised Canadian Constitution: Politics As Law* (Toronto: McGraw-Hill Ryerson, 1986).

B. Etherington, 'Arbitration, Labour Boards and the Courts in the 1980s: Romance Meets Realism' (1989) 68 *Canadian Bar Review*, 405.

J. Fudge, 'What Do We Mean by Law and Social Transformation?' (1990) 5 *Canadian Journal of Law and Society*, 47.

H. Glasbeek, 'A No-Frills Look at the Charter of Rights and Freedoms or How Politicians and Lawyers Hide Reality' (1989) 9 *Windsor Yearbook of Access to Justice*, 293.

A. Hutchinson, 'Charter Litigation and Social Change: Legal Battles and Social Wars' in R.J. Sharpe (ed.), *Charter Litigation* (Toronto: Butterworths, 1987).

T. Ison, 'The Sovereignty of the Judiciary', 10 *Adelaide Law Review*, 1 (1985).

R. Knopff and F.L. Morton, *supra*, note 6.

M. Mandel, *supra*, note 10.

L. Panitch and D. Swartz, *The Assault on Trade Union Freedoms: From Consent to Coercion Revisited* (Toronto: Garamond Press, 1988).

A. Petter, 'The Politics of the Charter' (1986) 8 *Supreme Court Law Review*, 473.

R. Romanow, 'Courts and Legislatures in the Age of the Charter' [1986] 9 *Canadian Parliamentary Review*, 2.

P. Russell, 'The Political Purposes of the Canadian Charter of Rights and Freedoms' (1983) 61 *Canadian Bar Review*, 30.

[61]The best example of this is probably the columns of Jeffrey Simpson: see, e.g., 'How the Courts Expand Rights and Whittle Away at Government', *The Globe and Mail*, 12 August 1992, A10; 'Priority Should Go to Protecting Minorities from Vicious Attacks', *The Globe and Mail*, 2 September 1992, A12; see also R. Fulford, 'The Charter of Wrongs', *Saturday Night*, December 1986, 7; and L. Martin, *Pledge of Allegiance* (Toronto: McClelland & Stewart, 1993): 42.

[62]Borovoy, *supra*, note 60 at 213.

[63]For instance, see Russell's brief but spirited defence of the judiciary and its protection of some civil liberties based on the 'pragmatic and empirical', a quote cited a number of places in this book: P. Russell, 'The Political Role of the Supreme Court of Canada in Its first Century' (1975) 53 *Canadian Bar Review*, 576, 592–3: 'Our judges have been at their best in the field of civil liberties when, instead of being asked to theorise about such abstractions as "equality before the law" or "due process of law", they have been called upon to identify the rights implicit in the working of our basic institutions of government. . . .'

Another instance of courts attempting to protect minorities occurred in the treatment of Franco-Manitobans: see K. Roach, 'The Role of Litigation and the Charter in Interest Advocacy' in F. Seidle (ed.), *Communities, the Charter and Interest Advocacy* (Montreal: Institute for Research on Public Policy, forthcoming).

[64]*Supra*, note 30 at 42–3.

[65]*Supra*, note 40 at 40. See also notes 30 and 31 at 197, and note 1 at 198 of Beatty's work. Beatty has, in fact, taken to excoriating the Supreme Court for its regressive decisions in labour matters: see, for example, 'A Conservative's Court: The Politicization of Law' (1991) 41 *University of Toronto Law Journal*, 147.

[66]H.W. Arthurs, 'Jonah and the Whale: The Appearance, Disappearance and Reappearance of Administrative Law (1980) 30 *University of Toronto Law Journal*, 225

at 225–6.

[67] J.M. Evans et al., (eds), *Administrative Law Cases, Text and Materials* (3d ed.) (Toronto: E. Montgomery, 1989): 12–14.

[68] For example, *Re Alberta Statutes* [1938] *Supreme Court Reports,* 100 and *Switzman v. Elbling,* [1957] *Supreme Court Reports,* 285.

[69] Cheffins and Johnson, *supra,* note 60 at 133, observe: 'It is absolutely clear that no Canadian court has ever based a decision on the implied bill of rights.'

[70] Borovoy, *supra,* note 60 at 208.

[71] *Edwards Books and Arts Ltd* v. R. [1986] 2 *Supreme Court Reports,* 713, 779: 'In interpreting and applying the Charter I believe that the courts must be cautious to ensure that it does not simply become an instrument of better situated individuals to roll back legislation which has as its object the improvement of the condition of less advantaged persons.'

[72] I. Abella and H. Troper, *None Is Too Many: Canada and the Jews of Europe, 1933–1948* (Toronto: Lester & Orpen Dennys, 1982).

[73] Monahan, *supra,* note 30 at 120, discussing some of the foibles.

[74] P. Russell, 'The Political Purposes of the Canadian Charter of Rights and Freedoms' (1983) 61 *Canadian Bar Review,* 30 at 52.

[75] G. Horowitz, *Canadian Labour in Politics* (Toronto: University of Toronto Press, 1968): 18.

[76] M. Valiante and W.A. Bogart, 'Helping "Concerned Volunteers Working Out of Their Kitchens": Funding Citizen Participation in Administrative Decision Making' (1992) 31 *Osgoode Hall Law Journal,* 1.

[77] Petter, *supra,* note 60 at 479 *et seq.*

[78] Ibid., 483, citing remarks made by Chief Justice Dickson to the mid-winter meeting of the Canadian Bar Association in Edmonton, 2 February 1985.

[79] A point in response might be that the problem of access is not as acute as it first appears because most Charter cases involve criminal matters where there is provision for legal aid. Assuming that the amount and scope of coverage in legal aid is otherwise adequate, there are still many problems with access. First, the preponderance of criminal cases under the Charter simply invites the question of what the statistical profile would look like if there were adequate access for other kinds of issues. Second, there can be many other interests implicated in criminal cases such that any number of groups and organizations may wish to participate through intervention. Here, again, problems of resources and access arise.

[80] L. Fox, 'Costs in Public-Interest Litigation' (1989) 10 *Advocates' Quarterly,* 385.

[81] K. Ruff, 'Final Appeal', *Canadian Forum,* June 1992, 14, and see the discussion concerning backlash in Chapter Two.

[82] T. Highway, *Dry Lips Oughta Move to Kapuskasing* (Saskatoon: Fifth House, 1989): 108.

[83] These various statistics are taken from P. Macklem, 'First Nations Self-Government and the Borders of the Canadian Legal Imagination' (1991) 36 *McGill Law Journal,* 383 at 386, and A.J. Piggner, 'The Socio-Demographic Conditions of Registered Indians' in J.R. Ponting (ed.), *Arduous Journey: Canadian Indians and Decolonization* (Toronto: McClelland & Stewart, 1986).

[84]G. York, 'Children Without a Life Seek Euphoria in Despair', *The Globe and Mail*, 6 February 1993, A3.

[85]*Supra*, note 44 at 454–5.

[86]W. Pentney, 'The Rights of the Aboriginal Peoples of Canada in the Constitution Act, 1982: Part I — The Interpretive Prison of Section 25' (1988) 22 *University of British Columbia Law Review*, 21, 22:

> [T]his article is founded on the supposition that it is legitimate and appropriate to articulate and interpret the rights of the aboriginal peoples of Canada in a language and in the context of an institutional structure that is non-aboriginal. Many aboriginal peoples reject this approach because they do not recognize the Canadian legal and political structure as legitimate. I do not seek to dispute that view. The modest assumption . . .

[87]Ibid., 59.

[88]W. Pentney, 'Part II — Section 35: The Substantive Guarantee' (1988) 22 *University of British Columbia Law Review*, 207, 278.

[89]P. Monture, 'Ka-Nin-Geh-Heh-Gah-E-Sa-Nonh-Yah-Gah' (1986) 2 *Canadian Journal of Women and the Law*, 159, 163–4.

[90]*Supra*, note 44 at 394–5; see also P. Macklem and R. Townshend 'Resorting to Court: Can the Judiciary Deliver Justice for First Nations?' in D. Engelstad and J. Bird (eds), *Nation to Nation — Aboriginal Sovereignty and the Future of Canada* (Toronto: Anansi, 1992).

[91]*Supra*, note 44 at 387.

[92]Ibid., 394.

[93]Ibid., 393.

[94]Ibid., 455.

[95]Ibid., 394.

[96]D. Shoalts, 'Natives Value Justice Differently', *The Globe and Mail*, 9 September 1991, A1. See also O. Dickason, *Canada's First Nations: A History of Founding Peoples from Earliest Times* (Toronto: McClelland & Stewart, 1992), especially Chapter XXIII, 'Canadian Courts and Aboriginal Rights'.

[97]For example, the recent British Columbia Court of Appeal's judgement in *Delgamuukw* v. *The Queen*: see F. Cassidy, 'On the Road to Recognition of Canadian Native Rights' *The Globe and Mail*, 9 July 1993, A21.

[98]M.E. Turpel, 'Aboriginal Peoples and the Canadian Charter: Interpretive Monopolies' Cultural Differences' (1989–90) 6 *Canadian Human Rights Yearbook*, 3.

[99]Ibid., 13.

[100]Ibid., 23.

[101]Ibid., 29.

[102]Ibid., 44.

[103]This analysis is based on the 'Text of the Charlottetown Agreement: Revised Draft: 2:30 p.m., 28 August 1992', *The Globe and Mail*, 1 September 1992, A1, A8–9.

[104]M. Cernetig, 'Natives Envision Breaking Vicious Cycle', *The Globe and Mail*, 14 July 1992, A1.

[105]Charlottetown text, *supra*, note 103 at s. IV, A42.

[106]Ibid., s. IV, A41.

[107]Ibid., s. IV, A43.

[108]S. Delacourt, 'Text Being Altered Native Women Say', *The Globe and Mail*, 19 September 1992, A4; M. Landsberg, 'Unity Deal Will Rob Native Women of Key Rights', *The Toronto Star*, 22 September 1992, B1; S. Fine, 'Native Women Aim to Block National Referendum in Court', *The Globe and Mail*, 13 October 1992, A10. For a discussion of these issues in a larger context, see S. Wesner, 'First Nations Women and Government Policy, 1970–92: Discrimination and Conflict' in S. Burt et al., *Changing Patterns — Women in Canada* (2d ed.) (Toronto: McClelland & Stewart, 1993): 92.

[109]*Supra*, note 103, s. IV, A41(a).

[110]Ibid., s. IV, C50.

[111]S. Venne, 'Treaty Indigenous Peoples and the Charlottetown Accord: The Message in the Breeze' (1993) 4 *Constitutional Studies*, 43.

[112]J. Simpson, 'Paying for Native Self-Government: If Nunavat's the Model, It's a Big Tab', *The Globe and Mail*, 4 February 1993, A20; T. Siddon, 'Nunavat: A Price Worth Paying', *The Globe and Mail*, 3 March 1993, A19.

[113]P. Russell, 'Canada's Charter of Rights and Freedoms: A Political Report' [1988] *Public Law* 385.

[114]Ibid., 389.

[115]A. Bryant et al., 'Public Attitudes Toward the Exclusion of Evidence: Section 24(2) of the Canadian Charter of Rights and Freedoms' (1990) 69 *Canadian Bar Review*, 1, 14–15.

[116]*Supra*, note 113 at 392.

[117]F. Morton and M. Withey, 'Charting the Charter, 1982–85: A Statistical Analysis' [1987] *Canadian Human Rights Yearbook*, 65.

[118]F. Morton et al., *Judicial Nullification of Statutes under the Charter of Rights and Freedoms, 1982–1988* (Calgary: Research Unit for Socio-Legal Studies, Faculty of Social Sciences, University of Calgary, 1989).

[119]F. Morton et al., *The Supreme Court's First One Hundred Charter of Rights Decisions: A Statistical Analysis* (1992) 30 *Osgoode Hall Law Journal*, 1.

[120]Ibid., 48.

[121]Ibid., 4.

[122]Ibid., 40.

[123]Ibid.

[124]G. Brodsky and S. Day, *Canadian Charter Equality Rights for Women: One Step Forward or Two Steps Back?* (Ottawa: Canadian Advisory Council on the Status of Women, 1989).

[125]Ibid., 103. The study involved decided cases (reported and unreported) to 17 April 1988. Notes on the database are included in Appendix B to the study.

[126]Ibid., 49.

[127]Ibid., 56.

[128]Ibid., 66 and Chapter Six 'Access to the Courts' in which the authors observe (140): 'The issue of access is the most basic one, and the state of access is, at present, shocking.'

[129] Ibid., 103.

[130] *Andrews* v. *Law Society of British Columbia* [1989] 1 *Supreme Court Reports*, 143 (rejecting 'similarly situated' test and accepting 'disadvantage' analysis).

[131] *Supra*, note 124 at 205 *et seq*. See also B. Baines, 'Law, Gender, Equality' in S. Burt *et al.* (eds), *supra*, note 108, 243 at 269–70.

[132] Ibid., 207 *et seq*.

[133] P. Russell, 'Canadian Constraints on Judicialization from Without', Conference on 'The Judicialization of Politics', address to the Interim Meeting of the International Political Science Association Research Committee on Comparative Judicial Studies, University of Bologna, Forli, Italy, June 1992, forthcoming in the *International Political Science Review*, 1993–4.

[134] Ibid., 17–18.

[135] Ibid., 7.

[136] Ibid.

[137] Ibid., 8.

[138] Ibid.

[139] Ibid.

[140] Ibid., 10. At 9–10: 'After a rollicking barrage of initial decisions in which the Court, citing John Marshall, expressed its determination to take Charter rights seriously and upheld three-quarters of the Charter claims brought to it, the Court settled down to a relatively moderate approach.'

[141] Ibid., 10.

[142] Ibid.

[143] *Retail, Wholesale and Department Store Union* v. *Dolphin Delivery Ltd* [1986] 2 *Supreme Court Reports*, 573.

[144] Russell, *supra*, note 133 at 10.

[145] *Edwards Books and Art Ltd* v. *The Queen* [1986] 2 *Supreme Court Reports*, 713.

[146] *Attorney-General for Quebec* v. *Irwin Toy* [1989] 1 *Supreme Court Reports*, 927.

[147] Russell, *supra*, note 133 at 11.

[148] *McKinney* v. *University of Guelph* [1990] 3 *Supreme Court Reports*, 229.

[149] *The Queen* v. *Askov* [1990] 2 *Supreme Court Reports*, 1199, and the second attempt at this question *Deepak Kumar Sharma* v. *The Queen* [1992] 1 *Supreme Court Reports*, 814.

[150] *The Queen* v. *Schwartz* [1988] 2 *Supreme Court Reports*, 443.

[151] *The Queen* v. *Hufsky* [1988] 1 *Supreme Court Reports*, 621; *The Queen* v. *Thomsen* [1988] 1 *Supreme Court Reports*, 640.

[152] Russell, *supra*, note 133 at 13.

[153] 'How the Charter Changes Justice', *Toronto Globe and Mail*, 17 April 1992, A1.

[154] Russell, *supra*, note 133 at 14.

[155] *Morgentaler* v. *The Queen* [1988] 1 *Supreme Court Reports*, 30.

[156] *The Queen* v. *Seaboyer; The Queen* v. *Gayme* [1991] 2 *Supreme Court Reports*, 577.

[157] *The Queen* v. *Keegstra* [1990] 3 *Supreme Court Reports*, 697.

[158] *Supra*, note 13.

[159] *The Queen* v. *Skinner* [1990] 1 *Supreme Court Reports*, 1235.

[160]*Butler* v. *The Queen* [1992] 1 *Supreme Court Reports*, 452.

[161]Russell, *supra*, note 133 at 15.

[162]Ibid., 16, quoting *Citizens Forum on Canada's Future, The Globe and Mail Condensed Version*, 2 July 1991, A9.

[163]Citing M. Jackman, 'When a Social Charter Isn't', *Canadian Forum*, April 1992, 8.

[164]Russell, *supra*, note 133 at 17.

[165]Ibid., 9.

[166]Ibid., 3.

[167]*Quebec* v. *Ford et al.* [1988] 2 *Supreme Court Reports*, 712.

[168]Russell, *supra*, note 133 at 4–5 quoting P. Monahan, *Meech Lake: The Inside Story* (Toronto: University of Toronto Press, 1991): 164.

[169]*Supra*, note 6 at 231.

[170]*R.* v. *Jones* [1986] 2 *Supreme Court Reports*, 284.

[171]*Supra*, note 143 and *Lavigne* v. OPSEU [1991] 2 *Supreme Court Reports*, 211.

[172]*Supra*, note 7.

[173]*Supra*, note 149.

[174][1992] 2 *Supreme Court Reports*, 679.

[175]*Supra*, note 15, note 17, and note 18.

[176]Russell, *supra*, note 133 at 8.

[177]*Reference re s. 94(2) of the British Columbia Motor Vehicle Act* [1985] 2 *Supreme Court Reports*, 486.

[178]*Supra*, note 30 at 76.

[179]See P. Hogg, *Constitutional Law of Canada* (3d ed.) (Toronto: Carswell, 1992): 44.7, citing in particular *Re ss. 193 and 195.1 of Criminal Code* (Prostitution Reference) [1990] 1 *Supreme Court Reports*, 1123, but see also *Minister of Employment and Immigration* v. *Chiarelli and Security Intelligence Review Committee* (1992) 2 *Administrative Law Review* (2d) 125 (SCC).

[180]*Supra*, note 124.

[181]Russell, *supra*, note 133 at 9, quoting his article, 'The Charter and the Future of Canadian Politics' in A. Gagnon and J. Bickerton (eds), *Canadian Politics: An Introduction to the Discipline* (Peterborough: Broadview Press, 1990): 246, 256.

[182]Notes for an Address by the Honourable A. Kim Campbell, minister of justice and Attorney-General of Canada on the Canadian Charter of Rights and Freedoms to the BC Civil Liberties Association, Vancouver, BC, 15 May 1992, 10–11.

[183]*Supra*, note 5.

[184]K. McRoberts, *Quebec: Social Change and Political Crisis* (3d ed.) (Toronto: McClelland & Stewart, 1988): 106, quoting C. Black, *Duplessis* (Toronto: McClelland & Stewart, 1976): 549.

[185]Even in the aftermath of the Charlottetown debacle and in the midst of so much confusion, for example, the uncertainty surrounding the continuing in politics of Premier Bourassa because of his health, there are some glimmerings of accommodations: see L. Gagnon, 'Most Francophones Favour a More Tolerant Approach to Language Laws', *The Globe and Mail*, 6 February 1993, D3.

[186]R.M. Dawson, *Dawson's the Government of Canada* (6th ed.), revised by N. Ward (Toronto: University of Toronto Press, 1987): 153.

[187]Ibid.

[188]C.E.S. Franks, 'The Senate and Its Reform' (1987) 12 *Queen's Law Journal*, 454, 454.

[189]L. Gagnon, 'A Word We Long to Hear from the Senate: Adieu', *The Globe and Mail*, 3 July 1993, D3.

[190]*Supra*, note 1: 'many of my colleagues at the bar who witnessed the Bork hearings would say "who needs it?"'

PART FOUR

Conclusions

CHAPTER TEN

The Courts
and the Country

. . . it is simply not true that a politician must lie or intrigue. That is utter nonsense, very often spread about by people who — for whatever reasons — wish to discourage others from taking an interest in public affairs.

— Vaclav Havel[1]

RIGHTS AND PARTICIPATION

Who better to instruct us about the aspirations of politics than Vaclav Havel? Imprisoned during the long darkness of the communist regime, elected president of his country on the return of democracy, he then came to preside over the eve of its dismemberment. He steadfastly opposed such division and its realization appears to have been a main reason for his withdrawal from the presidency. Only when the separation was complete did he then successfully run for president of the new Czech state.[2] Nevertheless, his powers as a writer have only increased and with them an abiding faith in democratic politics.[3] Throughout all the tumultuous events he has experienced and is living through in the 'post-communist nightmare',[4] he has been able to believe that 'genuine politics, politics worthy of the name . . . is simply serving those close to oneself: serving the community and serving those who come after us. Its deepest roots are moral because it is a responsibility expressed through action. . . .'[5]

Yet such sentiments seem a lofty dream, laudable but unrealizable as we come to this century's — indeed, the millennium's — end. The fall of a great enemy of democracy — totalitarian communism — seems not to have spurred us on to contemplate the potential of free societies but instead we rail at their limits while paradoxically reacting as if these confines are somehow preordained. That there is evidence that politicians and their craft have been placed on a sort of probation throughout the world is context but not comfort as we survey our own terrain. No one policy or program has been given notice but the entire federal and constitutional arrangement has been placed in a sort of suspended jeopardy, at least over the last decade: 'So corrosive is this mood that those who risk public life will be largely those who cannot think of anything better to do and who, elected, will earn more money than in any other job they might ever have.'[6]

Small wonder then that ways to bypass the process that seems immediately responsible for our collective sense of failure and betrayal are sought. Smaller wonder that many (by no means all) such searches come to focus on an existing element of our governance that yet stands apart from popular politics. Courts with their mechanisms that require response, that do not depend on deals (much less connivance), that can capture principle and command it to do the good seem to provide a whole new stream for a people to run its course, at least for some undetermined time. The aloofness, élitism, unrepresentativeness, and lack of accountability seem to be from this different view not foibles but attractive insulating factors from the debilitated, treacherous ground that has, it is everywhere sighed, become our politics.

This exit to the courts seems even more assured and right at some fundamental level when the litigation is channelled through the abstractions of the Charter. Now the judges are not reflecting their own predilections but are instead mirroring and implementing core values — free speech, fundamental justice, equality — to name but a few items on a long and attractive list. True, there is pause — quite a lot actually — about how the judges decide in any particular case, but still, we have an institution in society that looks at the big picture by focusing on basics. What a change from the horse trading — largely unsuccessful — these all too many years: 'The Charter has spawned a generation of rights-hungry but responsibility-wary citizens for whom the old totems of Canadian federalism — federal-provincial negotiations, inter-governmental compromise, French-English accommodation — mean next to nothing.'[7]

This sharp contrast between the retreat from our politics and the temptation to turn to the courts returns us to Charles Taylor's ideas and the contrast between the rights model's link with centralization and the participatory model's link with decentralization, which opened the discussion at the beginning of Chapter One. It is not, Taylor contends, that the participatory model does not respect rights or their enforcement. What is critical is that rights recognition — particularly through courts — is not the fundamental element of citizen dignity which, rather, focuses 'on having a voice in deciding the common laws by which members live. . . . Special importance attaches to the fact that we as a whole, or community, decide about ourselves as a whole community.'[8] Yet a much different effect is produced by the rights model with its 'atomist consciousness', which necessarily weakens the underpinnings of common purpose: '. . . I cannot be too willing to trump the collective decision in the name of individual rights if I haven't already moved some distance from the community which makes these decisions. . . .'[9]

The arguments for the rights model (and conversely against the participatory model) take much of their appeal from their claim to protect interests ignored by the political process. Participation as a paradigm is but a rosy depiction if affected interests conclude that — far from being heard — they are muffled in it. Rights, on the other hand, are there for the claiming, awaiting no political or bureaucratic agendas, which are unresponsive in any event. In particular, the assertion that the disadvantaged can exit a hostile political process and shelter in a forum that will respond to their pleas propels the case for courts and rights forward.

If invocation of the rights model actually worked in this way, the price it exacts on the workings of politics might indeed be justified. Society might be more divided, the lure of this new avenue might make everyone less committed to the general good, whether in terms of establishing new programs, invigorating old ones, or participating at all by actively taking a role or just voting. Yet it could be asserted to be a fairer society: more atomistic but more equally so. Ideally, the two models would be harmonized. Here rights would be attended to (again claims on behalf of the disadvantaged are the most sympathetic) as not only an end in themselves but also a means of instruction for the political process. Recognition — creation —of rights by the courts would be messages sent back to the bureaucratic and political processes, signalling ways for reconstruction and renewal.

But dreams stumble over reality. Try as they might, proponents of the rights model cannot point to any deep and enduring evidence that courts have ever been responsible for long-lasting and effective social or political change. In the United States, the homeland of such claims on behalf of courts, students of the consequences of litigation of these issues instead portray a much more ambiguous set of results. As we saw in Chapter Two, a number of studies on courts done by those sympathetic to progressive forces are not sanguine about the enthusiastic embrace of the rights model in the name of reform. Thus after an extensive study of such interests and their involvement with litigation in the 1970s, Handler concluded that such activity 'will not disturb the basic political and economic organization of modern American society'.[10] Meanwhile, Mary Ann Glendon points to the dangers that judicial intervention has in the aggregate on the political process: 'One danger is . . . that of atrophy in the democratic processes of bargaining, education and persuasion that take place in and around legislatures. Another is that by too readily preventing compromise and blocking the normal political avenues for change, courts leave the disappointed majority with no legitimate political outlet.'[11]

The most sobering account of public interest groups and their experience with litigation in the United States comes from Gerald Rosenberg in *The Hollow Hope*. He bluntly concludes: 'US courts can *almost never* be effective producers of significant social reform.'[12] While Rosenberg could find no substantial evidence that court decisions mobilized supporters of significant social reform, he contends that there is evidence that litigation may actually galvanize opponents. At the same time, litigation may 'lure' groups to expend more resources better spent in the electoral, legislative, and administrative processes. The last sentence of his book is a sharp and eloquent warning: '[W]hile romance and even naïveté have their charms, they are not best exhibited in court rooms.'[13] Even those who believe that Rosenberg is too categorical in his conclusions about litigation's inability to effect progressive change acknowledge that because of *The Hollow Hope*: 'there is room for much uncertainty about this matter [of consequences] . . . [Rosenberg] has put into question the assumption of people who now believe . . . that litigation is an especially promising approach to social reform.'[14]

Historically in Canada, courts' indifference to progressive issues can be readily established. We saw this when we looked at women's issues before the Charter.[15] Whether the issue was admission to the practice of law or the division of assets upon the breakdown of intimate relationships or discrimination based on pregnancy (among other issues), women almost invariably lost in the courts and almost always achieved some redress through the legislative process. The courts had a similar attitude to such issues as workers' compensation, labour relations, and human rights, among others. Those seeking reform were largely defeated in the courts, but achieved change in the legislature through the creation of the administrative state.[16] Nevertheless, judges persisted in exerting at least an ideological influence over the workings of these tribunals and programs created by the state through a review process — essentially fashioned by themselves — of these administrative decisions. Such a process was used to prune and corral programs inimical to judicial values.[17] More or less the same pattern emerges historically regarding similar issues with the courts in England, as evidenced by Griffith's discussion in *The Politics of the Judiciary*.[18] In all such instances, the courts were almost universally hostile to any progressive change. Animating these decisions was a commitment to traditional liberal values so that any initiatives that could possibly interfere with the market and minimalist government were eschewed.

There is no question that an account of judicial activity during the initial decade of the Charter is more complex. Progressives can point to a number of areas where courts have been responsive to those seeking reform. These initiatives have been discussed generally in conjunction with the Charter,[19] regarding litigation for progressive reform on behalf of women,[20] concerning the administration of criminal justice,[21] and in terms of remedies granted by courts.[22] On the other hand, there have been many other cases during this first decade that must give reformers pause. Reservations about the judiciary being involved in a range of complex political and social issues do not stem only from the possibility that those acting for the disadvantaged will lose. The reservations are much more extensive, focusing as well on problems of access to the courts because of the cost of litigation.[23]

Even more pointedly, such doubts focus on the ramifications of winning. Victories in litigation may elicit negative political reaction and actually cause the political process to withdraw from grappling with larger social and political issues. We saw the complexities of winning dramatically illustrated in the discussion of abortion and related issues.[24] Through a number of cases, the Supreme Court has established women's legal right to an abortion, but these victories do not address access to abortions. As well, access is now even more difficult. Meanwhile, solutions to related questions critical to addressing women's disadvantage, such as maternity leave, pre- and postnatal care, and day care appear even more remote.

The possibility of litigation causing the political process to back away from controversial issues was also raised by the consequences of the *Schachter*[25] decision, which allowed excluded groups to be read into legislation because their exclusion would be unconstitutional. Yet an immediate reaction to the decision was the legislature's curtailment of parental leave benefits.[26] Shortly thereafter, the federal government abandoned its commitment to day care. *Schachter* was also used to further gay rights' inclusion in the Canadian Human Rights Code by a lower court, but with the Supreme Court's decision in *Mossop*[27] curtailing gay and lesbian rights on other grounds[28] and politicians' ambivalence and hostility to the issues, gays and lesbians may now be actually worse off in their struggle to achieve legal protection.

The 'due process trajectory' and its impact on other values in the administration of criminal justice further illustrated how litigation can confound initiatives the political process might otherwise have taken. Theoretically, there is much to be said for accommodating due process and preventing crime. Yet as we saw, underestimating of the potential of due process to transform and control other interests and values can result in indifference regarding underlying concerns, as exemplified by the discussion of the controversies surrounding Supreme Court cases on speedy trials, on the 'rape-shield' law, and by an analysis of the largely unsuccessful criminal rights 'revolution' in the United States.[29]

A final illustration of the possibilities and the hazards of litigation in the name of reform are the complexities of using the courts on behalf of Amerindians.[30] While there is potential for improvement based in part on change already initiated by courts, there is also much evidence of failure, some of it extremely costly. More fundamentally, profound questions arise as to having the dominant culture's judiciary decide such issues at all. The worry is that even should there be a series of progressive decisions they would not 'transform' but instead contain the little that remains of a culture so different from our own, including substantial diversity within itself.

In any event, we can be certain about one thing. Judicial involvement (especially that of the Supreme Court) in important issues affecting this society is on the rise. This is obviously true regarding the Charter in the last decade. In addition, we have seen an enthusiastic return to federalism litigation[31] and an interventionist position on the part of the Supreme Court in judicial review of administrative action.[32] All these types of litigation involve governmental action as the target of the suit. Taken together they can send powerful messages about giving the courts some complex issues that the political process is too divided, confounded, or absorbed to answer. The politicians involved in constructing a new constitutional arrangement (abandoned for the undetermined moment) were sorely tempted to deal the courts into the very arrangements themselves. This is what occurred to a critical extent in terms of recognizing self-government for Aboriginals in the Charlottetown Accord where the right was incorporated but its application and meaning would have been ultimately left to the courts.[33]

At this point we have come back to Charles Taylor. Taylor is a philosopher who does not purport to canvass the detailed effects of embracing the rights model. Yet his depiction of the inevitable tension between the rights and the participatory models dealt with earlier is largely borne out by examining the accounts just summarized. The more of one model means the less of the other. As rights litigation and rights discourse flourish, they can loosen commitment to community and consensus. Such a loss can corral legislative, bureaucratic, and administrative initiatives that can be central to the improvement of society, perhaps particularly for the disadvantaged but also in terms of mediating among all legitimate interests.

But those who have responded to these arguments and evidence might ask what can be done. If in only a decade our habits of thought and our expectations of government have become so refocused in terms of the courts, can this advance ever be turned back? Conversely, will we ever have sufficient respect for our politics so that we see it as a driving force for realizing society's common good? Will there be a day when the mere mention of politics elicits some hope that it will not just be about the possible but, as Havel insists, also 'the impossible, that is the art of making both ourselves and the world better'?[34]

I would not be so foolish to hazard predictions about what is to become of us. Nevertheless, what may be useful is to point to a number of ways that litigation can be limited and yet still fulfil important functions. The hope is that this discussion could contribute to a widely held sense that the role for litigation in this society is a subject for reflection and debate as much as any other process or institution in our governance. To forego such debate is to run the risk that courts, through a series of steps each possibly justified on its own terms, will come to dominate social and political policy. The fear is that the discourse of rights, by default and by drift, will become the focus of our participation.

THE POSSIBILITY OF LIMITS

To begin to approach the limits of litigation, we should first consider the core functions of courts. If we can establish that, we might then examine a number of strategies for keeping lawsuits within these bounds while looking at the foibles of our politics that tempt groups and individuals to turn to the courts. To reduce any complex activity to one statement is to risk gross oversimplification, but it can also be enormously helpful in terms of focus: dispute resolution with norms generated incidentally and subject to legislative override.

Those familiar with the law may say that this core description of litigation is nothing but a terse account of the common law, the law made by the judges in the jurisdictions of that tradition, which was to focus on resolving disputes and only 'make' law to the extent necessary to resolve the myriad problems placed before them over time. Laws made by the judges could be augmented, modified, or overruled by legislatures who reached their own decisions concerning what rules and methods of resolving applicable disputes should prevail. In fact, in large measure they will be right because this core function of the common law (appropriately adapted for the civil law tradition of Quebec) points a way to steer between a parliamentary supremacy that is self-satisfied in its exercise of power and a judiciary whose exercise of power becomes not democracy's prod but its enervation.

To make the case for this core function for litigation, we can begin by thinking back to the chapters on the administrative state[35] and tort.[36] These sections cover a panorama of important issues from compensation of workers for injuries sustained while at work, to protection of the environment, to defence of human rights, to protection against defamation, to redress for damage caused as a result of medical malpractice, among others. There was nothing in the apparatus of the common law that precluded it from engaging virtually any issue of the human enterprise when such questions arise in specific disputes. That it frequently did not do so, so that the legislative process intervened with a range of solutions, does not blunt the fact that the core functions of courts could address such questions. Yet the judiciary's failure to respond does underscore that those seeking progressive solutions had much more cause historically to turn from the courts than they had to worry about unresponsive legislative processes and dulled bureaucracies. A similar depiction could be presented regarding women's issues — from the right of women to practise law to financial arrangements upon the breakdown of intimate relationships — at least until the Charter.[37]

Still, at this point readers may recall how the structure of a lawsuit (costs, class actions, etc.) was and still is unaccommodating (even hostile) to progressive interests, particularly when they assert collective, diffuse claims.[38] There are three points here. First, there is nothing about the structure of litigation or about courts themselves to prevent developing more welcoming structures for such interests. Some changes have been realized by the judges in terms of standing, intervention, and remedies. Second, it is open to legislatures to intervene to transform such rules and their workings. Class action legislation in Quebec and even more recently in Ontario are current examples of such activity by the politicians. The effectiveness of such activity may be the subject of scrutiny,[39] yet such an assessment simply underscores the fact that legislative efforts can be revised. They are compromises imperfectly arranged, subject to revision by those who can harness the political will, a fact that is the basis for their legitimacy. Third, it is also true that in the space of ten years, we have witnessed the initiation and then termination of the Court Challenges Program, a federal initiative that funded (to an extent) certain types of Charter challenges. It was the main program underwriting litigation for equality-seeking groups.[40] Its termination demonstrates the shifts and unreliability of politics. But the rights model has even greater difficulty with its cancellation since the more proponents rail against its termination (I am sympathetic to such protests) the more they underscore the lack of access inherent in the rights model, a central point made in the discussion of the case against the Charter.[41]

This model — dispute resolution with norms generated incidentally and subject to legislative override — would also accommodate federalism litigation. It is true that in federalism litigation the judges have a capacity to nullify legislation of one level of government on the grounds that it intrudes on the other. However, it remains the case that the legislation can be enacted by some level of government so, in that sense, the judges clearly do not have the last say. Moreover, as we saw, federalism decisions lead to complex effects that are used by governments as chips in bargaining with each other so that these consequences are very much returned to politics and the daily workings of legislators and their bureaucrats.[42]

Discussion of federalism litigation raises another point of particular application in this context but of broader relevance as well. We saw that American courts have virtually absented themselves from resolution of federalism questions.[43] There is a broad consensus about the wisdom of such withdrawal resting on agreement that regional interests are better represented by other institutions and mechanisms of government and that conflicts between the central and state governments are better resolved through overtly political processes.

While no such norms of abstention have ever been endorsed by our Supreme Court, it is the case that before the upswing in federalism litigation in the late seventies, the parties (federal and provincial governments and, to a large extent, 'private' actors) themselves reached informal norms of understanding that federalism questions should not be channelled through the courts but managed through ongoing negotiation and compromise.

True, such agreement rested on a set of terms and conditions obtaining during that period, for example, on Quebec's relative lack of ambition to regulate areas conceivably reserved for the central government and the federal authorities' willingness to accommodate the rise of provincial initiatives, particularly with regard to Quebec.

It is equally true that establishing a basis for such norms in today's climate of federal-provincial relations would be no easy task. But the fair question is to ask which route is likely to produce over the long term an atmosphere in which the intractable differences of geography, history, culture, and contemporary needs can be worked through. In this depiction, court pronouncements are not a solution. Further, they could easily become a source of deflection eroding even a minimal understanding that accommodation and reflection of these differences may be our only hope for survival. Taylor is eloquent about the need for accommodation as he links the participatory model with decentralization, urging us to embrace a 'deep diversity': 'Someone . . . might indeed feel Canadian as a bearer of individual rights in a multicultural mosaic. . . . But this person might nevertheless accept that a Quebecois, or a Cree, or a Dene, might belong in a very different way, that they were Canadian through being members of their national communities. And reciprocally, the Quebecois, Cree or Dene would accept the perfect legitimacy of the "mosaic" identity.'[44]

But suppose I have brought the reader along so far, at least to the point where such a relationship between the courts and the rest of government is plausible. Will the entire suggestion not stumble when we come to the Charter? How could the claim of legislatures having the last word — prominent in the proffered model — ever be reconcilable with the powers said to be conferred on the judiciary by the Charter? Is there not a fundamental clash here between the judges and the politicians that forces us to choose? Is there not a fundamental divide so that those favouring the Charter and the role it articulates for courts ought to declare themselves and those who are against the enterprise should be resolute in their antipathy?

I believe the Charter was a mistake because of all the hesitations about judicial power that this book has been at such pains to discuss and to demonstrate. That the Charter might someday disappear from the constitutional terrain is not implausible, given the conditional nature of our arrangements, perhaps particularly in terms of constitutional ordering, especially over the last decades. Yet given the outcry over Meech Lake and the Charlottetown Accord, any form of constitutional amendment is unlikely for a very long time.

In any event, given the central arguments here about the need to reinvigorate politics so as to forge a common commitment based on moderation and compromise to work through the problems and differences that beset us, it would be bitterly ironic for this book to take a do-or-die position on the Charter. Moreover, it has been the burden of this work not to claim to be able to describe precisely the consequences of litigation but to engender a widely held scepticism about them. It follows that I must allow that my prognostications, which are decidedly gloomy at times, may not turn out to be so bad. I freely admit that I could be wrong, on one condition: that those with high hopes for litigation, in turn, will allow that they could be left with hollow ones.

What would this terrain of suspended judgement look like where those focused on the bright promise of rights would coexist for at least some time with those hoping for a particular version of participatory democracy to fulfil their expectations? Of course there is no simple or easy answer to this question.[45] Yet there are several strands that such a truce can look towards in the hope that we achieve a balance that would reflect the aspirations that 'A society that cannot imagine its disadvantaged going to court to achieve reform will have an impoverished sense of justice; one that relies on such Herculean efforts will have an illusory one'[46] and that rights and the common good are not pitched as adversaries but partners in the 'dance of adjustment'.[47] Still, framing a means of compromise, while no simple exercise, is the easier part. Finding the will to implement and honour such measures is by far more difficult.

THE LIMITS OF COURTS, THE OBLIGATIONS OF POLITICS

We can begin with a fundamental proposition: if it is the case that the more we judicialize fundamental social and political questions, the more we enervate politics, then it is also likely that the more we limit the judiciary, the more politics will need to respond to the discontents that make recourse to the courts seem so tempting or at least necessary. If those who insist upon using the courts as the outlet for their discontents insist upon the right to gamble upon rights, then to that extent, the political process is forced to stand idly by. But by the same token, those who wish to assert the essentials of politics to respond to fundamental issues in society cannot hope to ignore these dissatisfactions. They may offer different solutions — preferably a range of them as a basis for consensus — but they cannot in any event ignore the claims.

In fact one can develop an inventory of possible initiatives that both courts and politicians could respond to. That response would acknowledge the important role courts have come to play in our social and political life and yet continue to have legislatures develop, implement, and assess programs and institutions so that 'we as a whole, or community, decide about ourselves as a whole community'.[48] That response would be respectful of and solicitous towards rights, but would not allow them (or at least any particular conception of them) to be used as trumps.

An obvious place to begin in terms of attempting a balance between courts and legislatures and their agents is with the text of the Charter itself, which contains two express limits on the judicialization of rights. The first is contained in s. 1 and is a direction to the courts that their recognition and protection of rights should strive for the common good. The second is contained within s. 33 and contemplates that the legislatures can have the final say between rights and the common good.

S. 1 instructs that the 'rights and freedoms' in the Charter are subject 'to such reasonable limits prescribed by law as can be demonstrably justified in a free and democratic society'. It is clear, therefore, that the Charter contemplates at least some constraints on rights in order to advance a greater purpose. But the extent to which s. 1 provides a defence to governmental acts that otherwise offend provisions in the Charter will depend on how it is interpreted and that exercise is one primarily for the courts. Yet however they interpret s. 1, it is clear that this provision requires that the courts formulate a view of the role legislatures have in balancing the claim of rights against the claims of the common good.

Initially, the Supreme Court articulated a very stringent test for governments to avail themselves of a s. 1 defence, an approach consistent with rights as trumps.[49] More recently, the Court has demonstrated a greater openness to arguments that infringement of rights may be tolerable to advance a governmental purpose and, in any event, legislatures should be accorded some leniency in making such judgements.[50] While there can be tortuous debates about the details of such a test of deference under s. 1, the vital aspect of it must be the courts recognizing in theory and in application governments' central role in balancing rights with an understanding of the common good: 'a margin of appreciation, a zone of discretion in which reasonable legislators could disagree. . . .'[51] Some members of the judiciary in speeches and writings (aside from their judgements) are demonstrating profound attempts to reconcile their role with an enlivened Canadian democracy.[52] Yet by definition under s. 1, such possibilities for recognizing the difficulties and complexities of political judgements, including fiscal implications — 'all roads cannot be paved at once'[53] — rest in the hands of the judges.[54]

For their part, legislatures have a means (housed in s. 33) to override judicial pronouncements in terms of the appropriate balance between assertion of rights and the realization of a common purpose. It is clear that s. 33 is not to be employed lightly. It requires that a legislature must expressly state in legislation that 'the Act or a provision thereof shall operate notwithstanding a provision included in section 2 or sections 7 to 15 of this Charter' and that such exclusion has a five-year limit unless renewed by that legislature. But at this point, readers may protest that I am taking them down blind alleys because, as was noted in Chapter Ten, s. 33 has been so excoriated that it is 'politically speaking . . . almost unusable'.[55]

Indeed, former Prime Minister Mulroney, in that very special way he had, proclaimed s. 33 to be the 'major flaw of [the constitutional settlement of] 1981, which reduces your individual rights and mine', making the Charter 'not worth the paper it is written on'.[56] Such a statement illustrates the fears expressed in this book. Behind it lie ideas that equate principle and rationality with the judiciary and collusion and connivance with insensitive legislatures. In this depiction, rights with their 'atomist consciousness'[57] (almost always left vague and unspecified so as to appeal to as wide a range of political aspirations as possible) are a bulwark; rights, in balance, are a capitulation.

A participatory model, in contrast, views s. 33 as an opportunity to fold the judicial enterprise back into the workings of democracy. This perspective attempts to use the courts to enliven and stimulate democracy as one component of democratic processes, not their detached overseer. From this perspective, comments like Mulroney's terse remarks are accurate only if one accepts a certain model for the judicial role, but such a role is in no sense inevitable or obviously superior and a participatory model urges instead that s. 33 become 'the foundation of an interinstitutional dialogue, in which courts and legislatures issue reasoned responses to each other's initiatives, thereby improving the quality of both public deliberation and its policy outcomes'.[58]

There is another reason for s. 33 to have vitality emerging from the actual effects of litigation seeking to bring about change.[59] Those efforts over the long haul were not conspicuously successful. Even when courts sided with those seeking reform, such orders often did not have the desired effects because they depended on the support of the political process for their implementation, which was not forthcoming; legislatures came to regard the results of litigation, however determined, as removing issues from their control and responsibility. In contrast, s. 33 with its capacity to require 'interinstitutional dialogue' could tie the two processes together. If a legislature has a true capacity to override judicial pronouncements with which it disagrees, it should follow that that legislature ought to honour the letter and spirit of any rulings with which it does not interfere.[60] Such a supposition rests on what must be bedrock: reform on behalf of the disadvantaged may use the courts as a spur, but they must return to legislative and bureaucratic processes for the programs and funds that are the mainstay for such efforts. Otherwise there may be judicial victories, but they will be pyrrhic and isolated.

The great stumbling block is that in our haste to embrace the culture of rights, we see s. 33 not as a means to bridge the gap between courts and politics but as a threat to judicial supremacy. We are so disgruntled with the legislators that we turn to the courts and give them unqualified judgement over complex social issues. Instead of seeing s. 33 as a means of careful and provisional experimentation with the rights model, while recognizing the necessity of vigorous politics, we rush head on into the proposition that judicial pronouncement is not an important perspective on difficult issues but the supreme and final disposition.[61]

A different tack in terms of confining the judicial role within democratic boundaries is to make the judiciary more democratic in the sense of more representative. The claim here is that, quite apart from dilemmas about the judiciary's proper relation to the other institutions of government, judicial decisions themselves will be more acceptable and more legitimate if judges are more representative of the citizenry subject to their orders. There is little doubt that the unrepresentative nature of the judiciary is counted as a grave weakness, even among those with high aspirations for the courts.[62]

Such concerns do not rest on mere speculation but are grounded on studies that demonstrate that judges are overwhelmingly white, able-bodied, and male, and that less than lofty reasons surround many of the appointments. A recent study of judicial appointments during the first Mulroney government reached the following conclusions:

> [P]atronage, or 'political favouritism', . . . continued to have a major influence on judicial appointments during the first Mulroney government. One hundred and eight appointees, just under half the total number (47.4 per cent), had a known political association with the Conservative Party. For just under a quarter (24.1), the involvement was considered strong. Mr. Mulroney's government, it would appear, so far as judicial appointments are concerned, did not exercise its options much differently from the Trudeau/Turner Liberal government.[63]

In fairness, prior political involvement should not by itself raise the spectre of patronage and to the contrary, it is possible that some such involvement could help judges to develop a sympathy for the tough choices that are sometimes made as a part of the political process. Still, one need not subscribe to extreme notions of determinacy to be persuaded that such an unrepresentative body will have difficulty coming to grips with claims that do not conform to a narrow range of attributes; the history of Canadian courts, as documented in this book, establishes that sad fact, a matter commented upon even by judges of the Supreme Court, particularly its female members.[64] Moreover, it is fair to suggest that the unrepresentative nature of the judiciary and the fact that political connections still play a prominent role are by no means unrelated.

The prescriptions offered for this problem vary.[65] One would focus on breaking the hold of the governing party in making the appointments by involving the legislature in some basic way, perhaps including some hearing process. The other places more hope in independent bodies that are more broadly representative, who would screen potential appointments, make recommendations to the government, and monitor and report the extent to which their recommendations were followed. Both routes have possibilities. Some initiatives with regard to the latter have begun.[66] The goal is clear: a more representative and capable judiciary freed of the taint of patronage.

Another charge that is made against the judiciary is that it is not accountable. The fundamental method of accountability (and legitimacy) is through the ballot. Some states in the United States elect their judges, but there is little enthusiasm in this country for attempting to achieve accountability so directly. Even the most enthusiastic of democrats need to acknowledge the limits of elections. A more straightforward method of furthering this goal of a more accountable judiciary would be to limit judges' terms of appointment. There is nothing radical or even novel about this proposal, as Beatty points out in his discussion of these issues,[67] since many countries in western Europe do this to confine the opportunity that any one individual has to wield such power. Of course it is important to preserve the judges' independence during their term of office by stipulating that a judge can only be removed for a very narrow set of circumstances, focused on moral culpability or clear incapacity, and by requiring that the decision for such removal be made (for federal appointments) by both houses. But an unlimited term is in no sense required for such independence and, conversely, '[g]iven the substantial powers that these individuals wield, it makes obvious sense, both theoretically and practically, to limit how long they will be able to monopolise such powerful positions of legal authority'.[68]

The last suggestion concerning the appointment of judges may be the most controversial. Must all judges be lawyers? Is this a necessary requirement for our highest Court where the questions posed and answered do not involve application of technical rules and doctrines of law but social and political questions of vital importance? One of the strongest counts against litigation, particularly under the Charter, is that it removes essential questions from public debate and puts them into the discourse of the law. This means that critical elements of the common interest come to be dominated by a handful of lawyers and judges. Even if this group were to become more representative, it would still be the case that to participate in this particular form of discourse and resolution, one needs to be a trained and certified legal practitioner, which is by no means a modest requirement in terms of time, financial, and other resources. Yet why need this be so?

One answer is to insist that a law degree or legal professional certification — to say nothing of the years of experience before one is appointed — does equip lawyers with special skills that are indeed necessary for determining legal issues. This is clearest at the trial level with its procedural and evidentiary rules pertinent to the fact-finding process. Moreover, most disputes at that level will not involve issues of high policy but the application of a body of doctrine, a task that is by no means beyond anyone of good intelligence and judgement, but is particularly suited for those legally trained (though even in making this point, we should be mindful of the number of hearings conducted by administrative agencies, some involving very elaborate procedural and evidentiary questions; many members of such tribunals are not lawyers). While the business of intermediate appellate bodies, such as the provincial appeal courts, moves them substantially towards policy making, here, too, arguments about the need for expertise associated with the legally trained could reasonably prevail.

However, at the highest Court a set of different needs and circumstances are at the forefront, especially regarding Charter litigation. Here policy making is to take place implicating fundamental values, ones that, it is claimed, affect us all and in which all of us have a stake. Of course, formidable intelligence must be brought to bear and, in addition, experience and compassion as broadly representative as possible of the strands that are a part of these fundamental (but frequently conflicting) values. Clearly, there are many distinguished lawyers with such attributes, but will anyone argue that these virtues are the exclusive preserve of that profession? On the other hand, it might be insisted that such questions have a special complexity and are embedded in a particular body of learning (constructed by lawyers) that dictates that they be decided only by the legally trained. Yet in asserting such a posture, are not its adherents necessarily conceding the argument made against moving such issues so directly into the courts: their removal from the participation (and responsibility) of the broader, more representative public to become the domain of an élite bounded by a limited set of ideas and discourse?

This brings us directly to the matter of participation. Notice that both the rights and the participatory model suggest that much of their respective appeal comes from involving the citizenry in the decision-making process. This appears to be a point of commonality, though its manifestation in each is substantially different. In the participatory model (notice the inclusion of this key ingredient in this model's name) the focus is on the democratic processes themselves. In the rights model, courts will ultimately decide, sending their judgements back to the legislatures and their agents for (it is hoped) incorporation so that this process can change in light of these instructions in principle. In an arrangement in which there is scepticism about the effects of litigation on the one hand and a commitment to revitalize the institutions of democracy on the other, what would this common claim to enhanced participation look like?

Some of the political processes' blights are easy to identify. What to do about them is another matter. A political arrangement that tolerates the chronic underrepresentation of women when they constitute over half of the population contains a substantial flaw manifested in everything from women's issues being ignored or mangled to a woman member in recent years being called a 'slut'.[69] As of January 1993, 13 per cent of the seats in Parliament were held by women, a figure that fell in between the representation in the legislatures from a high of 25 per cent in British Columbia and Prince Edward Island to a low of 6 per cent in Nova Scotia.[70] That we have finally had a woman prime minister — and not elected in her own right — simply throws such underrepresentation into relief.

Any theory that suggests that you must have a certain set of characteristics to represent a particular segment of the population is heading us towards a hopelessly divided society and, by definition, one in which minorities (and minorities within minorities) will have little chance in the wake of such fragmentation.[71] Yet a process that is so very unrepresentative (my specific example and statistics here focus on women, but the point has a depressing familiarity for visible minorities, the disabled, Aboriginals, etc.) is fraught with hazards almost anywhere on the political spectrum in terms of having claimed to attend to issues of the common good. Meanwhile, the expectations of those historically unrepresented in decision-making processes have developed such momentum (based on good cause shown) as to be unstoppable.

It is naïve to expect such interests to speak in a unified voice and there is already plenty of evidence that they do not. What they do share is a grievance about being excluded from political power, a bill of complaints that will only grow as long as they are outside the assemblies. Brought into the legislatures, their expectations will have to confront each other and mix with the ones already there: they will have a right to expect the common good to reflect their aspirations, they will be full partners in discharging the obligations to see that such a common good is realized.

Electing minorities will, of course, be no easy task. The history of women in Canadian politics has been a hard one.[72] Reasons for their low representation are complex, ranging from all the explanations about why women have not entered the full-time workforce to hostility in political parties to women's candidacy because they lack authority and they cannot raise money.[73]

Yet these very reasons raise a challenge to the political process to respond. The first New Democratic Party government in Ontario in 1990 had almost equal gender representation in the Cabinet; solutions clearly need to transcend left-right cleavage if they are to be enduring.[74] The Royal Commission on Electoral Reform and Party Financing recommends a number of critical initiatives to achieve more diverse representation among politicians.[75] To that end, it made a number of recommendations that would directly or indirectly increase the number of successful women candidates, such as child-care tax breaks for those who seek nomination or election; imposition of spending limits on nomination contests, allowing women to compete more equally against male candidates who are typically better off or have greater access to funding; more public funds for parties with more than 25 per cent women MPs. (The commission went further in terms of the Amerindians and recommended the creation of as many as eight seats to be held only by them. Their unique place in Canadian history, the fact that they were denied the vote until 1960, and because they are scattered and cannot pool their votes to elect their own representatives, underlay the commission's recommendations.[76])

In terms of courts, it might be thought that I am unconcerned about problems with access, given my plea for a reduced scope for their powers. After all, if the public interest groups who complain about lack of access are one of the primary elements responsible for pushing the courts to extend the boundaries, at least in terms of traditional notions of the business of courts, is not reducing — or in any event not encouraging — the groups' participation by invigorating the established costs rules a part of the solution? The same question could be put for other devices designed to broaden participation like standing, class actions, and intervention.[77]

Paradoxically, minimizing participation by erecting barriers through costs and these other devices would only make litigation more powerful. How? As we saw in Chapter Three, the traditional structure of litigation was designed to reflect liberal values of individualism, autonomy, and the limited state. The way litigation proceeded had a substantial effect in terms of the outcome of litigation and how legal rules were shaped: the form of litigation reflected the substance of the law. Insisting on that model would not stop judicial overreaching, but it would certainly buttress the depiction of the Charter, and indeed the whole enterprise of litigation, as centred upon this essential but limited range of values. Such a depiction would inevitably seep into our politics as the right and the good, as the depiction of constitutional arrangement.

In contrast, a model that at least tolerates a wider range of interests and even encourages them through a more accommodating costs regime[78] puts before the courts a range of interests and ideologies much more like the complexities that face legislatures and their agents as they make decisions. While such a range of interests will be no guarantee of judicial deference, it will be much more difficult for courts to convince themselves and the public that their decision making is and ought to be fundamentally different than the complexities that face politicians and their agents.[79]

Running through this entire discussion are questions of the role of lawyers as advocates, judges, policy-makers, and legislators and their ability to shape the relative influence of the rights and participatory models. Any discussion of that role inevitably turns to law schools and their devotion to a curriculum centred upon courts (particularly appellate courts) as the source of law. The established curriculum of law schools was dominated by an occupation with appellate court judgements in the construction and impact of the law taught as a body of neutral precepts set apart from larger political ideas or social influences. Much of that impulse remains today, though there is no doubt there has been some important evolution in at least some parts of the curriculum.

Yet much of the content and atmosphere of law schools still convey the message that what counts in the law is what courts do, with legislatures and administrative agencies as adjuncts that need the watchful eye of judges to ensure they do not stray too far from curial pronouncements about the good. Further, there are many ways that such an attitude is conveyed outside the formal curriculum itself. Virtually all law schools require first-year students to participate in a simulation exercise to convey a sense of what lawyering is actually like: they argue a case in an appeal court. (Indeed the largest hall in a law faculty is usually referred to as the 'moot court'.) The many other skills used by lawyers — negotiation, mediation, policy formulation, lobbying, advocating in settings other than courts where a different range of arguments and discourse might be employed — are treated as non-existent or, in any event, not within the special province of the law and lawyers. Students with the highest grades are encouraged to cap their law school careers by serving a clerkship with an appellate court, and the most prestigious positions are with the Supreme Court. The mere mention of a similar internship with a legislator (Cabinet member) or an administrative agency would be greeted with derision or 'no such position available'.

Small wonder that the view of democratic processes as the main source of social and political policy with law its reflection has a hard time with lawyers. This may have always been true. It is now overwhelmingly so with arguments and debates about the Charter flooding law faculties. If these institutions will not work to change so they become centres that honour the law of other democratic institutions as they do the law of the courts, they must be seen as one of the prime forces taking us away from any prospect for the participatory model so that Glendon's evocative description of America becomes ours: 'Court majorities with an expansive view of the judicial role, and their academic admirers propelled each other, like railway men on a handcar, along the line that led to the land of rights.'[80]

CONCLUSION:
WE OF THE 'PRAGMATIC AND EMPIRICAL'?

It will be recalled that in Chapter Two's discussion of the impact of litigation, there was a section discussing the role of ideology regarding such issues. In concluding that part, I looked to an article by Peter Russell in which he talked about how our political inheritance mostly came not from John Locke but from Edmund Burke. The article was written in 1975 and, in retrospect, seems even more accurate in describing ourselves then and highlighting the distance we have travelled since:

> [The approach] which is truest to our experience and most in keeping with our capabilities is that of Edmund Burke, not John Locke. Canadians — neither their judges, nor their politicians — are creatures of the Enlightenment. Their forte is not abstract, rationalist philosophising. The American Republic may be built on self-evident principles and universal rights, but Canadian political and legal thought is far more pragmatic and empirical.[81]

'Pragmatic and empirical' seems descriptive of how we have constructed our social and political life until the last years. Now very different forces are at work. The language of the courts and of rights courses through our national life and it is a discourse and a habit of mind that is far removed from the pragmatics of incremental change effected by consensus, negotiation, and settlement. Not so long ago John Kenneth Galbraith answered the question about what distinguished Canada on the world stage by singling out our politics and public administration: '[T]he greatest Canadian achievement has been in the conduct and purposes of government.'[82] That such an assertion would now be greeted with derision and anguish shows what these recent years have brought. Probably most of us would still shrink from Henry Adams's characterization of politics as 'the systematic organization of hatreds'[83] even while contemplating the accuracy of such a depiction for many scenes we are witnessing.

Of course there were many flaws to what we had before whether in terms of human rights, regional alienation, the divide between the English and the French, among others. Yet others saw us forging a truly enviable record in dealing with issues of central importance for citizens in their daily lives. As mentioned at the beginning of Chapter One, the UN Development Program recently gave Canada highest rankings for three consecutive years in a study of the best places to live. In these rankings there were criticisms of Canada having one of the widest gaps between the rich and poor for developed nations, a high incidence of drug crimes, and a high degree of sexual discrimination in our political system. Nevertheless, an official connected with the study underscored our formidable achievement because 'with the resources that Canada possesses it has managed to produce a human development which is much higher than its rank in terms of income should give it'.[84]

But such improvement through the political process is now out of fashion or perhaps it is more accurate to say that it is assumed that such attainments are the foundation on which the edifice of rights will rise. But that, of course, is the question. Will the Charter and its trail of litigation in other areas of the law take us to new successes in fashioning the common good? Or are we headed to a sort of atomistic consciousness and behaviour: each of us in some splendid isolation matched by official indifference abounding?

'We are in the rapids and must go on.'

— D'Arcy McGee in 1865, during the Confederation debates.[85]

NOTES

[1]V. Havel, 'Paradise Lost' (1992) *The New York Review of Books*, 9 April 1992, 6, 7.

[2]'Havel to head Czech Republic', *The Windsor Star*, 27 January 1993, A9.

[3]As, for example, V. Havel, *Summer Meditations* (New York: Knopf, 1992). Translated by P. Wilson. See the review of this book: G. Kennan, 'Keeping the Faith', *The New York Review of Books*, 24 September 1992, 3.

[4]V. Havel, 'The Post-Communist Nightmare', *The New York Review of Books*, 27 May 1993, 8.

[5]V. Havel, *supra*, note 1 at 6.

[6] J. Simpson, 'Who Would Be an Elected Politician in This Corrosive, Mean-Spirited Age?' *The Globe and Mail*, 28 October 1992, A26.

[7] Ibid.

[8] C. Taylor, 'Alternative Futures — Legitimacy, Identity, and Alienation in Late Twentieth Century Canada' in A. Cairns and C. Williams, *Constitutionalism, Citizenship, and Society in Canada* (Toronto: University of Toronto Press, 1986): 183, 211. See also C. Taylor, 'Can Canada Survive the Charter?' (1992) 30 *Alberta Law Review*, 427; C. Taylor, *Reconciling the Solitudes — Essays on Canadian Federalism and Nationalism* (Montreal-Kingston: McGill-Queen's University Press, 1993).

[9] Ibid., Taylor, 'Alternative Futures', 211.

[10] J. Handler, *Social Movements and the Legal System: A Theory of Law Reform and Social Change* (New York: Academic Press, 1978): 233.

[11] M.A. Glendon, 'A Beau Mentir Qui Vient De Loin: The 1988 Canadian Abortion Decision in Comparative Perspective' (1989) 83 *North Western University Law Review*, 569, 588.

[12] G. Rosenberg, *The Hollow Hope — Can Courts Bring About Social Change?* (Chicago: University of Chicago Press, 1991): 338.

[13] Ibid., 343

[14] C. Sunstein, 'How Independent Is the Court?' *The New York Review of Books*, 22 October 1992, 47.

[15] See Chapter Five.

[16] See Chapter Four.

[17] Ibid.

[18] J.A.G. Griffith, *The Politics of the Judiciary* (London: Fontana, 1981), discussed in Chapter Two.

[19] See Chapter Nine.

[20] See Chapter Five.

[21] See Chapter Seven.

[22] See Chapter Three.

[23] See Chapter Three.

[24] See Chapter Five.

[25] *The Queen* v. *Schachter* [1992] 2 *Supreme Court Reports*, 679.

[26] See Chapter Three.

[27] *Mossop and the Canadian Human Rights Commission* v. *Department of the Secretary of State* [1993] 1 *Supreme Court Reports*, 554.

[28] That is, as a matter of statutory interpretation, the Charter was not argued despite the fact that the Court explicitly invited the parties to do so.

[29] See Chapter Seven.

[30] See Chapter Nine.

[31] See Chapter Eight.

[32] See Chapter Four.

[33] See Chapter Nine.

[34] V. Havel, 'New Year's Day Address', Foreign Broadcasting Information Service, Eastern Europe, 90–001, 2 January 1990, 9–10, as quoted in M.A. Glendon,

Rights Talk — The Impoverishment of Political Discourse (New York: The Free Press, 1991): 183.

[35] See Chapter Four.

[36] See Chapter Six.

[37] See Chapter Five.

[38] See Chapter Three.

[39] See also Chapter Three for a discussion of how class actions have largely been ineffective in achieving progressive social reform while at the same time they can have a role in redressing mass harms.

[40] See Chapter Three.

[41] See Chapter Nine.

[42] See Chapter Eight.

[43] See Chapter Eight.

[44] Taylor, 'Can Canada Survive the Charter?' *supra*, note 8 at 446.

[45] For another attempt to grapple with this tension, particularly in comparision with American constitutional values, see J. Cameron, 'Cross Cultural Reflections: Teaching the Charter to Americans' (1990) 28 *Osgoode Hall Law Journal*, 613.

[46] K. Roach, 'Teaching Procedures: The Fiss/Weinrib Debate in Practice' (1991) 41 *University of Toronto Law Journal*, 247, 286 discussed in Chapter Seven.

[47] A phrase used by Barbara Frum to describe us before we became locked in the constitutional embrace: 'My view of Canada was that you shift it around and make it work. I liked the non-explicit adjustments we were making — but now we're into a cold, crass, explicit trading of advantages. We've lost that dance of adjustment.' See S. Godfrey, 'Frum on Frum', *The Globe and Mail*, 1 February 1992, C7.

[48] Taylor, 'Alternative Futures', *supra*, note 8 at 211.

[49] The test was articulated in *R. v. Oakes* [1986] 1 *Supreme Court Reports*, 103 (SCC). The Court stated that there were two basic criteria that governments had to meet before s. 1 can be successfully invoked. First, the objective of the assailed act had to 'relate to concerns which are pressing and substantial in a free and democratic society. . . .' Second, there had to be proportionality in the means chosen to respond to such concerns. Such proportionality was to be judged in three ways: the means had to be 'rationally connected to the objective'; such means had to impair individual rights as little as possible; there had to be a proportionality between the 'effects' of the means and the objective identified as of 'sufficient importance' (138–9). For more on this test and a criticism of it, see P. Monahan, *Politics and the Constitution — The Charter, Federalism and the Supreme Court of Canada* (Toronto: Carswell, 1987), 115.

[50] See, for example, *Rocket v. Royal College of Dental Surgeons of Ontario* [1990] 2 *Supreme Court Reports*, 232, 246, where the Court did not refer to the need for 'pressing and substantial' reasons for governmental action stating instead the less exacting formulation that the legislative objective 'must be of sufficient importance to warrant overriding a constitutionally protected right'. Similarly, courts have begun to ask whether an infringed right lies at the 'core' of a protected value or at the periphery with those towards the limit easier to override by invoking s. 1: see, for example, *United States v. Cotroni* [1989] 1 *Supreme Court Reports*, 1469 1481, 1492, where the Court held that although extradition violated the Charter's

s. 6 mobility rights, it 'lies at the outer edges of the core values sought to be protected by that provision' and, as such, could be justified under s. 1. For a discussion of the courts' willingness to alter their view of s. 1 in favour of deference to governments, see R. Knopff and F.L. Morton, *Charter Politics* (Toronto: Nelson Canada, 1992): 47–50.

[51]P. Hogg, *Canadian Constitutional Law* (3d ed.) (Toronto: Carswell,1992): 882.

[52]For example, Justice McLachlin, 'The Charter: A New Role for the Judiciary?' (1991) 29 *Alberta Law Review*, 540; Justice Iacobucci, 'The Evolution of Constitutional Rights and Corresponding Duties' (1992) 26 *University of British Columbia Law Review*, 1.

[53]*Supra*, note 51 at 875.

[54]See also A. Lokan, 'The Rise and Fall of Doctrine under Section 1 of the Charter' (1992) 24 *Ottawa Law Review*, 163.

[55]P. Russell, 'Canadian Constraints on Judicialization from Without', presented at the Interim Meeting of the International Political Science Association Research Committee on Comparative Judicial Studies, Forli, Italy, June 1992, 3.

[56]Quoted in R. Knopff and F.L. Morton, *Charter Politics* (Toronto: Nelson Canada, 1992): 231, in the context of an excellent discussion of s. 33.

[57]Here I am returning to Taylor's words, 'Alternative Futures', *supra*, note 8 at 211.

[58]*Supra*, note 56 at 229.

[59]See, in particular, Rosenberg, *supra*, note 12 and the discussion of his work in Chapter Two of this book.

[60]*Supra*, note 45 at 636–40.

[61]For a spirited defence of s. 33 along with further recommendations about how it ought to be legitimately invoked, see C. Manfredi, *Judicial Power and the Charter* (Toronto: McClelland & Stewart, 1993): Chapter 7.

[62]See, for example, Ontario Law Reform Commission, *Appointing Judges: Philosophy, Politics and Practice* (Toronto: Ministry of the Attorney-General, 1991).

[63]P. Russell and J. Ziegel, 'Federal Judicial Appointments: An Appraisal of the First Mulroney Government's Appointments and the New Judicial Advisory Committees' (1991) 41 *University of Toronto Law Journal*, 1, 19. See also R. Martin, 'Ideology and Judging in the Supreme Court of Canada' (1988) 26 *Osgoode Hall Law Journal*, 797.

[64]B. Wilson, 'Will Women Judges Really Make a Difference?' (1990) 28 *Osgoode Hall Law Journal*, 507.

[65]For example see the collection of papers in Ontario Law Reform Commission, *supra*, note 62, and D. Beatty, *Talking Heads and the Supremes — The Canadian Production of Constitutional Review* (Toronto: Carswell, 1990): Chapter 10, 'The Democratic Integrity of the Court'.

[66]For example, Minister of Justice and Attorney General of Canada, *Justice Information* (n.d.).

[67]Beatty, *supra*, note 65 at 271 *et seq*.

[68]Ibid., 271.

[69]S. Burt, 'The Changing Patterns of Public Policy' in S. Burt et al., *Changing*

Patterns — Women in Canada (2d ed.) (Toronto: McClelland & Stewart, 1993): 212.

[70] G. Fraser, 'Why So Few Women Run For Office', *The Globe and Mail*, 26 January 1993, A13.

[71] The statement in the text could be said to be a crude summary of post-modernism: its contribution is that we should never again make easy assertions about the common good; its danger is to make commonality itself ever suspect, perhaps particularly among progressives: see J. Handler's presidential address to the Law and Society Association and the response of his critics — 'Postmodernism, Protest, and the New Social Movements' (1992) 26 *Law and Society Review*, 697.

[72] S. Bashevkin, *Toeing the Lines — Women and Party Politics in English Canada* (Toronto: University of Toronto Press, 1985).

[73] Such problems are obviously not unique to Canadian women: W. Kaminer, 'Crashing the Locker Room', *The Atlantic*, vol. 270, July 1992, 59.

[74] B. Aarensteinsen, 'Rising to the Challenge', *The Toronto Star*, 14 March 1993, B1.

[75] *Royal Commission on Electoral Reform and Party Financing*, (Ottawa: Canada Communications Group, 1992). See also G. York and R. Howard, 'Royal Inquiry Urges Reforms for Elections', *The Globe and Mail*, 14 February 1992, A1.

[76] Ibid., Royal Commission.

[77] See Chapter Three.

[78] See Chapter Three.

[79] I am not suggesting that the specifics of opening up litigation to a broad range of interests would be easy. I am saying that such accommodation should be seen as both a legitimate and necessary subject for debate and realization. In this regard, see S. Fairley, 'Private Law Remedial Principles and the Charter: Can the Old Dog Wag His Tail?' in J. Berryman (ed.), *Remedies, Issues and Perspectives* (Toronto: Carswell, 1991): 313.

[80] Glendon, *supra*, note 34 at 9.

[81] P. Russell, 'The Political Role of the Supreme Court of Canada in Its First Century' (1975) 53 *Canadian Bar Review*, 576, 593.

[82] J.K. Galbraith, 'Canada Customs' (January 1987) *Saturday Night*, 113.

[83] As quoted in M. Lind, 'Buchanan, Conservatism's Ugly Face', *The New York Times*, 19 August 1992, A21.

[84] L. Schlein, 'Canada Second Only to Japan in Survey of Best Places to Live', *The Globe and Mail*, 23 May 1991, A1. See 'First Column', *The Globe and Mail*, 17 May 1993, A1; P. Lewis, 'New UN Index Measures Wealth as Quality of Life', *The New York Times*, 23 May 1993, A6.

[85] Quoted in D. Olive, 'An Honours List for Canada, on the Eve of Its 125th', *The Globe and Mail*, 27 June 1992, D4.

Index

Aboriginal people, xi, 4, 15; and Charlottetown Accord, 20, 275, 276, 306; and Charter of Rights, 271–7; and courts, xv, 21, 193, 274–5, 305; land claims, 20; and legislative authority, 273; and Quebec, 20; parliamentary representation, 316; and 'rights discourse', 275; self-government, 17, 20–1, 274, 275–6, 306; social conditions, 271–2; and Supreme Court, 274–5; title, 273; treaty rights, 273; women, 141–2
Abortion, ix, 135, 144, 146–54, 282, 305; absence of law, 149, 152; access to, xiii, 135, 150–1, 152–3; antiabortion movement, 147, 151, 153; see also 'Victory, paradox of'
Accused, rights of, xiii, 200–2, 204–5, 206, 207, 210; Canada–US comparison, 201–2; see also Due process model; Rights, legal
Action, affirmative, 114
Adams, G., 121–2
Adams, Henry, 319
Aid, legal, 92–3
Alberta, 16, 223; abortion, 152; Human Rights Commission, 89
Andrews v. *Law Society of BC*, 280
Anti-Americanism, 8
Arbitration, 93
Aristotle, 171
Arthurs, H.W., 269
Assembly of First Nations, 20
Atiyah, P.S., 166, 173, 185
Atlantic Canada, 145
Attorney-General, 78–9
Attorney-General of Canada v. *Lavell*, 142, 144
Attorney-General of Quebec v. *Attorney-General of Canada* (*Quebec Veto* case), 243, 246–7
Atwood, Margaret, 9, 192

Backhouse, C., 135
Baines, Beverley, 135–6, 141
Baker v. *Carr*, 48
Bankruptcy/receivership cases, 84
Bargaining, collective, 113–14, 125
Beatty, D., 126, 268–9, 314
Beetz, Justice, 123
Bell v. *Ontario Human Rights Commission*, 120, 125
Bill C–43, 151–2, 154
Bill C–55, 260
Bill of Rights, ix, 62, 141, 142, 147, 201, 263
Birth control, 146
Black, Conrad, 23
Bliss v. *Attorney-General of Canada*, 143, 144, 145
Bork, Robert, 288
Borovoy, Alan, 267, 269
British Columbia, 15, 152, 261
British North America (Constitution) Act (1867), 17, 225, 229–30, 245
Brodsky, G., and S. Day, 280, 285
Brooks v. *Canada Safeway*, 144–5
Brown, George, 18
Brown v. *Board of Education*, 43, 48, 50, 56–7, 58
Bureaucracy, 108, 109, 111
Burke, Edmund, 63, 194, 195, 318
Burns, Peter, 154–5
Burt, Sandra, 156
Bush, George, 7

Callbeck, Catherine, 152
Campbell, Kim, 89, 152, 210, 285–6
Canada: attitudes to law, 192–4; central, 13–14; cleavages (regional, French-English), 13–21, 22–3, 223, 228, 247; comparisons with US, 6, 22, 119, 149, 191; and competition, 11, 117; convergence with US, xi, xiv; deference to authority, 11–13;

economy, 10–11; 'English' Canada, 18; geography, 13; heartland/hinterland split, 13, 16; ideological diversity, x–xi, xv, 172 (*see also* Ideology, variegated); integration with US, 22, 23; literature, 9; national identity, x, 4–5, 6, 8–10; 'pragmatic and empirical', 57, 63, 110, 318; relations with US, xiv; as 'socialist monarchy', 7–8 (*see also* Socialism; Toryism); 'two nations' concept, 246; UN ranking, 3, 319

Canada Elections Act, 260

Canada Gazette, 40

Canadian Council on Social Development, 93

Canadian Human Rights Act, 143; Code, 88, 89; Commission, 90

Canadian Industrial Gas and Oil Ltd (CIGOl) v. *Government of Saskatchewan*, 242, 243

Canadian Panel on Violence, 153

Canadian Radio-television and Telecommunications Commission (CRTC), ix, 108

Capital punishment, 195

Causality (judicial/extrajudicial paths), 49–50

Central Canada Potash Co. Ltd v. *Government of Saskatchewan*, 243

Centralization, 5, 12, 233; and Charter, 266, 278; and regionalism, 13

Certification, motion for, 73

Charlottetown Accord, x, xiv, 4, 17, 20–1, 225, 238, 249; and Aboriginal people, 275, 276, 306; reasons for failure, 21

Charter of Rights and Freedoms: and Aboriginal people, 271–7; arguments against, 266–71; arguments for, 262–6; and Canada–US convergence, xiv, 191; and Canadian unity, 263; and centralization, 266, 278; challenges to legislation, ix–x, xiii, xiv–xv, 257, 259–61, 278, 282, 309; comparative effects on federal and provincial legislation, 278–9; and criminal justice, 200–11, 279–80, 282; decided cases, 258–61; and democracy, 285–6, 288; distinguished from judges' decisions, 258; and due process model, xiv, 13, 202, 282, 284; and education, 284; equality provisions, 87, 146, 147, 202, 281–2, 284–5; as experiment, 287–8; and FTA, 260–1; funding for challenges, 93; and gay/lesbian rights, 89; impact, 258, 277–80, 281–2; and judicial legitimacy, 261–2; and judicial power, 256–8; and judicial review, 264–5, 288; and judicial role, ix–x, 235, 277; and 'judicialization' of politics, xv, 262, 280–6; and 'judicialization' of rights, 4, 310–11; and labour relations, 122, 281, 284; left criticism, 61–2; and legal rights, 199–202, 203–4, 208–11, 278, 279–80; and liberal ideology, 259, 265, 266; minority access, 262–3; and 'moral issues', 282; not subject to legislative repeal, 256; origins, 266; and 'other' identities, 263; and property rights, 281, 284; public attitudes, 207, 277–8; 'reasonable time' provision, 208–9; restrictions on impact, 281–2; rights, 159, 265–6; s. 33 (override, 'notwithstanding' clause), xiv, xvi, 43, 144, 257, 264–5, 266, 283, 311–12; and sexual orientation, 90; and social welfare, 284; and Supreme Court, 279, 281–2; unequal access, 203; and victims of crime, 203; and women's issues, xii–xiii, 134–5, 144, 154, 176, 304; and workers' rights, 126

Cheffins, B., 118

Child care, xiii, 88, 148, 152, 153

Child support, 140

Choper, Jesse, 46–9, 59

Cité Libre, 245

Citizens' Forum on Canada's Future, 282

Citizens' Insurance Co. of Canada v. *Parsons*, 232

Clark, Joe, 20

Class actions, 91, 173; as 'burdensome', 76; deterrence function, 73; history,

73–5; legislation (Quebec), 308; for mass torts, 77; objectives, 73; procedural aspects, 73; and social progress, 77
Coase, R., 239
Collectivism, 7, 12, 80, 109
Compensation, 174, 177–8; fault system, 112, 170–1; health care, 181–3; no-fault, 113, 174, 175, 178, 179–81, 182, 183; three-level system, 168; workers', xii, 304
Competition: law, 11, 109, 117–19, 126, 242; Tribunal, 119
Compromise, xv, 90–1, 149, 156
Confession, involuntary, 198
Consent, informed, 44, 47
Constitution: and Aboriginal people, 273; federal amendment power, 246–7; and federal-provincial division of powers, 227, 228; reform (1982), 16–17; *see also* Charlottetown, Meech Lake Accord
Constitution Act: (1982), 17; *see also* British North America Act
Contract: breach of, 190; freedom of, 115, 118
Corporations, 77, 78, 83, 166, 175; Crown, 11
Cory, Justice, 209
Cotterrell, Roger, 40–1, 61
Court Challenges Program, 93, 271, 308
Courts: and Aboriginal people, xv, 21, 193, 274–5, 305; access/costs, xvi, 51, 82, 93, 95, 267, 268, 270–1, 305, 316–17; accountability, 4, 302; administration, 209; alternatives to, 112–19; arrogance, 122; and Bill of Rights, 141; budgeting, 209; and civil liberties, 13; and collective bargaining, 113–14; and collective values, 80; conditions for change, 51; and competition law/policy, 117–19; constrained/dynamic models, 50–1; deference to legislatures, tribunals, xvi, 122, 123, 124 , 141; and democracy, xvii, 54–6, 156, 256, 267, 268, 301–3 ; 'dialogue' with legislature, 265; and discrimination, 114–16; as federal-provincial referee, 225–9, 234, 249 (*see also* Litigation, federalism); focus on property rights, 125; formalism, 74, 75, 76; and group (nontraditional) claims, 79; and human rights cases, 117, 120–1; legislative override of, 259, 307; and legislative policy, 118, 120; legitimacy, 42; and liberal individualism, 8, 11, 268; and market principles, 111; 'one-time' disposition, 113; open to public scrutiny, 96; passivity, 113; philosophical foundations, 74; and policy-making, 144; and political/ economic leverage, 51; and public opinion, 200, 205–7; and regionalism, 17; resistance to state intervention, 111, 113, 114, 117; and social progress, 124–5, 256, 268–9, 303–5; as substitute for/brake on political/ legislative action, 5, 97, 125, 156, 212–13, 239, 262, 276, 282–3; and women (pre Charter), 134–8; *see also* Charter; Decisions, court; Judiciary; Review, judicial; Supreme Court
Criminal justice system, xiii, xiv, 13, 279–80; crime control model, ix, 13, 191–2, 194–5, 196–8, 203 (*see also* Due process model); and morality, 190–1; public nature, 190; and racism, 192
Cyr, Lizzie, 136

Damage awards, 85
Davies, Robertson, 7–8
Decentralization, 5, 13, 224, 232–3, 309
Decisions, court: as brake on political action, 150; compliance with, 47–8; enforcement of, 50; and legislative change, 176; legislative reactions to, 125–6, 139, 149, 155, 210–11; long-term impact, 55; and mobilization of opposition, 55–6; public awareness of, 44–5; real benefits, 48; regressive, 268; on federal-provincial powers, 230–1, 232–5, 239–41,

242–3, 244; symbolic impact, 50
Decrees, 83, 85, 86–7
Default judgements, 77, 84
Democracy, 269–70; and Charter, 285–6, 288; and courts, xvii, 156, 267, 268, 269–70, 301–3, 307; and regionalism, 224; social, 64, 80, 179, 264; two models, xiv, 256
Deterrence, 174, 178, 180, 182
Dickson, Chief Justice, 84, 122, 124, 145, 267, 269, 281
Diefenbaker, John G., 15
Disabled people, xi, 4, 57, 116
Discrimination, 114–16, 120–1, 123, 192–5; and Aboriginal women, 142; and Weinrib model, 174–5
Dispute resolution, 73, 77, 78; alternative (ADR), 73, 93–6
Divorce Act, 95, 139–40
Dominion Law Reports, 40
Dred Scott case, 59
Due process model, xiv, 13, 45, 191, 196, 200–7, 280, 305; Canada/US comparison, 213; and Charter, 284; drawbacks, 191–2; and liberal ideology, 194
Duplessis, Maurice, 245
Duress, defence of, 197

Eberts, Mary, 154
Economic Council of Canada, 107
Economy, x; government presence in, 10–11
Education, ix, 284
Electoral boundaries, 261
Electoral system, 260
Elitism, 11–12
England, 60–1, 166
Environment, 11, 57, 116
Equality, *see* Charter, equality provisions
Equity: horizontal, 178, 180; pay, 116, 154
Estey, Justice, 75, 279
Evidence, rules of, xiii, 197–200, 201, 206–7, 212 (*see also* Rape-shield law); Federal-Provincial Task Force on the Rules of Evidence, 199

Fairness doctrine, 85
Family: assets, 138–9; 'values', 149
Federalism, xiv, 263–4; cooperative, 224, 227, 233, 242; executive, 233, 263; and heartland/hinterland split, 223; nature of, 233; purposes, 225; review, 126 (*see also* Litigation, federalism)
Feeley, Malcolm, 46
Fees, contingency, 92
'Fellow servant' rule, 112
Felony murder rule, 197
Feminism, 135; *see also* Women
Fiss, Owen, 43, 44, 173–4
Ford v. *Quebec* (*Signs* case), 247, 278
Frankfurter, Justice, 58–9
'Free rider' problem, 91–2
Frum, Barbara, x
Frye, Northrop, 9, 23
Fuller, L., 86

Galanter, Marc, 40
Galbraith, John Kenneth, 318–19
Gays/lesbians, xi, 4, 123; protection for, 88–90, 115; rights, 259, 305
Ginsberg v. *New York*, 49
Ginsberg, Ruth Bader, 151
Glendon, Mary Ann, 148–9, 155–6, 303, 318
Glenn, P., 76–7, 173
Government: as 'aggregate of power', 77, 78, 83; growth of, 107–9; and nation building, 110, 111; presence in economy, 10–11, 107–8, 110–11, 117; regulatory activity, 108–9, 110–11; restraint of, xi; two views of, 107–8, 109, 125
Government, federal: conditional grants, 238–9, 248; declaratory power, 229; disallowance power, 224, 226, 229, 237, 248; reservation power, 237; spending power, 238–9, 248; taxing power, 237–8; *see also* Powers, federal-provincial division of
Grant, George, 23
Griffith, J.A.G., 60–1, 304

Hagan, J., 194, 195, 196
Hamilton, Alexander, 50, 58, 59
Handler, J., 52–3, 55
Harassment, sexual, 145
Harlan, Justice, 58
Havel, Vaclav, 301, 306
Health care, 181–3, 261
Highway, Tomson, 271
Hodge v. *The Queen*, 232
Hodgetts, J.E., 109
Hogg, P.W., 225–6
Holmes, O., 168
Horn, Kahn-Tineta, 142
Horowitz, G., 6, 270
Hutchinson, A., 175
'Hyperlexis', 93

Ideology, x–xi; litigation and, 57–63, 198–9, 318; 'new right', 15; variegated, x–xi, 6–8, 22, 72, 80, 110, 262, 270; *see also* Democracy, social; Individualism; Liberalism; Socialism; Toryism
Immigration Appeal Board, 108
Imprisonment, 206
Income Tax Act, 153
Indian Act, 4, 20, 141–2
Individualism, xi, 5, 6, 7, 8, 42, 61, 62–3, 80, 170–1; and abortion, 149; and class actions, 74; economic, 116; and torts, 78–9
Injunctions, structural, 83–7
Injury, personal, 177–8
Instrumentalism, 39
Insurance: automobile, 180; malpractice, 181; social, 182; unemployment, 142–3
Interest, legal, 79–80
Interest groups, public, 47, 52–6
Interests, competing, 48
International Covenant on Civil and Political Rights, 142
International Covenant on Economic, Social and Cultural Rights, 266
Intervention, third-party, 81–2
Intoxication defence, 196–7
Isaac v. *Bedard*, 142

Janzen v. *Platy Enterprises*, 145
'Judicialization', 126: of abortion, 148, 149; of politics, xv, 262, 280–6; of rights, 4, 276, 310–11
Judicial process: left criticisms, 61
Judiciary, 258, 259–61; accountability, 313–14; activism, 259; appointment process, xvi, 288, 313, 314–15; caution, 50; and class actions, 74, 75, 76; conservatism, 176; and democracy, 307; and governance, 255–6; impartiality, 60; independence, 86, 176, 314; and labour, 268–9; legitimacy, 261–2; liberalism, 8, 268; and public/expanded model of litigation, 97; and public interest, 61; subjectivity, 121–2, 206; term limitation, 314; unrepresentative nature, 4, 312–13, 314–15
Justice: and courts/legislatures, 267–8; corrective, 170–5; criminal, xiii, xiv, xv, 13, 279–80 (*see also* Criminal justice system); social, 172, 184

Kant, Immanuel, 171, 175
Keirans, Tom, 11
King, Mackenzie, 13
King, Martin Luther, 56
Knopff, R., and F.L. Morton, 259, 260–1, 283

Labatt Breweries of Canada v. *Attorney-General of Canada*, 240
Labour relations, 112–17, 122, 125, 268–9, 304; boards, 108–9; and Charter, 281, 284
Lajoie, A., et al., 244, 246, 247
Lamer, Chief Justice, 257, 279, 286
Laskin, Chief Justice, 137, 267
Lasser, William, 59
Law: attitudes towards, 192–4; common, 62, 71–2, 111, 112, 120, 268, 307; competition, xii, 11, 109, 117–18; constitutional, 42–3; criminal, ix, 178, 246, 247 (*see also* Criminal justice system); effects/impact, 40–2, 45–51; extension of legal activity, 40; journals, 40;

'private', 165–7; remedial, 58; schools, 317–18; and social change, 41; as state instrument, 190; substantive, 58
Law Reform Commission, 199
Lawyers, 39–40, 50, 52, 53, 314–15, 317–18
Leatherdale v. *Leatherdale*, 138–9
Legal Education and Action Fund (LEAF), 154
Legislatures: and collective interests, 62; 'communitarian perspective', 116; 'dialogue' with courts, 265; and justice, 267; override of courts, 259, 307; reactions to court decisions, 11, 125–6, 136, 139, 149, 155, 210–11; and social progress, 268–9; and women's issues, 135, 136
Lesage, Jean, 233
Lévesque, René, 243
L'Heureux-Dubé, Justice Claire, 279
Liberalism, xi–xiii, xvi, 6, 7, 58, 117–18, 178–9, 304; and abortion, 148–9; and Charter, 259, 265, 266; and courts, 8, 111, 268; and 'private' interests, 166; in US, 60, 109, 110
Liberties, civil, xiv, 12, 62–3, 267, 269
Linden, A., 175–7, 184
Lipset, S.M., 10, 191, 279
Liquidator of the Maritime Bank of Canada v. *Receiver-General of New Brunswick*, 232
Litigation: access/costs, 38, 72, 73, 79, 91–3; and accountability, 38; and Canadian identity, 4; civil, 71–2; and compromise, 90–1; constitutional/federalism, ix (*see also* Litigation, federalism, below); functions, ix, 307; increase in, 42; and leverage, 53; ; and liberal ideology, xiii, 72; 'one-shot', 92; and political change/social progress, xi, xv, 38, 45, 50–7, 149–50, 155, 156, 211–13, 307–8; private, 96, 166; proposed limits, 307–10; public/expanded model, 71, 72, 81, 83, 97; and publicity, 176; and public relations, 53; and public values, 173–4; social effects, xi, xv, 37–8; and social policy, 88; structure of, xi–xii, xv, 71–97, 96, 173, 307–8; test case, 52; 'win-lose' structure, xv, 63, 113; *see also* Courts; Torts
Litigation, federalism, xiv, 17, 306, 308–9; arguments for and against, 235–7, 242; decisions as 'bargaining chips', xiv, 239–41, 242–3, 308; court's role, 224–9; decision patterns, 230–5; increase in, 234; and Quebec, 245–6; as substitute for negotiation/compromise, 225, 227–8, 244, 248–9
Lobbying, 53
Locke, John, 60, 63, 194, 195, 270, 318
Long-arm provisions, 77
Loss distribution, 168
Lovelace, Sandra, 142
Lysyk, K., 233, 234, 247

Macdonald, Sir John A., 10–11, 224
Macdonald Commission, 11, 62, 199, 244, 247
MacKinnon, Catherine, 155
Macklem, Patrick, 273–4
McDonald, Lynn, 143–4
McDonald Commission, 199
McDougall, Barbara, 154
McGee, D'Arcy, 319
McIntyre, Justice, 279
McRoberts, Kenneth, 179
Malpractice, medical, 44, 45, 181; litigation, 182
Manitoba, 138; French minority, 18, 84; and Meech Lake, 17, 20
Market, free, xi, 113, 114–15
Marketing boards, 108
Marriage, 137
Martin, Clara Brett, 136
Mediation, 93, 94–6
Meech Lake Accord, xiv, xvi, 4, 16–17, 19–20, 225, 238, 249, 263, 283
Mercantilism, 16
Mill, J.S., 149
Minorities, ix, xi, 4, 57, 61–2, 269; and Charter, 203; political underrepresentation, 315–16
Miranda doctrine, 48, 203

Mirosh, Dianne, 89
Moge v. *Moge*, 140–1
Monahan, P., 231, 234, 239–40, 248
Monture, Patricia, 273
Morton, F.L., 278
Moss, J., 9
Mulroney, Brian, 7, 311, 312
Multiculturalism, 18, 309
Munro, Alice, 156
Murdoch v. *Murdoch*, 137–8, 256

Nader, Ralph, 52
Naken v. *General Motors of Canada*, 74–5
Nation building, 223, 224
National Abortion Rights Action League (NARAL), 151
National Action Committee on the Status of Women (NAC), 143, 147, 153
National Citizens' Coalition Inc. and Brown v. *Canada (Attorney-General)*, 260
National Energy Board, 108
National Energy Program (NEP), 16
Nationalism, 8–10
New Brunswick, 14, 18
New Democratic Party, 7
Newfoundland, 14, 20, 152
Northwest Territories, 14–15, 152
Nova Scotia, 14

October crisis (1970), 193
Oka crisis (1990), 20
Ontario, 260; abortion, 152–3; class actions, 308; Family Law Act, 95; Family Law Reform Act (1978), 138, 139; Human Rights Code, 89, 120, 121, 143; Law Reform Commission, 75–6, 82, 93; Municipal Board, ix; and Quebec, 13, 14; Workers' Compensation Board, 108
Ownership, foreign, 11

Packer, H., 194
Parliament: declining power, 107; regulatory activity, 107; *see also* Legislatures
Parti Québécois, 179, 247

'Persons' case, 115, 137
Political process, xvi–xvii, 38
Politicians, 282
Politics (Canadian): 'Americanization' of, 279; 'judicialization' of, xv, 262, 280–6; popular, xvi
Polycentrism, 86
Populism, 12
Pornography, 155
Poverty, 140
Powell, Justice, 58
Power, 'aggregates of', 77, 78, 91
Powers, federal-provincial, division of, 18–19, 224; in Constitution Act, 229–30; need for negotiation/compromise, 225, 227–8, 235; non-judicial shifts in, 237–9; paramountcy challenges, 235, 236; *see also* Litigation, federalism
Precedent, 176, 203–4, 205, 231
Prichard, R., 182–3, 184
Prince Edward Island, 14, 152
Privative clauses, 120, 125
Privy Council, Judicial Committee of, 115, 137, 224, 232–3
Probate cases, 77
Progressive Conservative party: Family Caucus, 149
Property: family, 137–8; rights, 281, 284
Protectionism, 118
Proulx, Justice, 155
Public utility boards, 108

Quebec, 12–13, 20, 223, 244, 287, 309; and abortion, 20; attitudes to crime, 194; Bill 101, 279, 283; and Charter, 266; civil law, 18, 307; and class actions, 75, 76, 308; as distinct society, 17, 20, 21; and federalism litigation, 244–8; legislation (1945–60), 245–6; nationalism, 228; no-fault compensation, 179, 180; and Ontario, 13, 14; political thought, 244–8; *Signs* case, *see Ford* v. *Quebec*; sovereignty movement, 3, 14; success in Supreme Court (1960–78), 246–7
Quebec Veto case, 243, 246–7

R. v. *Askov*, 208–9, 284
R. v. *Beaver*, 196
R. v. *Big M Drug Mart*, 260
R. v. *Butler*, 155
R. v. *Dominion Stores Ltd*, 240
R. v. *Dyment*, 104, 205
R. v. *Edwards Books and Art*, 260
R. v. *Hogan*, 199
R. v. *Lavallee*, 145, 146, 155
R. v. *Morgentaler*, 147, 149, 151, 278
R. v. *Mossop*, 89–90, 123, 305
R. v. *Schacter*, 87–9, 153, 259, 284, 305
R. v. *Seaboyer*, 209–10
R. v. *Wray*, 198, 199
Race, 114–15, 192
Rand, Justice, 267
Rape-shield law, xiv, 145, 209–11, 259, 282
'Reading-in', 87–91, 305
Reagan, Ronald, 7
REAL Women, 147
Reference re Amendment of the Constitution of Canada (Patriation Reference), 234, 242–3
Reference re Anti-Inflation Act, 233, 243, 246
Reference re Upper House, 234
Reform party, 16
Refugee status, 259–60
Regionalism, 4, 5, 13–17, 223–4, 228, 247; and decentralization, 13; and democracy, 224
Reibl v. *Hughes*, 44–5
Reimer, John, 89
Remedies, 83–91, 259
Responsibility, community, 178, 180
Review, judicial, 264–5, 288; of administrative decisions, xii, 112, 119–24; and federalism, 225–9, 237–49
Revolution, Industrial, 113
Rights, xv, 4, 53–4; and Charter, 259, 265–6; civil, 56; constitutional, 50; equality, 202, 280; gay/lesbian, 259, 305; group, 275; human, xii, 112–17, 120–1, 123, 304; individual, 165–6, 275; judicialization of, 4, 276, 310–11; judicially created, xi;

language, 84, 247, 278; legal, 200–2, 203–4; mobility, 278; 'private', 165–6; property, 281, 284; provincial, 18; resource, 11; 'rights discourse', 155–6, 213, 275, 306; victims', 208; workers', 126; *see also* Society, rights model of
Roach, K., 174, 203
Roberts, J., and A. Doob, 206
Robertson, G., 169
Rocher, Guy, 62, 194
Roe v. *Wade*, 50, 148, 149–50, 151
Rosenberg, Gerald, 49–50, 55–7, 86–7, 211–13, 303–4
Royal Commission on Aboriginal Peoples, 20
Royal Commission on Electoral Reform and Party Financing, 316
Royal Commission on the Economic Union and Development Prospects for Canada, *see* Macdonald Commission
Royal Commission on Reproductive Technology, 153
Royal Commission on the Status of Women, 142
Russell, Peter, 62–3, 195, 234–5, 242, 249, 277, 280–6, 318

Saskatchewan, 16, 152
Scheingold, S., 54
Schmerber v. *California*, 204–5
Scott, F.R., 224
Senate, 17, 152, 287–8
Sentencing, 206
Signs case, *see* Ford v. Quebec
Singh et al. v. *Minister of Employment and Immigration*, 259–60, 284
Smith, Goldwin, 23
Smiley, Donald, 228
Socialism, 6, 7, 110, 149; *see also* Democracy, social
Society: participatory model, 5, 302–3, 309, 312, 315; rights model, 5, 10, 302–3, 308, 312
Sopinka, Justice, 255, 288
Special Joint Committee on the Constitution, 143
Southam Newspapers, 270

liberalism, 60, 109, 110; litigation and social issues, 211–13; malpractice suits, 182; 'minimalism', 109, 110; 'no-cost' system, 92; policing, 195; political intolerance, 12; popular sovereignty, 58; prisons, 212; public awareness of court decisions, 44; public interest litigation, 303–4; regulatory activity, 111; reliance on courts, xi, 5; rights of accused, 201; and 'rights model', 5; structural injunctions, 85; Supreme Court, 47–50, 53, 58–60, 148, 203–5, 211, 279; term-limitation measures, 245; tort law, 166, 167, 172, 185; *see also* Due process model

'Victory, paradox of', xii–xiii, 135, 144, 149, 151, 305

War Measures Act, 12–13
Weiler, Paul, 230–1, 235–6
Weinrib, Ernest, 166, 171–5, 172, 184, 185
Welfare: social, 177, 284; welfare state, 9

Western provinces, 15–17; alienation, 16; and federalism, 223; as hinterland, 16
Whyte, John, 43
Wilson, Justice, 147, 148–9, 267, 279
Winnipeg General Strike, 192
Women, ix, xi, 4, 45, 57; Aboriginal, 141–2; in Canadian literature, 9; and Charlottetown Accord, 21; and Charter, xii–xiii, 144, 176, 203, 280, 304; competence, 136, 137; and courts (pre-Charter), 134–8, 154; judicial defeats, 145–6; legislative redress, 135, 136, 138; in marriage, 140; as persons, 136–7; political underrepresentation, xvi, 315, 316; pregnancy, 142–3, 144–5; property/support issues, 137–41; 'security of person' right, 147, 210; self-defence, 145, 146, 155; women's movement, 135
Workers: compensation, 112–17; right to organize, 113; *see also* Labour relations

Yukon, 14–15

Stanbury, W.T. 117
Stanfield, Robert, 8
Standing, 78–80
State, administrative, ix, 73, 96, 178; as alternative to tort litigation, 177; and compensation, 184–5; and courts, xii, 109 (*see also* Review, judicial; Government); and criminal justice, xiii
Sunstein, C., 56–7
Supreme Court, 20; and abortion, 135, 147–9, 152, 305; centralism, 245, 246–8; and child care, 153; and civil liberties, 62–3; and class actions, 75; and criminal justice, 192, 196–200, 201–2, 203, 205, 208–10; and discrimination, 114–15, 121; and federal-provincial division of powers, 224, 226, 228, 230–1, 233–5, 236, 237–8, 240, 241–3, 245–8; and gay/lesbian rights, 89–90; and human rights, 123; and intervention, 82; legislative reaction to, 121, 125; political role, 62–3; progressive judges, 267; and Quebec, 19, 21, 245–7, 283; 'self-restraint', 286; and standing, 80; and structural injunctions, 84–5; and US Supreme Court, 203–4, 279; and women, 115, 137, 138, 140–1, 142, 143–5, 154; *see also* Charter; Judiciary
Sweden, 148
Swinton, K., 231, 237, 248

Tariff Board, 108
Task Force on Canadian Unity, 228
Taylor, Charles, 5, 302, 306, 309
Thatcher, Margaret, 7
Toronto, 22
Torts: arguments against, 177–83, 184; and compensation, 171, 172; and 'consumer democracy', 176; costs, 177; defendant-plaintiff relationship, 171–2, 173, 174–5; definitions, xiii, 166, 167; and deterrence, 168–9, 170, 171–2, 178; and education, 169–70; effects, 167; in England, 166; functions, 167–70, 175–7; and government agencies, 176; and individualism, 171, 178–9; and liberalism, xiii; mass, 77; and morality, 171; 'normative immanence', 172–3, 175; 'ombudsman' function, 175–7; as 'private', 183; and public law, 172; reform of, xiii, 177; in US, 166, 172; and vengeance, 169; and victim compensation, 168;
Toryism, 6, 7, 11, 64, 80, 110, 149, 264
Trade, free, 22, 118; FTA/NAFTA, 8–9
Trade unions, 77, 78, 83, 143; *see also* Labour relations
Trebilcock, M., 180–1, 184
Tremblay, G., 241–2
Tribe, Lawrence, 42–3, 44
Tribunals, ix, 113, 230; as alternatives to courts, 73, 112–24; human rights, 121, 123; jurisdiction, xii, 109, 120, 121, 122; labour relations, 125; respect for persons, 124, 125; workers' compensation boards, 116
Trudeau, Pierre Elliott, 16, 245, 261, 266
Turpel, Mary Ellen, 273, 275

Unionization, xiii
United Kingdom, 182
United Nations Human Rights Committee, 142
United States: and abortion, 148, 149 (*see also* Roe v. Wade); Bill of Rights, 259, 262; and Canadian identity, 6, 8–9; capital punishment, 195; class actions, 74, 76, 77; compared with Canada, 6; competition policy, 117, 118; Constitution, 58, 83; constitutional law, 42–3; Congress, 60; court powers, 58, 59, 60; courts and social progress, 50–1; criminal justice, 191, 305; decrees, 86; elected judges, 313; federalism litigation, 225–6, 249, 308; Federal Rule 23, 74; 'fruit of the poisoned tree' doctrine, 198; 'government of laws', 58; ideology, 262; individualism, 60; judicial review, 264; judicial role, 262;

MARIANNE KAURIN

IRGENDWO IST IMMER SÜDEN

Aus dem Norwegischen von Franziska Hüther

Heute ist der letzte Tag. Nur noch ein paar Stunden. Dann ist Schluss.

Aber es ist kein Schluss, bei dem man weinen muss. Es kommen keine Axtmörder oder Meteoriten oder Epidemien. Das hier ist ein guter Schluss. Die meisten haben sich darauf gefreut. Haben die Wochen im Kalender durchgestrichen, ihre Koffer gepackt und Sandalen gekauft. Sich eine schicke Sommerfrisur schneiden lassen. Ich habe auch gesagt, dass ich mich freue. Das wird so cool, habe ich gesagt und ausgerechnet, wie lange es noch dauert.

Ich habe schon immer gern Dinge gezählt. Tage und Minuten. Haargummis, Farbstifte, Freunde. Irgendwie fange ich ganz automatisch damit an. In meinem Mäppchen stecken vierzehn lila Buntstifte, obwohl meine Lieblingsfarbe Blau ist. Es sind achtundsechzig Treppenstufen vom vierten Stock bis runter in den Hof, zweiundvierzig Schritte bis zu dem hässlichen Schild mit der Aufschrift *Willkommen im Tyllebakken Bauverein*.

Ich habe schon mehr als viertausend Tage gelebt. Ich habe in sechs Wohnungen gewohnt. In drei Städten. Bin in fünf verschiedene Klassen gegangen. Ich hatte drei Freunde, deren Namen mit einem M anfingen. Mit keinem von ihnen habe ich mehr Kontakt, aber M ist mein Lieblingsbuchstabe. Deshalb passt es auch so gut mit Maria.

Wenn mich jemand fragen würde, wie viele Schritte es von der Turnhalle bis zum Klassenzimmer sind, wüsste ich die Antwort. Und genau da bin ich gerade. Direkt vor der Turnhalle, auf dem Weg zum Klassenzimmer. Der Asphalt glüht, die Flagge am Mast ist gehisst. Mathilde und Regine lehnen sich gegen den Zaun der Mittelschule, als ob sie nicht schnell genug dort anfangen könnten. Sie stehen in der Gruppe, in der jeder gern stehen will. Sie *sind* die Gruppe. Alle tragen enge Tops und haben lange Haare. Regine hält ihr Handy hoch, um die ganze Clique auf ein Bild zu kriegen. Sie lachen, haben Spaß.

Ich schließe den Mund, als ich vorbeigehe. Es ist besser, nur im Kopf zu zählen, denke ich und beobachte Mathilde, die mit Kussmund vor der Kamera posiert, bevor sie sich wieder zu den anderen dreht.

Da drüben ist Markus, am Fahnenmast bei den Jungs. Er hat ein rotes T-Shirt an und ist schon richtig braun an den Armen und im Gesicht. Ich höre sein Lachen bis hierher, obwohl ich noch über sechzig Schritte von seiner schönen Stimme entfernt bin. Eigentlich sollte ich laut zählen, wenn ich an ihm vorbeigehe, einfach nur damit er meine Existenz bemerkt. Aber dann wäre ich für alle die Komische, und das wäre nicht wirklich besser, als die Neue zu sein.

Am Eingang stehen Johanne und ein paar andere Mädchen aus der Klasse und schauen sehnsüchtig zu den Schaukeln. Johanne hat noch ihren Fahrradhelm auf und eine Jacke an, obwohl es vierzig Grad sind. Sie reden von irgendeinem Pfadfinderlager, in das sie in den Sommerferien wollen, das wird so toll. Vielleicht könnte ich mich zu dieser Gruppe dazustellen. Im Lager dabei sein. Aber ich träume mich rüber zum Fahnenmast und zur Mittelschule, zu denen, die mich wirklich hochziehen könnten.

Also sage ich wieder einmal nur Hi und laufe schnell durch den Eingang, die Treppen hoch in den zweiten Stock und ins Klassenzimmer, dessen Fenster zum Schulhof zeigen. Das immer still ist, immer wartet.

Ich habe mich gerade ans Fenster gestellt, von wo aus ich einen perfekten Blick auf einen gewissen Fahnenmast habe, als plötzlich die Tür aufgeht und ein Kopf voller Locken erscheint. Ein Junge.

»Hi.«

Nur sein Kopf guckt herein, er lächelt mich mit großen Augen an. Ich habe ihn noch nie vorher gesehen und bleibe zögernd am Fenster stehen.

»Ist das hier die 6a?«

Er macht einen Schritt zurück, schließt die Tür und öffnet sie wieder. Wahrscheinlich hat er auf den Stundenplan geschaut, der draußen hängt.

Ich nicke. Gehe schnell zu meinem Platz und setze mich. Tue so, als ob ich mit etwas Wichtigem beschäftigt wäre, krame in meinem Mäppchen.

»Wie heißt du?«, fragt er und betritt das Klassenzimmer. Blickt sich um und lächelt. Als ob er noch nie zuvor in einem Klassenzimmer gewesen wäre, als wäre unseres vollkommen anders und tausendmal spannender als ein ganz normales norwegisches Durchschnittsklassenzimmer. Er hat eine Hand in der Hosentasche, in der anderen hält er eine Kappe. Das T-Shirt zeigt einen Aufdruck vom Zoo, und die kackbraunen Shorts sind ihm viel zu groß, hängen wie eine Baggy unter der Hüfte, aber auf uncoole Weise. Seine Füße stecken ohne Socken in irgendwelchen Stoffschuhen, die vor hundert Jahren bestimmt mal weiß waren. Die Beine und Arme sind dünn und bleich, die Locken tanzen auf seinem Kopf auf und ab, selbst wenn er sich nicht bewegt.

»Ina«, antworte ich.

»Aha«, sagt er und lächelt noch breiter. Sein einer Schneidezahn ist schief. »Ich bin Vilmer.«

Mehr sagt er nicht, guckt mich nur an. Als würde er darauf warten, dass ich ein Gespräch anfange, als wäre es meine Aufgabe.

Ich könnte fragen, was er in unserem Klassenzimmer macht oder ob er den Zoo mag und überdimensionale Shorts, aber ich komme nicht dazu. Denn jetzt klingelt es, und vier Sekunden später steigt der Lärmpegel in der Klasse bis in den Himmel. Vilmer lehnt sich ganz hinten gegen die Wand. Die anderen scheinen ihn nicht mal zu bemerken, alle lachen, albern herum und reden aufgeregt durcheinander. Denn heute ist der letzte Tag. Bald ist Schluss. Noch drei Stunden mit unserer Lehrerin Vigdis, und dann heißt es Sommerferien.

Die Sommerferien dauern vierundfünfzig Tage. Ich habe es im Kalender abgezählt, der am Kühlschrank hängt. Vierundfünfzig Tage entsprechen eintausendzweihundertsechsundneunzig Stunden. Oder siebenundsiebzigtausendsiebenhundertsechzig Minuten. Die Sekunden habe ich noch nicht ausgerechnet, aber es sind sicher viele. Vielleicht mehrere Millionen.

Jetzt steht Vigdis vor uns, am allerletzten Tag in der 6a. Zu diesem besonderen Anlass hat sie extra ein hellgelbes Kleid angezogen und reichlich Schminke aufgetragen. Die Lippen glänzen rosa, die Haare thronen als pilzartiges Knäuel auf dem Kopf.

»Willkommen, ihr Lieben, zu eurem letzten Tag als Sechstklässler«, sagt sie feierlich und lässt den Blick über das Klassenzimmer schweifen wie eine Königin, die zu ihren Untertanen spricht.

Sie nimmt ihre runde Brille ab und steckt sich den Bügel in den Mund, was sie ungefähr alle zwei Minuten tut. Und weil sie so oft an ihrem Brillengestell nuckelt und solche Unmengen von Lippenstift benutzt, ist sie oft rosa hinter den Ohren. Viele in der Klasse finden Vigdis blöd. Machen ihren schaukelnden Gang nach und lästern über ihre langweiligen Kleider. Vigdis scheint es nicht zu stören. Einmal hat sie Markus dabei erwischt, wie er sie nachmachte. Er watschelte im Klassenzimmer herum und gackerte wie ein Huhn, während Vigdis in der Tür stand und ihm zuguckte. Markus war ziemlich verlegen, aber Vigdis lachte nur.

»Kikeriki, kikeriku, das Huhn bist du«, sagte sie und lief in ihrer selbstreflektierenden Sicherheitsweste, unter der man deutlich ihre Hängebrüste sieht, zur Pausenaufsicht nach draußen.

Jetzt deutet sie zur Wand auf der gegenüberliegenden Seite des Klassenzimmers, und alle drehen sich um. Ein Flüstern geht durch die Reihen, als die anderen den unbekannten Jungen in seinen hässlichen Klamotten entdecken. Die Leute in meiner Klasse nehmen es sehr genau, was Kleidung betrifft.

»Da bist du ja«, sagt Vigdis zu dem Jungen, der sich als Vilmer vorgestellt hat. »Wie wunderbar, dass du kommen konntest.«

Sie geht zu ihm nach hinten, begrüßt ihn, zieht ihn hinter sich her zur Tafel und breitet die Arme aus.

»Wir haben Besuch«, verkündet sie und legt ihre

Hände mit festem Griff auf seine Schultern. Sie sieht stolz aus, als würde sie gerade ein neugeborenes Baby zum ersten Mal der Familie präsentieren.

»Und dieser junge Mann, meine Damen und Herren, wird nach den Ferien in unserer Klasse beginnen. Heute ist er nur hier, um kurz Hallo zu sagen.«

Sie beugt sich zu Vilmer vor.

»Du kannst ja selbst erzählen, wie du heißt.«

»Vilmer«, sagt er laut und deutlich.

Ein paar Leute kichern.

»Genau«, sagt Vigdis. »Vilmer ist neu hierhergezogen. Wo wohnst du noch mal?«

»Trostevejen 30«, sagt Vilmer. »Aufgang F.«

Er klingt wie ein kleines Kind, das eben erst gelernt hat, seine Adresse auswendig aufzusagen.

»Genau«, sagt Vigdis wieder. »Das ist nämlich im Tyllebakken Bauverein.«

Jetzt kichern noch mehr Leute aus der Klasse. Ich weiß nicht, was am Tyllebakken Bauverein so lustig ist, abgesehen davon, dass er einen Spitznamen hat, der sich auf Tylle reimt, und er bei einem Wettbewerb um die hässlichsten Wohnorte garantiert den ersten Platz gewinnen würde.

»Ina wohnt ja auch dort«, ergänzt Vigdis und zeigt auf mich. »Da könnt ihr nach den Sommerferien zusammen zur Schule laufen.«

Eigentlich mag ich Vigdis, sie ist nett. Aber jetzt ärgere ich mich über sie. Wieso bestimmt sie, dass ich zusammen mit einem Jungen in Schlabbershorts und einem T-Shirt vom Zoo zur Schule laufen soll, nur weil er zufällig auch in Tyllebakken wohnt? Warum muss sie überhaupt von Tyllebakken reden? Es ist ja schön und gut, dass Vigdis Freunde für mich finden will, das probiert sie schon, seit ich hier in der Sechsten angefangen habe. Aber ich brauche Freunde, die mich hochziehen, nicht runter. Und mit diesem Vilmer wäre garantiert Letzteres der Fall.

Schließlich darf Vilmer sich auf einen Stuhl in der allerletzten Reihe setzen. Er versucht, meinen Blick einzufangen, als er an meinem Tisch vorbeigeht, als ob wir schon beste Freunde wären. Bloß weil wir in der Nähe voneinander wohnen und uns zehn Sekunden vor den anderen getroffen haben. Ich schaue schnell woandershin.

»Vigdis, Vigdis!«

Mathilde wedelt mit dem Arm in der Luft herum und fängt direkt an zu reden, obwohl Vigdis immer noch mit Vilmer beschäftigt ist.

»Können wir nicht eine Runde machen, in der jeder erzählt, wohin er in den Ferien fährt?«

Der Vorschlag stößt sofort auf große Begeisterung. Mallorca, USA, Frankreich, rufen alle durcheinander.

Mathilde ist inzwischen aufgestanden und fuchtelt mit den Armen, um die Runde zu organisieren, bei der offensichtlich so viele dabei sein wollen. Vigdis schlägt vor, dass vielleicht nicht alle etwas erzählen müssen, aber Mathilde ist viel zu aufgeregt und hört gar nicht zu.

»Tuva fängt an!«, ruft sie und zeigt zum Fensterplatz in der ersten Reihe.

Mein Bein zittert, der Mund ist trocken. Und Tuva erzählt, dass sie für drei Wochen nach Italien fährt, in den südlichen Teil.

Mathilde deutet auf Teodor, damit alle verstehen, dass wir von vorne nach hinten vorgehen, Tisch für Tisch.

Ich zähle bis elf. Lege die Hand aufs Bein, um es ruhig zu halten. Elf Tische, bis ich an der Reihe bin.

Teodor fährt nach Kroatien. Selma für mehrere Wochen nach Spanien. Simen, der hinter Selma sitzt, fliegt nach Florida. Das erzählt er mit lauter und deutlicher Stimme, mehrere seufzen neidisch. Una, die nach Simen an der Reihe ist, würde auch viel lieber nach Florida reisen, doch bei ihr geht es nur nach Dänemark.

»Aber nächstes Jahr«, fügt sie hinzu, »fahren wir dafür vier Wochen nach Thailand.«

Noch sieben Tische, dann bin ich dran.

Mathias macht Urlaub auf Rhodos. Vilde in Dubai. Alle haben Pläne für die Sommerferien, alle werden sie davon erzählen. Alle verreisen. Ins Ausland. Die Leute in dieser Klasse sind total heiß aufs Ausland. Es gab sogar einen Wettstreit, wer schon in den meisten Ländern war. Regine führt mit siebenundzwanzig.

Ich schaue zu Vigdis und starre auf meinen Tisch, während Mathilde verkündet, dass sie zwei Wochen in einem Resort in Portugal verbringen wird. Ich weiß nicht genau, was ein Resort ist, aber es hört sich ziemlich schick an. Gleich bin ich dran. Gleich muss ich etwas erzählen. Es pocht in meinem Bauch, fast ganz oben beim Herzen.

»Du lieber Gott«, sagt Vigdis überwältigt. »Hier gibt es aber wirklich viele Weltenbummler. Wisst ihr, was ich in den Ferien vorhabe?«

Es sind nur noch drei vor mir, daher ist es gut, dass Vigdis kurz übernimmt und ich Zeit habe, etwas mehr über meine eigenen Reisepläne nachzudenken.

»Ich habe mir ein Sommerhäuschen gekauft. An einem See im Wald. Mein eigenes kleines Resort sozusagen. Da werde ich den ganzen Sommer sein und nichts tun außer Bücher lesen und gutes Essen kochen. Das wird sicher auch sehr schön, meint ihr nicht?«

Keiner antwortet, nur ein paar Leute nicken, und irgendjemand macht eine Art Grunzlaut. Als ob Vigdis' Ferienpläne ultra-lame wären. Ganz ehrlich, wer will schon an einem See im Wald hocken und Bücher lesen?

Markus ist der Nächste. Er sitzt zwei Tische vor mir. Ich verbringe jeden Tag vier Stunden damit, seinen Rücken zu betrachten. Das sind ganz schön viele Minuten, wenn man es auf ein volles Schuljahr hochrechnet. Ich kenne seinen Rücken quasi auswendig, weiß genau, wie es aussieht, wenn er hustet oder lacht, die feinen Bewegungen zwischen seinen Schulterblättern. Bemerke sofort, wenn er einen neuen Pulli anhat. Ich habe mir insgesamt bestimmt schon zweitausend Stunden vorgestellt, wie es wäre, mit der Hand über seinen Nacken zu streichen und den Rücken hinunterzufahren, den ich die ganze Zeit anstarre.

Markus erklärt, dass er erst mal im Sommerhaus in Sørland ist, gleich morgen geht es los. Dann fliegt er für zwei Wochen nach Spanien. Er nickt Selma zu.

»Aber worauf ich mich am meisten freue«, fährt er eifrig fort, »ist London.«

Er macht eine kurze Pause, vergewissert sich, dass er die volle Aufmerksamkeit hat.

»Denn da gehen mein Vater und ich zum Chelsea-Spiel. Das wird der Hammer, mein Vater ist nämlich genauso ein Chelsea-Fan wie ich.«

Er dreht sich lächelnd zu Julie um. Mein Gesicht wird heiß wie ein Wasserkocher, denn ich sitze direkt hinter Julie. Er schaut also fast zu mir. Nur ein paar Zentimeter, dann würden sich unsere Blicke kreuzen.

Julie beginnt zögernd, ihre Stimme ist rau. Vielleicht hat sie ja nichts zu erzählen, wird nicht vierundfünfzig Tage lang die aufregendsten Dinge erleben, sondern einfach nur zu Hause sein. Aber so ist es natürlich nicht. Kein Mensch ist im Sommer einfach nur *zu Hause.* Julie fährt nämlich nach Zypern. Mit ihrer Mutter. Und dann nach Frankreich, mit ihrem Vater.

»Das ist das Tolle daran, wenn man geschiedene Eltern hat«, erklärt sie hochzufrieden, »man fährt zweimal richtig in den Urlaub. Die Ferien werden sozusagen verdoppelt.«

Sie dreht sich auf ihrem Stuhl zu mir um und schaut mich an. Alle schauen mich an. Auch Vigdis. Es wird still. Vollkommen still. Ich weiß, dass ich den Mund aufmachen muss, weil alle hören wollen, was ich im Sommer unternehmen werde, welche spannenden Pläne ich mit meiner Familie habe, was ich alles erleben werde. Ich sehe von einem zum anderen, in die neugierigen Gesichter, aber mein Mund ist leer. Es ist kein einziges Wort darin. Ich räuspere mich, öffne den Mund und schließe ihn wieder, schlucke, und dann geben meine Stimmbänder einen schwachen Laut von sich.

»Im Sommer«, sage ich und schaue zu Markus. Er schaut zurück. Jetzt schaut er mich an!

»Im Sommer«, wiederhole ich und warte darauf, dass mir etwas einfällt.

»Im Sommer fahre ich in den Süden.«

Vigdis nickt ermutigend und lächelt. Markus schaut mich immer noch an. Alle schauen mich an, sie wollen mehr.

»Ich freue mich schon so«, sage ich und sehe die Schwimmbecken und Wasserrutschen und den ewig langen weißen Strand, die Sonnenschirme und den Kids Club vor mir. Für den ich natürlich zu groß bin.

»Ich werde schwimmen und in der Sonne liegen und mich entspannen. Einfach nur Südendinge machen. Viele Wochen lang. Morgen früh fahren wir los.«

Auf einmal höre ich ein Kichern. Oder besser gesagt zwei. Es kommt von der vorletzten Reihe am Fenster. Mathilde lehnt sich zu Regine, hält sich die Hand vor den Mund und flüstert ihr irgendwas ins Ohr.

»Es gibt keinen Ort, der Süden heißt«, sagt Regine sachlich.

Sie ist Zweite Vorsitzende im Schülerrat und will später Anwältin werden, genau wie ihre Mutter.

»*Süden*, also, das klingt echt bescheuert.«

Mein Bein fängt wieder an zu zittern. Und der linke Arm auch ein bisschen. Können wir jetzt nicht einfach weitermachen, kann nicht irgendwer anders übernehmen?

»Wo genau fährst du denn hin, Ina? Süden ist ja kein Land.«

Die beiden kichern wieder. Mehrere andere lachen ebenfalls. Aber da mischt sich glücklicherweise Vigdis ein.

»Es ist ganz normal, dass man Süden sagt, auch wenn es kein physischer Ort auf der Karte ist. So nennt man es eben, wenn man irgendwohin weiter südlich in Urlaub fährt, um sich zu entspannen und Spaß zu haben und schwimmen zu gehen. Genau wie Ina.«

Vigdis zeigt ganz merkwürdig auf mich. Als wären die anderen in der Klasse senil und hätten plötzlich vergessen, von wem eigentlich die Rede ist.

»Der Süden kann also theoretisch an jedem beliebigen Ort der Welt liegen.«

Vigdis sieht zu Marte, und dann geht die Runde weiter. Zum Glück. Genug vom Süden.

Auf Marte wartet Wanderurlaub in den Bergen, anschließend fährt sie den Rallarvegen mit dem Fahrrad. Patrick macht eine dreiwöchige Rundreise mit dem Auto durch Europa. Johanne besucht ihre Großeltern auf den Lofoten. Regine ist in den Ferien auf Kreta, einer Insel im Süden. Sie guckt zu mir, als sie Süden sagt, betont das Wort, als würde sie es einem Dreijährigen oder einer Person mit einem Hirnschaden erklären.

»Aber erst mal bin ich für eine Woche zum Shoppen in Paris«, verkündet sie stolz und schaut zu Mathilde.

Als alle von ihren Plänen erzählt haben, übernimmt Vigdis wieder.

»So, dann fangen wir jetzt an«, sagt sie. Aber da entdeckt sie Vilmer ganz hinten. »Huch, dich haben wir ja völlig vergessen zu fragen, Vilmer. Hast du irgendwelche spannenden Pläne?«

Alle drehen sich zu ihm um.

Er lächelt.

»Ich fahre auch in den Süden«, sagt er und wirft mir einen Blick zu.

Was meint er damit?

»Nee, Quatsch«, sagt er dann. »Ich bleibe zu Hause.«

Jetzt schaut er Vigdis an.

»Mein Vater ist nämlich pleite, deshalb wird es dieses Jahr nichts mit Urlaub.«

Er zuckt mit den Achseln und lehnt sich zurück.

Natürlich kichert jemand. Irgendjemand kichert immer.

»Kein Süden für mich«, sagt Vilmer mit breitem Lächeln.

Als ob es ihm völlig egal wäre, dass er nirgendwohin fährt. Es sieht aus, als würde er sich auf die Ferien freuen, obwohl er einfach nur zu Hause bleibt. Mit seinem Vater, der pleite ist. Im Tyllebakken Bauverein.

Dieses Jahr habe ich etwas Besonderes mit euch vor«, sagt Vigdis, als es zur letzten Stunde geklingelt hat.

Sie erinnert mich an einen eifrigen Hundewelpen, der jeden Moment ohne Leine in den Wald sausen darf. Ihr gelbes Kleid hat große Schweißflecken unter beiden Armen, die Haare kleben ihr auf der Stirn.

»Ich habe da etwas in einem Lehrermagazin gelesen und fand, dass es sich richtig lustig anhört. Nehmt euch bitte alle einen Stift, und dann bekommt jeder ein Blatt Papier.«

Sie eilt durch die Klasse, ihr starker Parfümgeruch beißt in der Nase. Ein leeres Blatt segelt auf meinen Tisch. Ich betrachte Markus' Rücken. Er sitzt ganz still auf seinem Stuhl, das Papier in der linken Hand.

»Jetzt schreibt ihr alle euren Namen oben auf euer Blatt«, sagt Vigdis. »Anschließend schreibt ihr drei Punkte auf – drei Dinge, von denen ihr hofft, dass sie in den Sommerferien passieren werden.«

Sie lächelt zufrieden. Klatscht in die Hände.

»Und man darf ruhig ein wenig träumen«, flötet sie. »Ihr sollt nicht nur Dinge aufschreiben, von denen ihr schon *wisst*, dass sie passieren werden, sonst wäre es ja witzlos. Seid ein bisschen verrückt. Lasst eurer Fantasie freien Lauf. Wenn ihr fertig seid, faltet ihr das Blatt zwei Mal.«

Sie demonstriert es mit ihrem eigenen Blatt.

»Danach gehe ich herum und sammle alle Zettel in diesem Korb. Die Zettel bleiben den ganzen Sommer über hier in der Schule. Und wenn die Ferien vorbei sind und ihr in der siebten Klasse seid, dürft ihr lesen, was ihr geschrieben habt. Klingt das nicht lustig? Dann könnt ihr sehen, ob etwas davon tatsächlich eingetroffen ist.«

Alle sitzen über ihre Blätter gebeugt und schreiben. Es ist eine schwierige Aufgabe. Ich schließe die Augen, so kann man besser denken. Wovon träume ich? Mein Kopf ist vollkommen leer, kein einziger Traum weit und breit. Ich mache die Augen wieder auf und sehe als Erstes Markus' rotes T-Shirt. Da fällt mir etwas ein. Ich lächle beim Schreiben, verdecke das Papier mit der Hand, damit niemand lesen kann, was da steht. Vigdis hat ja gesagt, dass wir träumen sollen. Also träume ich. Bis mir jemand auf die Schulter tippt.

»Hast du einen Stift?«

Es ist der Lockenkopf mit dem T-Shirt.

»Ich hab nämlich nichts mitgenommen«, erklärt er und lächelt mich mit seinem schiefen Schneidezahn an. Ich bin nicht sicher, ob es süß oder hässlich aussieht.

»Ich dachte, es macht keinen Sinn, meinen ganzen Kram mitzuschleppen, wenn ich ja eh nur zu Besuch bin.«

Ich nehme einen Bleistift aus dem Mäppchen und reiche ihn ihm.

Er lächelt wieder. Liest, was ich geschrieben habe, und lächelt noch breiter. Ich falte schnell das Blatt zusammen.

Vilmer geht zurück zu seinem Platz. Eigentlich hatte ich mir schon zwei weitere Punkte überlegt, aber jetzt habe ich alles wieder vergessen. Nur wegen Vilmer, der anscheinend ausgerechnet mich nach einem Stift fragen musste. Ich zerbreche mir den Kopf, bis Vigdis zum dritten Mal mahnt, dass nun wirklich alle zum Schluss kommen sollen. Also kritzele ich einfach irgendwas hin, was sowieso nie im Leben passieren wird, falte mein Blatt zusammen und gebe es Vigdis. Es mischt sich mit den Träumen der anderen. Vigdis drückt den Korb an sich, als hielte sie ein Katzenbaby in den Armen.

»Ich verspreche auch, dass ich nicht gucke«, sagt sie und lacht laut über sich selbst.

Sie hält garantiert den Norwegenrekord im Übersich-selbst-Lachen.

»Und wenn der Sommer vorbei ist, sehen wir ja, welche Träume sich bewahrheitet haben.«

Vigdis holt die Gitarre und schlägt ein paar Akkorde an. Mehrere Schüler winden sich auf ihren Stühlen, so wie immer, wenn die Gitarre auftaucht.

»Jetzt müsst ihr singen!«, ruft Vigdis in die Runde und klimpert eifrig drauflos.

»Glaub nicht, von allein würd' es So-ho-mmer, in Garten und Wiese und Wald. Den Sommer, den muss jemand we-hecken, dann blühen die Blumen schon bald.«

Es klingt total falsch und peinlich, aber Vigdis kann anscheinend nicht genug davon kriegen.

»Suuuuper!«, feuert sie uns an und zwingt uns durch sämtliche Strophen. Wir haben seit den Osterferien geübt, damit dieser Moment das wird, was Vigdis perfekt nennt.

»Da hüpf ich und renne und spri-hi-nge und spüre den Sommer in mir.«

Als wir endlich fertig sind, hat Vigdis Tränen in den Augen.

»Ihr habt euch wirklich verbessert«, sagt sie mit brüchiger Stimme. »Und das freut mich. Es freut mich aus tiefstem Herzen.«

Mathilde und Regine kriegen einen Lachkrampf. Als Markus die Augen verdreht, kichern sie noch mehr. Und dann ruft Vigdis, dass es nur noch zehn Minuten bis zum Ende der sechsten Klasse sind und wir uns jetzt ordentlich in einer Reihe aufstellen sollen, damit sie uns allen einen schönen Sommer wünschen kann.

Ich ergattere den Platz direkt hinter Markus. Schubse Johanne dafür ein klein bisschen zur Seite. Noch einmal sehe ich seinen Rücken, seinen Hinterkopf und das glatte Haar. Das rote T-Shirt und die braunen Arme. Er hat einen ganz besonderen Geruch. Ich beuge mich ein Stück nach vorne und atme den Duft ein. Er riecht nach Junge und Waschmittel, vielleicht auch nach einem Hauch Sonnencreme.

Vigdis beginnt ihre feierliche Abschiedsrunde. Einem nach dem anderen gibt sie die Hand, und jeder bekommt eine Umarmung. Sie lächelt und wünscht schöne Ferien. Das dauert. Zum Glück. Ich stehe absolut perfekt, fast ein bisschen zu dicht an Markus. Achte darauf, dass mein Arm leicht gegen seinen stößt, mein Kinn seinen Rücken berührt. Es sind die letzten Sekunden, bevor ich ihn für viele Millionen Sekunden nicht mehr sehe. Er ist ja den Sommer über kaum da, es ist also höchst unwahrscheinlich, dass ich ihm irgendwo über den Weg laufen werde. Außerdem wohnt er ziemlich weit weg von mir. Ich bin schon oft an seinem Haus vorbeigegangen, sein Zimmer liegt im zweiten Stock, er hat Chelsea-Vorhänge vor den Fenstern.

Vigdis drückt Markus. Seine braunen Arme legen sich um sie. Wie es nur wäre, wenn er mich so umarmen würde, wenn ich in diesem Moment Vigdis wäre.

»Genieß deine Ferien, Ina.«

Vigdis steht plötzlich vor mir.

»Ich hoffe, du hast einen schönen Sommer«, sagt sie und drückt mich fest. Sie schaut mich lange an, mustert mich, als wolle sie etwas sagen, was ihr nicht über die Lippen kommt.

»Du auch«, sage ich. »Es wird bestimmt toll im Wald.«

Vigdis zwinkert mir zu. Dann geht sie zum Nächsten.

Erst da bemerke ich Vilmer. Er steht direkt hinter mir und sagt zu Vigdis, wie sehr er sich schon darauf freue, in unsere Klasse zu kommen. Die Leute hier scheinen echt nett zu sein, fügt er hinzu. Und dieser Satz ist so verrückt, dass ich mich zu ihm umdrehen muss. Entweder ist er bekloppt oder einfach nur ein bisschen zu optimistisch.

»Vielleicht sehen wir uns ja«, sagt er auf einmal zu mir.

Und in diesem Augenblick entscheide ich mich. Der schiefe Schneidezahn ist hässlich. Solche schiefen Zähne haben nichts Charmantes. Er sieht einfach nur aus wie ein Loser. Wieso sollten wir uns *sehen*? Ich drehe mich wieder um und schaue zu Markus. Ich habe keine Lust, nett zu Vilmer zu sein, bloß weil er neu ist und den Sommer über zu Hause hocken wird.

Die ganze Klasse steht in Reih und Glied, während wir ungeduldig von einem Fuß auf den anderen treten und kichern und lachen und Quatsch machen und warten. Auf das Signal, dass Vigdis den Letzten umarmt hat und endlich, endlich Ferien sind, vierundfünfzig Tage lang frei. Darauf haben wir uns das ganze Schuljahr gefreut.

Und dann ist es so weit.

»Schöne Ferien, 6a!«, ruft Vigdis, so laut sie kann, und fuchtelt dabei mit den Armen wie ein Zirkusdirektor in der Manege.

Und da verwandelt sich das Klassenzimmer in einen ausbrechenden Vulkan. Zweiundzwanzig Sechstklässler schießen wie glühende Lava hinaus in die Sommerferien. Wir rennen zur Tür, den Gang entlang, die Treppen hinunter, durch den Ausgang und hinaus auf den sonnigen Schulhof. Rufen und schreien und jubeln. Es ist Sommer. Wir haben Ferien. Endlich kann es losgehen mit all den Plänen. Wenn man welche hat.

Am Haupttor hat sich plötzlich eine dichte Schülertraube gebildet. Wo vor gerade mal zwei Minuten noch alle in die Freiheit gerannt sind, stehen sie nun verschwitzt und außer Atem vor dem Ausgang und versperren den Weg, sodass man unmöglich in die Ferien kommt, ohne sich an ihnen vorbeizuschieben. Mathildes heller Kopf sticht aus der Menge heraus. Ihre Stimme ist laut und durchdringend, als würde sie einem Trupp Soldaten kurz vor Kriegseinsatz die letzten lebenswichtigen Befehle erteilen. Markus steht neben ihr und hört aufmerksam zu.

»Es geht um sechs los«, kommandiert Mathilde. »Und alle müssen kommen!«

Ich bleibe zögerlich stehen. Schaue mich um, sehe aber keine andere Möglichkeit, als mich zu den anderen dazuzuquetschen. Sonst müsste ich über den Zaun springen, und das wäre definitiv auffälliger, als einfach lautlos mit der hintersten Reihe zu verschmelzen.

Auf einmal erinnere ich mich wieder an die Einladung und die Fotos von Mathilde auf der Karte. In Badeanzug und mit Sonnenbrille, auf dem Boot und am Strand, ein Eis in der Hand. Jetzt lächelt sie jeden Einzelnen an. Macht ein hochzufriedenes Gesicht. Die Einladung liegt immer noch in meinem Rucksack, ich habe gar nicht erst nach dem Datum geschaut. Eigentlich gehe ich nie auf Geburtstage, Mama wird immer so gestresst, wenn Geschenke besorgt werden müssen. Diesen Geburtstag hatte ich daher auch nicht eingeplant. Vor allem nicht diesen.

Langsam löst sich die Schar auf, und die Leute strömen nach draußen auf die Straße.

»Du kommst doch, oder?«

Mathilde hat sich plötzlich vor mir aufgebaut. Regine steht neben ihr.

Ich zögere. Tausend Ausreden jagen durch meinen Kopf.

»Ich fahre richtig früh los morgen«, höre ich mich auf einmal sagen.

Markus tritt dazu. Das rote T-Shirt und die braunen Arme. Der Geruch von Sonnencreme und Waschmittel. Er steht so nah bei mir, dass ich nervös werde. Ich habe erst zweimal mit ihm gesprochen, und das eine Mal haben wir eine Gruppenarbeit über Vitamin D zusammen gemacht, das zählt also nicht. Schnell lasse ich die Hände in den Taschen meiner Shorts verschwinden.

So weiß ich wenigstens, wo sie sind und dass sie nichts Komisches tun.

Er lächelt.

Oh Mann, dieses Lächeln. Ich lächle zurück. Glaube ich jedenfalls. Meine Lippen pressen sich so fest aufeinander, dass ich fast einen Krampf kriege.

»Wann geht denn der Flug?«, fragt er.

Er spricht mit mir! Erkundigt sich nach einem Detail aus meinem Leben!

»Um halb sechs«, antworte ich hastig, und meine Wangen fangen an zu brennen. »Und vorher muss ich noch total viel packen, weil wir so lange weg sind.«

Ich traue mich nicht, ihm in die Augen zu schauen. Also starre ich auf den Boden und merke, wie meine Hände in den Taschen anfangen zu schwitzen und mein Gesicht bestimmt mindestens so rot wird wie sein T-Shirt. Gestern Abend vor dem Einschlafen habe ich erschrocken festgestellt, dass ich Markus jetzt volle vierundfünfzig Tage lang nicht sehen werde.

»Aber du liegst ja wohl nicht schon um sieben im Bett, oder?«

Mathilde und Regine prusten los. Er lächelt den beiden zu, dann wieder mir. Markus geht natürlich auf die Party. Alle wollen auf diese Party.

»Also, du kommst«, sagt Mathilde entschieden.

»Ja«, antworte ich und starre weiter auf meine Füße,

warte darauf, dass Markus etwas sagt wie »Super, dann sehen wir uns ja später«. Als ob er sich jemals darüber freuen und es auch noch vor Mathilde und Regine aussprechen würde.

»Was ist los?«

Der schon wieder. Vilmer mit dem Schneidezahn. Was will der denn jetzt hier?

Vilmer lächelt in die Runde. Hebt fragend die Augenbrauen.

Ich schaue zu Markus. In sein hübsches Gesicht. Und verdrehe die Augen. Vilmer ist dermaßen neugierig.

»Ich feiere heute Abend Geburtstag«, sagt Mathilde. »Mit der ganzen Klasse.«

»Oh, cool«, sagt Vilmer begeistert.

Anscheinend nimmt er an, er wäre auch eingeladen. Immerhin gehört er schon seit ungefähr fünf Minuten zur Klasse und hat mit seinen hässlichen Klamotten und genau null Ferienplänen einen ziemlich schlechten Eindruck hinterlassen.

»Vielleicht können wir ja zusammen hingehen?«, fragt er mich, als ob es die normalste Sache der Welt wäre. »Dann kannst du mir den Weg zeigen«, fügt er hinzu.

Mathilde und Regine tauschen Blicke mit Markus. Die drei sehen aus, als würden sie jeden Moment laut loslachen. Einen winzigen Augenblick lang hatte ich gedacht, die Sache könnte ein gutes Ende nehmen. Bis Vilmer sich einmischen musste. Ich verdrehe noch mal die Augen, einfach nur um zu unterstreichen, dass Vilmer sich aufdrängt und er ganz bestimmt kein Freundschaftsmaterial ist. Auf einmal stehen wir wie zwei Sonderlinge nebeneinander, die beide im Tyllebakken Bauverein wohnen und ganz wunderbar zusammenpassen. Und das ist wirklich das Letzte, was ich gebrauchen kann.

»Na, dann bis um sechs«, sagt Mathilde spöttisch und unterdrückt einen Lachanfall.

Anschließend machen sich die drei gemeinsam auf den Heimweg, Richtung Solvangtoppen, wo sie alle wohnen.

Ich spüre Vilmers Blick auf mir, aber ich marschiere einfach allein los. So schnell ich kann. Nach links, in Richtung Tyllebakken. Ohne zu antworten. Vilmer klebt mir an den Fersen wie eine Briefmarke.

Ich werde ganz bestimmt nicht mit dir nach Hause laufen, denke ich, während ich über den glühend heißen Asphalt stapfe.

Zu Hause in der Wohnung ist es still und heiß. Stickig. Die Fenster sind zu, und das Wohnzimmer brät in der Sonne. Ein paar braune Pflanzen verdursten auf der Fensterbank. Ein Strauß verwelkter Margeriten hängt in einer Vase. Der Staub wirbelt im Sonnenlicht. Die Tür zu Mamas Schlafzimmer steht einen Spaltbreit offen, die Bettdecke ist zu einem Haufen zusammengeknüllt, und es dauert einen Moment, bis ich erkenne, dass sie nicht dort liegt. Sonst ist Mama immer daheim, wenn ich von der Schule komme, meistens schläft sie. Soweit ich weiß, hatte sie heute nichts vor.

Mama ist seit einer Weile sehr müde. Seit November vielleicht. Jedenfalls fing es irgendwann vor Weihnachten an, ich habe die Tage nicht genau gezählt. »Das wird bald besser«, sagt sie jeden zweiten Tag mit einem optimistischen Lächeln und mit ihren braunen, schläfrigen Augen. »Für clevere Mädchen kommt schon alles in Ordnung, Ina.«

Ich öffne das Fenster in meinem Zimmer und lege mich aufs Bett. Ein paar Kinder spielen unten im Hof, lachen und johlen, die Möwen schreien um die Wette.

Mathildes Geburtstag. Sie hat die Einladungen schon vor mehreren Wochen verteilt, alle immer wieder daran erinnert, sich dieses Datum frei zu halten.

»Denn es ist so langweilig, in den Ferien Geburtstag zu haben«, sagte sie, »wenn alle weg sind und so.«

Vielleicht sollte ich heute Abend doch hingehen? Aber man braucht ein Geschenk, wenn man zu einem Geburtstag eingeladen ist, und Geschenke kosten Geld. Was sich schwer beschaffen lässt, ohne Mama zu fragen. Und Mama wird beim Thema Geld immer so gestresst. Deshalb bin ich normalerweise krank. Oder sage, dass wir ausgerechnet an diesem Tag Besuch kriegen. Vielen Dank für die Einladung, aber es klappt leider nicht.

Auf meiner Oberlippe bilden sich Schweißtröpfchen. Zum Teil wegen der stickigen Luft, vor allem aber wegen Markus. Wenn ich auf Mathildes Geburtstag gehe, habe ich drei Stunden extra mit Markus, bevor die vierundfünfzig Tage anfangen.

Ich rufe Mama an, doch ich höre nur ihre müde Stimme auf der Mailbox. *Hier ist Anja, ich bin gerade leider nicht zu erreichen, bitte hinterlassen Sie eine Nachricht nach dem Piepton.*

Ich lege auf, laufe in die Küche und werfe einen Blick in den Kühlschrank. Ein Glas Erdbeermarmelade, eine halbe Pizza, Ketchup und eine zusammengedrückte Tube Mayonnaise. Vielleicht ist Mama ja einkaufen. Ich esse die kalte Pizza und schaue aus dem Fenster in den Hof. Denke an den Süden. An Markus. Den Geburtstag. Beschließe hinzugehen.

Ich google *Geburtstag + 12 Jahre + Mädchen + Geschenk + Preis*. Entscheide mich um, mache mir ein Marmeladenbrot und schreibe Mama mit großen Buchstaben: *WO BIST DU?*

Manchmal liegt ein bisschen Geld in einer Dose im Küchenschrank. Zwanzigkronenstücke, Zehner oder ein Hunderter. Ich schiele zum Schrank. Vielleicht fällt es Mama gar nicht auf, wenn etwas fehlt.

Die Dose ist verdächtig leicht und gibt einen ziemlich mageren Laut von sich, als ich sie schüttele. Man taucht nicht ohne Geschenk auf einer Geburtstagsfeier auf. Ich werfe die Dose zurück in den Schrank.

Plötzlich sehe ich ihn. Einen Zettel. Auf dem Küchentisch, halb unter der Tischdecke versteckt. Komisch, dass ich ihn vorher nicht gesehen habe, ich hier gesessen und eine halbe Pizza verdrückt habe, ohne das Stück Papier mit Mamas Handschrift zu bemerken. Da steht, dass sie bei einem Kurs ist und um sechs nach Hause kommt. Dass wir heute Abend Tacos essen können. Darunter hat sie ein Herz gemalt. Schief und unförmig. Und in dem Herz steht *Ina*.

Ich überlege zwanzig Sekunden, dann schreibe ich zurück. Sie braucht keine Tacos zu kaufen, weil ich auf einen Geburtstag gehe. Ich lösche *Geburtstag* wieder und tippe stattdessen *Klassenfest*, bevor ich auf Senden drücke. Klassenfeste sind gut, Klassenfeste sind gratis.

Ich warte eine Weile auf eine Antwort von ihr, aber es kommt keine. Ob ich doch zu Hause bleiben soll? Aber dann schließe ich die Augen und stelle mir Markus in seinem roten T-Shirt vor. Und als ich die Augen wieder aufmache, habe ich mich entschieden. Ein für allemal. Ich habe einen Plan.

Mathilde wohnt in einem weißen Haus. Mit Garten und Büschen und großen Fenstern, offenen Gardinen und einer Mutter, die in der Tür steht und jeden begrüßt. Mathildes Mutter trägt eine enge Hose und hat rot lackierte Fingernägel, weiße Zähne und blonde Haare, die zu einem Pferdeschwanz zusammengebunden sind. Eine Sonnenbrille auf dem Kopf. Goldene Ohrstecker. Sie wirkt kein bisschen müde. Im Gegenteil, sie sieht richtig wach und froh aus.

»Wie schön, dass du da bist, Ina«, sagt sie und umarmt mich.

Sie riecht nach Parfüm. Süß und elegant. Nicht so aufdringlich wie das von Vigdis. Und sie kennt tatsächlich all unsere Namen. Sogar meinen, obwohl ich gerade mal seit einem Jahr in Mathildes Klasse gehe und man uns nicht gerade als beste Freundinnen bezeichnen kann. Sie ist eine von diesen Müttern, die immer auf dem Laufenden sind, die ihre Mails lesen. Auf

Elternabende gehen. Namen lernen und den Überblick haben.

»Hallo … du«, sage ich, während sie mich drückt, denn ich habe keine Ahnung, wie Mathildes Mutter heißt.

Viele sind schon da. Ein paar Leute stehen auf der Terrasse, andere quatschen drinnen miteinander.

Hinter mir höre ich, wie Vilmer sich Mathildes Mutter vorstellt. Er kenne die Klasse erst seit ein paar Stunden, sagt er, aber er hoffe, es sei trotzdem okay, dass er gekommen sei.

Vilmer stand draußen im Hof, als ich von zu Hause losgegangen bin, aber ich habe so getan, als würde ich ihn nicht sehen. Er war den ganzen Weg über circa drei Meter hinter mir.

Ich gehe auf die Terrasse zu. Über den Rasen, halte nach Markus Ausschau. Ist er nicht hier? Er muss da sein. Sonst bin ich völlig umsonst gekommen. Wenn er nur wüsste, was ich seinetwegen auf mich nehme.

»Heeeeeey«, sagt Mathilde.

Sie trägt ein helllila Kleid. Die Haare fallen ihr in perfekten Locken über die Schultern, sie hat sie bestimmt vier Stunden mit dem Lockenstab bearbeitet. Mindestens. Sie umarmt mich fest, als wären wir beste Freundinnen und sie hätte diesen Geburtstag auf keinen Fall überleben können, wenn nicht ausgerechnet *ich* hier erschienen wäre. Dann schaut sie mich an. Erwartungsvoll.

Und da beginne ich mit der Ausführung meines Plans.

»Oh nein!«, rufe ich so laut, dass möglichst alle es mitkriegen. »Das Geschenk! Ich habe dein Geschenk vergessen. Oh Mann, wie kann man nur so blöd sein!«

Mathilde reißt die Augen auf.

»Du hast mein Geschenk vergessen?«, fragt sie enttäuscht.

Ich nicke und setzte eine zutiefst betrübte Miene auf. Fast gelingt es mir sogar, noch ein paar Tränen hervorzupressen.

»Dabei habe ich so lange gesucht, um genau das Richtige für dich zu finden«, seufze ich.

»Ina hat mein Geschenk vergessen«, sagt Mathilde zu Regine, die auf einmal neben ihr aufgetaucht ist.

Regine mustert mich wie eine Bakterie, deren einziges Ziel es ist, jeden auf dem Fest anzustecken.

»Soll ich noch mal heimgehen und es holen?«, frage ich kleinlaut.

Ich weiß nicht, warum ich das vorschlage. Wenn sie Ja sagt, habe ich ein echtes Problem. Was genau soll denn dieses fabelhafte Geschenk sein, für das ich so irre viel Zeit aufgewendet habe? Unbewusst balle ich die Hände zu Fäusten. Bitte, bitte, mach, dass ich nicht nach Hause muss, um etwas zu holen, was es gar nicht gibt. Lass mich mit Markus auf dem Fest bleiben.

Mathilde sieht mich an. Auf einem Tisch direkt bei der Terrassentür liegt ein Haufen mit Geschenken. Sie braucht unmöglich noch mehr.

»Jeder kann mal was vergessen.«

Es ist Mathildes Mutter, sie lächelt freundlich.

»Mathilde kann das Geschenk ja einfach irgendwann bei dir abholen. Mach dir keine Sorgen, Ina.«

Sie klopft mir aufmunternd auf den Rücken und ruft alle nach drinnen ins Wohnzimmer. Zeit für die Geschenke.

Das Wohnzimmer ist größer als unsere gesamte Wohnung. Ein gigantischer Tisch ist mit einer Tischdecke, Namensschildchen und Blumen gedeckt. In den Fenstern hängen silberne Ballons: *Mathilde 12 Jahre*, jeweils ein Ballon pro Buchstabe und Zahl. Ein großer Kuchen steht auf dem Küchentresen.

Mathilde lässt uns einen Kreis um sie bilden. Sie setzt sich in die Mitte. Dann nimmt sie ein Päckchen nach dem anderen hoch, liest laut vor, was auf den Karten steht, bevor sie Geschenk für Geschenk auspackt. Darin sind Täschchen und Schminke. Umschläge mit Geld. Hundert- und Zweihundertkronenscheine. Mathilde präsentiert stolz, was sie alles bekommen hat, und bedankt sich bei jedem. Ihr Vater sammelt die Geldscheine ein, damit sie nicht im Haufen aus Geschenkpapier verloren gehen.

Dann klatscht Mathildes Mutter in die Hände und sagt, dass wir uns jetzt an den Tisch setzen sollen.

»Wer möchte Pizza?«, trällert sie.

Und plötzlich, während alle umherschwirren und ihren Namen auf den Schildchen suchen, steht er da. In blauen Shorts und einem weißen T-Shirt. Die braunen, supersüßen Augen lächeln, und ich spüre ein Kribbeln im Bauch oder weiter oben beim Herzen. Er beachtet mich nicht, doch er ist hier, im selben Raum wie ich.

Markus umarmt Mathilde, und dann setzen sie sich nebeneinander ans Kopfende des Tischs, weit weg von mir. Ich habe den Platz ganz außen. Neben Johanne. Aber wenigstens habe ich einen Platz.

Vilmer dagegen steht verloren neben dem Tisch. Keiner hat daran gedacht, ein Namensschild für jemanden vorzubereiten, der erst seit zwei Stunden in der Klasse ist. Mathildes Mutter bringt schnell noch ein Glas und einen Teller und entschuldigt sich mindestens vier Mal bei ihm.

Es ist nicht einfach, Pizza zu essen, sich mit Johanne zu unterhalten und gleichzeitig Markus zu beobachten. Zum Glück ist Johanne eine von denen, die gerne reden. Wenn ich mich nur darauf konzentriere, in regelmäßigen Abständen Ja und Nein und Echt und Wow zu sagen, reicht es eigentlich schon.

Markus rollt die Pizzastücke zusammen und kaut ausgiebig. Er wischt sich mit der Serviette über den Mund, unterhält sich mit seinen Sitznachbarn und lacht. Man kann unmöglich hören, worüber sie sprechen, aber was Mathilde sagt, ist ganz offensichtlich witzig. Er scheint sie auch ziemlich süß zu finden mit ihren Locken und dem lila Kleid, jedenfalls lehnt er sich mehrmals zu ihr rüber.

Johanne erzählt von einer Fischerhütte auf den Lofoten und dass sie zum ersten Mal Kanu fahren wird. Es ist total uninteressant, aber ich lächle trotzdem. Für den Fall, dass Markus plötzlich zu mir rübersieht. Was er nicht tut.

Vilmer sitzt mir genau gegenüber. Er scheint Spaß zu haben. Erzählt davon, wie er und sein Vater angeln waren, damit will er wohl an Johannes Geschichte von der Fischerhütte anknüpfen.

»Vierzehn Flundern«, sagt er zufrieden und führt aus, wie sein Vater die Wette verlor und mit all seinen Kleidern ins Wasser springen musste.

Am anderen Ende des Tischs scheinen sie sich prächtig zu amüsieren, ich würde alles dafür geben, bei ihnen sitzen zu können. Aber ich hocke hier fest. Weit weg, ganz unten. Ich brauche Freunde, die mich hochziehen, keine Leute mit Flundergeschichten und einer Vorliebe für Fischerhütten. Irgendetwas muss passieren.

Mathilde macht ein Selfie mit Markus. Ich kriege keinen Happen mehr runter. In unserer Ecke wird es still. Nur Vilmer lacht immer noch über die Angelgeschichte und schiebt sich ein weiteres Stück Pizza in den Mund.

Jetzt bin ich schon seit einer Stunde und fünfundvierzig Minuten hier, ohne ein einziges Wort mit Markus gesprochen zu haben. Ich habe ein Geschenk erfunden und versucht, mich für Flundern und die Lofoten zu interessieren. Aber er hat mich nicht mal bemerkt.

Ich schaue immer wieder auf die Uhr. Obwohl die Sommerferien viel zu viele Stunden und Minuten ohne Markus bedeuten, bin ich froh, als es schließlich nur noch zwanzig Minuten bis zum Ende des Festes sind.

»Hast du inzwischen rausgefunden, wohin genau du fährst?«, fragt Regine auf einmal, nachdem wir uns alle für den Rest der Feier auf das riesige Sofa gesetzt haben.

»Oder fährst du immer noch in den *Süden*?«

Das letzte Wort betont sie ganz besonders und schaut dabei kichernd zu Mathilde.

Mehrere andere hören aufmerksam zu. Es hören immer mehrere Leute zu, wenn Regine oder Mathilde reden.

»Mama war heute bei einem Kurs«, antworte ich,

und es ist offensichtlich, dass niemand versteht, was ich damit sagen will. »Deshalb konnte ich sie nicht fragen.«

Mathilde und Regine lachen wieder. Ein leises, irritierendes Lachen.

Ich habe während des Geburtstags hauptsächlich geschwiegen, aber jetzt fange ich an zu plappern. Erzähle von den Swimmingpools und dem Apartment, in dem wir wohnen werden – oder besser gesagt von dem Bungalow. Er liegt direkt am Strand. Einem langen weißen Sandstrand voller Palmen.

»Es gibt megacoole Wasserrutschen«, sage ich. »Und einen Spa-Bereich und tausend Geschäfte in der Nähe. Wir werden bestimmt ziemlich viel shoppen.«

Jetzt schauen fast alle zu mir. Auch Markus.

»Zum Glück haben wir all-inclusive«, erzähle ich weiter, »man braucht sich also null zu stressen, man kann einfach den ganzen Tag lang essen, so viel man will. Aber wir gehen natürlich auch ins Restaurant zwischendurch, wenn es uns im Hotel zu langweilig wird.«

Ich lächle zufrieden.

»Boah, ich will nicht wissen, wie braun ich werde«, prahle ich. »Wir sind da ja viele Wochen lang. Fünf oder sechs, glaube ich. Einfach nur zum Chillen. Morgen früh fahren wir los.«

Mathilde flüstert Regine etwas ins Ohr.

Regine grinst. »Denk dran, Bilder zu schicken«, sagt sie.

Ich schlucke. Nicke.

»Wir sind echt gespannt«, sagt Mathilde.

Ich nicke noch mal. Schaue auf den Boden. Höre, wie Mathilde alle dazu auffordert, jede Menge tolle Urlaubsbilder zu posten. In unserer Klassengruppe, damit alle sie sehen können.

Ich spüre ein Pochen hinter den Schläfen. Jetzt habe ich ein neues Problem. Könnte ich mein Handy zu Hause vergessen? Das würde erklären, wieso ich wochenlang im Südenurlaub bin, ohne ein einziges Foto zu machen.

Zum Glück werden wir von Mathildes Mutter unterbrochen.

»So, jetzt müssen wir leider zum Ende kommen«, sagt sie. »Vielen Dank, dass ihr alle da wart, und schöne Ferien!«

Mathilde stellt sich an der Haustür auf, um jeden zum Abschied zu umarmen. Sie bedankt sich für die tollen Geschenke. Ihre Eltern stehen hinter ihr und lächeln. Ich drücke sie hastig, sage kein Wort über das Geschenk, das ich leider vergessen habe.

Markus ist der Letzte in der Reihe. Ich gehe, so langsam ich nur kann, drehe mich bei jedem dritten Schritt um, um zu schauen, ob er nicht bald aus dem

Haus kommt. Und als ich schon fast beim Gartentor bin, sehe ich es. Mathilde gibt Markus einen Kuss auf die Backe.

Ich bin zu achtundneunzig Prozent sicher, dass es ein Kuss war.

Die Sommerferien hätten eindeutig besser anfangen können. Zum Beispiel hätte statt Mathilde ich diejenige sein können, die Markus auf die Backe küsst. Er hätte nach dem Fest mit mir nach Hause laufen können. Vielleicht nicht ganz bis nach Tyllebakken, aber wenigstens bis zur Kreuzung am Laden. Dann hätte ich den Rest des Wegs allein zurücklegen können. Über die Straße, durchs Tor und in den Hinterhof. Zu Aufgang A. Und dort, bevor ich in den dritten Stock hochgegangen wäre, hätte ich mein Handy nehmen und ihm eine Nachricht schicken können, oder auch nur ein Herz. Oder so was in der Art eben. Und vielleicht hätte Markus im Laufe der siebenundsiebzigtausendstündigen Sommerferien irgendwann mal Zeit gehabt, sich mit mir zu treffen. Ein Eis zu essen. Oder an der Badebucht abzuhängen. Oder eine Fahrradtour zu machen. Auch wenn er nach Spanien und Sørland und London fährt.

Als ich die Haustür aufschließe, sitzt Mama im Wohnzimmer. Sie steht auf, schaltet den Fernseher aus und kommt mir im Flur entgegen. Sie fährt sich durch die Haare und unterdrückt ein Gähnen. Sie trägt einen fleckigen Jogginganzug, dazu hat sie ein Paar blaue Schlappen an.

»War's schön?«, fragt sie mit leiser, müder Stimme.

»Ja«, lüge ich und lasse mich umarmen.

»Gegessen hast du ja bestimmt?«, fragt Mama.

Ich nicke. Nach der ganzen Sache eben habe ich keinen großen Appetit.

»Ich werde heute früh ins Bett gehen«, sagt Mama.

Als ob das eine Neuigkeit wäre. Wieso muss sie mich jeden Abend darüber informieren?

»Es ist Freitag«, erwidere ich.

Mama nickt. Lehnt sich gegen den Türrahmen.

»Aber ich war doch heute beim Kurs«, sagt sie. »Und das war wirklich wahnsinnig anstrengend.«

Ich würde ihr gern sagen, dass es ganz normal ist, als Erwachsener einen Job zu haben. Dass andere Leute immer früh aufstehen und arbeiten gehen, Abendessen kochen und die Nachrichten sehen. Dass sie enge Hosen tragen und ihre Haare zu Pferdeschwänzen binden und wissen, wie die Freunde ihrer Kinder heißen. Dass sie die ganze Klasse zum Geburtstag einladen. Aber dafür fehlt mir gerade die Energie.

»Gibt's noch irgendwas Süßes?«, frage ich, obwohl ich mich auf dem Fest schon mit Kuchen und Knabberzeug vollgestopft habe.

»Nein«, sagt Mama. »Ich bin nicht dazu gekommen, einkaufen zu gehen. Ich war doch beim Kurs, weißt du?«

Ich verdrehe die Augen, obwohl ich weiß, wie traurig sie das macht. Aber dieser *Kurs* geht mir allmählich auf die Nerven.

»Morgen machen wir's uns gemütlich«, sagt Mama. »Da muss ich nicht zum Kurs.«

Es ist echt nicht zu fassen. Als ob dieser Kurs so wichtig wäre. Was lernt man denn da? Italienisch? Stricken? Tango tanzen? Ich kann mir keinen einzigen Kurs vorstellen, der zu Mama passen würde. Abgesehen vielleicht von einem Kurs im Muttersein.

»Was ist das eigentlich für ein Kurs?«, frage ich.

»Puh«, antwortet Mama. »Komm, setz dich mal, Ina.«

Sie schlurft in ihren Schlappen zum Sofa. Ich lasse mich neben sie plumpsen, betrachte die tiefen Furchen auf der Stirn, die farblosen Lippen, das trockene Haar. Was ist denn jetzt los? Mama macht ein ernstes Gesicht. Ernst wie »Wir müssen uns mal unterhalten«. Sie holt tief Luft und atmet langsam wieder aus, bevor sie zu sprechen beginnt.

»Es ist ein Kurs, an dem ich teilnehmen muss. Um

zu versuchen, einen Job zu kriegen. Aber ich bin ja eigentlich nicht fit genug, das merke ich, deshalb wird es wirklich anstrengend werden.«

Ich denke wieder an ganz normale Erwachsene. Die arbeiten gehen *und* Kurse besuchen.

»Und was außerdem ein bisschen blöd ist«, fährt Mama fort, »das habe ich heute erst erfahren ... dieser Kurs dauert sechs Wochen.«

»Sechs Wochen?«, rufe ich.

Mama nickt.

»Und das findest du *ein bisschen* blöd?«

»Ich habe gesagt, dass ich ein Kind habe und der Kurs genau in die Sommerferien fällt. Aber es geht nicht anders, ich habe es schon so oft aufgeschoben. Sonst haben wir kein Geld.« Mama blinzelt hektisch.

Was meint sie damit? *Sonst* haben wir kein Geld.

»Das wird vielleicht ein bisschen langweilig für dich«, sagt sie und wirft mir einen unsicheren Blick zu.

Vor einer halben Stunde dachte ich, die Sommerferien könnten nicht schlimmer werden. Anscheinend habe ich mich geirrt. Sie können definitiv schlimmer werden.

»Aber ich habe mit Oma vereinbart«, sagt Mama, »dass du ab und zu bei ihr vorbeischaust oder sie wenigstens anrufst. Damit du das Gefühl hast, einen Erwachsenen in der Nähe zu haben.«

In der Nähe? Es dauert mehr als zwanzig Minuten mit dem Fahrrad bis zu Oma, wenn man schnell fährt. Und was soll ich da bitte schön machen? Zeitschriften lesen und fernsehen und stricken?

Ich schweige.

»Es sind bestimmt auch viele andere zu Hause.«

Mama peilt echt gar nichts. Sie sollte wissen, wie die Leute in meiner Klasse ihre Ferien verbringen.

»Maria zum Beispiel. Mit ihr kannst du dich doch treffen?«

Ich starre auf den Boden.

»Und dann gibt es ja viele schöne Plätze in der Nähe, wie die Badebucht, wo man mit dem Fahrrad hinfahren kann.«

Sie seufzt.

»Ja, hätte ich das alles etwas früher gewusst, hätte ich dich ja für ein Feriencamp oder so anmelden können. Das ist bestimmt toll, und außerdem kostet es nichts.«

Kein Laut kommt aus meinem Mund.

»Wir müssen halt das Beste daraus machen«, sagt Mama schwach. »Und dann unternehmen wir nachmittags was Schönes zusammen.«

Ich habe keine Lust, ihr zu antworten. Ich weiß, dass sie lügt. Wenn sie vom Kurs nach Hause kommt, wird sie direkt ins Bett gehen. Sie wird zu rein gar nichts die Kraft haben.

»Ich gebe mir wirklich Mühe«, sagt Mama sehr leise. Das sagt sie immer, um sich selbst zu trösten. Als ob Muttersein so dermaßen schwer wäre, dass es nur die wenigsten gut hinkriegen.

Jetzt schaue ich ihr ins Gesicht und stehe vom Sofa auf. Ich hasse diesen Kurs. Ich hasse die Sommerferien. Ich hasse Markus. Und Mathilde. Und Urlaubspläne.

»Wohin willst du?«, fragt Mama beunruhigt.

Es pocht und brennt und sticht – im Bauch, im Kopf. Am liebsten würde ich das Fenster aufreißen und all unsere Sachen nach draußen schmeißen. In den Hinterhof. Das Sofa, die Vorhänge, die vertrockneten Pflanzen auf der Fensterbank, das Foto von mir und Mama an der Wand, die Dose im Küchenschrank mit den Zweikronenstücken, die Stühle, die Tischdecke, Mama. Alles.

»IN DEN SÜDEN!«, schreie ich und laufe aus dem Wohnzimmer, durch den Flur. Reiße die Tür zu meinem Zimmer auf und knalle sie so fest zu, dass die Wand bebt. Werfe mich aufs Bett und presse mein Gesicht in die Decke.

»In den Süden«, schluchze ich ins Laken, während sich mein Herz zusammenzieht.

Der Strand ist weiß und endlos. Das Meer blau, beinah türkis. Eine sanfte Brise sorgt für angenehme Kühle. Streicht vorsichtig über meine warme, gebräunte Haut, während ich in der Sonne liege. Der Klang von Vogelgezwitscher und spielenden Kindern. Das Rauschen der Wellen. Sommerliche Musik von der Strandbar. Vor dem Mittagessen kann ich noch mal ins Wasser, denke ich. Und ein Eis essen. Ich habe jede Menge Zeit, das ist ja das Schöne. Ich denke an absolut gar nichts. Fürchte mich vor nichts. Freue mich auf absolut alles. Neben meiner Liege steht ein süßer rosa Cocktail mit einem Strohhalm, der so lang ist, dass ich mich nicht mal aufzurichten brauche. Ein gelbes Sonnenschirmchen schmückt das Glas. Es gibt sieben Swimmingpools. Mehrere Wasserrutschen. Heiß beliebt bei den Kleinsten ist das Becken mit dem Piratenschiff. Im Relaxbecken herrscht eine ruhigere, entspanntere Atmosphäre. Die Bungalows sind geschmackvoll eingerichtet und haben Meerblick. Bieten alles, was man sich für seinen Traumurlaub nur wünschen kann. So steht es hier.

Die Bilder sehen toll aus. Hell und sommerlich, man spürt richtig die Sonne und das Meer und den Sand, wenn man sie bloß anschaut. Jedenfalls, wenn man lange schaut. So wie ich.

In den ersten Tagen der Sommerferien herrscht eine Hitzewelle. Glühende Sonne und Temperaturrekorde im ganzen Land. Mindestens achtzig Grad in der Wohnung. Ich traue mich nicht, die Fenster zur Straße hin aufzumachen, falls irgendjemand aus der Klasse zufällig vorbeilaufen sollte und sich wundert, wieso wir lüften, während wir doch im Süden sind. Mit den Fenstern zum Hinterhof brauche ich es dagegen nicht so genau zu nehmen. Ich reiße sie jeden Tag weit auf, während ich allein zu Hause bin, aber die Luft steht trotzdem in der Wohnung. Da sitze ich also und schwitze wie eine wahre Südentouristin.

Jeden Morgen, nachdem Mama zu ihrem Kurs aufgebrochen ist, rufe ich Oma an. Sage, dass man bei dieser Hitze nur eins tun kann: zur Badebucht fahren und dort so lange abhängen, bis Mama heimkommt. Ich schaue lieber wann anders vorbei, wenn es nicht mehr ganz so warm ist, sage ich und versuche, fröhlich zu klingen.

»Ich kann gut verstehen, dass du mit deinen Freunden

zusammen sein willst«, sagt Oma. »In meiner Kindheit habe ich den Sommer immer auf dem Land verbracht, und da sind wir von morgens bis abends nur draußen herumgeschwirrt. Die Erwachsenen hatten keine Zeit, auf uns aufzupassen.«
Oma lacht ins Telefon.
»Viel Spaß«, sagt sie.
Und dann legen wir auf.

Ich bin fast ununterbrochen im Süden. Suche stundenlang nach dem perfekten Ort für Mama und mich. Lege Kriterien fest. Swimmingpool. Balkon. Meerblick. Allinclusive. Wasserrutschen. Sortiere nach Preis und wähle das allerteuerste Hotel. Mit den meisten Sternen. *Blue Lagoon Deluxe.* Wir haben die Suite, die direkt zum Strand geht, mit eigenem Swimmingpool auf der Terrasse. Falls wir keine Lust mehr haben, mit den anderen zu baden. Der Mann hinter der Rezeption sieht nett aus. Die Frau an der Strandbar lächelt in ihrem rosa T-Shirt, während sie ein Glas voller Schirmchen und Strohhalme hochhält. Im Spa-Bereich arbeiten zwei Frauen mit langen braunen Haaren und Make-up im Gesicht. Sie lächeln auch. Alle lächeln im Süden.

Sobald Mama nachmittags nach Hause kommt, zieht sie ihren Jogginganzug an. Sie sagt, der Kurs sei so furchtbar anstrengend, dass sie zu nichts mehr Energie habe. Jeden Tag stellt sie mir dieselben Fragen, bevor sie sich hinlegen muss.

»Hattest du einen schönen Tag? Warst du draußen?« Ich sage Ja, obwohl es nicht stimmt. Mama freut sich so, wenn sie hört, dass ich etwas unternommen habe. Schließlich tut man das in den Sommerferien. Dann stelle ich meine zwei Fragen.

»War der Kurs gut? Hast du was gelernt?«
Mama antwortet auf beides mit Nein, und damit ist das Gespräch beendet.

Abends schieben wir eine Pizza in den Ofen, und immer wieder redet Mama von Garnelen. Sie hat solche Lust auf Garnelen. Sie träumt von Garnelen. Hat Pläne, was sie alles mit Garnelen kochen will. Sobald sie nur ein kleines bisschen Geld übrig hat, um ordentlich einkaufen zu gehen. Schließlich isst man das im Sommer. Garnelen mit Weißbrot. Und man trinkt Weißwein. Auf einem Felsen oder auf der Veranda oder auf einem Boot.

»Man sitzt ja nicht in der Wohnung und isst Tiefkühlpizza«, sagt Mama niedergeschlagen in ihrem Jogginganzug.

Ich sage, dass Pizza super ist. Meinetwegen brauchen wir keine Garnelen.

»Ach, mein Schatz«, seufzt Mama mit dem Mund voller Pizza. »Dieses Jahr ist nicht gerade ein Traumsommer.«

Sie schaut aus dem Fenster auf den grauen Hinterhof des Tyllebakken Bauvereins.

»Da helfen Garnelen wohl auch nicht«, murmelt sie.

Tyllebakken ist eine hässliche Wohnanlage. Im Hinterhof wächst ein schmaler Streifen Gras, der Rest ist Asphalt. In der Mitte ist ein Bereich mit Wäschegestellen, wo kein Mensch etwas aufhängt. Direkt daneben stehen die Mülltonnen. Grüne Plastikcontainer, die oft so sehr überquellen, dass die Deckel nicht richtig schließen. Morgens liegen Essensreste und Papier und Plastiktüten, in die die Vögel Löcher gehackt haben, rundherum verteilt auf dem Boden. Bei den Wäschegestellen gibt es auch einen Sandkasten voller Laub, der nach Katzenpisse stinkt. Außerdem ein Klettergerüst, zwei Schaukeln und eine Wippe. Die Geräte sind verrostet und knirschen, wenn man sie benutzt. Was zum Glück nicht oft vorkommt, obwohl hier jede Menge Kinder wohnen.

Die Betonbauten sind gelb gestrichen. An vielen Stellen ist die Farbe abgeblättert, sodass man den grauen Zement darunter sehen kann. Jedes Gebäude hat vier Stockwerke. Im Hinterhof führen Türen zu den verschiedenen Aufgängen. Es fängt bei A an, wo Mama und ich wohnen, und geht weiter in alphabetischer Reihenfolge. Bis zum J. Es sind viele Türen. Zehn, um genau zu sein.

Unser Aufgang ist grün, darum ist es bei uns immer dunkel. Und irgendwas stimmt nicht mit der Lampe an der Decke, denn das Licht flackert andauernd. Dunkel, hell, dunkel, hell.

»Wie lange werden wir hier wohnen bleiben?«, habe ich Mama gefragt, als wir einzogen.

Ich mochte unsere alte Wohnung lieber. Da hatten wir einen Balkon. Und Aussicht auf einen Park. Jetzt gucken wir von der Küche und meinem Zimmer aus auf den Hinterhof. Und vom Wohnzimmer auf die Straße und die Tankstelle. Die rund um die Uhr geöffnet hat. Und gut besucht ist.

»Ich weiß nicht so genau«, sagte Mama. »Aber eine Weile wahrscheinlich schon.«

Am ersten Tag in der neuen Klasse machte ich einen Fehler. Vigdis bat mich zu erzählen, wie ich heiße, wo ich wohne und was meine Hobbys sind. Also sagte ich meinen Namen und übersprang die Frage nach den Hobbys, weil ich nicht richtig wusste, was ich sagen sollte. Stattdessen erzählte ich, ich sei in den Trostevejen 30 gezogen, und jemand aus der Klasse, ich glaube, es war Regine, fragte, ob das nicht zu Tyllebakken gehöre. Ich sagte Ja. Weil ich es nicht besser wusste. Erst hinterher wurde mir klar, dass man niemals Tyllebakken antworten darf, wenn jemand fragt. Mehrere in der Klasse kicherten, und dann hörte ich es. Zum allerersten Mal. Den Spitznamen meines neuen Zuhauses. Güllebakken.

Seitdem behaupte ich immer, ich würde in Solvangtoppen wohnen. Das liegt direkt hinter Tyllebakken, es ist also fast nicht gelogen. In Solvangtoppen gibt es schöne Häuser mit Kieswegen und Gärten und Garagen. Spielplätze mit neuen Klettergerüsten und Schaukeln, die nicht knirschen.

Der Name Güllebakken passt zu Tyllebakken. Jetzt habe ich hier einen Herbst und Winter und einen Frühling und bald auch einen Sommer gewohnt, und es ist zu jeder Jahreszeit gleich hässlich. Auf dem Schild mit der Aufschrift *Willkommen im Tyllebakken Bauverein* hat jemand die ersten beiden Buchstaben durchgestrichen und *Gü* hingesprayt. Mit schwarzem Graffiti. Keiner hat sich die Mühe gemacht, es wegzuwischen.

Es ist langweilig, in Güllebakken im Südenurlaub zu sein. Denn genau das bin ich. Ich kann nicht nach draußen, für den Fall, dass ich jemanden aus der Klasse treffe. Also muss ich den ganzen Tag lang drinnen hocken. Wie eine Gefangene.

Die Sommerferien sind vier Millionen sechshundertfünfundsechzigtausendsechshundert Sekunden lang. Fünfundzwanzig davon habe ich benutzt, um diese Zahl auszurechnen. Wie viele Sekunden ich auf YouTube verbracht habe, weiß ich nicht, aber ich habe bestimmt zweihundertfünfundachtzig Clips von Leuten gesehen, die Schleim herstellen. Schade, dass ich im Süden bin und nicht zum Supermarkt kann, um Linsenwasser und Rasierschaum zu kaufen.

Ich google *Gefangener + eigenes Zuhause* und lese Geschichten von Leuten, die im selben Boot sitzen wie ich. Von Straftätern, die eine Fußfessel tragen und ihr Haus nicht verlassen dürfen. Von einer deprimierten Mutter mit einem Baby, die sich daheim eingesperrt fühlt und nicht die Kraft aufbringt, mit dem Kind nach draußen zu gehen. Von einem Dichter, der seine Wohnung dreißig Jahre lang nicht verlassen hat. Wir sind viele, die auf unterschiedliche Weise in ihren eigenen vier Wänden eingeschlossen sind. Ich erfinde Geschichten darüber, warum ich gefangen bin. Es fühlt sich gut an, ein bisschen zu lügen, wenn die Wahrheit so peinlich ist wie in meinem Fall.

Davon abgesehen, dass ich eine Schleimexpertin geworden bin, habe ich sehr viel Zeit auf der Seite des *Blue Lagoon Deluxe* verbracht. Ich habe sämtlichen Leuten auf den Bildern Namen gegeben, es ist fast so, als ob ich sie kennen würde. Monica und Eliza im Spa-Bereich. Dordi mit der hohen Kochmütze. Jonathan und Aleksandra von der Rezeption. Leandra im Kids Club und Margarita mit den Schirmchendrinks. Das hat ein paar Tausend Sekunden gedauert. Es braucht Zeit, sich gute Namen auszudenken.

Ich verbringe sehr viel Zeit mit Zählen. Dabei ist es eigentlich sinnlos zu wissen, wie viele Gabeln in der Schublade liegen. Wie viele Unterhosen ich habe. Wie viele Autos im Laufe eines Vormittags an der Tankstelle halten. Wie viele Bilder in der Klassengruppe gepostet werden.

Mathilde postet Bilder von ihrem Resort in Portugal. Sie ist schon ultrabraun und lächelt in die Kamera, die Haare wehen im Wind. Regine teilt Fotos aus Paris, sie posiert mit großen Einkaufstüten in der Hand vor dem Eiffelturm und isst ein Eis. *Viel Spaß*, schreibt Mathilde. Julie postet Bilder aus Zypern. Der Strand ist weiß, das

Meer türkis, sie trägt einen Badeanzug und Sonnenbrille. Sie schreibt, dass es genial ist. Markus sitzt in einem großen Boot, er dürfte der Einzige auf der Welt sein, dem eine Rettungsweste steht. Mit geschlossenen Augen lässt er sich die Sonne ins Gesicht scheinen, er ist noch brauner, als er eh schon war. Johanne schickt Fotos aus der Fischerhütte auf den Lofoten. Sie hat nicht so viele Likes wie die anderen, keiner hat ihre Posts kommentiert.

Ich klicke mich stundenlang durch die Bilder. Es kommen ständig neue, mehrfach am Tag. Auf allen scheint die Sonne. Bei allen ist es genial. Keiner langweilt sich, keiner streitet oder hat schlechte Laune. Keine Wolken am Himmel. Und zum Glück hat noch keiner nach Fotos von meinem Südenurlaub gefragt.

Mir graut es jetzt schon davor, wenn die Schule wieder anfängt. Denn nach den Ferien sollen immer alle erzählen, wie toll es bei ihnen war.

Irgendwas muss passieren, denke ich. Das ist der schlimmste Südenurlaub, den ich je erlebt habe. Und ich war ja noch nicht mal wirklich im Süden.

Und dann passiert etwas.
Ich esse mit Mama in der Küche zu Abend. Sie sitzt mit untergeschlagenem Bein auf dem Stuhl und schlürft ihren Tee. Der Jogginganzug hat Flecken, sie lächelt müde.

»Ich habe mit Oma gesprochen. Sie sagt, du bist so viel unterwegs, dass du keine Zeit hast, sie zu besuchen.«

»Stimmt«, lüge ich.

Ich habe dreiundzwanzig Videos über Schleim gesehen, aber ich sage, ich sei an der Badebucht gewesen.

»Wie war das Wasser?«, fragt Mama.

»Kalt«, antworte ich kurz.

Ich brauche ja nicht unbedingt ins Detail zu gehen.

»Warst du allein da, oder …?«

»Nein«, lüge ich wieder. »Mit Maria.«

Mama lächelt. Es hört sich schön an, wie ich es erzähle. Wer würde schließlich nicht mit Maria zur Badebucht fahren wollen? Beste Freundinnen, den ganzen Tag am Strand.

»Du musst sie mal einladen«, sagt Mama. »Ich würde Maria gern kennenlernen.«

Ich nicke. Es pocht in der Brust. Direkt unter dem Herzen. Kribbelt.

»Vielleicht mag sie Garnelen«, sagt Mama.

Ich nicke wieder. »Ich kann sie ja mal fragen,« sage ich und lege die Hand auf mein Bein, das zu zittern begonnen hat.

»Das wäre schön«, sagt Mama träumerisch. »Ein richtiger Garnelenabend. Du und ich und Maria.«

Ich nicke zum dritten Mal. Versuche schnell, das Thema zu wechseln, um nicht länger über Maria reden zu müssen. Ich schaue Mama an.

»Wenn du dir aussuchen könntest, wohin du mit mir in den Urlaub fährst – wo würdest du hinfahren?«

Mama lächelt. Solche Fragen mag sie. Sie runzelt die Stirn, sieht aus, als ob sie angestrengt nachdenken würde.

»In den Süden«, sagt sie schließlich entschieden.

»In den Süden?«

»Ja. Irgendwohin, wo es Sonne gibt und Sand und Meer und wir an nichts denken müssten, sondern uns einfach nur entspannen könnten.«

Blue Lagoon Deluxe. Mama und ich in der großen Suite.

»Dir ist aber schon klar, dass der Süden kein Land ist«, ziehe ich sie auf.

Sie grinst.

»Du weißt, was ich meine, Ina. Kreta, Spanien, Portugal, Rhodos. Ganz egal, Hauptsache, in den Süden.«

Natürlich verstehe ich, was Mama meint. Keiner versteht es so gut wie ich.

Ich gehe gut gelaunt ins Bett. Mit Zahnpastageschmack im Mund und einem frischen Nachthemd. Mama sitzt im Wohnzimmer und guckt fern. Wir haben Chips gegessen und Limo getrunken, obwohl Dienstag ist. Mama hat bestimmt zwanzig Minuten lang darüber philosophiert, was sie machen würde, wenn sie zehn Millionen im Lotto gewinnen würde.

Der Himmel leuchtet rot. Als gelbrosa Ball versinkt die Sonne langsam hinter Aufgang F. Das Fenster steht einen Spaltbreit offen, und die warme Abendluft sickert in mein Zimmer.

Und da passiert es. Genau in dem Moment, als die Sonne hinter dem Hausdach verschwindet.

»Ina?«

Der Ruf kommt aus dem Hinterhof.

Ich erstarre. Halte den Atem an.

»Ina?«

Irgendwoher kenne ich die Stimme, kann sie aber nicht einordnen. Es klingt wie ein Junge.

»Hallo?«

Ich weiche rückwärts vom Fenster weg. Ducke mich. Bewege mich in gebückter Haltung zum Bett, obwohl es zum Verstecken längst zu spät ist.

»Ina?«

Es zieht in meinem Bauch. Sticht in der Brust. Ich schalte das Licht über meinem Bett aus, das einzige Licht, das ich anhatte.

Aber es wird nicht dunkel, es ist der hellste Monat des Jahres, man kann trotzdem alles erkennen. Geduckt schleiche ich zurück zum Fenster und schiele vorsichtig hinaus.

Da steht er und guckt zu meinem Fenster hoch, in einem blauen T-Shirt und mit lockigen Haaren.

Er hat mich gesehen! Ich hätte das Fenster zum Hinterhof nicht aufmachen dürfen. Wie konnte ich nur vergessen, dass er direkt gegenüber von mir eingezogen ist?

Vilmer. Der nervigste Nachbar der Welt. Jetzt weiß er, dass ich nicht im Süden bin.

Am nächsten Morgen wache ich nass geschwitzt auf. Ich habe mit geschlossenem Fenster geschlafen, und in meinem Zimmer herrscht eine Temperatur wie in der Sauna. Die Vorhänge habe ich zugezogen. Es soll den Anschein machen, als wäre ich nicht da, auch wenn ich ja schon aufgeflogen bin.

Eigentlich hatte ich vor, mich heute nach draußen zu schleichen und mit dem Fahrrad zu Oma zu fahren. Gestern habe ich einen ziemlich großen Strohhut in Mamas Schrank gefunden. Habe lange vor dem Spiegel gestanden und überlegt, ob ich ausreichend getarnt wäre, wenn ich ihn tief genug in die Stirn ziehen würde. Aber nach der Sache mit Vilmer lasse ich es besser nicht darauf ankommen. Also rufe ich Oma an und sage, dass ich zu Maria gehe.

»Ach, Inalein«, sagt Oma.

In ihrer Stimme schwingt Freude mit. Sie hat vollstes Verständnis dafür, dass ich mich lieber mit Maria als mit ihr treffe.

»Dieses Jahr ist ja nicht unbedingt ein Traumsommer für dich«, sagt sie und klingt genau wie Mama. Haben die zwei das zusammen einstudiert?

»Aber es ist wirklich schön, dass du so viel unterwegs bist. Du machst das Beste aus der Situation, das ist eine gute Eigenschaft, mein Schatz.«

Komisch, wie sie alle denken, mir ginge es so fantastisch. Ich scheine echt ganze Arbeit zu leisten, mit dem Lügen, meine ich. Was würde Oma sagen, wenn ich ihr die Wahrheit über mein angeblich so tolles Leben erzählen würde? Dass ich mein Leben nur erfinde? Sie ist froh, dass ich so viele Freunde habe, herumschwirre und beschäftigt bin, genau wie sie als Kind. Oma mag es, wenn die Dinge normal sind. Sie will nicht von traurigen Dingen reden. Als Mama müde wurde und ihren Job verlor und wir nach Tyllebakken ziehen mussten, war Oma total sauer, obwohl wir vorher viel weiter weg gewohnt haben. Sie kommt nur selten zu Besuch, und wenn sie es tut, weint Mama hinterher immer.

»Ich wünsch dir ganz viel Spaß«, sagt Oma und legt auf.

Am Abend steht Vilmer wieder im Hinterhof. Ich höre ihn meinen Namen zum Fenster hochrufen. Zum Fenster, das geschlossen ist. Ich sitze im Dunkeln auf dem Bett in meinem Zimmer. Ganz reglos, für den Fall, dass

Vilmer Superaugen hat und durch Wände sehen kann. Schweißtropfen bilden sich auf meiner Stirn, mein Top klebt am Rücken. Vier Mal ruft er meinen Namen. Dann wird es still. Ich bin gerade vom Bett aufgestanden, da höre ich ein neues Geräusch. Irgendetwas klickert mehrmals gegen meine Fensterscheibe. Ich kann gar nicht so schnell mitzählen. Vorsichtig ziehe ich den Vorhang ein Stück zur Seite, um durch den Spalt nach draußen schauen zu können. Vilmer holt weit aus, damit die kleinen Steinchen bis ganz nach oben in den dritten Stock fliegen. Es sieht komisch aus.

Nach einer Weile gibt er auf und geht zurück zu Aufgang F. Wenig später wird das Licht in einem der Fenster im dritten Stock angeschaltet, schräg gegenüber von mir. Ich beobachte Vilmer, wie er sich dort im Zimmer an den Schreibtisch setzt und auf den Computerbildschirm starrt. Einsam und allein. Genau wie ich.

In den nächsten Tagen lasse ich mein Fenster geschlossen und die Vorhänge zugezogen. Nur zur Sicherheit. Die Ferien waren ja eh schon versaut, aber jetzt ist alles noch viel schlimmer. Ich hocke in der brütend heißen Wohnung und hasse den Süden. Hasse mich selbst, weil ich gelogen habe. Wieso habe ich es nicht einfach wie Vilmer gemacht? Ich hätte ja nicht erwähnen brauchen, dass Mama pleite ist. Hätte einfach sagen können, dass wir es uns zu Hause gemütlich machen. So tun, als stünde das auf meiner Ferienwunschliste auf Platz eins.

Regine ist auf Kreta angekommen. Fast alle liken die Selfies vor dem riesigen Swimmingpool, die sie postet. Julie steht vor einer Wand voller lila Blumen und hält eine französische Flagge hoch. Auch ihr Bild wird von allen gelikt. Markus badet mit seinen Brüdern an einem Sandstrand in Spanien. Mathilde hat es mit einem Herz kommentiert. Vielleicht lassen mich die Hitze, die stickige Luft, die vertrockneten Pflanzen und der Anblick all dieser Fotos den Verstand verlieren, jedenfalls mache ich plötzlich etwas vollkommen Unkontrolliertes. Ich kopiere die Bilder vom *Blue Lagoon Deluxe*, wähle eines aus, auf dem der Swimmingpool in der strahlenden Sonne zu sehen ist, und öffne die Klassengruppe. *Relaxen am Pool*, schreibe ich. Und poste es. Bevor ich darüber nachdenken kann.

Mehrere Minuten lang geschieht gar nichts. Verkrampft halte ich mein Handy in der Hand und starre auf genau null Likes und null Kommentare. Bereue, was ich da gerade getan habe.

Aber dann kommen die Reaktionen. *Schöööön*, schreibt Johanne. *Genieß es*, schreibt Una. Teodor schickt eine Sonne. Mehrere liken mein Bild. Aber nicht Mathilde. Nicht Regine. Und nicht Markus.

Vilmer wirft weiter mit Steinchen, jeden Abend steht er vor meinem Fenster. Ich liege im Bett und zähle mit, wie viele Steinchen gegen die Scheibe klickern. Einmal sind es acht. Ein andermal sieben. Ich frage mich, was er sich dabei denkt, wieso er nicht damit aufhört. Ich hatte gleich den Verdacht, dass Vilmer ein paar entscheidende Antennen fehlen, jetzt habe ich die Bestätigung. Wenn er schließlich zurück ins Haus geht, beobachte ich ihn immer durch den Spalt in der Gardine. Sehe, wie das Licht in der Wohnung angeht. Seinen

Kopf hinter dem Fenster, die Locken. Ich schaue gern zu ihm rüber. Weiß nicht genau, warum eigentlich. Er sitzt am Schreibtisch, wahrscheinlich ist es sein Zimmer. Die Wände sind hellblau gestrichen, keine Bilder oder Poster. Es sieht aus, als ob er Computer spielt.

An diesem Abend zähle ich bis neun. Dann wird es still. Vorsichtig linse ich nach draußen. Er schaltet das Licht in seinem Zimmer an, stellt sich ans Fenster und guckt direkt zu mir rüber. Es ist schon nach elf. Im Bad brummt Mamas elektrische Zahnbürste. Und dann höre ich es plötzlich. Ein schwaches Piepsen meines Handys. Für einen Moment leuchtet das Display auf, strahlt wie der kalte Lichtkegel einer Taschenlampe in den Raum. Die Nachricht kommt von einer unbekannten Nummer. Sechs Wörter und ein Fragezeichen. *Was ist mit dem Süden passiert?*

A m nächsten Morgen wache ich früh auf. Höre, wie Mama Wasser aufsetzt und mit Gläsern hantiert, während im Radio eine Oper läuft. Ich checke mein Handy, um sicherzugehen, dass ich es nicht nur geträumt habe – aber die Nachricht ist immer noch da.

Mama sitzt am Küchentisch, nippt an ihrem Tee und kaut an einer Scheibe Brot mit Erdbeermarmelade.

»Hat er dich gestern noch erreicht?«, fragt sie, als ich in die Küche komme. »Wie hieß er noch mal?«

Ich starre sie an. Bestimmt sehe ich aus wie ein Alien, der erst vor ein paar Minuten auf der Erde gelandet ist und keine Ahnung hat, wie ihm geschieht.

»Da hat gestern ein Junge angerufen und nach deiner Nummer gefragt«, sagt Mama und lächelt mit Marmelade an den Zähnen. »Er kommt im Herbst in deine Klasse und wollte sich vorher schon mal mit dir bekannt machen.«

Vilmer. Hab ich mir doch gleich gedacht, dass die

Nachricht von ihm sein muss. Obwohl ich seinen Namen nicht finden konnte, als ich nach der Nummer gesucht habe.

»Er macht einen sehr netten Eindruck«, sagt Mama. »Ein richtig freundlicher, höflicher Junge.« Sie nimmt einen großen Bissen von ihrem Brot und fährt mit vollem Mund fort. »Ich weiß nicht mehr, wie er hieß. Es war irgendwas Ungewöhnliches.«
Ich sage den Namen nicht. Antworte nur, dass keiner angerufen hat. Dann wechsle ich schnell das Thema und erzähle von meinen Plänen für den Tag. Maria und ich wollen Fahrrad fahren.

Mama strahlt. Die perfekte Tochter, die das Beste aus einem nicht gerade perfekten Sommer macht.

»So, ich muss mich beeilen, sonst komme ich zu spät zum Kurs«, sagt sie und klingt zur Abwechslung mal beinahe fröhlich.

»Denk an den Helm!«, ruft Mama, während sie sich im Flur die Schuhe anzieht.

Ich lese die Nachricht acht Mal. Dann putze ich Zähne, kämme mir die Haare, binde mir einen Pferdeschwanz und betrachte mich im Spiegel. Und lese die Nachricht noch weitere fünf Mal. Ich weiß nicht, ob ich den kurzen Text nett oder unverschämt finden soll. *Was ist mit dem Süden passiert?* Ich habe keine Ahnung, was ich antworten soll. Natürlich könnte ich behaupten, Mama sei krank geworden oder dass der Flug wegen eines Sturms abgesagt wurde. Aber das wären nur noch mehr Lügen, über die ich den Überblick behalten müsste.

Also antworte ich einfach gar nicht.

Ich habe keine Lust, mich mit Vilmer anzufreunden. Will nicht zugeben, dass ich gelogen habe. Mir fällt keine einzige Sache ein, die ich gern mit ihm zusammen unternehmen würde. Er ist total langweilig. Überhaupt nicht mein Typ. Ich kann mir nicht vorstellen, dass wir auch nur *ein* gemeinsames Gesprächsthema hätten.

Ich gehe das Risiko ein und öffne das Fenster zur Tankstelle. Ich brauche Luft, um klar denken zu können, und das muss ich.

Anscheinend will er wirklich gern was mit mir machen. Sonst würde er wohl kaum den ganzen Aufwand betreiben, Steine gegen mein Fenster zu werfen und dann auch noch herauszufinden, wie Mama heißt, sie anzurufen, nach meiner Nummer zu fragen und mir eine merkwürdige Nachricht zu schicken. Ich bin schon fast beeindruckt von seinem Einsatz. Ich mache das Fenster wieder zu. Vielleicht könnten wir ja ein bisschen zusammen im Hinterhof abhängen, wo uns keiner sieht. Schließlich habe ich sonst niemanden. Außerdem ist es neun Tage her, seit ich zuletzt draußen war.

Abends brennt wie immer Licht in der Wohnung von Vilmer und seinem Vater. Ich weiß nicht, ob er Geschwister hat oder eine Mutter, die auch pleite ist, oder ein Haustier. Ich weiß gar nichts über ihn. Außer, dass er schon wieder unten im Hinterhof steht und meinen Namen ruft. Auch heute wirft er mit Steinchen. Still sitze ich in meinem Zimmer auf dem Bett und zähle das Klicken gegen die Scheibe. Spüre, wie sich meine Mundwinkel verziehen, zu einem Lächeln. Als das Klicken aufhört, gehe ich zum Fenster. Atme gegen den Stoff des Vorhangs. Schiebe ihn vorsichtig zur Seite.

Dort unten steht er. Reglos wie eine Statue. Ich stehe genauso versteinert am Fenster. Mein Herz klopft. Er schaut mich an. Ich schaue ihn an. Ich glaube nicht, dass ich lächle. Er trägt ein blaues T-Shirt. Die Haare sind verstrubbelt. Er lächelt auch nicht. Die Sekunden verstreichen. Ich zähle sie nicht. Stehe einfach nur da. Ertappt, ohne einen schützenden Vorhang, hinter dem ich mich verstecken könnte.

Dann hebe ich die linke Hand, wie ein Verkehrspolizist an der Kreuzung. Vilmer hebt die rechte. Er sieht aus wie ein Soldat, der vor dem König salutiert. Mir entschlüpft ein leises Lachen. Jetzt lächelt auch Vilmer. Er beginnt, mich mit einer Hand zu sich zu winken. Dann mit der anderen. Hüpft auf der Stelle. Zappelt. Es sieht total bescheuert aus. Wie ein merkwürdiger, unrhythmischer Tanz, als wäre er eine Aufziehpuppe.

Vilmer ist vielleicht der nervigste Nachbar der Welt, aber wenn man erst mal eine Zeit lang als Gefangener in seiner eigenen Wohnung gelebt hat, darf man keine großen Ansprüche stellen. Und irgendwie ist es schon witzig, wie er in Norwegens hässlichstem Hinterhof auf dem Asphalt herumspringt. Ich fische mein Handy aus der Tasche. Suche die Nachricht von der unbekannten Nummer, von dem Jungen, der da unten immer noch seinen Sommernachtstanz aufführt.

Und dann schicke ich eine Antwort. *Kein Süden*, schreibe ich und beobachte seine Reaktion durchs Fenster.

Er hört auf zu tanzen, holt sein Handy raus. Schaut zu mir hoch.

Es piepst.

Treffen wir uns morgen?, steht da auf meinem Display.

Vilmer wartet direkt vor der Tür, als ich am nächsten Morgen in den Hof komme.

»Da bist du ja!«, sagt er fröhlich, als hätte er die ersten zehn Tage der Sommerferien nur damit verbracht, hier auf mich zu warten.

Er hat dieselben Shorts an wie am letzten Schultag, die, die so uncool unter der Hüfte hängen. Darüber trägt er ein schwarzes, ausgewaschenes und viel zu großes T-Shirt, auf dem vier Männer mit langen Haaren und ein Totenkopf zu sehen sind.

»Das ist von meinem Vater«, erklärt Vilmer, weil ich ihm auf die Brust starre. »Er ist so ein Metal-Typ.«

Ich nicke. Als ob diese Information irgendwie aufschlussreich wäre. Vilmer scheint sich keine großen Gedanken um die Wahl seiner T-Shirts zu machen. Zoo oder Metal, quasi eins wie das andere. Plötzlich muss ich an Markus denken, der immer so perfekt angezogen ist, ganz anders als Vilmer.

»Sorry, dass ich so viele Steine gegen dein Fenster

geworfen habe«, sagt Vilmer. »Ich weiß eigentlich gar nicht, was ich mir dabei gedacht habe.« Er zuckt mit den Achseln. »Also, ich bin keiner von diesen Psychonachbarn, falls du das glaubst.« Beim letzten Satz verzieht er sein Gesicht zu einer Grimasse, versucht offenbar, creepy auszusehen. »Ich hab mich einfach gelangweilt.«

Die Sonne scheint ihm auf den Kopf, die Locken glänzen im Licht. Ich habe bis jetzt kein Wort gesagt. Weiß nicht, was ich sagen soll. Wieso habe ich bloß auf diese Nachricht geantwortet, wieso habe ich die Vorhänge zurückgezogen? Suche ich wirklich so verzweifelt nach einem Freund? Auf einmal bereue ich, dass ich nicht einfach in der heißen Wohnung geblieben bin. Da drinnen war es langweilig, aber wenigstens unkompliziert. Jetzt habe ich keine Ahnung, was mich erwartet.

Vilmer schaut zum leeren Sandkasten, zu den Wäschegestellen und den klapprigen Spielgeräten. Dann wieder zu mir. Seine Miene hellt sich auf, die Augen sind knallblau.

»Komm mit, ich zeig dir was.«

Ich folge Vilmer durch den Hinterhof. Ein Mann und eine Frau keifen sich an, ein kleiner Junge ist von seinem Dreirad gefallen und weint. Vilmer läuft mit schnellen, zielgerichteten Schritten vor mir her. Der hintere Teil des Hofs liegt im Schatten, die Sonne reicht hier nicht über die Hausdächer. Es riecht nach feuchtem Asphalt.

»Da«, sagt er und deutet auf eine kleine Treppe, die mir noch nie aufgefallen ist.

Sieben, acht Stufen führen nach unten und enden an einer Tür, die kaum zu sehen ist, wenn man nicht weiß, dass es sie gibt. Auf den letzten Stufen liegt verwelktes Laub. Die Wände sind mit Graffiti besprüht.

Vilmer geht vor.

»Komm, Ina«, sagt er.

Es klingt schön, wie er meinen Namen sagt. Als ob wir beste Freunde wären und gerade irgendwas Tolles unternehmen würden.

Vor der Tür bleibt er stehen und wartet auf mich. Ich nehme Stufe für Stufe, bis ich bei ihm bin. Hier ist nicht viel Platz, mein Arm berührt Vilmers T-Shirt. Ich spüre seinen Atem. Rieche den Duft seiner Locken.

Vilmer holt etwas aus seiner Hosentasche. Ein Werkzeug, irgendwas Spitzes aus Metall. Er drückt mit dem Oberkörper gegen die Tür und presst gleichzeitig das Werkzeug ins Schloss. Es macht klick. Dann öffnet sich die Tür.

»Willkommen in meinem Reich«, lächelt er und lässt mich zuerst eintreten.

Der Raum ist dunkel und riecht nach Keller. Feucht und muffig.

An der einen Wand steht ein Schreibtisch. Er war sicher mal weiß, aber die Farbe ist vergilbt und abgeblättert. Die oberste Schublade ist aufgezogen, ein paar Papiere gucken heraus. An der Seite klemmt eine metallene Lampe, der Schirm hängt schlapp und verdreht über der Tischplatte. Der dazugehörige Schreibtischstuhl hat nur noch drei Räder. Auf der anderen Seite des Zimmers steht ein Sofa mit einem niedrigen Tischchen davor. Es ist mit einer Art rotem Wollstoff bezogen, an ein paar Stellen quillt die Füllung heraus. Darauf liegt ein Kissen mit Stickereien, so wie alte Omas sie mögen. Auf dem Boden neben dem Schreibtisch steht ein großer Werkzeugkasten. Ein rostiger Gegenstand lugt daraus hervor. Von dem Zimmer gehen noch zwei Türen ab. Dunkelbraune Rahmen.

Ich schaue mich schweigend um. Was ist das für ein Ort?

Ein einsames kleines Fenster ist die einzige Lichtquelle. Dann schaltet Vilmer die Deckenlampe an und tritt in den Raum. Seine Schuhe machen ein komisches Geräusch. Als ob er auf etwas Klebriges treten würde.

»Hier unten war ich in der letzten Zeit ziemlich oft«, sagt er.

Ich antworte nicht. Vor ein paar Minuten hat Vilmer behauptet, er sei keiner von diesen Psychonachbarn, aber ich habe so meine Zweifel, ob das stimmt. Was hat er denn hier gemacht? Dieses dunkle Kellerloch ist ja wohl der Inbegriff der Gülle im Güllebakken Bauverein. Ich wüsste gern, wie es bei Vilmer daheim aussieht, wenn er sich lieber hier aufhält als zu Hause. Wie mies sind *seine* Sommerferien eigentlich?

Der schwarze T-Shirt-Rücken bewegt sich durch die Wohnung. Er öffnet eine der beiden Türen. Dahinter kommt ein kleiner Raum mit Klo und Waschbecken zum Vorschein.

»Alles funktioniert«, sagt er und dreht den Hahn auf.

Er erinnert mich an einen eifrigen Vertreter, der einem irgendeinen Dreck aufschwatzen will.

»Guck mal.«

Jetzt geht er zu der anderen Tür. Sie quietscht, als er sie öffnet. Er schaut in den Raum und schaltet das Licht an. Winkt mich zu sich.

Ganz hinten steht eine Küchenbank. Ein paar Gläser und ein Teller warten in der Spüle auf den Abwasch. Ein kleiner Kühlschrank brummt in der Ecke. Der Herd ist dreckig, als hätte jemand vor zwanzig Jahren Frikadellen gebraten und anschließend vergessen, die Platten sauber zu machen.

»Hier koche ich«, sagt Vilmer stolz.

Zwei leere Pizzaschachteln liegen in einer Ecke neben dem Herd. Speciale mit Hackbällchen. Er mag dieselbe Sorte wie ich. Mitten im Raum stehen ein kleiner Tisch und zwei Stühle. Sitzt er dort und isst, vollkommen allein?

»Er hieß Anton«, sagt Vilmer plötzlich. »Der, dem die Wohnung gehört hat. Anton Berntzen.«

Er kratzt sich am Kopf.

»Ich stelle gerade ein paar Nachforschungen an«, erklärt er. »Lese alte Papiere und so. Deshalb weiß ich, dass er in Tyllebakken Hausmeister war.«

Jetzt schaut er mich an.

»Aber ich habe den Verdacht, dass er nicht besonders gut in seinem Job war«, grinst er und geht zum Kühlschrank.

»Setz dich ruhig aufs Sofa«, sagt er und zeigt zum Wohnzimmer.

Das Sofa ist überraschend weich und bequem. Ich höre, wie Vilmer mit irgendwas in der Küche hantiert.

Vilmer, mit dem ich jetzt sozusagen befreundet bin. Zum Glück kann mich keiner sehen.

Er taucht im Türrahmen auf. Hält ein Tablett in den Händen, auf dem er zwei Gläser und eine Flasche Pepsi balanciert. In jedem der Gläser steckt ein Strohhalm, ein gelber und ein rosafarbener.

»Ta-taa«, sagt er und lächelt wie ein übertrieben freundlicher Kellner in einer trostlosen Poolbar.

Vilmer geht zu dem vergilbten Schreibtisch und zieht die oberste Schublade auf. Ein paar Blätter flattern wie in Zeitlupe zu Boden, er bückt sich und hebt sie auf.

»Ich habe einen Haufen Unterlagen von früher gefunden«, sagt er, zieht die ganze Schublade heraus und bringt sie zum Sofa, um mir den Inhalt zu zeigen.

»Das meiste ist so Hausmeisterkram. Anton hat Glühbirnen und Material bestellt.« Er hält mir ein Blatt hin. »Und dann hat er vergessen, dafür zu bezahlen.«

Es ist ein Brief von der Bank. *Wir bitten Sie freundlich darum, den Betrag umgehend zu bezahlen*, steht da in großen, fetten Buchstaben.

»Ich arbeite mich nach und nach durch den Stapel«, fährt Vilmer entschuldigend fort, als wäre ihm selbst klar, dass es ziemlich merkwürdig ist, seine Sommerferien mit dem Lesen alter Hausmeisterbriefe zu verbringen.

»Du glaubst gar nicht, wie viele Beschwerdebriefe darunter sind. Die Leute in Tyllebakken waren echt sauer auf Anton. Bei einigen ging der Strom nicht. Anton sollte die Treppe in Ordnung bringen. Grete Brattberg musste ins Krankenhaus, nachdem sie am Sicherheitskasten einen Stromschlag abgekriegt hatte.«

Vilmer balanciert die Schublade auf seinem Schoß und lehnt sich zu mir.

»Guck mal.«

Er deutet auf ein Blatt und liest vor, was darauf steht.

»Wir waren in all den Jahren sehr zufrieden mit Herrn Anton Berntzen. In der letzten Zeit aber ist unser sonst so freundlicher und pflichtbewusster Hausmeister faul, wenig entgegenkommend und nicht willens, seine Arbeit auszuführen. Sollte sich dies nicht bald ändern, sehen wir uns gezwungen, ihn darum zu bitten, von seiner Anstellung als Hausmeister des Tyllebakken Bauvereins zurückzutreten.«

Vilmer zieht die Augenbrauen hoch.

»Er hat wohl lieber auf dem Sofa gechillt«, sagt er und grinst. »Genau wie ich. Armer Anton, er tut mir leid.«

Vilmer holt eine neue Flasche Pepsi aus dem Kühlschrank.

Er erzählt, wie er diesen Ort entdeckt und die Tür aufgebrochen hat.

»Am Anfang sah es hier viel schlimmer aus«, sagt er.

»Aber ich hab sauber gemacht und ein paar Dinge repariert.«

Ich muss wieder an die Sache mit dem Psychonachbarn denken. Stelle mir vor, wie Vilmer nach Hause zu seinem Vater geht, Werkzeug holt und das Schloss aufknackt. Wie ein Dieb in die Wohnung einbricht und es sich auf dem Sofa gemütlich macht. Pepsi in den Kühlschrank stellt und Pizza in den Ofen schiebt. Den Kram des faulen Hausmeisters aufräumt.

»Ich bin einfach total neugierig«, erklärt Vilmer. »Und es ist halt echt ein bisschen langweilig, den ganzen Sommer über zu Hause zu sitzen.«

Seine Miene wird ernst, er schaut mich an, als würde er darauf warten, dass ich etwas sage. Ihm erzähle, wieso ich nicht im Süden bin.

Ich lenke das Thema schnell wieder auf Anton.

»Wie lange ist es her, dass er hier Hausmeister war?«, frage ich und ziehe die Schublade mit den Papieren auf meinen Schoß. Suche in dem Stapel nach der Datierung der Briefe. 1963. 1966.

»Was wohl aus ihm geworden ist?«

Ich greife nach einem Stapel und sehe plötzlich in einer Ecke der Schublade unter einigen Umschlägen etwas Goldenes glänzen.

»Krass, zeig mal«, sagt Vilmer. »Den hab ich noch gar nicht gesehen.«

Es ist ein Goldring. Klein und schmal, als wäre er für ein Kind. Vilmer nimmt ihn vorsichtig zwischen Daumen und Zeigefinger. Hält ihn ins Licht.

»Da ist was eingraviert«, sage ich und strecke die Hand aus.

Vilmer reicht mir den Ring.

»*Dein Anton*«, lese ich. »*Zur Verlobung, 16. August 1962.*«

Wir starren auf den Ring.

»Anton hatte eine Freundin«, sagt Vilmer erstaunt. Sein Mund weitet sich zu einem Lächeln.

»Aber scheinbar hat sie ihm den Verlobungsring zurückgegeben«, sage ich.

»Vielleicht hatte er deshalb keinen Bock mehr auf seinen Job«, seufzt Vilmer. »Jetzt hab ich noch mehr Mitleid mit ihm.«

Schweigend trinken wir unsere Pepsi. Vilmer hat sich den Verlobungsring von Antons Freundin angesteckt. Ich greife nach meinem Handy, um zu checken, ob Mama angerufen hat. Lasse es schnell wieder in der Tasche verschwinden, als Vilmers Blick auf mein Bildschirmfoto fällt. Es zeigt den Swimmingpool. Im *Blue Lagoon Deluxe*.

»Als wir bei Mathilde waren und du erzählt hast, dass du in den Süden fährst ...«, fängt Vilmer plötzlich an.

Mir wird heiß, und ich schaue weg. Habe keine Lust, darüber zu reden. Nicht jetzt. Ich schiebe die linke

Hand unter meinen Oberschenkel und kreuze die Finger.

»… da hab ich mich dermaßen wiedererkannt.«

Es sticht in meinem Bauch, ganz oben, direkt beim Herzen.

»Weil ich genau das Gleiche gemacht hab.«

Ich fühle seinen Blick auf mir, obwohl ich stur auf den Boden starre.

»Gelogen.«

Das Wort hängt in der Luft.

»Ich war letztes Jahr auf den Malediven«, sagt er und lacht. »Oder war es Malta? Ich weiß gar nicht mehr. Und es war genauso fantastisch wie der Südenurlaub, von dem du erzählt hast.«

Mein Blick wandert langsam nach oben, über Vilmers T-Shirt und weiter zu seinen Augen, hellblau und ernst. Lieb.

»Ich sag's keinem«, verspricht er und lächelt mich mit seinem schiefen Schneidezahn an.

In dieser Nacht träume ich von Markus. Er sitzt ganz dicht neben mir auf einem Sofa. Wir trinken Limonade mit Strohhalmen. Ich lehne mich gegen sein rotes T-Shirt, atme den Geruch von Sonnencreme und Waschpulver ein. Auf einmal wird das T-Shirt schwarz. Es ist Vilmers T-Shirt. Markus hat Locken und einen schiefen Schneidezahn. Er hält einen Goldring zwischen Daumen und Zeigefinger, fragt, ob wir uns verloben wollen. Es ist Vilmers Stimme. Plötzlich sitzen wir nebeneinander auf dem Sofa, während wir Limonade trinken.

Dann wache ich auf.

Mein Handy, das auf dem Nachttisch liegt, leuchtet auf. Ich erkenne die Nummer. *Wär cool, wenn du heute wieder kommst*, steht da. Dahinter grinsen drei Smileys mit Sonnenbrille.

Mama sitzt in der Küche. Sie hat Rührei gemacht und ist normal angezogen. Weißer Rock, lila Bluse. Die

Haare sehen frisch gekämmt aus. Aus dem Radio tönt fröhliche Musik, Mama summt die Melodie mit.

»Guten Morgen, Ina«, strahlt sie, als ich in die Küche komme.

Ich starre sie an. Andere finden vielleicht, Rührei und eine angezogene Mutter wären nichts Besonderes, auch wenn es erst halb acht ist. Aber für mich ist es ein Grund, sie anzustarren. Der Kurs zeigt anscheinend Wirkung, obwohl sie behauptet, dort nichts zu lernen.

»Hast du heute was vor, Ina?«

Ich schaue aus dem Fenster. Die Sonne scheint.

»Badebucht«, antworte ich kurz angebunden.

Mama lächelt immer noch.

»Mit Maria?«

»Mhm.« Ich nicke.

»Willst du sie nicht mal zu uns einladen?«, fragt Mama. Schon wieder. »Sie kann auch gern hier übernachten. Morgen würde zum Beispiel gut passen.«

Ich schaue Mama an. Ihre hellen Augen, ihr erwartungsvolles Lächeln. Vielleicht erträgt sie die Wahrheit, jetzt, wo sie ausnahmsweise einmal gut gelaunt ist.

Mama hebt die Augenbrauen, sie wartet auf eine Antwort. Ob Maria hier schlafen will. Meine beste Freundin. Die ich letzten Winter erfunden habe, weil Mama es so schade fand, dass ich keine Freunde in der neuen Klasse hatte. Wie soll ich jetzt wieder aus der

Nummer rauskommen? Maria ist praktisch, eigentlich würde ich sie gern noch eine Weile behalten. Außerdem will ich Mama nicht traurig machen, wo sie doch eh schon dauernd so niedergeschlagen ist.

Ich nehme mein Handy, tippe mit schnellen Bewegungen darauf herum, als würde ich eine Nachricht schicken.

Mama schaut mich gespannt an. Vielleicht wird sie durch den Kurs wacher.

Ich halte mein Handy abwartend in der Hand, tue so, als bekäme ich eine Antwort.

»Oh nein!«, rufe ich und setze eine betrübte Miene auf. »Maria ist krank.«

»Ach, wie schade«, sagt Mama tröstend. »Aber du kannst sie ja auch nächste Woche einladen. Zum Glück sind die Sommerferien noch lang.«

Da ich offiziell im Süden bin und sonst keinen zum Abhängen habe, kann ich mich genauso gut mit Vilmer treffen. Er ist cooler, als ich gedacht habe. Ziemlich witzig, um ehrlich zu sein. Echt seltsam, aber auf eine nette Weise. Außerdem ist es ja nur für jetzt, während der Ferien, danach werde ich nichts mehr mit ihm machen. Und es sieht uns zum Glück keiner zusammen, solange wir in Tyllebakken bleiben.

Um den anderen zu beweisen, dass ich immer noch

im Süden bin, poste ich ein Bild vom Strand vor dem *Blue Lagoon Deluxe.*

Den ganzen Tag im Wasser, schreibe ich und werfe noch ein Herz dazu.

Während ich auf die Reaktionen der anderen warte, kommentiere ich ein paar ihrer Bilder. Regine hat eine Fotoserie von sich selbst vor dem Meer hochgeladen, die untergehende Sonne im Hintergrund. Sie sieht echt hübsch aus in dem rosa Licht.

Tolles Bild, schreibe ich, als ob wir Freundinnen wären.

Wenige Sekunden später kommentiert sie mein Strandbild. *So schön!*

Mathilde schickt auch einen Kommentar: *Glückspilz.*

Es ist das erste Mal, dass jemand ein Foto von mir kommentiert. Auf einmal fühle ich mich federleicht. Ich schwebe die Treppe hinunter und in den Hinterhof.

Vilmer sitzt auf dem roten Sofa. Er spielt auf seinem Handy und merkt nicht, dass ich direkt neben ihm stehe und auf den Bildschirm schaue. Seine Daumen bewegen sich in einem irren Tempo, er steuert einen Typ, der irgendwelche anderen Typen in einem dunklen Keller abknallt.

»Hi«, sage ich nach einer Weile vorsichtig.

Vilmer zuckt zusammen.

»Mann, hast du mich erschreckt«, sagt er. »Jetzt bin ich tot.« Er legt das Handy weg und lächelt mich an.

Was ist das eigentlich für ein Ding mit seinen Klamotten? Heute steckt er in einem schlammgrünen T-Shirt mit der Aufschrift *Get a life* über der Brust.

»Du, ich hab ziemlich viel über den Süden nachgedacht«, sagt er.

Meine Brust zieht sich zusammen. Er hatte doch versprochen, es niemandem zu verraten. Dass ich gelogen habe. Wieso fängt er jetzt wieder damit an? Können wir nicht einfach über irgendwas anderes reden?

»Was hat diese Halldis noch mal gesagt?«

»Vigdis«, korrigiere ich ihn.

»Dass der Süden gar kein bestimmter Punkt auf der Karte ist, sondern wir das bloß so sagen, wenn wir einen Ort meinen, wo man sich entspannen und Spaß haben und chillen kann.«

Vilmer sieht mich eifrig an.

»Das Wort *Süden* bezeichnet ja eigentlich jeden Ort, der von uns aus gesehen weiter südlich liegt, oder? Das heißt, wenn man zum Beispiel von Oslo nach Kristiansand fährt, reist man quasi in den Süden.«

Ich erwidere nichts. Weiß nicht, worauf er hinauswill.

»Frøydis hat gesagt, man kann selbst entscheiden, wo der Süden ist.«

Er sieht mich an, als hätte er eine Riesenentdeckung gemacht.

»Also kann der Süden doch auch hier sein.«

»Hier?«, frage ich.

»Ja, hier in der Wohnung. Denn die liegt am südlichsten. Vom Hinterhof aus betrachtet, meine ich.«

Ich glaube, meine Lippen haben sich ein klein bisschen verzogen. Ein Muskel in meinem Mundwinkel zuckt.

»Wir können es doch einfach Süden *nennen*, oder nicht? Schließlich ist das hier ein Ort, an den man geht, um sich zu entspannen und Spaß zu haben und zu chillen. Jedenfalls tue *ich* das.«

Ich schaue mich um. In dem Fall wäre es die langweiligste Südenreise, von der ich je gehört habe, denn diese Kellerwohnung hat nicht die geringste Ähnlichkeit mit dem *Blue Lagoon Deluxe*.

Vilmer lächelt immer noch. Er erinnert mich schon wieder an einen eifrigen Verkäufer, der für irgendwas Bescheuertes Werbung macht.

»Win-win«, sagt er. »Du musst nach den Ferien in der Schule nicht mehr lügen, weil du ja sozusagen wirklich im Süden warst! Und ich kann behaupten, ich wäre auch noch in den Süden gefahren und gar nicht nur zu Hause gewesen.«

Kann es sein, dass ich ihn anlächle? Ich habe fast so das Gefühl.

»Es braucht doch keiner zu wissen, wo genau der *Süden* ist.« Er setzt das Wort mit den Fingern in Gänsefüßchen. »Oder?«

Jetzt lächle ich ganz sicher. Das ist ein echt bekloppter Vorschlag. So ziemlich der bekloppteste, den ich seit Langem gehört habe, um ehrlich zu sein. Und trotzdem gefällt er mir.

»Lust auf Pepsi?«, fragt er und geht zum Kühlschrank, bevor ich nicken kann.

Die Hitze von draußen dringt bis in die Kellerwohnung. Das kleine Fenster bei der Tür brutzelt in der Sonne. Die Sonnenstrahlen legen sich auf das Sofa, auf dem wir beide mit einem Glas kalter Pepsi sitzen.

Wir reden über den Süden und was wir alles dafür brauchen. Damit Antons alte Hausmeisterwohnung ihm möglichst nahekommt. Wir haben ziemlich viel zu tun, um es milde auszudrücken. Ich zeige Vilmer die Bilder auf dem Handy. Die Screenshots vom *Blue Lagoon Deluxe*, die ich gepostet habe. Vilmer ist nicht in der Klassengruppe, darum kennt er sie noch nicht.

»Hmm«, sagt er und studiert die Fotos – die Swimmingpools und die Wasserrutschen, den Mann mit der Kochmütze und den Sonnenuntergang über dem Strand, die aufgereihten Sonnenschirme, das türkisfarbene Meer.

Er holt ein Blatt Papier aus Antons altem Schreibtisch. Sucht zwischen den Sachen nach etwas zum

Schreiben. Rüttelt und zieht an der verschlossenen Schublade. Gibt auf und findet schließlich in Antons verstaubter Werkzeugkiste einen Bleistift. *Was wir im Süden brauchen*, notiert er ganz oben auf dem Blatt und steckt sich den Bleistift in den Mund.

»Swimmingpool«, sage ich.

Vilmer schreibt es auf.

»Sonnenschirme? Und Strand?«

Ich nicke.

»Spa-Bereich«, sage ich. »Und Kids Club. Auch wenn wir natürlich zu groß dafür sind.«

Vilmer setzt alles auf die Liste. *Kids Club für die Kleinen*. Und in Klammern dahinter: *Nicht für uns*.

»Musik?«

Ich nicke wieder.

»Jeden Abend muss es Tanz auf der Terrasse geben«, füge ich hinzu. »Bei Sonnenuntergang.«

Vilmer notiert *Tanz* und *Sonnenuntergang* als zwei Punkte. Schreibt auch *Terrasse* dazu.

»Cocktails«, sage ich. »Mit Schirmchen im Glas.«

Ich zeige ihm das Bild von Margarita an der Poolbar.

»Ja«, sagt Vilmer eifrig. »Das brauchen wir.«

»Und wir müssen in einem Bungalow wohnen. Direkt am Strand.«

All meine Träume, all die Bilder, die ich stundenlang angeschaut habe. Was rede ich da? Hier in der Hausmeisterwohnung erinnert absolut gar nichts an den Süden. Trotzdem mache ich einfach weiter.

»Der Strand muss weiß sein. Mit blauen Sonnenliegen.«

»Ist es wichtig, dass sie blau sind?«, fragt Vilmer, während er schreibt.

»Eigentlich nicht«, sage ich. »Aber die im *Blue Lagoon Deluxe* sind blau.«

»Südenessen«, schlägt Vilmer vor. »Pizza und Hamburger und Pommes.«

Das hört sich gut an.

»Badesachen und Handtücher«, fällt mir noch ein.

»Und Sonnenhüte.«

Endlich mal etwas, was sich leicht besorgen lässt.

»Ich glaube, eine Kappe steht mir besser«, sagt Vilmer trocken und fügt der Liste die neuen Punkte hinzu.

Als wir fertig sind, ist Vilmers Blatt voll.

»Womit fangen wir an?«, frage ich mutlos.

Plötzlich scheint es vollkommen unmöglich, diesen gammeligen Keller in ein Südenparadies zu verwandeln. Wo sollen wir einen Strand und einen Pool und einen Sonnenuntergang herkriegen? Wo soll der Spa-Bereich sein? Und der Kids Club für die Kleinen, für den wir aber schon zu groß sind?

Vilmer sieht aus, als würde er unter den Locken angestrengt nachdenken. Seine hellen Augen wandern von einer Wand zur anderen, prüfen das Zimmer.

»Wir müssen mit dem Einfachsten beginnen«, sagt er entschlossen.

Und dann machen wir einen Plan.

Das Wichtigste ist, sich zu entscheiden«, sagt Vilmer ein paar Stunden später.

Er begutachtet unsere Ausbeute. Sie ist nicht besonders groß. Ich habe den Strohhut aus Mamas Schrank geholt, Vilmer eine Kappe. Außerdem haben wir beide ein paar Spiele für den Kids Club zusammengesucht. Einen Teddy, ein rosa Kaninchen, ein Puzzle und eine Schachtel mit Buntstiften. Und natürlich Badesachen und Handtücher. Wir müssen zwar noch überlegen, wo der Pool und der Strand hinsollen, aber so haben wir wenigstens schon mal ein paar Dinge beisammen.

»Wir müssen einfach *entscheiden*, dass hier der Süden ist.«

Er geht wieder zum Schreibtisch, angelt einen Filzstift heraus. Dann verschwindet er in der Küche und kommt mit einer leeren Pizzaschachtel zurück. Reißt den Deckel ab, glättet die Seiten und legt sich zum Schreiben auf den Boden.

Ich studiere unsere Liste, krame in den hintersten Ecken meines Gehirns nach Ideen, wie man die schwierigen Punkte lösen könnte.

»Ich gehe noch mal heim und suche weiter«, sage ich.

Zu Hause finde ich zwei hohe Gläser. Ich durchforste den Küchenschrank und einige Schubladen, in der Hoffnung, dass Mama zufällig Schirmchen für die Cocktails hat. Leider Fehlanzeige. Aus der Abstellkammer im Flur hole ich Mamas alte Sonnenliege. Sie hat sie schon länger nicht benutzt, und jetzt mit dem Kurs hat sie eh keine Zeit, sich zu sonnen. Der Bezug ist türkis – das kann als Blau durchgehen.

In Mamas Kleiderschrank entdecke ich ein bunt gemustertes Kleid aus dünnem Stoff. Es sieht aus wie so ein typisches Kleid, in dem man im Sonnenuntergang am Strand entlangwandert. Auf einem Kleiderbügel hängt ein weißes Kleid. Ich denke an die Frauen im Spa-Bereich. In ihren weißen Arbeitsuniformen.

Ich lasse Bodylotion und Seife aus dem Badezimmerschrank mitgehen. Außerdem finde ich eine eingetrocknete Fußcreme und eine Nagelfeile in einem Körbchen. Dann nehme ich noch eine Packung Wattepads mit. Benutzen die so was nicht immer im Spa?

Als ich fertig bin, stopfe ich alles in eine große Papiertüte. Die Sonnenliege klemme ich mir unter den

Arm. Ich laufe die Treppe runter in den Hinterhof, über die kleine Grasfläche, an den Wäschegestellen und dem Sandkasten vorbei, über den Asphalt und die Treppe nach unten zur Kellerwohnung.

Und da sehe ich es. Vilmer hat ein Schild aufgehängt. Man kann fast nicht mehr erkennen, dass es mal eine Pizzaschachtel war. Er hat sie rund geschnitten. Zu einem perfekten Kreis. Mit roter Farbe hat er in großen, geschwungenen Buchstaben daraufgeschrieben: *Willkommen im Süden.*

Wir beschließen, dass der Spa-Bereich ins Badezimmer kommt.

»Sollen wir ihm einen Namen geben?«, ruft mir Vilmer aus dem Wohnzimmer ins Bad zu, wo ich gerade die Pflegeprodukte auf dem kleinen Waschbecken aufreihe.

»Wie wär's mit *Paradies*?«, rufe ich zurück und höre Vilmer lachen.

Er taucht mit einem neuen Schild auf, das er wieder aus einer Pizzaschachtel ausgeschnitten hat. *Paradise Spa*, hat er in blauer Schrift geschrieben. *Where dreams come true.*

»Stand das nicht auf der Seite von deinem Luxushotel?«, fragt er.

Ich nicke. Denn so ist es tatsächlich im Spa des *Blue Lagoon Deluxe*. Träume gehen in Erfüllung.

Das Restaurant kommt natürlich in die Küche. Hier gibt es einiges zu tun. Kein Mensch auf der Welt würde seinen Fuß jemals in dieses Restaurant setzen, und wenn er noch so ausgehungert wäre. Wir versuchen, den Herd zu putzen, aber die braunen Ränder gehen einfach nicht ab. Als wir die Küchenschränke öffnen, finden wir ein paar Teller, die richtig zusammenkleben, so lange haben sie hier schon gestanden. Wir räumen alles aus dem Schrank, Gläser, Teller, einen Kerzenständer und eine Kaffeetasse mit dem Logo der Olympischen Winterspiele in Lillehammer 1994. Ich fülle Wasser in die Spüle und fange mit dem Abwasch an, während Vilmer weitersucht.

»Guck mal«, sagt er. Er hat ein Tischtuch in einer Schublade entdeckt. Es ist zerknittert und hat braune Streifen. Vilmer versucht es zu glätten, allerdings ohne großen Erfolg. Er platziert den Kerzenständer in der Mitte des Tischs, als ob er für ein Festessen decken würde.

»Wenn wir irgendwo eine Kerze herkriegen, sieht es richtig schick aus«, sagt er. Dann fragt er mich noch mal nach einem Namensvorschlag. Diesmal für das Restaurant.

»Wie heißt das im *Blue Lagoon Deluxe*?«, fragt er.

Ich muss lächeln. Es tut so gut, jemanden den Namen laut aussprechen zu hören. Lange habe ich ihn ja immer nur im Kopf gehabt, wie in einem Traum. Es ist schön, ihn mit Vilmer zu teilen.

»*Sunlight Taverna*«, sage ich. »Klingt das nicht toll?«

Den Kids Club haben wir an der einen Längsseite des Wohnzimmers eingerichtet und dort unser Spielzeug aufgereiht. Einen eigenen Namen hat er nicht, er heißt einfach *Kids Club für die Jüngsten*. Vilmer hat ein Krokodil, eine Puppe, ein rotes Auto und einen Teddy auf das Schild gemalt. Wir haben alles so kinderfreundlich gestaltet wie nur möglich, auch wenn uns leider nur begrenzte Mittel zur Verfügung standen. Wir sind ja sowieso zu groß für den Kids Club, und es werden sich wohl kaum irgendwelche Kinder hierher verirren.

Mamas Sonnenliege lehnt zusammengeklappt an der Wand. Sobald wir wissen, wo der Strand hinsoll, stellen wir sie auf. Der Sonnenhut und die Kappe liegen daneben, bereit für den Strandspaziergang.

Swimmingpool, Strand und Sonnenuntergang müssen noch ein bisschen warten. Wir haben stundenlang gearbeitet, bald kommt Mama heim, und ich habe versprochen, bis dahin von der Badebucht zurück zu sein.

»Der Süden wurde nicht an einem Tag erbaut«, sagt Vilmer und lässt die Tür zur Hausmeisterwohnung hinter uns ins Schloss fallen.

Wir gehen die kleine Kellertreppe hoch und merken erst jetzt, wie heiß es immer noch ist. Die Sonne glüht am Himmel. Der Geruch von Asphalt und Grillwürstchen hängt in der Luft. Ein paar Leute spritzen sich auf dem Rasen mit dem Gartenschlauch ab. Sie laufen lachend durcheinander.

Drei Frauen sitzen auf Liegestühlen neben einem aufblasbaren Schwimmbecken, in dem zwei kleine Kinder wild herumplanschen.

Auf einmal ist es richtig nett. Hier. Im Güllebakken Bauverein. Oder liegt das nur an mir? Nehme ich die Dinge plötzlich anders wahr als sonst?

Ich gehe zu Aufgang A und drehe mich noch einmal um. Sehe, wie Vilmer die Tür zu Aufgang F öffnet. Seinen Rücken in dem grünen T-Shirt, die vielen Locken.

»Vilmer!«, rufe ich laut.

Er wendet den Kopf in meine Richtung.

Eigentlich gibt es gar nichts mehr zu sagen, keinen Grund zu rufen. Ich stehe einfach bloß da und schaue zu ihm rüber.

Vilmer winkt.

Dann schlägt die Tür hinter ihm zu, und er ist verschwunden.

Der Süden ist sehr viel besser als Schleim. Ich habe echt Lust weiterzumachen. Dinge zusammenzusuchen, die wir brauchen, um die Hausmeisterwohnung in ein Südenparadies zu verwandeln. Zwischendurch denke ich darüber nach, wie kindisch dieses Spiel eigentlich ist. Wie peinlich es wäre, wenn mich jemand hierbei sehen würde, zusammen mit Vilmer. Ihn scheint es nicht groß zu kümmern, er hat einfach Spaß und kommt mit einer Idee nach der anderen. Deshalb vergesse ich oft, wie albern die ganze Sache ist.

Nach dem Abendessen, bei dem ich Mama von dem fantastischen Wasser in der Badebucht erzählt habe, fange ich an.

Ich habe unsere Liste abfotografiert und gehe sie Punkt für Punkt durch. Der Swimmingpool ist eindeutig eine Herausforderung. Ich google ziemlich lange. Finde Firmen, die zu einem nach Hause kommen und den Garten aufgraben. Runde Schwimmbecken. Viereckige. Längliche. Umweltfreundliche. Lauter Bilder von fröhlichen Leuten, die mit Wasser spritzen und sich am Beckenrand sonnen. Pools in Kellerwohnungen sehe ich keine.

Aber dann fällt mir das aufblasbare Planschbecken im Hinterhof ein. Mir fällt ein, was Vilmer gesagt hat: Dass es am wichtigsten ist, sich für Dinge zu entscheiden.

Ich suche ein bisschen weiter im Internet. Ein Planschbecken kostet zwischen hundert und fünfhundert Kronen, je nachdem, welches Modell man möchte. Hundert Kronen habe ich nicht, und Vilmer wohl auch kaum. Mama will ich nicht fragen, und Vilmers Vater ist pleite. Ich gehe auf eine Seite mit gebrauchten Sachen und klicke auf *Zu verschenken*. Schreibe *Schwimmbecken* in das Suchfeld und grenze die Treffer so ein, dass nur Ergebnisse in der Nähe erscheinen. Ich bekomme ein einziges. Ein kleines rosa Hello-Kitty-Becken. In Solvangtoppen!

Als Nächstes gebe ich *Sonnenschirm* ein. Finde einen knallroten, den jemand loswerden will. Leider kann er nicht mehr zusammengeklappt werden, steht in der Anzeige.

Sonnenuntergang, tippe ich in das Suchfeld. Es kommen mehrere Treffer. Alles, was irgendwie auf *Sonne* passt. Und auf *Gang*. Ein Buch, mit dem Wort *Sonnenuntergang* im Titel. Ich scrolle nach unten. Suche und suche. Und dann finde ich es. Eine große Rolle Tapete. Es ist ein riesiges Foto von einem Strand mit Palmen und weißem Sand. Vor einem fantastischen rosa Sonnenuntergang.

Ich speichere meine Resultate und schicke Nachrichten an die Besitzer. Dann schreibe ich Vilmer. *Wichtige Dinge gefunden.*

Er antwortet ungefähr drei Sekunden später. *Ich auch*, steht dort. Und ein großes Daumenhoch.

Vilmer ist schon da, als ich am nächsten Tag nach unten komme. Ich frage mich, wie lange er bereits auf dem roten Sofa sitzt und auf seinem Handy spielt. Es sieht nicht so aus, als ob außer seinem Vater noch jemand auf ihn aufpassen würde. Und es sieht nicht so aus, als ob sein Vater sonderlich gut auf ihn aufpassen würde.

Heute hat Vilmer ein komplett weißes T-Shirt an – ausnahmsweise mal ohne Aufdruck. Und es passt ihm sogar. In der Mitte des Zimmers steht eine große blaue Ikea-Tüte. Ein Kabel guckt heraus.

»Yes«, sagt er und beendet das Spiel. »Gewonnen!«

Vilmer schaut mich prüfend an.

»Wo sind die Sachen, die du gefunden hast?«, fragt er, weil ich mit leeren Händen dastehe.

»Im Internet«, sage ich.

»Im Internet?«

Er macht ein enttäuschtes Gesicht. Deutet auf die blaue Ikea-Tüte. »Meine sind hier.«

Er zeigt mir eine gelbe Strandmatte, eine Packung Adventskerzen und einen kleinen Lautsprecher. Außerdem hat er eine Playlist für uns erstellt, mit Südenmusik.

»Gib dir das mal.«

Er zieht an dem Kabel, das aus der Tüte hervorlugt. Ein Haufen bunter Glühbirnchen kommt zum Vorschein. Grün, lila, blau, rosa, gelb.

»Na, ist das Süden, oder was?«, fragt Vilmer zufrieden. Er hält die Lichterkette in der Hand und schaut sich nach einem geeigneten Platz dafür um.

»Da vielleicht?«, fragt er und deutet aufs Fenster.

Ich nicke.

Vilmer holt Nägel aus Antons Werkzeugkasten und schlägt sie in die Wand. Wir hängen die Lichterkette an den Nägeln auf, drapieren sie in einem Bogen um das kleine Fenster und weiter bis fast zur Tür.

»Hast du schon probiert, ob sie geht?«, frage ich.

Vilmer zieht das Kabel zur nächsten Steckdose.

»Auf die Plätze, fertig, los!«, ruft er und steckt den Stecker in die Dose.

Die Lichterkette leuchtet. Beinahe alle Birnchen sind noch heil. Die Hausmeisterwohnung sieht aus wie eine Strandbar, die in ein warmes, gemütliches Licht getaucht ist.

»Woow«, sage ich begeistert, und auf einmal streicht mein Arm über Vilmers Rücken.

Er grinst.

»Jetzt können wir aber wirklich von Süden reden, oder was meinst du?«

Wir beschließen, Sand aus einem der Sandkästen im Hinterhof zu holen.

»Aber nur, wenn er nicht nach Pisse riecht«, sage ich.

Er ist nicht besonders sauber und südenhaft, aber keiner verschenkt Sand. Ich habe extra im Internet nachgeschaut. Und wir sind uns einig, dass wir sowieso nicht so viel brauchen.

»Wir *entscheiden* einfach, dass es ein Strand ist«, sagt Vilmer und geht voraus in den Hinterhof.

Unser kleiner Sandstrand sieht ziemlich traurig aus. Er ist weder weiß. Noch lang. Noch endet er in einem türkisfarbenen Meer. Das Aufstellen der Sonnenliege macht es auch nicht besser.

Wir legen eine Pause auf dem Sofa ein und trinken Pepsi.

»Ob Anton Berntzen noch lebt?«, überlege ich und betrachte den Ring, der nach wie vor an Vilmers Finger steckt. »Hast du ihn schon gegoogelt?«

Ohne auf seine Antwort zu warten, greife ich zum Handy. Wenn ich eins kann, dann ist es Googeln. Vilmer beugt sich zu mir rüber, um zu sehen, was ich schreibe.

Er riecht nach Sonnencreme, was ein bisschen merkwürdig ist, schließlich verbringt er seine Ferien in einer Kellerwohnung. Ich versuche es mit verschiedenen Varianten. *Anton Berntzen + Hausmeister* ergibt keine Resultate. Ich probiere *Tyllebakken + 60er,* füge *Trostevejen 30* hinzu. Aber nichts passt.

»Ich habe mir mal die Namen auf den Briefkästen durchgelesen, als ich nichts zu tun hatte«, sagt Vilmer. »Und auf einem stand *Grete Brattberg.*«

Er wirft mir einen vielsagenden Blick zu.

»Du weißt schon, diese Frau, die sich über ihn beschwert hat, weil sie sich einen Schlag am Sicherungskasten geholt hat und ins Krankenhaus musste.«

Ich lache.

»Ich glaube, sie wohnt immer noch hier.«

»Wir könnten zu ihr gehen«, sage ich eifrig. »Vielleicht weiß sie ja, was mit Anton Berntzen passiert ist.«

Am Türschild von Aufgang H steht G. *Brattberg*. Sie wohnt im dritten Stock. Im Treppenhaus riecht es süß, nach Pfannkuchen, meint Vilmer.

Er klopft an ihre Tür, und wir warten geduldig. Hören Geräusche aus der Wohnung, schlurfende Schritte, die langsam näher kommen. Endlich öffnet sich die Tür, und ein Kopf erscheint im Spalt.

»Ja, bitte?«

Sie hat ein Sicherheitsschloss vor der Tür, eine dicke Kette, die ihr Gesicht teilt, während sie uns anstarrt.

»Wir wohnen hier in Tyllebakken«, erklärt Vilmer. »Und wollten gern mit Ihnen reden.«

»Ich kaufe nichts!«, sagt Grete Brattberg entschieden. »Nicht das kleinste Garnknäuel kaufe ich euch ab!«

»Wir möchten mit Ihnen über alte Zeiten sprechen«, sage ich und lächle das Gesicht im Türspalt an.

Ihre Augen weiten sich, und sie schließt die Tür. Wir hören ein Klicken, dann öffnet sich die Tür wieder, und der Pfannkuchengeruch schlägt uns entgegen.

»Ich liebe alte Zeiten«, sagt Grete Brattberg. Auf einmal hellt sich ihre Miene auf, als hätte jemand eine Glühbirne angeschaltet. »Kommt rein.«

Wir betreten einen Flur, der genau wie der bei uns zu Hause aussieht. Grete Brattberg ist kleiner als Vilmer und dünner als ich. Sie hat braune, lebhafte Augen, ihre Haare sind zu einem Knoten mitten auf dem Kopf zusammengebunden.

»Macht euch nichts aus der Unordnung«, sagt sie und deutet ins Wohnzimmer, wo überall auf dem Boden Zeitungen und Papiere verstreut liegen. Vor den Fenstern hängen schwere dunkelblaue Vorhänge. Eine schwarze Katze streicht ums Sofa.

»Er heißt Terje«, sagt Grete Brattberg. »Nicht unbedingt ein Katzenname, aber mir ist nichts Besseres eingefallen.«

Vilmer bückt sich und streichelt Terje.

»Was wollt ihr denn über die alten Zeiten wissen?«, fragt Grete Brattberg eifrig und lädt uns mit einer Handbewegung ein, uns zu setzen.

Wir zögern. Als ob keiner von uns gleich mit dem Wichtigsten anfangen will.

»Wohnen Sie hier schon lange?«, frage ich, und Grete nickt.

»Geboren und aufgewachsen in Tyllebakken.«

»Wir haben uns gefragt, ob Sie vielleicht einen Hausmeister kennen? Er hieß Anton Berntzen. Wahrscheinlich ist es schon etwas länger her, dass er hier gearbeitet hat.«

Grete schaut erst mich an und dann Vilmer.

»Wollt ihr Waffeln?«, fragt sie plötzlich und steht auf, bevor wir antworten können.

Sie geht in die Küche, wir hören Tellerklappern.

»Waffeln«, sagt Vilmer und lächelt mir zu. »Riechen fast genauso wie Pfannkuchen, oder?«

Grete kommt mit einem Berg Waffeln zurück.

»Anton Berntzen«, sagt sie und schiebt uns die Marmelade zu, »war ein großartiger Hausmeister. Er konnte alles, was ein Hausmeister können muss. Und nicht nur das. Er war freundlich. Klug. Sympathisch. Und er spielte Akkordeon.«

Sie verteilt Marmelade auf einer Waffel. Isst und lächelt uns an.

»Wissen Sie, wo er jetzt wohnt?«, frage ich.

Grete macht ein ernstes Gesicht. »Im Himmel, hoffentlich«, sagt sie leise.

»Also ist er tot?«

Sie nickt. »In den letzten Jahren war er nur noch ein Schatten seiner selbst. Er saß die meiste Zeit in seiner Hausmeisterwohnung und las. Ich glaube, er mochte Gedichte.«

Sie klappt eine Waffel zusammen und schlingt sie herunter, während sie weitererzählt.

»Ich weiß noch, dass er mit der Schönen zusammenkam. So nannten wir sie immer. *Die Schöne.* Ihren Namen habe ich vergessen. Irgendwas mit Vögeln vielleicht?«

Vilmer wirft mir einen Blick zu, legt die Hand mit dem Ring auf sein Knie.

»Und Anton war so verliebt. Er spazierte mit ihr in Tyllebakken umher, um sie vorzuzeigen. Sie war groß und schlank, er dagegen klein und dick. Das war vielleicht ein Paar.«

»Aber was ist passiert?«, fragt Vilmer ungeduldig, nachdem Grete ein paar Sekunden geschwiegen hat.

Sie atmet langsam ein. »Paris«, sagt sie. »Da ist die Schöne hin, wie ich gehört habe. Auf alle Fälle bot man ihr einen Job als Mannequin an. Wie es eben so läuft, wenn man sehr hübsch ist. Und da war es aus und vorbei mit Anton.«

Vilmer streicht über den Ring, der möglicherweise einem Mannequin in Paris gehört hat.

»Ich glaube, der Hausmeister litt für den Rest seines Lebens an Liebeskummer.«

Grete Brattberg schaut wieder erst mich und dann Vilmer an.

»Ihr seid so jung, vielleicht wisst ihr noch nicht richtig, was Verliebtsein bedeutet«, sagt sie. »Aber es kann sehr unheimlich sein.«

Vilmer kichert.

Grete macht große Augen. »Bist du in jemanden verliebt?«, fragt sie. »Sei ehrlich.«

Mein Bauch zieht sich zusammen, oder vielleicht ist es auch mein Herz. Ja, es muss das Herz sein. Ich traue mich nicht, Vilmer ins Gesicht zu sehen. Stattdessen richte ich den Blick nach unten, auf die hübschen Hände in seinem Schoß. Der Zeigefinger der rechten Hand tippt unruhig gegen das Knie.

»Ich glaub nicht«, sagt Vilmer leise.

Ich habe Schwierigkeiten, die drei Wörter zu verstehen, dabei sitzt er so nah bei mir, dass ich seinen Atem an meiner Wange spüren kann. Er ist knallrot angelaufen. Rutscht auf dem Stuhl hin und her.

»Aber wenn es eines Tages so weit ist«, sagt Grete Brattberg mit erhobenem Zeigefinger, »dann musst du dich in Acht nehmen. Sich zu verlieben kann lebensgefährlich sein.«

Vilmer nickt. Ein paar Locken kleben ihm an der Stirn. Er schaut mich nicht an. Aber ich schaue ihn an. Meine Augen wandern zu seiner Brust. Als würde ich versuchen, direkt in sein Herz zu sehen, um herauszufinden, wie es zusammengeschraubt ist.

Auf dem Weg nach Solvangtoppen, wo ich das Schwimmbecken abholen will, fällt mir plötzlich ein, dass ich ja eigentlich immer noch im Süden bin. Erst gestern habe ich in unserer Klassengruppe ein Foto vom *Blue Lagoon Deluxe* gepostet und geschrieben, wie heiß es ist. Sogar Markus hat es gelikt. Was, wenn ich jemanden aus der Klasse treffe, während ich hier mit Vilmer auf der Jagd nach einem Schwimmbecken durch die Stadt laufe? Wie, bitte schön, soll ich das erklären?

Vilmer läuft schweigend neben mir her. Ich wünsche mir so, dass er beeindruckt ist. Von all den Sachen, die ich organisiert habe. Vielleicht findet er ein aufblasbares Hello-Kitty-Becken total blöd? Und die Tapete mit dem Sonnenuntergang und den roten Sonnenschirm, der sich nicht zusammenklappen lässt?

Wir klingeln bei den Leuten, die das Schwimmbecken verschenken. Ihr Haus gleicht dem von Mathilde. Es ist groß und weiß, wie die meisten Häuser hier.

Eine Frau öffnet die Tür und schaut uns freundlich an.

»Meine Mutter hat mich hergeschickt, um ein Hello-Kitty-Becken abzuholen«, sage ich so höflich, wie ich nur kann. »Es ist für meine kleine Schwester.«

Die Frau in der Türöffnung lächelt.

»Das Planschbecken liegt im Carport«, sagt sie und zeigt neben das Haus, wo das Heck eines riesigen Autos aus einer Garage ragt.

Wir holen das Ding, das aussieht wie eine Plastiktüte, aus der Garage.

Ich ziehe daran und versuche es auszubreiten, sodass Vilmer einen Eindruck von unserem neuen Swimmingpool bekommt.

»Cool«, sagt er. »Ein Punkt weniger auf der Liste.«

Von der Tapete ist Vilmer auch ziemlich beeindruckt, das merke ich. Vorsichtig rollen wir sie auf dem Gehweg aus, damit er schon mal sieht, wie schön der Sonnenuntergang im Süden wird. In unserem Süden. Wie weiß der Strand ist, wie sich die Palme sozusagen richtig im Abendwind hin und her wiegt. Wir beschließen, dass sie an die Wand mit der Lichterkette kommt.

»Das wird der Hammer«, sagt Vilmer.

Und dann streift er meinen Arm, ich spüre seine warme Haut auf meiner.

Um den Sonnenschirm abzuholen, müssen wir ein ganzes Stück laufen. Vilmer trägt die zusammengerollte Tapete, ich das kleine Planschbecken. Die Sonne verschwindet hinter einer Wolke. Es wird kühl. Eine Schar Vögel fliegt von einem Baum auf, als wollten sie sich schon auf den Weg nach Süden machen.

»Ist es der da?«, fragt Vilmer und zeigt auf einen roten Sonnenschirm, der wie ein umgefallener Fliegenpilz in einer Garageneinfahrt liegt.

Ich überprüfe die Adresse und nicke.

»Er lässt sich nicht zusammenklappen«, erkläre ich Vilmer. »Also müssen wir ihn so tragen.«

Wir gehen unter dem roten Sonnenschirm nach Hause. Die Leute gucken uns an und lächeln. Wir lächeln zurück und grüßen alle, denen wir begegnen. Vilmers Gesicht hat so eine schöne Farbe unter dem roten Stoff. Er sieht südenbraun aus, fast ein bisschen verbrannt von der Sonne.

Wir haben noch den halben Heimweg in den Süden vor uns, als wir es hören. Donner. Ein lautes Krachen. Kurz darauf fängt es an zu regnen. Erst fallen nur ein paar leise Tropfen auf die Oberfläche des Schirms. Dann schwillt der Regen an, bis er auf das Dach über unseren Köpfen trommelt. Wir kauern uns unter dem Schirm zusammen. Vilmer presst sich die Tapete an die Brust, damit sie nicht nass wird. Das Wasser dringt durch meine Stoffschuhe. Meine Füße werden kalt. Es donnert und knallt. Blitzt und zuckt. Wir zählen. Einundzwanzig. Zweiundzwanzig. Dreiundzwanzig. Schauen einander an, wenn der Donner kracht, als würde jemand den Himmel mit einer Motorsäge zerteilen.

»Hast du Angst vor Gewitter?«, fragt Vilmer.

»Nein«, lüge ich.

Eng aneinandergedrückt stehen wir unter unserem roten Dach, bis das Schlimmste vorbei ist. Halten beide den Schirm fest. Vilmer legt seine Hand auf meine. Ich traue mich nicht, ihn anzusehen. Es pocht und sticht in meiner Brust, als ob ein Teil des Gewitters in meinen Körper gezogen wäre. Mein Gesicht hat bestimmt dasselbe Rot wie der Sonnenschirm angenommen. Das Wasser strömt über die Gehwege. Der Schirm ist schwer vor Nässe. Und Vilmers Gesicht ist so nah. Die Lippen, die Augen, das Haar.

Dann wird es still. Vilmer steckt den Kopf unter dem Schirm hervor.

Wir gehen weiter. Nach Hause in den Süden.

Den Rest des Tages arbeiten wir. Blasen das Planschbecken auf, füllen es mit Wasser. Überlegen uns, wo der Poolbereich hinsoll, und drapieren Badesachen und Handtücher auf einem Stuhl neben dem Becken. Stellen Gläser mit leuchtend pinken Strohhalmen auf.

»Für die Poolbar«, sagt Vilmer.

Für die Tapete bräuchten wir eigentlich Kleber, aber Anton hat keinen in seiner Werkzeugkiste. Stattdessen müssen wir Reißwecken nehmen, was ziemlich schwierig ist. Wir stehen jeweils auf einem Stuhl und arbeiten uns von den Seiten bis zur Mitte vor. Befestigen die Tapete direkt unter der Decke und streichen sie dann nach unten, sodass sie keine Wellen schlägt. Als wir fertig sind, treten wir ein paar Schritte zurück, um den Sonnenuntergang im bunten Schein der Lichterkette zu bewundern.

»Das ist echt der schönste Sonnenuntergang, den ich je gesehen habe«, sagt Vilmer mit verträumtem Gesichtsausdruck.

Der Sonnenschirm ist zu nass, um ihn drinnen am Strand aufzustellen, deshalb bleibt er erst mal zum Trocknen auf der Kellertreppe. Wir gehen die Südenliste durch und stellen fest, dass wir eigentlich fast alles beisammenhaben.

»Und was machen wir jetzt?«, frage ich Vilmer.

Er schaut mich überrascht an. Als ob er noch nie im Leben so eine dumme Frage gehört hätte.

»Na, wir genießen den Süden!«, sagt er.

Und grinst.

Jeden Morgen, sobald Mama zum Kurs gegangen ist, laufe ich die Treppe nach unten in den Hinterhof. Und wenn ich das Schild mit der Aufschrift *Willkommen im Süden* sehe, fängt mein Herz wie wild an zu klopfen.

Vilmer sitzt immer schon auf dem roten Sofa und spielt. Und jedes Mal hellt sich seine Miene auf, wenn er durch mich unterbrochen wird, auch wenn er dadurch ein Leben verliert.

Normalerweise sitzen wir erst mal eine Weile nebeneinander auf dem Sofa und unterhalten uns, bevor wir uns überlegen, was wir machen wollen. Und dann machen wir Südendinge.

Wir baden im Pool. Das Becken ist so klein, dass darin immer nur einer von uns Platz findet. Und das auch nur, wenn man sich mit angewinkelten Beinen ins Wasser setzt. Der andere relaxt in der Zwischenzeit an der Poolbar. Mit Pepsi und Schirmchen im hohen Glas. Anschließend tauschen wir.

Wir essen Südengerichte in der *Sunlight Taverna*. Pizza oder Würstchen, das geht am einfachsten. Manchmal, wenn wir kein Geld haben, um etwas zu kaufen, essen wir einfach nur Brot. Aber wir nennen es *Club Sandwich*. Vilmer zündet die Adventskerzen an und spielt den Kellner.

»Darf es noch ein Latte macchiato sein?«, fragt er und hält die Tasse von den Olympischen Winterspielen hoch.

Ich gehe ins *Paradise Spa* und bekomme eine Hautpflegebehandlung von Vilmer. Er hat Mamas weißes Kleid angezogen und eine Playlist mit Entspannungsmusik runtergeladen, Panflöten und Geige.

»Relax, relax«, sagt er mit heller Stimme und taucht Wattepads in Wasser, mit denen er mir sanft übers Gesicht streicht.

Keiner von uns schlägt vor, im Sonnenuntergang zu tanzen, obwohl es zu den typischen Südendingen gehört, die wir uns eigentlich vorgenommen hatten. Aber das wäre einfach zu peinlich, egal ob wir allein oder zusammen tanzen würden. Stattdessen sitzen wir auf dem roten Sofa mit Blick auf den Sonnenuntergang und hören die Playlist.

Wir sind auch nicht sehr viel am Strand, weil der wirklich nicht besonders toll geworden ist. Doch ab und zu tun wir so, als ob wir uns sonnen, einfach nur um es mal gemacht zu haben. Ich liege auf Mamas türkisfarbenem Sonnenstuhl, Vilmer auf der gelben Strandmatratze. Wir schließen die Augen, weil die Sonne so grell ist, und zwischendurch schlafen wir ein bisschen. Ich jedenfalls.

»Warst du eigentlich schon mal im Süden, Ina?«, fragt Vilmer, als wir eines Tages so daliegen.

»Nein«, antworte ich. »Du?«

»Ja«, sagt er. »Ein Mal.«

Ich drehe mich auf die Seite und schaue ihn an. Er hat die Arme unter dem Kopf verschränkt, sie verschwinden in seinen Locken. Sein T-Shirt ist hellblau und macht Werbung für ein Elektrogeschäft.

»Aber unser Südenurlaub gefällt mir viel besser«, sagt er und blinzelt mich mit einem Auge an. Als ob er tatsächlich vom hellen Sonnenlicht am Strand geblendet würde.

»Ehrlich?«, frage ich.

»Ja.«

Er schweigt eine Weile. Schließt wieder die Augen.

»Hier ist nämlich keiner betrunken.«

Abends vor dem Schlafengehen stehe ich am Fenster. Schaue rüber zu Aufgang F. Zu seinem Fenster im dritten Stock. An manchen Abenden winkt er mir von seinem Zimmer aus zu. Ich winke zurück, lege die Hände unter die Wange, als ob ich darauf schlafen würde, und halte den Daumen hoch. Um ihm eine gute Nacht zu wünschen.

Ich denke oft vor dem Einschlafen an Vilmer. Und träume von ihm. Im Traum hat er immer ein rotes T-Shirt an. Ich weiß nicht, warum es ausgerechnet diese Farbe ist, denn ich habe Vilmer noch nie in Rot gesehen.

Wir haben darüber gesprochen, was aus dem Süden wird, wenn die Sommerferien vorbei sind. Sollen wir alles zusammenpacken, jetzt, wo es so schön geworden ist?

»Die Leute fahren ja auch im Herbst in den Süden«, sagt Vilmer und schielt zu mir rüber.

Ich erzähle ihm nicht, was ich dachte, bevor wir mit dem Süden anfingen. Dass ich nur mit ihm abhänge, weil es sonst keinen gibt. Dass wir nach den Ferien nicht länger Freunde sein werden. Dass eine Südenreise im Herbst sehr unwahrscheinlich ist.

Wir haben eine Abmachung getroffen: Alles, was im Süden gesagt wird, bleibt auch im Süden. Es ist wie ein Pakt. Eine heimliche Vereinbarung. Vielleicht fällt es uns deshalb so leicht, miteinander zu reden? Ich erzähle von Mama, die immer müde ist, und von ihrem blöden Kurs. Von unseren Geldsorgen, den vielen Umzügen und meinen genau null Freundschaften. Ich erzähle von meinen Lügen. Der Badebucht und Maria. Dem Geschenk für Mathilde. Den Bildern, die ich von meinen Ferien im *Blue Lagoon Deluxe* gepostet habe. Vilmer sitzt auf dem roten Sofa und hört zu. Es macht nicht den Anschein, als ob er mich für bescheuert halten würde.

Dann erzählt er. Warum sie hierhergezogen sind. Von seinem Vater, der cool und ziemlich lustig ist, aber ein bisschen zu gerne Bier trinkt. Von seiner Mutter, die jetzt in Schweden wohnt, wo sie ein Kind mit Sture hat. Sie ruft jeden Dienstag und Freitag an, über Facetime.

Es ist komisch mit Vilmer, der nur ein Südenfreund ist. Ich weiß plötzlich gar nicht mehr, wie alles werden soll nach den Ferien. Will einfach nur im Süden sein. Auf dem Sonnenstuhl liegen, in der *Sunlight Taverna* essen, den Sonnenuntergang anschauen. Zusammen mit ihm. Vilmer fühlt sich an wie ein richtiger Freund. Vielleicht ein bester Freund. Vielleicht mehr.

Ich habe keinen Überblick mehr darüber, wie viele Tage der Sommerferien schon vergangen sind. Habe aufgehört, die Stunden zu zählen. Die Minuten. Sekunden. Der beste Moment des Tages ist, wenn ich in den Süden komme und Vilmer auf dem roten Sofa sehe. Wenn er aufblickt und mir zulächelt.

An diesem Morgen aber sitzt er nicht an seinem gewohnten Platz. Stattdessen steht er mit dem Rücken zu mir vor dem Schreibtisch. Rüttelt und zieht an der verschlossenen Schublade, in der Hand hat er irgendein Werkzeug, eine Art Stange, die an der Spitze gebogen ist.

»Hi«, sagt er und dreht sich mit einem Lächeln zu mir um.

Er hat wieder das T-Shirt vom Zoo an. Das vom allerersten Tag. Damals fand ich es hässlich. Jetzt gefällt mir die grüne Farbe.

»Heute kriege ich diese Schublade auf«, sagt er außer Puste und hält das Werkzeug hoch. »Ich hab's aufgegeben, den Schlüssel zu finden.«

Er platziert die Spitze der Stange an der Schublade und zieht mit voller Kraft. Das Holz knirscht, und die Schublade bewegt sich ein Stück. Ich gehe zu ihm hinüber und greife das Werkzeug über seiner Hand am Schaft, ziehe und rüttle gemeinsam mit Vilmer. Auf einmal löst sich die Schublade mit einem Ruck, und wir taumeln zurück.

Die Schublade ist so gut wie leer. Vilmer macht ein enttäuschtes Gesicht. Er nimmt einen Umschlag und ein rotes Buch heraus.

Wir setzen uns mit unserer bescheidenen Ausbeute aufs Sofa. Der Umschlag wurde bereits geöffnet und die Adresse mit einem dicken schwarzen Stift durchgestrichen. Vilmer zieht den Brief heraus und streicht einen Bogen glatt, auf dem nur ein paar wenige Sätze stehen. Die Schrift ist krumm und schief.

»*Liebe Frida*«, liest Vilmer vor. »*Heute habe ich dein Bild und einen Artikel über dich in der Zeitung gesehen. Schön, dass es so gut für dich läuft. Hier zu Hause geht so weit alles seinen Gang. Ich …*«

Der Rest des kurzen Textes ist durchgekritzelt. Vilmer dreht das Blatt, versucht, die Wortfetzen zu entziffern, die noch zu erkennen sind.

»*… denke an dich. Ständig. Liebe. Viel zu sehr. Jeden einzelnen Tag. Bereue. Wieder nach Hause. Liebste.*«

»Das ist ein Liebesbrief!«

Ich schaue Vilmer an, seine süßen Augen, seine Haare. »Aber er hat ihn ja gar nicht abgeschickt«, sagt er und hält den Umschlag hoch. »Da ist keine Briefmarke.«

Ich greife nach dem roten Buch, das auch in der Schublade lag. Es knistert leise, als ich es aufschlage. Zwischen den Seiten steckt ein Foto. Die Frau darauf hat dunkle halblange Haare und braune Augen, ein Muttermal auf der Wange. Sie lächelt, sodass man ihre weißen, geraden Zähne sieht. Das Bild sieht aus, als ob es bei einem Fotografen gemacht worden wäre.

»Die Schöne!«, flüstert Vilmer aufgeregt. »Frida.«

Das rote Buch ist voller Gedichte. Die Anton geschrieben hat. Manche handeln von Sonnenuntergängen und Vögeln und den Wellen des Meeres. Aber die meisten handeln von Frida.

Wir lesen uns gegenseitig ein paar davon vor. Es ist ziemlich peinlich. Erstens, weil die Gedichte schlecht sind, und zweitens, weil es um Liebe geht. Wir bemühen uns, nicht zu lachen, schließlich hat Anton sie geschrieben. Und wenn man mit jemandem Mitleid haben muss, dann mit ihm. Aber manchmal ist es echt schwierig, ernst zu bleiben. Anton vergleicht Frida mit Kartoffeleintopf, voller himmlischer Zutaten, spannend, weich und köstlich. Sagt, sie sei interessant wie ein Werkzeugkasten.

»Wahrscheinlich war es ganz gut, dass er Hausmeister wurde«, murmelt Vilmer.

Wir hängen das Bild von Frida auf. Stehen lange davor und betrachten ihr schönes Gesicht, das in unser Südenparadies lächelt.

»Man kann schon verstehen, dass Anton in sie verliebt war«, sagt Vilmer und schaut mich an.

Ich merke, wie mein Gesicht heiß wird, mir das Blut in die Wangen schießt, unter der Haut prickelt.

»Stell dir vor, vielleicht haben sie hier gesessen«, fährt er gedankenversunken fort. »Hier auf dem roten Sofa, genau wie wir jetzt. Und waren verliebt. Haben sich geküsst und so. Stell dir mal vor, Ina.«

Vilmer ist ebenfalls ein bisschen rot geworden.

Ich greife schnell nach dem Handy und tippe hektisch darauf herum. »Ob Frida noch lebt?«, überlege ich.

Es ist gut, etwas zu tun zu haben, wenn man rot im Gesicht ist und nicht weiß, was man sagen soll. Ich gehe auf Google und gebe *Frida + Mannequin + Paris* ein. Keine Ergebnisse. Ich versuche es mit *Verlobung 1962. Frida + Anton Berntzen*, aber es kommt nichts, was uns irgendwie weiterbringt.

»Wenn wir nur wüssten, wie sie mit Nachnamen hieß«, sage ich.

Ratlos stehen wir vor dem Bild an der Wand und betrachten die Schöne. Frida ohne Nachnamen. Antons große Liebe.

»Erinnerst du dich noch an die Sache mit den Bungalows?«, fragt Vilmer, kurz bevor ich mich abends auf den Heimweg mache.

Er greift nach meinem Arm, als ob er mich plötzlich nicht gehen lassen will.

»Das haben wir irgendwie vergessen.«

Ich nicke. An die Bungalows habe ich keine Sekunde mehr gedacht.

»Wir könnten ja mal probieren, hier zu übernachten. Nur wenn du willst, natürlich.« Er zieht fragend die Augenbrauen hoch. »Aber dafür bräuchten wir vielleicht einen Bungalow.«

Hier lässt sich unmöglich ein Bungalow reinstopfen.

»Wie wäre es, wenn wir einfach auf dem Sofa schlafen?«, schlage ich vor. Und denke auf einmal an Mama. Wenn ich ihr erzähle, dass ich in einer Kellerwohnung im Hinterhof übernachten will, flippt sie garantiert aus.

»Einer von uns könnte auch die Matratze auf dem Boden nehmen«, füge ich hinzu, als ob die Sache mit Mama schon wieder vergessen wäre.

»Ja«, sagt Vilmer aufgeregt. »Ich kann auf der Matratze schlafen, und du kriegst das Sofa.«

Er schaut mich an.
»Morgen vielleicht?«
»Vielleicht«, sage ich.

Irgendetwas ist anders. Ich fühle es in der Brust, direkt unter dem Herzen. Oder darin.

Was finde ich nur auf einmal an Vilmer? Ich will sein T-Shirt berühren, eng neben ihm auf dem roten Sofa sitzen. Seine Stimme und sein Lachen hören, auf seinen Rücken schauen, wenn er in die *Sunlight Taverna* geht, um mir eine Pepsi zu holen.

Mama ruft mich zum Essen. Ich antworte, dass ich gleich komme, bleibe aber im Bett liegen, um noch ein bisschen nachzudenken. Es prickelt in meinem Gesicht, eine heiße Welle schwappt durch meinen Körper.

Der nervigste Nachbar der Welt. Ich will über die Haut auf seinem Arm streichen, seine Hand halten, so wie Pärchen es tun.

Oh Mann. Ich setze mich ruckartig auf. Vilmer ist ein Freund, den ich echt gar nicht gebrauchen kann. Ich brauche Freunde, die mich hochziehen, nicht runter. Jemanden wie Markus. Und Vilmer wird niemals so jemand sein. Er ist zu merkwürdig, trägt peinliche T-Shirts und hat kein Gefühl für die sozialen Regeln, sagt einfach, was ihm in den Sinn kommt, und kümmert sich nicht darum, was die Leute über ihn denken könnten. Der Plan war, nur während der Sommerferien mit Vilmer befreundet zu sein, weil ich sonst gar niemanden gehabt hätte. Er sollte ein Südenfreund sein. Einer, den man nach den Ferien wieder vergisst. Das war der Plan.

Mama hat Kerzen angezündet und eine Tischdecke ausgebreitet. In einer Vase stehen Blumen.

»Ja, ja«, sagt sie und schenkt mir Saft ins Glas ein. »Es ist ja nicht gerade ein Traumsommer geworden, aber wir müssen das Beste daraus machen.«

Ich antworte nicht. Traumsommer. Bevor die Ferien anfingen, hatte ich eine ziemlich genaue Vorstellung davon, was *Traumsommer* bedeutet. Jetzt habe ich meine Meinung geändert.

»Aber du kannst dich ja ganz toll allein beschäftigen«, fährt Mama fort. »Das sagt Oma auch. Um dich muss man sich keine Sorgen machen. Und darauf bin ich wirklich stolz.«

Sie setzt den Pizzaschneider an und fährt durch den Teig. Legt ein Stück auf meinen Teller, ein langer Streifen Käse hängt an der Seite herunter.

»Ach so, übrigens«, sagt Mama, als sie sich gesetzt hat. »Eine Frau aus dem Kurs hat mich für morgen Abend zu sich nach Hause eingeladen.«
Sie lächelt unsicher.
»Auf ein Glas Wein. Aber ich weiß nicht so richtig. Es könnte spät werden.« Mama sieht aus wie eine Siebenjährige, die unter der Woche Süßigkeiten essen will. Als ob ich plötzlich die Erwachsene wäre.
Es dauert einen Moment, bis ich begreife, was sie da eigentlich sagt. Als ich den Schock überwunden habe, dass Mama nicht nur eine Freundin gefunden hat, sondern auch noch eingeladen wurde und zur Abwechslung mal glücklich aussieht, wird mir klar, welche Möglichkeiten sich mir hier eröffnen.
»Ich finde, du solltest gehen«, sage ich und bemühe mich, nicht allzu begeistert auszusehen. »Das klingt doch toll.«
»Ja, oder?«, meint Mama. »Sie heißt Janne und ist echt nett. Aber sie wohnt ein Stück weiter weg.«
Mama hat keinen Jogginganzug an, sie sitzt in normalen Kleidern am Tisch. Ziemlich schicken Kleidern. Weiße Bluse und blaue Hose, große Silberohrringe. Sie lächelt mir immer noch unsicher zu, und da setze ich zum Stoß an.
»Kann ich dann bei Maria schlafen?«, frage ich und

denke an Vilmer. »Sie hat ihre Eltern schon gefragt, und bei ihnen passt es super.«

Mama strahlt.

»Na klar«, sagt sie mit Erleichterung in der Stimme. »Von mir aus gern. Das ist doch schön, Ina. Wirklich schön.«

»Cool«, sage ich. »Dann brauchst du dir um mich jedenfalls keine Gedanken zu machen.«

»Ja, ja«, sagt Mama und lehnt sich über den Tisch, um nach meiner Hand zu greifen. »Aber ich denke doch immer an dich, mein Schatz.«

Ich kann nicht fassen, wie gut es gelaufen ist. Ich liege mit meinem Handy auf dem Bett und überlege, wie ich es Vilmer sagen soll. Probiere verschiedene Varianten aus. *Morgen klappt. Wir können übernachten. Mama hat Ja gesagt.* Aber ich lösche alle gleich wieder, sobald ich sie geschrieben habe. Und dann schicke ich einfach nur ein Daumenhoch und das Wort *Bungalow*.

Mama hat mir Geld gegeben. Das macht sie so gut wie nie, aber jetzt habe ich hundert Kronen, um mir und Maria etwas zu kaufen. So froh ist Mama darüber, mit Janne ein Glas Wein trinken zu können.

Ich gehe in den Laden und kaufe Süßigkeiten und Käseflips. Vilmer will Pizza besorgen. Außerdem hat er Pepsi geholt. Bald haben wir alles, was wir brauchen.

Ich traue mich nicht, meine Decke mitzunehmen. Es wäre schon auffällig, wenn es in Marias Haus keine Gästedecke gäbe. Und Mama kommt ja irgendwann nach Hause und sieht, dass mein Bett leer ist. Also schreibe ich Vilmer und frage, ob er eine Decke für mich mitbringen kann.

Ich spüre ein leichtes Pochen hinter den Schläfen, als ich nach unten in den Hinterhof laufe. Als ob heute alles irgendwie anders wäre. Es ist nicht einfach bloß ein ganz normaler Tag im Süden. Die Spielgeräte, die Wäschegestelle, die kleine Grasfläche, die gelben Betonwände. Alles, was sonst so hässlich ist, wirkt heute auf einmal schön. Güllebakken hat sich verändert.

Vor der Tür bleibe ich stehen und muss lächeln, als ich das Willkommensschild sehe. Vilmer hat einen neuen Satz dazugeschrieben, mit blauer Farbe: *Fridas und Antons Paradies.*

Wie immer sitzt Vilmer auf dem roten Sofa, und wie immer ist er mitten in einem Kampf. Er tippt völlig besessen auf seinem Handy herum, es sieht aus, als wollte er es killen. Heute hat er ein rotes T-Shirt an. Was ist so Besonderes daran? Wieso werde ich selber rot, nur weil er zufällig ein rotes T-Shirt trägt?

»Hi«, sage ich, obwohl ich weiß, dass Vilmer nicht gern erschreckt wird.

Er spielt weiter, aber dann antwortet er.

»Kacke, jetzt bin ich gestorben.«

Vilmer dreht sich um und lächelt. Und ich weiß nicht, was ich sagen soll. Also sage ich nichts. Stehe nur da und schaue dumm auf meinen Südenfreund. Mit seinem roten T-Shirt und dem Lockenkopf. Ich lächle zurück. Auf einmal fällt mir ein, dass ich mich sonst immer neben ihn setze, darum beeile ich mich, das auch heute zu tun.

Dann sitzen wir ziemlich lange auf dem roten Sofa und schweigen uns an. Das Rot steht ihm wirklich gut. Vilmer kommt mir darin ganz verändert vor. Erst sagt er nichts. Plötzlich fängt er an, sehr viel zu reden. Allen möglichen uninteressanten Kram. Bis er wieder verstummt. Jedes Mal, wenn ich zu ihm rübergucke, schaut er woandershin.

Wir machen unsere normalen Südensachen, genau wie sonst. Schieben die Pizza in den Ofen und essen in der *Sunlight Taverna*. Futtern die ganze Packung Käseflips, obwohl wir längst pappsatt sind. Vilmer liegt auf der gelben Strandmatratze, ich auf der Sonnenliege. Ich glaube, wir sind beide fast eingeschlafen. Jedenfalls bin ich so weggedämmert, dass ich nicht weiß, wo auf einmal das Geräusch herkommt. Von irgendwoher höre ich es piepsen und vibrieren, und ich setze mich auf.

Mein Handy liegt direkt neben dem Sand auf dem Boden. Das Display blinkt, ich habe eine Nachricht bekommen, also beuge ich mich nach unten und angle danach.

Sie ist von Mathilde! Ich habe noch nie eine persönliche Nachricht von ihr bekommen. Sie schickt natürlich die ganze Zeit Nachrichten und Bilder an die Klassengruppe, aber die hier ist nur an mich.

Und? Immer noch im Süden? Dahinter ein zwinkernder Smiley.

»Guck mal«, sage ich überrascht zu Vilmer.

Er steht von der gelben Strandmatratze auf und kommt zu mir rüber, beugt sich über das Display, um zu sehen, was da steht. Seine Locken kitzeln mich an der Wange.

»Komisch«, sagt er. »Seid ihr Freundinnen?«

Ich schüttle den Kopf. »Kein bisschen. Sie kann mich nicht ausstehen.«

Es ist merkwürdig mit Mathilde und Regine und Markus und all den anderen. Die sonst immer so wichtig für mich sind. An die ich ständig denke, vor denen ich Angst habe und mit denen ich gleichzeitig so gern befreundet wäre. In der letzten Zeit habe ich sie völlig vergessen. Aber jetzt ist es, als ob sie plötzlich wieder aufgetaucht wären, ein komisches Gefühl.

Ich halte das Handy eine Weile ratlos in der Hand, überlege, was ich antworten soll. Wie lange wollte ich angeblich noch mal im Süden sein? Vor zwei Tagen erst habe ich das Bild mit dem Koch und der hohen Mütze vor dem riesigen Büfett gepostet und geschrieben, dass es alles zu essen gäbe, was man sich nur wünschen kann. Markus hat es gelikt. Mathilde und Regine auch. Ich könnte einfach *Ja* antworten. Bräuchte nicht ins Detail zu gehen. Außerdem bin ich ja wirklich im Süden. Es ist eben eine andere Art von Süden, als Mathilde gewohnt ist.

Bevor ich groß nachdenken kann, habe ich schon

auf Senden gedrückt. *Ja, steht da nur in der Nachricht, und dahinter ein Smiley, der nicht zwinkert.*

Es dauert ungefähr fünf Sekunden, bis es wieder piepst. *Dann schick doch ein Bild. Von dir selbst! Diesmal ohne Smiley.*

»Was soll ich jetzt machen?«, frage ich kleinlaut.

Vilmer streckt die Hand aus.

»Gib mir mal das Handy«, sagt er entschieden.

Ich reiche es ihm widerwillig, habe keine Lust, dass er irgendwas Kreatives erfindet. Er versteht nicht, wie wichtig das mit Mathilde und Regine ist.

»Stell dich da drüben hin«, sagt er.

»Hier?«, frage ich und nähere mich dem Sonnenuntergang.

Vilmer hält das Handy hoch, starrt auf den Bildschirm.

»Perfekt«, sagt er. »Aber du musst dir was anderes anziehen.«

Plötzlich verstehe ich, was Vilmer vorhat, und hole meinen Badeanzug, der drüben bei dem kleinen Hello-Kitty-Becken liegt. Gehe in den Spa-Bereich und ziehe mich um. Stelle mich wieder vor den Sonnenuntergang.

»Sieht ziemlich echt aus«, sagt Vilmer und knipst los.

»Die werden nicht merken, dass es Fake ist.«

Wir schicken zwei Bilder von dem weißen Strand

im Sonnenuntergang, ich mit einem Lächeln im Badeanzug vor den Palmen, die sich leicht im Wind wiegen. *Das Blue Lagoon Deluxe ist ein Paradies,* schreibe ich.

Und dann schalte ich das Handy schnell wieder aus, bevor Mathilde antworten kann.

Es ist ein warmer, schöner Sommerabend. Ein Traumsommerabend. Wir müssen das kleine Fenster öffnen, um frische Luft hereinzulassen. Dann machen wir auch die Tür auf und sitzen für eine Weile an die warme Mauer gelehnt auf der Kellertreppe. Ich denke an Mama, die bei Janne Wein trinkt, bestimmt amüsiert sie sich. Vielleicht wird sie langsam eine Mama, die die Dinge auf die Reihe kriegt.

Es ist still und schwül, gewittrig. Ich betrachte Vilmer in seinem roten T-Shirt. Fühle mich glücklich. Mein Knie stößt gegen seins. Seine warme Haut an meiner.

Das Gute an Vilmer ist, dass man einfach so mit ihm dasitzen kann. Ganz still. Ohne dass es komisch ist. Und es ist auch nicht komisch, als Vilmer irgendwann wieder zu reden anfängt, nachdem wir lange so auf der Treppe gesessen haben, Knie an Knie.

»Wie lange sind eigentlich noch Sommerferien?«, fragt er.

Und ich, die normalerweise den vollen Überblick

über Stunden und Minuten und Sekunden hat, kann beim besten Willen nicht sagen, wann die Schule wieder anfängt.

»Ich finde, die Ferien sind ultraschnell rumgegangen«, fährt er fort, als er merkt, dass ich seine Frage nicht beantworten kann.

»Ich auch«, sage ich und denke an den Tag, als Mama mir von dem Kurs erzählt hat. Als ich noch geglaubt habe, ich müsste absolut jede einzelne Sekunde der Ferien drinnen hocken und mich langweilen. Und dann kam alles ganz anders. Nur seinetwegen.

Als es langsam kühler wird, gehen wir nach drinnen. Sitzen auf dem roten Sofa und hören Musik von Vilmers Playlist. Plötzlich steht er auf und tritt hinüber zum roten Sonnenuntergang. Beginnt, sich davor zu bewegen. Hin und her. Mit merkwürdigen weichen Bewegungen zum Rhythmus der Musik. Tanzt er etwa?

»Steht doch auf der Liste«, sagt er, als ich lachen muss.

Und dann streckt er den Arm aus, wie um mich zum Tanz aufzufordern. Vor der Tapete mit dem Sonnenuntergang.

Das Gute an Vilmer ist, dass man tatsächlich mit ihm vor dem Sonnenuntergang tanzen kann. Ohne dass es komisch ist. Wir albern rum und lachen. Machen übertriebene Bewegungen, singen lauthals mit. Vilmer probiert, in den Herrenspagat zu gehen. Ich versuche mich an klassischem Ballett, drehe Pirouetten. Wir hüpfen herum, als wären wir total übergeschnappt.

Bis das ruhige Lied kommt, das von *Love* und *Heart* und *Pain* handelt.

»Ich glaube, jetzt müssen wir anders tanzen«, sagt Vilmer und streckt die Arme aus.

Ich gehe zu ihm, und er fängt mich wie ein Tintenfisch. Legt seine Arme auf meine, zieht mich ein bisschen näher zu sich heran, sodass es oben bei meinem Herzen wieder zu pochen anfängt. Und dann tanzen wir, so wie Erwachsene tanzen. Wiegen uns sanft hin und her. Ohne zu reden oder Quatsch zu machen. Vilmers Arme sind warm und fühlen sich angenehm an. Alles ist warm und angenehm.

Vor dem Schlafengehen putzen wir uns im *Paradise Spa* die Zähne. Vilmer hat eine Decke und Laken mitgebracht, aber er hat die Matratze und den Schlafsack vergessen, also beschließen wir, zusammen auf dem roten Sofa zu schlafen.

Wir liegen uns schweigend gegenüber. Die Füße jeweils auf Kopfhöhe des anderen. Es ist fast dunkel im Raum. Nur ein schwacher Streifen Licht fällt durch das kleine Fenster und teilt den Süden in zwei Hälften.

»Vilmer?«, sage ich.

»Ja?«

»Schläfst du schon?«

Es ist ziemlich sinnlos, jemandem diese Frage zu stellen, der gerade geantwortet hat.

»Was ist?«, fragt er und dreht sich um.

Ich überlege. Denke an das, was ich ihn fragen möchte. Was ich mich aber nicht so richtig traue.

»Als wir bei Grete Brattberg waren«, stottere ich schließlich und mache eine lange Pause. »Da hast du gesagt, dass du glaubst, du wärst in niemanden verliebt.«

Es wird still.

»Ja?«, sagt Vilmer nach viel zu vielen Sekunden.

Ich richte mich auf, um ihn anzusehen. Es ist merkwürdig, über so ernste Dinge zu reden, wenn man Kopf an Fuß auf einem Sofa liegt. Vilmer hat sein Gesicht in einem Kissen vergraben, es ist fast nicht zu erkennen.

Ich weiß nicht, was ich als Nächstes sagen soll. Mein Gehirn hat sich noch keine Worte zurechtgelegt. Jedenfalls keine, die irgendwie zu gebrauchen wären. Mehrere Sekunden verstreichen. Wäre ich in diesem Moment ich selbst, hätte ich sie gezählt, aber ich bin nicht ich selbst. Ich bin schon eine ganze Weile nicht mehr ich selbst.

»Ich glaube, das war gelogen.«

Er liegt noch immer reglos da, ohne sich aufzurichten oder auch nur den Kopf zu heben. Als ob er im Schlaf sprechen würde.

»Wie meinst du das?«, frage ich leise.

Vilmer legt sich den Arm übers Gesicht, sodass er noch schwieriger zu erkennen ist.

»Das war gelogen«, sagt er.

Ich schlucke. Was soll das heißen? Ich stoße ihn mit dem Fuß an, damit er reagiert. Er muss erklären, was er damit meint. Ich mag keine Rätsel. Hasse Rätsel. Zumindest, wenn es um so wichtige Dinge geht.

»Ich glaube, jetzt bin ich es.«

Er setzt sich auf und sieht mich an. Seine Augen sind lieb und kreisrund. Wie bei einem Labrador. Es klopft in meinem Herzen, nicht im Bauch. Lange, harte Schläge.

Es ist still und schön im Süden. Er holt die Hand unter der Decke hervor und legt sie auf meine. Unsere Finger verflechten sich miteinander. Er fragt nicht, ob ich verliebt in jemanden bin, aber ich glaube, man kann es sehen. Vielleicht an der Haut über meinem Herzen oder an meinem roten Gesicht oder an meinen Lippen, die nicht aufhören können zu lächeln.

»Du bist süß«, flüstert Vilmer.

Und ich werde so knallrot wie sämtliche roten T-Shirts der Welt.

Er rückt zu mir rüber. Wir sitzen eng nebeneinander, ohne etwas zu sagen. Atmen nur. Vilmer legt seinen

Kopf auf meine Schulter. Seine Locken kitzeln mich am Kinn. Und dann passiert es. Wir küssen uns. Halten einander im Arm. Sein warmer Atem auf meiner Wange, seine weichen Lippen auf meinen. Er riecht nach Vilmer. Es ist ein guter Geruch.

Wir schlafen nebeneinander auf dem Sofa. Vilmers Atem in meinem Ohr. Seine Hand auf meinem Rücken. Ich denke an alles Mögliche, bevor ich einschlafe. Das Küssen. Das Tanzen im Sonnenuntergang. Das Bild, das ich Mathilde geschickt habe. Mama bei Janne. Maria, bei der ich angeblich übernachte. Den Traumsommer. Und was passieren wird, wenn die Ferien vorbei sind.

A ls ich am nächsten Morgen aufwache, ist Vilmer verschwunden. Im Zimmer ist es kalt, draußen höre ich es tröpfeln. Ich strecke mich, mein Körper fühlt sich irgendwie anders an als sonst. Als ob alles neu zusammengesetzt wäre. Muskeln und Glieder. Haut. Haare und Nägel. Ich lege den Zeigefinger auf meinen Mund und fahre mir damit über die Lippen. Sie sind rau. An ein paar Stellen ist die Haut aufgesprungen. Ob das vom Küssen kommt, denke ich und spüre allein durch die Frage ein Ziehen bis in die Zehenspitzen. Als ob sich etwas in meinem Bauch lösen und sich als ein Kribbeln im ganzen Körper ausbreiten würde. Mein Herz klopft so heftig, dass ich mich auf die Seite drehen muss. Ich schließe die Augen und spüre den Puls an meinem Hals pochen. Meine Arme und Beine sind steif vom zusammengekrümmten Liegen. Zu zweit auf einem Sofa.

Wo ist er eigentlich? Ich setze mich auf, und da höre ich es. Er klappert mit irgendwas in der *Sunlight Taverna*. Ein leckerer Geruch zieht zu mir herüber.

Ich angele nach meinem Handy, das auf dem Boden liegt. Schalte es an und warte ungeduldig darauf, dass es hochfährt. Es dauert eine Ewigkeit, bis das Display aufleuchtet. In der Küche klirren Gläser.

Und dann erscheint die Mitteilung. Jemand hat mich angerufen. Zwölf Mal. Was ist passiert? Ich klicke auf den grünen Telefonhörer. Mathilde! Sie hat zwölfmal versucht, mich anzurufen! Mein Magen krampft sich zusammen. Meine Lippen werden noch trockener. Wieso nur hat mich Mathilde so oft angerufen? Sie hat mich noch nie angerufen.

Ich gehe zurück zum Startbildschirm und sehe sieben neue Nachrichten. Ich zögere einen Moment, bevor ich sie anklicke.

Wir sind auf dem Weg zu dir nach Hause. Nur damit du's weißt.

Ich springe auf. Halte das Handy in der Hand, als wäre es eine Waffe. Etwas Gefährliches. Am liebsten würde ich es weit von mir schleudern, es wie eine Granate an der Wand explodieren lassen, sodass ich möglichst wenig Schaden nehme. Aber es liegt schwer in meiner Hand, und ich schaffe es nicht, es wegzuwerfen. Sie sind auf dem Weg. Was wollen sie bloß bei mir?

Ich scrolle im Chatfenster nach oben, lese nicht alle Nachrichten, nehme nur einzelne Wörter wahr, die aus Mathildes grünen Sprechblasen hervorploppen.

Wir wissen alles. Lügnerin.

Ich arbeite mich weiter zurück. Bis zu dem Bild, das ich Mathilde gestern geschickt habe. Es sticht in meiner Brust, als ich es sehe. Mich selbst im Badeanzug vor dem Sonnenuntergang. Vor unserem Sonnenuntergang. Vilmers und meinem. Er wirkt plötzlich so lächerlich. Ich wirke plötzlich so lächerlich. So kindisch in dem Badeanzug. Vor dem falschen Sonnenuntergang, der nur eine Tapete ist. Plötzlich bin ich wieder Ina. Die alte Ina. Alles kommt zurück. Plötzlich habe ich wieder Angst. Vor Mathilde und Regine und Markus. Vor den Gruppen auf dem Schulhof. Vor Geburtstagsfeiern und Ferien und dem Lügen und So-tun-als-ob. All dem, was sie entdecken könnten. Wenn sie bloß ordentlich hinschauen.

Wir wissen, dass du nicht im Süden bist!

Ich starre auf die erste Nachricht. Sie wurde direkt, nachdem ich das Telefon ausgeschaltet habe, gesendet. Direkt nach dem Foto vor dem Sonnenuntergang.

Warum lügst du?

Es sticht in meinen Augen, brennt. Ich kann nicht schlucken, mein Kopf wird heiß und neblig.

Regine und ich waren bei dir zu Hause, um mein Geburtstagsgeschenk abzuholen, das du vergessen hattest. Und deine Mutter hat gesagt, du schläfst bei Maria!

Ich blinzele mehrmals, bevor ich weiterlese.

Deiner besten Freundin Maria, die in unsere Klasse geht!
Mein Herz. Es hat noch nie so schnell geschlagen. Ich sterbe. Es wird aus meiner Brust springen. Über den Boden davonhüpfen. Mir steigen die Tränen in die Augen, ich blinzele sie weg, sie kommen wieder.
Wir haben deiner Mutter nichts gesagt, aber das werden wir jetzt tun. Sie hat so eine Lügentochter wie dich nicht verdient.
Wir werden der ganzen Klasse erzählen, dass alles nur gelogen war.
Wo bist du?
Nimm endlich ab!
Und dann die letzte Nachricht.
Wir sind auf dem Weg zu dir nach Hause. Nur damit du's weißt.
Der Arm mit dem Telefon in der Hand zittert. Meine Beine zittern auch. Ich kann kaum noch stehen. Die letzte Nachricht wurde vor zehn Minuten geschickt! Es dauert fünfzehn Minuten von Mathildes Haus bis zu mir!

Ich schnappe meine Shorts, die in einem Haufen Klamotten auf dem Boden liegen. Springe hinein, reiße mir das Schlafshirt runter und ziehe hastig das Top von gestern über. Schließe im Laufen den Reißverschluss meiner Hose, während ich nach meinen Schuhen suche. Wo sind sie bloß?

Plötzlich steht Vilmer im Zimmer.

»Frühstück«, sagt er fröhlich und hält mir zwei Teller mit Eiern und Speck entgegen. Er hat das bescheuertste T-Shirt ever an, hellblau und eng anliegend, mit einem gigantischen Bild von Elsa und Anna und dem Schriftzug *Sisters Forever* auf der Brust. Er lächelt.

Ich sehe ihn nur eine hundertstel Sekunde an, aber das reicht schon. Auf einmal ist er wieder Vilmer. Der alte Vilmer. Mit dem schiefen Schneidezahn und null sozialen Antennen. Der offen zugibt, dass sein Vater pleite ist und er nicht in Urlaub fährt. Der seltsame Typ aus dem Klassenzimmer, der ungebeten auf Mathildes Geburtstag aufgetaucht ist. Der Psychonachbar, der Steine gegen die Fenster von Leuten wirft, die er nicht kennt. Es kann nicht wahr sein, dass ich neben ihm auf dem Sofa geschlafen habe, ihn geküsst habe. Dass wir wochenlang hier unten gespielt haben wie zwei Kleinkinder. Alles von früher kommt zurück. Denn jetzt sind Mathilde und die anderen auf dem Weg hierher! Und es gibt nichts Schlimmeres, als von ihnen entlarvt zu werden.

»Ich kann nicht mehr mit dir spielen!«, rufe ich Vilmer zu und halte das Telefon hoch. »Kapierst du nicht, wie bescheuert das ist? Das ist echt so megakindisch.«

Ein dumpfer Laut kommt aus meiner Kehle.

Vilmers Augen verdüstern sich.

»Du musst nach Hause gehen! Jetzt sofort. Das Spiel ist aus. Es ist vorbei!«

Und dann renne ich zur Tür, reiße sie auf, nehme immer zwei Treppenstufen auf einmal. Hoch in den Hinterhof. Es regnet. Vorbei am Sandkasten und den Wäschegestellen und dem Grasfleck. Blutgeschmack im Mund. Vor Aufgang A steht niemand. Ich mache kehrt und renne zum Torweg. Stoppe unter dem Schild mit der Aufschrift *Willkommen im Güllebakken Bauverein*. Wähle Mathildes Nummer und halte mir das Handy ans Ohr. Sie nimmt nicht ab. Ich schicke eine Nachricht.

Geht nicht zu meiner Mutter. Ich werde euch alles erklären.

Drei Minuten nachdem ich die Nachricht abgeschickt habe, tauchen sie am Ende der Straße auf. Der Blutgeschmack im Mund ist weg. Ich atme wieder normal. Hoffentlich kann man nicht sehen, dass ich geweint habe. Während ich im Torweg stehe und warte, versuche ich mir Mut zu machen. Mir einen Plan auszudenken. Aber da kommen sie schon. Mathilde und Regine. Mit festen, entschiedenen Schritten. Sie betreten den Torweg, bleiben vor dem Schild stehen, auf dem *Willkommen im Güllebakken Bauverein* steht. Schauen mich an. Mit wütendem Blick. Ich bin die Gefangene, die ein Geständnis abgelegt hat. Sie sind hier, um mich zu holen.

»Hi«, sage ich und setze ein Lächeln auf. »Hattet ihr schöne Ferien bis jetzt?«

Sie ignorieren meine Frage.

»Echt 'ne ganz schön schwache Nummer, die du da abziehst, Ina«, sagt Mathilde. »Wieso lügst du eigentlich so viel?«

Ich schweige. Habe keine Antwort parat. Habe eine Antwort im Kopf, kann sie aber nicht aussprechen. Es gibt keinen Grund, mich noch kleiner zu machen, als ich ohnehin schon bin.

»Wir sind gestern hier vorbeigelaufen, und die Fenster deiner Wohnung standen offen. Da hab ich beschlossen, mein Geschenk abzuholen. Wir haben deine Mutter gefragt, wie es im Süden war, und sie hat gesagt, ihr wärt die ganzen Ferien nur zu Hause gewesen.«

»Also haben wir dir die Nachricht geschickt und gefragt, ob es schön ist im Süden, nur um zu sehen, was du darauf antwortest«, erklärt Regine. »Und du hast weitergelogen!«

Sie schüttelt den Kopf.

»Du hast die ganze Klasse belogen!«, sagt sie fassungslos. »Die Bilder, die du gepostet hast, waren ja nur Fake.«

»Und deine Mutter glaubt, du hättest eine Freundin namens Maria!«, fügt Mathilde hinzu.

Die beiden starren mich an wie zwei Polizistinnen bei einem Verhör. Wieso steigern sie sich so da rein?

»Es ist echt ätzend, wenn einem die Leute direkt ins Gesicht lügen«, sagt Regine scharf, als hätte sie meine Gedanken gelesen.

»Wo warst du eigentlich?«

Der Blutgeschmack ist zurück. Obwohl ich gar nicht gerannt bin.

»Und diesmal wollen wir die Wahrheit hören! Wir haben gestern sogar überlegt, die Polizei anzurufen!«

Ich kreuze die Finger hinter dem Rücken, auch wenn ich weiß, dass es nichts helfen wird. Nichts kann mir jetzt helfen.

»Ich war irgendwie schon im Süden«, murmele ich und bereue meine Worte sofort.

»Im Ernst jetzt?«, sagen Mathilde und Regine im Chor.

Ich starre auf meine Füße, weiß nicht, was ich tun soll. Sie gewinnen so oder so.

»Es war Vilmer«, höre ich mich auf einmal stammeln. »Der Neue.«

Ich zeige zu Aufgang F.

»Er wohnt da drüben. Irgendwie haben wir angefangen, uns zu unterhalten, und dann hatte er eine Idee.«

Meine Stimme ist kaum mehr als ein Flüstern. Ich verstumme.

Sie schauen mich neugierig an.

»Was für eine Idee?«, fragt Regine.

Ich antworte nicht.

»Hallo?«

»Das mit dem Süden«, murmele ich und merke erst jetzt, dass meine Füße nass sind. Dass ich ohne Schuhe nach draußen gerannt bin und friere.

»Ich hab nur mitgemacht, weil ich nichts Besseres zu tun hatte.«

Meine Stimme wird ein bisschen fester. »Er hat eine leere Hausmeisterwohnung entdeckt«, erkläre ich, weil ich merke, dass es keinen anderen Ausweg gibt. »Und dann hat er da so eine Art Süden aufgebaut. Mit einem Planschbecken als Swimmingpool und so.«

Die beiden starren mich an.

»Ein Planschbecken?«

»Er ist echt komisch«, sage ich.

Und plötzlich lächeln sie. Als ob ihr Verdacht bestätigt worden wäre.

»Irgendwie kindisch.«

Mathilde und Regine wechseln einen Blick.

»Er tut so, als wäre er im Süden. Da unten im Keller«, sage ich und deute mit dem Finger in die Richtung.

»Zeig's uns«, sagt Mathilde und marschiert los.

»Sonst erzählen wir allen, dass du gelogen hast.«

Wir gehen am Klettergerüst und dem Sandkasten und dem Grasfleck vorbei. Ein Mann steht bei den Wäschegestellen und spricht mit sich selbst, schlägt die Hände vors Gesicht und schimpft vor sich hin.

»Ich war noch nie hier«, flüstert Regine. »Ist ja voll asozial.«

»Es heißt nicht umsonst Güllebakken«, sagt Mathilde. »Der Name passt.«

Meine Socken klatschen über den nassen Asphalt. Ich friere in dem Top und den dünnen Shorts. Spüre einen Druck hinter den Augen und beiße mir fest auf die Unterlippe. Jetzt bloß nicht anfangen zu heulen.

Wir sind am anderen Ende des Hinterhofs angekommen.

»Da«, sage ich und zeige auf die Treppe. »Da unten ist es.«

Mathilde und Regine steigen eng nebeneinander die Stufen hinab. Als ob sie sich gegenseitig vor Gefahren schützen müssten, die möglicherweise am Ende der Kellertreppe auf sie lauern.

Ich denke an Vilmer, der völlig ahnungslos ist. Vilmer, der Spiegeleier mit Speck gemacht hat. Fühle ein Stechen, beiße noch fester. Auf die Unterlippe. Denn jetzt bin ich die alte Ina. Die unsichere, ängstliche.

Sie lesen das Schild, auf dem *Willkommen im Süden. Fridas und Antons Paradies* steht.

»Wer sind Frida und Anton?«, fragt Mathilde und lacht.

Ich antworte nicht. Sie würden es eh nur lächerlich finden. Wer interessiert sich schon für Geschichten über einen alten Hausmeister mit Liebeskummer?

Die Tür ist zugefallen, aber Vilmer hat mir gezeigt, wie man sie öffnet. Man braucht das Schloss nur mit einer Münze oder etwas Ähnlichem aufzudrücken. Ich habe eine Krone in der Hosentasche und stecke sie in das Schloss, bis es aufspringt. Lasse die beiden hinein. In den Süden. Der leer und still ist. Der Geruch von gebratenem Speck hängt noch in der Luft. Mein Magen knurrt.

»Hallo?«, rufe ich.

Keiner antwortet. Vilmer muss meiner Aufforderung gefolgt und nach Hause gegangen sein. Zum Glück, dann sehen Mathilde und Regine ihn nicht in seinem bescheuerten T-Shirt.

Sie stehen mit fassungslosen Gesichtern beim Sofa. Schauen sich um, zeigen mit den Fingern auf die Sachen. Tuscheln. Alles, was geheim war, wird ans Tageslicht gezerrt.

»Was ist das hier, dieses ganze Zeug?«

Sie starren auf das rosa Planschbecken mit dem Hello-Kitty-Motiv. Den Sand auf dem Boden. Die Sonnenliege. Meinen Badeanzug und Vilmers Badehose, die wir zum Trocknen aufgehängt haben. Sie starren auf den Sonnenuntergang und die Kerzen. Den roten Sonnenschirm. Das Schild am Eingang zum *Paradise Spa – where dreams come true.*

»Oh Mann, wie arm ist das denn.«

Ich bin die alte Ina. Die sich mit neuen Augen umsieht. Mit Mathildes und Regines Augen. Es ist so erbärmlich. Alles hier. Der gesamte dämliche Ort, den wir uns da zusammengebaut haben. Der Süden, als ob! Ich wusste die ganze Zeit, dass es total kindisch ist, auch wenn es schön war. Die Drinks mit den Schirmchen von gestern stehen immer noch auf dem Tisch. Es scheint mir, als wäre gestern schon hundert Jahre her. Kein Laut ist zu hören.

»Hast du hier das Bild gemacht?«, fragt Mathilde und zeigt auf die Tapete.

Ich nicke. Fühle die Tränen aufsteigen. Sie dürfen jetzt nicht kommen. Heulen kann ich später.

»Vilmer hat mich fotografiert«, sage ich und spüre, wie die Tränen verschwinden. Meine Muskeln spannen sich an, ich werde stärker. Habe jemanden, hinter dem ich mich verstecken kann. Eine Art Schutzschild. Ich deute auf das Planschbecken, die Sonnenliege, den Sonnenschirm und die hässliche Tapete.

»Er hat das Zeug auf dem Sperrmüll gefunden«, sage ich und lache. Lachen hilft.

Ich verdrehe die Augen. Schließlich *war* es ursprünglich Vilmers Idee. *Er* wollte die alte Hausmeisterwohnung in ein Südenparadies verwandeln. *Er* hat die Tür aufgebrochen, um im Keller abzuhängen.

»Ich war hier nur ab und zu«, lüge ich.

»Der muss ja echt ein ziemlicher Nerd sein«, sagt Regine.

Ich nicke. »Total.«

Plötzlich heißt es wir gegen Vilmer. Er passt nicht dazu, und das wusste ich eigentlich von Anfang an.

»Er ist sozusagen ein Südenfreund«, fahre ich fort, denn die Sache läuft besser als erwartet. »Einer, mit dem man nur in den Ferien zusammen ist, weil man sonst keinen hat.«

Sie scheinen zu verstehen, was ich meine. Die beiden hatten bestimmt schon selbst eine ganze Reihe von Südenfreunden, so oft, wie sie bereits dort waren. Und es war ja auch mein ursprünglicher Plan, nur während der Ferien etwas mit Vilmer zu machen. Ich hatte nie vor, weiter mit ihm befreundet zu sein, wenn die Schule wieder anfängt und jeder uns sehen kann.

»Ich glaube, es ist nicht so toll bei ihm zu Hause«, sage ich. »Er ist hier nämlich andauernd.«

Sie schauen mich neugierig an. Wollen offenbar mehr. Mehr über Vilmer hören. Er ist spannender als ich und meine Lügen.

»Erzähl schon«, sagt Regine eifrig.

»Ich glaube, sein Vater trinkt ziemlich viel«, sage ich und denke daran, was Vilmer mir über seinen bisher einzigen Südenurlaub erzählt hat. »Und seine Mutter hat die Familie verlassen und irgendwo in Schweden ein Kind mit einem Typ gekriegt. Deshalb redet er nur über Facetime mit ihr.«

Diese Blicke. Sie wollen mehr. Noch mehr. Sie lechzen förmlich danach.

»Er hat kein Geld«, sage ich. »Trägt hässliche T-Shirts und viel zu große Shorts von seinem Vater. Und dann hat er so ein altes Gammelhandy, bei dem der Akku alle fünf Minuten schlappmacht und die Kamera total mies ist.«

Sie lachen. Hängen an meinen Lippen, als ob ich der weltbeste Komiker wäre. Ich hole tief Atem, fülle mich mit Luft.

»Er war nur ein einziges Mal in seinem Leben im Urlaub. Im Süden. Und da war sein Vater die ganze Zeit besoffen, es war also nicht gerade ein Traumurlaub.«

Jetzt schauen sie sich an. Ungläubig. Nur ein einziges Mal im Süden? In sämtlichen Oster- und Sommer- und Herbst- und Weihnachtsferien? Wie ist das bitte möglich?

»Oh Mann«, sagt Mathilde. »Was für ein Loser.«

»Ich weiß«, sage ich.

Und fühle ein Stechen in der Brust.

Es wird still, meine Rede ist zu Ende. Der Komiker hat die Bühne verlassen. Die Angst kommt zurück.

»Tut mir leid, dass ich gelogen habe«, sage ich wie ein Hund. Bittend und schwanzwedelnd. Sie könnten ein Stöckchen werfen, und ich würde hinterherrennen, um es zu holen.

Mathilde und Regine wechseln wieder Blicke, als würden sie wortlos diskutieren, ob sie mir vergeben sollen oder nicht.

»Ist schon okay«, meint Mathilde schließlich. »Aber du musst versprechen, von jetzt an die Wahrheit zu sagen.«

Ich nicke mit meinem Hundekopf. Die Zunge hängt mir aus dem Maul.

»Auch deiner Mutter.«

Wieder nicke ich. Ich hatte ja eh vor, Mama das mit Maria zu sagen, nur gab es bisher keine passende Gelegenheit.

Es wird wieder still.

Aber auf einmal höre ich in der Küche ein Rumpeln. Ein Stuhl ist umgefallen.

Mir wird eiskalt.

Mathilde und Regine schauen mich überrascht an. Ich halte den Atem an. Bitte lass es nicht wahr sein. Denn dann sterbe ich.

Ich gehe mit schnellen Schritten durch den Raum. Zur *Sunlight Taverna*. Die Tür steht offen. Ich betrete die Küche. Es ist vollkommen still. Vollkommen leer. Die beiden Teller mit Spiegelei und Speck stehen unberührt auf dem Tisch. Ein Stuhl liegt auf dem Küchenboden.

Ich atme in kurzen Stößen. Und jetzt sehe ich ihn. Er hockt zwischen der Wand und dem verdreckten Herd. Zusammengekauert. Umschlingt die Knie mit seinen Armen, den Blick starr nach unten gerichtet. Die Locken auf seinem Kopf bewegen sich nicht im Geringsten. Die Augen sind weit aufgerissen. Wie eine Muschel.

Er hat es gehört. Alles. Alles, was ich gesagt habe. Jedes einzelne Wort.

Ich renne aus dem Süden, die Treppe hoch. Mathilde und Regine laufen mir nach. Mit der Hand reibe ich mir übers Gesicht. Als könnte ich Vilmer und das, was ich eben gesehen habe, einfach wegwischen.

»Was war das für ein Geräusch?«, fragt Mathilde atemlos.

Sein Körper hinter dem Herd. Der Kopf mit den Locken. Sein starr nach unten gerichteter Blick.

»Nichts«, sage ich und spüre einen Kloß im Hals. »Nur ein Fenster, das zugeschlagen ist.«

Ich gehe mit schnellen Schritten über den Hinterhof. Immer noch auf Strümpfen. Mathilde und Regine schnaufen hinter mir. Sie sollen mein Gesicht nicht sehen, denn es hat sich garantiert verändert.

Vilmer hinter dem Herd. Regungslos wie ein Soldat im Krieg. Ich kann jetzt nicht an ihn denken. Es tut zu weh. Seine Locken, seine Ohren. Ich kann nicht an ihn denken!

Der Hinterhof ist grau und nass. Der komische Typ

von vorhin ist zum Glück nicht mehr da. Im Sandkasten liegt Müll, ein paar leere Flaschen und eine Plastiktüte. Im ersten Stock von Aufgang C hat jemand eine Wolldecke vors Fenster gehängt. Die großen Häuser mit Terrasse und hellen Vorhängen tauchen vor meinem inneren Auge auf. Die Garagen und die Mütter mit engen weißen Hosen.

»Was ist los?«, fragt Regine außer Puste. »Hast du es dermaßen eilig, oder was?«

Wir sind bei Aufgang A angekommen. Wollen sie nicht langsam mal heimgehen?

Ich reiße die Tür auf, sie folgen mir ins Treppenhaus. Ohne ein Wort zu sagen, laufe ich die Treppe hoch. In meinem Hals sitzt ein dicker Klumpen. Ein Ton, und ich breche in Tränen aus. Ich merke, wie Mathilde und Regine die Risse in den Wänden anstarren, die Reihen verbeulter Briefkästen. Es stinkt nach gebratenem Essen. Die Lampe an der Decke flackert wie in der trostlosesten Disco der Welt. Auf dem Treppenabsatz zwischen erstem und zweitem Stock liegt eine leere Styroporschachtel. Daneben sind die Reste eines Döners verstreut. Die Leute im zweiten Stock streiten und keifen wie immer, ein Mann brüllt irgendwas. Mathilde und Regine zucken zusammen. Im dritten Stock riecht es nach Rauch. Am Fenster liegen Zigarettenstummel.

Mit großen Augen schauen sie sich um. Als wären sie auf einer Safari im Slum.

Vor unserer Tür mache ich halt und schließe auf. Mein Herz hämmert.

»Wir kommen mit rein«, sagt Regine entschieden und öffnet die Tür zu unserem winzigen Flur.

»Hallo, Ina!«, ruft Mama aus dem Wohnzimmer.

Klingt sie sanft oder müde oder wütend? Ich kenne Mamas Stimme so gut, aber gerade kann ich sie gar nicht einordnen. Zu viel wirbelt durch meinen Kopf. Vilmer hinter dem Herd. All das, was ich gesagt habe.

Mama taucht in der Tür zum Wohnzimmer auf. Im Schlabberlook, die fettigen Haare zu einem losen Knoten im Nacken zusammengebunden. Nichts, was im Entferntesten an enge Hosen und rote Lippen erinnern würde. Sie passt perfekt nach Güllebakken.

»Oh«, sagt sie und macht schnell das Haargummi raus. »Hast du Freunde mitgebracht?«

Nervös fährt sie sich mit den Fingern durch die Haare, versucht sie glatt zu kämmen.

»Hallo noch mal«, begrüßt sie Mathilde und Regine. Sie riecht komisch. Irgendwie säuerlich. Vielleicht ist es der Wein von gestern.

»War es schön bei Maria?«, fragt sie mich.

Im Flur wird es vollkommen still.

Mathilde dreht sich zu mir, stößt mich mit dem Ellbogen in die Seite, als wollte sie mir ein Zeichen geben. Regine hüstelt.

Ich beiße mir auf die Lippen. Die Lippen, die gestern noch Vilmer geküsst haben. Die Lippen, die so viele Worte gesagt haben, so viel Gemeines. Und trotzdem ist es immer noch nicht vorbei.

Ich schaue Mama an. Schaue ihr in die Augen. In das fragende Gesicht. Was, wenn sie anfängt zu weinen?

»Setz dich lieber hin«, sage ich und schiebe Mama vorsichtig ins Wohnzimmer, während sie mich unverwandt anstarrt.

Mathilde und Regine folgen uns. Sie sehen sich um. In unserer Wohnung, die halb so groß ist wie Mathildes Wohnzimmer. Wir haben keine großen Tische mit gefüllten Blumenvasen, keine grauen Sofas, auf denen eine ganze Klasse Platz findet. Wir haben eine abgenutzte Couch mit einer Decke über der Rückenlehne, und darauf sitzt Mama in ihrem Jogginganzug und sieht nervös aus.

Ich hole Luft.

»Es gibt keine Maria.«

Meine Stimme ist heiser und schwach. Als ob ich bald keine Worte mehr in mir hätte.

Mama lacht auf. Es ist ein merkwürdiges, kurzes Lachen, das schnell wieder erstirbt. Dann blickt sie mich an.

»Ina?«, fragt sie ernst. »Was hast du da gesagt?«

»Es gibt sie nicht«, wiederhole ich.

Meine Stimme wird noch schwächer. Bald habe ich auch keinen Atem mehr.

»Ich hab sie erfunden.«

Mama öffnet den Mund. Sie sinkt in sich zusammen. Es sieht aus, als würden eine Million Gedanken durch ihren Kopf schießen.

»Aber«, sagt sie und macht den Mund wieder zu.

»Es ist wirklich wichtig, dass endlich die Wahrheit ans Licht kommt«, bemerkt Regine. Es klingt, als würde sie schon für das Amt der Schülersprecherin trainieren. »Ina hat ziemlich viel gelogen in der letzten Zeit.«

Mamas Augen werden grau und durchsichtig. Es tut weh, sie anzuschauen.

»Aber. Wo bist du denn jeden Tag gewesen, wenn du nicht mit Maria zusammen warst?«, flüstert sie.

Ich höre, wie ihre Stimme zittert. Sehe, wie sie blinzelt und versucht, sich zusammenzureißen.

»Im Süden«, schluchze ich.

Denn jetzt kann ich nicht mehr. Jetzt lässt mich der Klumpen in meinem Hals nicht mehr atmen, und tausend kleine Tränen steigen in meinen Augen auf.

»Im Süden?«, fragt Mama bestürzt.

Es gibt keine Worte. Nicht mehr. Es gibt nur noch Tränen. Für Vilmer. Für Mama. Für alles, was ich gesagt und getan und erlogen habe.

»Nach den Ferien fängt ein Junge bei uns in der Klasse an«, höre ich Mathilde sagen. »Er wohnt hier in Tyllebakken. Und er hat sich irgendwie seinen eigenen Süden gebaut, in einer leeren Kellerwohnung im Hinterhof. Mit lauter Kram, den er auf dem Sperrmüll gefunden hat. Und dann hat er Ina überredet mitzumachen.«

Mamas Gesicht verschwimmt hinter meinen Tränen. Ich blinzele und sehe, dass sie vom Sofa aufsteht. Plötzlich steht sie wie ein Riese im Jogginganzug vor uns. Die Arme in die Hüfte gestemmt. Der Blick fest.

»Ist er denn nett?«, fragt sie mit lauter Stimme. »Dieser Junge. Ist er nett?«

»Ja«, piepse ich. »Er heißt Vilmer. Er ist nett.«

Und mein Herz schrumpft in meiner Brust zusammen.

Mathilde und Regine lächeln, als sie wieder draußen im Flur stehen, sie wirken sehr zufrieden mit sich selbst. Endlich haben sie die Lügnerin überführt. Endlich sind sie dieser ganzen dreckigen Angelegenheit auf den Grund gekommen. Die Gefangene hat gestanden. Die Gefangene bereut ihre Taten. Sie können triumphierend nach Hause gehen.

Mama hat sich zurück aufs Sofa gesetzt. Sie hat die Haare zusammengebunden, und ihre Augen sind wieder normal. Ich habe versprochen, dass ich ihr später den Süden zeige. Keine Geheimnisse mehr. Und keine Lügen. Das habe ich laut und deutlich gesagt, damit Regine und Mathilde es auch hören. Ab jetzt erzähle ich nur noch die Wahrheit. Egal, worum es geht.

»Eins noch«, sagt Mathilde. »Mein Geburtstagsgeschenk, hast du das, oder …?«

Ich schüttele den Kopf.

»Das gibt es auch nicht«, sage ich.

Denn jetzt bin ich so nackt, dass es eh keinen Unterschied mehr macht.

»Ich hatte kein Geld. Und Mama wollte ich nicht fragen, weil sie immer so gestresst wird von Geburtstagen und Sachen, die etwas kosten. Also hab ich so getan, als hätte ich ein Geschenk für dich gekauft und es bloß zu Hause vergessen.«

Mathilde starrt mich entsetzt an. Als ob dies das absolut Schlimmste wäre von all dem, was sie heute erfahren hat. In ihren Augen glänzen Tränen, womöglich hat sie nie zuvor etwas so Schreckliches erlebt. Regine legt beschützend den Arm um sie.

»So, jetzt wisst ihr alles«, sage ich.

Ich schließe die Tür und fühle mich vollkommen leer.

Nachmittags folgt mir Mama nach unten in den Süden.

Wir haben lange geredet. Ich habe ihr Dinge erzählt, die ich vorher nur mit einem einzigen Menschen geteilt habe. Dass ich keine Freundinnen habe. Dass ich nicht nach Geld frage, selbst wenn ich es brauche, weil ich sie nicht traurig machen will. Dass alle anderen teure Klamotten und lauter Sachen haben und Geburtstagsgeschenke kaufen können. Dass sie in den Ferien ins Ausland fahren. Dass sie schöne Häuser in Solvangtoppen haben, während ich hier wohne, im Güllebakken Bauverein, in einer Wohnung, die kleiner ist als die Wohnzimmer der meisten meiner Klassenkameraden. Dass die anderen nie an Geld denken. Weil sie immer Geld haben. Und dass ich fast die ganze Zeit daran denke.

»Wem außer mir hast du das alles erzählt?«, hat Mama gefragt, und da musste ich wieder losheulen.

Weil es unmöglich ist, seinen Namen auszusprechen,

ohne mich an das Bild von ihm hinter dem Herd zu erinnern. Ohne mich an all das zu erinnern, was er gehört hat.

Jetzt fühle ich meinen Herzschlag. Nur noch ein paar Meter. Ich habe nicht die leiseste Ahnung, was ich sagen soll, falls Vilmer auf dem roten Sofa sitzt. Keine Worte der Welt können wiedergutmachen, was passiert ist. Ich kann ihm nicht in die Augen sehen. Ich bin der schrecklichste Mensch im Universum. Ich habe einen heimlichen Pakt gebrochen. Auf die absolut grausamst-vorstellbare Weise.

Oben auf der Treppe liegt etwas. Etwas Rosafarbenes. Es dauert einen Moment, bis ich begreife, was es ist: das Hello-Kitty-Planschbecken. Die eine Seite hängt schlaff herunter, in der Ecke hat sich eine kleine Pfütze Regenwasser gesammelt.

Mama und ich gehen nach unten. Mein Magen zieht sich zusammen, als ich das Schild sehe. Es ist in der Mitte durchgerissen. Auf der einen Hälfte steht *Frida* und auf der anderen *Anton*, sie liegen auf unterschiedlichen Treppenstufen. Ein paar Tesareste und ein Fetzen Pizzakarton kleben noch an der Tür.

»Wo sind wir hier?«, flüstert Mama.

Ich fische das Kronenstück aus meiner Hosentasche, stecke es ins Schloss und stemme mich gegen die Tür. Sie öffnet sich mit einem Klicken.

Mama geht mit unsicheren Schritten hinein. Als ob ich sie in eine Falle locken würde, wo jeden Augenblick ein Haufen unheimlicher Leute auftauchen könnte.

Ich schalte das grelle Deckenlicht an. Vor unseren Augen erscheint der Süden. Aber es ist nicht mehr Vilmers und mein Süden. Es ist ein völlig anderer Ort. Der Sonnenschirm ist umgefallen. Mamas Liegestuhl krümmt sich neben Antons Schreibtisch. Der Sandstrand ist über den ganzen Fußboden verschmiert. Die Lichterkette wurde in eine Ecke geschmissen, die Nägel ragen wie Stacheldraht aus der Wand heraus. Das Bild von Frida ist weg. Das Buch mit den Gedichten und der Umschlag mit dem Brief, der niemals abgeschickt wurde, liegen neben dem Sofa auf dem Boden. Und der Sonnenuntergang hängt in Fetzen von der Wand. Mitten entzweigerissen, genau dort, wo die schönen Sonnenstrahlen auf die Palmen fallen.

Ich betrete die *Sunlight Taverna*. Zwei leere Teller auf dem Tisch, gelbe Spiegeleierreste. Ein Stück Speck auf der Tischdecke. Auf dem Boden liegen Scherben. Ich bücke mich. Es ist der zerbrochene Becher von den Olympischen Winterspielen in Lillehammer. Ich schaue hinter den Herd. Nur um sicherzugehen, dass er dort nicht mehr sitzt. Der leere Platz macht mich unendlich traurig.

Im *Paradise Spa* liegen alle Schönheitsprodukte im

Waschbecken. Eines von Vilmers Handtüchern hängt halb im Klo. Der Boden ist dreckig.

Mama steht immer noch wie angewurzelt im Wohnzimmer. Es scheint, als würde sie jeden Moment wieder anfangen zu weinen. Ich dachte, sie könnte sich den Süden etwas besser vorstellen, wenn ich ihn ihr zeige. Aber jetzt, so, wie es hier aussieht, lässt sich schwer dafür Werbung machen.

»Bin ich die schlechteste Mutter der Welt?«, flüstert sie.

Ich antworte nicht. Kapiere nicht, wieso es plötzlich um sie geht.

»Es kommt mir vor, als hätte ich geschlafen«, fährt sie fort. »Und plötzlich ist es wieder Morgen.«

»Du bist ja schon ziemlich lange sehr müde«, sage ich vorsichtig.

Mama nickt.

»Ich verstehe nur nicht«, sagt sie und blickt sich um, »wieso du den ganzen Sommer lang *hier* warst. Ich war so sicher, dass du an der Badebucht bist und dort Spaß hast. Mit Maria.«

Ich schweige, gehe einfach zu ihr und lege die Arme um sie. Höre ihr Herz in meinem Ohr schlagen. So stehen wir lange da.

Dann sehe ich den Ring. Er liegt auf dem Schreibtisch. Ich gehe hinüber und stecke ihn an. Hebe das

Buch mit den Gedichten und den Brief vom Boden auf, presse beides gegen die Brust. Es sticht und schneidet mir ins Herz. Es ist zerstört. All das Schöne ist zerstört.

Ich rufe Vilmer nicht an. Ich schreibe ihm nicht. Klingele nicht bei Aufgang F. Gehe nicht zurück in den Süden.

Sein Fenster ist dunkel. Die ganze Wohnung ist dunkel. Von meinem Fenster aus schaue ich über den Hinterhof auf das Haus gegenüber. Suche nach einem Zeichen, dass es ihn noch gibt. Dass ich ihn nicht bloß erfunden habe, so wie Maria.

Ich zerbreche mir den Kopf darüber, was ich zu ihm sagen soll, wenn ich ihn wiedersehe. Falls ich ihn wiedersehe. Es gibt keine Worte, die groß genug sind. Keine Worte, die passen. Ich habe unseren Südenpakt gebrochen. Es reicht nicht, sich einfach zu entschuldigen und zu glauben, damit sei alles wieder gut. Zu sagen, dass es mir leidtut. Er will garantiert nie mehr mit mir reden.

Die Tage verstreichen.

Ich denke jede dritte Sekunde an ihn. Fange wieder an zu zählen – die Tage und Stunden, die noch übrig sind von den Sommerferien. Von den besten und schlimmsten Sommerferien der Welt. Dreizehn Tage werden zu zwölf, werden zu elf und zu zehn. Ich halte das Handy in der Hand und starre auf seine Nummer. Um es dann wieder wegzulegen.

Mehrfach träume ich von ihm. Er läuft eine Straße voller Autos entlang und wird immer kleiner und kleiner, bis er schließlich als Punkt am Horizont verschwindet. Er lehnt sich mir entgegen, lacht sein Lachen, das ich so mag, die Locken hüpfen auf seinem Kopf. Und dann küssen wir uns. Er sitzt auf dem roten Sofa im Süden, das plötzlich ein Boot ist, draußen auf dem offenen Meer. Er segelt davon, taucht in den Wellen ab, die Locken werden nass und kleben ihm am Kopf.

Ich lese in Antons Gedichtbuch. Lache über seine Reime und das hoffnungslos schlechte Gedicht über den Kartoffeleintopf. Es bringt mich zum Weinen. Als ob Vilmer es geschrieben hätte. Für mich. Als ob ich Frida wäre. Eines der Gedichte heißt *Verzeih mir*. Ich schreibe es ab und hänge es an die Wand über meinem Bett. Es ist das Erste und Letzte, was ich an jedem einzelnen Tag sehe.

Jetzt, wo es weder Maria noch den Süden mehr gibt, muss ich jeden Tag mit dem Fahrrad zu Oma fahren, während Mama bei ihrem Kurs ist. Oma scheint nicht so zufrieden mit dieser Lösung zu sein. »Willst du dich denn nicht mit deinen Freunden treffen?«, fragt sie immer wieder, obwohl ich jedes Mal dieselbe Antwort gebe. »Ich habe keine Freunde, Oma. Das weißt du doch.« Und Oma dreht sich um, schaut in den Fernseher und schaltet die Lautstärke hoch. Sie mag es, wenn die Dinge normal sind.

Mama macht jetzt jeden Morgen Frühstück. Legt mir Kleider zum Anziehen raus. Mittags kocht sie, es gibt nicht mehr nur Tiefkühlpizza. Außerdem erkundigt sie sich etliche Male, wie es mir geht und ob alles in Ordnung ist. Ihr Blick ist klar und durchdringend. Sie scheint nicht mehr so müde zu sein, redet nicht über den Kurs, schlüpft nicht in den Jogginganzug, sobald sie zur Tür hereinkommt.

Mama sagt, es sei, als ob sie aus einem tiefen Schlaf erwacht wäre. Für mich ist es genau andersherum. Ich war wach, und jetzt schlafe ich. Alles zieht an mir vorbei, ohne mich zu berühren.

Mamas Garnelentraum geht endlich in Erfüllung. Eines Tages kommt sie mit einer dicken Tüte nach Hause. Trällert in der Küche, während sie Weißbrot aufschneidet, Butter und Mayonnaise aus dem Kühlschrank nimmt, die Garnelen in eine Schüssel legt. Sogar Dill hat sie mitgebracht, sie hackt ihn mit schwungvollen Bewegungen. Es klingelt, und Mama bittet mich aufzumachen. Mein Herz klopft. Was, wenn …

Oma steht vor der Tür. Sie lächelt und umarmt mich fest. Mein Herz fällt.

»Ina, Ina«, sagt Oma und drückt sich an mir vorbei in den engen Flur. »Jetzt gibt's Garnelen!«

Ich lege mich aufs Bett und lausche, wie Mama und Oma im Wohnzimmer den Tisch decken, sie unterhalten sich mit gedämpften Stimmen.

»Hat sie wirklich keine Freunde?«, fragt Oma. »Als ich in ihrem Alter war, bin ich den ganzen Tag draußen herumgesprungen. Es ist doch nicht normal für eine Zwölfjährige, keine Freunde zu haben.«

»Schsch«, macht Mama. Dann sagt sie: »Ich versuche, etwas zu deichseln.«

Sie lächeln mich an, als ich ins Wohnzimmer komme. Die Garnelen stehen bereit, der Tisch ist mit einer weißen Decke und rosa Servietten gedeckt. Limo in meinem Glas, Weißwein für Mama und Oma.

»Es gibt nichts Besseres als Garnelen im Sommer«, sagt Oma und häuft sich eine fette Portion auf den Teller.

Was haben Erwachsene nur mit Garnelen, frage ich mich, während Mama und Oma drauflosschälen, als gelte es ihr Leben. Sie mampfen hochgetürmte Garnelenbrote, wischen sich die Mayonnaise vom Mund. Ein Haufen mit Garnelenschalen nach dem nächsten. Ist das normal? Sind *sie* normal? Wer bestimmt eigentlich, was für Zwölfjährige normal ist und was nicht? Und was versucht Mama zu deichseln?

Ich könnte sie fragen, habe aber nicht die Energie. Lasse einfach alles an mir vorbeiziehen. Esse zwei Garnelen und gehe ins Bett.

Am nächsten Morgen weckt mich das Piepsen meines Handys. Die Sonne knallt durchs Fenster, in der Wohnung riecht es nach Kaffee. Mein Herz klopft wieder, genau wie gestern, als es an der Tür geklingelt hat. Was, wenn es Vilmer ist?! Das Handy liegt auf dem Boden und leuchtet. Ich sehe eine Nachricht auf dem Bildschirm, einen einzigen Satz.

Kommst du mit zur Badebucht?

Sie ist von Mathilde. Ich lese den kurzen Text mehrere Male, das Handy liegt schwer in meiner Hand. Was soll ich antworten? Noch vor ein paar Wochen wäre ich vor Freude ausgeflippt. Über eine Nachricht von Mathilde. Dass ich mich ausgerechnet mit *ihr* an der Badebucht treffen darf.

Vielleicht hat sie mir das mit dem Geschenk inzwischen verziehen. Vielleicht sind sie und Regine zu dem Schluss gekommen, dass ich eigentlich doch ganz nett bin und in die Clique aufgenommen werden kann. Einen Moment lang stelle ich mir die Gruppen auf dem

Schulhof vor. Die Siebtklässlergruppen. Die wichtigsten Gruppen von allen. Inmitten der allerwichtigsten steht natürlich Mathilde. Und vielleicht auch ich. Ich weiß ja, dass ich Freunde brauche, die mich hochziehen, nicht runter. Überhaupt brauche ich ganz einfach Freunde.

Also öffne ich das Chatfenster und fange an zu tippen. *Ja*, schreibe ich und lösche es wieder. *Wann?*, schreibe ich und lösche es wieder. *Nur wir zwei?*, schreibe ich und lösche es wieder. *Klingt gut*, schreibe ich. Aber bevor ich es abschicken kann, kommt eine weitere Nachricht.

Sind ab 11 da.

Mein Badeanzug liegt noch im Süden, deshalb muss ich einen alten Bikini nehmen, der mir zu klein geworden ist. Ich brauche mich ja nicht unbedingt zu sonnen, denke ich und ziehe die Vorhänge auf, draußen sind bestimmt dreißig Grad.

Mama sitzt am Küchentisch und frühstückt.

»Ich fahre zur Badebucht«, sage ich.

Mama zieht die Augenbrauen hoch.

»Keine Sorge«, sage ich, »diesmal stimmt es. Ich bin mit Mathilde und Regine verabredet, den beiden, die neulich hier waren.«

Ich habe bisher gar nicht an Markus gedacht. Ob er auch kommt. Oder ob noch andere da sind. Und wie viele normalerweise immer an der Badebucht abhängen. Was sie anhaben und worüber sie reden. Und ob Mathilde und Regine ihnen von meinen Lügen erzählen werden, vom Süden und von Vilmer. Die altbekannte Angst steigt in mir auf. Am liebsten würde ich stattdessen wieder zu Oma fahren. Aber Mama lächelt zufrieden. Sie trägt ein rotes Sommerkleid und sieht wach aus. Und ich bin so froh, wenn sie lächelt.

»Hab ganz viel Spaß, Ina«, sagt sie und zwinkert mir zu, während sie ihren Kaffee austrinkt.

Sie sitzen im Gras. Mathilde hat sonnengebräunte Haut, sie trägt einen weißen Bikini und eine große Sonnenbrille. Regines Haare sind zu einem zerzausten Dutt hochgesteckt, ihr Bikini ist rot. Ein Stückchen entfernt sitzen die Jungs. Ich erkenne mehrere von ihnen, sie gehen auf die Mittelschule. Mathilde flüstert Regine etwas ins Ohr, dann winken sie mir zu.

»Hi«, sagen sie im Chor, wechseln Blicke und umarmen mich kurz und vorsichtig.

Es ist, als ob ich sie bei irgendetwas unterbrochen hätte, als ob sie gerade etwas Supergeheimes besprochen hätten, bevor ich aufgetaucht bin. Mathilde rückt zur Seite, um mir Platz auf ihrer Decke zu machen.

Es ist schön, an der Badebucht mit Mathilde und Regine auf einer Decke zu sitzen. Zu spüren, wie die Jungs von der Mittelschule mich anschauen. Sie haben mich bestimmt vorher noch nie bemerkt. Aber jetzt sehen sie mich, einfach nur, weil ich hier sitze.

»Alles gut?«, fragt Mathilde, und ich nicke, obwohl ich versprochen habe, nicht mehr zu lügen.

Regine und Mathilde sagen nichts, lächeln nur. Und Mathilde fragt, ob ich eine Zimtschnecke will.

Ich nicke wieder. Und dann essen wir alle drei genüsslich unsere Zimtschnecken, bevor wir uns hinlegen, um uns zu sonnen.

»Da kommt Markus«, sagt Regine nach einer Weile.

Ich drehe mich um und sehe, wie Markus in weißen Shorts und einem dunkelblauen T-Shirt in unsere Richtung schlendert. Warte darauf, dass mir das Herz aus der Brust springt, so wie immer, wenn er in der Nähe ist.

»Hi, Mädels«, sagt Markus mit einem Lächeln.

Er lässt seinen Rucksack fallen und setzt sich zu uns auf die Decke, direkt neben mich. Er riecht wie immer: nach Sonnencreme und Waschmittel. Seine Haare sind länger, und er ist noch brauner als vor den Ferien. Sein Arm berührt meinen Oberschenkel. Aber mein Herz bleibt ruhig.

Markus legt sich auf den Rücken. Dicht neben mich. Irgendwie kann ich es gar nicht so richtig fassen, dass ich auf einmal zur Clique gehöre. Dass ich auf derselben Decke liege wie Markus und die beliebtesten Mädchen der Klasse. Dass wir in wenigen Tagen in die Siebte kommen und ich Teil von etwas Neuem bin. Sollte ich nicht eigentlich ziemlich glücklich sein?

»War's schön im Süden?«

Markus schaut mich an und lacht.

Alle lachen.

»Ja«, sage ich.

Schließlich habe ich versprochen, die Wahrheit zu sagen.

»Cool«, sagt Markus und grinst Mathilde und Regine an.

»Wir haben es Markus erzählt«, sagt Regine. »Hoffe, das ist okay.«

»Hast du Vilmer noch mal gesehen?«, fragt Mathilde.

Ich habe keine Lust, über Vilmer zu reden.

»Nein«, antworte ich kurz.

»Er ist wahrscheinlich noch im *Süden*«, sagt Markus und macht Gänsefüßchen in die Luft. »Ich freue mich schon darauf, wenn er nach den Ferien vom Urlaub erzählen soll.«

Sie lachen wieder. Die Sonne verschwindet hinter einer dünnen Wolke.

»Aber wie ist das denn jetzt genau, seid ihr Freunde?«, fragt Mathilde und setzt sich auf. »Das ist schon wichtig für uns zu wissen. Warst du gern mit ihm zusammen?«

Es passt gerade wirklich schlecht, dass ich die Wahrheit sagen soll. Aber wenn ich nicht lüge, fange ich an zu weinen. Und wenn ich anfange zu weinen, halten sie mich für eine Loserin. Und wenn sie mich für eine

Loserin halten, bin ich nach den Ferien doch wieder in keiner Gruppe. Jedenfalls in keiner, die cool ist.

Deshalb schüttele ich den Kopf. Und ziehe eine Grimasse. Damit sie verstehen, wie kindisch und bescheuert die Sache mit Vilmer einfach nur war. Ohne dass ich es explizit sagen muss.

Da lächeln sie.

Und wir lachen.

Mathilde wechselt einen Blick mit Regine.

»Denn jetzt versuchen wir ja sozusagen, mit dir befreundet zu sein«, erklärt sie. »Und da wollen wir diesen Vilmer nach Möglichkeit nicht unbedingt dabeihaben.«

Ich nicke. Beiße mir auf die Unterlippe.

»Super«, sagt Mathilde. »Wir haben deiner Mutter nämlich versprochen, nett zu dir zu sein.«

Ich starre sie an.

»Meiner Mutter?«, frage ich verständnislos.

»Ja«, sagt Regine. »Sie wünscht sich doch so sehr, dass du ein paar Freunde hast, die tatsächlich existieren.«

»Sie hat mir eine Nachricht geschickt und mich gebeten, dich mitzunehmen«, erklärt Mathilde.

Sie hat die Sonnenbrille auf den Kopf geschoben, in ihren Mundwinkeln zuckt ein kleines Lächeln.

Ich versuche, etwas zu deichseln. Mama, die mit Oma tuschelt. Wie konnte ich nur glauben, dass sie mich einfach so einladen würden? Dass sie mich tatsächlich gern an der Badebucht dabeihaben wollten?

»Erzähl noch was über Vilmer«, sagt Markus. »Das muss ja echt voll der Loser sein.«

Sie schauen mich alle drei erwartungsvoll an. Genau wie unten im Süden, als Mathilde und Regine immer noch mehr hören wollten und ich den Pakt gebrochen habe.

Ich schaue Markus an, der mit offenem Mund dasitzt. Mathilde und Regine, die lächeln und sich aneinanderdrücken. Und da wird mir alles klar. Einfach alles. Welche Freunde einen hochziehen und welche runter.

»Nein«, sage ich laut.

Denn das ist das beste Wort, das mir einfällt. Das einzige Wort.

Und dann stehe ich auf, packe meine Sachen zusammen und gehe.

So schnell ich kann, fahre ich nach Hause. Strample die Hügel hoch. Im Hinterhof springe ich vom Rad und setze den Helm ab. Da höre ich es.

»Fuglesang!«, ruft mir eine Stimme zu. »Fuglesang war es!«

Ich drehe mich um und sehe Grete Brattberg, die mir eilig entgegentrippelt.

»Ihr Name war Fuglesang! Jetzt weiß ich es wieder!«

Sie fuchtelt aufgeregt mit den Händen, bis sie außer Atem vor mir zum Stehen kommt.

»Ich habe mir den Kopf zerbrochen, wie die Schöne denn noch mal hieß. Die Verlobte von Anton Berntzen. Seit du und dein netter Freund bei mir wart und wir von alten Zeiten gesprochen haben.«

Ich schweige. Mein netter Freund. Das kommt mir auch wie alte Zeiten vor, so lange scheint es her zu sein.

»Und jetzt ist es mir endlich wieder eingefallen«, sagt Grete Brattberg zufrieden. »Frida Fuglesang.« Sie trällert den Namen.

»Anscheinend wurde sie in Paris ziemlich berühmt. War mit irgendeinem Filmstar oder so zusammen.«

Grete Brattberg schaut mich an. Als ob sie auf eine Antwort von mir wartet.

»Dein Freund hat mir erzählt, dass ihr ein paar Dinge gefunden habt. Unten in Antons Wohnung. Briefe und ein Gedichtbuch und ein altes Foto«, fährt sie eifrig fort.

Plötzlich beugt sie sich zu mir.

»Es sollte nicht so schwer sein, sie zu finden«, flüstert sie geheimnisvoll und drückt mir einen Zettel in die Hand.

»Wer weiß, vielleicht freut sie sich ja, die Sachen zurückzubekommen. Auch wenn es schon so lange her ist.« Sie zwinkert mir zu.

Was will sie mir damit sagen?

»Ich fände es jedenfalls schön, ein Buch mit Gedichten zu kriegen, in denen es um mich geht.«

Grete Brattberg schlendert in Richtung Aufgang H davon.

»Du musst den netten Jungen mitnehmen!«, ruft sie mir von den Wäschegestellen aus zu.

Ich falte den Zettel auf und lese den kurzen Text. Unter Frida Fuglesangs Namen stehen nur zwei Wörter. *Solvangtunet Seniorenzentrum.* Na, das klingt aber nicht nach Paris!

Es hätten Vilmer und ich sein sollen. Die zusammen mit den Fahrrädern losfahren. Vilmer vorneweg und ich hinterher. Die Straßen entlang, um eine alte Liebesgeschichte in Ordnung zu bringen. Vilmer hätte den Verlobungsring anhaben sollen, und ich hätte den Brief und das Gedichtbuch in einer Tasche am Lenker gehabt. Es hätten wir zwei sein sollen.

Stattdessen bin es nur ich. Ich werde die Liebesgeschichte allein reparieren. Die alte und die neue.

Vor dem Solvangtunet Seniorenzentrum stelle ich mein Fahrrad ab. Zwei Männer sitzen in Rollstühlen und rauchen, folgen mir mit ernsten Blicken.

Drinnen im Eingangsbereich riecht es nach Mittagessen, nach irgendetwas Gebratenem. Meine Augen gleiten über die Namensliste. Mein Herz klopft schneller. *Frida Fuglesang* steht da neben drei Ziffern. 515.

Ich gehe einen langen Gang mit hellgrünen Wänden entlang. Eine Tür folgt auf die andere. 501, 503.

Plötzlich taucht eine Frau in blauer Uniform vor mir auf.

»Wohin willst du?«, fragt sie mit resoluter Stimme. Ich antworte nicht, denke stattdessen wieder an Vilmer. Wenn er doch nur hier wäre.

Die Frau in der Uniform runzelt die Stirn. Auf einem Schild über ihrer Brust steht *Wenche*.

»Zu Frida Fuglesang«, murmele ich.

»Frida Fuglesang?«, wiederholt sie und mustert mich skeptisch. »Frida bekommt sonst nie Besuch. Und wer bist du, wenn man fragen darf?«

»Eine Freundin«, stammle ich und schiele zur Tür mit der Nummer 515.

»Soso«, sagt Wenche.

Es ist wahrscheinlich ein bisschen unglaubwürdig, dass Frida Fuglesang auf einmal eine Freundin von elfeinhalb Jahren haben soll. Wo sie doch sonst nie Besuch kriegt.

»Genauer gesagt ist sie eine Freundin von meiner Oma«, füge ich hinzu und lächle, so lieb ich nur kann.

»Und du warst schon mal hier?«, fragt Wenche, immer noch mit gerunzelter Stirn.

»Ja klar«, erwidere ich schnell.

Wenche sieht nicht so richtig überzeugt aus.

»Sie ist auf ihrem Zimmer«, sagt sie säuerlich. »Aber sie schafft wahrscheinlich keinen allzu langen Besuch.«

Fridas Zimmer ist weiß und still. Ein riesiges Bett thront in der Mitte des Raums. Darauf liegen schwere Decken und ein rosa Überwurf. Zwei graue Sessel stehen beim Fenster. Die Vorhänge sind zugezogen, an den Wänden hängen keine Bilder.

Einen Moment lang schaue ich mich ratlos um und frage mich, wo Frida eigentlich ist. Die Tür zum Bad steht offen, aber auf dem Klo und in der Dusche ist niemand zu sehen.

Da höre ich plötzlich ein Husten aus Richtung des Betts. Unter dem rosa Überwurf liegen gar keine schweren Decken, sondern Frida Fuglesang höchstpersönlich. Ich halte den Atem an. Was habe ich mir überhaupt gedacht? Schleiche einfach so ins Zimmer einer wildfremden Frau, die in einem rosa Bett liegt und hustet! Um ihr einen alten Liebesbrief und ein Buch mit schlechten Gedichten zu überreichen.

Frida Fuglesang setzt sich in ihrem Bett auf. Sie hat kurze dunkle Haare und sieht zierlich aus. Die Augen in ihrem schmalen Gesicht sind groß und braun, wie bei einem neugierigen Hund. Es ist schwer vorstellbar, dass diese Gestalt früher einmal Mannequin in Paris gewesen sein soll. Aber das Muttermal auf der Wange verrät, dass es wirklich Frida Fuglesang ist. Sie hat schon eine gewisse Ähnlichkeit mit der Frau auf dem Foto.

»Was machst du hier?«, fragt Frida Fuglesang mit schwacher, eingerosteter Stimme.

Vilmer und ich hätten zusammen hier sein sollen, aber ich bin allein. Ich räuspere mich.

»Ich suche Frida Fuglesang«, sage ich leise.

Sie hebt die Augenbrauen.

»Das bin ich«, erwidert sie.

Ich nicke und beschließe, direkt zur Sache zu kommen.

»Ich wollte fragen, ob Sie schon mal was von einem Anton Berntzen gehört haben?«

»Anton Berntzen?«, wiederholt Frida überrascht. »Ob ich schon mal von Anton Berntzen *gehört* habe?«

»Er war vor vielen Jahren Hausmeister im Tyllebakken Bauverein.«

Es macht nicht den Eindruck, als hätte Frida Fuglesang auch nur die leiseste Ahnung, von wem ich da rede. Sie sitzt mit offenem Mund im Bett und starrt mich mit kugelrunden Augen an. Ihre Hände liegen auf dem rosa Überwurf. Sie trägt keinen Ring.

Ich halte den Umschlag hoch.

»Wir haben einen Brief gefunden. Vilmer und ich. Aber er wurde nie abgeschickt.«

Fridas Mund öffnet sich noch weiter.

Ich gebe ihr den Brief. Frida Fuglesang faltet ihn auf und beginnt zu lesen. Schließt den Mund. Ihre Augen wandern die Zeilen entlang. Ihre Mundwinkel ziehen sich nach oben. Sie lächelt.

»Ich glaub, ich werd verrückt«, murmelt sie.

»Also haben Sie schon einmal von Anton Berntzen gehört?«, frage ich eifrig.

»Gehört?«, antwortet sie. »Ich habe mein ganzes Leben lang an Anton Berntzen gedacht.«

Wir lächeln uns an.

Ich vermisse Vilmer. Sehr sogar.

»Er hat auch an Sie gedacht«, sage ich und reiche ihr das rote Büchlein mit den Gedichten.

Frida Fuglesang wirft mir einen unsicheren Blick zu, bevor sie vorsichtig beginnt, darin zu blättern. Sie liest und lächelt. Lacht. Wischt sich die Tränen aus dem Gesicht.

»Ich hatte keine Ahnung, dass Anton so gut dichten konnte«, sagt sie nach einer Weile. »Er hat mich mit Kartoffeleintopf verglichen!«, ruft sie begeistert. Eine Träne tropft aus ihrem linken Auge und läuft die Wange hinunter. »Das hat noch keiner getan.«

Ich lächle zufrieden. Endlich ist Antons Ehre wiederhergestellt.

»Wo in aller Welt hast du denn nur dieses Buch gefunden?«, fragt Frida aufgeregt.

Vilmer. Ich erzähle von Vilmer. Es ist, als würde ich Frida Fuglesang schon sehr lange kennen. Aus alten

Zeiten. Ich erzähle ihr von der Hausmeisterwohnung, die Vilmer entdeckt hat. Wie es dort aussah. Was Anton alles hinterlassen hat. Dass ich alle angelogen habe. Und wie aus der Kellerwohnung ein Südenparadies wurde.

Frida Fuglesang macht ein nachdenkliches Gesicht.

»Anton Berntzen war gewissermaßen nicht gut genug für mich. Er war ja *nur* Hausmeister. Das haben meine Eltern immer gesagt. Sie meinten, ich könnte jemand Besseren kriegen.«

Sie seufzt.

»Und zum Schluss hab ich es selbst geglaubt. So leicht war ich zu beeinflussen. Ich war so damit beschäftigt, was andere dachten, dass ich vollkommen vergaß, was ich selber dachte.«

Sie sieht mich an.

»Und als dann das Angebot aus Paris kam, rieten mir alle, es unbedingt anzunehmen. Statt mit Anton in einer Hausmeisterwohnung zu versauern.«

Sie lächelt vorsichtig.

»Er war sehr traurig, als ich fortging«, erzählt sie leise. »Sagte, er wolle mich nie mehr wiedersehen. Tat so, als ob ich ihm egal wäre. Deshalb habe ich mich nicht getraut, wieder Kontakt zu ihm aufzunehmen. Ich kam mir vor wie der schrecklichste Mensch auf der Welt.«

Sie schweigt, streicht gedankenverloren über das Buch.

»Ich konnte ja nicht wissen, dass er die ganze Zeit in Tyllebakken saß und Gedichte über mich schrieb«, sagt sie. »Hätte ich das geahnt, wäre ich auf der Stelle zurück nach Hause gefahren.«

Mir fällt plötzlich der Ring ein. Vilmer hatte ihn am Finger, jetzt steckt er an meinem.

»Vielleicht möchten Sie den hier wiederhaben?«

Frida reißt die Augen auf. Sie nimmt den Ring aus meiner Hand, liest die Gravur. *Dein Anton.*

»Hast du auch seinen Ring gefunden?«, fragt sie. »Darin war *Deine Frida* eingraviert. Wir haben uns die Ringe in seiner Wohnung angesteckt.«

»Vielleicht hat er ihn nie abgenommen«, sage ich.

Frida lächelt.

»Vielleicht«, murmelt sie nachdenklich.

Ich zeige Frida die Fotos auf meinem Handy. Vom Süden. Sie seufzt und lächelt. Es sticht in meiner Brust. Vilmer und ich auf dem roten Sofa, vor dem Sonnenuntergang. Er hat den Arm um mich gelegt, wir stehen eng zusammen, um beide aufs Bild zu passen.

Plötzlich geht die Tür auf, und Wenche in ihrer blauen Uniform steckt den Kopf herein.

»Jetzt sind Sie aber bestimmt müde, nicht?«, fragt sie Frida. Es hört sich an, als ob sie mit einer Zweijährigen spricht. »Soll ich das Mädchen bitten zu gehen?«

Frida Fuglesang wedelt irritiert mit der Hand.

»Kommt nicht in die Tüte«, sagt sie laut. »Das hier ist der beste Besuch seit Langem.«

»Sie hatten lange keinen Besuch«, korrigiert Wenche.

»Das weiß ich wohl«, sagt Frida verärgert. »Aber jetzt habe ich jedenfalls Besuch.«

Sie funkelt Wenche an.

»Und Sie können sich schon mal darauf einstellen, dass ich bald noch mehr Besuch bekomme. Wie hieß dein Freund noch gleich?«

»Vilmer.« Mir wird ganz warm, wenn ich nur seinen schönen Namen sage.

Meine Augen brennen, und ich starre schnell auf den Boden, denn sonst fange ich garantiert an zu weinen.

Wenche schließt die Tür, und es wird vollkommen still im Raum. Ich spüre Fridas Blick auf mir.

»Der Junge ist etwas Besonderes, nicht wahr?«, fragt sie leise.

Ich blinzele die Tränen weg, höre sie Atem holen.

»Bist du in ihn verliebt?«

»Verliebt?« Ich schaue auf.

Frida sieht mich ernst an. Und obwohl ich sie noch nie zuvor getroffen habe, ist es, als würde sie mich ganz genau kennen. Als würde sie alles verstehen.

»Wieso ist er heute nicht mit dabei?«, fragt Frida Fuglesang und schiebt sich ein Kissen hinter den Rücken.

Und zum ersten Mal schütte ich jemand völlig Fremdem mein Herz aus. Ich erzähle von Vilmer. Wie schön es ist, mit ihm zusammen zu sein, wie süß er in seinen bescheuerten T-Shirts aussieht.

»Er ist so viel mehr als nur ein Südenfreund«, schluchze ich, und nun ist es mir egal, dass ich weine.

Ich schildere Frida, wie Vilmer hinter dem Herd gekauert und alles mit angehört hat. All die schrecklichen Dinge, die ich gesagt und gar nicht so gemeint habe. Und dass es jetzt hinter seinem Fenster immer dunkel ist. Dass jetzt alles nur noch dunkel ist.

Frida Fuglesang hält mir ein Taschentuch hin und schaut mich lange an.

»Du musst Entschuldigung tun«, sagt sie.

»Entschuldigung tun?«, frage ich verwirrt. »Das gibt es doch gar nicht?«

»Nein«, sagt Frida Fuglesang. »Sollte es aber. Es ist ein großer Unterschied, ob man Entschuldigung tut oder Entschuldigung sagt.«

Sie lächelt mich an.

»Ich zum Beispiel habe mein ganzes Leben lang bereut, dass ich nie bei Anton Entschuldigung getan habe«, sagt sie. »Denn vielleicht habe ich ihn so sehr verletzt, dass er bis zum Ende seines Lebens nicht mehr richtig glücklich wurde.«

Plötzlich nimmt sie meine Hand.

»Aber du hast die Möglichkeit, Entschuldigung zu tun.«

Sie drückt meine Hand und lächelt aufgeregt. »Und diese Chance musst du nutzen«, fährt sie fort. »Glaub mir, ich weiß, wovon ich rede. Du *musst* Entschuldigung tun, Ina. Und zwar schnell. Bevor es zu spät ist.«

Auf dem Weg nach Hause fängt es an zu donnern. Ein dunkles Grollen rollt über den schwarzen Himmel. Ein Blitz zuckt auf, ich komme nur bis zweiundzwanzig, bevor es erneut kracht. Wenn Vilmer hier wäre, hätte ich nicht solche Angst. Der rote Sonnenschirm, seine Hand in meiner, die lieben Augen. Ich denke an Vilmer. Den ganzen Heimweg lang sage ich immer wieder laut seinen Namen, um den Donner zu übertönen.

Entschuldigung tun. Wie *tut* man Entschuldigung?

Noch acht Tage, bis die Schule wieder anfängt. Acht Tage entsprechen einhundertzweiundneunzig Stunden. Ich habe noch elftausendfünfhundertzwanzig Sekunden.

Ich schreibe eine Liste mit Ideen. Genau wie Vilmer und ich, als wir den Süden gebaut haben. Überlege lange, bevor ich entscheide, wo ich anfangen will.

Ich laufe über den Hinterhof. Freue mich auf den Süden, auch wenn ich weiß, dass Vilmer nicht auf dem roten Sofa sitzt.

Ich knacke das Schloss. Die Luft in der Wohnung ist stickig. Es herrscht nach wie vor Chaos. Seit dem schrecklichen Tag scheint er nicht mehr hier gewesen zu sein.

Ich schaufle den Strand zurück an seinen Platz. Mache mich mit einem Eimer auf den Weg in den Hof, um neuen Sand zu holen. Das Pärchen, das dauernd streitet, steht direkt beim Sandkasten. Ich setze mich in den Sand und beginne, den Eimer zu füllen. Merke, dass sie mich komisch anschauen, aber beachte sie gar nicht, gehe einfach an ihnen vorbei, zurück nach unten in den Süden. Streue Sand auf den Strand. Lächle.

Ich räume die ganze *Sunlight Taverna* auf. Werfe die

zerbrochene Tasse weg. Wasche die Teller, an denen immer noch getrocknetes Fett vom Bacon und gelbe Spiegeleiflecken kleben. Ich entsorge die leeren Pizza-Speciale-Kartons. Schüttle die Tischdecke aus. Setze neue Adventslichter in den Kerzenständer. Ich mache im *Paradise Spa* sauber. Leere das Waschbecken und reihe die Beautyartikel auf. Hänge Mamas Kleid an einen Haken und putze den Spiegel. Ich schraube den Deckel der Fußcreme ab und ziehe den Duft ein. Höre Vilmers Stimme im Kopf. *Relax, relax.*

Ich wische das Hello-Kitty-Becken sauber und bringe den Poolbereich in Ordnung. Lege die Handtücher und unsere Badesachen zurück an ihren Platz. Bestücke die Poolbar mit zwei sauberen Gläsern, dekoriere jedes davon mit einem rosa Strohhalm.

Das Türschild ist weg. Im Kühlfach in der *Sunlight Taverna* liegt eine Pizza. Ich nehme sie aus der Schachtel und lege sie zurück ins Kühlfach. Stehe mit der kalten Schachtel in den Händen da und schaue mich suchend nach einer Schere um. Entdecke eine in Antons Werkzeugkiste. Während ich einen Kreis ausschneide, denke ich an Frida Fuglesang. *Willkommen im Süden*, schreibe ich in großen roten Buchstaben und hänge das Schild draußen an der Tür auf. Überlege lange. *Vilmers und Inas Paradies*, schreibe ich. Es sieht hübsch aus.

In Antons Schublade finde ich Klebeband. Damit befestige ich die heruntergerissenen Tapetenstreifen an der Wand, sodass das Foto von der Palme am Strand wieder aussieht wie vorher. Es dauert, einen Sonnenuntergang zu reparieren.

Zum Schluss hänge ich die Lichterkette zurück an die Nägel. Die Birnchen funktionieren noch. Gelb, grün, blau. Der Süden leuchtet wieder. Zufrieden setze ich mich auf das rote Sofa und schaue über das Paradies.

Allmählich wird es abends früher dunkel. Die Augustluft ist kühl und klar. Ich stehe lange vor Aufgang F und atme in tiefen Zügen ein und aus, lege den Kopf in den Nacken und schaue hoch zum Fenster im dritten Stock. Heute Abend flimmert dahinter ein schwaches Licht. Vielleicht sitzt Vilmer vor dem Computer. Ich kreuze die Finger hinter dem Rücken und gehe zu der Reihe mit den Klingelschildern. *Vilmer und Tommy.* Die Namen sind mit blauem Kugelschreiber geschrieben. In großen, leicht schiefen Buchstaben. Mein Finger liegt unbeweglich auf dem Knopf. Ich räuspere mich. Für den Fall, dass ich etwas in die Sprechanlage sagen muss.

Dann drücke ich fest auf die Klingel. Drei Mal. Stehe stocksteif da, fühle, wie sämtliche Zellen in meinem Körper miteinander Krieg führen. Was soll ich sagen?

Keine Reaktion.

Ich klingle erneut. Jetzt viermal, kurz und sachte. Lautlos zähle ich die Sekunden, die verstreichen. Einundzwanzig. Zweiundzwanzig. Wie bei Gewitter, wenn ich den Abstand zwischen Donner und Blitz messe. Neunundzwanzig. Nichts.

Ich gehe die kleine Treppe hinunter. Zurück in den Hinterhof. Sehe ein letztes Mal zu seinem Fenster hoch. Und da höre ich es.

»Hallo?«

Ich laufe wieder zur Tür.

»Hallo?«

Es ist seine Stimme! Es ist Vilmer! Ich bin so froh, dass es mir die Kehle zuschnürt.

»Hi«, sage ich in die Sprechanlage. »Ich bin's, Ina. Hi.«

Er antwortet nicht. Aber ich höre ihn atmen.

»Ich wollte dir nur was zeigen, Vilmer.«

Nichts. Er legt auf.

Meine Kehle schnürt sich noch enger zusammen. Ich gehe die kleine Treppe wieder hinunter. Lege den Kopf in den Nacken und schaue zu seinem Fenster hoch. Er hat das Licht ausgeschaltet. Jetzt ist es nur noch ein schwarzes Viereck. Vielleicht steht er hinter dem schwarzen Viereck und schaut zu mir in die Dunkelheit herunter. Vorsichtig hebe ich die Hand. Für den Fall, dass er mich sehen kann. Ich bücke mich und hebe ein paar Kieselsteine vom Boden auf. Ziele mit einem der Steinchen auf sein Fenster und werfe es so hoch wie möglich. Aber es reicht nicht. Ich kann nicht so gut werfen wie Vilmer. Auf seinem Weg zurück zur Erde landet der Stein auf meinem Kopf. Ich versuche es erneut. Wieder und wieder. Doch vergebens.

Hinter seinem Fenster bleibt es dunkel. Ich gehe nach Hause.

Noch einhundertzwanzig Stunden, bis die Schule wieder anfängt. Ich stecke einen Zettel in seinen Briefkasten. Vilmers und Tommys Briefkasten. Auf dem Umschlag steht Vilmers Name.

Ich habe gestern den ganzen Tag lang in meinem Zimmer gesessen und geschrieben. Insgesamt bestimmt tausend Wörter. Vielleicht mehr. Meine Finger sind steif nach all den Seiten, die ich geschrieben, zusammengeknüllt und in den Papierkorb geworfen habe.

Der Umschlag landet mit einem dumpfen Laut auf dem Boden des Briefkastens. Ich möchte Vilmer tausend Worte sagen, aber nur fünf davon stehen auf dem Zettel. Die allerwichtigsten. *Es tut mir so leid.*

Noch vier Tage, bis die Schule anfängt.

Der Regen trommelt auf den Asphalt im Hinterhof. Ich stehe am weit geöffneten Fenster in meinem Zimmer, die feuchte Luft lässt mich frösteln. Trotzdem schaue ich unverwandt zu Vilmer hinüber. Denn bei ihm brennt Licht. Ich habe seinen Kopf gesehen. Jetzt brauche ich nur noch zu warten.

Und plötzlich ist da sein Gesicht. Die Locken. Der schiefe Schneidezahn, den ich von hier natürlich nicht erkennen kann, aber von dem ich weiß, dass er hinter den geschlossenen Lippen sitzt. Er steht am Fenster. Reglos wie eine Statue. Ebenso reglos wie ich. Ich höre meinen Herzschlag. Er schaut mich an. Ich schaue ihn an. Dann hebe ich die linke Hand. Wie ein Verkehrspolizist an der Kreuzung. Genau wie letztes Mal. Aber Vilmer rührt sich nicht.

Ich greife nach dem Handy auf dem Nachttisch. Versuche, den Blick auf Vilmer gerichtet zu halten, während ich tippe. Drücke auf Senden.

Es tut mir leid.

Erst steht er weiter wie versteinert da. Doch dann sehe ich, dass er die Nachricht liest. Er blickt wieder hoch, zu mir. Als warte er auf weitere Worte. Als sei diese kümmerliche Entschuldigung viel zu wenig.

Ich bin der furchtbarste Mensch der Welt, schreibe ich. *Ich wollte den Südenpakt nicht brechen. Bitte. Verzeih mir.*

Meine Nachrichten fliegen wie Pfeile über den Hinterhof. Aber sie treffen auf einen Schild. Vilmer rührt sich immer noch nicht. Ich kreuze die Finger meiner linken Hand. Warte und warte darauf, dass mein Handy piepst.

Vilmer hält sein Handy in der Hand. Tippt er etwas? Es pocht in meinem Bauch, direkt unter dem Herzen. Was schreibt er? Es muss mehr sein als nur *ok*, wenn es so lange dauert.

Sind die Coolen nicht mehr deine Freunde?

Ich starre lange auf den kurzen Text. Es piepst erneut.

Und du brauchst wieder einen Südenfreund?

Vilmer schaut reglos zu mir herüber.

Sie sind mir egal, schreibe ich und sehe ihn an. *Nur du bist mir wichtig.*

Er liest. Und dann verschwindet er plötzlich vom Fenster. Das Licht in seinem Zimmer geht aus.

Noch zwei Tage, bis die Schule wieder anfängt. Mama kommt vom Kurs nach Hause und ruft mir vom Flur aus zu. Sie sieht ganz verändert aus. Die Haare sind kürzer, die Lippen rot. Sie trägt eine neue weiße Hose. Große Goldohrringe.

»Zieh dir was Hübsches an!«, sagt sie aufgeregt. »Ich verrate nicht, wo es hingeht.«

Draußen vor Güllebakken steht ein Taxi und wartet. Mama lächelt geheimnisvoll.

Wir fahren zur anderen Seite der Stadt.

»Sie können hier anhalten«, sagt Mama nach einer Weile zum Taxifahrer und zieht den Geldbeutel heraus.

Wir stehen vor einem Restaurant. Es leuchtet einladend hinter den Fenstern.

»Jetzt machen wir uns einen richtig schönen Abend, Ina«, sagt Mama und schiebt mich durch die Tür.

Wir suchen uns einen Platz am Fenster. Mama trinkt Wein. Wir bestellen jeder drei Gänge.

»Ich muss dir etwas erzählen«, sagt Mama.

Sie sieht kein bisschen müde aus. Ihre Augen sind groß und leuchten. Der Mund verzieht sich zu einem breiten Lächeln. Sie hat Lippenstift am Zahn.

»Ich habe einen Job!«

Sie schaut mich gespannt an. Ich lächle.

»In einem Blumenladen«, fährt sie begeistert fort. »Ich hab mich doch schon immer so für Blumen und Pflanzen interessiert.«

Ich denke an die braunen, vertrockneten Pflanzen im Wohnzimmer. All die leeren Vasen.

»Jetzt werden es andere Zeiten für uns«, sagt Mama und hebt ihr Glas. »Vielleicht können wir in den Süden fahren.«

Sie räuspert sich.

»Also, in den richtigen Süden, meine ich.«

»*Blue Lagoon Deluxe?*«, frage ich.

Wir lachen.

»So was in der Art«, sagt sie.

Ich frage Mama, ob sie mir ein bisschen Geld leihen kann.

»Na klar«, sagt sie. »Brauchst du es für etwas Bestimmtes?«

Ich nicke.

»Ich muss Entschuldigung tun«, sage ich. »Bei Vilmer.«

Mama lächelt mit Schokomousse an der Nasenspitze. »Für clevere Mädchen kommt schon alles in Ordnung, Ina«, sagt sie. »Denk immer daran.«

Noch fünfzehn Stunden, bis die Schule wieder anfängt. Ich stehe vor dem Spiegel und betrachte mein neues T-Shirt. Ich war in einem Geschäft, wo sie T-Shirts bedrucken. Erst wurde ich ein bisschen komisch angeguckt, als ich gesagt habe, was für ein Text darauf stehen soll. Aber ein paar Stunden später war das T-Shirt fertig. Ich habe es mit dem Geld von Mama bezahlt.

Mein Herz klopft hinter dem knallgelben Baumwollstoff. Ich sehe aus wie ein verzweifeltes Osterküken, das nicht weiß, wo es hinsoll.

Ich habe für über dreihundert Kronen eingekauft. Lauter Sachen, die Vilmer mag. Pepsi und Käseflips und Pizza Speciale. Alles ist vorbereitet.

Als ich vor dem Schlafengehen noch einmal nach draußen schaue, ist es dunkel hinter seinem Fenster. Mit weit aufgerissenen Augen liege ich unter der Decke und denke an morgen. Den Beginn von etwas Neuem. Oder das Ende.

Im Traum hat Vilmer ein rotes T-Shirt an. Rot wie der Sonnenuntergang im Süden.

Noch zwölf Minuten, bis die Schule wieder anfängt. Der Asphalt auf dem Schulhof glüht. Die Flagge am Mast ist gehisst. Die altbekannten Grüppchen haben sich schon zusammengefunden. Mathilde und Regine hängen bei den Mittelschülern ab. Markus und ein paar von den Jungs stehen bei den Bänken unter der Flagge. Als ob sich in den letzten vierundfünfzig Tagen nichts geändert hätte. Es sind dreihundertachtzehn Schritte von der Turnhalle bis zur Klasse. Ich gehe in meinem gelben T-Shirt geradewegs an Mathilde und Regine vorbei. Höre sie lachen. Sehe, dass Markus mich anstarrt. Aber ich laufe einfach weiter, auf den Eingang zu, die Treppe hinauf in den zweiten Stock und in unser neues Klassenzimmer, ein ganz gewöhnliches norwegisches Klassenzimmer mit Blick zum Schulhof.

Er ist nirgends zu sehen. Nicht im Hof. Nicht hier. In dreißig Sekunden klingelt es. Zwanzig. Zehn. Jetzt.

Vigdis steht vor uns, an unserem allerersten Tag in der 7a. Sie hat einen grünen Rock und eine geblümte Bluse an, die Haare hängen ihr offen über die Schultern, die Lippen glänzen rosa, die Haut auf der Nase pellt sich nach einem Sonnenbrand.

»Willkommen, ihr Lieben! Zu eurem ersten Tag als Siebtklässler«, ruft sie freudestrahlend und breitet wie gewöhnlich die Arme aus.

Anscheinend hat sie sich in ihrer Waldhütte bestens erholt, denn jetzt schnattert sie, ohne Luft zu holen, drauflos und watschelt dabei wie eine überglückliche Henne durchs Klassenzimmer.

»Als Erstes«, sagt sie und geht zum Schrank, »wollen wir schauen, ob eure Träume für den Sommer in Erfüllung gegangen sind.«

Sie nimmt den Korb heraus und drückt ihn an ihre Hängebrüste. Und dann verteilt sie die Zettel, die wir am letzten Schultag vor den Ferien geschrieben haben.

Der Tisch an der Tür ist frei. Zwei Reihen vor mir.

Vilmers Tisch. Was, wenn er nicht kommt? Was, wenn er die Schule gewechselt hat? Was, wenn ich niemals die Chance bekomme, Entschuldigung zu tun?

Mein Zettel landet auf meinem Tisch. Ich falte ihn auf. Lese die drei Punkte, von denen ich niemals gedacht hätte, dass sie eintreffen.

Urlaub machen. Einen Freund finden. Küssen.

»Ich werde euch nicht fragen, ob eure Träume in Erfüllung gegangen sind«, sagt Vigdis und lacht so laut über sich selbst, dass sie sich damit garantiert für den Norwegenrekord qualifiziert.

Und dann passiert es. Endlich. Die Tür öffnet sich. Er steht auf der Schwelle und schaut ängstlich ins Klassenzimmer. Seine Lippen sind zusammengepresst. Die Locken auf seinem Kopf bewegen sich nicht. Er schweigt. Lächelt nicht.

»Da bist du ja«, sagt Vigdis und geht zur Tür, um Vilmer abzuholen, als wäre er ein Zweijähriger, der von einem Erwachsenen geführt werden muss.

»Herzlich willkommen in unserer Klasse!«

Hunderttausend Blitzeinschläge in meinem Bauch. Vilmer! Meine Beine zittern, und es hämmert in meinem Herzen und in der Brust. Mein Mund ist trocken, meine Haut prickelt.

Wortlos läuft er zu dem freien Tisch und schiebt

den Stuhl zurück. Sieht mich nicht an. Sieht nicht mein T-Shirt.

Vigdis nuckelt an ihrer Brille und lässt ihren Königinnenblick über die Klasse schweifen. Und da setze ich ihn in Gang. Meinen Plan. Jetzt geht es los.

»Vigdis! Vigdis!«, rufe ich und wedele mit dem Arm in der Luft.

»Können wir nicht eine Runde machen, in der jeder von seinen Ferien erzählt?«

Ein Wispern geht durch die Reihen. Viele lachen. Inzwischen wissen bestimmt die meisten, dass meine Bilder in der Gruppe nur Fake waren.

Vigdis sieht mich verblüfft an.

»Hm, ja, warum eigentlich nicht?«, erwidert sie unsicher. »Wir können gern erst ein bisschen über die Ferien sprechen.«

Ich richte mich ein Stück auf und deute auf Tuva, die immer noch am Fenster in der ersten Reihe sitzt, um die Runde genauso zu organisieren wie vor den Ferien. Ich muss die Sache nur in Gang bringen, dann wird alles von selbst laufen. Dann kann sich mein Plan entfalten, so wie ich es mir ausgedacht habe.

Tuva hatte einen fantastischen Urlaub in Italien. Und Teodor hinter ihr eine tolle Zeit in Kroatien. Simen hat die unglaublichsten Dinge in Florida erlebt, und Unas Meinung nach ist Dänemark das Traumferienland, auch wenn sie sich natürlich auf Thailand nächsten Sommer freut.

Ich schaue zu Vilmer. Seinem regungslosen Rücken. Seinen Ohren, die meine scheußlichen Worte gehört haben. Gerade erzählt Mathilde von dem großartigen Resort in Portugal. Regine beschreibt ausführlich, was sie alles in Paris gekauft hat.

Und gleich bin ich dran. Gleich muss ich erzählen. Ich bin vorbereitet.

Markus schwärmt von Sørland und Spanien und dem Chelsea-Spiel, auch wenn sie verloren haben. Es ist langweilig, ihm zuzuhören. Uninteressant. Stattdessen beobachte ich Vilmer. Seine Locken. Ich weiß, wie sie riechen, denke ich lächelnd, während Julie eine Ewigkeit damit zubringt, Zypern und Frankreich zu vergleichen.

Vigdis setzt sich die Brille auf und schaut mich an.

»Du bist an der Reihe, Ina«, sagt sie nervös.

Alle drehen sich zu mir um. Absolut alle. Außer Vilmer. Der immer noch regungslos auf die Tischplatte starrt.

Jemand kichert. Oder besser gesagt, viele kichern. Anscheinend haben Mathilde und Regine den Großteil der Klasse über meine Lügen informiert.

»Im Sommer«, beginne ich.

Meine Stimme ist klar und deutlich. Ich setze mich

kerzengerade hin, sodass alle lesen können, was auf meinem T-Shirt steht.

»Im Sommer war ich im Süden.«

Ein Raunen geht durch die Reihen.

»Das ist doch wohl nicht ihr Ernst«, schnaubt Mathilde und schaut zu Regine und Markus.

»Und es war der beste Urlaub meines Lebens«, fahre ich fort. »Ich habe wochenlang nur Südendinge gemacht. Zusammen mit dem besten Südenfreund der Welt.«

Vilmer. Sein Rücken in dem weißen T-Shirt. Plötzlich dreht er sich um. Die Locken auf seinem Kopf bewegen sich. Seine Augen sind weit geöffnet.

Regine meldet sich und fängt an zu reden, noch bevor Vigdis sie drangenommen hat.

»Kannst du nicht endlich die Wahrheit sagen? Dass du den ganzen Sommer lang in Güllebakken warst!«

Sie funkelt mich wütend an. Zum Glück sitze ich nicht im Schülerrat und muss mit ihr diskutieren.

Ich stehe ruckartig auf. Es fühlt sich ganz natürlich an.

»Ich *war* im Süden«, wiederhole ich ruhig an Regine gewandt. Als wäre sie ein Kleinkind, dem man etwas sehr Kompliziertes erklären muss.

»Es war einfach nur eine andere Art von Süden, als du gewohnt bist.«

Ich spreche mit sanfter, geduldiger Stimme. Die Beine stehen fest auf dem Boden.

»Denn der Süden ist kein Land«, erkläre ich. »Das hast du selbst gesagt.«

Regine und Mathilde starren mich ungläubig an.

»Es ist nur ein Ort, an den man fährt, um sich zu entspannen und Spaß zu haben, richtig? Also kann ich doch wohl selbst entscheiden, ob ich im Süden war, oder?«

Ich schaue zu Vilmer.

Er lächelt! Sein Mund hat sich leicht geöffnet, sein schiefer Schneidezahn sieht so süß aus. Er starrt auf den Text auf meinem T-Shirt.

Willkommen im Süden.

Vilmers und Inas Paradies.

Es ist das uncoolste T-Shirt der Welt, uncooler als alle von Vilmers T-Shirts zusammen. Und Gelb steht mir wirklich überhaupt nicht.

»Es war ein Traumsommer«, sage ich zufrieden und wedele mit meinem Zettel. »Alles, was ich aufgeschrieben habe, ist wahr geworden.«

Ich lächle Vilmer an.

»Ich habe einen Südenfreund fürs Leben gefunden.«

Vilmer erwidert meinen Blick. Mit einem breiten Lächeln. Den tollsten Augen. Dem zweituncoolsten T-Shirt der Welt.

»Nein, nicht nur einen Südenfreund«, verbessere ich mich. »Einen besten Freund. Oder so was in der Art.«
Ich setze mich ruhig auf meinen Stuhl. Kein Laut ist zu hören.

Niemand kichert. Zum ersten Mal ist die gesamte Klasse mucksmäuschenstill.

Und was machen wir jetzt?«, fragt Vilmer, als der erste Schultag vorbei ist und wir über den Hof gehen.

Ich sage nichts, obwohl ich die Antwort weiß. Sie liegt auf der Hand.

»Erst zeige ich dir etwas«, sage ich und ziehe mein Handy aus der Tasche, öffne die Bildergalerie und klicke eins der Fotos an.

»Rate mal, wer das hier ist!«

Ich reiche Vilmer das Handy. Er bleibt stehen und beugt sich über das Display. Dann schnappt er nach Luft.

»Du verarschst mich!«

Ich grinse, schüttele den Kopf.

»Das ist Antons Freundin!«, rufe ich.

»Die Schöne«, flüstert Vilmer.

Der Ring an Fridas Finger, das Gedichtbuch in ihrer Hand. Das Muttermal auf der Wange. Ich sitze neben ihr, mit ausgestrecktem Arm, um das Selfie zu machen. Wir lächeln in die Kamera.

»Sie heißt Frida Fuglesang und möchte dich unbedingt kennenlernen!«

Vilmer starrt mich mit offenem Mund an.

»Frida Fuglesang«, sagt er ehrfurchtsvoll. »Der leckere Kartoffeleintopf.«

Ich lache. »Sie wohnt in Solvangtunet«, sage ich. »Und hat jeden einzelnen Tag an Anton gedacht. Ist das nicht unheimlich traurig – und schön?«

Ich greife Vilmers Hand. Halte sie fest, während wir an den Grüppchen vorbeischlendern. All die Köpfe, die sich zu uns umdrehen. Viele lachen. Über den Text auf meinem T-Shirt oder über uns. Es kann uns egal sein. Ich blicke geradeaus. Vilmers Hand fühlt sich trocken und angenehm an, sie passt perfekt in meine.

Wir gehen vom Schulhof, in Richtung Güllebakken. Es ist heiß und schwül. Drückend. Vielleicht zieht ein Gewitter auf, aber das macht nichts, wenn wir, so wie jetzt, nebeneinanderlaufen.

Ich habe alles vorbereitet. Die Pepsi liegt im Kühlschrank. Auf der Playlist sind neue Songs. Der Tisch in der *Sunlight Taverna* ist für zwei gedeckt. Ich habe die Sonnenliegen unter dem roten Schirm aufgestellt. Das Schild aufgehängt, auf dem derselbe Text steht wie auf meinem T-Shirt, das ich gerade der gesamten Schule präsentiert habe.

Ich schaue zu Vilmer. Meinem wunderbaren Südenfreund, der vielleicht mehr ist als das. Und dann antworte ich endlich auf seine Frage. Denn ich weiß ganz genau, was wir jetzt machen werden.

»Na, wir genießen den Süden«, sage ich.

Und grinse.

Die Autorin
Marianne Kaurin, geboren 1974, studierte am Norwegischen Kinderbuchinstitut in Oslo. 2012 debütierte sie mit ihrem Jugendroman *Beinahe Herbst*, für den sie großartige Kritiken und zwei der wichtigsten Jugendliteraturpreise des Landes erhielt. Marianne wohnt mit ihrer Familie in Oslo.

Die Übersetzerin
Franziska Hüther, geboren 1988 bei Darmstadt, studierte Skandinavistik und Germanistik in Frankfurt am Main und Reykjavík. Nach mehreren Aufenthalten in Skandinavien lebt und arbeitet sie nun wieder in Deutschland, wo sie als Übersetzerin für die Sprachen Dänisch, Schwedisch und Norwegisch tätig ist.

Die Illustratorin
Friederike Ablang wurde 1977 geboren und studierte in Großbritannien und Deutschland Fotografie und Gestaltung. 2004 machte sie ihr Diplom an der Kunsthochschule Berlin-Weißensee und arbeitet seitdem als freie Illustratorin. Friederike lebt mit ihrer Familie, einer Katze und vielen Wollmäusen in Berlin.

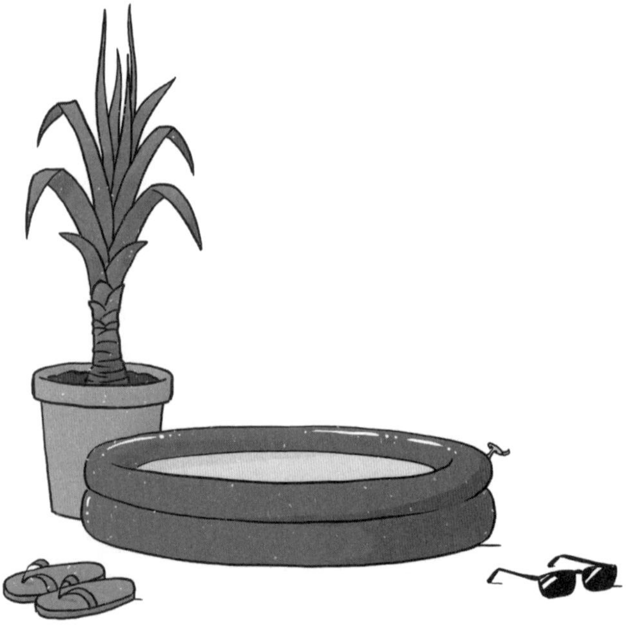

Die Übersetzung wurde gefördert von NORLA,
Norwegian Literature Abroad

NORLA
NORWEGIAN LITERATURE ABROAD

MIX
Papier aus verantwortungsvollen Quellen
FSC® C083411

Deutsche Erstausgabe
2. Auflage 2020
© Atrium Verlag, Imprint WooW Books, Zürich 2020
Alle Rechte vorbehalten
© Text: Marianne Kaurin
Aus dem Norwegischen von Franziska Hüther
Die Arbeit der Übersetzerin wurde vom Europäischen Übersetzer-Kollegium Nordrhein-Westfalen in Straelen e. V. gefördert
Die Originalausgabe erschien unter dem Titel *Syden* bei H. Aschehoug & Co. (W. Nygaard) AS, Oslo 2018
Published by agreement with Oslo Literary Agency
Cover-Illustration: Friederike Ablang
Satz: Pinkuin Satz und Datentechnik, Berlin
Druck und Bindung: CPI books GmbH, Leck
ISBN 978-3-96177-050-2

www.woow-books.de
www.instagram.com/woowbooks_verlag

DAS ABENTEUER IM LAND DES WILDEN VOLKES BEGINNT!

Sylvia V. Linsteadt
Das Wilde Volk (Bd. 1)
Deutsche Erstausgabe
Aus dem Englischen von Alexandra Rak
Gebunden | 448 Seiten
18,00 € [D] | 18,50 € [A]
ISBN 978-3-96177-051-9

Auf der Insel Farallone ist das zerbrechliche Gleichgewicht zwischen Mensch und Natur in Gefahr. Die grenzenlose Gier der Stadtbewohner nach dem kostbaren Sternengold bedroht das geheimnisumwobene Wilde Volk. Dessen einzige Hoffnung ruht nun auf Tin, einem Jungen aus der Stadt, und Comfrey, einem Mädchen vom Land. In Begleitung von zwei jungen Hasen begeben sie sich auf eine abenteuerliche Reise – um das Land zu retten, das sie alle lieben.

MAN NEHME: EINE FLIEGENDE TASCHE, EINEN ZAUBERSPIEGEL UND EINE MAGISCHE PUPPE

Michelle Harrison
Eine Prise Magie (Bd. 1)
Deutsche Erstausgabe
Aus dem Englischen von Mareike Weber
Gebunden | 448 Seiten
18,00 € [D] | 18,50 € [A]
ISBN 978-3-96177-044-1

Drei Schwestern, gefangen durch einen uralten Fluch.
Drei magische Gegenstände, mit der Kraft, alles zu verändern.
Ein Wettlauf gegen die Zeit beginnt, denn sobald die Sonne aufgeht, nimmt das Schicksal seinen Lauf …

LChoice App kostenlos laden,
dann Code scannen und jederzeit
die neuesten WooW Books finden.